I0814560

The Honourable John

NORQUAY

The Honourable John NORQUAY

Indigenous Premier, Canadian Statesman

GERALD FRIESEN

UNIVERSITY OF MANITOBA PRESS

The Honourable John Norquay: Indigenous Premier, Canadian Statesman

28 27 26 25 24 1 2 3 4 5

University of Manitoba Press
Winnipeg, Manitoba, Canada
Treaty 1 Territory
uofmpress.ca

Cataloguing data available from Library and Archives Canada
ISBN 978-1-77284-058-2 (BOUND)
ISBN 978-1-77284-059-9 (PDF)
ISBN 978-1-77284-060-5 (EPUB)

Front and back cover photographs: Kennedy Street, parliament building, and Government House, Winnipeg, c. 1888, Archives of Manitoba, P78925; Hon. John Norquay, Montreal, 1882, #208259; and The Forks c. 1884, #131575, McCord Stewart Museum.
Cover design by Frank Reimer
Interior design by Jess Koroscil

Printed in Canada

This book has been published with the help of a grant from the Federation for the Humanities and Social Sciences, through the Awards to Scholarly Publications Program, using funds provided by the Social Sciences and Humanities Research Council of Canada.

The University of Manitoba Press acknowledges the financial support for its publication program provided by the Government of Canada through the Canada Book Fund, the Canada Council for the Arts, the Manitoba Department of Sport, Culture, and Heritage, the Manitoba Arts Council, and the Manitoba Book Publishing Tax Credit.

Funded by the Government of Canada | Canada

To Jean, Joe, Alex

Contents

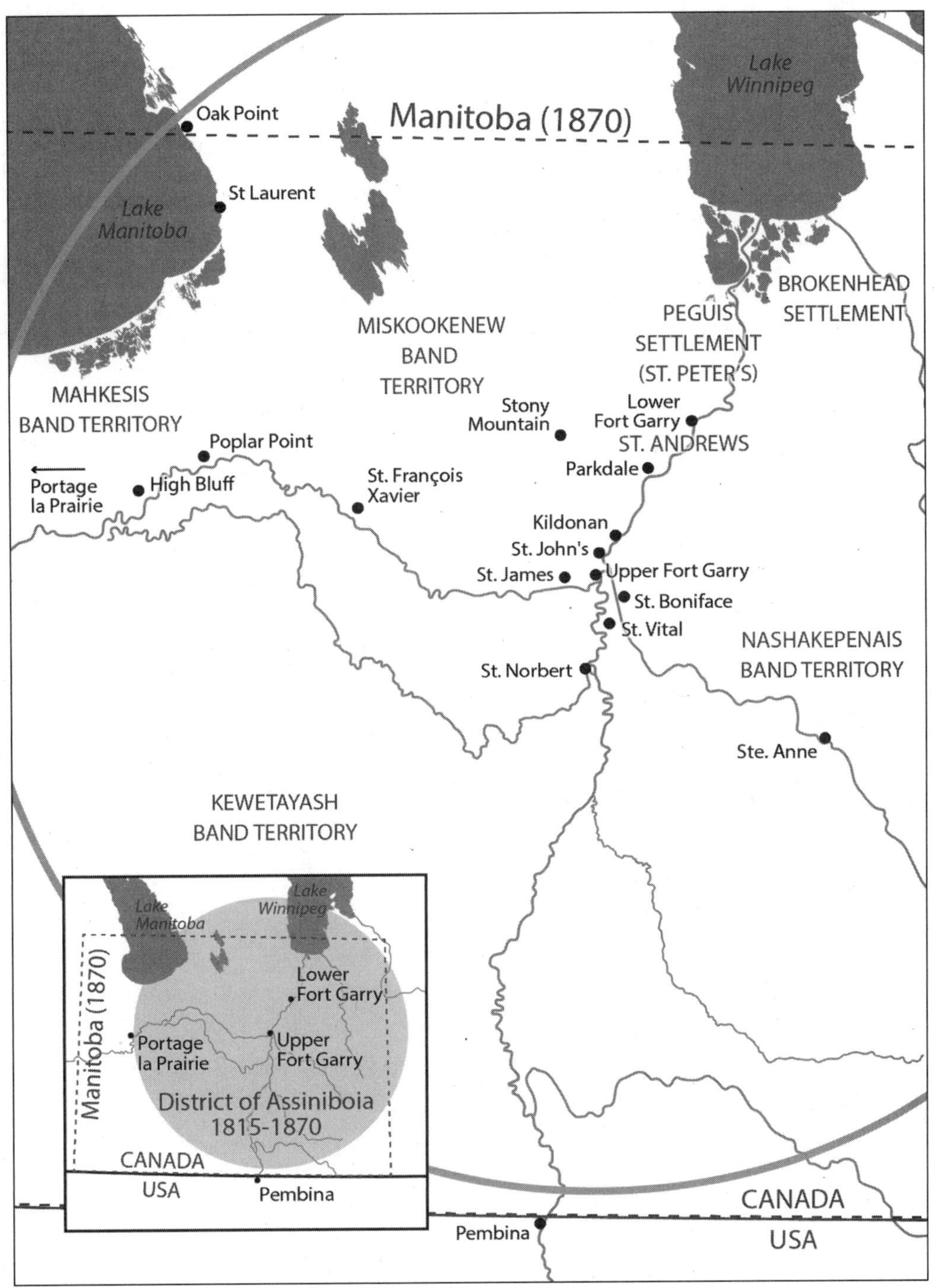

Map 1. Red River Settlement.

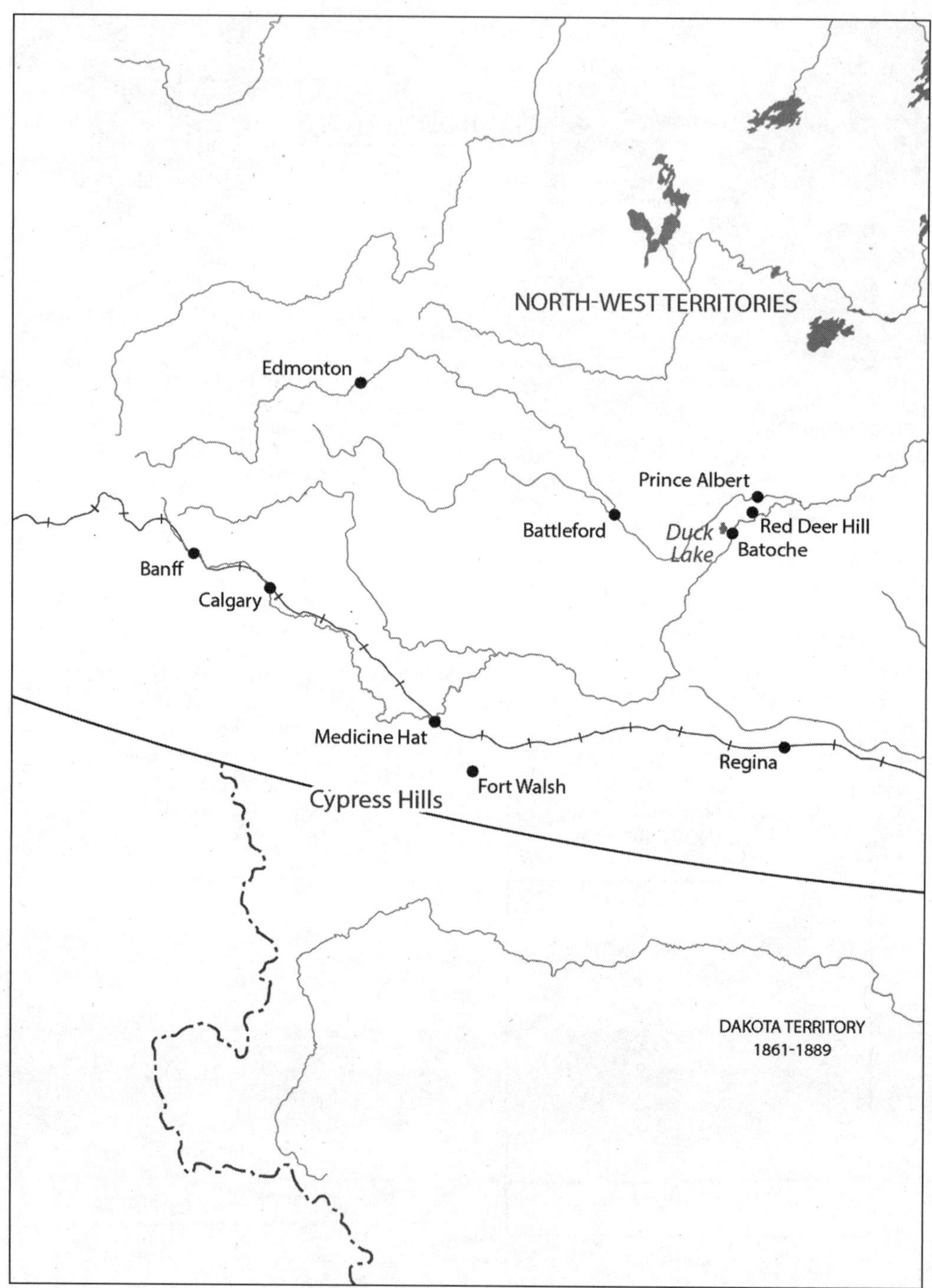

Map 2A. Western Interior.

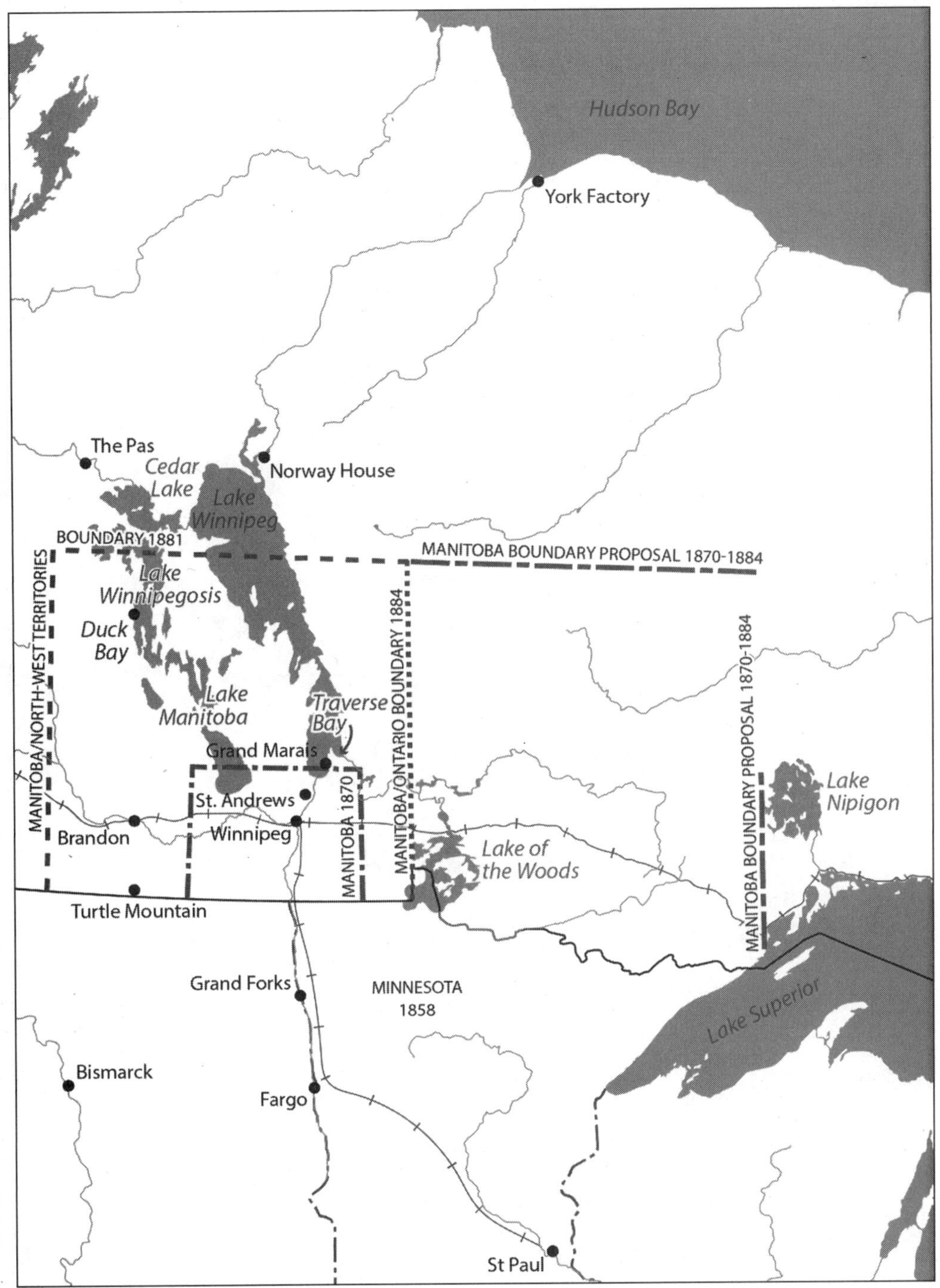

Map 2B. Western Interior.

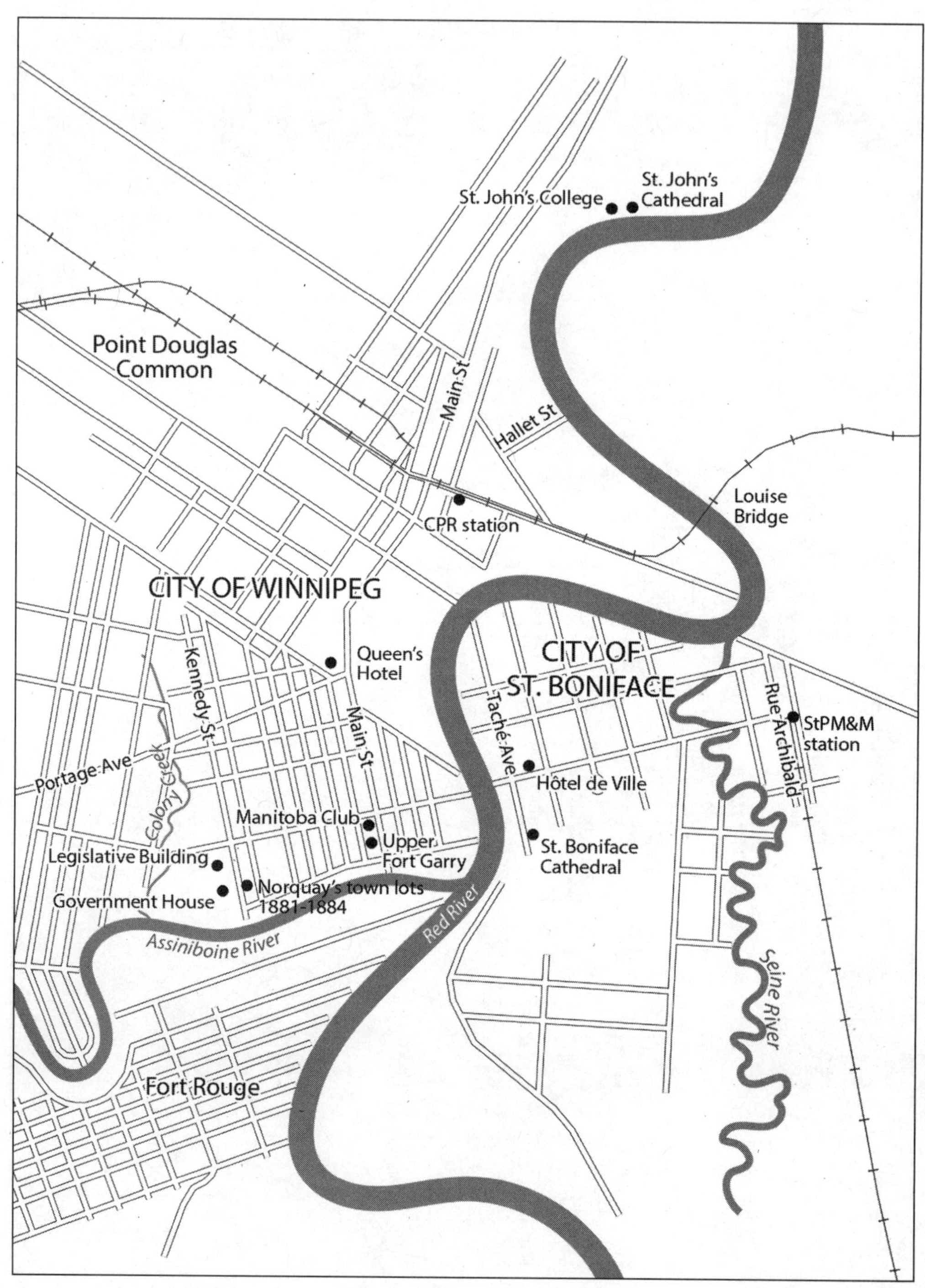

Map 3. Winnipeg Capital Region, 1886.

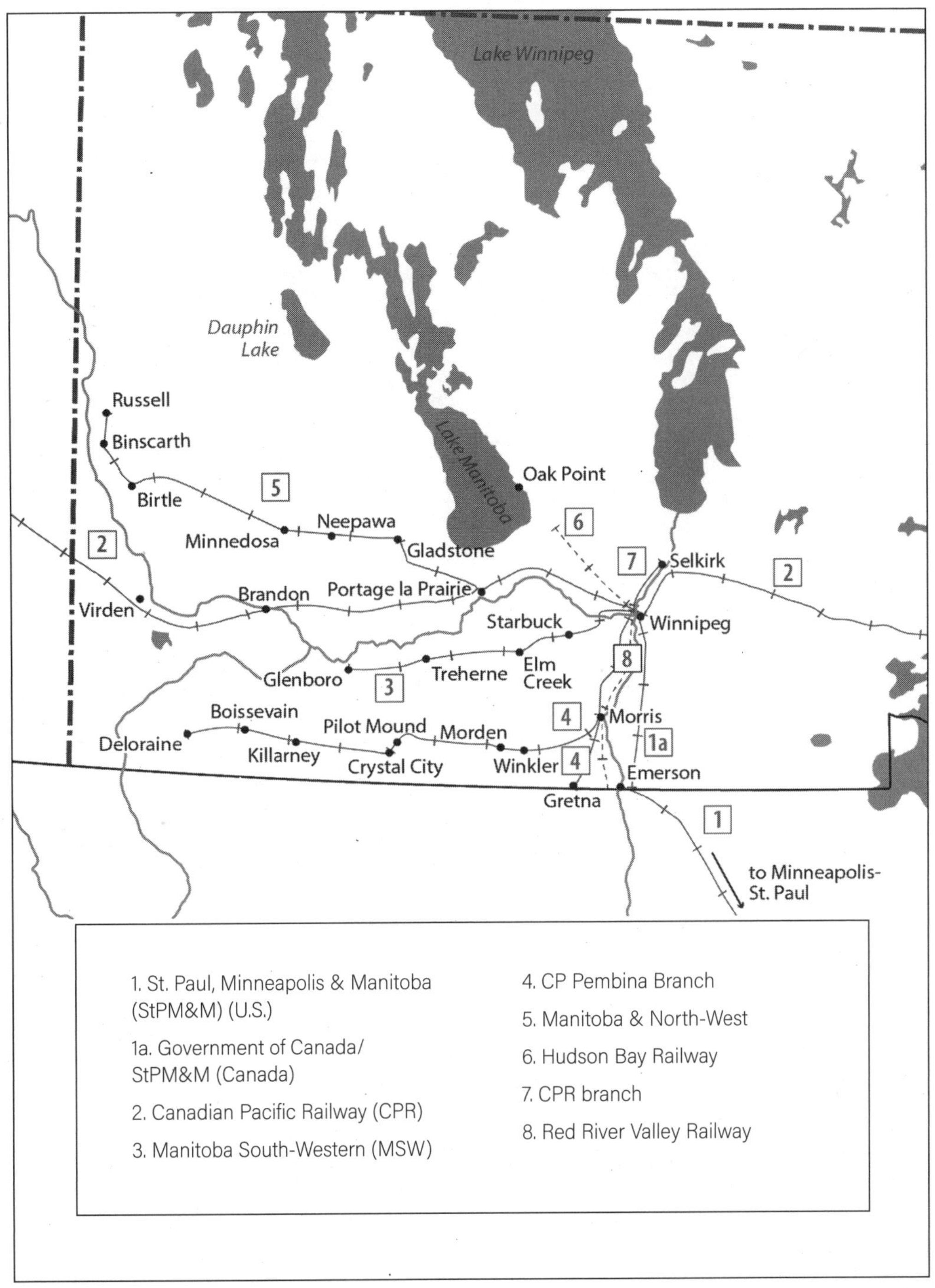

Map 4. Manitoba Railways, 1886.

ISABELLA TRUTHWAITE'S
FAMILY TREE

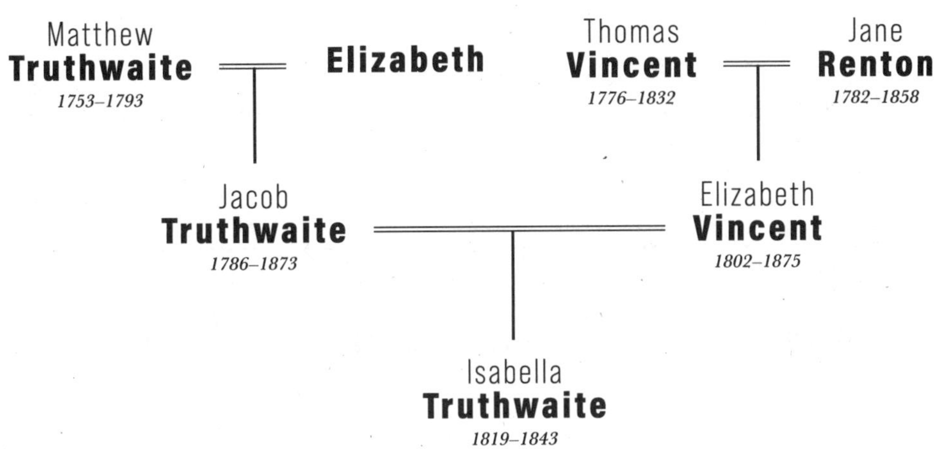

ELIZABETH SETTER'S
FAMILY TREE

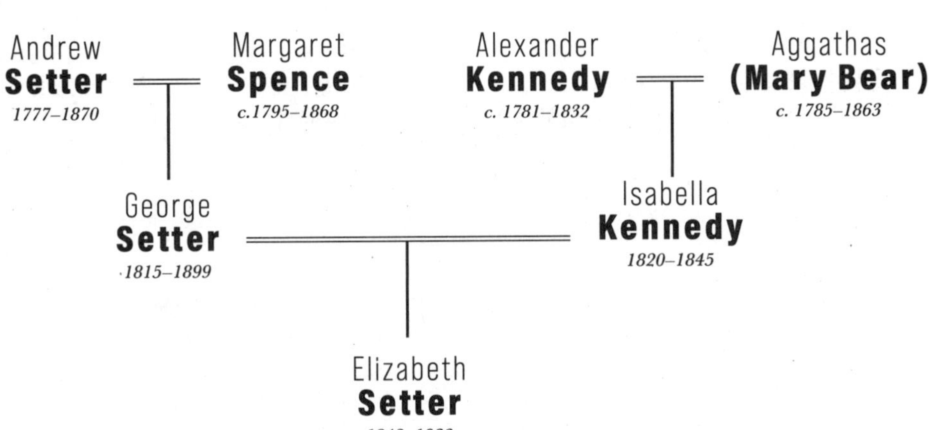

JOHN NORQUAY'S
FAMILY TREE

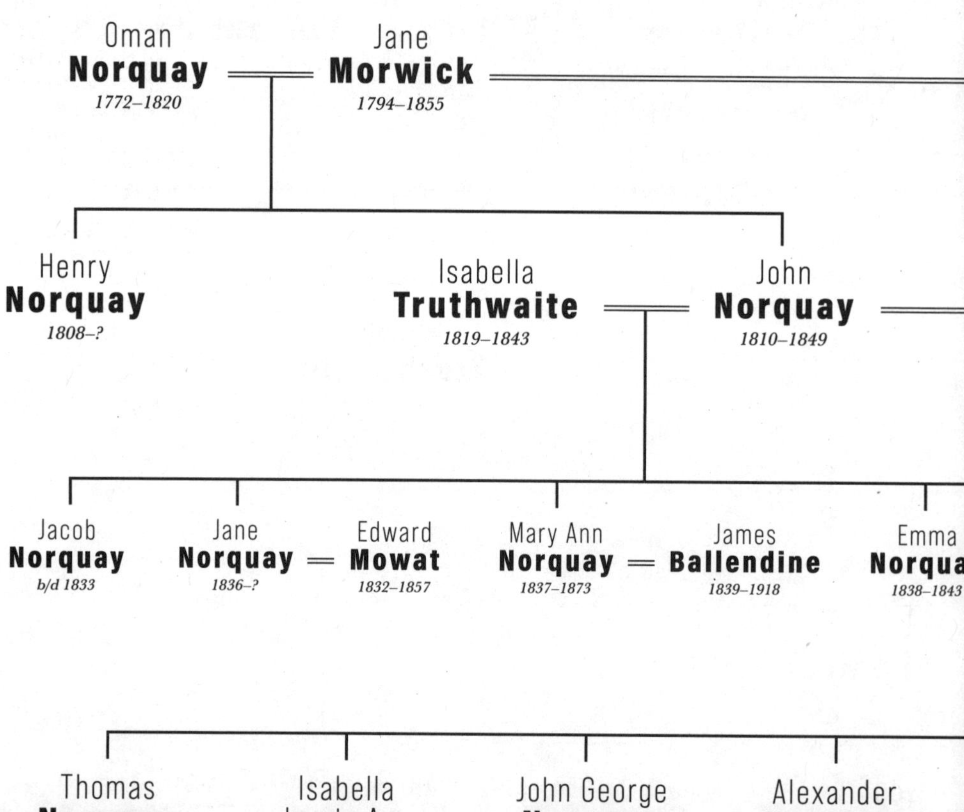

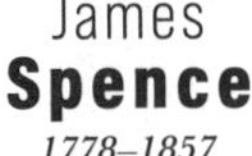

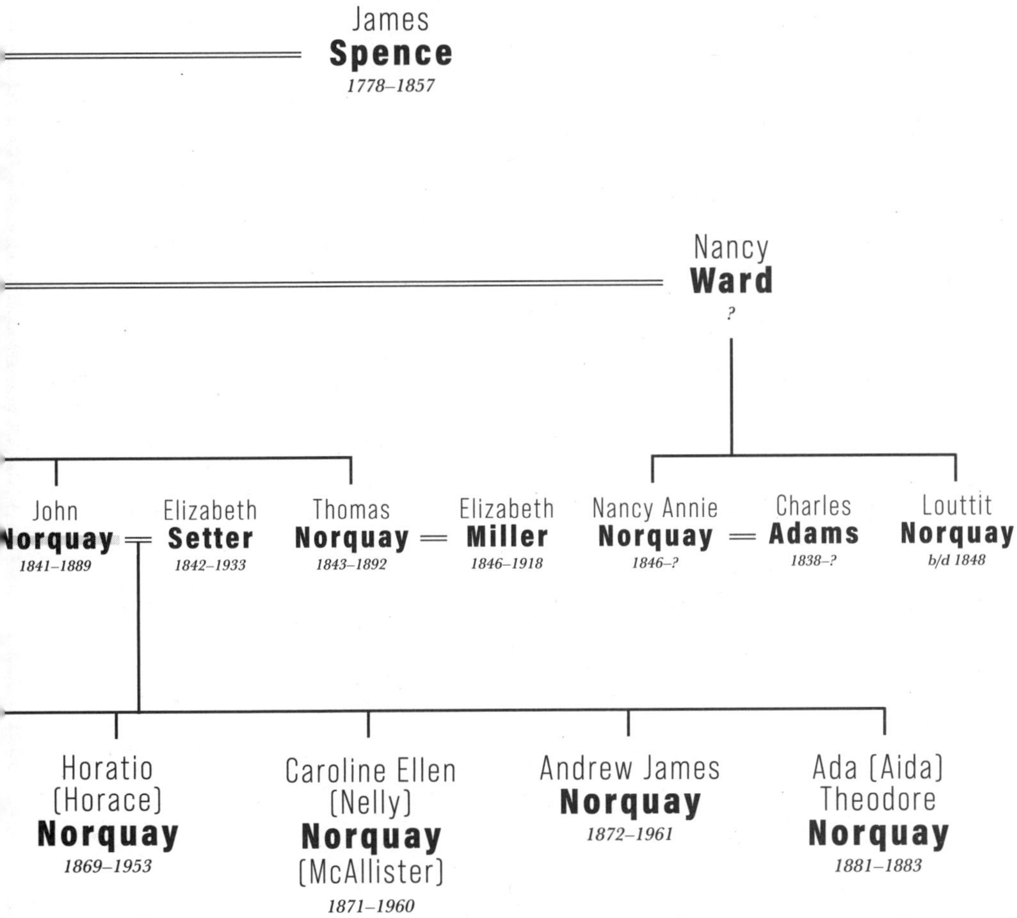
James
Spence
1778–1857
Nancy
Ward
?
John
orquay
1841–1889
Elizabeth
Setter
1842–1933
Thomas
Norquay
1843–1892
Elizabeth
Miller
1846–1918
Nancy Annie
Norquay
1846–?
Charles
Adams
1838–?
Louttit
Norquay
b/d 1848
Horatio
(Horace)
Norquay
1869–1953
Caroline Ellen
(Nelly)
Norquay
(McAllister)
1871–1960
Andrew James
Norquay
1872–1961
Ada (Aida)
Theodore
Norquay
1881–1883

The Honourable John NORQUAY

Introduction

The name of John Norquay is not instantly recognizable today, but in his time he was a force to be reckoned with in Canadian public life and a central figure in prairie society. In his early years, the middle decades of the nineteenth century, he farmed, fished, and hunted in the Red River Settlement, a majority Métis community in the northwestern interior of North America. He was Indigenous, was fluent in Cree (Inninumowin) and Saulteaux (Anishinaabemowin) as well as French and English, and he had some familiarity with Latin and Greek. Norquay possessed a remarkable memory and was unusually able in mathematics. His quick mind and good education enabled him to take jobs as a teacher and fur trader while he and his wife were raising eight children. He loved to dance, entertained his friends with jokes and stories, and revelled in card games and political debates. He participated in numerous business ventures, including land purchases, a gold mine, and a coal mine. When Manitoba entered the Canadian federation in 1870, he was elected by acclamation to the Legislative Assembly. A year later he was invited to join the cabinet as the leading political representative of about one-third of the provincial population, the "English," Rupert's Land–born portion. In 1878 he became premier of the province, an office he held for the next nine years while winning four general elections. In that role he was widely acknowledged to be a maker of policy, a source of stability, and the principal defender of the prairie west against the colonial inclinations of the federal government and "eastern Canada."

Norquay experienced fiercely partisan criticism within the province during his premiership but his sudden death brought a brief moment of generous recollection. Local commentators expressed admiration for his personality, his integrity, and even his relative poverty. This positive judgement became the Manitoba norm during the next two generations.[1] Almost all the popular treatments of the prairie past mention that Norquay was born in Red River, and most refer to Scottish or Orkney and "Indian" ancestry. His name was attached to a school, street, park, and government building in Winnipeg, a town in Saskatchewan, a district in Alberta, a school in Vancouver, and most famously a Rocky Mountain peak, Mount Norquay, overlooking the townsite in Banff National Park. Despite these memorial gestures, he has been forgotten by present-day citizens, along with almost every other political leader of his era.

Norquay has not fared well at the hands of national historians. In a book published in 1920, Chester Martin criticized Canada's "definite 'colonial' subordination" of Manitoba and said that Norquay had waged a "courageous but ineffectual attempt to cope with conditions that were too strong for him or perhaps any man."[2] Sympathy, in short, but not applause. George Stanley devoted little space to him in his 1936 survey of two resistance movements on the prairies, those of 1869–70 and 1885, but was generous in his estimate, saying that Canada might have avoided the latter conflict had John A. Macdonald taken Norquay into the federal cabinet.[3] The major provincial histories, including William Morton's authoritative *Manitoba*, defended Norquay's integrity and praised his advocacy of the province's interests while judging that his administration fell short of the ideal.[4]

Partisan Liberals tended to be less kind. *Winnipeg Free Press* editor John Dafoe's assessment, written in 1931 when Dafoe was a journalist of international stature, reflected opinions that he had gathered during his days as a cub reporter in the 1880s. He said that some of Norquay's ministerial appointments were unwise, his "great abilities were largely nullified by indolence and excessive good nature," and his government "got into serious financial difficulties."[5] With these damning phrases, Dafoe established an historical interpretation of Norquay hinting at faulty judgement, corruption, and laziness that has cropped up regularly in the intervening century.[6] In the following pages Dafoe's criticisms will be shown to be unfair and, in important ways, mistaken.

Many Canadians know of Norquay's contemporary, Louis Riel, the Métis leader who guided Manitoba into the Canadian federation in 1869–70 and then, in 1885, was hanged after leading a second armed uprising. Norquay was once described as Riel's alter-ego.[7] Both had "mixed" First Nation/European ancestry and both passed their childhood years in the Red River Settlement. Norquay's home parish was the Anglican St. Andrews, Riel's the Catholic St. Boniface and St. Vital. (The three parishes are now located within the capital region of greater Winnipeg.) Like Riel, Norquay had the advantage of more intensive formal schooling than most of his prairie contemporaries. Like Riel, he was bright, articulate, eager to lead, and able to command. As prominent figures in their communities, the two leaders faced the same challenge: how to ease their peoples' entry into a world very different from the one they had known.

To place the unknown John Norquay beside the famous Louis Riel is to raise questions about the vagaries of historical memory and collective remembering.[8] Where does Norquay, the so-called Métis premier, whom some might describe as Canada's most successful leader of mixed ancestry, fit in a narrative about his community's past? Why have Canadians forgotten him? Did he fail his people? Was he merely a collaborator, a quisling? The following pages will make clear that Riel and Norquay represented different ways of thinking about people of mixed ancestry, about "nation," and about Canada's confederation.

Norquay chose the path of negotiation and compromise in his political career and in his personal life. He rejected what he regarded as Louis Riel's extreme path, instead working within the economic and political constraints imposed on their homeland by big money and big government. Living through the phases of the west's transition from Indigenous to Canadian sovereignty, he managed to maintain his perch atop Manitoba politics while adjusting to a new nation-state and global capital movements.

Describing Norquay as a "statesman" might appear to be a stretch. I defend the claim on three grounds: first, in the belief that provincial leaders have a responsibility equal to that of their national counterparts for the conduct of public affairs in Canada, and Norquay stood tall among them during his years in power; second, because he developed an interpretation of peoples' history in prairie Canada that gave evidence of his intellectual capacities and his wisdom; and third, because he dealt wisely with "the state," an entity of crucial importance in the reshaping of his society. Norquay was the state's leading advocate among Manitobans during his lifetime. He led his Red River contemporaries, and then a much larger and more populous Manitoba, in adapting to its dictates.

Norquay's life is remarkable, made more so because so many letters written to and about him have survived. As many students of the times have commented, he lived in an age of correspondence and correspondents. After his death, almost all the missives that he received between the mid-1870s and the late 1880s were tied with ribbon in neat bundles by his secretaries, placed in a trunk, and given to his family, where they rested for half a century. The family then gave the trunk and its contents to a young historian, Ellen Cooke, who typed copies of many of the letters written by Norquay that were fading into oblivion on the pages of onionskin letterbooks. Cooke increased the significance of this collection in the following forty years through her own extensive research, including notes on her interviews with Norquay's descendants. Although she never completed a biography of Norquay, the collection that she tended has since been catalogued, as she requested in her will, and is now available in the Archives of Manitoba, complete with an invaluable index compiled by historian Lee Gibson.[9] The files contain about one thousand letters composed by Norquay and his secretaries as well as about four thousand letters from people in all walks of life, ranging from the prime minister in Ottawa to fur traders and farmers scattered across the west.

The Norquay archive establishes the limits of the life I have been able to recover. It contains no documents on the influence of his parents, his private worries, or his response to Indigenous and Christian faiths. Nor are women's experiences and his relationships with women represented in this collection. His children wrote to him from time to time, and some of their letters are extant, but not a single note from his wife has survived. In the public record, including newspaper stories and official papers, we see Norquay as a political actor. Buried in his private accounts are cheque stubs, bills, investment records, and a household's patterns of consumption. In short, the range of research materials is wide but it is not complete.

Biography, as a literary form, is said to be "the dominant narrative mode of our times."[10] It offers an accessible version of the past organized by milestones—school, marriage, children—that we all know well. Norquay is an ideal subject for a life story. In his day, he was known for his intellect, the range of his experience, the depth of his concern for others, and his capacity for enjoying life. Those details alone are sufficient to make an interesting biography. Beneath his life story lies a second narrative, the "times" portion of a "life and times" volume. Norquay lived during an era when the globe was transformed. The great developments he had to deal with included the emergence of disciplined political parties as ambitious politicians forged a competitive party system; the increasing power of investment bankers and entrepreneurs as their syndicates pursued profits around the globe; the maturation of a federal system of government in Canada as provinces and the central government worked out their respective roles; and the country's evolving response to Indigeneity, as "race," treaties, and the new category of "Métis" complicated national life. Norquay handled the provincial government's response to these big questions and influenced the thinking of his community in the process. As an individual in a Red River, Manitoba, Canadian, and British imperial setting, he merits sustained attention and reflection.

CHAPTER 1

"A Merry Prankish Youngster," 1841–58

John Norquay was born on a farm in the Red River Settlement, British North America, on 8 May 1841.[1] He grew up in a parish of river-lot farms, canoed and fished on the lakes and rivers, and travelled the plains on the great bison hunts. He learned very early that trade in furs and Sundays at church bound him to a wider world centred on Britain and the Bible as well as to the plains and parkland environment of the northwestern interior of the continent. He encountered people who spoke Bungee and Michif, Inninumowin (Cree) and Anishinaabemowin (Saulteaux/Ojibwa) and Dakota, French, Gaelic, and English.[2] He built rafts, crafted bows and arrows, snared rabbits, learned to handle a canoe, and helped his father with farm animals. He also survived an onslaught of epidemic diseases.

Like most of his childhood friends, John belonged to a family embedded in the North American fur trade. Both his father and his mother grew up in households connected to the Hudson's Bay Company (HBC). One of his grandfathers was an Orkneyman who had come to North America as a low-level HBC servant.[3] The other was an England-born officer in the company. Both of John's grandmothers had been born in the region. One of his great-grandmothers was English. The other three were born in northwestern British North America, descended from Europeans, Métis, Cree, and Saulteaux.[4]

John's birthplace, the family's river lot, was situated on the west bank of the Red River midway between St. Andrews Church and Lower Fort Garry (near present-day Lockport and a few kilometres north of present-day Winnipeg). The land had been sold to John's parents by the Hudson's Bay Company. Perhaps just as important as the sale contract was the permission granted by Peguis, the leading Saulteaux (Anishinaabe) chief in the district. According to Norquay family lore, the chief had given permission to Thomas Truthwaite, patriarch of John's mother's family, to settle there: "Peguis jammed a spear into the ground and said anyone interfering with Thomas would be dealt with that way."[5]

The Norquay family lived beside rather than within the communities of Cree and Saulteaux peoples. Next to the family's small log house was a burial mound where, during John's adult years, Indigenous artifacts were unearthed.[6] The discovery made plain what John knew implicitly: this district had been occupied by many generations of Indigenous peoples. The broader settlement that formed around the forks of the Assiniboine and Red Rivers in the first half of the nineteenth century was built upon peaceable relations among Indigenous and incoming groups.[7]

In 1832 John's father, about twenty-two years of age, married Isabella Truthwaite, about thirteen.[8] Their first child, Jacob, born in 1833, died within a year. The elder Norquay had signed by then a five-year contract with the Hudson's Bay Company to serve as a labourer. He was assigned to Norway House, 400 kilometres north of the Red River Settlement in the forests just beyond the north end of Lake Winnipeg, where he earned seventeen pounds per year (about eighty-five dollars in the Canadian or American currency of that era). A mention of him in a post journal in August 1834 noted that the general labourers, all named and presumably all on annual contracts, of whom he was one, did various jobs: three were making clay chimneys in the buildings, one baked bread at the outdoor oven, and two, including Norquay, had been dispatched with six unnamed Cree labourers to a nearby grassy area to cut hay.[9] In late September he was part of a crew of six who took axes and saws to a "wooding tent" located in a stand of spruce and pine some kilometres away. There they camped for several weeks while they felled trees, limbed them, and tore off the bark in long strips. Having hauled the tree trunks out of the woods with the aid of an ox, they loaded them into capacious York boats and sailed back to the post. Norquay returned to the deep forest with a similar crew and lived for nearly three winter months in hide tents with pine bough floors. The men cut trees, squared timber, and sawed boards that would be used to refurbish the Norway House establishment.[10]

The rhythm of the year was shaped by the seasons and the various tasks that Norquay shared with Métis employees hired on contracts, and crews of local Métis and Cree labourers paid on a casual basis. Isabella probably joined him at Norway House a year or two later. They had two more children during their stay, Jane in 1836 and Emma in 1838. Both were baptized in St. Andrews Church when the family made summer expeditions to the Red River Settlement.

The elder Norquay was expected to have a number of practical skills, including fishing, haying, lumbering, fur packing, and animal husbandry. He studied how to construct log buildings weatherproofed with clay daubing. He learned how to survive weeks at a time in a forest camp, whether in the searing heat and insect-ridden days of high summer or in the snowdrifts and ice of deep winter. He helped to raise garden plants and prepare wild food for the table. Above all, he dealt with a range of colleagues, Métis and Cree, who cut hay and hauled logs and worked in the garden with him. He was part of a closely knit, diverse community of nearly 100 souls, including thirty-five male employees of various ranks led by formidable, well-educated Scottish Chief Factor Donald Ross, and fifty-three women and children. Norquay spoke several languages, refined the many skills that fit under the general heading of manual labour, accepted the challenges presented by climate and resources, and participated in the life of a growing family.

There is little information beyond entries in census and church registers about young John's mother, Isabella Truthwaite Norquay. It is clear from church records that she married as a young teen. The births of her children are recorded in a baptismal register. Her presence on the farm is apparent in several censuses. Beyond those sparse accounts, two letters from her grandmother offer the only other insights into the family's history. In October 1843, Jane Vincent wrote from Moose Factory on James Bay to her daughter, Elizabeth Truthwaite (Isabella's mother), in the Red River Settlement. She told the family of the deaths of several acquaintances, the success of Elizabeth's brother in London, and the travels of famed surgeon and explorer Dr. John Rae. She also noted that "Mooshoom," an elder (in Cree), was "going on a Fall Trip to his own Country." The letter made special mention of Elizabeth's daughter (John's mother), twenty-five-year-old Isabella, whom Jane knew to be ill, and added the hope that the still-young mother "may long ere this be reinstated and she has risen from a Bed of Sickness, and able again to attend to her family Affairs."[11]

John and Isabella had returned to the settlement in 1838 to take up the land that they had purchased from the Hudson's Bay Company a year before.[12] Their fourth child, Mary Ann, joined her two sisters in 1839; John was born in 1841 and Thomas in 1843. Thus, in the first eleven years of marriage, Isabella and her husband had six children. Their 100-acre farmstead was coupled with another lot directly across the river on the east bank that supplied the farm with wood for fuel, fencing, and lumber. The land transactions were entered in the company books as sales, not as free grants. The household soon comprised a house, barn, stable, and eleven animals: a mare, two oxen, three cows, two calves, and three pigs. Crops had been planted on four cultivated acres. All the family members, children as well as parents, contributed their labour to an enterprise that produced milk, meat, and cereals. Young John, like his siblings, was acquiring the knowledge and skills by which he in turn could become a farmer.[13]

The census taker recorded in 1840 in the column for "country of birth" that the elder John Norquay was a "Native," a category that distinguished him from European-born residents of the settlement. This designation hinted at distinctions among the population that cropped up more frequently in later years. One of these distinctions was evident to everyone and helped to create social hierarchies. John, like all the children along River Road, grew up with two versions of English. He heard and understood the standard English of the parish school and church, but he also spoke with a local accent and rhythm and learned local words. His version of this "people's language" came to be known as Bungee, a distinctive dialect, a variant of Scots English, Inninumowin (Cree), and Anishinaabemowin (Ojibwa), with a little French, Norn, and Gaelic added. The vocabulary, rhythm, and accent of this unique "English" became not only a prominent part of the Red River Settlement but also a lingua franca that travelled across the far-flung HBC trading territory of northwestern North America.[14]

Languages did not separate groups in quite the same fashion as they do today. John learned to speak Cree and Saulteaux as a child and continued to use words and phrases from those Algonquian languages throughout his life. Archbishop Taché, writing to thank Premier Norquay for his assistance in the 1880s, ended with a carefully inscribed phrase in Cree: "ki nanaskomitin," meaning "thank you from the bottom of my heart."[15] Charles Adams, who married Nancy (Annie) Norquay, John's sister, opened his letters to John with the salutation "Dear Neestaw" ("brother-in-law" in Cree) and once sent him a telegram in Cree: "Ke nanaskomitinan mistapeneya mena kesee," meaning "I am grateful for and I really miss your sister."[16] Although Adams used a dialect of English as his first language, he told John that the newest Adams family member was beginning to speak and, like the baby's three-year-old brother, was doing so in Cree, the language of the community surrounding the HBC post at The Pas.[17] Mixes of Cree, Saulteaux, and European were represented in parishioners' family trees, in short, and in their conversations.

The sound of Red River Bungee differed in several ways from that of standard English. In his early years John said sawl (shawl), pitser (picture), wis (wish), soot (shoot), and dzudz (judge). He spoke in a lilting rhythm, a cadence stemming in part from placing equal stress on all syllables, as in kunn-oo (canoe) or ban-nock (an unleavened bread). His vocabulary included many words that never made it into English dictionaries or did so with other definitions. John shared the local dislike of "skitters," the term applied to western kingbirds (not mosquitoes), a species known for harassing other birds. He loved the excitement of night-time "scooping," which took place when sturgeon, jackfish, and pickerel moved from Lake Winnipeg to spawn in the Red River and settlers built fires on the bank to lure them into nets looped on the ends of long poles. His speech marked him as different, for example, from the English-born children of the Anglican bishop who became his classmates.[18]

Although John started out in life speaking the Bungee dialect of English, he picked up enough Cree, Saulteaux, and Dakota in these years to enable him to conduct trade or conversation in any of those three languages when he was an adult. In his teen years, he acquired some of the vocabulary and accent of southern England. His distinctive Bungee did not disappear, and his ability to speak in the dialect was mentioned by several colleagues in later years. Throughout his life his family employed Cree terms for relatives: "mooshoom" for an honoured elder, "neestaw" for a brother-in-law. One of the family stories about John as an adult turned on the Cree term "appichiquani."

His five-year-old niece was turning somersaults on a summer's day, and the premier, by then a huge man, tried to join her. When he failed to duplicate her feat, she laughed at his attempted "appifanie," a mispronunciation that provoked laughter and was handed down through the generations.[19]

The pivotal moments in John Norquay's first decade involved epidemics. Although the phenomena were not well understood in the Red River Settlement, settlers perceived the passage of deadly illnesses and feared their effects. There had been only a few disastrous epidemics in this relatively isolated region between 1600 and 1820, the period when European diseases first assaulted North America's Indigenous populations. As late as the mid-1830s, the effects of a dangerous smallpox epidemic in the northwestern interior were somewhat reduced by HBC officials, who imported the vaccine and ensured that hunting families in a few districts were vaccinated and rendered immune. There was no such antidote for the flu and whooping cough and similar lung-based "crowd diseases," let alone for deadly dysentery. What is more, such diseases were entering populations that had not yet acquired resistance to them.

The Norquay family felt the blows of these epidemics as severely as any other family in the settlement. John's mother, Isabella, just twenty-four years old, died in October 1843 and was buried in the cemetery at what was then called Grand Rapids, Red River Settlement. Three weeks later Emma, aged six, followed her. To judge from the timing, the cause was a virulent form of scarlet fever that arrived in the settlement in the summer and killed more than 100 people, many of them children. The presiding HBC officer commented that the illness hit the most crowded homes, those possessing the fewest resources, especially hard.[20]

John's father remarried in October 1845. His union with Nancy Ward, daughter of a freeman or independent hunter-trader and an anglophone of mixed ancestry, was conducted at the Rapids (St. Andrews) Church by Reverend William Cockran.[21] The elder Norquay was sufficiently literate to sign his name in the marriage register, and Nancy entered an x. Their first daughter, Nancy (later known as Annie), was baptized in September 1846, and another baby, "Louttit Norquay, son of John and Nancy, settlers," arrived on 1 October 1848.[22] Three weeks later, on 25 October, an entry in the church register recorded the infant Louttit's burial. The family's survival rate should be noted: three of the eight children died in infancy or early childhood.[23]

Although some family memories suggest that John Sr. was unable to care for all the children after his first wife died in 1843, the census offers convincing evidence that the family stayed together on the farm. In 1846–47, the enumerator visited the household and recorded that John Norquay, born in Rupert's Land, a Protestant, was living with his wife and "2 sons under 16, 3 daughters under 15." The boys would have been John and Thomas, the girls Jane and Mary Ann and their recently arrived half-sister, Annie. And his wife would have been the former Nancy Ward. The Norquay household possessed a house, a barn, a stable, two and a half acres of cultivated land, and fifteen animals, including horses, cows, and pigs. The 1849 census noted the addition of a second stable and a few more animals, including a horse, some pigs, and five sheep. They now cultivated five acres with a plow and harrow. For transportation, they owned three carts and a canoe.[24]

Several months after the visit of the census taker, disease struck the Norquay family yet again. John's father was buried on 10 June 1849. At thirty-nine years, his life was even shorter than that of Oman, John's Orcadian grandfather (1773–1820).[25]

Young John, then eight years old, probably left his stepmother and the St. Andrews farm after his father's death. Accompanied by his older sister, Jane, then thirteen, he moved to the home of his anglophone grandmother, a woman of mixed European and Indigenous ancestry known in the settlement as Widow Spence and in the family as Granny Spence. The other set of grandparents, the Truthwaites, whose land lay farther down the river and closer to Lower Fort Garry, probably took in Tom, Mary Ann, and Annie. The siblings lived a substantial distance from each other—about twenty kilometres—but the two households did not lose contact. John's relationship with sister Annie and brother Tom, in particular, continued to be close, then and throughout their lives.[26]

St. John's Collegiate School: "God Has Created All of One Blood"

Norquay might have attended St. Andrews parish school briefly in the late 1840s, and after moving to Granny Spence's house he certainly went to the junior school in St. John's parish in the early 1850s. The small log buildings were crammed with students, sixty in St. Andrews in 1852, sixty in St. John's in 1853. Books, paper, and equipment were in short supply. Still, the men who served as teachers were able to introduce the elements of literacy and the church's view of a good life. The Anglican bishop, David Anderson, who arrived in the settlement in the fall of 1849, was delighted with the quality of both students and teachers. He placed church teachings at the centre of the curriculum and expected the children to learn how their community fit into the wider world. His report on an opening day at St. Andrews school illustrated his priorities: "We formed in singing some hymns, after which I read a portion of God's word, Proverbs III, and addressed the children from it. After a short prayer, we commenced the actual business of the school, inspecting first the beautiful maps and examining [the students] . . . in their knowledge of Geography." The pupils were enthusiastic, Anderson reported, and the teacher, Mr. Kirkby, was "a great favorite with both parents & children." Anderson concluded that the parish schools provided "a solid, substantial, and scriptural education."[27]

Red River students typically stayed in class for just a few seasons because the cost of tuition, added to the lost labour at home, was more than most families could bear. Norquay escaped that fate because, at both schools, he excelled in academic competitions and encountered excellent teachers. Like Kirkby at St. Andrews, Peter Jacobs, his teacher at St. John's, was a local star, having graduated from Red River schools and studied in London under the sponsorship of the (Anglican) Church Missionary Society. Bishop Anderson testified to the school's excellence after attending an "admirable examination" in 1853. He said that the progress of the sixty students in Jacobs's care "was such as quite to astonish me." Norquay, then twelve years old, was almost certainly one of these admirable students.[28]

Bishop Anderson hoped to develop a group of clergy as well as secular leaders in northwest North America. To that end, he founded St. John's Collegiate School and recruited the children of fur trade officers and wealthy merchants who could afford to enrol their children in an institution offering a superior level of education. They paid a set fee that covered tuition, meals, and "Bedroom, service, and Laundry." This enterprise underwrote a second category of student, exceptional local boys who excelled in their studies. To identify these potential scholars, Anderson encouraged competitive examinations in the parish schools that would "stimulate both masters and pupils to exertion." He ensured that in each year between 1850 and roughly 1857 or 1858, when the Collegiate School was in full operation, two of the best students in the parish schools received scholarships at St. John's. An unknown number of young men, perhaps thirty or forty, attended the school in these years, of whom about sixteen received scholarships or "exhibitions."[29]

The Collegiate School differed from its parish counterparts in both nature and ambition. It comprised a mismatched collection of log, frame, and stone buildings on the banks of the Red River at the heart of St. John's parish. Its main building, a huge, rambling, two-storey frame structure topped by a cupola, contained classrooms, offices, and rooms for student boarders. It was adjacent to the Anglican cathedral and Bishop's Court, the house where Anderson and his family resided during their fourteen years in the Red River Settlement. The school's facilities were respectable. The main rooms were heated by wood stoves. In the winter a servant lit fires in the students' bedroom fireplaces. The library contained a large and growing collection of books, nearly 1,000 volumes by the mid-1850s, ranging from religious works drawn from Anderson's own collection such as *Essays on the Church* to works on the wider world, including Robertson's *Scotland*, McFarlane's *Mountains*, Oliphant's *Black Sea*, Strive's *Key to Uncle Tom's Cabin*, and *Gospels in Syllabic Cree*, a writing variant that had just been developed in the HBC territory.[30]

The school day was crammed with lessons and silent study sessions, a schedule that probably varied little for the next half century. A Cree boy who attended St. John's College in a later decade said that he rose at 6:30, studied until 8:00, then ate breakfast with all the other boys and teachers, followed by prayers in the chapel. He engaged in classes and individual study until 12:30, when dinner was served. Classes resumed at 1:30, followed by an hour of individual study from 3:30, and then free time for "a game of football, or walk till tea time (5:45); after tea, I go into one or two of the students' rooms for a half-hour, and then go into my room and study; at 10, go to prayers (short) after prayers go back to my books, and study till 11; then retire for the night." Weekends were a little more relaxed and included time for visits outside the college as well as for church services.[31]

In today's terms St. John's resembled an advanced secondary school, not a university or college but much more than a parish school. Bishop Anderson claimed that "the instruction is fully equal to that of most English Preparatory Schools."[32] A distinguished graduate reinforced this judgement half a century later during a visit to Winnipeg. By then master of Corpus Christi College at the University of Cambridge, Robert Townley Caldwell told the *Free Press* that "I got my early education in St. John's College from Bishop Anderson.

From him I learned to read my first Greek play and to solve my first quadratic equation. When we went back to England I found myself grounded by Bishop Anderson.... [W]hen I went to Cambridge, I got a fellowship at my college, Corpus Christi." At least five St. John's Collegiate School graduates went to the University of Cambridge and one to the University of Toronto. Other classmates of Norquay's—indeed most of the young men, several dozen in total—made important contributions in the prairie west.[33]

In leading the school, David Anderson saw himself as a pioneer of the British Empire. His years in the Red River Settlement coincided with an exceptional moment in the history of the Church of England. Anderson's diocese of Rupert's Land (the HBC territory), was founded in 1849 in the same era as Freetown (British West Africa, now Sierra Leone, 1849), Victoria (now Hong Kong, 1849), Natal (southeast Africa, 1850) and Wellington and Nelson (New Zealand, 1858). Travelling alongside British military and economic power, and galvanized by the competition of Roman Catholics, Anglican leaders at mid-century canvassed wealthy donors in rapidly expanding imperial metropolises to fund parishes, build churches, and found schools. In his first formal address in Rupert's Land, Anderson celebrated "a glowing thought, that the Church of the British Isles should span the world!" The life and energy of the church "must come from Britain. England must still be regarded by us as the heart and centre of life." He asked in a later address, "Is not Britain's a moral weight among the nations—the weight of Christian character and Christian influence: Is not her greatest glory the guardianship of the truth of God—is not her high vocation its dissemination throughout the world?"[34]

The bishop managed the school with the aid of his sister, Margaret, a candid, starchy, and practical administrator. She spoke in a no-nonsense way, knew how to handle the details of a large establishment, and possessed strong views on a proper life. She described having to "civilize & reform" HBC officers' children, who might not have been able to speak English, "who have grown up without the slightest notion of restraint or order," and who have been "all as wild & untamed as the Buffalo on the prairies."[35]

The bishop shared his sister's views on morality and deportment. In one of his formal addresses to clergy and settlers, he expressed concern about what he saw as looseness in the settlers' living arrangements. All family members should not sleep in the same room, he argued, and to separate them would be a matter of "comfort" that contributed to "the moral well-being of the household." Anderson criticized boisterous weddings attended by the entire settlement as "the prolific source of much evil." He probably talked to everyone, clergymen and settlers and students, about church matters, the British Empire, and the future of the settlement, subjects that recurred frequently in his many published addresses. He was more informal, less given to scolding, than his sister and was beloved among the students and those to whom he ministered. One of Norquay's classmates, Benjamin Mackenzie, described Anderson as "a truly loving and lovable man who quietly busied himself in initiating plans and efforts for the future progress and development of the Diocese."[36]

The most profound and complex lessons delivered by Bishop Anderson, and observed by Norquay, concerned matters of "race." There is no way now to tell what the student made of the teacher's words on this theme, but it is possible to be clear about the bishop's point of view. Anderson did not accept the notion of separate human races, a view that he ascribed to the Cree and Saulteaux whom he met in the Red River Settlement. Rather, like evangelical leaders such as Reverend Henry Venn, he believed that "God has created all of one blood." Anderson said in his first charge to the clergy at Red River that "we all behold the Indian, we gaze upon him as a fellow-creature, possessing the same immortality with ourselves, we notice him as he passes, and he gives and receives the usual salutation of his countrymen. He proceeds onwards, and thinks that God has created different races for different ends, and that an insuperable barrier divides the White from the Red man." This view Anderson rejected completely. However, while presuming humankind's single origin, he was concerned that language issues—the words of the faith, the print medium by which they were communicated, the implicit rules embedded in different cultures—made it difficult to convey the church's teachings to Indigenous peoples.[37]

Anderson suggested, nevertheless, that the goal of the Anglican mission should be to ensure the preservation of Indigenous cultures as well as to convert people to Christianity and provide access to the rewards of a "civilized life." Although he saw the Cree and Saulteaux as equal to the British in their humanity and potential abilities, he believed that they had to acquire the tools of literacy and to deal squarely with holy writ before they could develop the "depth and solidity of character"—what he called "spiritual progress"—that undergirded a reliable and consistent faith. The difference between Indigenous peoples and newcomers from Europe, in his view, rested on the fact that the former lived in a migratory, oral culture, whereas the latter possessed fixed places of residence and an enduring—because text-based—Christian faith. Indigenous society had to rely on speech and memory alone to communicate its insights, whereas the British church possessed print that preserved, sharpened, and disseminated its understanding of what it believed to be Christianity's unique and transcendent truths.[38]

Anderson's estimation of the local Cree and Saulteaux did not apply to Norquay and his Bungee/English-speaking countrymen of mixed ancestry. Whereas the "pure natives" (Venn's phrase) required special attention, church officials taught that the people whom they called "half-breeds" or "half-caste" possessed, or could readily develop, what Venn described as "mature Christian character." Although Bishop Anderson recognized that the English-speaking parishioners of mixed ancestry belonged to a social category distinct from that of Europeans, he advocated on their behalf and defended their abilities against European presumptions of superiority. Young John Norquay, in this view, possessed the keys to what Anderson saw as "civilization," including talent sufficient to take on roles that a European might fill and literacy sufficient to grasp biblical, classical, and contemporary literature. Anderson assumed that Norquay could acquire fixed property and achieve the mature Christian character that, in the view of the church, might flow from such attainments.[39]

Anderson knew of the abilities of Norquay and placed him in the company of the best students in the parish schools. In February 1854, in a letter to former top student James Ross, who had moved from the Red River schools to the University of Toronto, the bishop picked out young John as a leader in the next crop of scholars: "I shall give the prizes at Jacobs' School next week, when I intend to allude to your [James Ross's] success, & that of A. Isbister [then gaining public attention in England].—John Norquay is by a good deal the head boy. Next to him comes David Tait." Not yet thirteen, John had reached one of those moments in life when crucial choices are made: should he stay in school for a few more years? Or should he take advantage of his strength and wits by heading out immediately to the hunt, the trade, and manual labour?[40]

Norquay won a scholarship in 1854. The prize probably enabled him to live in the St. John's residence. According to a contemporary, it also required him to care for the horse belonging to Thomas Cochrane, one of the school's masters. The award included free tuition for three years, plus ten pounds sterling annually as pocket money, and a seat at a separate table with the teacher, "where much better fare was provided than could reasonably be accorded the ordinary school boy." The total value of the scholarship was said to be thirty pounds per year (or $150), a large sum in that era and nearly double John's father's yearly wage at Norway House twenty years earlier. The generosity of Reverend Cochrane and Bishop Anderson enabled John to receive an education typically reserved for the most privileged children in his community.[41]

The schooling changed the course of his life. For the next three or four years, John followed an advanced curriculum that included classical languages (both Latin and Greek) as well as French, three different types of mathematics, including calculus, and a range of histories. John moved on from the parish school's slates and chalk to quill pens. He worked on translations of various classical texts, including the Greek testament, three or four excerpts from the works of Greek historian Herodotus, three plays by the Athenian tragedian Euripides, and works by Virgil, the Roman poet and scholar. His program emphasized the classics partly because of university admission requirements and partly because, as Anderson told one parent, "another language quickens the powers for all other studies."[42] A note that survives in Norquay's papers, one that John might have written himself, records that he "plodded through . . . Caesar Sallust Ovid Horace Virgil Xenophon Homer & Sophocles."[43]

A passing comment in Bishop Anderson's letter to the London office of the Church Missionary Society in the summer of 1855 suggested that Norquay was doing well: "We had lately a most satisfactory Examination of the Collegiate School, at which our good Governor Caldwell, & Judge Johnson were present." Norquay would have participated in this day of examinations. At the start of the next school year, Anderson told James Ross, then studying at the University of Toronto, "I have now a very good French Class: Norquay, Budd [Henry Budd Jr.], Archy [Anderson], Boyd, D[avid] Tait, & David [Anderson]" (David and Archy were the bishop's sons); "they will be very good Grammarians." Given that this would have been the class of 1855–56, and that Norquay had at least a three-year scholarship, he might have continued his studies until the spring of 1857 or even 1858, when he turned seventeen. With the others, he took a program that attempted to attain, as Anderson later commented, a "collegiate school level" in mathematics and classics.[44]

It is impossible to know precisely what Norquay took from Anderson's example. Because the scholarship students were few in number and shared a lunch table as well as daily lessons and chapel services, they probably spoke frequently with their teachers informally as well as in formal classroom settings. Several of the young men recalled in later years that they were very impressed by the bishop's oratory. His chatty letters suggest that Anderson was close to his students and informal in his relations with colleagues. He was said to have "a soft pleasing voice and a gentle manner." Both became part of Norquay's personal style in later life. There was no question about the clergyman's loyalty to the Church of England; Norquay never wavered in his Anglican Church membership and regularly said a blessing at meals and observed family prayers on Sunday evenings. The bishop was British in every fibre of his being; to judge from John's later statements, the young student absorbed this perspective and adopted aspects of it as a supplement to his Red River experience.[45] Bishop Anderson hoped to alter many Red River customs and campaigned consistently for such reforms; Norquay would have heard and pondered these strictures. Like other Anglican parishioners in the Red River Settlement, he recognized that the bishop preferred a way of life somewhat different from the one that had developed in his little community during the preceding half century.

As in any such school, there were moments of discovery, of drudgery, and of fun. One of Norquay's classmates recalled the excitement of tobogganing, a favourite recreation in winter, when a group of young boys packed onto a sled and rode at high speed down the steep bank of the Red River and out onto the ice. The boys skated on a nearby swamp in winter, helped to plant and cultivate vegetables in the collegiate garden in spring, and picked berries at the swamp edge in summer.[46]

One might question whether Norquay adopted the school's teachings as his model for life. The experience of one of his classmates demonstrated, if any such example was necessary, that students reached their own conclusions about a good life. Peter Erasmus joined the Collegiate School as a mature student in 1855. Fully twenty years of age, bigger and stronger and more worldly than his classmates, he had been teaching Cree students at The Pas and Nepowewin (Nipawin) for several years. Bishop Anderson hoped that Erasmus would become a missionary. The young man reluctantly agreed to study at the Red River school, but he did not let its rules control his behaviour. He loved dances, played the fiddle, and on several evenings stole away from the residence with "a chum" to attend parties in the settlement. He acknowledged that many of his classmates did not share his wish to rebel: they "were fun-loving friends, who looked upon the work of the church as a great opportunity, and were happy and contented."[47]

Norquay could not have missed the critical views that Erasmus held of the English churchmen, but did he share them? Many years later one of the legislator's classmates recalled that Norquay was "a merry prankish youngster and that his schoolmates had coined a name to fit his disposition, 'ROGWEECE,' probably the local (Bungee) pronunciation of the word Roguish."[48] The image fits but it is unlikely that Norquay was the chum who ducked out of residence in the evenings with Erasmus. Given his demeanour in his adult years, including Bible reading and prayers within the family, membership in church congregations, and consistent service on church committees, Norquay identified as a Christian and an Anglican. He readily associated his successes in life with Bishop Anderson and St. John's Collegiate School. When he left the school, probably at Easter in 1858, he moved into another clergyman's parish and taught the same Bible-and church-based lessons that he had begun as a child just a few years before. Unlike Erasmus, Norquay did not leave the school in a huff. He understood that he possessed the qualifications listed by the bishop as essential for full citizenship in both state and church.

St. James Parish School

In January 1858, the Reverend William Henry Taylor of St. James parish, Red River Settlement, reported to the London office of the Society for the Propagation of the Gospel (SPG, Church of England) that he had encountered a problem and solved it: "During the last year, we had a Daily School only part of the year & at this present time it is not in operation. We cannot raise a Master's Salary.—But I trust we shall start again soon—and that with an efficient Teacher." Three months later he had better news: "Our daily school has reopened today under the teaching of a young man from the coll[egia]te school[.] I hope it may be carried on with greater advantage and profit than formerly. I think there is every reason to expect it." The young man was John Norquay.[49]

At seventeen, Norquay was taking his first steps into adult employment. He was accepting a new and demanding assignment, moving to a relatively unfamiliar district, and living in yet another clergy-run environment. It was not unusual in that era to begin teaching at such a young age, but the job would impose constraints. His supervisor, William Taylor, worked closely with Bishop Anderson, so one can assume that Norquay's appointment came with the bishop's blessing.

St. James was one of the first settlements of English-speaking farmers to be established west of Upper Fort Garry. By the late 1850s it extended eight kilometres along the Assiniboine River and contained a population of 500, including Europeans, French Canadians, Cree, Saulteaux, and Métis. The Anglican congregation numbered between 100 and 200, of whom 32 were adult communicants. The parish had an Anglican school, an Anglican church building (the log structure stands in Winnipeg to this day), and an "efficient library." Taylor explained to the secretary of the London SPG in mid-decade that the school served "very young students" and that an adult evening class met on two evenings per week in winter. The school was short of supplies, he said: "For proper class books, slates, pencils, copybooks &c &c we feel a great and an increasing want."[50] The new teacher's pay would present a problem because money was not easily wrung from St. James households.

The day class was about twenty strong, split equally between boys and girls. Although Taylor was not enthusiastic about these young charges, he probably dropped in on the school from time to time to provide encouragement and give a lesson.[51] On a quiet winter Sunday when Norquay might have been residing with him, the clergyman wrote that "what is so lamentable is the want of solidity in their [the students'] character generally. They are too flighty fickle and inconstant."[52] Whether Norquay found the students difficult was not recorded.

In the year that he lived in St. James, Norquay learned a great deal about the rhythm of the settlement calendar. No longer viewing the world through the filters of the Collegiate School, he met the full range of Red River citizenry for the first time as an adult. He arrived just as the snow was melting in spring and had to listen to Taylor's complaints about the wet, muddy conditions. The congregation in these weeks was smaller since the typical "Indian moccasin" (Taylor's term) became so soaked and cold that women chose not to go to church for fear that they would "lay the seeds of consumption [tuberculosis]." The month of May was farm and garden time, and by early June Norquay was dealing with heat, humidity, and swarms of mosquitoes. The quiet was punctuated one extraordinary day when the "rasping screech" of hundreds of ox-drawn Red River carts assaulted the residents for hours as hunters and their families filed westward through St. James on the way to the plains bison hunt.[53] This was also the moment when brigades departed from the Red River Settlement by water for York Factory to the north and, a relatively new phenomenon, headed overland to St. Paul, Minnesota, on the Mississippi River in the United States.

Summer was dedicated to agriculture in the parish, at least for those who had remained behind when the hunt brigade and the transport teams departed. By August the young women were harvesting Taylor's barley with a sickle, binding it, and standing the bundles in stooks. In some years the parish endured a plague of grasshoppers, a "sadly disgusting sight" according to Taylor. The creatures swarmed through the settlement, "getting into clothes and houses, holding onto the outside walls and ravaging all before them." What is worse, they deposited eggs that carried the promise of another year of disaster to follow. In the late summer of 1857, just months before Norquay started to teach in St. James, Taylor wrote that "it is reported that miles and miles of the plains are quite blackened with devastations and that at Pembina they were, in places, 3 inches thick."[54]

Autumn often brought beautiful weather and dangers of a different kind. The clergymen reported that, every fall, settlers set fields alight to remove old grass. Almost inevitably, the fires leaped the bounds of the backfires. Taylor described the practice as "a barbarous plan & full of danger to the homesteads & terror to the inhabitants. In some cases it was observed that the burning fragments made extensive leaps—50 or 60 yards—setting on fire the dry grass & stubble in every direction."[55]

Winter slowed work in the settlement, but only a blizzard could shut down the regular round of activities. The hunters typically returned in November, carrying tallow and fresh meat. Soon enough, the arrival of snow ensured that the screech of wooden axle on wooden cartwheel was replaced by the smooth glide of sleighs. New Year was marked by special services in the churches and by dances and weddings in the houses.[56] The season could be bitterly cold but also beautiful. Bishop Anderson described his travel to the new stone church at St. Andrews on the day of its consecration in 1850:

> The sight on the River was a very pretty one, and if it could have [been] witnessed from the [river]bank by friends at home, it would I am sure have yielded them much gratification. We were quite a cavalcade—the [horse-drawn] carioles travelled [on the river ice] one after another from this end of the Settlement and as we approached the Church many more fell into the line. At times the sun shone brightly on the pure surface of the snow, and caused a dazzling reflection—and all this was heightened by the pleasing sound of the bells on many of the horses.[57]

Norquay was learning much more about the diversity of the settlement. He knew his own St. Andrews, the most populous of the mainly English/Bungee-speaking farming parishes (over 1,000 residents in 1849), but he knew less about the Michif/francophone parish of St. François Xavier (over 900 residents), a few kilometres west of his new home in St. James. Taken together the two parishes contained the largest fractions of the community, accounting for nearly 40 percent of the population. Norquay had probably travelled many times through the Cree and Saulteaux parish of St. Peter's (just under 500 Cree and 100 Saulteaux) and the largely Scots community of Kildonan (around 300), but he was less frequently among the Michif/French-speaking residents of St. Boniface, St. Norbert, and Ste. Anne. He certainly knew the Hudson's Bay Company and must have strolled within its two imposing garrisons, Upper Fort Garry and Lower Fort Garry. According to the 1849 census, the total population of the settlement, which now extended 160 kilometres from the American boundary to Lake Winnipeg, and over 100 kilometres from Ste. Anne in the east to Portage la Prairie in the west, was around 5,000. There were 2,100 Protestants in the settlement, 2,500 Roman Catholics, among whom were some Canadians (largely French speaking), some retired HBC officers, some British army pensioners, and from 1857 to 1861 the soldiers of the Royal Canadian Rifles, a British army regiment.[58]

It was a relatively quiet and peaceful community, an extended ribbon of farm lots bordering the Red and Assiniboine Rivers. Governor Alexander Ramsey of Minnesota described it as

> a long suburban village [with] . . . spires of several large churches peeping above the foliage . . . whitewashed school houses . . .

> gentlemen's houses of pretentious dimensions and grassy lawns and elaborate fencing . . . an English Bishop's Parsonage, with a Boarding or High School nearby; and over there a Catholic Bishop's massive Cathedral, with a Convent of the Sisters of Charity attached; whilst the two large stone forts . . . helped to give additional picturesqueness to the scene. I had almost forgotten to mention, what is after all the most prominent and peculiar feature of that singular landscape . . . the numerous wind mills, nearly twenty in all, which on every point of land made by the turns and bends in the river, stretched out their huge sails athwart the horizon.[59]

In St. James Norquay encountered a question that would concern him for the rest of his life: the place of Indigenous peoples in the community. The question arose because Taylor expressed ambivalent and at times anxious opinions on the subject. Although the clergyman was relatively unruffled by his dealings with the few Cree and Saulteaux who lived in St. James, he was not so calm in his assessment of the settlement's military and political circumstances. He often expressed a fear that the district was situated only "24 hours hard ride" from the Dakota communities in Minnesota. He worried that the Dakota "may surprise the Colony at any time."[60] In 1855 he shared the settlement's "state of great fear & excitement" after a Dakota attack "on the Plain Hunters, as they are called—& the robbery & loss of life which attended it." He claimed that the "panic" about the Dakota developed annually because they were "worse than barbarians—worse than Kaffir [the British term for Africans, mainly Xhosas, in the Eastern Cape of South Africa]."[61] Such concerns about the Dakota must have been communicated to Norquay. They were part of an attitude that Taylor had developed in the face of the rough, sometimes violent, atmosphere of western North America.

Taylor disliked the uncertainty that lay beneath the surface of his daily life. He blamed the Dakota, was critical of the behaviour of some settlers, and believed that the military personnel, though necessary, were no better than they needed to be. He told the church office in London that "the cruelty of people is shocking as we see & hear of it here.—Such scenes as men witness on the Plains must make them very indifferent to human suffering & life. The Sioux & Saulteaux get the scalp of those they kill."[62] In the year that Norquay spent with Taylor, he would have heard this tone of disapproval expressed frequently. He also perceived that Taylor saw Indigenous peoples as very different from "civilized" Britons, the term that Taylor used.[63] Norquay had to deal with the clergyman's categories of humankind and to decide where he placed himself in such hierarchies.

In March 1859 a brief note in Taylor's journal suggested that Norquay had come to another turning point. "Kept daily School all this week," the clergyman wrote. It was an unusual declaration given that he had been at the school so rarely earlier in the year. Seven days later he recorded that he had "attended the school every morning this week—have the prospect of a Teacher for a time, till we can again make engagements for a year or so."[64] It is likely that, one year after he had begun to teach in St. James parish, John Norquay had moved on.

The year in St. James had been an important one. Norquay had earned income as a teacher and lived as an adult, observing for the first time the patterns of the Red River Settlement as one who had to take some responsibility for them. He had dealt with twenty children and taught them the basics of literacy and a few passages from the Bible. He had worked closely with an Anglican clergyman of British stock and listened to that man's opinions on the church's mission. Norquay had also been exposed to countless moments when Taylor pronounced on the sins and virtues of the settlement's inhabitants. The perspective was so unlike that in most settlement households, so fearful of anticipated violence and critical of rough deeds, so concerned about "barbarous" behaviour and convinced of "civilization's" virtues, so full of concern about pacific and ordered behaviour, that Norquay could not help but see the contrast to attitudes in other circles. Now, about eighteen years of age, he was moving on.

John Norquay's first eight years were difficult. He lost his mother and then his father and, as will become clear, was conscious forever after of the dismaying precariousness of life. He also found much that was positive. Relatives along River Road in St. Andrews parish made him welcome within an extended family. The farm was his anchor. The animals, the seasons, the parish neighbourhood, and the river expressed nature's rhythms and the passing of the years. John attended sessions in a primary school near the church and stood with other children on the periphery of crowded worship services when the congregation, drawn seemingly from every household up and down the road, constituted a bustling, diverse throng. He was part of the haying and watched the seeding and the threshing. He knew the joys of snowfall on mild days as well as the trials that came with bitter cold. And John talked about these events in a distinctive dialect while picking up the speech of the church ministers as well as phrases in Cree and Saulteaux. Although he would not have perceived the connection between improvements in transportation hundreds of kilometres away and the arrival of epidemic diseases in the Red River Settlement, he knew their effects firsthand after two siblings and both parents died in his first eight years.

Details of the years when John lived with Granny Spence and attended St. John's schools are scarce. The only certainty is that his work impressed his teachers and soon the bishop. The three or four years as a teenager at St. John's Collegiate School, from 1854 to 1858, were decisive in shaping the course of his life. John devoted himself to his studies and shared in the substitute families created by his teachers and fellow students. During this time he would have recognized Miss Anderson's strictures and Bishop Anderson's delight in and ambitions for the Red River Settlement. He moved some distance away from the river-lot farm as well as from the Cree and Saulteaux peoples of the settlement. He learned the standard English that was already superseding Bungee in the settlement. He acquired advanced skills in literacy and numeracy that placed him in a different position from that of almost all his contemporaries in the region. John discovered the power of reading and learned far more about the world—commencing with exposure to math, language, history, and geography—than the students who attended a few sessions in the parochial schools. Only a handful of his classmates and a few young men in the French-language community across the Red River, including Louis Riel, who had been sent to Montreal to study, could match his training.

The late historian John Foster has argued that the Bungee/anglophone peoples of the Red River Settlement, the category in which Norquay belonged, played a special role as bridge builders and mediators in the settlement. While they "nurtured British institutions such as churches, schools and government, they also served as the amalgam that held the Settlement together.... Their relations with the different communities constituted the cultural bridges that made the Red River historical experience possible. The mosaic of peoples there could not function in relative harmony without the activities of individuals whose actions served to breach ethnocentric barriers."[65] Norquay grew up among people who modelled these British imperial habits of authority. He benefited from contact with the self-styled elite of the settlement, individuals such as Dr. John Bunn, British army officer Major William Caldwell, and HBC officer Eden Colvile. Thanks to the opportunities provided by his teachers, Norquay became confident as an orator and learned what was meant by leadership in European institutions. Implicit in the lessons of St. John's Collegiate School were British expectations about citizenship, law, and government.

Like Peter Erasmus, Norquay recognized that some of the settlement's leaders, both White and Métis, saw him as different, not of their world. He absorbed the Whites' subtle and not-so-subtle judgements of local house styles, clothing styles, and customs. He perceived the social distinctions that accompanied their version of self-discipline and deportment. What Norquay made of their generosity and their race-based thinking was not recorded, but as comments by Erasmus illustrate, such impressions would endure. Of the Michif/francophone Catholics, Norquay probably knew less. He would have met them at the forts and on the hunts but not in the churches or the schools. What he made of them in his first two decades cannot be determined. It is clear that Norquay was not a rebel. As events were to demonstrate over and over, he stayed within the lines. But he was more than just a cypher. That was the message contained in the classmates' label for him: he was "roguish."

CHAPTER 2

Red River Family, 1859–70

A young adult now living on his own, John Norquay moved to the river-lot community of his birth in the spring of 1859. He stayed in St. Andrews parish for seven years. Listed in church records as a schoolmaster at Park's Creek (later called Parkdale), on the southern border of the parish, and as a farmer, he acquired the experience that young men had to bring to Red River households. During these years John met Elizabeth Setter, a young woman whose ancestry and childhood experience were similar to his. They married in 1862 when she was nineteen, he twenty-one. In the autumn of 1866, having concluded that their small river lot and the schoolmaster's wage in St. Andrews produced meagre returns, the Norquays moved west to High Bluff, near Elizabeth's parents' home, to try farming on a larger scale. Once again they ran into food shortages. During the grasshopper plague and near famine of 1868–69, they were forced to move north to Lake Manitoba, where they could fish. John also worked as a fur trader. By the spring of 1870, they were back at their High Bluff farm and taking a small part in the dramatic political events that marked the founding of Manitoba.

Teacher

The school in South St. Andrews (about six kilometres from the parish church, on the border of St. Paul's parish) provided John with a church stipend and levies paid by parents for each student.[1] He enjoyed the work and was said to be a fine teacher. In 1860 the newly founded Red River Settlement newspaper, the *Nor'Wester*, spoke generously of the "excellent school-room" where Norquay, the "very able teacher," had been instructing a large group of aspiring scholars. The story covered the annual examination day in May, during which his forty-nine pupils were put through their paces by examiners, clergymen all, in front of an attentive audience of parents and younger children. The fact that forty-nine students took the tests suggests that this teaching assignment was far better paid than the school of twenty students that John had left in St. James.

The examination began with the first grades, concentrating on the alphabet, mental arithmetic, and tables. For the upper-school pupils, it included the recitation of a hymn. These older children then turned to grammar, geography, the history of England, and the Bible. The oldest students spent most of the day writing essays on biblical "worthies" and completed the test by reading their compositions aloud. At about three o'clock, the six-hour ordeal over, Archdeacon James Hunter gave out prizes to the most advanced scholars and then delivered a short address on Proverbs 22:6: "Train up a child in the way he should go; and when he is old he will not depart from it." The group then sang a hymn, Andrew Setter led in prayer, and the archdeacon pronounced his benediction.[2]

Norquay was only a few years older than his students, but he had spent many hours in classrooms and in reading. As the report about examination day suggested, he taught the alphabet and a little arithmetic, a little about the church and the Bible, and a little about the wider world and its past. Above all, his students learned to read and write. About twenty years later, among the letters arriving in the premier's office was a note on a ragged sheet of paper, in shaky handwriting, from Joe Favell Jr., then living near The Pas: "Dear Sir: I now take the pleasure of writing you a few lines to let you know that I am quite well @ present thank the Lord for his goodness wishing you all the same I aught to be very thankfull to you for being able to set down and write as I do whereas if I had been brought out here when a child on this part of the world I soppose I would be seting along side of somebody telling him what to write as I see lots of men do out here."[3] It was a student's testimonial to a teacher and a measure of what could be accomplished in crowded parish schools.

Norquay's classroom was closely connected to the United Kingdom, the British Empire, and the Anglican Church. Students read English literature and sang English hymns, learned the geography of Britain's global possessions, and memorized a potted history of English kings and queens. Bungee might have prevailed in the schoolyard, but in class Norquay would have tried to adhere to standard English. The Bible was the foundation of every day's reading. The educational attainments of his students, and the curriculum itself, testified to the ambition and standards of the parish's founding citizens. The Roman Catholic–run, French-language schools in other parts of the settlement would have appeared quite different, but their cultural foundations—literacy, Christianity, European laws, and work discipline—were much the same.

Thanks to several dozen men and a few women, the proportion of literates in the settlement was "fully as large as in any other community," the *Nor'Wester* claimed, though its editor did admit that there were a "very few who could not read and write." Nevertheless, teachers in the Red River Settlement faced a crisis in the 1860s because their pay was low and uncertain and the burden of collecting fees unending. Bishop David Anderson recognized the problems: "I regret to say that education of a higher stamp has rather fallen behind. The want of openings in the country for those trained, the growing nearness to the superior advantages of Canada and England, leave few on the spot willing to devote the necessary time to the prosecution of more advanced studies: education in consequence languishes; schoolmasters are scarce, and remain but a short time at their posts."[4]

The crisis concerned not just teaching. In a sermon in 1860 Anderson admitted that the settlement could not hold its educated young people. It provided no outlets or rewards to "those who have passed from their years of education, and have just entered on the freedom of life." He could have been speaking directly to Norquay when he lamented that local young people "are a source of deep anxiety to us all. The object is to retain a hold upon them—to promote in every way self-improvement—and to lead to the cultivation of domestic habits." Anderson hoped that a new hymn book might lead to a few becoming interested in church music, that discussions in newly founded Young Men's Christian Associations might encourage "a taste for reading and the promotion of study," and that lectures in a number of schoolrooms (including at Norquay's school in Parkdale, where Reverend James Hunter gave a series of talks) might inspire Christian endeavour. None of these initiatives was a great success. The bishop lamented that "in this, however, we are so dependent on the clergy, and so devoid of the means of illustration or experiment, that comparatively little can be done."[5]

Four years later, disenchanted with his surroundings and about to leave for England, Anderson returned to what he saw as the Red River Settlement's economic and intellectual stagnation. In his parting address he said that schools had not become the engines of development that he had hoped: "The desire for higher education has much diminished; the dispersion of the settlers over a wider area has made it impossible to overtake them with Schools. As a consequence, the attendance on the individual Schools is smaller, the School is less remunerative, and in itself less interesting to the Master; and, as other more lucrative openings present themselves, few comparatively are willing to undertake the necessary toil and drudgery of tuition." He seemed to be addressing Norquay's own disappointments.[6]

Farmer

Norquay probably accepted as a matter of course that most of his time and labour had to be dedicated to animals, crops, the hunt, and the fishery. Given his relative youth when his parents died, he possessed only the rudiments of a farm education. At school he curried, watered, and harnessed Reverend Thomas Cochrane's horses. At his grandmother's home he might have driven cows to the hay lands, observed the business of slaughtering and butchering, and joined neighbours as they worked at the haying, fishing, and ice cutting that punctuated the yearly cycle. By the time Norquay reached his late teens and commenced his teaching career, he had devoted a good deal of effort to the study of local agriculture.

Red River farms grew in size during these decades, and their productivity increased.[7] A soldier who had served in many theatres of war throughout the Atlantic world enthused about the district's advantages: "The red river settlement itself is one of the finest countries in the World[—]it will Grow anything[.] The Land is so rich it never requires any Manure. . . . I have Grown potatoes in the one spot for four years & have Got potatoes from it as big as a mans Head & never put any manure to it—we have a Sergeant named Balmer who [h]as Grown Turnips in his garden that whed [weighed] 19 lbs—in fact all this place wants is emigration . . . plenty of land for every one for nothing."[8]

The records of a neighbour suggest the outline of Norquay's labouring year in rural St. Andrews. Like Norquay, Samuel Taylor, a farmer and quarryman, cut cordwood for fuel, erected fences to keep wandering animals out of his crops, laid flooring in the house, thatched the roof, and set nets in the river to catch fish. He gathered birch for the manufacture of snowshoes and sleds, shot geese and ducks, killed and butchered cattle and oxen and pigs, cut and stacked hay, cut and threshed wheat and barley, spread dung on the garden, planted and harvested potatoes and other garden produce, and made whitewash from a lime-rice-glue concoction to brighten the exterior walls of his home. Because he had to mud the walls, he might have shared a neighbour's delight with the "fine mud" discovered below the riverbank on Henry Fidler's farm. Taylor cut ice on the river and squared logs for the icehouse that would preserve food in summer. And he joined expeditions heading northward to Lake Winnipeg to bring in fish or logs or firewood or sturgeon oil. Norquay would have laboured similarly most days of the year. Elizabeth's work would have been just as demanding but with the added burden of newborn children, five in the seven years between 1863 and 1869, two more in the next four years, and another some years later.[9]

There were pleasures as well as trials and endless labour in the ordinary male settler's life. Taylor, a stonemason and middling-level farmer, wrote that, after having completed a task in the woods, "it gives one a good appetite to partake of a good plum pudding and a glass of Brandy sitting beside the blink [flickering] of his own fireside." His sketch of one trip illustrated how prairie expeditions were both demanding and pleasurable. In mid-December 1859 he and a friend took fat pork, cakes, milk, potatoes, and bison meat with them on a long, slow, overnight journey by horse and sleigh to Grand Marais, about seventy kilometres north of his farm. They then followed the Lake Winnipeg–Traverse Bay portage, where at sunrise they observed fresh moose and deer tracks:

> We had dinner in a tent at the farthest end of the portage, and then crossed over [the narrows of the lake] to the point of Metass and had [a] hearty dram under the fish stage, and then commensed loading [fish] and then had something to eat in an Indian tent and then start[ed] and got back soon after dayset, to the portage again and put up for the night, I sleeped warm in the tent, beside [the friend] E. Pruden's at one side and an Indian Woman at the other, we start[ed] again in the morning about sunrise, and had dinner more than halfway across the portage of Fat Pork[,] potatoes, butter, cakes, buffalo [bison] meat, and then came to the end of the portage just as the sun was setting.

A job well done, Taylor then drank "as usual a good glass of rum." The trip was long and cold, but it offered new sights, material gain, comradeship, and a sense of accomplishment.[10]

The St. Andrews parish families all attended weddings and stayed for the parties and dances that followed. They enjoyed celebrating the queen's birthday, "which was kept up in grand stile at the Stone Fort." They watched races on the river ice near Lower Fort Garry, such as the exciting contest between Edward Harriott's and Thomas Folster's fastest horses. They attended school examination days and temperance meetings. When, in early November 1862, the river ice was "getting strong [and] now people is skating . . . we walked up and down on the ice and it was smooth as glass, no snow on it."[11] Their jokes frequently centred on death. When a long-time resident died, the McKay boys hesitated to tell their father because he, too, was dying. Finally, one son said, "'Father, did you know that Robie died this morning?' 'Oh,' he replied calmly, 'he's a slow traveler. I'll catch up.'"[12] They took a little time to get into their stories: "Sofie—her now—she," a three-subject phrase of the sort common in Bungee, introduced a joke that turned on the scarcity of matches. A man sat up in bed, according to Nellie Norquay McAllister, and said to Sofie, his wife, "'Laightt the lamp I think I'm gonna die.'—[Sofie, her now, she] couldn't find a match—'Arh Sam, can't ya die in the dark?'"[13] Both stories were passed on from generation to generation.

St. Andrews contemporaries would have distinguished Norquay, and almost all Bungee/English-speaking settlers of mixed ancestry, from Cree, Saulteaux, and Dakota individuals. In the daily journal kept by Samuel Taylor, those of European and mixed ancestry were mentioned by name—John Flett, John Fidler, Thomas Truthwaite, Mr. Corrigal (who merited the "Mr.," perhaps, because he was a schoolmaster)—but many of the Cree and Saulteaux people who supplied casual labour were not. Thus, Taylor recorded that Peter Moar left the farm, "Indians along with him," James Ellison "and two Indians came with the Packet," or simply Mr. Beads "and an Indian."[14] Taylor worried about the consequences of the 1862 Dakota-settler conflict in Minnesota. He recorded the presence of ninety First Nations people at Upper Fort Garry in December 1862 and noted several months later that there was "great fear of the Sioux [Dakota] coming into the settlement about this time." The same concern cropped up in the summer of 1864. In June and July 1866, he reported that "some Sioux [have been] killed by Red Lake Indians a day or two since at the upper Fort" and that "the five following days I keeped watch all night, owing to a great many Indians being about."[15] Uncertainty about the Dakota aside, the people of the settlement lived peaceably and generally accepted the rulings of local courts.[16]

John Norquay adjusted easily to the calendar of work and leisure, but his position in local society was nonetheless elusive. In the estimation of those at the top, the social scale within the community included, in descending order, fur trade and military officers and senior clergy, prosperous merchants and settlers, junior clergy and teachers, HBC clerks, and middling and poor farmers. Where did Norquay belong? As an orphan who had moved away from St. Andrews parish at the age of eight, he had to find his place again upon his return from St. John's and St. James at the age of eighteen. His education and his teaching position marked him as a well-educated citizen compared with most of the settlers around him. He would have been able to speak to the clergy as one who belonged in their company and understood their language. As a relatively young man who had yet to make his mark in the world and possessed little material wealth, though, he would not have been on equal terms with the HBC officers or the Anglican bishop. Despite his stipend as a part-time schoolmaster, Norquay remained a farmer and belonged on a level closer to farmers like Taylor, the diarist, than to the great gentlemen who governed the colony, captained the military, guided the churches, and grew steadily richer in the fur trade.

When a local man froze to death in the winter of 1860, and many gathered at St. Andrews Church to pay their respects, Samuel Taylor noted, perhaps with sarcasm, that "a great number of the nobility attended his funeral."[17] He would not have placed Norquay among the nobility. Both maintained modest farms, conversed familiarly in the Bungee dialect, and attended the Anglican church, but they did not venture into the family pews rented by the fur trade elite. Their work practices and food sources and views on domestic architecture were shared by several thousand others in the settlement. As became evident in the years that followed, Norquay was one of the people. He made his living not just in the school but also in the hunt, at the mill, and on the lakes. The key difference between him and his neighbours was his exceptional schooling, which set him apart in ways that became more significant in the following decade.

Betsy

Elizabeth Setter Norquay said that she met her future husband when she was keeping house for her brother on the family farm near Portage la Prairie.[18] John might have been teaching in one of the local schools to supplement his income at Park's Creek school and perhaps helping with someone's farm work. Elizabeth was tiny, not 100 pounds (45 kilograms) and not five feet (153 centimetres) in height; John was huge, at least six feet, one inch tall (186 centimetres) and over 200 pounds (90 kilograms). Among the few surviving stories about their courtship are several claiming that he walked the seventy kilometres from St. Andrews to visit her. He is said to have carried extra moccasins to dances because he could count on wearing out several pairs in his enthusiastic stepping. As proof of his agility, according to one such tale, he planted a footprint above a door frame more than six feet (183 centimetres) above the floor.[19]

John Norquay of St. Andrews parish, twenty-one, married Elizabeth Setter of Portage la Prairie, nineteen, in the plain wooden Anglican church at St. Mary's la Prairie in June 1862.[20] Reverend Thomas Cochrane, his benefactor when John first entered St. John's Collegiate School, performed the ceremony. Like her husband, Elizabeth could connect her family in Portage la Prairie to relatives in the fur trade. She knew that her ancestors included Orkney employees of the Hudson's Bay Company and their country wives. Her mother, Isabella (Kennedy) Setter, was the child of a Cree woman, Aggathas, and HBC Chief Trader Alexander Kennedy, an Orcadian, who set up a household near The Pas in 1804.[21] Isabella married at fifteen in 1835 and died in 1845, leaving four children, including Elizabeth, then three years old. Her father, George Setter, remarried and had seven children with his new wife. In the early 1850s the Setters moved seventy kilometres westward to the vast, fertile, flat-as-a-tabletop plain along the Assiniboine River, where the new community of Portage la Prairie was taking form.[22]

Elizabeth's background and upbringing were similar in many respects to those of John. Like him, Elizabeth grew up with a stepmother, in a large family, in a Church of England parish, in a circumstance that required her to care for younger siblings. Her farm-based childhood, her family's Scottish and Indigenous ancestry, her mother's death and father's remarriage, and her literacy were important matters that she shared with her husband. But, unlike him, she had only limited opportunities to attend school after her family's move west, and she was never able to compete for a scholarship or secure an advanced education.

It is possible that Elizabeth had a few sessions in a Portage la Prairie school to supplement her limited exposure to formal education in St. Andrews parish. She remembered her school days vividly to the end of her life. She told an interviewer many years later that she took a wedge of bannock for lunch at the noon hour and played games in the schoolyard, including cross-tag, wolf, and button, and in winter she slid down the riverbank on an old bison robe. Elizabeth also remembered the religious tenor of the day: "The first thing every morning at school was the reading of a chapter of the Bible.... After recess there would be another chapter. And school closed in the afternoon with prayer." She recalled the physical arrangements that seemed so strange at first: "The desks were sloping boards along the wall. The little children who were beginners had cards with the alphabet and little words on them." And she recalled the clothing that they all wore: "In the winter most of the girls used to come wearing coats made with two-point 'H.B.' [HBC] blankets, with a leather cord to hold them together. And we wore woolen caps and moccasins, of course, outside of duffels made of the white or blue blanket-cloth and coming up to the knees and tied there to keep the snow out." She was sensitive to the differing circumstances of the wealthier and the poorer families around her: "At the school we had slates and slate-pencils. A boy or girl who had no pencil used a lump of clay instead, and if there were little pieces of stone in it they scratched the slate and you could rub the writing off, but not the scratches."[23]

Elizabeth recalled vividly the exceptional flood of 1852 when the family had to drive cattle to Stony Mountain, the highest land in the district. She retained a clear picture of her home life: "When we came home from school at four in the afternoon there was always work for us to do, such work as teasing a great bunch of wool for the women to card next day. Our clothes were made out of homespun. Everybody had sheep." She also knew intimately the details of domestic architecture: "On the floor of the house where I was born... were Indian mats, as we used to call them. The Indians wove them with rushes, and stained them with vegetable dyes which they made themselves. We made all our own furniture. In my father's old house when we came in at the front door we were in the dining-room, and the kitchen was back of it. The other rooms in the house were bedrooms. The fireplace was made with mud and so was the chimney. Whole logs of white poplar used to burn in the fireplace." Elizabeth never forgot the work that accompanied almost all of her waking minutes: "The girls had chores to do every evening and every morning, too, before school. We all used to get up very early, and the men would go out to the barns to thresh with a flail, or to do other work, and the girls would help in milking the cows and feeding them, and in feeding the calves and pigs." And the religious observances: "Then, when everybody came in for breakfast, the Bible was read and we had prayers before we sat down to eat."[24]

From the year of her marriage, Elizabeth's waking hours were filled with the needs of a growing family. She was pregnant for more than half the months during the next decade and nursed babies continuously. As with all young wives in this era, one of the greatest risks to her health lay in childbirth. Every year there were stories of the death of a mother in labour or of a mother and child. Elizabeth likely relied on local midwives for the seven births between 1863 and 1872, but not a word about this support has survived. The first child of the young couple, Thomas, named after John's brother, was baptized in November 1863. Isabella (or Bella, named after her grandmother) was born twenty months later, in July 1865. John, the third child in the family, arrived another year later, in August 1866. Each child was baptized in the Anglican church at St. Andrews. Their fourth child, Alexander, was born in November 1867 and baptized in St. Mary's Church in Portage la Prairie. Horace (Horatio), their fifth child, was born in November 1869, at either High Bluff or Duck Bay, and baptized at St. Anne's Church in Poplar Point. In each of these years, the parents were described as "John and Elizabeth Norquay, St. Margaret's, Settlers." Caroline Ellen (Nellie) followed in March 1871 and Andrew in August 1872, probably at Sturgeon Creek, a settlement closer to Winnipeg.[25]

Elizabeth's recollection of life on her father's farm would have applied to the first decade of her married life as well. Their log houses in St. Andrews and High Bluff were small, the interiors dark, though whitewashed inside as well as outside. Window openings in some houses of this type might have been covered with parchment of fish or animal skin if the household budget did not extend to the use of glass. The Norquays made some of their own furniture. Their fireplace and chimney were handmade of local mud and clay. They kept a few sheep, and Elizabeth made some of the family's clothing out of homespun cloth. She undertook as a child and then supervised as a parent the milking of cows and the feeding of animals. She managed the making and mending of clothes and helped with the fieldwork, including the haying, and gathered plant foods such as wild potatoes, the inner bark of poplar, buffalo root, and all the wild fruits—saskatoon, blueberry, chokecherry, cranberry, plum. With a few exceptions, such as tea and tobacco (which nonetheless had locally produced substitutes), she relied on local food. Meat came from domestic birds and animals as well as the hunt, and cereals were harvested in the fields.

Elizabeth prepared almost all the meals. She remembered "knocking barley" as a child, pounding the grain in a wooden bowl with a mallet until, fully winnowed, it was ready to be boiled into barley broth, a practice that continued in her new home. She recalled the water mill at Park's Creek and even occasions when, wind and water having failed to turn the stones at the mills, she had to sift unbolted grist to make flour. "[Maple] sugar was scarce, too, and we had no cakes or pies in those days, and we had to preserve our berries by drying. We used to dry raspberries, saskatoons, and blueberries . . . in a cake, and when we wanted some for the table we would break a piece off the cake and put sugar with it."[26] The sweetener was maple sugar from the sap of maples harvested at Sugar Point on the Red River by Cree and Saulteaux families and sold to homes along River Road.

Decades later, asked to reflect on the Red River experience, Elizabeth spoke fondly of her years as a young mother. She acknowledged the centrality of church and Bible in community life and recalled the rules of hay cutting, the locations of roots and barks used by the Cree and Saulteaux to ward off scurvy, and how to make the least greasy pemmican: "We worked hard and were happy. We did not have much but our wants were simple."[27]

High Bluff

In the mid-1860s, significant changes seemed to be just around the corner for the Red River Settlement. Steamboats from the United States now docked at Upper Fort Garry every summer. The American Civil War had just ended, and railways promised to transform the continent. Large-scale British emigration to Canada appeared to be increasingly likely. Surely a new system of government and vastly expanded trade would soon commence, and larger, well-situated farms would be rewarded.

John and Elizabeth decided to move from St. Andrews to a river lot along the Assiniboine River in the autumn of 1866.[28] Their reasoning went unrecorded, but economic and domestic factors would have played parts.

The land near Portage la Prairie had been proven wonderfully fertile in the preceding fifteen years and was considered to be free for the taking. By settling closer to Elizabeth's parents and siblings, they would gain emotional support and perhaps some additional domestic help. The first documents establishing their departure are dated October and November 1866 and record the sale of a parcel of land near Park's Creek. This might have been the tract that they lived on after their marriage. They treated it as private property, sold it as a commodity, and seemed to be aware of its value as real estate.[29]

Despite publicists' promises, field crops could not be relied on, as the Norquays knew well. The growing season was short, the maturing period of spring wheat and corn was long, and the danger of killing frosts in late August or early September was high.[30] Grasshopper plagues destroyed the hopes of farm families in several years during the decade. These voracious pests invaded the entire settlement in 1867, just as the Norquays were raising their first crops at High Bluff. The following year's devastation was even worse. Sister Curran of the Grey Nuns wrote in her journal in June 1868 that "crowds of grasshoppers [were] devouring the fields, which had looked so promising. In the gardens there is nothing but cabbage and shallots left."[31] The Red River Settlement residents set up a relief committee in the fall of 1868 and sent out appeals for help. According to Sister Curran, 1,000 carts left the settlement to purchase or beg for flour in neighbouring American communities.[32] The people of St. Paul, Minnesota, dispatched donations of seed grain and money. Faced with the grasshopper famine, the Norquays could not survive on their farm.

To supplement farm crops, a family could join the annual settlement bison hunts, the expeditions to the plains that involved hundreds of carts, horses, and dogs and several months of hard work. The hunts, typically one in spring and another in fall, absorbed large fractions of the Red River Settlement population and required sufficient supplies to maintain a moving community (one-third women, one-third children) for several months. An expedition processed several thousand bison, each weighing nearly 450 kilograms, into pemmican. It consumed more in the form of fresh (or "green") meat. It also brought in hundreds of robes or hides that were cured and processed by the women. For several decades, products of the hunt constituted the settlement's main exports.

By the 1860s as many as 2,000 of the 10,000 residents of the settlement joined the hunt in any given year, and many more participated at some point in their lives. One expedition, described by a reporter in the Red River newspaper, the *Nor'Wester*, saw the families gather at the edge of the settlement in the late summer of 1860. Moving south and west, they stopped briefly near Pembina Mountain to gather wood for the fires that would dry the meat on the plains. Standing on an elevation the reporter looked back on a long, winding, noisy line of animals and people, riders to the fore, white canvas and skin coverings on the carts standing out like beacons. He wrote that the sound of the "diabolical" barking of 1,000 dogs and the smell of effluvia made the regular camp moves a relief rather than a burden.[33]

John Norquay left a brief essay in which he described how a typical day on the expedition commenced with the women preparing bannock and meat over a fire in the early morning while men smoked and children played among the carts. Around 7 or 8 a.m. the flag was raised at the guide's cart, announcing that the camp was moving out. Tents were struck and carts packed, cattle driven onward by groups of boys, and extra horses roped behind the families' carts. They stopped twice daily around noon and toward evening. When the sun began to descend in the sky, tents were again pitched, fires lit under the cooking pots, and oxen unyoked and placed inside the ring of carts. There might be a fiddle tune, a jig, a song, a game of cards, and talk.[34]

Elizabeth spoke knowledgeably about pemmican, the flesh of bison shredded to powder and fibre, a crucial food product of the settlement's hunts. She explained that "the women used to pound choke cherries and put them with the pemmican, just as we use currant jelly with mutton." She knew the best ways to prepare pemmican, including "rubaboo . . . made by boiling the pemmican with potatoes, and with onions and any other vegetables," and "rowshow [probably a corruption of *réchauffé*], . . . made by shredding the pemmican and mixing flour and water with it and frying the mixture in a pan." Elizabeth knew the history of such foods in the region and observed that shredding and frying pemmican "was the voyageur's favourite way of cooking" the food. She also knew the different ways of making pemmican during the hunt: "Of course, there were several grades of pemmican. It was made on the plains by the women who accompanied the buffalo hunters. They pounded the buffalo meat and then poured melted buffalo fat over it and sewed it up in buffalo hide. Some pemmican was made carelessly. Pemmican made carefully from the best parts of the buffalo, with the right mixture of sugar and berries to correct the greasiness, was very good." Pemmican might have been the fuel of the fur trade, but Elizabeth, like any connoisseur, recognized that the superior meal featured "tongues and bosses [humps] . . . [as] the most delicate buffalo meat."[35]

As the destruction of the bison population proceeded relentlessly on both sides of the border, and the remaining herds concentrated in territories to the west, the hunt ceased to be a major annual preoccupation of the settlement. Some Métis moved west to follow the last of the once numberless herds. Others, including the Norquays and many of their neighbours, abandoned the economic strategy of combining subsistence farming with bison hunting.[36] They had to turn to new ways of feeding their families.

Lake Manitoba became an alternative in the famine of 1868. Elizabeth recalled the family's straitened circumstances: "I had never believed that I could live on fish, as we had to do when the grasshoppers came and ate everything green. We had a farm at High Bluff then. Before our supply of flour was all used, we moved up to Lake Manitoba, so that we could get fish. We mixed our flour with fish, and made what we called fish rolls."[37] In the wake of food shortages, Norquay took a job as a fur trader in the employ of local entrepreneurs, the House brothers.[38] The family spent one or two winters in the trade, probably at Duck Bay, a northerly post on the shore of Lake Winnipegosis where John dealt with Métis, Cree, and Saulteaux families. All the hunters took credit to pay for the goods that they promised to repay with furs at the end of the season. John spoke to them using his schoolroom French and learned their Michif. He spoke to the neighbouring Scotch Cree and Scotch Saulteaux in his own childhood dialect, Bungee. In all likelihood the family relied on hunting expeditions conducted by John and their new neighbours in the surrounding bush country. The family returned to the farm in the High Bluff district near Portage la Prairie in the late winter or early spring of 1870. These events help to explain Norquay's absence during the first crucial months of the resistance movement of 1869–70. But they do not make more precise his place in the political forces then taking shape in the settlement.

Leadership

The Red River Settlement's two central economic activities, farming and bison hunting, were administered by distinctive institutions that shaped

Norquay's view of public affairs. Although not an active participant in the colony's governance, Norquay was interested in the process. A family story, perhaps burnished with the passage of time, sounds plausible: "John Norquay, Andrew Spence and Peter Henderson were batching in a cabin on the north bank of the Assiniboine in the High Bluff area about 1863 and formed a debating society. Some of the neighbours later inquired how the debating was progressing. Spence and Henderson said Norquay was not debating any more. 'He is making speeches and when he gets the floor we can't get it from him.'"[39]

Public discussion about community affairs was normal practice in the Red River Settlement, especially regarding its great enterprise, the bison hunt. The male hunters met daily during the hunt, and a succession of brief speeches set out alternatives. The most senior speakers, including the captain of the day and the chief of the hunt, spoke last, and their views usually prevailed.[40] Norquay did not possess the status of an elder in these years. Although he might not have addressed the assembly, he would have listened to and learned from it.

This governmental practice acquired legitimacy over the course of the nineteenth century. Peter Erasmus, Norquay's schoolmate, described a hunt in which three candidates ran for leadership, each conducting his campaign by informal conversations with the other hunters. After one candidate dropped out, every voter was given two sticks, one short and one long, representing the two remaining nominees, and each voter placed one of the sticks in the ballot sack. What Erasmus called the "unwritten law of the hunt" then prevailed, and the victor was elected to govern the group's activities. No one "in my experience," he said, "ever disputed the rules and regulations that were enforced by the leader." They shared the animals killed, no matter whether an individual shot many or few. According to Erasmus, when one man slipped out of the camp the evening before a hunt, scattering the animals, his property was confiscated. "These rules of the hunt were necessary and important for the well-being of the majority," he concluded.[41]

Formal discussions enabled Indigenous groups to reach clear understandings about peace and war. A meeting in 1860 between Red River hunters and a Dakota band involved three days of feasting and dancing as well as formal speeches. The conclusion of the negotiations stipulated that there would be "no sly approaches to each other's camp by night, and that if any infringed the rule, those molested were at liberty to shoot the culprits." This was one of the forms of government—politics in the style of the bison hunt—that Norquay would have recognized as appropriate and effective. Decision making depended on public speeches by individual leaders and public agreement within groups. Leadership pivoted on quiet conversations and an individual's ability to express ideas in a forceful, convincing manner.[42]

In contrast, the Red River Settlement's farming and commercial activities were administered by the territory's ostensible owner, the Hudson's Bay Company. It defined the boundary of its legal sway as a circle of eighty kilometres radius centred on Upper Fort Garry.[43] The governing council of this "District of Assiniboia," first established in 1815, became a more representative government when reorganized by the company in 1835. Thereafter the council included the leading fur trade, church, and military figures (when British troops were in the district) and a few other prosperous settlers and merchants. Not elected, its members were named on the advice of local officers by the company's governing body in London. Norquay was never a member of this charmed circle.

He attended a public meeting in January 1863 that indicated his own and many others' dissatisfaction with political affairs in the settlement. The discussion centred on options for the replacement of HBC rule and how to achieve British Crown colony status. The group also called for the establishment of regular communications with the united Canadas, the British colony 1,600 kilometres to the east, and lamented the community's vulnerability given the departure of British troops and the recent Dakota-settler conflicts in Minnesota. The petition developed at the meeting was signed by about 500 settlers, including Norquay.[44]

Beginning in 1866 he belonged to another political community, the growing farm- and hunt-based neighbourhoods on the western edge of the settlement. The District of Assiniboia's eighty-kilometre radius meant that the parish developed under Reverend William Cockran's ministry at Portage la Prairie, like Grand Marais on the south shore of Lake Winnipeg, did not come under the jurisdiction of the HBC Council of Assiniboia. Portage la Prairie and its adjacent parishes therefore presented legal and administrative problems. This English- and Bungee-speaking community contained about 120 souls in the 1850s, perhaps 400 by the late 1860s, as a younger generation of Red River families, including the Norquays, moved west to cultivate larger plots than could be obtained in the original parishes.[45] Although High Bluff, Poplar Point, and St. Margaret's parishes were mostly within the roughly calculated boundary of the District of Assiniboia, the settlers often took their lead from and joined conversations in Portage la Prairie rather than Upper Fort Garry.

During the winter of 1867–68, before the grasshopper infestation had ruined crops and pushed his family into the fishery and fur trade, Norquay and some of his neighbours participated in an unusual political adventure led by the mercurial Thomas Spence. Born in Edinburgh in 1832, Spence came to Canada in the early 1850s and moved to the Red River Settlement in 1866. A year later he opened a store in Portage la Prairie. Talkative, energetic, and impractical, Spence had some education and a fair degree of political experience. He proposed that their little group send a petition to Lord Monck, governor general of the newly confederated Canada, asking to be constituted as a new political jurisdiction with headquarters at "LaPrairie, Rupert's Land, British North America." He and his group of visionaries hoped to cooperate with "the adjoining Colony of Assiniboia" and proposed that William Mactavish, its governor, oversee their state. Norquay was one of eight who signed the petition.[46]

Spence's group was articulating thoughts similar to those of the Red River Métis resistance movement launched a year later, but the men at Portage la Prairie did not mobilize military power as Louis Riel did. Rather, they asked Britain for official recognition and imposed a tariff on goods arriving from the Red River Settlement, claiming that a locally run justice system would be funded by the proceeds. They soon ran into objections from an obstinate shoemaker who accused them of spending the revenue on booze. Official Britain stepped in, rejecting their claims out of hand and saying that the local agitators had "no authority to create or organize a Government or even to set up Municipal Institutions." The famine of 1868–69 ended the enterprise. In the difficult days of food shortages, Spence, like Norquay and others, moved north to Lakes Manitoba and Winnipegosis, where he fished and gathered salt alongside the Métis salt makers.[47] His initiative came to nothing, but it did give evidence that Norquay was ready to participate in public affairs and to seek alternatives to the rule of the Hudson's Bay Company.

A worldly American who visited the Red River Settlement in this period was surprised to discover that its organizing structures were far distant from the political conventions in his own community. The polity that he encountered was "slow," he thought, "50 years behind our times." He perceived that the "government has but little to act upon, and the influence of leaders must be almost wholly *personal*. There can exist no power over the people that are not of such a nature that it will gain strength by close and intimate association of ruler and ruled, and a governor must be a hero to his *valet de chambre*, or he can be no hero at all."[48] His estimate fit with the realities of a small community accustomed to the dual governing structures of farm municipality and bison hunt.

Norquay had the skills to lead. As Spence's Portage la Prairie experiment demonstrated, he also had some interest in doing so. But his family faced a crisis in 1868–69 because of serious food shortages. The famine and his fur trade job probably accounted for his absence from the events associated with Louis Riel and the founding of Manitoba during the winter of 1869–70. Late in the fall or early in the winter of 1869, the family headed back to the fur trade post for another session of three or four months. They returned to High Bluff at the beginning of March 1870 to discover a settlement in turmoil and, in his own family, talk of war.[49]

Mediator

Canada's acquisition of the HBC territories in 1869–70 and the Red River Settlement's resistance to it were decisive moments in the history of the continent's northwest. Loyalties forged among individuals and communities during this year endured not just for the next decade but for generations to come. They also established the context of John Norquay's political career. Norquay faced two very different options. Louis Riel, a twenty-five-year-old Métis, having recently returned from a decade of study and political apprenticeship in Quebec, offered one path forward. John Christian Schultz led the alternative. He was thirty years old, an Ontarian, nominally a medical doctor, but more obviously an ambitious business promoter. Schultz had arrived in the settlement in the early 1860s and become an outspoken advocate of Canadian annexation, a critic of the Hudson's Bay Company, and no friend of the Métis. Norquay would have to navigate in waters defined by these opposites.

The Red River Settlement's population of 12,000 in 1869–70 included about 4,400 who, like Norquay, identified as Bungee/English-speaking,

Protestant, and "mixed" ancestry. Another 5,700 were Michif/French-speaking Métis. They were joined by about 700 Cree and Saulteaux residents, mainly in St. Peter's parish ("the Indian Settlement"), and 1,200 people of Canadian and European ("White") heritage. The "mixed" peoples, over 80 percent of the total population, recognized that the political transition from British and HBC to Canadian administration presented significant issues for them that had to be addressed if they were to flourish in the new order.

At a pivotal meeting of settlers in July 1869, some Métis argued that the £300,000 Canada was offering the Hudson's Bay Company as part of the transfer agreement should be paid instead to the Cree, Saulteaux, and "mixed" settlers as rightful owners of the soil.[50] But that discussion, and the reasoning behind it, faded as new factions seized the initiative in the following months. Riel entered the political struggle at this stage. Alone among the contending groups, he and a small group of Michif/French-speaking Métis decided on a strategy of direct action. After several symbolic acts of resistance, they seized control of Upper Fort Garry, the only easily defended military redoubt in the settlement. Their pre-emptive strike, accomplished initially without the spilling of blood, sustained a provisional administration for nine months, the duration of negotiations with Canada. The resistance movement's standing among the residents of the settlement waxed and waned, but Riel and his Métis adherents, though sometimes under threat, were never deposed. Norquay, who had been trading at Lake Winnipegosis with Michif-speaking hunters, whose High Bluff farm was located just a few kilometres west of the large Métis settlement St. François Xavier, and who participated in its bison hunts, might not have agreed with their strategy but understood their concerns.

John Schultz, the other pole in Assiniboia politics, led a small but vociferous English-speaking faction, the "Canadian party," that favoured Canada's immediate annexation of "the North-West." Many of these recently arrived Canadians behaved as though they were superior beings from a superior civilization. A few, mostly English-speaking farmers from Ontario, settled on the rich Portage la Prairie plains just behind the pioneers' river lots along the Assiniboine River. They immediately provoked confrontations with Cree and Saulteaux who had lived in the area for decades if not generations and with the Dakota who had arrived in 1863–64 in the aftermath of Indigenous-White conflicts in Minnesota. In particular the Ontario newcomers infringed the hay lands of the "mixed" settlers' river lots.[51] They also fed conspiracy theories about the Hudson's Bay Company, the Roman Catholic Church, and the Michif-speaking residents of nearby parishes, in the process winning favour among some of the Bungee/English-speaking old settlers.[52] The Ontario nationalist Charles Mair, in particular, attracted a following with his anti-French, anti-Catholic views. Among his followers was Norquay's brother-in-law, John James Setter. In mid-February 1870 they formed a military force aiming to defeat the Riel forces, an initiative that nearly provoked a civil war. Norquay understood their perspective too.

Although some families joined the Canadian party in opposition to Riel, and a second group supported the resistance wholeheartedly, there was a third group in Assiniboia that tried to stay aloof from both. Those in the so-called moderate camp accepted that the Métis resistance movement was defending their interests, particularly their claims to land and resources. These people found the aggressive language employed by the Ontarians offensive. Neither Michif nor Ontarian, they urged both sides to steer clear of armed conflict. As William Tait, a Scot "Halfbreed" settler, said in November to those Canadian hotheads who opposed Riel, "you may talk, but in the convention we sit opposite those who were born and brought up among us, ate with us, slept with us, hunted with us, traded with us, and are our own flesh and blood. . . . Gentlemen, I for one cannot fight them. I will not imbrue my hands in their blood."[53]

Norquay belonged to this third camp. He saw the risks associated with the vocal Orange Order Ontarians. He was doubtful about the leadership of the mercurial Louis Riel, leader of the resistance. Rather than opt for one side or the other, Norquay chose the role of intermediary and acted as a conciliator in public debates. Many years later a brief biographical sketch, perhaps drafted by Norquay himself, noted that he "took a prominent part in all the discussion relating to the Red River Rebellion of 1870, and by the moderation of his views secured the confidence of all parties."[54] The statement was made well after the fact and probably exaggerated his role, but the assertion fit the person. Like many of the Red River Settlement's residents, Norquay believed that the interests of long-time settlers should be protected as they entered a political arrangement with Canada.

His growing reputation as a public figure also received partial confirmation during the resistance. In the spring of 1870, Norquay was one of two magistrates appointed by the Riel administration to serve in a Portage la Prairie district court.[55] The appointment acknowledged his standing in the parishes on the western edge of Assiniboia.

The clearest evidence of Norquay's interest in the politics then roiling Red River was the record of a public meeting on 1 March 1870 in St. Margaret's district. A nominee, his cousin John Lazarus Norquay Sr., was "duly elected by public meeting of the parishioners of St. Margaret's Parish" to represent the community in the council of the provisional government. The signatories to this letter were "John Norquay, Jun., and George Adams."[56] In short, Norquay was present in the parish on 1 March and attended the official nominating meeting but was not chosen to be its representative in the Legislative Assembly of Assiniboia.

More than five months later, just after Christmas 1870, and after Manitoba had been securely lodged within Canada's confederation, the constituency of High Bluff held a nomination meeting to select candidates for the first election in the new province. John Norquay Jr. was nominated first, then his cousin, John Lazarus Norquay Sr. The latter resigned in favour of the former, there were no further nominations, and John Jr. was declared elected by acclamation. He was to sit in the provincial legislature for the next nineteen years. The confusion concerning two men of the same name residing in the same district and seeking the same office ended almost as soon as it began.[57]

Why did John Lazarus Norquay Sr. step back?[58] He was literate but not a well-educated man. Likely he was less articulate and forceful in public debate than his cousin. A letter from the older Norquay to the younger, written five years later, gives evidence that he formed the letters of the alphabet with difficulty and was aware of the contrast between their levels of schooling. Later on the elder cousin wrote to the younger cousin, now in the premier's office: "Excuse my bad penmanship for I can hardly make it out but no doubt you will as you are a better schollar."[59] At the time of the nomination meeting in December 1870, facing the prospect of some months away from his household, and having seen what the work entailed during the spring session of the Legislative Assembly of Assiniboia, John Sr. might have wished to concentrate on the needs of his family and farm. He might have doubted the security of a politician's life. He might have disliked the pressures that he had experienced in High Bluff as tensions over race and religion increased. And he might have believed that his younger cousin had qualities he lacked and ambition he did not possess.

Innocent Bystander or Knowing Collaborator?

Young John Norquay, member designate of the Legislative Assembly of Manitoba, knew only a little about the political institutions in which he would work. He might not even have understood that some of the most important policy decisions shaping the future of his new province had already been made. The outline of Manitoba politics for his entire political career rested on clauses in the Manitoba Act that determined the fate of the province's public lands and natural resources and, in the process, created distinct categories of people. Norquay bumped against them frequently in the next two decades.

The great purpose of confederation in 1867—as envisaged by Sir John A. Macdonald and his colleagues—was the creation of a transcontinental nation-state in the northern half of North America. To that end they would assume outright ownership of all the territory previously held by the Hudson's Bay Company, a territory twice as large as the Canadian nation-state at that time. Riel's resistance movement meant that Ottawa eventually and reluctantly had to negotiate the terms of entry with representatives of the 12,000 residents of the District of Assiniboia. Macdonald acquiesced to Riel's condition of provincial rather than territorial status for the new entity. But Manitoba would not be a province like the others, nor would the lands surrounding it that became the North-West Territories and, decades later (in 1905), portions of which became Saskatchewan and Alberta. Rather, the national government would control the lands and resources of this huge tract. Whereas British Columbia and the original four provinces owned the lands and natural resources, and benefited from the taxation revenues associated with them, Manitoba and its prairie siblings would not. Overnight the Ottawa government became the possessor of an empire, and the vast HBC lands became its colony.

Historian John Weaver treats this chapter in the history of the modern world under the title "Great Land Rush." He suggests that there were "no long-lasting, profound differences" in the experience of taking land from Indigenous peoples in the "neo-Europes" of Australia, New Zealand, South Africa, Argentina, the United States, and Canada, though these far-flung territories encountered "countless variations in specific policies and practices."[60] One such variation, the Hudson's Bay Company's Rupert's Land, took the form of a single, vast, quasi-colony and a single transaction. This despite the fact that a small but influential portion of the whole, the District of Assiniboia, had developed its own property rules—a blend of Indigenous, British, and French practices—during preceding decades. The Red River Settlement's flexible customs, adapted to the resources of the land and the needs and customs of the families living off them, were overwritten by Canada's empire builders within just a few years, at most half a decade after July 1870. The informal, consensus-based practices of earlier days then largely disappeared.[61]

Two potential alternatives for landholding rules during the era of transition were discussed in the Assiniboia assembly and at other venues during 1869–70, the year when decisions were set in stone. The first was a Michif/French proposal for a large, contiguous reserve for the Métis community as outlined by Father Noel-Joseph Ritchot, the lead Assiniboia negotiator in the Ottawa talks between Red River delegates and the Canadian government. Ritchot wanted to "establish . . . not less than 50 or 75 years in which children not yet born will have a right to land." Such an enclave could be ensured, he suggested, by allocating control of public lands to the new provincial government. The second was James McKay's suggestion to the Assiniboia assembly that they reserve a portion of the land as commons where Cree and Saulteaux families could continue to harvest resources in some sort of collective arrangement. McKay was an influential trader and merchant whose opinion carried weight. His approach, like Ritchot's, would prevent the implementation of a single, overriding principle of the Canadian and British type in which all land would be subdivided into individual parcels controlled by the Crown and available for private ownership. Canada rejected both Ritchot's proposal for local management of a large parcel of land and, by implication, McKay's suggestion that a system of collective resource ownership be permitted to the Métis as well as the Cree and Saulteaux. Instead, the crucial bargaining chip ceded by Prime Minister Macdonald and Minister George-Étienne Cartier, one that Ritchot accepted, was a grant of land—1.4 million acres—to Métis children. This grant would be doled out as individually owned parcels, not a community enclave.[62] It is fair to say that the people of Assiniboia, through their representatives in the Legislative Assembly, accepted this approach by endorsing the terms of the Manitoba Act in their sittings of 23–24 June 1870. Red River's alternative answers to the question of who owned the land, the answers proposed by at least some locals, based on collective as well as individual rights in some sort of mixed system, did not prevail. Edward Hay, England-born assembly member and mill-owner, welcomed the new, individualist, Canadian system in an 1872 assembly debate, saying: "His people desired that each one should be allowed his choice of location."[63]

Although Norquay inherited these rules, he had no voice in their creation. Did he acquiesce? Yes. Ever the practical modernizer, he accepted the new property regime.

The next step in his own family's land history gave further evidence of his willingness to engage with private land markets. John and Elizabeth sold their St. Andrews lot in 1871.[64] This was an important decision and probably had a simple explanation: they did not need and could not manage a second farm eighty kilometres from their new High Bluff home. They probably recognized that the tract in St. Andrews, situated near the centre of a lively community, had considerable market value. The couple received an infusion of cash as they adjusted to moves between the farm at High Bluff and temporary residences nearer to the centre of government in Winnipeg. The sale of the land might also have provided funds for John's brother and sisters. But a business deal involving a significant plot of land, especially land that had family meaning, had broader significance: selling land and making profit were part of the Norquays' worldview. The sale was a sign of things to come.

John Norquay's circumstances in 1870 might have seemed little different from those of several thousand other mixed-ancestry householders in the settlement trying to make ends meet and to care for growing numbers of children. The appearance was deceiving. Despite his Indigenous and Orkney heritage, he did not conform to the pattern set out in the few surviving memoirs of men who had grown up in the Red River Settlement and laboured in the bison hunt and fur trade. Those who have left extended records of their lives—Peter Erasmus, Louis Goulet, Johnny Grant, Norbert Welsh—were the quintessential "free men" of Métis myth, the ones who evaded the grasp of "bosses" and made their own rules while working at pace, dancing with gusto, fighting when necessary. Welsh gloried in his freedom and adventures. Erasmus refused to bow before the elites. Grant made and lost fortunes. Although sharing some of their qualities, Norquay was more restrained and, as will become apparent, more willing to accommodate the newcomers.[65] He was a teacher and a farmer, not an entrepreneur, not a revolutionary, and he possessed talents as well as training that would open opportunities not accessible to the others.

The most distinctive aspect of his life to this moment was his education. As a teenager, he learned about Greek wars, Roman myths, industrialists' triumphs, and the imperial Anglican Church. Communicated exclusively by teachers and by print, such knowledge remained abstract, far removed from his daily experience. But the schooling and reading kindled his ambition. As a young adult, Norquay experienced first-hand the conduct of public affairs in the homegrown institutions of western North America, including the Cree and Saulteaux lodge, the Métis hunt, the courtrooms of Assiniboia, and the printed laws circulated by the Assiniboia district council. He learned that leadership in these forums depended on oratory and that he could hold his own in parish discussions.

His victory by acclamation in the 1870 election marked a turning point. Norquay willingly accepted the challenges posed by his new political role. He had the intellectual training to deal with debates and statutes and government accounts and complex legal arrangements. Among the last category, the most important were the Manitoba Act clauses on land allocations. These sections of the federal legislation creating the province shaped the course of Canada's western territories and of the national government itself and, perhaps surprisingly, even contributed to what has been described as "ethnogenesis," the emergence of a new ethnicity or peoplehood. Where Norquay stood on that subject remained to be seen.

CHAPTER 3

"The Transfer Made Us Wise," the 1870s

The 1870s required drastic adjustments in the Norquay family. Living in four different homes during the first half of the decade, raising seven children, balancing the domestic budget, and staying on top of the changing political scene imposed many pressures on John and Elizabeth. They had to deal with the stresses just as they had to cope with the changes in diet and the financial demands that accompanied their new roles. Elizabeth managed the household while dealing with bouts of illness and the death of several close relatives. John continued to farm and hunt, but attendance at regular cabinet meetings and supervision of a government department meant that he had become more than an assembly member and farmer.

In this decade the family encountered newcomers from eastern Canada, Britain, and Europe who conveyed attitudes strikingly different from those held in old Red River. Both "Métis" and "Indian" acquired meanings and significance in local society that differed from previous usage. A rhyme of that era captured the wrenching change:

> Oh, for the times that men despise
> At least I liked them, me whatever,
> Before the Transfer made us wise,
> Or politics . . . made us clever.[1]

The "politics" referred to factional conflicts within the community. The "Transfer" meant Canada's assumption of control over the Red River Settlement. Henceforth, sovereignty over the western interior resided in a different location, the Canadian Crown as opposed to Indigenous peoples and the British Crown. In the view of most newly arrived Whites, this was a distinction without a difference. In the view of settlers of old Red River, however, a proud heritage—a combination of Indigenous, British, and French customs—was being superseded. They were prepared to accommodate the new reality but they found the "clever" debates jarring. Working out a reconciliation would impose demands on every individual and family. Norquay, like Riel, steeped in the old ways of Red River, tried to help them ride out the "Transfer."

At Home

The Norquay family occupied river lots of the customary Red River type for most of the twenty-three years between 1862 and 1885. Despite the importance of politics and government in John's experience, Elizabeth and the children continued to see themselves as members of a farm household. Daily work followed the time-honoured routines attached to cereal crops and animal husbandry. They fed and watered horses, cows, and pigs on a regular schedule. They fixed harnesses and sleighs and cutters and wagons. They shovelled manure out of the stable and barn. They planted and harvested crops. Horse-related purchases—of whips and trotting plates, of sleigh runners and carriage springs, of shoeing and reshoeing services at the blacksmith's, of livery barn charges in the city ("one horse, two feeds" each day that John worked in the office)—represented a sizable proportion of the yearly budget. He bought the farm equipment, organized the construction work, looked after the animals, and spent some weeks each year cultivating fields and gathering wood and hay.[2]

The farm loomed large in the lives of the children when they were young. Seventy years later they provided a few details to an interviewer. They recalled with pleasure walking in the fields with their father on Sunday mornings during the growing season, especially the times when he filled his pockets with candy and let them help themselves. They said that he seeded broadcast, a sack over his shoulder full of the grain that he cast on the plowed land.[3] The family gathered for prayers, and John himself "often wrote the prayer for Sunday evening." Andrew remembered that his father was "very fond of the voyageur's song, 'En roulant ma boule' [about a prince, a maiden, and a duck hunt], and sang it often." They recalled, too, that he played cricket and participated in gun club events.[4] His children described Norquay as a "jolly father." One of his sons said he was "easy to meet and interesting to talk to. He was good company, and he enjoyed parties and dancing . . . [and was] fond of all kinds of reading." But the same son, Dr. H.C. Norquay, also said that, until the family moved to Winnipeg in 1885, the children saw little of him after he became premier except on weekends. A granddaughter said that "when he came home late at night he woke up the whole family and they would sing and dance. [He] was a very kindly person—he had warmth, gaiety, and happiness. . . . [He] played, laughed, and had fun."[5] These brief recollections gathered many years later offer hints but not more about the man and his family in the 1870s.

Formal instruction was an important part of the year for the children. They started out in local parish schools and then, as they entered their teens, awaited parental decisions about their future. Norquay spoke to the bishop of Rupert's Land in the winter of 1875 about sending Tom, the eldest, then aged twelve, to St. John's College. The bishop replied, "I shd be glad to have him for he is a clever & good boy though requiring to be kept to his work." Tom performed adequately in the school. He came in "first in his Form of 15 boys in Religious Instruction & equal at First with another boy in English," according to the bishop's end-of-term report. "In Latin he did not do so well & there lost place in his Form. He has very good abilities & I daresay will study well if in College [residence]. In all his conduct he gives the fullest satisfaction & is a nice, hearty, pleasant boy."[6]

Bella (Isabella) was next. The patchwork of her early schooling included sessions at "the parish school of St. Andrew's . . . [and then] old St. Mary's academy, which she attended as a very little girl, and where she was a great favourite of Bishop Taché . . . [and then] St. Andrew's school again." Bishop Machray stepped in at just the right moment with a plan to organize the St. John's Ladies School in the fall of 1876. As a clergyman said, this school was designed for "the daughters of the upper classes in the Province of Rupert's Land." John Norquay was invited to become a member of the school's board. Bella attended the school from at least 1879, when she turned thirteen, through the early 1880s. She took classes in English, French, German, arithmetic, art, and music. Caroline Ellen followed her to the Ladies School when she was of age.[7] A measure of the style in both the boys' and girls' branches of St. John's was a rule requiring the young men to "wear Academical Dress at all lectures & at meals and at Morning and evening prayer and when they call on the Warden or any of the Professors on any business." Students were expected to be in their rooms by 8:30 p.m.[8]

Bella got on very well with her father. Not yet fourteen, and a resident student at St. John's Ladies School, she wrote to him about arrangements for a friend's wedding:

> My dear papa I hope you are quite well and I hope mamma is better[;] let me know soon please for I feel very uneasy about her[.] I hope she will be better before Wednesday and if you come for me please come on Thursday so that I will be down [to St. Andrews] in time and please get me a pair of slippers to wear for I am going to wear my white dress and I nead slippers with it[.] The number that I take in slippers are 5[.] If I go I am going to be Bella's bridesmaid she told me so[,] that is if she did not cho[o]se one already[.] Give my love to all at home and tell mamma I am quite well[.] I remain your loving Daughter Bella.[9]

Concern about her mother's health; an interest in clothing; sensitivity to the pecking order among friends; attentiveness to social events; matter-of-fact dealings with her father: the letter hints at Isabella's confidence and her easy relationship with her parents.

The Norquay home exhibited the gender divide of that era. The father and older boys had to have skills in farming and house construction, the mother and daughters in making clothing and furnishing and feeding the household. The farm equipment and lumber bills indicated men's work. Elizabeth ordered the tweed, velveteen, damask, and dress goods, and Bella received lace, cotton, embroidery, spools, hose, and a sunshade. One grandchild claimed, much later, that John favoured the boys: "In the Premier's family the girls had to give way to the boys; the boys were spoiled. The Premier had pillow fights with his sons."[10] Farm work fell to the older children as well as to their father, but the family could not meet the farm's demand for labour without additional help. When Tom Adams, the son of John's sister, was staying with them in the late 1870s, he acted as an unpaid member of the workforce. They also employed at least one adult male labourer from the mid-decade and possibly a maid.[11]

John's preoccupation with agriculture was shared by most other residents of Manitoba. John knew the problems and the equipment and could join with farm dwellers in taking offence at city jokes about rural life. His decision in 1877 to pay $250 for a wagon, harness, and mule team (rather than horses or oxen), to carry out the basic field and yard work, became the butt of opponents' mocking commentary. In an age when horses were the pride of a farm, Norquay's decision to work with mules for a brief period stood out as quixotic and easily scorned. What was more, one of the mules then strayed from the stable. The animal was eventually found but not before Winnipeg's new satirical newspaper, *Quiz*, published a long poem on the subject and added that any animal fleeing its warm quarters at the start of winter was making "a perfect ass of itself."[12]

The Norquay farm had to adjust to the rapid industrialization of the continent in these decades. By the 1870s, standardized production techniques and farm equipment had become part of everyday life. Each new product had its brand name. Norquay soon abandoned the homemade Red River carts and implements of the previous generation in favour of a Snowball wagon, a Lion rake, and a Mohawk plow.[13] Although he might have been slower to do so than his Ontario-born neighbours, he was acquiring the equipment of a modern farm.

In contrast to the log homes of the 1830s–60s era, the Parkdale house was constructed with glass windows and milled lumber, shingles, and doors. The furniture within was not produced locally. Rather, purchases of a sideboard, secretary table, Brussels carpet, washstands, and hanging lamps, just a few of the invoices sent to John's office, underlined the Norquays' adoption of contemporary Victorian fashion.[14] By the early 1880s the house and even the farm looked much like those being established by incoming Canadians. Branded goods and cash purchases had become parts of family life. Although every family member's labour ensured that the Parkdale home was a viable economic unit, the steady arrival of bills required that John find the cash to pay for them.

The lives of the family members were changing because money and stores and grocery bills now figured prominently in their weekly regimen.

The household diet changed substantially in these modernizing surroundings. In the 1860s it had mirrored that of other Red River families by relying almost exclusively on foods they gathered themselves. John's time-consuming office work in the 1870s meant that, because his and Elizabeth's labour could not supply all the food needs, the family had to adapt to new kitchen habits while continuing to rely on field crops and garden vegetables. John continued to go to the steam mill in St. Andrews for cracked wheat, bran, and flour, presumably ground from his own crops.[15] And, to judge from the bills for guns and ammunition, he hunted as often as possible. By the closing years of the decade, however, the Norquays were spending more than $100 annually at the Bannatyne store alone. In one year, 1877, they ordered rice, sugar, lard, ham, macaroni, coconut, biscuits, white buns, apples, figs, raisins, various beverages, and a can of lobster, at a total cost of $152.80. Considering that a hired hand might expect to work six months to earn an equal sum, and that Bannatyne's was just one of the grocery stores patronized by the family, they were immersed in a cash economy and retail food sources.[16]

In 1878, John and Elizabeth were raising seven children, ranging in age from fifteen to six. That responsibility in itself worried him. He was now thirty-seven. He must have been very conscious that Omy Norquay, his grandfather, died at forty-seven, his father at forty, and his mother at twenty-four. Coincidentally the 1870s marked the emergence of the retail life insurance industry in Canada. John became an avid consumer of its wares. At one point or another between 1877 and 1882, he had active policies with Sun Life, Standard Life, Canada Life, Confederation Life, Lion Life, and North American Life. Two other companies refused to cover him: in 1877 his insurance policy with Provincial Life was cancelled because he had a policy with another company, a duplication contrary to Provincial's regulations. And Equitable Life rejected him point blank: "Dear Sir: The issuing of a policy on the life of Mr. Jno. Norquay is declined by our Medical Directors a/c overweight."[17] The range of contacts—eight companies in five years—suggests the depth of his concern about health and mortality as John approached his fortieth birthday.

A comment by his friend William Kennedy offered insight into prevailing thoughts on the end of life in gospel-conscious homes. Kennedy, a one-time missionary and now a distinguished figure in St. Andrews, wrote to Norquay while he was in Ottawa in 1879: "Your family are well but I regret to tell you poor Bella Setter the wife of young Adam McDonald died suddenly yesterday & is likely to be buried today. She had got safely over child birth but some trouble stept in some days after & took away this usually strong & healthy girl as she appeared. Hoping that in the midst of life we may always remember that death is always at hand & therefore that we diligently prepare for it[,] I remain, very truly yrs."[18] Bella's passing came as a shock and, as Kennedy said, demanded contemplation.

Despite his interest in life insurance, and Kennedy's talk of death, one should not exaggerate Norquay's frailty. John had not stopped growing, though he now grew outward rather than upward. He towered over most of the people around him.[19] He was also heavier. It is likely that he started the decade at a figure closer to 200 pounds and ended it nearer 300. Rumours of his increasing girth travelled as far as his sister and her family in The Pas. When they caught word of his changing dimensions, they urged brother-in-law Charles Adams to write that "Nancy [John's sister?] wishes very much for you to send her your likeness [since] we hear that you are getting so fearfully big."[20] John was a large man who lived in an era when physical demands were considerable. He hunted often, travelled by horseback and wagon, worked on a farm regularly, was accustomed to walking everywhere, and was said to cut a fine figure when dancing.

Elizabeth was quiet, whereas John was a performer. Although frequently unable to attend her husband's official appearances, her presence was recorded from time to time. At the opening of the legislature in February 1873, the first session presided over by Lieutenant Governor Alexander Morris, Elizabeth sat in the gallery along with Eleanor Kennedy, the wife of family friend Captain William Kennedy, and "Mrs. Dr. Schultz," the wife of Norquay's most irritating detractor. Given that Eleanor Kennedy was English, and that the Schultz family's distaste for Métis was widely known, they would have made an unusual and awkward party.[21] The strain of managing a family of seven children, John's frequent stays in the city, and the moves from district to district took a toll on Elizabeth's health. What was to become a constant worry emerged in the winter of 1874–75. The illness had no obvious origin, but several correspondents expressed their concern. Her brother, John James, observed in one letter that Elizabeth had been unwell, and John's old friend (and her relative) Andrew Spence expressed pleasure in hearing that she was recovering from a "serious illness."[22]

Then, in 1876, just as Elizabeth was recovering, she faced a greater sorrow. The death of a newborn child in her care hit her hard. George Peter McDonald, the son of her sister, Bella, was born on 22 January 1876. The McDonalds turned to provide the boy's feeding and care. A note beside his name in a list of dates of death in the Norquay family Bible records that George was "taken charge of by Mrs. A. McBeth" on 10 February. She probably served as wet nurse and caregiver for his first three months, at which time he was transferred to Elizabeth's care at Parkdale. George died at the end of summer, aged seven months. The tragedy was mentioned in a letter from Elizabeth's brother: "My Dear Neestaw [brother-in-law]: Yours of the 4th inst was recd[.] I am sorry to learn that you have lost that sweet little baby[.] I am sure that poor Betsy [Elizabeth] must feel lowly as you state." The episode is not part of any other account in the family's history, nor was the cause of the child's death clear.[23]

Mentions of Elizabeth's health appeared in Norquay's correspondence in the following years. Charles Adams, writing from The Pas in 1878 and inquiring about the welfare of his two sons then boarding in the Norquay household, added "only I feel for poor Betsy—how much she must be bothered with so large a family to look after, & she too, being not one of the strongest." He returned to the same thought, "poor Elizabeth," in a letter twenty months later. Bella, then thirteen, wrote to her father during his Ottawa trip in 1879 to say that "mamma is sick again." Expressions of concern came from several other friends in 1879, an indication that her health was a continuing question.[24] A doctor visited the house for "medical attendance" on at least five occasions in 1879–80. The kind wishes and worries about Elizabeth's illness appeared for at least the next five years. So did a consistent pattern of reliance on the drugstore for "capsules," "sulfur," "salicylic acid cachets," "pyretic saline," and "milk of magnesia."[25]

In material terms, the Norquay family was challenged by new realities and attracted by convenient shortcuts. As they adopted factory-made equipment, store-bought foods, and milled lumber, they followed patterns prevailing not just in Manitoba but also across Canada's provinces and America's states. With the destruction of the great bison herds, the collective effort of prairie hunts disappeared from the calendar. In the short term, while people dealt with grasshopper infestations and crop failures, the very survival of families was placed in the balance. The Norquays saw uncertainty and risk but also opportunity in the new approaches to diet, field crops, and animal husbandry. If only they could find sufficient income.

Money

By the closing years of the decade, household bills had to be paid in legal tender, not by barter and credit as was the case in old Red River. The Norquays knew from experience that river-lot farms were no passport to wealth. Still, they should have been able to flourish. John received a ministerial stipend in almost every year, starting in 1872, as well as the sessional indemnity paid to MLAs, for an average of nearly $1,600 per year. An ordinary working man earned $300–$600 yearly. Given that he took in several times as much, Norquay was potentially well off.[26] Despite a government salary, country foods, and river-lot fields and a garden, however, family finances were never in good shape.

Although John's earnings far exceeded those of the hostler who cared for his horse in the city stable, they did not cover all the family's spending. The education of seven children, at first in parish schools and later in elite private schools, was an enormous burden for the family.[27] So was the creation of a modern Victorian home in the style to which they now aspired. His tastes increased in sophistication after John encountered the fashions of eastern Canada. His favourite clothier, though not the only source of his clothes, was Bernard Saunders of Toronto. There John purchased in 1879 a blue serge suit with a vest (twenty-five dollars) and a brown Devon overcoat lined with angora (thirty-eight dollars). Saunders wrote to say that the overcoat had been shipped: "Your garment is one of the best you or anyone else ever saw & one of the finest pieces of stuff ever made. You can't help but like it."[28] The life insurance bills, perhaps $100 per year between 1875 and 1885, also weighed heavily. John faced many requests for money that grew out of his role as a government minister. Then there were the requests for help from members of his extended family. And the small, voluntary subscriptions: the church, the Masons, the curling club, the Manitoba Club, and many others.[29] His finances were precarious at best.

How could Norquay balance the domestic budget? One solution was to turn to the land market. This strategy first emerged in his 1866 and 1871 land deals and became a frequent resort in the following decade. When the family moved in 1873 to a large log house facing the "Main Highway," or Main Street, near Point Douglas Common in North Winnipeg, his expenses dropped because he could commute easily to his legislative offices. When he moved to Park's Creek several years later, he retained ownership of the Main Street house, probably because it was large and centrally located. Within weeks the city's medical committee struck a deal with him to rent it for about $100 per year and to turn it into the city's general hospital. Several years later, when the hospital moved to a more appropriate building, he rented the decaying log structure to a less exacting customer.[30] It had become a revenue property, intended to relieve some of the pressure on the family purse.

Norquay also participated in a small way in the burgeoning market for Métis scrips. These government certificates were given to children of mixed-ancestry households born before 15 July 1870 under Section 31 of the Manitoba Act. If a person wanted to make money quickly in Manitoba in the late 1870s, the fastest route to wealth was speculation in scrip. Between June 1878 and December 1879, in company with some other speculators, Norquay signed six power of attorney documents giving him the right to receive the lands or scrips allocated to six individuals who expected to receive a grant under the Manitoba Act or subsequent legislation. Not one of the six was from St. Andrews, all had French names, and none appeared in any other connection in Norquay's correspondence. In two of the six cases he collaborated with Andrew Strang, a Winnipeg merchant. In another, A.G.B. Bannatyne, also a Winnipeg merchant, participated with Norquay in the purchase. Both businessmen were known to be active participants in the speculative land and scrip markets that reached a peak of activity during this eighteen-month period. The deputy minister of the Department of the Interior in the federal government signed a document enumerating these six claims, adding a note that the power of attorney documents had been "received this day from the Hon. Jno. Norquay."[31] Assuming that he had hand-delivered the documents to the office of the top bureaucrat in the Ottawa department, Norquay clearly wanted to complete these deals, did not shrink from using his position to ensure that they went through, and was prepared to participate, if only in a small way, in the speculative market. The transactions suggest that he had moved some distance from his thinking at the beginning of the decade.

Despite these various sources of revenue, John was always behind in his bill payments and regularly faced appeals from merchants. Extreme measures kept the household afloat financially. From the spring of 1876 to the fall of

1880, merchants granted John at least nine promissory notes, amounting to a total indebtedness in just these vehicles of nearly $600 on which he was paying substantial interest. The several hundred bills from commercial businesses now filed in his office papers, most of them from Winnipeg firms, must have weighed on his conscience. His tactic of paying small amounts on larger bills might have avoided an immediate crisis, and ensured continuing credit at various merchants, but could only postpone a day of reckoning.[32]

Whatever the shortfalls in domestic finances, the Norquays were seen as well-to-do by other members of their extended family and frequently were called on for help. The appeals came from the family of John's brother, Tom Norquay, who taught school in St. Andrews for some years and maintained a river-lot farm in the parish, and from John's cousin, John Lazarus Norquay, who asked for aid with a land question and a government job. Members of the Setter clan, including Elizabeth's sisters, brothers, nephews, and their families, turned to the Norquays frequently, especially in relation to business ventures. John also supported his sister and her husband, Charles Adams, at the HBC post in The Pas, who sent at least two of their children to reside in the Norquay household and attend school.[33]

The income from the Parkdale farm varied with the year. The government stipend depended on electors' whims. Speculation in land sales could be lucrative but also brought risks and potential losses. Relatives' appeals for help could not be ignored. It was not easy to strike a balance in the family accounts. Those were only the most immediate sources of stress. Norquay also had to deal with dozens of other acquaintances and their problems, typically related to land. Could he address all these uncertainties with one stroke by finding a more secure job that paid well and offered the opportunity to serve others? A federal government appointment looked increasingly attractive, and his strengths as an experienced teacher who spoke Cree, Saulteaux, and some Dakota seemingly qualified Norquay to become a civil service intermediary between Indigenous peoples and the Canadian state. That remained an aspiration throughout the decade.

Cree, Saulteaux, Dakota, and "Natives"

Today genomic science has concluded that "the concept of race has no genetic or scientific basis."[34] In the late nineteenth century, in contrast, many people believed that humanity was divided into races. By observations of cranium, hair, skin colour, and other physical characteristics, they discerned what they supposed to be categories of biological traits. Some citizens then associated groups' cultural differences, and individuals' behavioural differences, with these physical contrasts.[35] These notions of "race" informed government policy. The numbered treaties of the 1870s that Ottawa negotiated with Cree, Saulteaux, Assiniboine, and Blackfoot peoples imposed a legal definition of "Indians" and reinforced the pseudo-scientific categorization of "races" in Canadian society. Canada's federal administration, charged with responsibility under the British North America Act for "Indians and lands reserved for Indians," then undertook what it regarded as legitimate transfers of sovereignty over the prairie lands occupied by Indigenous peoples to its own control.

Such thinking also led to the ranking of putative ethnic groups in a hierarchy. People who claimed to be "White" declared their superiority over those said to be different in "colour" on the basis of this spurious notion. British historian Catherine Hall has gone so far as to say that "ways of thinking about race are the most destructive legacy of Britain's imperial past." She writes that, as a consequence, many of the British Empire's Indigenous peoples, including Indians, Aboriginals, and East Asians, lost the status of adults within their societies: "All were defined as racialized others, inferior to white Britons." British history became a "story of exclusion," she concludes, and race became associated with "terrible disparities of wealth and power."[36] This was the world Norquay and his countrymen were joining.

Norquay did not accept that some groups in society were doomed to inferior status by their biological inheritance or that members of another supposed group, people with "white skin," possessed a blood-related superiority. He believed in the ability of Cree, Saulteaux, and Dakota to adapt to changing circumstances. He thought in terms of the challenge presented to all prairie Canadians by a revolutionized economy and modern state. As a youth he had absorbed Bishop Anderson's teachings about the common roots of all humans. As a novice politician he had listened to Lieutenant Governor Archibald describe the Cree and Saulteaux leaders as able negotiators. While attending Anglican synod meetings he would have heard Archbishop Machray say that "the Indian has quite sufficient capacity for civilisation."[37] These convictions underlay his decision to secure an appointment in the Indian branch of the federal government.

On four occasions in six years between 1873 and 1879, Norquay applied for positions in the federal civil service. He submitted the first application in the spring of 1873, immediately after his trip to the Palestine (Gladstone) district, where he helped to organize a militia group and to calm anti-Dakota agitation. Having failed to secure that job, he applied for another in 1875. Premier Robert Davis, conducting a lobbying trip to Ottawa, acted as an intermediary. He wrote to Norquay that the request had been presented squarely to Alexander Mackenzie (Liberal prime minister, 1873–1878) and that he had "a fair chance." Nothing came of that proposal either.[38]

Norquay applied to be the Manitoba superintendent of Indian Affairs in the autumn of 1877. Rumours of the opening had been precipitated by charges involving purchases of cattle for Cree and Saulteaux communities by Norquay's cabinet colleague Joseph Royal and disgraced civil servant Joseph Provencher, yet another of the eastern Canadian lawyer-journalists who had received a federal post in the west. Surviving documents suggest that Norquay conducted a full-scale campaign for Provencher's position and that his application was supported by a number of local citizens, including merchant and Member of Parliament Andrew Bannatyne and clergyman-professor George Bryce. The federal minister wrote to Bryce to advise him on government procedures: "Mr. Norquay has been recommended to me by a great many of our friends as a good man to put in place of [Mr.] Provencher and if the members for Manitoba would only support him, I believe he would make an excellent agent. His knowledge of the French and Indian languages would be of great consequence to him in that capacity. . . . Personally, I should be very glad to meet your wishes."[39]

Norquay's ability to recruit such prominent citizens as supporters illustrated his growing reputation in Winnipeg. Unfortunately his case would have to be supported by Donald Smith, the local Member of Parliament. Although not at daggers drawn, Norquay and Smith were not close. A friend asked in a letter in mid-March 1878 "have you heard anything of the Indian Supty yet?"[40] Norquay had heard nothing, nor would he. The Mackenzie government in Ottawa was headed for defeat.

The job applications underlined Norquay's readiness to trade the risks of politics for a steady paycheque in the civil service. They also attested to his own estimate of his experience and abilities. He was aware of conditions in Cree and Saulteaux communities and fully prepared to put his energy into working with them. Taken together with a fourth application, submitted the following year, the initiatives represented an alternative path in life.[41] These apparent departures from what seems in retrospect to have been his obvious, even inevitable, career in electoral politics also raise the spectre of racism: was Norquay passed over because he had clashed with powerful individuals in government; or was he the victim of Ontarians' distrust of Red River people of mixed ancestry? Either way he was confronted by federal politicians' reluctance to hand appointments to him or other inhabitants of old Red River when there were plenty of eastern Canadian party workers seeking government paycheques.

Constrained by his cabinet responsibilities and not wanting to speak bluntly for fear that his words would be circulated widely, Norquay was nonetheless concerned by the growing gulf between Indigenous peoples and other inhabitants of Manitoba. The evidence of the divide was increasing. Within months of the "transfer" to Canadian control, for example, the Métis of St. Laurent pushed some Cree and Saulteaux families out of the lands alongside Lake Manitoba. Those who signed treaties, the Métis argued, must confine themselves to the reserves that had been selected. A federal government surveyor, William Wagner, was surprised by the aggressive stance of the Métis: "It appears to me as where all Halfbreeds up here [near Lake Manitoba] are of the opinion that a full-bred Indian had no right to hold any property amongst whites, if I may call the settlers at Oak Point [the Métis] by that name."[42] There is no evidence to suggest that Norquay wished to confine the Cree, Saulteaux, or Dakota to reserves as did these Michif/francophone countrymen.

When he heard calls for the removal of the Dakota from the Portage la Prairie district a few years later, he came closer to endorsing the idea.[43] His caution reflected the ambivalence with which long-time Red River settlers viewed the agitation regarding Indigenous peoples. William Luxton, the *Free Press* editor, moved that the Legislative Assembly send an address to the governor general "praying for the immediate removal of the Sioux [Dakota] Indians within this Province, to their reserves, as such Indians are a continual annoyance to the settlements, by reason of their pillaging and other evil habits."[44] Norquay was one of four assigned to draft the measure. In these conversations it appears that he and a few of his colleagues had come to an understanding that the Dakota had to settle permanently on a fixed tract of land. As James McKay, Norquay's influential countryman, said in the legislative council debates, "it would, no doubt, be very desirable that these and all the other Indians should be removed to their reserves."[45]

Norquay was concerned about Canada's approach to prairie First Nations. The evidence lies in his own words, in the speeches of several allies, and in letters that he received from his closest friends. Working with a few colleagues, he was developing a defence of Cree, Saulteaux, and Dakota in the face of what they saw as unwise government policies and racist talk among some newcomers. Among these colleagues, James McKay, in particular, condemned eastern Canadians' assumptions of superiority. He advised the administrators to deal with Indigenous peoples as equals or, as he put it, "like men." McKay was Norquay's friend and political ally. He knew the Dakota situation well, sympathized with the Dakota, and believed that thus far the federal government had acted generously and appropriately. What is more, McKay argued that only an approach that respected the Dakota and supported them with gifts of food and clothing would be appropriate. Although he was careful to conceal his tracks, Norquay agreed with McKay. They believed that diplomacy with prairie First Nations must adhere to previously agreed conventions if peace and trust were to be maintained.[46]

Several of Norquay's friends spoke in scathing terms about the administrators imported from eastern Canada to handle western affairs. One of these friends was William Kennedy, Cumberland House–born, Orkney-educated resident of St. Andrews parish. The child of a fur trade officer and a Cree woman, Kennedy was about fifty years of age when his attractive stone house, Maple Grove, was constructed near St. Andrews Church in the 1860s and he became active in local affairs. He had traded furs in Ontario and Labrador, sailed on the Great Lakes as a ship's captain, conducted two expeditions from England as part of the search for Sir John Franklin, and served briefly as a Church of England missionary in a Saulteaux community before settling at Red River. During the decade that their families lived in St. Andrews, the Kennedy and Norquay girls became friends, and their elders established ties that endured. William Kennedy believed that Canadian federal government policies were reducing the Cree and Saulteaux to the status of "parasites of civilization," as he wrote to Norquay. If nothing was done to change their lives, he said, then those who lived farther west, in the Saskatchewan river country, would find that their land had become "a valley of death & pestilence—a pestilence of two kinds—a natural as well as a moral one." Kennedy's motivation as a stern Christian was "to recover a class of British subjects [the First Nations of the west] who were elements of progress before Confederation so ruthlessly took hold of them."[47] Norquay never said on the record that he agreed with Kennedy. As in his relations with McKay, he was careful not to be quoted supporting his colleagues' outbursts. But given their close ties, it is almost certain that they shared an outlook. In these years, too, like Norquay, Kennedy decided that he could do better than the incumbent agents on First Nations reserves and applied for positions in the Indian branch of the Canadian government. He never received an appointment.

A decade later Norquay wrote a short essay for the *Dominion Illustrated* on "Sauteaux Indians." It provides important insights into his view not just of the Saulteaux but of all the prairie Indigenous communities. Recognizing that most of his readers would regard his subjects as exotic, he pandered to their prejudices by mimicking contemporary adventure novels of the era. Such condescending words might seem to have been portents of a harsh estimate of Indigenous peoples, but that was not the case. Drawn in by familiar language, his readers soon discovered that he offered positive assessments of the Saulteaux's adaptation to farming and of their lake and forest life in the northwestern interior of the continent.[48]

Norquay clearly knew a great deal about the Saulteaux. Synthesizing his wide experience, his reading, and his ability with languages, he explained in this brief (about 500 words) article that the Saulteaux constituted "some of the remains of the Great Algonquin nation which at one time spread over British America and a great portion of the United States." He pointed out that the many Saulteaux communities spoke a language "derived from one parent stock." He then distinguished between two broad cultural categories within the group, the northern forest/lake peoples and the southerners living on the margin of the plains. The two branches differed in their economic foundation, Norquay said, the one reliant especially on fish and the other on bison. They also differed in the degree of their integration within European Canadian society during the 1870s and 1880s. The prairie people were giving up their previous patterns of life while adapting to the near extinction of the bison. However reluctantly, in the case of the men in this group, they were now engaging successfully in farming. Those who dwelt in the northern forests had much less need to reconstruct an economy or culture because they were relatively less affected by the newcomers. They still encountered life-enhancing daily and seasonal change that Norquay judged to be "so delightful" and rewarding.[49]

In this article and in a manuscript that probably served as notes for a public lecture, Norquay acknowledged the Cree and Saulteaux claim to the land, an interest that preceded any HBC or French or British title. He also defended the First Peoples against the charge of hostility to incoming strangers. He wrote of the early weeks after the Selkirk colonists' arrival in 1812: "[The colonists] secured the services of some Indians and halfbreeds to take their children along [to Pembina] & found that when removed from the hostile influences of the North West Company these children of nature were not insensible to the dictates of kindness & humanity."[50]

Throughout the 1870s Norquay continued to acknowledge his connection to Cree, Saulteaux, and Dakota neighbours while asserting the distinctive claims of the peoples of mixed ancestry. His correspondence with John Setter, Elizabeth's nephew, hired by the North-West Mounted Police as an interpreter, illustrates the complications that accompanied his outlook. Writing from Fort Walsh in the Cypress Hills, 800 kilometres west of Upper Fort Garry, Setter reported to his uncle that he had conversed with Cree and Saulteaux who were hunting the few remaining bison: "I have several visits from the Crees and Saltose Indians[;] every day I am speeking to them I am continuley telling them that the sooner thay settle down the better for themselves and thay would find the benefit of it in lase [less] than two years." The Cree expressed an interest in Setter's self-declared kinship with them and in turn imposed a kind of race-based judgement on him: "The Crees is quite taking up with me being a native and explaining to them for their Intrest—as I told them that it was a native that was at the head of government at Winipeg thay ware soprisd [surprised]."[51] The conversations between Setter and his Cree visitors reflected a shared awareness of the difficulties posed by the disappearance of the bison. In speaking to them as he did, Setter was urging them to act in their own interests and asserting that he and they both possessed claims to the territory. But, in the very act of offering advice, he was also saying that their circumstance did not resemble his own.

Although Norquay might have been amused to hear that his name came up in such conversations on the western prairies, he would have recognized the reality of such discussions and applauded Setter for his approach. He would have accepted Setter's distinguishing, as in this letter, among three social identities: the Cree and Saulteaux "Indians" of the plains; the "natives" of settled Manitoba, mainly but not exclusively of mixed ancestry; and the "Whites" now arriving in great numbers. Norquay also knew that, like Setter, he was seen by many Whites, and most Cree and Saulteaux, as "native." However, he would have put the distinction in a more precise and less racialized manner than Whites would have done: he belonged to a "native" community whose members possessed shared interests and a shared past distinct from those of the Cree and Saulteaux. But, unlike Louis Riel, Norquay did not say that he belonged to a distinct race or nation carrying the label of "Métis" or "Halfbreed." The implications of such a position would have to be clarified in the coming years.

The rare pieces of his own writing illustrate his interest in and rapport with the Indigenous peoples who were his neighbours. Although he recognized a degree of kinship with them, a kinship understood in the sense of mutuality and human fellowship, he also knew that their education and economy differed substantially from his own. Like James McKay and William Kennedy, Norquay believed that his Red River Settlement experience would be invaluable in enabling him to lead his family through a comfortable transition. He assumed that he and most other Manitobans, including the Cree and Saulteaux in St. Peter's parish, were better prepared for the coming of a new way of life than the Indigenous hunters of the plains. Would those in Ottawa who had full authority over "Indians and lands reserved for Indians" see the advantage in appointing people of his knowledge and understanding to intermediary positions? And what role would the fraught issues of "race" and "Métis-ness" play in the government's decisions about using his expertise?

Coming to Terms with Métis-ness

A Métis "nation" acquired much clearer articulation in the 1870s. Norquay had no hand in its birth and did not desire national standing for himself or his followers but had to come to terms with the idea. He also had to deal with the White racism and racializing practices that contributed to its currency. He developed his own approaches and borrowed from the thinking of others as he encountered expressions of prejudice and ignorance. But Norquay could not change the basic facts of Canada's annexation of the prairie west: Manitoba Act clauses on land allocations shaped the course of Canada's western territories and contributed to "ethnogenesis," the emergence of an ethnic group or peoplehood.

His understanding of Métis-ness drew from predecessors whose thinking had resounded in public discussions during the years before Norquay became a public figure. Talk of the Métis as a "new nation" acquired prominence in relation to conflicts between the North-West Company and the Hudson's Bay Company, culminating in the battle at Seven Oaks in 1816. Pierre Falcon's "Chanson de la Grenouillère" found a ready audience among the Michif/French-speaking Métis at that time and lived on in public memory. A related but distinct view of national aspirations unfolded after the Hudson's Bay Company and the North-West Company merged in 1821. Developed mainly by the Bungee/English-speaking peoples of the district, this line of thought focused on who had the right to conduct trade: was it the chartered company alone or any Indigenous person? Could local people of mixed ancestry also set up shop as merchants? Insightful leaders wove the strands together in the half century between 1820 and 1870. They insisted on their freedoms both as British subjects and as Indigenous people.

Norquay understood that his childhood years had been passed in a unique setting and among members of a supportive extended family. Three aspects of his life experience shaped his social and political thought. First, the boundaries of his homeland, as he perceived it, coincided with the Indigenous territories of the continental northwestern interior. The residents who could trace family ties to the distant past referred to the land as their "country" and saw each other in relation to it, using phrases such as "my countrymen," "our country friends," and simply "natives."[52] Second, his personal and family history helped Norquay to define the dimensions of historical time and, in particular, to distinguish new arrivals in Manitoba, those who came after the "transfer" to Canada, from people who had lived in the original settlement along the Red and Assiniboine Rivers. Thus, he referred consistently during the 1870s to "old settlers," the people whom he saw as his special responsibility, thereby distinguishing them from those who arrived after the transfer.[53] A third element of his sense of self, his extended family, derived from the obvious fact that marriage and adoption and support networks in the Red River Settlement had knit his own clan together—despite the deaths of both his parents—across parishes and districts. As Mr. Fraser of Kildonan said of the Red River parishes, "go through the length and breadth of the Settlement, and you will find the people forming a long link of family connection."[54] These were the people with whom Norquay identified, and these were the activities—on river-lot farms, in hunts, during travels on land and water—that wove a web of relationships spanning the generations.[55]

Over the first half of the nineteenth century, it became common to refer to people who had both Indigenous and European ancestry as "natives of the country." Thus, when the Canadian Anglican bishop George Mountain visited the settlement in the 1840s, he encountered what he took to be three human types: "The great body of the population at the Rapids [St. Andrews parish] consists of Half-breeds, a term comprehending every shade of mixed blood among the Natives"; St. Peter's, the northernmost parish on the Red River, "with some exceptions [was] a pure Indian body"; and at the Middle and Upper Churches [St. Paul's and St. John's] he detected "a greater infusion of Europeans."[56] These were the conventional assumptions about three social categories—Half-breeds/Métis, Indians, Europeans—when Norquay was growing up. How deep were the divides separating the three named groups? Could the fissures be easily bridged? The questions probably did not cause him much concern in his first thirty years, but they demanded closer attention during the time of his prominence in public life.

A fundamental aspect of Norquay's thinking about the differences between settlers in the District of Assiniboia and members of Cree, Saulteaux, and Dakota societies concerned claims to land. The subject had preoccupied some of the leading thinkers in the Red River Settlement. In the 1840s, Alexander Isbister, the lawyer-educator of mixed ancestry who had been born in the North-West and was now living in London, associated his people with two political propositions: they possessed an Aboriginal right to the lands and resources of northwestern North America, and they had a right to be treated as political equals of all other British subjects.[57] During the 1850s and 1860s these principles were widely disseminated within the settlement, and Norquay would have been familiar with them.[58] Then, during the debates in the Assiniboia assembly in 1870, James McKay outlined the question of Métis and First Nations differences over land and resource claims: "As Half-breeds we require wood and hay quite as much as the Indian does his rights; and if we take a reserve [such as a bluff of trees, hay-filled pasture, or river lot, presumably] for our own use, I do not think for a moment that we are thereby depriving the Indian of any title." He concluded that "I am not at all afraid but that in my dealings with the Indians, I can satisfy them without robbing them of any of their titles (cheers)." The assembly record of debates then added that "(the hon. gentleman repeated his address in Indian [Cree, Saulteaux, Michif?] in which he is a very fluent and eloquent speaker)."[59] A right to resources and the use of land—rights that inhered in those of mixed ancestry and were distinct from the rights of First Nations and of Whites—lay at the heart of McKay's argument. It also was a part of Norquay's thought. It is important to note that this claim had been developed in their own councils because what happened next introduced complications they may not have anticipated.[60]

The intense events in 1869–70 and the passionate debates of the next decade, years when Norquay was contributing to the public conversation, pushed him to refine his thinking. One key source of inspiration was the leader of the Red River Resistance, Louis Riel. Twenty-six years old in 1870, three years younger than Norquay, Riel had been absent from the settlement since he was fourteen. He could not claim to be deeply embedded in Assiniboia's main institutions or to have won respect in the bison hunt. During the resistance crisis, Riel managed to maintain a fragile peace across the parishes. He also provoked opposition—in every language community—but most of his critics either withdrew from the settlement or held their opinions in check. No one, except perhaps a few Canadian hotheads, wanted to see blood spilled. Whether Riel's version of the ideal Métis nation, one that appealed mostly, but not exclusively, to the Michif/French-speaking group, could win wider support had yet to be resolved.

In the half decade that followed the resistance, Riel pictured himself as his people's philosopher, prophet, and political leader. He outlined a vision that changed the course of his community's history, though almost none of the vision's tenets, except the concept of a Métis nation and his own central place in it, survived. Hampered by his limited knowledge of the Red River Settlement's Métis past, he stressed themes that he believed to be of greater contemporary relevance, including the French language, Roman Catholic religion, Quebec state, and historical American and British political ideals.[61]

While sketching this peoplehood, Riel was also attempting to maintain a foothold in Manitoba politics. He moved in and out of the province for four years as bounty hunters and Orange Ontarians tried to capture him. Then in 1875, having received word of his official five-year exile decreed by Alexander Mackenzie's federal administration, his health gave way. When Riel lost control of his emotions in public on several occasions, his friends placed him in one and then another asylum in Quebec, where he remained for a year and a half.[62] He left Quebec in 1877 and travelled through the United States to the Montana Territory. His connections to Manitoba politics having frayed, their restoration seemed to be unlikely.

Riel's importance for Norquay lay in an absence: the Riel vision of the Métis nation offered little room in its ranks for Bungee/English-speaking Protestants or for a single, multilingual, "Halfbreed"/Métis community.[63] Norquay never endorsed Riel's vision. Moreover, as the decade progressed, he was unable to make a suitable political alliance with Charles Nolin or some other acknowledged leader of the Michif/French-speaking Métis. Although not accepting Riel's use of "race" and "nation" claims for the Métis, Norquay did agree with one aspect of the resistance leader's approach: the people of mixed ancestry, whatever their language or location or religion, belonged on a social and political plane equal to that of Whites. He rejected Riel's corollaries: where the French leader used the term "civilized" to describe the Métis and to distinguish them from the Cree and Saulteaux, and relied on church, economy, and material culture as markers of "national" difference, Norquay did not. Riel followed a different line of reasoning about race, a line that accepted a "blood" and "national" foundation for a distinct peoplehood. Norquay worked from an initial assumption of shared political interests among all Indigenous peoples.

Norquay put a sharp point on his thinking about these matters at a St. Andrews society dinner in Winnipeg before several hundred male partygoers in December 1872. It was an important occasion because the new lieutenant governor, Alexander Morris, was delivering one of his first major speeches as Manitoba's political leader. Flags adorned the room, a military band and bagpiper provided entertainment, and numerous toasts extended the evening into the early hours. In offering a very Ontarian vision of his plans, Morris's language and references differed radically from the norm in old Red River, notably when he praised the "British provinces" and Canada's great future.[64]

Among the many toasts that followed was one to "the Army and Navy," to which Norquay and a young army officer of mixed ancestry, Captain Allan Macdonald, replied. Macdonald, speaking first, regretted that more senior officers were not present but said that he was honoured to have the opportunity to speak, "more especially as in his younger days the feeling was to some extent prevalent that the Half-breed need never hope to attain the same social position as others." That "state of feeling had passed away," he said, "and now they could uphold with pride a Government which showed equal justice to all." The newspaper report contained his concluding words of "pleasure at seeing one of his own countrymen, Hon. Mr. Norquay, present—a gentleman who had obtained a position in the administration of the affairs of the country—the Captain resumed his seat amid cheers."[65]

It is likely that many of the members of this new organization had not heard Norquay deliver a formal speech before, but in the next few minutes he showed that he could win the attention of even this rowdy audience. He said that on many occasions he had been placed in a false position but never "such a false position as at this moment, when called on to respond to the toast of the Navy . . . (loud laughter). My forefathers may have been sailors, for aught I know to the contrary (renewed laughter). They came originally from the Island of Orkney, and before they could get from Orkney to the mainland, they must have done a little sailing—so perhaps the toast might have a little appropriateness in it so far as I am concerned (laughter)." He closed his remarks with a more serious point: "I cannot sit down without expressing the pleasure I feel at being amongst you this evening. This is the first time I have been present at the gathering of a society such as this; and it is perfectly evident to me that the hospitality characteristic of Scotchmen follows them to the land of their adoption (cheers). I am only sorry that I do not see here tonight more of the native Scots (hear, hear)."[66]

Norquay amused them, won their attention, and then posed a challenge that—if they were listening closely—should have taken them aback. He was saying that in the coming years they would all have to deal with an important disjuncture between "Scotchmen," for whom this was an adopted land, and "native Scots," who regarded the country as their own. Implicit in his message was a warning: "native Scots" might belong in different social networks but were the equals of his listeners. However discreetly, Norquay was taking note of the issue of "race" in Manitoba. The evening can be seen as one moment among many when Canadian priorities, as expressed by Canadian emissaries (Alexander Morris in this case), took precedence in the public sphere. Norquay would have to respond more and more frequently, given his increasing prominence and responsibility, in the years to come. He never resorted to threats of violence or armed resistance in his many speeches during the 1870s. Rather, he accepted the particular version of law that accompanied Canada's annexation of the prairie west.[67]

Norquay also had to accept that Canada's census reinforced blood definitions of his presumed "race." In providing numbers for the total population and breakdowns of its composition, census takers counted people under the rubrics of "White," defined as "those who are white or with no admission of Indian blood," "Indians," and "Métis or Halfbreed" (with subcategories for "French" and "English").[68] The same categories appeared in the Manitoba Act clauses that allocated land to "the children of the half-breed heads of families residing in the Province at the time of the said transfer to Canada." Introduced by Ottawa as a means to retain control of prairie—and national—development, the allocation actually cemented a category of citizenship and of social identification. Those who applied for the promised tracts of land found that they also acquired, willy-nilly, an inescapable label. The bureaucracy of the state would not permit them to enjoy any category other than "Métis/Halfbreed." Viewed from the vantage point of many Canadian Whites, the classification carried with it not just the fact of a land grant but also a connection with a history rooted in what some Whites saw as "unchurched" marriages, "illegitimate" births, and inferior "races."[69]

In his daily political duties, Norquay worked within the legal categories and land regulations created by the federal government. He received appeals from individuals and lobbied officials to secure favourable rulings on individuals' claims to land "grants."[70] He also ensured that his wife, whose father was alive and thus eligible under Section 31 rules, and their five children born before the transfer in 1870, ranging in age from seven to twelve in 1876, all received such land allocations. Each child signed a form that listed date and place of birth, named the parents as "Halfbreeds," and asserted: "nor have I claimed or received as an Indian any annuity monies from the Government of the said Dominion [of Canada]." Similarly, when applying for his parcel of land under a parallel legal process under Section 32, John filled out and signed forms declaring his standing as a "Halfbreed" head of a family. He also provided his date and place of birth and swore that he had not received any scrip for land, that his parents were "Halfbreeds," and that they had not sought annuity money as "Indians." For the claims of both the children and the adults, neighbours signed supporting affidavits.[71]

The Norquay family undoubtedly welcomed the additions to their landholdings. The total acreage acquired in the children's allocations, about 1,200 acres, eventually brought in considerable income.[72] Just as important, if not more so, was the fact that these allocations carried social and cultural implications. For the Norquays, as for everyone else in their circumstances, the allotment established permanently, in official registers and in the minds of recipients and observers alike, that they were "Halfbreeds."[73] What had once been informal and fluid was now made an official legal category. For outsiders who believed that the term possessed biological relevance, and for insiders who accepted land that came with the label, the state's definition of a Métis/Halfbreed peoplehood seemed to be inescapable. In this light Norquay would be expected to define himself forever as belonging within that category of citizen. Furthermore, the notion of "mixed blood" placed French/Michif-speaking and English/Bungee-speaking people together on one side of a boundary while locating those of "unmixed blood" on the other.[74]

Some Whites wielded the labels "Métis" and "Halfbreed" as terms of abuse. They imputed inferiority by a variety of gauges, all of which Norquay encountered in the Red River Settlement.[75] Henrietta Ross Black, a woman of mixed ancestry, voiced the most common examples when, in a letter to her brother, she cited her skin colour and lack of formal education as factors counting against a family move to Toronto: "How would [I,] an uneducated dark halfbreed[,] look among the fair & accomplished ladies of that civilised country?"[76] The Métis of St. Laurent provided another illustration, one based upon language, when they rejected the church's preferred candidate in an election. Rather than the priest's proposed nominee, a French-speaking man recently arrived from Quebec, they chose a person who was "Métis like us. He speaks our language [Michif]. When we want to speak to him, we won't have difficulty in making him understand us."[77] Skin colour, education, and language were just three of many factors that came to distinguish Whites and Métis in public conversation.[78] Such criteria made personal, and often painful, what was written by governments and courts in census and law. Norquay would have to address the issues raised by them.

He was not alone in pushing back against racist behaviour. Many thoughtful, open-minded citizens refused to see their Métis neighbours as lesser members of society. Donald Smith, an HBC officer who became one of the most influential business leaders in the British Empire, and whose wife had mixed ancestry, belonged in this company. In the Legislative Assembly of Manitoba, where he sat for one term, Smith spoke on his proposal for a "Halfbreed Land Protection Act": "I think the Half-breeds equal to other people in intelligence . . . but had from custom been confiding and therefore were liable to fall an easy prey to designing persons."[79] He meant well, but his generalizing about an entire group did not please some of the people whom he sought to help.

Norquay opposed Smith's legislation, arguing that land sale contracts must be fulfilled: "What right have we to cancel the bargain of any man, and what right have we to set up a rate of interest for a man's money?" Although Norquay supported Smith's goal, he rejected the proposed measure that would cancel contracts already completed: "The verdict of the people will be that this Bill is an insult to the Half-breeds themselves. . . . When I state my opinion I state it as a Half-breed myself."[80] His defence of property contracts offered a resounding assertion of his people's equality with the new arrivals.

Smith was only one among a number of Whites happy to meet those of mixed ancestry as equals in the Legislative Assembly. Kenneth McKenzie, a wealthy Scots immigrant who farmed near Portage la Prairie, was another. Although he sat as an independent and often voted against the government, he respected Norquay. However, he confessed to feeling frustrated by the conundrum of Métis identity. Writing in his diary after a late-evening debate, and perhaps feeling a little embarrassed, he said that he had pressed Norquay in the assembly discussion because he "wanted to know whether we are to look on them [Métis] as Indians or white men[.] I said I considered they as good as any other when educated &c[.] What provoked this reply was Norquay continually legislating for them[.] To night was the half breed scrip case again."[81] McKenzie was challenging the provincial government's policy on Métis land sales because it shielded individual Métis from the consequences of their decisions. He made no distinction between those whose first language was Michif/French and those who spoke Bungee/English. He accepted that Métis who had received an education were "as good as any other." They were not "Indians," however, and as "white men"—the alternative in McKenzie's picture of Manitoba society—they should accept the same market rules and contract law.

To counter the racist language, some Canadians moved to a new defence of the Métis and "Halfbreeds." Their argument drew upon an allegedly sharp contrast between the western policies of the American government and those of the Canadian government. The difference, they argued, was the result of Canada's legal and political circumstances, including the effectiveness of the North-West Mounted Police, of British institutions, and of the intermediary services provided by the mixed-ancestry peoples. Provoked by stories about American Indian wars, the argument gained public sway in the 1870s.[82] Canada's governor general endorsed this line of thought in a speech delivered in Winnipeg: "There is no doubt that a great deal of the good feeling thus subsisting between the red men and ourselves," Lord Dufferin said, "is due to the influence and interposition of that invaluable class of men, the half-breed settlers and pioneers of Manitoba—(loud applause)—who, combining as they do the hardihood, the endurance, and love of enterprise generated by the strain of Indian blood within their veins, with the civilization, the instruction, and the intellectual power derived from their fathers have preached the Gospel of peace and goodwill, and mutual respect, with equally beneficent results to the Indian chieftain in his lodge and to the British settler in the shanty. (Great applause)." The "Halfbreed" peoples, he said, were mediators between two ways of life: "They have been the ambassadors between the east and the west, the interpreters of civilization and its exigencies to the dwellers on the prairie as well as the exponents to the white men of the consideration justly due to the sensibilities, the sensitive self-respect, the prejudice, the innate craving for justice of the Indian race. (Loud applause)."[83]

Norquay was in the audience. He would have recoiled at Lord Dufferin's paternalistic, complacent depiction of Manitoba. Although the governor general meant to praise those of mixed ancestry, he actually diminished them. Which group provided the intellect and civilization? Which the endurance and hardihood? Norquay would have seen the paradox: by praising the contributions of mixed peoples, Dufferin was also repeating the prevailing White British assumptions about a global ranking of cultural achievement. The governor general's casual reliance on concepts of blood and race reinforced the very sentiments that, as a representative of the Crown, Norquay wished to rebut.

Still, the words offered an opening. Norquay could take from the statements a more inclusive approach to Manitoba society than that being noised by the Orange Ontarians with whom he so frequently clashed.[84] He could use the sentiments in later speeches to win the approval of newcomers. Most of all he could envision a greater future for the community. Manitobans had been insular in the province's first years, focused on their differences. Dufferin painted a canvas featuring thousands of immigrants, millions of fertile acres, great rivers, railways connecting prairie farms to city markets and the world.

Norquay could share these hopes and ambitions while imagining an equal role for his "native" countrymen.

Cockies, Political Scum, and Kit Atumiskatinan: The Tenor of the "Transfer"

Was Norquay a Canadian? Was he a Manitoban? What did such ideas mean when the entities themselves were just beginning to take shape? Seen from his perspective, the "transfer" was closer to an occupation than a partnership in the first few years after 1870. He encountered stories of White racism in conversations with his friends. He knew able individuals who failed to get government jobs for which they had superior qualifications. And others who lost land to eastern speculators or federal agents. He heard the unhappiness when he returned each week to his Parkdale home. Canada, in the form of Ontario Orangemen and federal government bureaucrats, had not endeared itself to the people of old Red River.

One of Norquay's most outspoken informants was William Kennedy. Although he had once campaigned for Canadian annexation of the North-West, Kennedy now depicted the incoming Canadian civil servants as "the political scum of other Provinces." In a letter to Norquay he argued that westerners should hold these jobs and administer the crucial land policies: "The Dominion has assumed the right to have the whole dictation in these matters & so long as we allow her to take this position she will continue to impose on us . . . thus acting towards us exactly in the way that England acted towards her [American] colonies till her colonists were driven to take up arms against her." Kennedy was incensed when land speculators "stole" Métis scrip. He reminded Norquay that "your own late sister Mrs. James Ballenden[']s was one of those stolen. I was told last week there is to be no redress for this stolen scrip & that we must just sit down with the loss which would be a disgrace to the Govt."[85]

Kennedy's scathing estimate of Orange Ontarians' behaviour in the prairie west included special criticism of John Schultz, a Member of Parliament for a Manitoba riding, who amassed dozens of river lots and scrip certificates. Kennedy attributed Schultz's wealth to federal government corruption:

> It [the federal administration] *gave* to the perjured swindler Dr. Schultz the means of buying his way to political power [by way of a huge compensation payment for alleged losses in 1870]. As one result of this one of his nominees gets into the Land Office

> in Winnipeg & forthwith [Métis] Scrip passes out of the proper hands & the man who steals them goes scot free perhaps only to await a still better opportunity for doing the same in a better field. It is to the disgrace of the Dominion that such men should have thus the opportunity to multiply themselves. [Kennedy feared that one of the new bureaucrats was cheating him.] Depend on it whatever value they put on this lot [a tract that Kennedy owned] it will not be in favor of the "Breed."[86]

The term—which Kennedy placed in quotation marks—jumped from the page, a slighting label for mixed-ancestry people. Norquay, the recipient of these letters, had to deal with his friend's frustration and anger as well as with the racial category that offended them both.

Canada did have its eloquent defenders, particularly among a few recent arrivals who had been elected to the Legislative Assembly. They offered the promise that land policy and support for railways would transform the economy and bring prosperity for everyone. In Manitoba's first years, Norquay's cabinet colleague Henry Clarke often introduced Canadian nationalist sentiments into debates. Born in Ireland, raised in Lower Canada (Quebec), bilingual, Roman Catholic, and an associate of Thomas D'Arcy McGee, Clarke was recruited by Montreal church and political leaders as a potential leader of Manitoba. Although often condemned as inconsistent and self-serving, he spoke convincingly about the development of a Canadian national feeling, as McGee had done in the 1860s when he became the eloquent champion of confederation. One of Clarke's strategies was to raise fears about a potential American annexation of the prairie west. Introducing an assembly resolution concerning a railway from Manitoba to eastern North America, Clarke admitted that a line through the United States might be built sooner and more cheaply than a Canada-only route, but it "would not be better, [and] it would be suicidal to our national interest if not to our national life (cheers)." He preferred a line from Winnipeg to Lake Superior on Canadian territory that "will in the not very far distant future make Canada one of the most powerful nations of modern times—(cheers)—a nation that will yet dictate terms to America."[87]

This Canadian nationalist sentiment figured prominently in the visions of vastness and potential evoked by the governor general during his thirty-day visit to Manitoba in 1877. Lord Dufferin referred frequently to Britain as the founder of the world's dominant empire and promised that Canada could achieve global prominence as its offspring.[88] Norquay had a walk-on role in this tour when he welcomed the vice-regal family—Lord Dufferin, Lady Dufferin, and their twelve-year-old daughter, Nellie (Helen)—to St. Andrews parish. The visit commenced with Norquay's speech of welcome and included a luncheon and a tour of the girls' school. In terms that resembled Dufferin's, Norquay told his guests that the first settlers in St. Andrews "were proud of belonging to that fatherland which has scattered its children more widely over the world than any other, and we their descendants, who share their feelings of pride and loyalty, welcome this opportunity of expressing to your Excellency our attachment and devotion to her most gracious Majesty, whose honored representative your Excellency is in the Dominion of Canada."[89] Norquay and Elizabeth received gifts from their guests, she a bracelet from Lady Dufferin, he a portrait that he later passed on to James McKay.[90]

On the following day the Dufferins took a short carriage ride from Lower Fort Garry to the town of Selkirk, where not one but two receptions awaited them. The town ceremony, including speeches and games, was preceded by a brief event staged by 100 residents of the Cree and Saulteaux communities of St. Peter's, Brokenhead, and Fort Alexander. The Cree and Saulteaux welcoming party, men on one side, women and children on the other, lined the road leading to a "triumphal arch." At the summit of the arch they had placed a birchbark canoe with paddles and a Union Jack flag. Attached to the supporting columns were medicine bags, papoose cases, pipes, cradles, birchbark tenting, quillwork, and a drum. Phrases in Algonkian, including "welcome to the great chief" and "God save the Queen," spelled out their good wishes. The crowd gave "three really hearty cheers" and then fell in behind the leading carriages of the procession, creating a "cortege nearly a mile long and including fifty or sixty vehicles of various descriptions" that proceeded into the town centre for the next event.[91]

In retrospect, the vice-regal visit to St. Andrews and Selkirk marked a turning point in the history of Norquay's home district. The change could be seen in several different spheres, starting with languages in the classroom. In a letter to family in England, Lady Dufferin explained that the St. Andrews schoolroom wall featured two banners. One read "Kit Atumiskatinan" ("we welcome you") in Cree; the other bore a three-line rhyme: "Native, or English,

Canadian we, / Teuton, or Celt, or whatever we be, / We are all of us loyal in our welcome to thee."[92] Lady Dufferin's striking mention of the banners in English and Cree captured a bilingualism soon to disappear from the schools. Norquay's reference to ancestry underlined a Britishness among Bungee/English-speaking residents that increased as awareness of specific Cree and Saulteaux family connections declined. The delegations from nearby First Nations reserves, having mounted their own welcome event at a place separate from the town's festivities, asserted a direct relationship with the British Crown that continued in later years. And pervasive tensions—the assurance of the aristocrats and their White acolytes, the uncertainty of the Bungee/English-speaking commoners—offered hints of social differences that became more entrenched as the years passed.

For Norquay, the events of that day and the months surrounding it seem to have inspired thoughts of wider horizons. Not only did he consolidate his position as a district political leader, but he began to think in grander terms about his own life. In the following year he talked of taking a senior administrative post in the federal Indian branch, then of running for a seat in the House of Commons, and finally of seeking the premiership of the province. The vice-regal visit gave him direct contact with Ottawa, London, and the British Empire. It enabled John, Elizabeth, their children, and their neighbours to put faces and voices to the abstractions that had been a part of throne speeches and political meetings for the past seven years. The charm of Frederick, Hariot, and Nellie Dufferin placed Canada and Britain in a positive light and brought Queen Victoria closer than ever before. Their presence enabled the Norquays, and so many other families, to see their own parish in a new light. Canada, too, appeared in a more favourable perspective because of its place in the British Empire. John might not have become 100 percent Canadian by the end of 1877, but he was far closer to that position than he had been seven years before. First and foremost, nonetheless, he remained a Red River Manitoban.

The decade of the 1870s, roughly coinciding with the years when John and Elizabeth Norquay were in their thirties, was challenging, disappointing, and exciting for the couple. They observed the breakup of the familiar parish communities of old Assiniboia. They saw old friends less frequently. Their growing children, the changes in their diet and clothing and furnishings, the moves from one church congregation to another, the demands of social gatherings among the highest social circles in the province, all required careful attention. They became central figures in an extended family and, as John's ability as a speaker became more widely known, a couple in demand in ceremonial roles and on public occasions.

One of his political challenges was to deal with the matter of race. Norquay did not see himself as part of Cree or Saulteaux communities, but neither was he regarded by all and sundry as fully a member of White society. He had to address the menace of Orange Ontarian prejudice and smooth the transition of "old settlers" into the new Canadian nation. In discouraging moments, Norquay was supported by his extended family and his countrymen. William Kennedy, Charles Adams, and James Sanderson were just three of many former Assiniboians who expressed pride in his achievements. As Sanderson, then at the Mounted Police redoubt of Fort Walsh in the Cypress Hills, put it, "so i thought i would sit down and drope you tis few lines to so [show] you that i have not forget old frands [friends] yet[.] Tho [you are] hily [highly] getting up in life and Hon [Honorable] i feel Proudness every tim i take the *Free Press* and see how your getting along and can give it to the cockies in the nose."[93] Another old friend who had risen within the ranks of the Hudson's Bay Company wrote from La Cloche on the northern shore of Lake Huron to say that he was "proud to see your name figuring at the head of the Ministry of the Manitoba Parliament. May you long enjoy the confidence of the natives of 'Red River Settlement,' for its few natives that have made their marks in the new order of things."[94] Norquay had become their representative, their support, and their last resort in difficult moments. He had navigated the political shoals of "the transfer" and had become "wise" to the racializing forces it unleashed. Was he sufficiently "clever," to return to the rhyme with which the decade started, to win security, equality, and prosperity for his countrymen? Would the "politics" of the decade even permit such an achievement?

CHAPTER 4

Public Life: An Introduction, 1871–74

John Norquay's greatest task in the decade of the 1870s was to learn to be a politician. At the start merely one of twenty-four novice assembly members, he became a cabinet minister before the year was out. In that role he administered two departments, served as a spokesperson for the Bungee/English-speaking community, liaised with a Dakota community, guided Russian-origin Mennonites looking for a new home, and shared duties at the cabinet table. His thinking evolved as he learned to use the powers of government. Having concluded that the "extreme Canadian party . . . the Orange or extreme Ontario opposition" (words employed by American consul James Wickes Taylor) must not be permitted to disrupt public order, Norquay struck a distinctively moderate position in public affairs that sustained his political fortunes in succeeding years.[1] Neither an opponent of the institutions that accompanied the new arrivals from eastern Canada nor a supporter of extreme anti-French sentiments, he was becoming a thoroughly modern intermediary.

The Assembly

The opening of the legislature in mid-March 1871 gave Norquay his first taste of ceremonial politics in the British imperial style. The British flag flew above 100 military personnel as they paraded down Main Street, the artillery fired a salute, and the band played "God Save the Queen" while

Lieutenant Governor Adams Archibald's horse-drawn sleigh travelled the few blocks from his official residence in Upper Fort Garry to the large private house that served as temporary accommodation for the legislature.[2] Two large rooms had been made into one chamber for the twenty-four assembly members. Another smaller room served the seven members of the upper house, the legislative council. Archibald read Manitoba's first throne speech in French and English, appealing for calm and asking his new colleagues to forget the troubles of the preceding year.

The fifty-seven-year-old Nova Scotian, a "firm Presbyterian," was a lawyer and an experienced, bilingual politician. He knew that he faced an uphill struggle. He stood between two hostile factions, Orange Ontarian "loyalists" determined to take control of the province and Michif/French-speaking farmers and bison hunters who would not shrink from combat. When Prime Minister John A. Macdonald criticized him on one occasion, Archibald replied bluntly that "with you it is a question of popularity—of newspaper criticism—with me it is one of life and death."[3] He did not exaggerate.

Norquay stood out in public affairs from the beginning. He was big and calm and genial. He prepared his speeches, using a list of headings on a piece of paper as a guide, speaking softly and fluently. He excelled in the give and take of debate. During the assembly's first week, when a motion on election irregularities threatened to become heated, he teased his colleagues: "It is not wise I think to surrender ourselves to such nice intricacies at the outset. We might get beyond our depth of judgment. (Laughter)."[4] Norquay accepted appointments to four assembly committees, including the Rules and Sessional Regulations committee, on which he learned parliamentary procedure.[5] At the first opportunity, he asked that specific boundaries be set out for parish lots in the "Assiniboine and Portage districts." This broad definition of his community, one that covered several other members' ridings, hinted at his ambition. Norquay warned the government that "strangers are coming in behind the old settlers [outside the river-lot "hay privilege" boundaries], and as there are no proper limits allowing what belongs to the old settlers and what is open to others, newcomers do not know where to take up claims." One of the cabinet ministers tried to evade the issue by palming it off on Ottawa, but Norquay did not relent and introduced a motion a week later calling for the creation of a special committee to deal with such limits.[6]

In these early days he sided most often with those who opposed Archibald's government party. He and a few like-minded English-speaking members were said to constitute an opposition faction. The most outspoken of their number, Edward Hay, an English immigrant who operated a mill in St. Andrews parish, was determined to punish Louis Riel and those who had joined the resisters in 1869–70. In his first statement in the house, Hay welcomed Archibald's support for economic growth but added that "there is one point on which some of us must disagree—the forgetting the past [which the lieutenant governor had urged legislators to do]. If we look for any justice . . . we cannot forget what has passed. I hope that in justice to what has passed, the House will some day take into consideration certain events which have taken place in this country, and thoroughly investigate them."[7]

Norquay shared Hay's concerns but not his passion for revenge. Rather, in seconding the motion, he advocated a careful review of the events of the preceding year. Where Hay's resolution referred to "guilty parties" and "bands of armed men" (meaning the Métis supporters of Riel), Norquay spoke of "even-handed justice to all. It is but right that the suffering should be recompensed, and that those on whom a stigma has been cast should have an opportunity of clearing themselves and appearing in their true colors. For this reason I desire an investigation—not for the purpose of reviving old grievances or animosities, but to establish the Settlement in the old peaceful, friendly position it occupied before the troubles arose." The government party accepted his gesture and amended its resolution by asking Ottawa to pay for an inquiry; Norquay then split with Hay and voted in favour of the amended measure. The vote marked him as a calm conciliator in a community racked by continuing tensions.

While finding his feet as a representative of old Red River, Norquay came to recognize that a stable ministry was a necessity. As he told his brother-in-law, it would be easy to defeat the government party, but no alternative administration existed. He said that their little opposition group "won't think of coalition." So he remained an opposition member, loosely aligned with Hay and the other critics of Archibald, as Ontarian newcomers wished, but brokering compromises when he could.[8]

The session turned out to be much longer—over six weeks—than anyone anticipated. As it closed members agreed to pay themselves an indemnity of $300 to cover their hotel and living costs rather than the $200 originally allocated. Norquay supported the increase. The next day, 3 May 1871, the sitting finally ended, and Archibald congratulated everyone on the creation of a legislative framework within which the province could operate for years to come.[9] Norquay emerged from the session with an enhanced reputation and an enigmatic voting record given that he had sided on occasion both with the Ontarian oppositionists and the Red River mediators.

The State and the Dakota

The Norquay family remained on the High Bluff farm during 1871. Caroline Ellen (called Nellie in her early years) was born there at the end of March, when the Legislative Assembly was in session. Elizabeth was busy with the baby, her sixth child in nine years, and probably needed some help, perhaps from a neighbour's daughter, to manage the five others, now aged between eight years (Tom) and one and a half (Horace). When the assembly meetings ended in the first week of May, Norquay returned home in time to work the fields.

Late on a mid-May afternoon, he was at home when Corporal Greenlay of the Quebec Rifles drove into the farmyard in a dusty buggy drawn by a weary horse. The soldier's mission was an official one. Upon receiving instructions from Archibald, Greenlay had rented the conveyance and hastened along sixty kilometres of rutted tracks to deliver an urgent request: a trader heading down the Assiniboine River toward the Red River must be stopped. The furs carried by the trader had been purchased from an Indigenous band farther west that, someone claimed, had been "infected with Smallpox." Norquay and Greenlay ate supper quickly, walked about five kilometres to a neighbour's farm, where they hired a rested horse, and travelled to the Portage la Prairie home of Francis Ogletree, a leading citizen and member of the legislative council, arriving at ten in the evening. Norquay and Ogletree arranged to set up a watch on the Assiniboine River. Two days later the pelt- and robe-laden boats were stopped and the furs impounded. A brief entry in a soldier's diary, written a month later, records the end of the story: "17 June—Robes released today." The disease had not spread, and the cargo was judged to be free of contamination. An effective response to a great public concern had been mobilized within forty-eight hours.[10]

The episode, in which the rookie assemblyman had taken a lead, signalled the beginning of a far-reaching development in his thinking in the 1870s.

As an elected representative, and with the delegated authority of the lieutenant governor, Norquay had been given the legal power to stop a fur-laden and possibly disease-carrying boat. His clout originated in a centuries-old institution, "the state," an expression of people's desire for shared action that combined the authority of law with the threat of force. The power of the state represented a very important addition to life in Manitoba. This intervention was much more extensive than the desultory police powers exercised in the District of Assiniboia. It derived from the development of governments over the preceding millennium, from laws passed in the Canadian Parliament, and more immediately from the troops who marched into Upper Fort Garry at the end of August 1870. Now a little of that power was being wielded by Norquay himself.[11]

Although he might have had a few qualms as he approached the Assiniboine River that May evening, he performed his new duties well. He chose to exceed the authority that he had been given, responding to local residents' agitation by moving the furs and robes to a location outside town and away from a large encampment of Dakota and Saulteaux families. Writing to the Board of Health, Norquay added that "we are sorry that this is contrary to instructions from Bd of Health, but zeal for protection of health of province is our best excuse."[12]

Familiarity with these Indigenous people placed Norquay in a new state-sanctioned role just a few months later. His responsibility arose because of issues surrounding Dakota (Sioux) families in the Portage la Prairie district. The Dakota had been historical enemies of the Saulteaux and a source of concern in the Red River Settlement. When Norquay was teaching in St. James, he listened to Reverend Taylor's expressions of fear about Dakota raids. Upon his return to St. Andrews, he heard frequently about the enmity between Dakota and Saulteaux and observed Red River settlers' anxieties, such as those of journal writer Samuel Taylor. John and Elizabeth then heard the shocking news of the battles in 1862 between Whites and the Dakota in Minnesota and the gallows erected in a Minnesota town square to hang thirty-eight Dakota men in a tragic spectacle. When the Norquays moved to High Bluff, they encountered Dakota who had moved to the district after the Minnesota disaster. John learned to converse in their language, and he might have employed them, as his neighbours did, to clear stumps, cut hay, and harvest cereal crops.[13]

The Dakota became his special responsibility in the winter of 1871–72 when Archibald asked him to investigate their clash with settlers along the Assiniboine River over the right to cut increasingly scarce firewood. Norquay concluded that wood for fuel was indeed in short supply, though he placed no blame for it, and he reported positively about the Dakota: "I have the honor to inform your Excellency that there are about 600 Sioux Indians in the Province that is men women & children all told[.] They are peaceable industrious & as a general thing honest[.] In the latter respect they compare favorably with any other tribe that I have come in contact." This amounted to an expression of trust. Norquay also took their side, pointing out that the Dakota wished to be allocated reserve lands. Rather than dismissing their concerns or opposing their interests, he urged a quick response to their request.[14]

Norquay was becoming an agent of the state. Within a few months he joined the province's Board of Education, agreed to be a justice of the peace for the County of Marquette, and organized a meeting of the "half-breed population of High Bluff" in which local settlers' land claims were discussed. Each of these roles—involving school administration, legal services, and land grants—marked a step in the evolution of the Manitoba state. Yet they constituted just a tiny fraction of its activities. Norquay was learning that the new regime would be regulating numerous relationships—buyer-seller, master-servant, husband-wife, child-school, hunter-prey, farmer-land, First Nations-government—that had been dealt with much less formally in previous decades.[15] The state defined the parties in each case and converted them into abstractions in order to guide people's behaviour with written rules. It also acquired, through a shipment to Donald Smith, the HBC officer and assembly member, no fewer than fifty Snider rifles and fifty bayonets, waist belts, slings, cartouches, and oil bottles, as well as 2,000 ball cartridges.[16] If necessary, it could enforce its rules by physical means. The state required different ways of thinking, and Norquay adjusted to those ways quickly.

He also learned that the government of Manitoba, like the Council of Assiniboia, was a small and weak example of a state compared with governments in Ottawa and the "original four" Canadian provinces. The local administration could spend only about $80,000 annually at the beginning of the decade and about $135,000 at the close. Although this was more than the Hudson's Bay Company had allotted to public arrangements and regulations, pre-1870, the sums remained risible. Public officials (Legislative Assembly and legislative council, civil service, Government House, printing) alone absorbed half of the total. The other half included equal sums for each of schools, roads, and the justice system (courts and jails). The assembly had almost no prospect of increasing the province's revenues. The government was so tightly constrained by the Manitoba Act that it could not build infrastructure or offer bonuses to promote more rapid growth.[17]

Norquay supported state paramountcy and private land ownership in his first forays into policy debates. His approach relied on surveyed property and an open market in which individuals bought and sold tracts of land and registered their ownership for all to see. He opposed the Catholic Church taking over huge acreages that might have enabled it to serve as the guardian of its flock. In a debate concerning incorporation of the bishop of St. Boniface, Norquay urged his colleagues to limit the quantity of land that could be held either by the Catholic leader or his Anglican counterpart: he did not think "that either of the Bishops in the Province should be allowed to buy up land in unlimited quantities." In the case of church involvement in schools, he hoped that education would "become part of the care of the Government in the Province, and the sooner the better." As for the argument that the two churches were unable to live off individuals' donations and required government grants, he questioned that assertion: "In my opinion, the sooner we all learn to be independent, the better."[18]

Norquay wanted to be a modernizer who worked within the rules of the new property system. The approach was not alien to the people of the Red River Settlement, where families had been trading furs for generations and knew the injunctions about helping a neighbour and paying one's debts. But the old property rules were flexible and derived from practices that had evolved over decades and centuries. They permitted parties to claim particular berry patches or salt flats on the basis of traditional usage, and the principles of open access ("first come, first served") had to be worked into the equation. They allocated hay lands according to carefully delineated rules. They distributed the harvest of the bison hunt widely, seemingly according to "moral economy" principles.[19]

Norquay was taking a giant step away from the past and toward a society in which the market would be king and tracts of land would be bought and sold by individual owners. He could have selected another path, one that placed him in the company of leaders such as Father Ritchot, who proposed an exclusive enclave for the Métis. Or he could have sided with James McKay, who proposed to set aside "reserves" of hay and trees and other resources for the use of those already resident in the district. Instead, Norquay chose to side with Prime Minister Macdonald and Lieutenant Governors Archibald and Morris. He accepted the state's control of western lands and worked within the individualist, private property approach that came with it.[20] Henceforth owners would control the resources on their properties, could prevent others from enjoying those resources, and even choose not to utilize or harvest them. Although his views on many topics evolved during the decade, on no subject did Norquay move as much as he did in softening this initial hard line on land law and property.

A test of his principles arose when the Legislative Assembly received a request from Lake Manitoba Métis for government aid in leaving "the chase" and starting farms. Although the problem stemmed from a grasshopper invasion, and though the Hudson's Bay Company had customarily supplied seed wheat on such occasions, Norquay and many of his faction voted against a monetary grant to the community. He preferred that each household deal with its own problems without government aid. His bias in support of unimpeded markets and commodification of land did not apply in all matters, however, for Norquay also wanted to side with underdogs in their encounters with the wealthy. Thus, when confronted with another version of the capitalist economy's rules, a draft of a law on master-servant relations, he proposed an amendment to provide "safeguards to the servant." Despite some opposition, a version of his amendment was adopted.[21]

Norquay had encountered the state only rarely in the Red River Settlement before 1870, but now he found that it could extend its powers in many directions.[22] He was far more prepared for its arrival than were most of his contemporaries, whether First Nations or Métis. As was apparent in the Portage la Prairie fur blockade and again in the Dakota controversy, he came to regard obedience to official commands as expected behaviour. In the crucial matter of lands, he supported the private property regime that had been introduced by the Hudson's Bay Company and now, with the Canadian takeover, was erasing Red River's customary variations.

Cabinet Crisis, 1871

Adams Archibald spotted Norquay as a potential leader in the early days of the assembly's opening session. He might have wondered about the depth of Norquay's moderation, but he respected the new member's courage in the hurly-burly of debate. Although attracted to the political advantages of an ally from the English-speaking parishes along the Assiniboine River, the lieutenant governor did not woo Norquay until a political crisis made such a step essential.

The crisis grew out of rumours of a "Fenian raid" aimed at Manitoba. The Fenians, Irish Catholics wishing to damage the British government, had attacked Canadian territories from American centres several times in the 1860s. Now, in the autumn of 1871, dreaming of an alliance with Métis sympathetic to the Catholic Church, a Fenian corps gathered in Dakota. Archibald immediately organized a defence force. He appealed for Métis support, agreed to inspect the group that assembled, and in so doing, whether knowingly or not, shook the hand of its leader, Louis Riel.[23] The Fenian assault never happened, but reports of the handshake lived on. The alleged outrage became a rallying cry for John Schultz, who wanted to accelerate Ontario's takeover of the west and regarded the moderate Archibald as an opponent to be defeated.

In these crucial months of late autumn 1871, Norquay tried to steer between the Orange Ontarians and the group gathered around Archibald. In the assembly he represented High Bluff, an area that contained many of the "Portage men" who had nearly precipitated a shootout with Riel's forces in February 1870 during the reign of the provisional government. One of these Portage la Prairie district residents was Elizabeth Norquay's brother, John James Setter, who claimed to have joined neighbours "to set aside the plough for the gun, and never rest until every Jesuite [*sic*] would be driven out of the country, & first and foremost *Smooth Archy* [Lieutenant Governor Archibald] would have been marched out of the country very unceremoniously."[24] Norquay, caught between Archibald's soft words and the hard language of Setter and others in Schultz's camp, had to choose. If the comments of the lieutenant governor suggest that he was studying the younger man carefully, then Norquay in turn was learning what leadership in the assembly might entail.

In response to the governor's proclamation about the Fenian danger, Norquay convened a meeting in the High Bluff schoolhouse. Community members came out in numbers and decided to request guns from the lieutenant governor. Norquay and Mr. Cadman, the latter designated captain of the local company, hurried to Upper Fort Garry with the appeal. Upon their return they explained at a second meeting in "a crowded house" that they had not been able to obtain weapons, an indication of Archibald's caution. In his report Norquay gave a stirring speech on the spirit of the Winnipeg men who had marched off to meet the Fenians, an oration that "so graphically described" what he had seen in Winnipeg that "the spirit of enthusiasm spread not only to the young men . . . [but also to] old grey headed grandfathers, who had lived all their lives under the Red, White, and Blue, [Britain's Union Jack flag, and who now] came forward and enrolled their names." News of Norquay's eloquence travelled far.[25]

When Archibald shook Riel's hand, he doomed his own administration. Schultz convened meetings throughout the English-speaking parishes, each of which declared its lack of confidence in the lieutenant governor. At these gatherings Schultz and a few allies directed the discussion by asserting that the previous election had been unfair and calling for a new ballot. Norquay signed the High Bluff petition.[26]

These gatherings in the "English" constituencies set the stage for a confrontation with the lieutenant governor on 1 December 1871. Schultz and representatives of the eleven other English-speaking parishes, Norquay among them, presented a document to the lieutenant governor expressing dissatisfaction with what they described as his "undignified partiality" in his appointments to public office and his sympathy for the Métis. Having conducted public votes at each constituency meeting, the document declared, the group would "respectfully request the Lieutenant Governor to at once dissolve the House and cause a new Election to be made."[27] Schultz had mounted an impressive resistance movement, though his goal was private gain as much as Orange Ontarian advantage. Norquay's support for this extraordinary request was evidence of the pressure exerted by Schultz's Orange faction during these tension-filled weeks.

Archibald claimed in a letter to Ottawa that he had responded courteously to his visitors but refused to be intimidated. Rather, he had explained patiently to the delegates why it would be unwise for him to deal with them as representatives of public opinion when there existed a body of elected assembly members. The delegates carried this message back to the people, and public anger intensified. Yet another public meeting was called, and this time some citizens threatened to topple the government by force. A man who had come to Manitoba with the volunteer troops and was now a saloon keeper went so far as to call for the pacification of the French "by extermination." Others alleged that Catholic Fenians loyal to Ireland, at that very moment, were negotiating an alliance with "the French" in St. Boniface. Prominent Winnipeg citizens, allies of the Orange faction, founded a home guard and patrolled the town at night. The American consul, James Wickes Taylor, mused in a letter to Washington that the Archibald administration might not survive.[28]

Three days later Schultz's father-in-law, James Farquharson, and a dozen others stole across the Red River under cover of darkness and entered the small log dwelling in St. Vital where Riel's mother lived. Guns drawn, they demanded to know her son's whereabouts. They told the frightened women that Riel would not live through the night. Although the incident did not end in bloodshed, Archibald was obliged to respond.

The lieutenant governor believed that Schultz's talk was designed for public consumption. Schultz wanted a seat in the government, Archibald told Prime Minister Macdonald, and was merely using the protest meetings to that end, "as he admits to me. He says he has no quarrel with the French, could combine with them, permitting them the same numerical representation on the Executive as they now have, and redistributing the English portion of the Government offices." On another occasion Archibald expressed his frustration with Schultz more baldly: "He would take anything that will give him office or fill his pocket."[29]

Who would stand beside the lieutenant governor in this moment of crisis? When he had first set up his administration, Archibald, following the prime minister's instructions, selected a cabinet from among apparent leaders in the various community factions. He expected ministers to be "secretaries rather than advisors," meaning that he, as the lieutenant governor, would act as the premier and that his government would not be a responsible one. Several of his choices had proved to be less than helpful. In particular the two representatives of the aggrieved English-speaking portion of the population—Alfred Boyd, a prosperous English merchant, and Thomas Howard, a twenty-six-year-old volunteer in the military expedition and now an aspiring merchant—failed to stand up to the Orange Ontarian leaders at the stormy public forums. As Archibald stated bluntly, they were not men of vigour and had no force in debate.[30]

Given the failings of Boyd and Howard, Archibald had to rely on a third English-speaking cabinet member, Henry Joseph Clarke. A journalist and lawyer, Clarke was expected to be Archibald's second in command, the bilingual ally who spoke for the administration in the assembly and defined the moderate centre in the province. Clarke, unfortunately for Archibald, was erratic and self-serving. By the end of the first session, Archibald concluded that his key minister was rash, knew little law, and had "little ballast": "I have seldom seen a man so void of anything like discretion—or common sense." The lieutenant governor feared that Clarke, an English-speaking Catholic, might be plotting secretly with Schultz. Even if that rumour proved to be false, it was evident that Clarke despised Boyd and Howard. Archibald simply could not rely on the cabinet that he had assembled.[31]

His quest for better English-speaking allies began and ended with Norquay, whom Archibald described as the "leading man in the exclusively English parishes of the Upper Assiniboine."[32] The young assemblyman was probably flattered by the lieutenant governor's appeal. Norquay had shown that he desired peace and opposed the violent talk of his opposition colleagues. In the second week of December 1871, the lieutenant governor spoke to Boyd, who probably welcomed the invitation to resign. Within days Boyd was gone, and Norquay joined the cabinet.[33]

The clerk of the executive council administered the oaths of office on 14 December 1871. Swearing to "be faithful and bear true witness to Her Majesty Queen Victoria," and to "defend her to the utmost of my power against all traitorous conspiracies," Norquay signed his name with a flourish. A second oath confirmed his appointment to the offices of minister of public works and minister of agriculture.[34]

Not everyone was happy with his appointment. His elevation gave John Schultz nothing, and as long as Schultz remained angry the Orange Ontarian camp would not be appeased. Critics swore that Norquay had betrayed them.[35] But his promotion provided the balance that the initial cabinet lacked. The lieutenant governor had taken account of realities and was prepared to work with the young man who spoke softly and with wit. As he said to officials in

Ottawa, he appreciated Norquay's "fair education" and even more perhaps his "force of character."[36] Archibald judged that Norquay possessed sufficient self-confidence to defend his countrymen against the broadsides from Schultz and his Orange Ontarians.

The cabinet appointment became just another important step in Norquay's education. As was apparent in the Portage la Prairie fur blockade, he was learning that the public's obedience to official commands could be enforced with police action. Whatever he might think in private moments, he could act effectively in public as the embodiment of the state's power.

The Minister and the State

In welcoming Norquay to the cabinet, the government organ, the *Manitoban*, said that he had been "the white-headed boy" of the opposition. It claimed that he "enjoyed largely the confidence of the English section of the population; least of all would he be suspected of any tender feelings towards the class of which Mr. Mulvey [Schultz's leading subordinate] has an insane hatred." Norquay had avoided factiousness in debate, had opposed the government fairly, and would be "a source of strength" in the cabinet. Reflecting Archibald's devout hope, the *Manitoban* described the reconstructed government as closer to a coalition, which it said was the only possible form of government at the moment, party lines being out of the question. Reaction on the French side of the river was less optimistic. *Le Métis* likened Norquay's appointment to a minor wintertime replastering job on a Red River log house. The implication was that the repair would have to be done again, properly, when spring arrived.[37]

Within hours Norquay was at work. Aside from the oath itself, the only document to survive from his first week in cabinet is a letter in Norquay's hand to Messrs. Barber and Sinclair reminding them to fulfill their contract for delivery of a quantity of wood, presumably fuel for public buildings, during the forthcoming winter. Norquay attended a gala event at which he received three cheers and an address celebrating his "honest and independent course" in public affairs. He also joined 300 citizens, many of them in Masonic regalia, celebrating St. John's Day at a supper and ball. He might not have seen the brief note from John A. Macdonald, whom he would not meet for some years, to Adams Archibald: "I congratulate you on the accession of Mr. Norquay to your Government." It was the first acknowledgement of a relationship between the prime minister and the Manitoban that would become increasingly important to both leaders. Norquay had arrived in the front ranks of the little community's public life at the age of thirty.[38]

For the next two and a half years, he sat in the executive council as a minister and settled into the steady routine of cabinet meetings and departmental business. The minutes of these first years of cabinet, which record only topics and decisions rather than discussions, demonstrate that Norquay was usually present at the weekly sessions but offer no insight into the role that he played. James McKay was listed by the contemporary *Canadian Parliamentary Companion* as the cabinet chair, but everyone understood that Archibald ran the government during its first two years.[39] Like his colleagues, Norquay acted as administrator, secretary, and advisor to the governor. He faced many challenges, of which the most pressing was his own political survival. In a province still hampered by language and religious differences, he tried to calm the belligerents in the English-speaking parishes while staying on a middle path that would reconcile lieutenant governor, cabinet colleagues, constituents, and conscience.

After Norquay entered the cabinet, a role that required his presence at many meetings in Winnipeg, he and Elizabeth probably decided that High Bluff, nearly eighty kilometres away, could no longer be their winter residence. The entire family moved to Sturgeon Creek, a rural district adjacent to St. James and much closer to the seat of government. An entry in the family Bible records that Andrew, the seventh child, was born at Sturgeon Creek in August 1872. The family might then have had two homes and two ways of life. It was becoming clearer with every passing month, however, that the demands of politics took precedence and that farming would have to accommodate the government's timetable. The Norquay family then moved to a house on North Main Street in Winnipeg, probably in 1873.[40]

The Department of Agriculture was small, simply requiring the allocation of grants to local agricultural societies and, in hard times, the distribution of seed grain. When Mennonites, Low German–speaking Protestants who had farmed on the steppes of southern Russia for a century, dispatched a delegation to Manitoba, Norquay became their host as the official representative of the government. He took the delegates on a tour of the Headingley area (just west of Winnipeg and near his old home in High Bluff), then southeast through Métis lands near Ste. Anne, and then to the northwest, past Portage la Prairie and toward the Whitemud River. A year later, in the summer of 1874, the first of some 5,000 Mennonite immigrants arrived. Their choice of Manitoba represented a triumph for the state. Norquay had had a hand in their migration.[41]

The Department of Public Works demanded more of his attention because it accounted for a large proportion of the provincial budget and came in for regular criticism. Norquay thus took responsibility for roadways and bridges in a country that had little infrastructure. Increasing numbers of migrants moving into more distant districts multiplied the demand for better roads. In winter, blizzards and thaws blocked routes for days at a time. In spring, rains made trails impassable. River crossings could be treacherous: Norquay's friend Thomas Spence twice fell through rubbery ice on the Assiniboine River, dramatically demonstrating the need for bridges and ferries.[42]

In the session in 1873 Norquay was criticized in the assembly because he had overspent his Public Works budget. He blamed unforeseen problems such as the spring floods in the previous year. He was able to disarm his critics by telling them that he regretted the need to rebuild a bridge in St. James that, "much against the will of the Government, yielded to the pressure of the spring freshets (laughter) and fell in."[43] A new Public Accounts committee promised to introduce a stricter regimen, and the cabinet launched what became known as a "better terms" campaign to secure a larger federal subsidy, a case that Norquay made almost annually for the next fifteen years. He was learning to be an administrator. In the manner of the times, he also found ways to benefit personally: in one year he received over $200 for supplying the government with lumber, firewood, and sundries from his own land.[44]

Although Norquay never spoke on the public record about the state as an entity, he absorbed its implications as he lived them. He was affected especially by several key institutions that fell within the state's authority. Each had evolved over centuries and arrived in Manitoba as an accomplished fact. Under England's distinctive approach to the state, these institutions included, first, citizenship, especially rules about who could and who could not take advantage of its privileges; second, land law, particularly England's view of land as a personal possession that could be sold; third, economic practice, given England's (and Canada's) assumptions about markets, master-servant law, and contracts; and fourth, democracy, especially elections and the functioning of a representative assembly. Each was intertwined with the others in a complex fabric. It would be some years before many of the residents of the former District of Assiniboia fully understood the implications. Like his fellow Manitobans, but sooner than most of them, Norquay learned from experience how the state redefined political community and distinguished among categories of citizenship.

Archibald's Departure

The legislative session of 1872 commenced just a month after Norquay entered the cabinet. The lieutenant governor's throne speech welcomed the assembly members, and expressed relief that a smallpox outbreak on the prairies had not reached Manitoba and that rain had averted the danger of drought. Bison herds had returned "to the plains, in numbers unequalled since 1859," a boon that reassured everyone. Despite all the positive words Archibald knew that his days were numbered.[45] He had already submitted his resignation, a consequence of Orange Ontarians' reaction to his meeting with Louis Riel, and awaited the prime minister's decision on a departure date.

No positive news could distract the opposition, represented by Edward Hay, from expressing its dismay that "the outlaw" Riel had not been captured. The "murderers" should be brought to trial, said Hay. John Schultz led the applause from the gallery and was ejected by the sergeant at arms. Hay perceived the events of the resistance as a conflict between French and English, Catholic and Protestant. He shared Schultz's hostility toward the Hudson's Bay Company and agreed that Quebec should be seen as an adversary.[46]

The government's defence rested on the shoulders of cabinet ministers and of one other assembly member in particular, the powerful Donald Smith of the Hudson's Bay Company. Smith had played an important role in the affairs of the Red River Settlement during the resistance in 1870 and was now a member of both the provincial assembly and the federal House of Commons. Soon to be made chief commissioner of the entire HBC operations in North America, he exercised a great deal of influence in the legislature. In the debate provoked by Hay on the events of 1869–70, he argued that Archibald had done well in difficult circumstances: "Again, even were it in our power, would it be wise for us to deal with this matter of the death of [Thomas] Scott [whom the Riel administration had executed]? There is not one man in this House who does not, equally with his fellow citizens in other

Provinces, deplore this sad event; and all would equally wish to see justice done." Smith's solution to the impasse was an evasive motion: given the need to address these "very serious troubles," and given that this was "a question that only the Imperial Govt is competent to deal with," the House should ask Queen Victoria what action had or would be taken "with the view of satisfying justice and the best interests of this country."[47]

Norquay joined Smith in urging calm. Now a cabinet minister sitting on the same side of the aisle, he was nonetheless careful not to endorse Smith's exact position. Norquay had served a brief stint as a "free" fur trader and sympathized with critics of the Hudson's Bay Company, the independent merchants who detested its claim in earlier days that it should have a monopoly on trade. His statement to the assembly adhered to his position staked out the year before:

> I am sorry to see the remarks made on this resolution, declining to so low an ebb. The [Hay] resolution before the House is certainly called for, and I am happy to believe it will be endorsed by every member. There is no doubt that the insurrection of 1869 left a legacy of heart-burnings and angry feelings, much of which remains to this day. It is nothing but right, then, that an effort should be made to allay these hard feelings, that such an investigation should be made as will enable the innocent to clear themselves at the bar of public opinion, and place the burden of responsibility for guilt on the right shoulders. The step [Smith's motion], I think, is a judicious one, the only thing I have to complain of respecting it, being that it falls short. There does not seem to be any request to Her Majesty to make the investigation.[48]

In taking this path, Norquay parted company with Smith by expressing sympathy for the opposition's concerns. But in the practical matter of how to respond to their campaign, he criticized Hay's proposal and agreed with Smith while putting a sharper point on Smith's suggestion: an inquiry into the resistance should be set up; it should function as a public forum; the testimony of all the participants should be heard; the commission should rule on the matter of guilt and innocence. Orange Ontarians did not like the

Smith-Norquay compromise. In the end Hay's resolution was defeated, and Smith's amended proposal for an imperial investigation carried unanimously. Because it failed to mollify Schultz and his followers, the confrontation between Orange Ontarians and the Michif/French-speaking followers of Riel had not been resolved.[49]

Archibald submitted his resignation within a few months of the handshake with Riel. His departure was then postponed for what must have seemed an eternity to the Nova Scotian, but finally he was permitted to leave Manitoba in October 1872. He expressed his frustration in a pithy note to his successor: "What are you to do with a people to whom no politics are of any consequence as compared with the politics of St. Vital [the Riel family's parish]?"[50] The lieutenant governor's eclipse must have been a source of sadness for Norquay, who had flourished under Archibald's guidance. It would have caused the young assemblyman some anxiety, too, given that Ottawa's acceptance of the resignation led to joyous celebrations in Winnipeg during which a crowd burned effigies of Archibald and Riel.

Electoral Support in High Bluff

If he was to remain in politics, Norquay would have to find a constituency that consistently supported him. For the moment, he represented his English-speaking countrymen in High Bluff, who had been his neighbours since 1866. The parish started in the 1850s as a river-lot community, mainly Bungee/English-speaking, situated along the winding Assiniboine River just east of Portage la Prairie. The 100-odd families constituted a small, closely knit community. Everyone knew a good deal about everyone else's business. And all knew their political representative. Although one critic charged that Norquay had never done an honest day's work in his life, a High Bluff man came to his defence in the *Manitoba Free Press*, arguing that his "demeanor . . . while occupying a humble sphere" had not changed when he became a minister of the Crown.[51]

With the arrival of Ontarians in the early 1870s, the parish changed in character. An Anglican clergyman told his supervisors about a growing community called Westbourne, just to the north of High Bluff: his Bungee/English-speaking parishioners, he wrote, "are taking every available opportunity to sell out, . . . the Indians of that place will be on the reserve," and the district was "now occupied by Emigrants." It was not long before the new residents recruited a few old-timers and founded a chapter of the Orange Lodge. Norquay wondered about his own political future, given the growing Ontarian presence in his High Bluff constituency.[52]

Thinking of these changes, his brother-in-law, John James Setter, put Norquay in the mix for the next federal election. "[He] is already spoken of as the next opponent of [Donald] Smith for the Dominion Parliament . . . & if he holds his ground as he has done there will be little fear for him."[53] The federal election took place in September 1872, just before Archibald's departure. The campaign in Manitoba illustrated Norquay's dilemma. He had been encouraged by Setter and his friends to run in the westernmost riding, Marquette, the seat that included new English-speaking settlers around Portage la Prairie and old settlers, Michif/French-speaking and Bungee/English-speaking, along the Assiniboine River and the shores of Lake Manitoba. Having worked with Métis hunters on Lake Winnipegosis and knowing many of the old settlers in the district, Norquay believed that he had a chance and agreed to stand. The prospect of a grander setting and the combined stipends of two parliaments would have interested him. He faced four opponents, including two Michif/francophone Métis, the Ontarian Schultzite Dr. Lynch, and the prominent moderate Robert Cunningham, editor of the government organ the *Manitoban*. Cunningham had the support of the Catholic hierarchy and Protestant moderates.[54]

Although Norquay canvassed widely in the riding, he was soundly defeated. Cunningham won 393 votes, Norquay 170, Dr. Lynch 71. In the French Catholic Métis section of the riding, according to a fragmentary return, Cunningham won 339 votes to Norquay's 5. The lesson was an important one. Norquay had to find a provincial constituency that would give him much greater support.[55] The idea of moving home to St. Andrews probably took root after this federal campaign.

Alexander Morris and Henry Clarke

The new lieutenant governor, Alexander Morris, assumed office at the beginning of December 1872. Then forty-seven years old, born and raised in Upper Canada (Ontario), he had been pressing for Canada to annex the west since the 1850s. In his well-publicized lectures he had sketched grand pictures of a British nation stretching across northern North America.[56] Morris had good reason to tread cautiously in his new role. His priority, like that of Archibald before him, had to be to prevent the outbreak of violence between the Orange Ontarians and their adversaries.

The first throne speech by Morris, read to a crowded assembly and many invited citizens in February 1873, struck the same optimistic notes as Archibald had done, but it lacked his predecessor's readiness to accommodate local realities. In one telltale sentence Morris expressed the wish that "the two great races who have mainly peopled this Province will unite in earnest, harmonious efforts to secure the advancement of the general interests."[57] He just assumed that the society and conflicts of the Canadas, Upper (Canada West) and Lower (Canada East), were mirrored in Manitoban society. He had missed or refused to acknowledge that the community was divided more by "old versus new" sentiments. Tensions between French and English did exist in Manitoba, but the province was still largely composed of mixed-ancestry peoples, and the previous half century's understanding between the two language groups still transcended the conflicts generated by newly arrived Ontarians and Quebecers. His experience in Parliament led Morris to believe that eastern Canada's preoccupations mattered more, even in this different province.

The community remained volatile. Ten days after the lieutenant governor's swearing in, Sister Curran reported in her journal that "on the 11th [of December 1872] we were advised that Mr. Dubuc had almost been assassinated in the city of Winnipeg by an Orangeman." This was a targeted attack. Joseph Dubuc was a brilliant young man, a former classmate of Louis Riel, a member of the Legislative Assembly, and recruited by Taché and Riel to serve as a leader in the French-speaking community. Walking down a Winnipeg street, he was assaulted by several men. As Sister Curran said, "the first blow which he received had been hard enough to make him lose consciousness, and stretched out thus on the ground he received in the face and on the head blows of the feet, the marks of which were only too visible, while the blood ran from one eye, from which he is still suffering." In an extraordinary dénouement, when the assailant returned to face charges some months later, he asked Dubuc to request that he be treated with mercy. Dubuc did so. The man later became Winnipeg's chief of police. Beyond the generosity of Dubuc's act, the incident illustrated the tensions that continued to plague public life.[58] The central parishes of the old Red River endured a state of siege, due in part to the undisciplined, riotous behaviour of the former members of the Canadian militia who occupied the district during these years.

Although he badly needed allies who could calm the waters, Morris did not have full confidence in Norquay. The clearest evidence of his lukewarm regard was his refusal to support Norquay's appointment to important federal administrative roles in the North-West. Urging the creation of posts for an "Indian commissioner" and two assistants to draw up treaties and to aid in the administration of Indian Affairs, Morris told Ottawa that the assistants should be "natives of the Country, familiar with the Indian dialects, and in whom they have confidence, and taken from the ranks of the English and French Half Breeds—Such a man as . . . for instance the Hon. James McKay, who has great influence with the Indian tribes, and who gives largely to them of his own means." Neither in that instance nor in considering the membership of the North-West council, in which Archibald had favoured Norquay, did Morris advise his appointment.[59] Rather, the lieutenant governor relied on others to restore social and political peace.

The reason for his lack of trust probably lay in discussions around the cabinet table. The lieutenant governor, acting as the premier, had to rely on the coalition that his predecessor had created. At its centre, for better or worse, was Henry Clarke: "With all his faults," Morris wrote to Macdonald in February 1873, "he is the best man I have, & has a strange streak of good & chivalrous loyalty running through his strange composition. In other words he is an Irishman." But Clarke was constantly creating political difficulties for the ministry, especially by his erratic responses to issues pitting French Catholics against Ontario Protestants. What was worse, said an unsympathetic observer, "the miserable wretch . . . foments the timber-hound in Norquay whom he leads by the nose."[60] It was not a fair judgement, but it encapsulated Norquay's problem: distrusted by Morris, the real head of the cabinet, Norquay accepted the lead of McKay, an honourable man, and Clarke, an attractive, unpredictable rogue. McKay, as a member of the appointed upper house, could afford to support his countrymen. Norquay, elected in a fickle constituency, had to navigate more cautiously.

Norquay was caught between two extremes. When responding to French- and Michif-speakers, he was critical of the Riel party and more likely to listen to the Métis who challenged Riel's leadership. In the English-speaking parishes, Norquay not only opposed Donald Smith and his HBC-based empire but also had to deal with attacks from Ed Hay and John Schultz. His choices reflected moderation and a quest for a consistent path between these polar opposites, but he risked alienating those on either side who saw compromise as betrayal.[61] By force of speech and quick wit, he managed to disarm critics in the assembly, but he suffered from the criticisms of Winnipeg's Orange Ontarian newspapers.

Norquay compounded his troubles by offending a cabinet colleague, Joseph Royal, the aspirant to leadership of French-speaking, Catholic Manitobans. Royal objected vigorously to a redistribution act that would have given English-speaking Manitobans more representatives than allocated to the Michif/French-speaking districts. Norquay was included in his denunciation. The legislation was due for review in the next assembly session, so the cabinet split mattered only a little, but it did warn of conflict in the future.[62] Norquay risked falling between stools as the assembly neared its closing term. Could he find supporters in some other part of the community? The Saulteaux, Cree, and Dakota, for example?

The Dakota, Cree, and Saulteaux

In his first years in the Legislative Assembly, Norquay dealt frequently with Cree, Saulteaux, and Dakota residents of the province. He and his assembly colleagues understood that the First Peoples possessed a prior claim to the land and that their acquiescence to a formal transfer of Indigenous sovereignty, as required by King George III's Royal Proclamation of 1763, would have to be secured before Canada's legal system of private property and land law could be set in place. Norquay approved of this process. As he explained years later in a lecture on prairie history, "in 1817 His Lordship [Selkirk] concluded a treaty with the Indian chiefs of the Saulteaux and Cree nations whereby he extinguished the Indian title to as much of the lands as he deemed necessary for settlement."[63] This approach, involving essentially state-to-state or people-to-people relations (though Selkirk was not "the Crown"), was followed when Canada's first numbered treaties, 1 and 2, were signed in the summer of 1871.

A dozen communities, about 1,000 individuals according to Lieutenant Governor Adams Archibald, were present at the treaty negotiations in Lower Fort Garry. The Crown was represented by Archibald, who acted with the support of an Indian commissioner and some leading citizens, including several members of the legislature. The Cree and Saulteaux selected their own representatives, seven for Treaty 1 and twenty-three for Treaty 2.[64] Norquay might have been present, but he had no part in the official negotiations and signed none of the documents. He knew many of these people and recognized the many interests at stake. Because the federal government had exclusive jurisdiction over "Indians and land reserved for Indians," the province had little role to play in their affairs, and Norquay rarely dealt formally with their concerns.[65] Like several of his close friends, nevertheless, he worried about the Canadian government's attempts to impose its rules on them.

The Dakota, perceived to be recent arrivals in the province, occupied a different position in the minds of officials. Their presence was complicated by a renewed migration, about 200 Siouan-speaking people in total, into prairie Canada in the autumn of 1872. These families were "Missouri Sioux," Lakota and Yanktonai rather than Dakota. Within months Norquay was warning the new lieutenant governor, Alexander Morris, about local gossip concerning these new arrivals. He said that rumours spoke of "the depredations of a band of Sioux Indians," including the stealing of horses and the killing of animals, "though I must say that this but rarely occurred." Norquay also suggested that the newcomers "are beginning to assume a defiant attitude." His opinions now seemed to be blunter than they had been twelve months earlier: "It is unnecessary for me to mention what amount of damage is done by these savages to the properties of the residents of these parishes, and the feeling with which they [the White settlers] contemplate a continuance of this state of affairs is anything but satisfactory." His choice of the word *savages* and the harsher judgement of at least some of the Sioux bands constituted an important change in language. But his defence of the Dakota families around Portage la Prairie—"this but rarely occurred"—should not be missed. Norquay attributed the critical sentiments expressed to "the residents of these parishes" and did not adopt them himself. Instead, he spoke cautiously about the local gossip and expressed opinions more supportive of the Dakota than White newcomers might have approved.[66]

In early spring 1873 rumours reached western Manitoba from the North-West Territories that more Sioux might be heading toward the province. Morris dispatched several community leaders, including Norquay, to assess the situation.[67] Norquay travelled to Palestine [Gladstone, MB] by sleigh in late winter, interviewing settlers at several farms en route. When he arrived at the little town, sixty kilometres northwest of High Bluff, he organized a public meeting to elect leaders of a defensive force. The people "readily enrolled themselves," he told Morris. But Norquay also concluded that there was reason to be concerned. Several local people had suggested to him that Sioux around Fort Ellice (300 kilometres west of Upper Fort Garry)—part of the Lakota, Yankton, and Yanktonai groups that moved back and forth between that district and the Missouri River—were threatening to "make a raid" on the province and that their manner "has considerably changed, instead of their former quiet deportment, they are now opening an arrogant tone, and behaving in a manner calculated to provoke a quarrel." Moreover, he wrote, those Dakota who lived closer to High Bluff had held councils "very frequently" during the winter and had even threatened that they would soon have the numbers "to do whatever they pleased."[68]

Norquay seemed to be distancing himself from some of the Dakota bands and to be categorizing them as a danger to Whites. But he was not arguing that the Dakota around Portage la Prairie should be pushed out of the community. Moreover, he maintained close relations with members of the Legislative Assembly who wanted to keep this valued labour force nearby. Norquay was acting as a perceptive, flexible politician who saw his task as conducting negotiations between groups that viewed the world differently.

Defeat of the Government and Repeal of the First Nation Franchise

In June 1874, a month before the session opened, Morris predicted a ministerial crisis. He no longer trusted Henry Clarke. Nor did Archbishop Taché. It was said that Clarke and others were seeking a warrant to arrest Ambroise-Didyme Lépine, leader of the court that sentenced Thomas Scott to death in 1870. Even more damaging was the widespread rumour that Clarke had left his wife and taken up residence with another man's wife. Then, in the first days of the session, an able opposition member, Robert Davis, raised damning questions about large sums of money paid by the provincial government to Clarke for his services as a lawyer. *Le Métis* declared that no one wanted Clarke, and therefore the ministry in which he was so prominent, to remain in office. Assembly members "wanted to get rid of him—at any price," the weekly said. The government faced a non-confidence motion tabled by Ed Hay and Joseph Dubuc, representatives of the English-speaking and French-speaking communities. Norquay spoke in defence of the administration's record and what he described as the moderate legislation to be considered during the session, but it was to no avail. Despite Clarke's vehement denunciations of this "most astonishing combination, concocted in the back room of a city tavern," the ministry was defeated by fifteen votes to seven. A new cabinet was sworn into office, led by a francophone Quebecer, Marc Girard, and an Englishman, Edward Hay.[69]

The new government would be calling an election within weeks but, before the assembly was dissolved, it tackled an important issue: should First Nations possess the right to vote? The Manitoba Act, the federal law admitting the province into confederation, contained a clause on the organization of the province's first election. It restricted the vote to male resident householders who were twenty-one and older, who owned property valued at $100 (or who rented property for at least twenty dollars per year), who had resided in the province for at least one year, and who were the queen's subjects "by birth or naturalization."[70] The franchise clause excluded women, the very poor, and recently arrived or transient individuals. But it did ensure that many Cree and Saulteaux men possessed the vote, a testament to the cultural legacy of old Red River. This right of full citizenship for Cree and Saulteaux householders (but perhaps not Dakota, who would have been seen by government officials as refugees or temporary immigrants) was the case in the general provincial election of 1870 and for several years thereafter. The principle underscored their status as responsible adults in possession of rights identical in character to those of any other adult. Dr. John Harrison O'Donnell, a member of the province's legislative council, observed in one council debate that the residents of St. Peter's parish, a district known as "the Indian settlement," were perceived to be "to all intents and purposes a civilized people. The rights of franchise has been extended to them, and they have their representative not only on the floor of the House but absolutely in the Executive Council."[71]

Attorney General Henry Clarke first mentioned the possibility of eliminating Cree and Saulteaux voting rights during the throne speech debate in 1872. He mused that a new election bill would be introduced eventually because, "under the law as it stands," after one year of residence "every householder . . . is entitled to vote, and by that law an Indian householder has as clearly the right to vote as any other householder." Clarke noted that the cabinet had yet to deal with the subject but that a federal law then in force would "settle the matter in future." That law declared that "an Indian receiving an annual allowance" must be considered a minor and therefore did not have the right to vote.[72] Though no law had been introduced in Manitoba, it was clear that Clarke at least was thinking about taking away the votes of Cree and Saulteaux individuals based upon a racial criterion.

The discussion resumed in 1873. Ed Hay, the English miller representing St. Andrews, proposed "a disqualification of the Indians . . . who received annuities and were in other respects treated as minors." Thomas Howard, who represented the "Indian settlement" of St. Peter's, interjected, shouting "Kaween" in Saulteaux, meaning "No." Hay replied that First Nations in other provinces did not have the vote and should not be permitted to vote in Manitoba. His case was built upon tenets related to fixed property and property values. Hay said that "many of the Indian people in this country had nothing to qualify them but a birch bark tent," a dwelling that would never meet the property qualification of $100 as stated in the Manitoba Act. Moreover, these families travelled through resource zones, harvesting food and supplies rather than remaining in one place. They did not cultivate the soil or participate in the life of a sedentary community. In Hay's words, "they might be here today, and in a very short time at Norway House," 450 kilometres north. Henry Clarke, speaking as the attorney general, agreed. In responding to Hay's speech, he added an additional qualification, saying that "the time must come when the Indian would have to determine between receiving Government bounties, and exercising the franchise."[73] His opinion was remarkable for two reasons: it defied the federal enfranchisement act of 1869, which stated specifically that an enfranchised Indian might retain annuities, and it seemed to assume that the right to vote depended on whether an individual received any sort of payment from the government.

The McKay-Clarke government never did introduce electoral legislation. That cabinet, including Norquay, fell from office in July 1874. The new administration led by Marc Girard and Robert Davis took the initiative on Cree and Saulteaux voting rights. With an election in the offing, it introduced a "registration of voters act." The bill disfranchised "any Indian or person receiving an annuity from the Dominion Government." In other words, the restriction would deny the vote both to federal government employees and to individuals who held membership in a treaty-signatory band and, as a consequence, received a treaty payment from the Crown.[74]

In the assembly Thomas Howard, the member for St. Peter's, objected to this clause "depriving the people that he had been representing for the last four years of the elective franchise." He told the assembly that he had "strenuously" opposed the same measure when it was placed before the McKay-Clarke cabinet. He was not happy about going back on the promises of the Manitoba Act that gave First Nations people the right to vote. He pointed out that the Church Missionary Society (Anglican) had been working among the people of St. Peter's parish for years and had "raised them to appreciate the benefits of an elective franchise." To take it away at this point would be to "place them in a very unenviable position." Having adopted this firm stand, he then made a reluctant but important observation about the assembly's collective opinion: "Judging from the expressions of members of this House I believe that a majority is in favour of such an enactment."[75]

Thomas Bunn, an assemblyman of mixed ancestry, spoke in support of the clause abolishing the Cree and Saulteaux franchise. But he argued that it should be presented to the legislature as a separate bill. He explained that it was "a new clause, not printed, and therefore one the members were not in a position to legislate upon." Bunn's claim that it was a "new" clause placed responsibility for the denial of the First Nation franchise exclusively on the Girard-Davis administration. The vote on the legislation was not recorded, and no document listing supporters and opponents has been found.

Where was Norquay at this fateful juncture? The answer is complicated. In the debate he supported Bunn's suggestion that the clause removing the Cree and Saulteaux right to vote should become a separate bill. He preferred that members be permitted to vote on the principle of First Nation suffrage without having to throw out the rest of the bill, which dealt with voter registration. Speaking directly to the disfranchisement of treaty First Nations citizens, Norquay affirmed that Howard had "opposed the measure in the late Government." In other words the idea was raised during the McKay-Clarke cabinet's reign but had not been implemented. It is likely, given his speeches to the assembly in 1872 and 1873, that Clarke had proposed the removal of the Cree and Saulteaux right to vote in cabinet meetings that Norquay attended. In the end, the McKay-Clarke cabinet, including Norquay, chose not to terminate the right of Cree and Saulteaux male householders to vote. But it is impossible to know who besides Howard opposed the idea.

In his speech on the new franchise act, Norquay also condemned its treatment of the "old settlers . . . the pioneers of this western country."[76] His objection was related not to Cree and Saulteaux peoples but to the circumstances of mixed-ancestry voters. Norquay disputed the Girard government's decision to reduce the number of seats allocated to the historic Red River parishes and to assign more seats to outlying districts populated by incoming settlers. His comments might have been evasive, given that he did not directly defend the rights of his Cree and Saulteaux neighbours. But his words conveyed a crucial nuance. While omitting reference to one difficult problem, the First Nations franchise, Norquay tackled a second directly. He was opposing the new Girard-Hay government on the issue of representation for Bungee/English-speaking Métis. These were carefully calibrated choices. In electoral terms—an election was coming within six months—he was appealing for the support of Bungee/English-speaking voters at a time when he was about to move back to St. Andrews. Norquay well knew that he would need every such vote in an election against Hay, a formidable opponent. Without spending any of his own political capital, Norquay simply reinforced the case made by Howard concerning the Cree and Saulteaux right to vote.[77]

The franchise legislation of 1874 marked a turning point in Manitoba. An entire way of life, one that had been viable for centuries, was not permitted to be reconciled with the incoming state. Legislators in Manitoba opted to exclude First Nations from the list of citizens who possessed "the right to have rights," in philosopher Hannah Arendt's phrase.[78] Henceforth the state, or more precisely its male political leaders, by excluding Cree and Saulteaux individuals, drafted laws and imposed conventions that shaped the operations of government without their participation. Norquay's position on the issue remains opaque. Norquay sympathized with Howard's objections, but whether he supported Howard in the assembly vote cannot be known. Still, he was present when the Manitoba government debated and eventually passed a law denying the franchise to Cree and Saulteaux people in provincial elections and, because provincial rules in that decade determined the federal franchise, by extension in federal elections. The decision on who could vote and who could not—that is, who had full rights as a citizen—was a matter of enormous significance in the history of Canada.[79] Norquay's part in these policy choices, an important aspect of his career, was undocumented and remains unknown.

Although he fell from office in 1874, Norquay did not suffer from the condemnation directed at Henry Clarke. Robert Davis, who had forcefully criticized the former attorney general, acknowledged that "some [members] of the late Ministry were honest." The *Manitoba Free Press* returned to Davis's statement a few months later: "It is a fact worthy of remark that even his bitterest enemies have never dared to charge Mr. Norquay with any of the crimes so frequently charged upon political rivals. Even Mr. Davis himself was heard to remark on the floor of the House . . . that there was one honest man (referring to Mr. Norquay) in the Government that he was at the time denouncing."[80]

John Norquay left the cabinet with a mixed reputation. As an administrator of government departments, he had performed well, though inevitably his performance was criticized by individuals who did not receive the favours for which they had hoped. His strong advocacy of a rapid economic transition and support for state interventions such as road and bridge construction were welcomed by many newcomers. The same strategic principles were rejected by those who had hoped for a continuation of Métis collective rights and the flexible property arrangements of old Assiniboia. On language and faith issues Norquay did not find favour among Orange Ontarians, especially those who supported John Schultz. Nor did Norquay have a following in the Michif/francophone districts east of the Red River and south of the Assiniboine River, where he was little known. As so often in politics, the positions that he had chosen in the Legislative Assembly could be interpreted as principled consistency or craven betrayal. The *Nor'Wester*, the newspaper of Orange Ontarians, called him a "somewhat slippery politician" who "infamously betrayed" his opposition colleagues by joining the Archibald cabinet: "We might, if we chose, go on to show that in honesty of purpose and political morality the least among them [assembly members] is greater than he."[81] William Luxton, another recent arrival from Ontario, disagreed strongly with that judgement. As editor of the *Manitoba Free Press*, he praised the independence and incisive reasoning shown by Norquay. Luxton argued that "during the four years that he has been member of Parliament no speech or act of his can be singled out as savoring of sectionalism." He concluded that Norquay "being a native may be pre-eminently regarded as the representative man of the English Half-breeds" and "the leader of the English-speaking element in this province."[82] At the end of the assembly's first term, with a general election in the offing, Norquay stood out as a public figure. Despite his critics, he had built a reputation as a reliable legislator and the spokesperson for old Red River's Bungee/anglophone parishes.

CHAPTER 5

Senior Minister, 1875–78

Public debates became shrill in the autumn of 1874. The government newspaper in Winnipeg painted some of the candidates in the forthcoming provincial general election as zealous Orangemen who would cause renewed violence in the streets. The man who sentenced Thomas Scott to death in 1870, Ambroise Lépine, was found guilty of murder after a dramatic trial. Louis Riel again won the Provencher constituency in the federal Parliament, his third victory in the riding in two years. The federal government still had not fulfilled its promise to transfer tracts of land to Métis children. Farther afield, the forces of Protestant Canada were rallying against French Catholics, notably in a battle over schools in New Brunswick. Little wonder that Manitobans felt threatened by sectarian conflict.

John Norquay rose above these hostile sentiments and maintained his pacific stance on public questions. The most difficult political issues that he faced during the next four years concerned Métis resistance to eastern Canadian administrators. He spoke cautiously about these public policy matters, sometimes urging adaptation and sometimes looking for ways to aid his countrymen. He had become a senior politician, a sympathetic listener in hard times.

Provincial Election, 1874

During the waning days of the session in 1874, Norquay sat on the opposition benches. His seatmates welcomed his arrival and hoped that he would bolster their anti-French, anti-Catholic positions. The government newspaper, the *Manitoban*, went so far as to say that Norquay was aligning himself with the Orange Ontarians and that his career had been "too strongly marked by the stains of avarice and self interest."[1] In fact, Norquay was defining a "third way" as he approached the coming election. The new government under Marc Girard had revised the previous electoral boundaries in a bill that Norquay described as "an attempt to crush out the old settlers in certain localities. The members of this House were elected by the men who bore the burden and heat of the day; they were elected by the pioneers of this western country, and yet we find them [the government] in three short years attempting to crush out the very men who elected them." His defence of the old boundaries was designed to appeal to the Bungee/English-speaking community. Norquay was defining an electoral base, setting out his claim for support, and employing emotionally charged language to fortify his position. From that time forward his last line of defence—it came up whenever he was under pressure—was the assertion that he belonged to and represented the people of old Red River.[2]

After his defeat in the federal campaign of 1872, Norquay knew that he could not count on victory in his old riding of High Bluff, a district that had changed markedly in social composition. His obvious supporters were Bungee/English-speaking countrymen whose interests he had represented effectively. In that district they now were outnumbered by newcomers from Ontario. The Cree and Saulteaux whom he had defended could no longer vote. His best bet was to return to St. Andrews, where his friend Alfred Boyd was planning to retire from public life.

The Norquay family moved to a house on Park's Creek, their fourth in four years, situated near the school where John had taught and about six kilometres from the river lot where he had been born. They were rejoining St. Andrews neighbours whom they had left less than a decade before. The lot on the west side of the river might have been Elizabeth's earliest home or part of her extended family's holdings. It was purchased for the princely sum of $2,000 and the mortgage may have been financed in part by the sale of her 160-acre Métis grant in 1876.[3] The two-storey house, in the children's experience, became the most familiar of all the Norquay homes because the entire family was based there for nearly a decade. It also made plausible another step in the formation of the new Manitoba government.

Norquay ran against Edward Hay, a Yorkshire-born machinist and mill owner, in the South St. Andrews constituency. At several public meetings he promised to stand up to "the French" and declared that Hay would be dominated by politicians with Quebec origins. Norquay canvassed diligently. The riding contained only 100 voters, many of whom were Bungee/English-speaking, and he knew them all. Hay, as the proprietor of a mill, also knew everyone, but his business and his English accent placed him in a different relationship with those of mixed ancestry. Norquay won by sixty-four votes to thirty-seven for Hay.[4] The provincial result was less clear. Observers concluded that the "French party" under Joseph Royal held eight seats, the "Canadian party" led by Francis Cornish held eight, and the "English party" under John Norquay held seven. But this guess was far from certain and, even if only partly right, presented serious problems for an incoming government.[5]

Robert Davis, a Winnipeg resident who had grown up in the Eastern Townships of Quebec, agreed to serve as premier. Born in 1841, the same year as Norquay, he had briefly taught school and tried his hand as a freighter on the American mining frontier before arriving in Winnipeg in 1870. He took over a hotel and saloon, set up a barbershop, pool room, and store, and became a popular business figure in the growing village. Fluent in French as well as English, and sympathetic to the French-speaking population, he faced the difficult task of putting together a cabinet that would represent the contending forces in a divided province.[6] Many leaders in the English-speaking community opposed any administration that would be reliant on francophone Catholic votes. This suspicion could be found among the more moderate activists as well as Orange Ontarians. William Luxton, of the *Free Press*, spoke for the moderates when he questioned whether Davis could "act honestly in the interests of the English-speaking people when he is dependent upon the French contingent for support and political existence?"[7]

The English-speaking assembly members met during these weeks. Within just a few hours they had decided that Norquay should head their group in the assembly and accept the title of opposition leader.[8] But, fearing a continuation of hostilities between factions, a small group of community leaders resolved to intervene. Secret conversations aimed at creating a broader, more representative cabinet commenced in early February 1875. The participants included Lieutenant Governor Alexander Morris, Premier Robert Davis, *Free Press* editor William Luxton, and *Le Métis* editor Joseph Royal, the senior French-language cabinet minister. They faced considerable pressure. The fate of Ambroise Lépine was once more on the table, causing much stress in the community. Alexander Mackenzie's Liberal government in Ottawa overruled a Manitoba court and decided that Lépine should not be hanged for the murder of Thomas Scott. Instead, Mackenzie invited the governor general to devise a compromise. Lord Dufferin decided to impose a prison sentence of two years and to take away Lépine's right to participate in public affairs. The Michif/French were unhappy, having desired full restoration of his citizenship rights. The "English or Orange party" still clamoured for his execution. So fragile was the peace that the American consul, James Wickes Taylor, reported to the State Department in Washington that Lépine was being "protected from an Winnipeg mob by a double guard of soldiery."[9] The moderate leaders simply had to find a way to bridge the political divide.

Their solution was to pull Norquay into the cabinet once again. He later told a public meeting that "negotiations had been carried to considerable length before he knew anything about it." In exchange for Norquay's support, a step that made the government much more representative of the population, Davis guaranteed a future redistribution of seats to ensure that English-speaking districts had sixteen representatives and French-speaking districts only eight rather than the fourteen/ten split of the 1874 election and the twelve/twelve split of 1870. Davis also conceded several sweeteners that would appeal to Portage la Prairie's English-speaking residents, including a grant of money for the local agricultural society, seed wheat to assist farmers devastated by a grasshopper invasion, and a guarantee that Portage la Prairie would receive a "considerable amount for county buildings." He might also have agreed that the French language would not be used in official communications in western Manitoba.[10]

The switch from opposition leader to minister made Norquay the key figure in the reconstitution of the cabinet. His appointment was just one of two key moves made by Premier Davis. The second was the appointment of Charles Nolin, a prosperous Michif/French-speaking Métis farmer from Ste. Anne, southeast of Winnipeg, to a cabinet portfolio. Both Nolin and

Norquay had to resign their seats and run for re-election, as was the custom in that era, and they were duly returned in mid-March.[11]

Their presence in the new government as representatives of the still powerful mixed-ancestry communities in the province took the "Canadian party," or "English and Orange party," by surprise. When news of the coalition broke, Donald Gunn, an aging member of the legislative council, wrote to his friend John Schultz to tell him the story: "There is some talk in town that *greasy John* has made another somersault—given his friends of the intended opposition the slip and is to have a seat in Mr. Davis' new ministry." Gunn could see that the old battles of 1869–70 concerning the alleged evils of Riel's provisional government and the death of Scott had been eclipsed. But he did not like the concessions being made to people whom he regarded as disloyal turncoats, and he fixed the blame on Norquay.[12] One of the Orange Ontarian newspapers, the *Nor'Wester*, argued that Norquay was not honest "in purpose or political morality." Another paper with the same outlook, the *Winnipeg Standard*, argued that he had been "bought up by a seat in the Cabinet" and was guilty of "desertion."[13]

His friends were much kinder. In praising the cabinet appointments, the *Manitoba Free Press* said that Norquay thought about public issues carefully and showed considerable strength of character in choosing his path. John James Setter, his brother-in-law, who had been in the Ontarian camp in previous years, congratulated Norquay on his election victory and accession to the cabinet: "I am sure that few public men hold so high in the estimation of both friends & foes as you do."[14] Norquay himself believed that the arrangement bridged the gulf between the French- and English-speaking communities and brought Bungee- and Michif-speaking leaders into positions of influence. It had been approved by four leading members of the opposition, and it would have the support of the *Free Press*. The Orange Ontarians had once again been left out in the cold. Norquay would have to live with their criticisms, as he had when he chose to join the cabinet of Adams Archibald in 1871.

French and English

The legislature opened at the end of March 1875. Alexander Morris, outfitted in a Windsor uniform, rode in an open carriage from Upper Fort Garry to the courthouse, where the session commenced. He read a throne speech prepared by Premier Robert Davis and his cabinet—this was Manitoba's second responsible government in two years—that outlined what the ambitious administration hoped to achieve in the legislative session: more Crown prosecutors and justices of the peace, more jails and courthouses and registry offices, more municipalities that in turn would carry out more public works in local districts. A "more advantageous route" for the dreamed-of railway to eastern Canada. Better schools that respected "the views and conscientious convictions of all classes of the community." Better rules for balloting in elections and composing electoral lists. Plus, if negotiations in Ottawa were successful, then expanded boundaries for the province and better financial terms.[15] There was much to be done but little money with which to do it.

In the assembly debates, it fell to Premier Davis to defend Norquay's entry into the cabinet. Davis referred to the election that had returned only a few government supporters in English-speaking ridings. In the circumstance, he said, he thought it preferable to secure fair representation from those areas, and to that end he had initiated conversations with members of the opposition. They agreed on the goals to be achieved, "and the leader of the Opposition with their (the Opposition's) advice and consent . . . had accepted a seat in the Cabinet." Davis spoke of his wish to reduce sectarian conflict and attributed the success of his coalition talks "mainly" to William Luxton and John Norquay.[16]

When it was his turn to speak, Norquay, the new provincial secretary, vigorously defended his entry into the cabinet. Following Premier Davis's tack, he explained that "as leader of the Opposition I was at the head of an element representing only one section of the community of this Province, which gave the Opposition the appearance of a sectional rather than a political Opposition, in fact it looked more like nationality pitted against nationality than anything else." He said that "I am willing to be member of an Opposition composed of both sections of the community in this Province when parties will divide on political principles and not on national differences."[17] The leaders of the coalition had decided to draw a line under the battles of previous years. They had come together in the interests of community harmony.

The inherited conflicts would not be buried so easily. The adversaries simply found new issues to enliven the old prejudices. In matters of education Orange Ontarians criticized the autonomy and public funding of Roman Catholic schools. Their grievance dated from 1870 when government money for education was split equally between two school boards, one Protestant and one Catholic. William Luxton preferred "thoroughly non-sectarian schools. . . . The principle of church and state ought to be and must be wiped out in all British countries." Francis Cornish declared that "we had got quite enough of separate schools without making it worse. The sooner we become one people the better." Norquay replied that both the Board of Education in Manitoba and the federal government in Ottawa supported the system, so "we must continue it for the present." But the funding arrangements could be adjusted, he said, to take Ontarian criticisms into account.[18] His defence was worded in pragmatic terms, not in the language of principles and rights.

The Ontarians added a second, equally contentious issue, that of language rights. Manitoba, they argued, should be more English-speaking and less bilingual. Luxton moved that all schools receiving government support must offer instruction in English: "Schools should prepare men to battle with the world, and a knowledge of English was indispensable. A knowledge of French is not so." A measure to incorporate a society of colonization to recruit French Canadian emigrants in New England provided another occasion for conflict. Its supporters proposed that a reserve be designated for these newcomers because they would want to live near compatriots and establish schools and churches of their own. Ontarian critics objected, arguing that in restricting access to a large block of land the reserve would deter settlement by other groups. Joseph Royal responded impatiently: "The members should remember one thing, that although we speak French, we are loyal British subjects, we are in fact the oldest British subjects [within the boundaries of Canada], and have never given doubts of our loyalty."[19]

The Davis government faced a continuing drumbeat of anti-French and anti-Catholic sentiments in the assembly. Ministers adopted a consistent strategy in response. Rather than high-minded appeals to generosity and cooperation, or legalistic statements about the constitutional settlements of 1867 and 1870–71, they explained their choices in terms of necessity. Thus, Norquay's defence of French-language printing in the 1875 session stressed not fairness but political reality: "The Government would be willing to bring in such measures [reducing the use of French in public affairs] when a good part of the French themselves would be willing for the change. The government had no desire to make asses of themselves in passing measures that would be disallowed by the Governor General at Ottawa."[20]

In other matters that divided English and French, such as redrawing the electoral map, the cabinet also took a pragmatic and moderate line. But it could not escape its own commitments to the coalition makers. Rather than wait for the cabinet to enact a redistribution measure, Luxton introduced a bill as soon as the assembly opened in 1875. It called for the creation of sixteen "English" and eight "French" seats. The *Free Press* editor congratulated the cabinet on its representative character and said that, "if the good feeling and good understanding so far exhibited in this House this session . . . were continued, the conflict of nationalities would soon be a matter of the past." The Davis government temporized, promising only that a revised electoral map would be presented by the government before the end of its term. Luxton was not satisfied with this vague promise and reminded Norquay of his original commitment: "If the legislation of the government was obnoxious to his [Norquay's] party, he was to withdraw at their united request." The *Free Press* claimed that Norquay had broken faith and that opposition members who had entered the original arrangement were thus freed from their obligations. Norquay accepted this description of the terms and agreed that Luxton was free to vote as he wished. But Norquay also promised that a new bill would come at the appropriate time. Indeed, two years later, well before the next general election, the government introduced a redistribution measure.[21]

French-English relations remained delicate during the session of 1876. The previous year had been disastrous for Manitobans. As the throne speech declared, a "locust scourge . . . [had] devastated the crops, and brought penury and suffering into many a household within our borders." Lieutenant Governor Alexander Morris and his cabinet went to the extraordinary length of proclaiming a "day of public humiliation and prayer" in the hope of averting further disaster. A crucial piece of reform legislation abolished the seven-member upper chamber (the legislative council). Norquay participated in the discussion, though not as a leading actor. He recalled the temper of previous debates, reminding his colleagues that those who resisted Canada's initial advances in 1869–70 had asked for a second chamber as a safeguard against a popularly elected assembly. The legislative council's defenders, he said, sought protection on matters "which were dearer to them than any other right that they claimed," a reference to language and religion and the continuation of the French-speaking Catholic community itself. Norquay argued that the French no longer needed such protections. Because the council had fulfilled its purpose, the French could "accede to the reasonable demands of a majority of the people of this Province and consent to its abolition."[22]

Despite supporting the abolition of the legislative council, Norquay stood against Orange Ontarians when they challenged the official use of French in assembly debates and printed proceedings. The clause protecting this linguistic right should not be abandoned, he said, and he was sorry to hear other members harping on it: "No doubt the time will come when the privilege claimed by those speaking the French language will be waived, but he, for his part, would never like to see them deprived of the privilege of speaking their language on the floor of the House and in the Courts of Justice." He believed, too, that Manitoba's statutes should be published in French as well as English.[23]

A by-election in the fall of 1876 gave Norquay an opportunity to articulate his own position in these culture wars. He suggested at a public meeting that the Manitoba government's first leader, Lieutenant Governor Archibald, had worked hard to maintain peace but eventually "leaned too much to one side" in his attempts "to screen offenders from justice." Lieutenant Governor Morris, in contrast, introduced "the first dawn of light on civilization in this country" by introducing the principle of responsible government and declaring that crimes should be punished. Norquay also told the meeting that the people of the Red River Settlement had had no training in government before 1870 and would not have managed public lands well if they had possessed that power. But times had changed, the present cabinet was managing affairs effectively, and "the day is not far distant when we will have control" of public lands. (His optimism outpaced events: the handover took place fifty-five years later.)[24]

In short, Norquay continued to act as a mediator and a defender of compromise in public affairs. He supported a "law and order" approach to the alleged crimes of 1869–70 and would have prosecuted only a few participants. Although he named no one, he left open the possibility of trying Riel. As for provincial rights, he stood with those who sought local control of public lands. While Liberals remained in power in Ottawa, this stand placed Norquay comfortably within the ranks of the federal Conservative party, a group then languishing in the wilderness of opposition. But should the national government change, it would portend strains not just between Winnipeg and Ottawa but also among local Conservatives.

FIGURE 1. A two-storey log house, c. 1875, chinked with mud, in the Red River frame style, with an addition that may have served as a byre. Log structures and fences, Red River carts and oxen were part of Norquay's farm life in the 1860s and '70s.

FIGURE 2A. Old St. John's College, Winnipeg, c. 1885. Completed in the 1840s, the building contained classrooms, kitchen, dining room, and residence rooms. Norquay lived here for three or four school years, 1854–57.

FIGURE 2B. St. John's College (detail). Premier John Norquay's sons are probably in this photo, along with classmates drawn from across Winnipeg and farther afield.

FIGURE 3. Andrew Spence and John Norquay, c. 1871. Note the Red River business attire, Norquay's trim build, and his moccasins.

DOMINION OF CANADA.
PROVINCE OF MANITOBA.
County of Lisgar.

I, ______ of the Parish of ______ in the County of Lisgar, ______ in said Province, ______ make oath and say as follows:

1. I am a Half-breed head of a family resident in the Parish of ______ in the said Province, on the 15th day of July, A.D. 1870, and consisting of myself and ______ and I claim to be entitled as such head of family to receive a grant of one hundred and sixty acres of land, or to receive Scrip for one hundred and sixty dollars pursuant to the Statute in that behalf.

2. I was born on or about the ______ day of ______ A.D. 18 ______ in the Parish of ______ in said Province.

3. ______ my father; and ______ my mother.

Elizabeth Norquay

Sworn before me at the Parish of ______ in the County of Lisgar

FIGURE 4. Elizabeth Norquay's Scrip application, 1875 (detail). In this affidavit, Elizabeth swore that she was a "Half-breed head of family resident in the Parish of High Bluff . . . on the 15th day of July, AD 1870" and was entitled "to receive Scrip for one hundred and sixty dollars." She also swore that her parents were "halfbreeds" and that she had not "received as an Indian any annuity moneys from the Government of the said Dominion." Annotation: "Scrip issued on 2nd Oct. 1876." Note Elizabeth's uncertainty in forming letters.

FIGURE 5. Elizabeth Norquay, c. 1882, was about to turn forty when this picture was taken.

FIGURE 6. Scrip. No. 11002, Dominion of Canada, Department of the Interior, Dominion Lands Branch: "The bearer hereof is entitled to an allowance of one hundred and sixty dollars in any purchase of Dominion Lands."

FIGURE 7. Photograph of Louis Riel, c. 1878, probably taken during his return journey westward after hospital stays in Quebec.

CORNER OF SPARKS AND ELGIN STREETS,
and UNION SQUARE,
OTTAWA, ONT.

THIS HOTEL which is unrivalled for size, style and locality in Ottawa, is open throughout the year for Pleasure and Business Travel. It is eligibly situated, being in the Immediate Vicinity of the Houses of Parliament and Departmental Buildings, in the heart of the business portion of the city, and within easy access of many places of interest which strangers delight to visit.

RUSSELL HOUSE.

RUSSELL HOUSE.

THE Proprietor in returning thanks for the very liberal patronage which he has hitherto received, informs the public that this Hotel has been thoroughly RENOVATED, EMBELLISHED and ENLARGED, and can now accommodate 350 Visitors, and he assures them that nothing will be wanting on his part that will conduce to the comfort and enjoyment of his Guests.

J. A. GOUIN, Proprietor.

F. X. ST. JACQUES, Manager.

SMITH & STEWART, Stationers, Ottawa.

A. S. WOODBURN, Printer, Ottawa.

FIGURE 8. Advertisement for Russell House, Ottawa, 1875. The hotel was usually Norquay's residence during his diplomatic excursions to the Canadian capital between 1878 and 1887. Its smoking rooms and dining room provided the setting for many of his informal meetings.

FIGURE 9. The view from The Forks, c. 1884, where the Assiniboine River (left) flows into the Red River. On the east bank of the Red River stands the institutional centre of the francophone community in prairie Canada: from the right, Grey Nuns' hospital, Collège Saint-Boniface, the Roman Catholic Cathedral, the Archbishop's Palace, and, farther north, a cluster of business buildings. Its population was about 1,500 in 1885–86.

FIGURE 10. Horace Norquay (age ten) and his father, Ottawa, 1880. Horace's outfit and the photo itself attest to his father's determination to cut a fine figure during expeditions to the national capital.

FIGURE 11. Winnipeg, Main Street, 1887, showing board sidewalks, rail lines for horse-drawn streetcars, telephone service, and multi-storey commercial buildings. This is the same stretch of Main Street as in the 1881 photograph (Figure 12). The camera is situated at the south end of the street, looking north from Portage Avenue toward City Hall (tower in centre of frame). The contrast between the two photos illustrates dramatically the changes that took place in Manitoba during Norquay's years as premier. The city's population in 1886 was 20,000.

FIGURE 12. Winnipeg, Main Street, c. 1881, at the start of the boom, looking south from the site of the City Hall. The decision on the railway route through Winnipeg having been taken, the village was beginning to assume its present layout. Its muddy main thoroughfare was lined mostly by one- and two-storey frame buildings.

FIGURE 13A. Brandon and the CPR, 1884. Selected as one of the transcontinental railway's divisional points on the prairies, the town on the Assiniboine River near the sites of fur trade posts known as Brandon House (1790s–1820s) was home to nearly 4,000 people in 1891.

FIGURE 13B. Brandon, Rosser Avenue, 1884. Manitoba's second city was less than three years old when Notman of Montreal took this photo of the main business street. Its population was about 2,400 in 1885–86.

FIGURE 14. Manitoba Legislative Assembly members, c. 1883–86. Norquay and LaRivière (front and centre), William Wagner (behind Norquay's right shoulder), Corydon Brown (behind his left shoulder), and Thomas Greenway (second from left in front row).

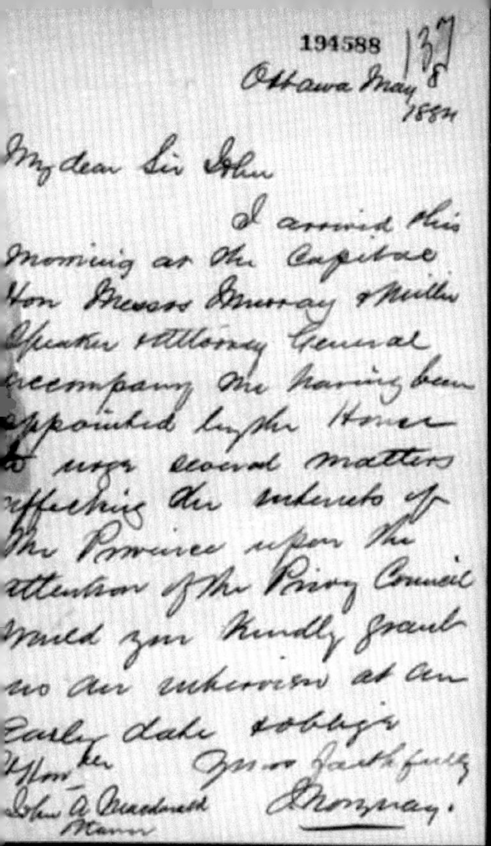

194588 137

Ottawa May 8 1884

My dear Sir John

I arrived this morning at the Capital Hon Messrs Murray & Miller Speaker & Attorney General accompany me having been appointed by the House to urge several matters affecting the interests of the Province upon the attention of the Privy Council

Would you kindly grant us an interview at an early date & oblige

Yours faithfully

J Norquay.

Hon.ble Sir John A Macdonald

Mann

138 194589 file

8 May 1884

Mr J. Norquay

Hon.ble

for interview

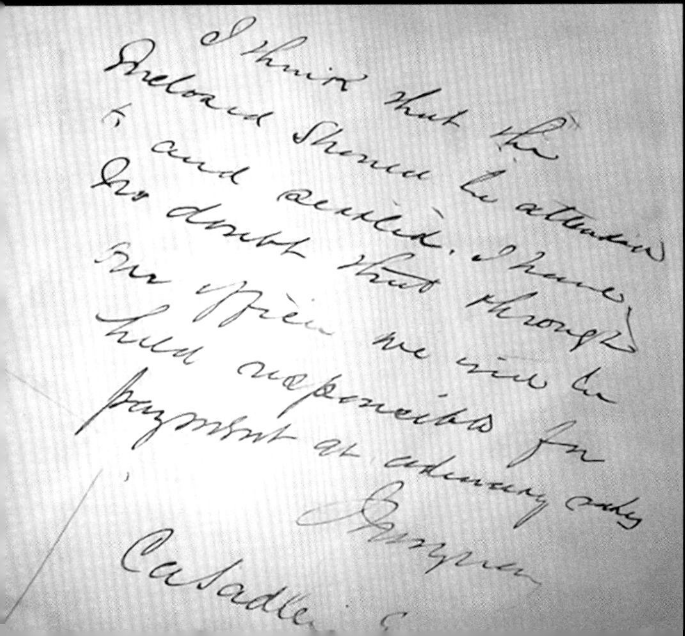

I think that the enclosed should be attended to and settled. I have no doubt that through our offices we will be held responsible for payment at ordinary rates

J Norquay

C A Sadleir

FIGURE 15A. Norquay's letter to John A. Macdonald, 8 May 1884, asking for "an interview" on "several matters affecting the interests of the Province."

FIGURE 15B. Norquay's incisive instructions on a government document, written in a firm, clear hand: "I think that the enclosed should be attended to and settled. I have no doubt that through our offices we will be held responsible for payment at ordinary rates. J. Norquay." The message was addressed to "C.A. Sadleir Exec. Council" who added the note: "done."

FIGURE 16. Kennedy Street, parliament building, and Government House, Winnipeg, c. 1888. Government House (top left) opened in 1883 and the legislative building (centre right) just before the spring session of 1884. Mounted troops heading for the barracks (bottom right), and the trappings of the street itself illustrate the development of a "government precinct" in Winnipeg.

FIGURE 17. Norquay (light suit and straw hat) stands among a large proportion of the Manitoba civil service, c. 1886. His friend, provincial auditor Walter Nursey, stands behind his right shoulder.

FIGURE 18. Norquay with Senator William Eli Sanford, a Hamilton business leader involved in Manitoba business ventures. He was appointed by Macdonald to the Canadian Senate in 1887.

FIGURE 19. George Stephen, later the president of the CPR, 1871.

FIGURE 20. Macdonald, Norquay, and other Conservative leaders, 1886. Norquay is seated on the left, John A. Macdonald and Charles Tupper are seated to the right. John Henry Pope is seated behind Macdonald and Tupper. As provincial Conservative party leaders, Norquay and Ontario's William Meredith (standing between Norquay and Macdonald) have been given top billing, perhaps representing cartoonist J.W. Bengough's estimate of their potential as replacements for the aging prime minister.

FIGURE 21. Turning the first sod for the Red River Valley Railway, 2 July 1887. The marquee in the background shaded the platform party (not visible), including Norquay, Thomas Greenway, and the contractors. This was the moment when, in Norquay's mind, Manitoba broke irrevocably with the federal Conservative government's railway policy.

FIGURE 22. The First Provincial Premiers' Conference, October 1887. Seated at the table: Premiers Andrew Blair (New Brunswick), Honoré Mercier (Quebec), Oliver Mowat (Ontario), William Fielding (Nova Scotia), and John Norquay (Manitoba). Minister delegates and civil servants stand behind them. Prime Minister Macdonald rejected an invitation to the meeting and, on the strength of his alliance with George Stephen of the CPR and his differences with the Manitoba government over railways, then decided that Norquay must go.

FIGURE 23. The Norquay monument at St. John's Cathedral in Winnipeg, c. 1900. The monument, funded by one-dollar donations from 2,000 Manitobans, was designed by Samuel Hooper, who later became the provincial architect. The base of the memorial is of "native stone from East Selkirk," and the central column is polished red granite from St. George, New Brunswick. The provincial coat of arms above the central plaque was sculpted by Hooper.

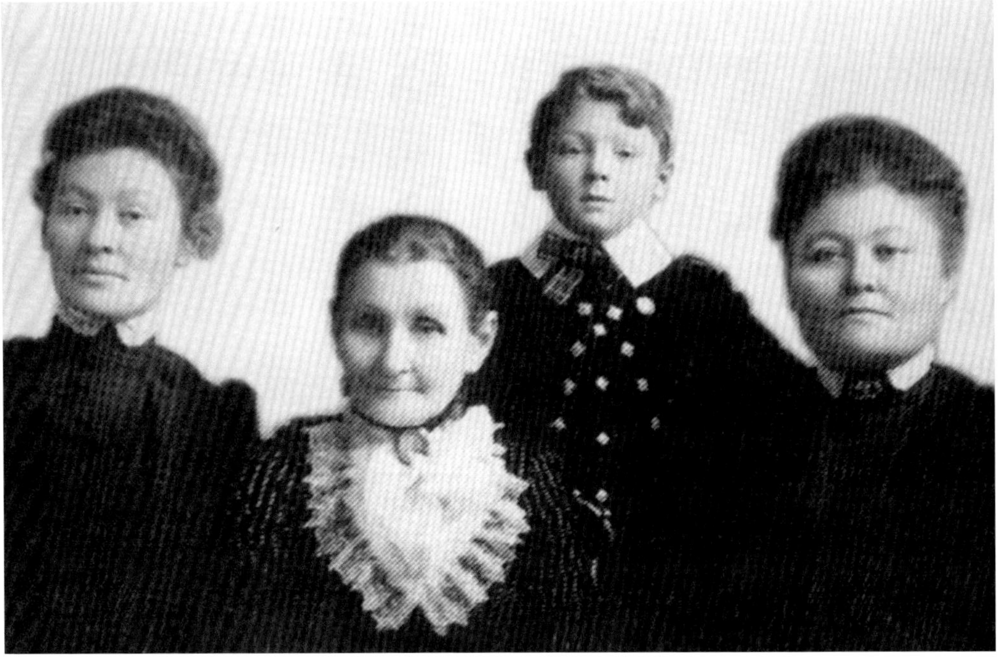

FIGURE 24. Elizabeth with her two daughters, Caroline (left), and Bella (right), with Caroline's son, John McAllister, c. 1905. Bella died in 1915, John in 1917 while serving in the First World War, Elizabeth in 1933, and Caroline (Nellie), in 1960.

FIGURE 25. Hon. John Norquay, Montreal, 1882.

FIGURE 26. Drawing of Norquay, *Grip* Supplement, 17 January 1885.

FIGURE 27. *Dominion Illustrated* portraits (clockwise from top left): Thomas Greenway, John Schultz, Henry Clarke, and Joseph Royal.

The passing of another year put a little more distance between assembly members and the events of 1869–70. The throne speech of January 1877, the last to be read by Alexander Morris, hinted that progress had been made in areas where conflict had once been the norm. It expressed delight in the abundant harvest of the preceding autumn, spoke of legislation to permit the incorporation of towns, and again hoped for a rail connection to Lake Superior. Venturing onto more contentious terrain, it outlined plans to establish a university and to hasten Ottawa's distribution of Métis lands. If the speech promised some important initiatives, it also suggested that many of the major questions of earlier days remained to be addressed, including some delicate matters in French-English relations.

In the throne speech debate, Norquay entertained and joked with confidence. He taunted the opposition, suggesting that "the policy enunciated by the Government had been, so far, universally endorsed. (Cheers)." He acknowledged that it was now time to consider the thorny issue of electoral district boundaries: "The Government were always anxious to meet the growing requirements of the Province, but were not at all anxious to endorse any buncombe resolution proposed by members merely to curry favour with their constituents (laughter and cheers). He defied any member of the House to show that the Government had ever shirked their duty in meeting the growing requirements of the Province of which they were the executive body (cheers)." Norquay enjoyed the limelight, taunted the opposition, and rallied his own team.[25]

Founding a university posed special problems for a government dedicated to French-English entente. Joseph Royal and John Norquay became part of a compromise that made the University of Manitoba an unusual product of the Davis era's balancing act. There had been differences in the cabinet about founding the institution. Norquay spoke in the throne speech debate in defence of the plan, saying that students should not be forced to travel to the older provinces "but should have facilities for this purpose offered them here (cheers). He flattered himself that sufficient educational talent and ability would be found in the Province to enable them to cope successfully with any difficulties which might arise in furthering this measure."[26]

The initial question was how to create a fully fledged institution of higher learning in which scholars could pursue knowledge in all directions and without church-imposed limits. Given the conflicts over these subjects in other Canadian provinces, the existing church-based colleges in Manitoba—Saint Boniface (Roman Catholic), St. John's (Anglican), and Manitoba (Presbyterian)—harboured suspicions about the partnership. But under the auspices of Roman Catholic Archbishop Alexandre Taché and Anglican Bishop Robert Machray, a representative committee debated differences of language, shades of philosophical opinion, and approaches to advanced education, and eventually found common ground. The new institution, an innovative solution to Manitoba's cultural dilemma, illustrated how far the community had moved from the tense days of seven years earlier. Norquay, who sat on the board of the Anglican college, St. John's, and his cabinet colleague Royal, who became the university's first vice-chancellor, carried the plan through the assembly. No one would claim that the two politicians had originated this aspect of the French-English entente, but everyone understood that they were its midwives. Not surprisingly, when the St. John's College leaders met in June 1877 to choose seven members to represent the college on the university council, Norquay was elected alongside six Anglican clergymen.[27]

The same pattern prevailed in the organization of the elementary and secondary education system, but because of its greater scale it attracted much more public attention. Lieutenant Governor Morris and the Davis government were successful in reducing the tensions between the two groups. Still, a pattern of behaviour developed in which French-speaking Catholics and English-speaking Protestants watched each other like hawks for fear that the other side might gain an undue advantage.[28] Norquay played an important part in the calming process. Despite frequent accusations by opponents that he sacrificed principle for personal gain, he justified his support for compromises on language and school issues as being in the best interests of the community.

Did this mean that he would support an alliance between his own followers and Michif/French-speaking Métis? Norquay encountered one moment during this parliament when Manitoba's mixed-ancestry peoples might have united to resist the newcomers. That moment came when Charles Nolin seized the initiative in a short-lived expression of frustration and defiance.

Charles Nolin's Ultimatum

In the spring of 1875, as a result of the new coalition, the Manitoba cabinet contained five ministers: Premier Robert Davis, a capable, business-savvy moderate who could find favour with francophone as well as anglophone electors; Joseph Royal, Archbishop Taché's ally and leader of the Michif/French-language group in the assembly; Charles Nolin, an impatient Michif/French-speaking Métis trader in Ste. Anne, a parish southeast of and different in character from that of St. Boniface; Colin Inkster, a Scots Métis member of the soon-to-be-eliminated legislative council; and John Norquay, who had been Inkster's classmate at St. John's Collegiate School. An alliance between Michif/French-speaking and Bungee/English-speaking peoples in Manitoba and the North-West Territories might have been forged at this turning point in Métis history. It would have depended on new leaders who possessed a wide vision and could fill the gap left by Riel's departure. Such an alliance grew increasingly plausible as Ontarian assaults, and the government's inability to deal with such openly expressed prejudice, made Métis living conditions nearly intolerable.

The Orange Ontarian hostility might not have struck the various mixed-ancestry communities equally, but it did torment them all. John A. Macdonald's informant in Manitoba, Gilbert McMicken, warned the prime minister in 1872 that, if the Orange Ontarians continued their harassment of Indigenous peoples, English/Bungee-speaking citizens might well side with the Michif/French and provoke another uprising.[29] At the close of 1874 William Coldwell, a Winnipeg journalist, cautioned Archbishop Taché that the "extreme" Canadian party was on a rampage; it was important to ensure that men of moderate views were elected to the assembly, he wrote.[30] By 1875 those classified as Métis/Halfbreed for land grant purposes, whether in French Catholic or in English Protestant parishes, were engaged in a common struggle with the federal bureaucracy to secure their hay privileges and children's grants. During these years of instability, a huge gulf opened between Michif/French Manitobans and Quebec-origin Manitobans.

At that moment Riel could not provide leadership for anyone. Where his presence had once been a source of unity and inspiration, his absence now emphasized the split between the St. Boniface elite, dominated by church and Quebec perspectives, and the Michif/French communities situated outside that circle. Three possible leaders of the Métis emerged in the Legislative Assembly: Charles Nolin, Michif/Métis, of Ste. Anne's parish; Joseph Royal, Quebecer, of St. Boniface; and John Norquay, Bungee/English-speaking member for St. Andrews.[31]

If the Manitoba Métis were to develop their own approach to the province's development, then they would have to do so through an alliance between Norquay and Nolin. Such a collaboration would not be easy to achieve because Nolin was a difficult person to work with. Like his two brothers, he was a prosperous farmer and trader, had at least some education, and was forceful in debate.[32] He was also independent minded. Nolin had opposed Riel, his cousin by marriage, on several occasions during the resistance of 1869–70. Despite his influential place in the parish, the clergy regarded him as too violent and quick tempered to be a political representative. In 1870 Nolin had acquiesced in the nomination of Archbishop Taché's choice for the Ste. Anne riding in the legislature. In the election of 1874, however, Nolin took the seat for himself, allegedly dispensing money and whiskey in order to win. According to the local priest, a college classmate of Riel, Father Louis-Raymond Giroux, Nolin exploited "le motif de nationnalité" during the campaign, meaning that he denounced the Quebecers' assumption that they could properly represent Michif/French-speaking Métis. Nolin set out a more aggressive defence of Métis rights and a call for immediate reforms. He intended to become an alternative to Riel and the increasingly Quebec-oriented leadership in Manitoba's Roman Catholic communities.[33]

Because of his prominence among the Métis, Nolin became the minister of agriculture in the reconstructed Davis government of 1875, the first Michif/French-speaking Métis to sit in the cabinet. There he joined Norquay as a spokesperson for mixed-ancestry settlers. Within a month of his appointment, Nolin launched a Métis rights campaign and called for a provincial resolution urging Ottawa to distribute Métis lands immediately.[34] He went much further six months later when he demanded that five recently arrived, French-speaking, Quebec-origin civil servants be required to resign from their offices (they included the land registrar and the clerks of the county courts) and that "qualified" French Métis take their places. His proposal also declared "that in future all offices falling vacant within the french speaking counties, or to which french speaking persons should of right be appointed should be filled by the *Métis* as far as possible, while they remain in a majority." To accompany these dramatic measures, Nolin was submitting his resignation from the cabinet "unless his views be acceded to."[35] His stand placed a great deal of pressure on his cabinet colleagues, particularly Norquay.

In this crucial moment, the cabinet had to weigh not just fairness to new appointees but also the ability and education of local Métis against the merits and shortcomings of Quebec-origin imports. Had Nolin prepared the ground for his attack on the Quebecers? It seems unlikely. Differing opinions must have been aired across the cabinet table, but the conversation ended quickly. Not one of Nolin's colleagues supported his proposal. Instead, the cabinet's other four members, including Norquay, decided "that Mr. Nolin's resignation be accepted." Within two days James McKay returned to the cabinet table as Nolin's replacement.[36]

The cabinet's decision to reject the Nolin motion marked a decisive moment both in Métis history and in Norquay's place in public affairs. If Norquay and Nolin had acted in concert on a "Métis rights" platform, they might have taken control of government policy and created a mixed-ancestry coalition in post-Riel Manitoba. But divided they had no hope of overturning federal land policy or controlling the influx of newcomers. McKay's willingness to rejoin the cabinet as a representative of the Michif/French-speaking Catholic community doomed hopes of creating a resistance movement that united the two language groups.

Why did a Nolin-Norquay alliance not occur? As would become even clearer during subsequent events, Nolin was not the person upon whom a stable, persuasive political movement could be built. His proposal on firing and hiring was hasty and short-sighted. When asked in the assembly session of January 1876 why he had resigned, Nolin replied that he had made demands in the interest of the Métis that had been refused by the government. He said that he would continue to support his former cabinet colleagues when they introduced good measures but as an independent.[37]

Norquay and McKay had done the larger Métis community no favour by torpedoing one of the few proposals that carried the prospect of unity in Manitoba in opposition to policies and appointments decided by, and likely to serve the interests of, eastern Canadians. Everyone recognized that newcomers were promoting their own welfare. Anti-eastern sentiment was in the Manitoba air. But in this important cabinet vote, Norquay declared that he would not accept Nolin's manner of governing. The decision sidelined a potential redefinition of mixed-ancestry people. Nolin continued to regard Norquay as a distant ally, but the two men did not unite in a common front against the incoming Canadians.[38]

Free Enterprise

In 1875 Norquay sent a petition to Canada's Department of the Interior lamenting Ottawa's painfully slow implementation of Métis/Halfbreed land grants. In this document he and his neighbours pointed out that newcomers, as "parties having no interest or claim therein," were taking timber from lands that did not belong to them. These tracts were supposed to be reserved for old settlers "in order that they might locate in the vicinity of their friends." Instead, such arrangements were becoming "daily more difficult owing to the fact that the greater part of the province is already out of the market." The petition insisted that the hay lands and outer two miles (three kilometres) of riverside parish lots (the so-called hay privilege) should be transferred to the owners of the river lots "in fee simple," as an official inquiry had concluded in 1874. Norquay's point was that trees crucial for building, fencing, and fuel had become a scarce commodity.[39]

Aside from the obvious interest in specific lands and resources, Norquay's words had a second message. The petition, signed by hundreds of landowners, marked their recognition of the universal application of Canada's legal approach to private property. By citing such concepts as "out of the market" and "fee simple," they were acknowledging that the former mixed property regime of Red River had ended. Norquay, as the organizer and petitioner, was leading his fellow citizens in an assertion of property rights and, by implication, in their acceptance of the new land system.

In mid-decade, he was becoming more concerned about the difficulties experienced by old settlers. The economic crisis, the severe grasshopper infestation, and the shortages of food and seed grain oppressed Norquay and his fellow cabinet members. With no obvious solution in sight, poor farm families turned to land and scrip sales for income. The strategy surfaced in a letter from Andrew Spence, stepbrother and childhood friend, who asked Norquay whether old settlers could sell the scrip being distributed by Ottawa: "The natives up this way [meaning Bungee/English-speaking residents] would like to know what about the grants to be given in script [scrip]. They ask me can they sell this scrip to the Gov and get $160?"[40] The provincial government had no money to make such cash grants, so presumably Norquay told Spence that scrip sales could take place only in the open market and be negotiated by willing sellers and buyers. He would worry, however, that Spence's family was in dire straits. Although he defended land speculation and open sales, Norquay also was concerned about the welfare of his countrymen, and Spence's hardships influenced his view of the government's social responsibilities.

Norquay addressed the land issue in the assembly session in 1876. Children's land grants having been delayed by Ottawa yet again, the Manitoba cabinet passed a resolution arguing that children old enough to sign contracts "should have the right to sell the land allotted to them, so soon as the allotment has been made and confirmed." The cabinet's concern was that the issue of legal patents for the allocated plot could take a long time. Such a delay would handicap speculators and further impoverish farm families.[41] Here was Norquay's initial approach enshrined in a cabinet motion. It favoured early sales and accommodated the speculative market.

In 1877, as children's grants finally were being readied for distribution, a new proposal to loosen restrictions on land deals was placed on the legislative agenda by development-minded legislators. On this occasion Norquay spoke more cautiously than before. Now he was willing to acknowledge that some Métis had been exploited by speculators and that Ottawa's bureaucratic approach during the previous seven years had caused delay and hardship. He did not want to encourage people to be dishonest, Norquay told the legislature, but he believed that his initial view had been mistaken: "Some people took advantage of half-breeds who sold their claims from necessity. It was unreasonable to force a man to sell 240 acres of land which is worth one, two and even four dollars an acre for twenty-five dollars and in a few cases the enormous sum of fifty dollars." The sarcastic comment about "enormous" sums underlined his affiliation with and sympathy for his countrymen. He now proposed that the federal government allocate specific tracts of land to individuals immediately after the issuing of scrip and to impose a defined period when sales could not be made. As guardians of known, tangible parcels, recipients of the grants would have time and opportunity to consider the land's value and to adapt their thinking to the new reality. Then, after this cooling-off period, the sale of property, including sales by minors, could resume.[42]

Norquay had modified his position, but he remained a supporter of individual enterprise and contracts. Métis should be able to sell their lands on the market, improvements should be paid for, and sale contracts should be regarded as definitive. He suggested that the allocation of land should immediately follow the government's drawing of lots "so as to enable those to whom this 240-acre grant had been given to become the guardians of their own property. At present the reserves were a sort of commonwealth—no one looked after them because no one had a special right to do so. Consequently the lands were going to ruin, and what might otherwise prove a very valuable patrimony was being wasted (hear and cheers)." Norquay had good reason to be concerned. He was receiving queries from friends and even strangers about scrip purchases and land sales. Reports came in from many directions of extensive speculation in land.[43]

Norquay moved still further away from unrestricted free enterprise as the years passed. In 1878 he tried to defend the poor and the poorly informed in their relations with speculators. In this skirmish an Orange Ontarian, Francis Cornish, moved that Métis minors over the age of eighteen be permitted to sell their lands without their parents' consent. This would prevent lands from being tied up, he said, because "we daily find them anxious to sell; but they can only do so by the father giving a mortgage on his property as security." Leading French-speaking assembly members Marc Girard and Joseph Royal opposed the motion. Norquay agreed with them. The motion would "open the door to fraud," he said: "Even now there are instances where men have been made drunk and sacrificed the noble patrimony given them. If this is the case with men, how much more will a young man of eighteen, who, as it has been remarked, will in all probability be sowing his wild oats, be liable to be victimized. It behoved every man who desired to see justice done to the half-breed to oppose the measure. He had no objection to a law enabling lands to be conveyed with parental consent." An amendment, passed into law, altered Cornish's motion by accepting Norquay's alternative that permitted sales by minors over eighteen with parental consent.[44]

Norquay started the decade as a free trader and capitalist. By 1878, worried about his countrymen and -women, finding it difficult to deal with the implications of the transfer to Canadian rule, he legislated to protect them from the full onslaught of the market's operations. But he still endorsed the property system. He wanted his Red River contemporaries to adapt to it as quickly, but also as carefully, as possible. Adaptation to a new norm had become a basic principle in all his assembly activities.

Assembly Life

The day after delivering the throne speech in 1875, Alexander Morris dispatched printed copies to his Canadian counterparts, the other six lieutenant governors. The impressive stationery and elaborate penmanship of the cover letter demonstrated that the province was now a full partner in a network of relationships built upon common understandings and rituals. The web extended across Canada, but Norquay and his colleagues knew that it also encompassed far-flung corners of the British Empire. They were learning that the system itself shaped people's behaviours and expectations, including those of assembly and cabinet members. As Morris explained when the session closed a few weeks later, members had been "providing in advance by wise legislation for the reception of a largely increasing population." They were creating "all the advantages, in this new land, of an older civilization."[45]

Norquay was happy to rely on the experiences of other jurisdictions and to work within the formal processes of British parliamentary institutions. In a debate on election rules, he opened his speech with a reference to British precedent and the broader Canadian setting: "Of course much of the bill has been copied from the laws in force in the other Provinces, but that is something not to be regretted. Much of our legislation requires to be the same and I see no reason why we should not avail ourselves of all the help we can get from their experience and assimilate our legislation to theirs, so that one general law shall prevail throughout the Dominion."[46]

Norquay enjoyed these days in the assembly. He participated regularly in debates, tried to keep the peace when members' language got out of hand, and smoked cigars with his colleagues in the speaker's private chamber as the night wore on and talk became expansive. The twenty-four assembly members, seven legislative councillors (until the council's abolition in 1876), plus assorted civil servants, such as the sergeant at arms and clerk, as well as members of the press, worked in a legislative building peopled almost entirely by men. Although guided by British parliamentary practices and Canadian conventions, their heckling and disputation reflected Manitoba's social divisions. Talk was blunt. Members applauded, laughed, cheered, and jeered. No one seemed to be exempt from having to engage in physical contests. Joseph Royal, the most sedate of members, explained to his colleagues that he had been confronted "at the foot of the stairs by a person named Thibaudeau who applied to him (Royal) an epithet no gentleman would submit tamely to, and he therefore placed his signature on that person's face." Charles Nolin accosted Alphonse Martin of Ste. Agathe outside the assembly and took him "by the nose for using insulting language." Consumption of strong drink led to unpleasant quarrels. William Luxton of the *Free Press* said that Martin and several of his colleagues had participated in "such disgraceful scenes [as] had never occurred in the annals of Canada." Norquay intervened as peacemaker, expressing the hope that "the House would be generous and not blight the prospects of a young man just starting in life and who had been partly led astray by older members who were perhaps more deserving of censure." Having been subdued by a motion condemning "his disorderly conduct in the House," Martin, then twenty-six years of age, later apologized. Norquay, the diplomat calming the waters, was a ripe old thirty-four.[47]

When the dispensing of free drinks in the speaker's chamber tested their patience again, the cabinet decided to call a halt to the practice. Premier Davis noted that members had been accustomed to retire to the speaker's room adjoining the assembly for cigars and drinks "whenever they saw fit." He and the speaker were tired of paying "$200 or $300 or more every session out of their private pockets to pay these expenses." They told the sergeant at arms, Alex Begg, to end the practice. Begg, who also enjoyed a drink, continued to supply members with liquor and cigars, despite the order, though he "naturally supposed they would repay him for them." They did not pay, however, and the premier, with Norquay agreeing, decided to place the items in the public accounts "so that the country could see how the money had been used." Norquay joined this discussion enthusiastically, picking up on "that famous item of $381 (a labourer's pay for a year) which had so much scandalized those who had helped to consume the cigars and champagne (laughter)." Some assemblymen, he said, "would not pay their bills themselves but made the public pay them (cheers and laughter, and cries of 'name! name!')." Norquay did not hesitate: "The member for Kildonan was one (cheers and renewed laughter). But no doubt such members had received a lesson by this publication which they would not forget in a hurry (hear, hear)."[48]

Alcohol figured prominently in Norquay's thinking during these years. The *Manitoba Free Press* reported in March 1875 that Norquay had been elected a councillor at the first annual general meeting of the British American (also known as the Independent) Order of Good Templars temperance organization. The group had been founded in the United States and was then spreading across the Western world. Dedicated to "the sacred pledge of temperance," its opening ode declared "Here we pledge ourselves anew /

Not to touch the drunkard's drink; / Proving faithful, proving true, / We will make the demon shrink." When asked formally, probably in 1874 or early 1875, "Will you take a solemn pledge to abstain from the use of all that can intoxicate, as a beverage?" Norquay would have declared his faith in God and answered "I will." The pledge itself, taken with the left hand on the Bible and the right hand on the heart, was a promise not to "make, buy, sell, or use any spirituous or malt liquors, wine, cider, or any other intoxicating drinks." He also would have sworn to obey the rules of the Templars organization, never to reveal its secrets, and to accept the Bible as "a true and safe chart for the whole voyage of life." Although Norquay did not honour the temperance pledge for the rest of his life, he probably did so for a few years.[49]

The matter of his consumption of alcohol was important, given the quantities of liquor purchased on the family account and the damage wrought by drunkenness in late-nineteenth-century communities. Norquay was at ease with liquor. In some years of the 1870s, his liquor bills were prodigious. In just six months in 1878, he bought alcohol at Bannatyne's store on thirteen occasions.[50] The existence of bills does not say that he drank the liquor. He might have been one of the cabinet members who accepted the obligation to supply his fellow assemblymen with strong drink during sittings, a practice that smoothed the passage of legislation. What is more, everyone knew that booze encouraged support during election campaigns. A hospitable man who enjoyed a wide circle of acquaintances and many social obligations, he provided support to his extended family members when relatives fell into alcoholism, but his own association with liquor came in political campaigns and normal social settings, not in the private trials that befell, for example, John A. Macdonald, or Norquay's brother, Thomas.

The Sessions of 1877 and 1878

Norquay was given the task of redrawing electoral boundaries in 1877. His draft embodied the compromises of the Davis years and ensured the continuing electoral significance of the former Red River Settlement. The province was divided into three elements, the "French" (largely Michif/French-speaking districts), the "old settlers" (Bungee/English-speaking districts), and the "new settlers" (mainly Ontario immigrants), and each was given eight seats in the areas where they predominated. Norquay's speech introducing the bill contained more blather than reason. He said that he wanted "to give to every party represented in the Province a just representation—that is, with regard to interests and elements." He assured his colleagues that he would deliver to those "unfairly represented . . . their just dues (cheers)." But he also wanted to ensure "the least possible interference with existing arrangements." Norquay did not aim for a purely equal allocation of seats as the principle of representation by population would require. And that meant one special consideration: "A full representation had been accorded to the old residents of the Province—who were, as hon. members were aware—the pioneers of the country (cheers). He stood there as the representative of that element, and maintained that it was nothing but fair that they should be amply represented (hear, hear)." The old settlers had "always been liberal towards the new settlers. . . . And now that the numbers and wealth of the newcomers would bring about a new era, this attitude of the old settlers would no doubt be remembered to their advantage (cheers)." Norquay claimed that his constituents, the old settlers, had earned this consideration by their sacrifices as pioneers, their unique interests as river-lot farmers, and the welcome they had extended to new arrivals.[51]

The law was passed by the coalition members over the protests of the opposition. And Norquay's definition of the bill's principles, distinguishing the components of the provincial population by their "interests and elements," lived on in public speech. Dr. Cowan thought that the "new scheme" of interests and elements, "more especially, he supposed, . . . interests (laughter)," ignored the important principle of equality among the province's residents. His arguments were endorsed by several English-speaking newcomers, but they were voted down by a margin of fifteen to five.[52] Norquay knew that the new electoral map served his own interests very well.

The legislative session of 1878 was opened by the new lieutenant governor, Joseph-Édouard Cauchon. Despite his Quebec background, and relatively recent switch from the Conservatives to the Liberals, Cauchon was acknowledged to be an individual of experience and political insight. As the months passed, he proved to be a reliable advisor to Ottawa on Manitoba affairs. The throne speech read by Cauchon, the last to be prepared under Robert Davis's direction, claimed that the province's agricultural fortunes were improving and that the railway from eastern North America was coming ever closer. It also listed a few pieces of legislation, including the planned consolidation of provincial statutes, underlining thereby how quickly and thoroughly Manitobans had become reliant on the state.[53]

Norquay spoke many times during the session. His interventions could be counted on to raise the temperature in the chamber and to rally government support. He opposed the continuing Orange Ontarian campaign against French Catholic schools that would have removed religious teaching from the classroom. In rejecting arguments for a "common school system," Norquay suggested that "secular schools" were likely to take away "the very book [the Bible] which of all others teaches and inculcates those social and moral principles which tend to make good and loyal subjects. Yes, Mr. Speaker, that book which it is intended should be excluded from our schools is the foundation of truth, honesty and loyalty, and is now talked of lightly by the sons of those who in their day were willing not only to fight but to bleed and die for it if necessary." His embellishments might have distracted his listeners, but the message itself drew from evangelical Bishop Anderson's classes of twenty years before.[54]

The government entered the session with considerable public support, and its position became nearly unassailable as the debates unfolded. Norquay delivered one of the major speeches of the session, a spirited defence of the government's record. Early in his cabinet career he had discovered that he could disarm his opponents by seeming to agree and then turning the tables on them. In one instance, he admitted that the roads from Kildonan to Winnipeg had been in a terrible state and, in mock horror, repeated that the member for Kildonan

> invited members to be astonished with him that such things should be (loud laughter). Why, even if the Government had had millions at their disposal, they could not have kept the highways in good order last summer. Men who could not see beyond their noses might require the Government to keep the rain away—(laughter)—might order them to procure snow immediately for the benefit of the country—(renewed laughter)—but such a course was the veriest trifling and unworthy of those who had a seat in that House. They only had a subsidy of $90,000 to spend, and no public land to sell, so what could the Government do more than they had done? The Opposition comments in this

> direction were, it would be seen, but the merest buncome and clap-trap (laughter and cheers).[55]

Norquay was just warming up. In the days that followed he delivered several more colourful speeches. Assembly members enjoyed the oratory. Former lieutenant governor Alexander Morris, no mean rhetorician himself, who left office in 1877, now referred to Norquay as "the best educated of the English halfbreeds and a *capital speaker*."[56]

Norquay's team loved his jokes at the opposition's expense and praised his stout defences of the government. Even opponents had to admit that he commanded the attention of the house. What is more, the local government's policy choices were winning public support. When the sitting ended in early February 1878, Norquay made a brief western swing with Premier Davis to take soundings. They were told that "the Government has never been so strong since it was formed as it is now." Davis made one further observation. Noting that a government member must travel east to negotiate a minor financial concession, he suggested that the task might fall to Norquay "as he has never been to Ottawa." It was a small indication of the preparations that the premier was making to train a successor.[57]

Setback: The Federal Election of 1878

With the approach of a national election, political campaigning intensified. Alexander Mackenzie's Liberal government had had to deal with an economic downturn during its four years in office, and John A. Macdonald was back in stride, promising a "National Policy" to restore growth and prosperity. Many western Canadians professed dissatisfaction with Mackenzie, a change from the situation in 1873–74, when revelations of Macdonald's corrupt dealings over a planned Pacific railway drove people into the arms of the Liberals. Federal party organizations became a fact of life in the Manitoba capital. In July 1878 the Conservative association in Winnipeg announced the convening of regular weekly meetings in a newly established free reading room. A Reform Club (Liberal), similarly, had begun to meet.[58]

Norquay shunned all talk of party lines in local politics, but he was an avowed Conservative in federal elections. He decided that he had a good chance of becoming a Member of Parliament for one of the Manitoba seats. He was now sufficiently sure of himself that he began to intrigue against the candidacy of Alexander Morris. As late as mid-summer 1878, still harbouring hopes of running for the Conservatives, he wrote to John A. Macdonald to say that, in the Selkirk constituency, "it is more than probable that I may be the Opp[ositio]n Candidate" and that Morris would run in Marquette. Norquay was doubtful about the Catholic vote, however, given that he had long been on the Bungee/English-speaking Protestant side of the Red River Settlement. He wondered if Sir John might intervene: "Even [the Catholics] ... will probably support me ... unless they are instructed to the contrary."[59]

Norquay could not overcome the hostility of John Schultz and the Orange Ontarians who dominated the Conservative party in Winnipeg. He eventually withdrew from the nomination contest, and Morris was acclaimed as the Tory candidate in Selkirk. Letters to the *Free Press* from a correspondent who took the name "Manitoba" criticized "a certain clique" in Winnipeg that had treated Norquay badly. Norquay made matters worse by complaining about his fate.[60] Suddenly he was in the Conservative party's bad books.

Everything changed when John A. Macdonald himself was defeated in Kingston. In an era when federal elections took place across several weeks, and riding nominations frequently occurred on election day itself, it was possible—if the party moved quickly—to find alternative seats in which to place a defeated candidate. One of these seats was Marquette in Manitoba, an ideal spot for Macdonald. The telegraph carrying news of his defeat to Winnipeg caused the rousting of Norquay and Royal from their beds. They "left town between two & three o'clock in the morning & arrived in Marquette in time." That is, they travelled eighty kilometres by horse-drawn carriage through the night and early morning, arriving at the Portage la Prairie poll before the nomination deadline at noon and in time to speak to the Liberal candidate, William Luxton, and the Conservative candidate, Joseph Ryan. They convinced both to withdraw in favour of Sir John: "They told Luxton that the aspect of things had changed and he must retire or else they would oppose him which meant defeat to him."[61]

Sir John was then elected by acclamation while his party was winning a sweeping victory in the national campaign. Norquay presumed that he was back in the new prime minister's good books. He wrote to the prime minister-elect with the jaunty warning that, if Sir John remained their Member of Parliament, he could rest assured that Manitoba matters would keep him busy. When Macdonald eventually chose to represent Victoria, British Columbia,

Norquay lost the leverage he had hoped for. Moreover, as the terms of Luxton's withdrawal came to be known, the antagonism between his allies and the Orange Ontarian Tories increased. Norquay, who was close to Luxton, "the Grittiest of Grits," was once again positioned on the wrong side of prominent figures in the Winnipeg Conservative party. What was worse, in making the deal on Macdonald's behalf, and getting Luxton to withdraw from the contest, he had committed the Manitoba government to long-term support of Luxton's *Free Press* through printing contracts. Ontarian Tories in Winnipeg regarded that price as far too high.[62]

The Provincial Election of 1878

Premier Robert Davis retired from politics in October 1878, citing "private affairs" as the reason for his departure.[63] There were two logical successors. One, Joseph Royal, the Quebecer who was both the editor of the local French-language newspaper and an effective ally of Archbishop Taché, became enmeshed in a political scandal during these months. The charges, combined with predictable Orange Ontarian opposition to a francophone Catholic, convinced Royal to accept second place in a new cabinet. The alternative, because of his ability in the house and his years in office, was John Norquay, the first Indigenous political figure to have reached such prominence in a Canadian legislature, let alone to find a place in the premier's chair. His elevation to the office represented an exceptional moment in Canadian parliamentary history.

In taking the premiership, Norquay appointed Royal to the cabinet and added two others, lawyer David Walker and businessman Corydon Brown. He postponed the choice of a Michif/French-speaking Métis minister until after the general election.[64] News of his choices received a warm welcome from the *Manitoba Free Press*. The enthusiasm was not simply the result of the editor's expectation of generous treatment. Rather, well before that moment, William Luxton had declared that Manitoba was better for Norquay's decision to stay in local politics. He praised Norquay as "able," "educated," and a "man of quality." He argued that Norquay, among all his peers, saw the importance of ensuring that Manitoba institutions matched the quality prevailing in older provinces. This statement probably referred to language and school laws but also to parliamentary practice and the role of the state in dealing with the market and labour-capital relations. Luxton also referred to Norquay as a "halfbreed" and "native of the country" and said that he constituted "a worthy tribute to native talent and worth." The *Free Press* editor regarded the new premier's heritage as a positive rather than a negative.[65]

Norquay turned immediately to the preparation of a letter to newly elected Prime Minister Macdonald outlining the needs of the province. This list included an enlarged boundary and a subsidy commensurate with Manitoba's needs and size. It enumerated drainage projects that would open up rich agricultural land around Winnipeg. It also included a new legislative building. These issues fell under the heading of "Better Terms," already a chestnut in Manitoba-Ottawa relations.[66]

Having reconstructed the cabinet, Norquay issued a manifesto in mid-November to launch the provincial election campaign. In it he emphasized that Manitoba needed railway access to eastern North America. If elected his government would assist the incorporation of municipalities that would then be able to offer bonuses for the construction of branch rail lines. As always the province would seek better financial terms from the federal government. It would propose to Ottawa the sale of at least some of the lands reserved for schools. It would also pass a drainage act that would permit the settlement of a vast acreage now covered by shallow water every spring. Norquay explained his platform at a public meeting at The Rapids schoolhouse in St. Andrews, where it was well received.[67]

News of the manifesto circulated widely. Norquay's brother-in-law, John James Setter, wrote to Norquay two weeks later to say that Portage la Prairie had yet to see the text but that "the reputation you gained from that speech is something to be proud of. I hope that it is only the beginning of a long, high & prosperous career as a public man." But Setter also acknowledged "the anxiety caused you by your high position"—presumably a reference to thoughts expressed by Norquay in a private letter—that Setter said was "nothing to be surprized at especially as there are so many conflicting interests & prejudices to surmount."[68]

As part of the election campaign, the *Free Press* prepared a special publication comparing the financial records of the "Clarke" government (1870–74) and the "Davis" government (1875–78). The comparison worked entirely in favour of the latter. The newspaper also published a bald statement declaring that Norquay was a poor man, no doubt to separate him from Clarke's profiting through government payments. These helpful statements were designed to blunt opposition criticisms that, as ever, claimed the government was hopeless at managing public affairs.[69]

The campaign in English-speaking districts resembled the two earlier elections. In the areas where newcomers, mostly from Ontario, predominated, the result was complicated by eastern Canada's party loyalties and religious or linguistic prejudices. A candidate in southern Manitoba, Julius Galbraith, spoke in favour of abolishing French printing because, he claimed, the French translations of bills were never used. He also argued for yet another redistribution of ridings, this time on the basis of representation by population and not, as in Norquay's act, by "interests." Yet Galbraith claimed that he was not a "Canadian party member" because those Orange Ontarians were truly anti-French. Instead, he ran as a supporter of the Norquay government. In Winnipeg, another prominent candidate assumed that the official status of French would be abolished soon. Even the French wanted it abolished, he said.[70]

Norquay relied on old friends to support his cause. One of them was the influential James McKay, who had a sterling reputation among Red River descendants, whether French or English speaking. As election day approached, McKay wrote to say that he had received Norquay's recent appeal for help and would "try to be at polling place early, even the evening before." He said that "I might be able to see some of my old friends, and those that are on a balance I might be able to bring over to the right side. . . . I wish you all success."[71]

Norquay's reputation for honesty and reliability remained intact among those who had supported him in previous years. A High Bluff friend wrote to correct a false impression that he opposed him: "There is neither McKenzie, Cowan nor any other man in this country that I hold in as great esteem as I do you. . . . I think that you may count on old [MLA] Kenneth McKenzie giving you a very fair support. You stand high in his estimation yet, though he has been in opposition to the Government for the last two years[.] He passed a night here last week and expressed himself as having every confidence in your honesty."[72] Alexander Murray of St. Charles wrote to Norquay to say that "I hope your election is sure, in fact I know it is, because surely our countrymen are possessed of more patriotism than to go back on themselves."[73] These were the positive voices.

In contrast to such encouraging sentiments, racism also surfaced in public discussion, particularly in the statements of some Orange Ontarians.

In mid-December, just before the vote, Luxton commented that Norquay was opposed by people who "pretend to think a 'Native' incapable of filling the position [of premier]." The most blatant negative reference to race came from a new Winnipeg satirical newspaper, *Quiz*. In Manitoba's first political cartoon, or so it claimed, the paper depicted "Norquay's Troupe." The sketch included four cabinet members—Norquay, Brown, Walker, and Royal—dressed formally in business suits. Although Norquay's attire resembled the clothing of his three European Canadian colleagues, a mule (at that time Norquay farmed with two mules) romped in the background, a fool astride him facing backward in the saddle. The fifth cabinet minister, who carried a sheaf of papers labelled "Agriculture," was portrayed quite differently. His face was much darker, he smoked a long, First Nations–style, ceremonial pipe, a blanket was draped around his shoulders, and, in contrast to the top hats of his colleagues, he wore a feather headdress. The fifth cabinet member had yet to be named when the cartoon appeared. Several days later, Métis Pierre Delorme's appointment having been announced, the *Quiz* editor commented that "the likeness is not bad." The editor might have said that the cartoon was just a joke, a matter of satire and free speech, but the crude image of a Métis legislator underlined the arrogance and prejudice that existed in some circles.[74]

The election was called for 18 December 1878. Norquay was not a shoo-in, even in St. Andrews. A public meeting there descended into a whiskey-fuelled scuffle; the chairman lost control of the assembled crowd and then he threw a chair at the hotheads. A general melee followed, the lights were put out, and benches were broken. When the polls closed, Norquay's winning margin was only three votes. One hostile resident, who described the new premier as a "political humbug," claimed that "about fifteen" outsiders, taking advantage of the electoral law permitting individuals to cast ballots in any riding in which they owned property, had nullified the preference of the actual residents of St. Andrews.[75]

The campaign in French ridings followed its own rhythm. *Le Métis*, the French-language weekly owned and operated by Joseph Royal, reported rumours in mid-October that some candidates were inviting voters home for drinks in exchange for votes. This practice, the newspaper warned, was illegal. Archbishop Taché and the priests of the Roman Catholic Church worked tirelessly to maintain peace between Quebecers and Métis. Their influence delivered results as it had in the two previous general contests.[76]

An extraordinary election battle in the village of Ste. Agathe, forty kilometres south of Winnipeg, warned of future trouble in French-speaking districts. The returning officer rejected two sets of nomination papers, one belonging to a candidate who allegedly had not taken the oath before a properly appointed magistrate, the other for tendering his deposit in foreign currency. The officer then declared that the winner, by acclamation, was Quebec-born farmer and lawyer Joseph Taillefer. That night the returning officer and the victorious Taillefer were guests at the home of two local priests. The house was visited twice by a "gang," and at 6:30 in the morning six men seized one of the priests and pushed him outside. When Taillefer intervened, he was shot at several times, one bullet hitting him in the thigh and causing him to fall to the ground. The men then dragged the captive priest through the snow to a sleigh and raced off toward the town of Morris, where they locked him in a hotel room. Although Taillefer's election was declared official, the tensions remained unresolved. The story, at bottom, concerned Métis discontent with Quebecers' leadership in Manitoba. It would return in a more significant form within months.[77]

The people of Manitoba elected sixteen candidates said to be likely to back the Norquay administration, six who were clearly opposition members and two who claimed to be independents. Orange Ontarians disputed whether the new majority should be called the "Norquay government." The *Manitoba Gazette*, an opposition newspaper, thought that Norquay was merely Royal's "cats-paw to be used for a short time, till the French Canadian clique of St. Boniface can mature their plan of future operations to secure another four years lease of the treasury of the province." The *Gazette* had a very low opinion of Royal himself, whom it described as "the hero of the Indian frauds," a reference to his alleged misuse of funds intended for Cree and Saulteaux reserves.[78]

The new Manitoba administration's most unusual aspect was its leader. John Norquay had become the foremost representative of his countrymen in northwest North America. His superior education and intellectual gifts, command of several languages, fluent speech and remarkable ease in public moments, had won a loyal following. Supportive of bilingualism, drawing on both Métis and newcomer voting support, neither Orange Ontarian nor Riel-affiliated, Norquay was urging Manitobans to adapt quickly to Canadian conventions. In the local culture wars—French vs. English, Catholic vs. Protestant, Red River-origin vs. European-origin peoples—he was avoiding extremes. In his view, public schools should be administered by the state rather than the church; Canadian property law should prevail but speculators must respect limits set by the legislature; eastern party lines must be avoided. He could anticipate serving in the premier's office for the next four years. But that expectation underestimated the uncertainties of politics and the Manitoba assembly's capacity to generate surprises. Within eleven months, voters would have to return to the polls because of the unrest generated by individual ambition and community cultural divides.

CHAPTER 6

Premier, 1879

The year 1879 marked the end of the bison era and the end of the old Northwest. In a matter of months, eastern people and products flooded every corner of Manitoba life. The St. Paul, Minneapolis & Manitoba railway ran more or less regularly from the Minnesota capital to St. Boniface from December 1878, ensuring year-round passenger and goods traffic with the wider world. Winnipeg merchants announced that they would deal only in cash rather than extending credit in the fashion of the fur trade, thus putting a formal end to the days of old Red River when "everyone and everyone's means were known to his neighbour," and people "seldom thought of repudiating a debt they had willingly incurred."[1] The year brought a dramatic political crisis that ensured newcomers would exert much greater influence in the province's public affairs. Henceforth, John Norquay would have to deal carefully with political party organizations imported from "down east" if he was to defend the interests of his Red River countrymen.

His new government was dealing with a much larger and more diverse population. More than half of Manitoba residents (about 30,000 of the 50,000) had arrived within the decade. Norquay also had to deal with huge changes in political practice. In 1870 the various political groupings in Canada were fluid. A decade later the two national organizations, John A. Macdonald's Conservatives (with the formal name of Liberal Conservatives) and Alexander Mackenzie's Liberals (also known as Reformers), behaved as more disciplined groups. These party lines had not invaded the Legislative Assembly of Manitoba, where majorities coalesced and fell apart as unaligned legislators approved or opposed the cabinet's offerings. Until 1874 Manitoba's lieutenant governor had provided the glue that held a majority together. Between 1875 and 1878 this role fell to Premier Robert Davis and his ministers. In both eras the rivalries between French and English, between Métis and Quebecers, and between Orange Ontarians and Bungee/English speakers figured in debates. Now, with talk of eastern Canada–style party allegiance in the air, Norquay's new provincial government had to respond to those who wanted party lines in local politics. Despite being a Conservative in the federal sphere, Norquay had friends in both national parties and believed that Manitoba benefited from standing outside the federal party system. Only by uniting in favour of better terms within confederation could they avoid being divided by the vagaries of federal politics.

The debate over partisan loyalties unfolded while Norquay dealt with other pressing issues. He had to face a new session of the legislature and win a vote of confidence. He had to pay a crucial visit to Ottawa to plead for financial help from John A. Macdonald, who had just returned to the prime minister's office after four years in opposition. The most pressing priority was to quell conspiracies among Manitoba Conservatives, including plots that would put a quick end to his days as premier.

Joseph Royal and Ottawa

The new premier toured western Manitoba in January 1879 with his two English-speaking cabinet colleagues, rural business owner Corydon Brown and Winnipeg lawyer David Walker. The tour went well, particularly because it gave Norquay a clearer picture of the sentiment among recent arrivals in the province, almost all of whom were English speaking and from Ontario. He then prepared a throne speech promising land drainage, Court of Queen's Bench sittings in western Manitoba, steps toward the incorporation of towns, and construction of branch railways.[2] Would the assembly approve of his leadership and support the ministry he had created? And could he provide effective leadership for Manitoba when he stepped onto the national stage?

The cabinet's support in the new legislature consisted of a strong contingent of Michif/French-speaking members (nine or ten in total, including at least seven backbenchers and two cabinet ministers) and five English-speaking allies, three of whom were cabinet ministers. That made at least fourteen votes in the house of twenty-four. The margin was sufficient to govern, though it depended on the Michif/French-speaking contingent.[3] That faction was led by the forceful journalist from Quebec, Joseph Royal, who frequently had alienated his Michif allies and clearly harboured an ambition to become premier of the province.

Royal became the focus of political events in the first months of 1879. A man of many accomplishments, he had trained as a lawyer in Quebec, founded several journals, written several books, and helped to dispatch volunteers to join the papal state's military force, the Zouaves, in Rome. Royal moved west in 1870 at the urging of Bishop Alexandre-Antonin Taché and George-Étienne Cartier when they were recruiting likely leaders to support French-language and Roman Catholic interests in the west. He founded a French-language weekly, entered the Manitoba cabinet, and served in public life for the next two decades, first as a Member of the Legislative Assembly, later as a Member of Parliament, and later still as the lieutenant governor of the North-West Territories. Having written a biography of Louis-Hippolyte La Fontaine, the leader of an earlier generation in Lower Canada, Royal understood and supported La Fontaine's concept of a "double majority," according to which French and English sections of the assembly were empowered to choose their own leaders. He had recently been musing that bills in the legislature should be permitted to pass only if they were supported by a majority in each section and that a French-English administration, built upon "moderate" Protestants and the double majority principle, was both desirable and possible.[4]

Royal's loyalties could not conceal his prejudices, notably his distrust of Protestants and his superior airs when dealing with Métis. Although he defended Métis interests consistently in the assembly and in his newspaper, he never won their affection.[5] Norquay recognized and shared the Métis' view of Royal. He nevertheless relied on the Quebecer both as a cabinet ally and as an effective advocate in negotiations with the federal government.

The house adjourned after just a few days in February to permit Norquay and Royal to visit Ottawa for crucial negotiations with the newly elected federal government led by John A. Macdonald. The premier's foremost concern was that Manitoba did not own the public lands and natural resources within its borders. It could not sell, lease, or otherwise profit from this crucial asset, nor could it extract revenue by means of generally accepted taxes on minerals, forests, and water rights. To win control over these revenue sources, Norquay would have to appeal to the prime minister's sense of fairness while reminding Macdonald that Manitoba's status was constitutionally anomalous since the other six provinces administered their own lands. His other priority was the transcontinental railway. The province needed improved access to eastern markets. Norquay wanted to ensure that the line would be built soon and, if possible, to influence the choice of its route.[6]

In late February 1879, accompanied by Royal, Norquay departed from St. Boniface on the recently completed railway that connected the Manitoba capital to St. Paul, Minnesota. In addition to a full three weeks of business meetings in Ottawa, he enjoyed brief visits to Montreal, Toronto, Port Dover, and Chicago. On these side trips he saw some friends from Red River days, chatted with investors, and charmed the family of mill owner and new Manitoba investor William Ogilvie.[7] Norquay wrote home to his family each week. In return daughter Bella kept him abreast of Elizabeth's latest illness and reported on events in St. Andrews, including news of a successful concert, the parish social event of the season, that she had missed: "I was to[o] late[.] I came down when the people were going away." She added that her brothers, Tom and John, were working, probably on the farm and the house.[8]

The two delegates on the Ottawa mission were accompanied by Alexander Begg, who acted as secretary, and Thomas Spence, Norquay's old friend from Portage la Prairie, who was now clerk of the Legislative Assembly. They enjoyed the capital's finest food and accommodation at Russell House, the famed hotel frequented by parliamentarians. They took part in Ottawa's social scene, including receptions and dinners and carriage rides and an evening at the theatre. The premier was learning to be a lobbyist and to dress as lobbyists did. His files contain bills for several ties, a pair of gloves, and a pair of shoes. His hotel bill included charges for a travelling cap, baths, shaving for one month, and cigars. His expenses for meals and sundries and laundry added up to over eighty dollars, two months' pay for a worker in Manitoba.[9]

In a letter to the prime minister dated Wednesday, 5 March, the Manitobans announced their arrival in the capital. Sir John responded immediately, and they met him, in company with Louis-Rodrigue Masson, on Friday. The inclusion of Masson illustrated Macdonald's canny ways. As the minister of militia and defence, Masson had no direct interest in the talks, but he had defended the Red River Métis resistance movement in Parliament in 1870 and could be expected to get on well with the Manitobans.[10]

Macdonald treated the negotiations with great seriousness. He had spent over four years, a full parliamentary term, in the political wilderness after his government's fall from power in the Pacific railway scandal of 1873. For two of those years, he drank to excess, shirked his duties as opposition and party leader, and considered retiring from politics. At the age of sixty-one, well past the life expectancy of men in that generation, he stopped drinking and found new energy in the encouragement of some exceptional allies, notably Charles Tupper of Nova Scotia. His team developed the so-called National Policy, including protective tariffs and the hastening of a railway to the Pacific Ocean, that might better integrate Canada's ill-fitting communities into a viable nation-state. Armed with this promising platform, his Conservatives won the election of 1878 and carried three of the four seats in Manitoba.

Now, six months later, the talks with Norquay and Royal mattered a great deal to the prime minister because they were preliminary to decisions on the national railway. Tupper would handle the details, but Macdonald wanted to ensure that the Manitobans cooperated with his policies. Begg's memorandum on the talks recorded that, within minutes of the opening pleasantries, "Sir John evinced a disposition to meet the wishes of the deputation and considered that no demand made [in Manitoba's official dispatch] was unreasonable." The prime minister accepted Norquay's claim that Ottawa's commitments dating from the negotiations in 1870 on Manitoba had not been fulfilled in the intervening years. His government would pay, he promised, for the erection of some public buildings in the province. The Manitobans were off to a good start.[11]

On Saturday the delegates met with Colonel John Stoughton Dennis, deputy minister of the Department of the Interior, the official responsible for implementing prairie land policy, to discuss school lands and drainage. The Manitobans asserted that a distant Ottawa bureaucracy did not grasp Manitoba's circumstances. In the case of the lands set aside for educational purposes, the provincial and local governments were responsible for the provision of schools. But Ottawa had not begun to sell lands in the areas where schools were required, thus imposing greater financial burdens on the province and local taxpayers. In the case of drainage, federal officials seemed to believe that Manitoba was like the rest of the prairies, flat and dry. That just was not true, the delegates said. Much of "postage stamp" Manitoba's land was covered with water, closer to marsh than wheat-field-in-waiting. Dennis listened to their appeals, explained his own views, and promised "to acquaint the delegates with the conclusion arrived at as soon as possible."[12]

Sunday was a quiet day, reserved for church services and a review of the delegation's strategy. A busy and productive week began on Monday, 10 March, when Norquay, Royal, and Spence presented the Manitoba assembly's address of welcome to the new governor general, the Marquis of Lorne, at Rideau Hall. On Monday, too, they opened negotiations with the Department of Justice concerning compensation for the cost of trials conducted in Manitoba arising from charges laid in the North-West Territories.[13] The next day they fulfilled the assembly's promise to Charles Nolin by asking the federal government to report on "all native appointees from Residents of Manitoba & the North West Territories to permanent salaried positions under the Crown."[14] On Wednesday morning, 12 March, the Select Standing Committee on Railways met to consider a branch railway in Manitoba. A senior minister, Hector Langevin, chaired the session, and Charles Tupper attended the meeting, a sign of its importance to the federal cabinet. Norquay emphasized that Manitoba needed "railway communication" and that he and his colleagues "had come to Ottawa for the purpose of watching such railway legislation as might affect Manitoba."[15]

The talks proceeded amicably and at a stately pace for another two weeks. On his last day in the city, having tried and failed to see the prime minister, Norquay left a cheerful note for John A. Macdonald to say that "I will do what I can to make matters run smoothly in Manitoba and N West. Many thanks for the consideration paid to our representatives."[16]

Both sides looked upon the results with satisfaction. The prime minister had agreed to a substantial increase in the provincial grant, including aid for land drainage, roads, and the construction of government buildings. He had also committed to an expansion of the size of the province, though this would not be announced immediately. He would revise the federal approach to the sale of school lands. He agreed to adjust the process for repayment of relief debts arising from the grasshopper scourge of 1873–75. Reflecting on the month's work, Norquay and Royal believed the federal government had been open and generous. This positive conclusion could not conceal two important failures. Nothing was concluded about Norquay's biggest concern, ownership of public lands and resources. On Macdonald's key concern, railways, their agreement covered only a portion of the potential issues that might arise and left one important detail unresolved, the duration of their agreement.

Railway Policy

Norquay's years in office coincided with the moment when railways caused a revolution in the economy of northwestern North America. Three major trunk lines—the Canadian Pacific in Canada, and the Great Northern and the Northern Pacific in the United States—played a part in deciding his fortunes. So did branch lines within the province. His administration had to deal with not one or two but several dozen proposals from these smaller companies. Although seemingly unrelated, the policies that shaped transcontinental transport and local short lines had to be dealt with during the Ottawa expedition. They shaped Manitoba's settlement map forever and they introduced problems that dogged the premier to his grave.

On branch lines, Norquay faced four competing proposals in 1879. One of the four, the Manitoba South-Western Colonization Railway (MSWR), aimed to secure a federal company charter, establish its base in Winnipeg, and connect fertile farmlands to the proposed transcontinental line. John Schultz, Norquay's nemesis in local Conservative politics, led this project. The other three all planned to build from Selkirk, where the Mackenzie government had decided the transcontinental line would cross the Red River before heading northwest through the Interlake and northern prairies to Edmonton. Rather than choose from among the four, Norquay's cabinet decided to postpone discussion until it knew more about Macdonald's plans. As Norquay put it, he wanted to "obtain an intelligent knowledge" of Ottawa's policy and "preferably to influence" the decisions that affected Manitoba.[17]

Branch line charter applications, taken in conjunction with the selection of a transcontinental route, would seal the fate of four Manitoba districts whose business leaders aspired to metropolitan status. They included the village of Emerson, on the American border where the Red River crossed into Canada; St. Boniface, on the east bank of the Red River at its junction with the Assiniboine River, the centre of francophone and Catholic institutions in prairie Canada and the terminus of the just-opened railway connection with St. Paul; Winnipeg, St. Boniface's twin city on the west bank of the Red

River, where for half a century Upper Fort Garry had served as a fur trade hub and military garrison; and Selkirk, the closest to Lake Winnipeg, where the Red River's higher banks were believed to be less prone to flooding. Which of the four sites would become the metropolis of the prairie west?

Norquay did not want to choose, and neutrality became his maxim. He represented a riding adjacent to Selkirk and owned land there. He also owned land in the Emerson district. He faced vigorous lobbying by clergy and business leaders in St. Boniface. Land speculators in Winnipeg, the largest population centre by far (about 5,000), were voluble and influential. Confronted at a mass meeting in Winnipeg, Norquay defended his support for one of the Selkirk syndicates by saying that he "was never grudging in giving assistance to those who wanted it, and if he helped his own people, he never begrudged it to others."[18] But, just as the negotiations in Ottawa opened, he was forced to make a decision by none other than his long-time critic, John Schultz, a proponent of the Manitoba South-Western line.

Schultz feared Norquay's opposition, confessing that he was on "fairly bad terms" with the premier. His dislike of Norquay originated in the latter's selection as a cabinet minister in 1871 and was reinforced by Norquay's success in politics thereafter. It also might have included a degree of racism. Or Schultz simply might have preferred that the limelight be his alone. Born in Kingston, he was a year older than Norquay, slightly taller, much leaner, better educated, and certainly richer. He had studied medicine in Ontario and, though he never completed a medical degree, practised in Red River from his arrival in 1861 while engaging in a number of businesses. He had opposed the HBC administration, raged against Riel's provisional government, and then won a seat in the House of Commons in 1871. Schultz held the seat through three subsequent general elections. Having filed for nearly $70,000 in compensation for his losses in the resistance, he received an award of $32,000, about fifteen times Norquay's annual ministerial salary, from his friends in Ottawa. Schultz was loved and hated in equal measure in Manitoba.[19]

Norquay surprised everyone by supporting Schultz's proposed branch line. The decision was wise, if unexpected, and easily explained. The premier could gain by having Schultz work the parliamentary corridors on his behalf. The South-Western line was seeking a federal charter, meaning that Norquay could do little to prevent its approval. Schultz's consortium wielded more lobbying power than the others, having recruited to its side an influential

Conservative Member of Parliament, future prime minister John Joseph Caldwell Abbott of Montreal, and a long list of Winnipeg business leaders.[20] Interestingly, Norquay demonstrated that he did not harbour grudges that might blur his vision.

When he and Royal entertained the province's federal representatives at a dinner on 11 March, all those in attendance, both the provincial cabinet members and the federal Members of Parliament from Manitoba, signed a recommendation in favour of Schultz's railway.[21] The next morning Norquay provided valuable testimony on Manitoba's outlook to federal ministers. His gift to Schultz was his statement that, of all the options, the proposed South-Western line "would best serve the interests of the people as a whole." Joseph Dubuc, the Member of Parliament for St. Boniface (Provencher constituency), observed that Schultz was relieved to have Norquay's support and gained much from the premier's testimony.[22] The committee meeting created one big winner in Manitoba's local affairs: Schultz secured a valuable federal railway charter and the accompanying 6,400 acres per mile of land grant that would multiply his considerable wealth.

The second aspect of Norquay's railway moment concerned the imminent construction of a trunk line from eastern Canada to the Pacific Ocean. Macdonald wanted to ensure that his government had a free hand in making the arrangements. On his side, Norquay did not like the rail route as it had been set out in the preceding four years by the Alexander Mackenzie government. Pushing north from Selkirk through the Manitoba Interlake, that route skirted the rich lands of the Red River valley and the Portage la Prairie plains, where most voters resided. Norquay was fortunate that plans for the Pacific railway rested with Minister of Public Works Charles Tupper, the able Nova Scotian, father of confederation, and godfather of the Conservatives' "National Policy." Tupper attended the two sessions on railways in the first week of the Manitoba talks and listened carefully to western perceptions of the territory, the route, the timing, and the broader competitive context of the transcontinental railway project. On 8 April 1879, just days after Norquay left Ottawa, Tupper announced that the proposed transcontinental railway would travel south of Lake Manitoba.[23]

Norquay was very pleased. As he explained to *Free Press* editor William Luxton, "their views were received [in Ottawa], and a policy determined upon, which it is expected, for the present at least, will entirely relieve the

Province of responsibility." They had the desired southern route for the transcontinental and had made a crucial decision on branch lines.[24] The federal cabinet's eventual order-in-council covering the talks declared that the Manitoba government "will oppose the granting of a charter for the present session at least for any Railway in Manitoba other than the one recommended by them from Winnipeg southwesterly towards Rock Lake [the MSWR]." The phrase "for the present session at least" was not included in the first draft but added later by Minister of Justice Alexander Campbell, who placed his initials "A.C." beside the addition. Both parties were aware of the issue raised by this wording: Macdonald wanted to avoid a time limit on the agreement, and Norquay was willing to use the vagueness for his own purposes.[25]

The wording haunted them for years to come. Manitoba possessed the constitutional right, and the credibility in international markets, to build or charter local railways. Norquay did not anticipate that a deal concerning the route of the transcontinental railway would have implications for the provincial power over such branch railway charters in the future. By giving the federal government an open field in contracting for a transcontinental line, and postponing provincial action on branch lines, however, he was relinquishing control of a policy area that came to matter very much. He had limited Manitoba's railway options in a manner as important to the future of the province as the 1870 Manitoba Act clause that gave the dominion government control over the province's public lands.

The premier enjoyed his Ottawa experience, though it left him more uncertain about his future than ever. He took home a memento of his journey, a photographic portrait taken in the Notman studio.[26] A week after his return to Winnipeg he and Elizabeth attended a grand ball at City Hall, where the council chamber was decorated with British and American flags, shields bearing Masonic emblems and deer trophies, and a buffet table bearing fruits, wines, salads, and trifles. Three weeks later the Norquays were invited to St. Mary's Academy in Winnipeg for a "Festal Entertainment" in honour of Archbishop Taché.[27] Norquay seemed to be riding high, having won significant gains and even personal recognition in Ottawa. One crucial piece of information had eluded the happy premier: just when he was winning plaudits for his success in the negotiations, some of his colleagues were planning to remove him from office.

Springtime Conspiracies

After the Ottawa trip, Norquay understood better how distant he was from the Conservative party's inner circles. He could see that not even his wholehearted support for Macdonald made any difference to the prime minister's Orange Ontarian partisans in Manitoba. Moreover, he perceived that Macdonald, despite his kindness toward Norquay personally and his generous reception of the Manitoba delegation, had many other sources of information in the west, as did the prime minister's Quebec lieutenants.

Recognizing the fragility of his hold on office and the conflicting demands of friends and party, Norquay began to think again of resigning from the office of premier. He tried to meet Sir John privately in the lobby of the House of Commons, probably in pursuit of a job in the federal civil service. He restated his interest in an appointment immediately upon his return to Winnipeg, emphasizing that "I am well & favorably known to most of the Halfbreeds in that portion of the Territories who I imagine will exercise a great influence in securing the allegiance of the aborigines." Besides, he added, he knew Indigenous languages and French, had a good acquaintance with the Cree and Saulteaux peoples, was a native of the country, and could build confidence between the federal government and prairie residents.[28]

A week later Norquay wrote to the influential William Ogilvie in Montreal on the same subject, evidence that federal employment was no passing fancy. Ogilvie replied with surprise: "I did not dream of your leaving your present position." He doubted that Norquay would get such a job: "I have really no means of knowing what your chances are of getting the position, but do not put much faith in it." The businessman was right. Macdonald would not give up a recently re-elected ally with whom he had just reached deals that would be pivotal in the coming years. Instead, the prime minister temporized: "My dear Norquay: I have yours of the 10th inst. The subject of appointing an Indian Commission in the North West [is] under consideration, but will probably not be settled until the hurry of the session is over." He promised to keep Norquay's letter "as a memorandum."[29] Once again the scheme was overtaken by events: Canada's policies on First Nations foundered in the swamp created by Alexander Mackenzie's Indian Act of 1876. Although Norquay remained a politician and a farmer, his interest in the federal civil service provided further evidence of his doubts about Ottawa's policies and his confidence in his own abilities at this difficult time in prairie Indigenous history.

While the Orange Ontarian Tories' impatience with Norquay bubbled in Winnipeg, politicians across the river in St. Boniface were concocting an even more dangerous brew. Their plan drew from the deepening distrust between Manitoba Métis and Quebecers. Although this divide might be called today a matter of "race" and "class," the labels do not precisely describe the concerns of the Métis. The relevant differences between the two camps included family ancestry, income, occupation, and formal education but also language and parish. The Métis, like their English-speaking counterparts, perceived that they were not respected by many incoming settlers of exclusively European heritage. They also recognized that language differences—the dialect and accent and vocabulary of Michif versus the distinctive tones of Quebec—marked them as inferior in the eyes of these newcomers. Such tensions were closer to the surface than Quebec-origin elites were prepared to admit in public. Although the conflicts within the French-speaking parishes were not directed at Norquay, Métis unhappiness with the politicians imported from Quebec, combined with the ambitions of Royal, produced an explosive mix.

The Michif/French-speaking Métis parish of Ste. Anne became a pivotal battleground.[30] One of its leading residents, Charles Nolin, did not appreciate the condescending attitude of his assembly colleague Joseph Royal and some of the others who came from Quebec. Nolin was not alone in thinking about Royal in this way. Norquay himself said that Royal "had the air and hauteur of the Grand Seigneur, his manner . . . more or less dictatorial."[31] Archbishop Taché had tried to neutralize this Métis discontent in the election campaign of 1878 with a pastoral letter insisting that parish priests had a right to speak on political subjects. They were disinterested, he wrote, better educated, and more desirous of the good of the country than were the mass of voters. Taché defined a good candidate as one who sought the aid of God and of wise, discreet advisors. Editorials in Royal's *Le Métis* struck a similar note. These appeals to unity implied their opposite: that dissent was increasing in some of the Michif/French-speaking communities and especially in areas where Nolin was well known.[32]

Nolin ran for re-election in Ste. Anne in 1878. He said that he would ally with the English, if necessary, to prevent the election in his riding of a "Canadien" (meaning a Quebecer). Nolin again asserted, as he had in cabinet discussions two years earlier, that Quebecers should not be placed in government jobs when Métis candidates were available. His brother declared publicly that he wanted to be rid of the "Canadiennerie," the Quebec-origin leaders in Manitoba.[33]

Despite appeals in *Le Métis* for a liquor-free campaign, the contest in 1878 was filled with bribery and treating. A respected, prosperous Quebecer, J.B. Lapointe, received the church's support in Ste. Anne but could not beat Nolin. The official tally, ninety-two votes to seventy-six, was immediately challenged on the ground of illegal treating. Nolin was charged and faced trial for offering bribes in the election. The French elite in St. Boniface supported the prosecution.[34]

When the results of the general election became known at the end of December 1878, Nolin wrote to Norquay to offer the new premier congratulations on the victory. He also made a promise: "You can always count on my support, in as much as the Government measures would not be detrimental to the Country."[35] The phrase could be seen as a warning to the leaders of the "French and Catholic party" as well as the Norquay government. During the week-long sitting in February 1879, Nolin and his Métis colleagues talked of overthrowing the Norquay-Royal administration in order to rid the province of the Quebec-origin leaders. Bishop Taché reported with relief that "our people," the nine Catholic representatives, remained united during those few days of sitting.[36]

Royal appeared to be increasingly confident in the months after the election. He enjoyed the diplomatic mission to Ottawa, visited Montreal, and in both cities renewed old friendships and enjoyed conversations about faith and nation. Now forty-two years of age, Royal believed that he, rather than Norquay, should have become premier when Robert Davis stepped down. According to gossip in St. Boniface, his daughter was bragging that her father would soon occupy the premier's office. As for relations with the Métis, Royal stood fast: the "French and Catholic party," as he labelled it, had to remain united in the face of English Protestant enmity. He declared that what they had in common as Métis and "Lower Canadians" (Quebecers) was far greater than their differences.[37]

While Royal was dreaming of higher office, Nolin was winning support within the French caucus and making its leaders appear to be out of touch and out of sympathy with the Michif/French-speaking constituencies. Nolin's own sense of grievance was multiplied because cabinet ministers Royal and Pierre Delorme did not back Nolin in his court case. Thus, while the provincial delegation members enjoyed themselves in Ottawa, several Métis assemblymen in Manitoba were reconsidering their loyalties. Four—Charles Nolin, Maxime Goulet, Andrew Bourke, and Louis Schmidt—plotted to overturn the ministry.

The plotters decided that Delorme should be replaced. They then won the support of two other influential Métis leaders, Maxime and Ambroise Lépine. One of the Lépine brothers, in turn, travelled south to St. Joe, the Métis settlement in the Dakota Territory, and there talked with Louis Riel, who had been released recently from a Quebec asylum. Rumours reached St. Boniface that Riel was advising the discontented Métis. Gossip attributed their anti-Quebecer rhetoric to Riel's inspiration because Ambroise Lépine was said to be incapable of serious thought (he "ne raisonne pas"), whereas "what comes from Riel is greater than gospel."[38]

The Ste. Anne election trial took place as the Métis intrigue was maturing and the postponed sitting of the assembly was about to convene. Nolin had lined up numerous witnesses in his defence. Before the morning session he even rallied his troops on the steps of the court, warning them to defend themselves against these attacks by outsiders. If he was guilty of stealing the seat, Nolin warned, then his friends were guilty of helping him, so they had better support him now or they, too, would face charges. Father Louis-Raymond Giroux wrote to Bishop Alexandre-Antonin Taché to tell him about the testimony: "Truly, drink flowed in this election and in the trial we heard of nothing but bottles." The presiding judge, Louis Bétournay, told Father Giroux that he had never seen such a disgusting trial or one in which the same witnesses came forward time and again to contradict the prosecution's testimony. That Bétournay was yet another Quebecer would not have been lost on Nolin and his supporters.[39]

Norquay now faced challenges on three fronts that could easily lead to his ejection from office. John Schultz, whose railway charter elevated him above all other Manitoba business leaders, would never be reconciled to Norquay's leadership. Joseph Royal had enjoyed his month in the national capital and believed that he would be a better premier than his colleague. Charles Nolin was preparing to lead Michif/French-speaking Métis in a revolt against the Quebecers' leadership. Then, at the end of May, just hours before the session reconvened after its four-month adjournment, Royal pulled the rug from under Norquay's feet.

A Ten-Day Crisis

The time-honoured warning "be careful what you wish for" has always had a special resonance in politics. It was never truer than during the ten-day ministerial crisis of 1879. Although it had been bubbling for months, the trouble exploded with unanticipated force. Nolin threatened to defeat the government. Royal threatened to unseat the premier and take the top job. In response, Norquay rallied the English. None of the actors could have predicted the result. The turmoil ended with champagne for the victors, chagrin among the defeated. Decisions made by the Michif- and French-speaking leaders during this fateful week, and by Norquay and his newfound allies, shaped events in the following decade and beyond.

The day before the Manitoba legislative session resumed, gossip concerning Métis disaffection was rife among assembly members. Because the verdict in the Ste. Anne election trial had not yet been announced, Nolin would be sitting in the assembly. He was rumoured to be planning a vote of non-confidence in the government in the hope of securing Pierre Delorme's ouster from the cabinet and his own return to high office. The Quebecers in St. Boniface were on edge. Although they would have denied accusations of racism, even the most well-disposed among them had become impatient with the Métis in the assembly.

Member of Parliament Joseph Dubuc, once Riel's classmate in Montreal and formerly sympathetic to the Métis cause, mocked his one-time Métis colleagues whose thinking was "so profound" (he wrote derisively) that they could see no way to attain their goals except by overthrowing the entire government.[40] Dubuc's long letters during the next month, which provide a ringside seat on the crisis, betrayed the frustration that Dubuc and Royal felt as they contemplated Nolin's challenge. Those who followed Nolin, Dubuc wrote, had behaved foolishly; those who followed Norquay had accepted the lead of a "coarse, unscrupulous, shameless animal who had already betrayed his friends."[41] Dubuc's intemperate language painted a stark picture of the gulf between mixed-ancestry peoples, whether Michif or Bungee-speaking, and White Canadians, as well as between French- and English-speaking Manitobans.

Joseph Royal's later, self-serving account of the crisis emphasized his innocent desire to preserve democracy and to introduce Louis-Hippolyte La Fontaine's "double majority" principle. Blaming Norquay above all others for the ensuing crisis, Royal claimed to have asked the premier on at least three occasions—in January, February, and April 1879—to increase the number of English-speaking representatives on the government benches. His worry, Royal said, was that English Manitobans were not properly represented in the administration. When it became apparent that Norquay would not act, he claimed, the Quebecers secretly approached Thomas Scott, an English-speaking Conservative, to join them in a new Royal-led government. They would then adopt the Conservative party label and affiliate with the federal Conservative organization. Federal party discipline would reshape provincial politics, and the double majority principle would operate henceforth in the legislature.

The session opened on 27 May at 3 p.m. This formal occasion, the first sitting after the adjournment in early February, offered nothing out of the ordinary. Nolin's threat to overthrow the government was not carried out. Dubuc, becoming increasingly caustic about the Métis, scoffed that Nolin probably did not know how to do it. The next morning the final witnesses in Nolin's Ste. Anne election case took the stand. That phase of the trial completed, the judge promised that he would deliver his decision quickly. Meanwhile, the French-speaking assembly representatives met in caucus. Nolin's complaints were the first order of business. Arguing that the Ste. Anne election trial was not an issue on which to overturn a ministry, Royal took control of the group by condemning Norquay's failure to win more English support. On this the French, whether Métis or Quebecer, could agree. Alphonse LaRivière was dispatched to discuss the situation further with Thomas Scott and, presumably, to complete arrangements for the overthrow of the Norquay administration.

Or so Royal's version of the story goes. As cover for this extraordinary move, Royal claimed that the French were facing an imminent Ontarian assault on their constitutional right to use their language in the public arena and to control their own confessional schools. He wrote to Archbishop Taché to say that the "orangistes" were stirring and would soon cause a storm of fanaticism that would "crush everything in its path." His plan, he said, was to unite the "French party," and show them the real situation: that the French, now a minority in the province, faced great danger when they supported a government that the English majority did not want.[42] Norquay probably did not know about the plotting by Nolin and Royal or that Thomas Scott, a leading Orangeman, might ally with French-speaking Catholics.[43]

Royal, having secured Scott's support, then took a fateful step that he would have depicted as honourable: he visited Norquay in his office and told him that, given the premier's failure to secure a majority of English-speaking representatives, the French would vote against his administration the following day. The Royal-Norquay confrontation took place late on Wednesday afternoon, 28 May. No report of this conversation survives, but in his own account of these events, as reported by his son, Norquay spoke of Royal's arrogance at this meeting.[44]

Norquay met at 7 p.m. with his two English-speaking cabinet colleagues, David Walker and Corydon Brown. Given that this conversation was recorded by a minute in the executive council register, the three regarded it as an official cabinet meeting. The cabinet minute contains this spare account: "Report from Mr. Norquay re protest of French representatives, Messrs. Walker and Brown offer to resign."[45] During this discussion, and in addition to their offers of resignation, the two ministers allegedly declared that no English member would support Royal. Their argument was that, contrary to expectations, he had not cleared his name of the charges levied against him in the Indian Affairs fraud case that had been bubbling in the background for months.[46]

What happened during the rest of the evening cannot be documented precisely. Norquay and his two cabinet colleagues seem to have convoked a meeting, perhaps at Walker's house, of the English-speaking assembly members. There, the premier outlined Royal's threat, presumably arguing that Royal's personal ambition and French Catholic loyalties would take the province in directions he, and they, must oppose. He then asked them to support an "English" platform that proposed cuts in French-language government printing and Roman Catholic school funds as well as fewer French-dominated assembly seats. Several participants described the meeting as excited and enthusiastic. Dr. James Cowan, an advocate of Orange Ontarian positions, whom Dubuc described as "narrow and ordinary" and "always fanatical and venomous," allegedly said that the political configuration might be brief but that the English speakers should seize the opportunity to end the quasi-official standing of the French language. The others "followed in his footsteps, several with reluctance," according to Dubuc. Those who attended signed a "round-robin" document setting out their proposed platform. Scott, erstwhile ally of the French, was present but did not attempt to turn the tide in the direction of Royal and the Conservative party. With the apparently unanimous support of the English-speaking members, Norquay carried the day.[47]

Royal's newspaper account of his position, and of Norquay's alleged treachery, was ready for distribution within hours. Norquay had thrown himself into the arms of people who had been his enemies for the past five years, it said, and he must be unseated: "Everyone distrusts this ambitious man, unrefined, uneducated, unprincipled, lazy, reckless, and willing to do anything to remain in power." The list of Norquay's alleged failings spoke volumes about Royal's own attitudes toward those of mixed ancestry. The article concluded dramatically with Norquay's (alleged) peroration at the English members' meeting: "Let us govern the country without them [the French], in spite of them, and against them, he [Norquay] cried in finishing his harangue."[48] There is no other evidence supporting the account in *Le Métis*. Just as the French newspaper was being prepared for printing in the morning of Thursday, 29 May, Norquay was writing to Royal, requesting his resignation.

Once again the French caucus assembled to discuss strategy and, after a brief consultation, agreed that both Royal and Pierre Delorme would send letters of resignation to the premier with copies to the press. As far as they knew this would put into motion their arrangement with Scott and set the stage for the formation of a new government. The letters were delivered to the premier's office around 1 p.m., and by 3 p.m. Norquay had announced his acceptance of Royal's resignation, though he said nothing about Delorme.[49]

In the afternoon sitting, Royal set forth his view that a genuinely representative Manitoba government must have support in both language communities. He turned to his seatmate, Norquay, saying that he had agreed with Royal when they talked of this on three different occasions. The business of the assembly continued for several uninterrupted hours and included the tabling of the Norquay-Royal report on their recent Ottawa negotiations. In a recorded vote, the Norquay cabinet (without Royal) was sustained by thirteen votes to six. All the English-speaking representatives stood with the premier. The six dissenters included three restive Métis (Nolin, Bourke, and Goulet) and three Quebecers (Royal, LaRivière, and Taillefer). Five members of the house apparently were not present or chose not to vote. It was clear that, in establishing an "English" majority, Norquay had lost the support of those who spoke Michif and French.[50]

A *Free Press* editorial said that the crisis was totally unexpected and left the house divided along French/English lines: "From that moment," Luxton wrote, "it became a matter of diplomacy and tactics who should come out ahead. . . . The French party have over-reached themselves—they have committed political suicide." In his view, compromise had become impossible because the English were now united on more radical measures than the French could accept. Luxton believed that some among the English group in the assembly "did not court what is likely to be evolved, and who rather regret than otherwise that they should have been forced to adopt severe defensive war measures." This was a fair summary of Norquay's position. Others in the English camp, wrote Luxton, deserved no credit: they had been cowardly supporters of intrigue who would not stand by their cause in adversity. The target here was undoubtedly Thomas Scott.[51]

The Michif/French assembly members lost battle after battle. On Saturday, 31 May, Judge Louis Bétournay ruled that Nolin was guilty of electoral fraud. The sentence disqualified him from political office for seven years and from any Crown appointment. Nolin was to pay all costs. He appealed the ruling immediately, and several weeks later the disqualification portion of the verdict was reversed. But the nullification of his original election remained. Nolin angrily told his friends that he was leaving the province forever. He threatened to nominate an English candidate to run in his stead, promising that he would deliver the Métis vote to an "Englishman." Burdened with debt, Charles and his brothers headed west to Saskatchewan, never to return. They left a vacant Ste. Anne seat and a leadership vacuum in the Métis community.[52]

Norquay was very busy during the next five days as he sought to consolidate his position. He had to fill the two empty cabinet portfolios by finding new allies in the Michif/French-speaking caucus, if possible, and to win the confidence of the assembly. On Saturday, Maxime Goulet, a Métis newcomer to the assembly, went to see Norquay. At this point the premier was ready to dispense with Pierre Delorme as representative of the Métis in the cabinet. Norquay assured Goulet that he wanted to govern with French-speaking allies, but he wished to choose his own ministers rather than permit the French caucus to impose their choice upon him. He would not hear of Royal's return or the promotion of LaRivière. He proposed instead Alex Murray, a competent debater and one-time scholarship student at St. John's Collegiate School. Goulet dismissed this idea as absurd because Murray was not Michif/French speaking. "Oh well," said Norquay in dismissing him, "it's take it or leave it; I don't need you people [vous autres]."[53]

On Monday, 2 June, the premier invited able young Quebecer Joseph Dubuc to join the provincial cabinet. Offering words of praise, Norquay depicted Dubuc and Marc Girard as the only French leaders popular among both French and English voters. Dubuc shrugged off the compliment with the observation that, if so, then English sentiment must have changed radically, since it had forced his resignation and that of the Girard-Davis government in 1874. Despite his cool response, Dubuc called a meeting of the French group in his office on Tuesday morning and outlined Norquay's offer. After a brief discussion, he was sent back to the premier's office for further talks. Norquay explained the new ministry's program to him, including curtailment of French printing and reduction of seats in the Michif/French-language parishes, and his wish to have at least one representative of that community in the cabinet. Dubuc returned to his colleagues in a gloomy mood. Several of his compatriots were anxious that he accept Norquay's offer, but the risk of a by-election loss in Dubuc's federal seat, and their wish to avoid "English" selection of the "French" leader, made Dubuc's agreement impossible. No, Dubuc replied to Norquay on 4 June, he would stand on the side of the church and defend the French language and the institutions that supported it.

The Quebecer leaders recognized that they had made a disastrous mistake. Dubuc summarized this phase of the crisis several weeks later: "Those who launched the movement [Royal and his allies] now repent it." They did not blame Scott, recognizing that Norquay had simply outflanked him, but they were chagrined by the rapid change in their fortunes. When Dubuc wrote to his friend Élie Tassé on Sunday, he opened his eighteen-page letter with "we are in a complete crisis in local politics, a crisis unforeseen, stunning, stupid, of an unimaginable stupidity, such as Manitoba knew in its infancy." The fortunes of French and Catholic Manitoba had been gambled away based upon a calculation that now seemed to be foolish in the extreme.[54]

On Tuesday, 3 June, Norquay finally decided that he would have to accept the resignation of Pierre Delorme. Having had little success with the French, and still awaiting Dubuc's reply, he was now negotiating with other members of his new English caucus to fill the remaining cabinet seats. The minutes of the executive council formally noted the departures of Delorme and Royal on Wednesday, 4 June. The same entry recorded that Samuel Biggs, a lawyer, was taking over the Department of Public Works and John Taylor, a teacher and farmer, the Department of Agriculture.[55] The new cabinet members and their supporters in the assembly agreed that they would continue to serve in a non-partisan capacity and ignore federal party lines when they were addressing local affairs.

That day the assembly witnessed two moments when the leading characters crossed swords. Royal won applause by comparing Norquay to the king of Belgium, the latter having faced a crisis during the European uprisings of 1848. When Belgians called for abolition of the monarchy, Royal told the assembly, the king "threw open his window and joined the crowd in shouting for a republic. (Laughter)." Royal's conclusion: "Norquay had known about the [French] printing for five years and said nothing—now he says, 'down with the printing.' (Laughter)." Norquay, in return, hinted at the racial connotations of the crisis: "Indeed there may be room for congratulation in the fact of a native of the country showing himself equal to the occasion and doing his share to help forward the progress of events." He then extended an olive branch: the French, he said, will have "justice . . . given them in ample measure."[56]

On Thursday, 5 June, before a packed gallery, the new cabinet arrangements were finally debated fully in the house. Royal defended his course over the preceding months, arguing that he was the prey, not the predator. The key issue in the present crisis, said Royal, was the "compact" between the two founding language groups, an assertion that ignored the multiplicity of languages in the Red River Settlement. In his view, the compact would function best if assembly motions had to be passed by majorities in each of the two language groups. As he explained, such a convention had been "very generously" proposed by "the French," and renewed through repeated requests, but had not been acted on by the premier, who had rushed into the arms of his long-time opponents instead. Royal said that his own actions were neither illiberal nor treasonous. After all, the minority sought justice for the majority! Norquay, he said, could not be trusted. He had "sold every party he was associated with." The French had been expelled "because we are French Canadians—because our language is French."[57] It was a strong speech, delivered to a silent, respectful audience. Dubuc, with whom Royal had gone over the main points ahead of time, believed that Royal's case was "assez fort" (quite strong).[58]

No one mentioned an inconvenient fact: the assertion that Royal led a solid French-speaking contingent in the assembly, a group with at least ten members, was suspect.[59] The crisis had begun because Charles Nolin did not wish to be subordinated to Royal's control in the house and did not see himself as simply a francophone. Nolin spoke Michif as well as French, represented a Michif-speaking parish, saw himself as Métis in heritage and culture, and found Royal's airs distasteful. When Nolin was unseated, however, the Michif/French-speaking members lacked a leader of equal force and turned back to their reliance on Royal.

Norquay had prepared his response carefully, knowing that a strong statement was necessary to hold his new English-speaking caucus together. He spoke in a "slow, well measured, deliberate style, which ha[d] great force," according to the *Winnipeg Times*, and used fewer words than usual to make his points: "I know my duty to the country whether in the Govt or out of it & it is necessary that if any compromise is made between the two factions that have unfortunately arisen out of this exigency that the English members be as united as their French friends always are." The issues were "as dear to them as are those defended by their French friends. Much as I deplore the unhappy circumstance of seeing one side pitted against another[,] for the purpose of carrying [the] legislature I will consider any man who proves renegade to the policy as submitted by the Govt not only a traitor to his professions but as willing for personal considerations to drag into the dust the interests that have ever been advocated over & over again & for which the Government has been so often blamed."[60] This warning was aimed directly at Thomas Scott, who would receive more criticism later, but it was also designed to shock the English-speaking representatives who might have been flirting with the idea of a "Conservative" Scott-Royal government.

Norquay spoke critically of Joseph Royal, saying that many assembly members had objected to the Quebecer's continuing presence in the cabinet but that "I stood by him." And then, he said, Royal and the French-speaking members whom he led "became dissatisfied without cause." Norquay dismissed the notion that Royal had insisted that he recruit English supporters, saying the idea might have come up "as a passing remark" but he had preferred to postpone such changes until the session was over, by which time the promises made in the election campaign would have been fulfilled. Royal might have become premier the past November, he acknowledged, but many voters would not have trusted him. Norquay then asked a rhetorical question: why had he not told Royal about the English caucus that he had suddenly convoked? Since a game evidently was being played, he said, he had withheld from the man who was betraying him both the news of the meeting and the names of attendees.[61]

Referring presumably to English dissatisfaction with his government, Norquay said that the cabinet had frequently heard statements that its policy did not go far enough in supporting some elements of the population. Given the wishes of what was now an English majority in the province, the only recourse was to develop a policy responding to that community's concerns: "I would have been to blame if the members were again sent home and no legislation enacted & the measures foreshadowed being among those in a political sense most urgently demanded by the public. It behoved the Govt in its duty to the country to see that they were carried."[62] His fundamental defence was one of necessity: the province had changed, the people demanded a revision of the arrangements made in 1870, and he was accommodating them.

Norquay insisted that the new cabinet was not anti-French: "I have been accused by nearly every member who criticised the Govt policy that it was enunciated merely for the purpose of retaining power & for that reason that I have appealed to the prejudices of race. It is for no consideration of the kind that I have done so." He claimed that none of the meetings of the newly created English group, despite rumours, had been strident, nor had harsh measures been advocated. And he would ensure that the French minority was "handsomely treated and need fear nothing."[63]

Under the rules of the house, open debate was permitted after the two leaders had completed their statements. Royal spoke immediately. The province had two "important elements," the French and the English; the country had been discovered, settled, and defended by "French from Canada . . . and they are as able and patriotic as the ancestors of the hon. Gentleman. (Cheers and laughter)." On the surface an innocent statement about several centuries of French and English competition, such a reading was belied by the laughter. Rather, it was probably a racist jibe. Norquay replied immediately: "I made no remark reflecting in any way against French Canadians (hear, hear)." He went on: "I did not criticize French Canadians and our legislation will not do violence to them."[64]

The debate continued during the next few days. The basic English argument was articulated by James Cowan, the blunt-speaking doctor and entrepreneur who consistently irritated the Quebecers. Born in County Tyrone, Ireland, a resident of Ontario for twenty years, and a Manitoban since 1871, Cowan had been a member of the assembly for five years, long enough to conclude that both Norquay and Royal were good leaders. He told his colleagues that both ministers constituted "an honour to the country they represented. . . . [Yet] men in politics are placed in such a position that occasionally their course appears to be crooked when it is in reality straight, and their doings wear an evil aspect, whereas they are not bad. During the Premier's career of six or seven years, he did not seem in all cases politically honest; and yet I can make excuses for him, owing to his surroundings." Norquay had never appropriated public funds for personal gain, Cowan said, and was "strictly honest in all matters," whereas Royal still had to face the charges of fraud against him. The main issue, as Cowan saw it, was that the old government would not give the voters whom he represented the policies sought by English-speaking people.[65]

Assembly members were wondering when constituency boundaries would be changed. Would there be another general election? These matters bothered everyone, particularly Thomas Scott, who raised it in debate. The premier countered him immediately, mocking Scott by calling him "the French member for Winnipeg." Norquay committed the government to hold an election soon rather than permitting the assembly to live out the normal term of three more years. If the assembly would complete the legislative agenda and redraw the electoral map, he said, then an election could be held before the close of the year. Scott, said the *Free Press*, had been caught out again.[66]

The crisis was over. It had consumed ten days, inspired dramatic scenes, and reduced some observers to despair. Certainly, it moved the province away from its original foundations. As the *Free Press* declared in an editorial, "the session . . . will be an epoch in the history of Manitoba." In the evening of 5 June, his cabinet making complete, Norquay purchased a great deal of champagne destined for consumption at a large party.[67] Several weeks later all the assembly members attended a ball where they could gossip to their hearts' content about what had happened in the session. At the same moment the satirical newspaper *Grip*, in its latest cartoon, returned to the theme of Norquay's famous mule. In this drawing, which has survived only in a prose description in the *Free Press*, the mule carries the name "English Cabinet" on its flank; Norquay stands beside the animal, asking "will he carry me through?"[68] But, in the end, a Michif/French alliance with the Bungee/English, an alliance personified by Norquay himself, an understanding that had sustained the resistance of 1869–70 under the leadership of Louis Riel and been renewed in the intervening years, had ceased to matter.

Round-Robin Session

Norquay found the storm occasioned by the proposed legislative changes unpleasant.[69] He did not want to eliminate French language or school rights, and—what made things worse—he now had to accommodate long-time opponents, including some Orange Ontarian firebrands. Thomas Scott argued correctly and with effect that the new cabinet did not represent all the people of the province, meaning that it omitted the Michif and French speakers. What is more, Scott and Royal opened old wounds by saying that Norquay had betrayed friends and his own principles, implying that this had become a pattern.[70]

Responses to the dramatic events divided along predictable lines. The premier's friends expressed pride in his victory, his brother-in-law depicting it as a "master stroke of diplomacy." His opponents, especially the Quebecers, reviled Norquay. Observers in the rest of Canada expressed surprise and, in the case of several friends, dismay.[71] When Norquay wrote to Prime Minister John A. Macdonald on Wednesday, 4 June, the day that the new cabinet appointments were formalized, he expressed no misgiving. The public interest would not suffer under the new cabinet, he told the prime minister. What was more, he would follow Macdonald's advice in his dealings with Luxton and the *Free Press* and would soon "be clear of" the Liberal newspaper. Then came an intriguing statement: "I regret very much that I had to adopt such extreme measures with Royal but his treachery left me no alternative." Regret over the French unhappiness? Probably. Regret over "extreme measures" in relation to Royal? Surely not.[72]

Norquay's new government soon implemented the promises made to the round-robin group of English-speaking assembly members. Before a week had passed, ministers were introducing legislation to redraw constituency boundaries and to require the organization of municipalities. Decisions on printing followed quickly. The assault on the French community, as it was described by the St. Boniface elite, was less sweeping than they had anticipated or than their rhetoric declared. But the political and social authority of the church would be undermined by elected municipal organizations, and the quasi-official status of the French language was under siege.[73] According to Joseph Royal, French in Manitoba differed from German (the language of Mennonite immigrants) because French speakers had lived in the region for sixty years and German speakers only five. The French had sacrificed much, had preserved this region "for civilization," and now possessed "vested rights," almost a treaty, with the federal government and the imperial parliament. Royal reminded his colleagues that, during the debate on abolition of the legislative council three years earlier, the French were told that they could maintain their language in public institutions, including the legislature and courts, until they voluntarily chose to give up such guarantees. Royal blamed Norquay, saying that the premier had gone back on his earlier protestations of concern.[74]

In his carefully drafted reply Norquay admitted that he had helped to devise the round-robin document. He opposed extreme views, he told his colleagues, and did not wish to abolish French rights. The printing act aimed only to curtail unnecessary printing, and he hoped to appoint French representatives to the cabinet. Norquay acknowledged the continued relevance of entrenched legal and moral guarantees for the French language in Manitoba while insisting that he did not wish to limit these rights.[75]

Amazingly, the language legislation then disappeared. Lieutenant Governor Joseph Cauchon exercised his constitutional power to reserve the act for review by the federal government, doing so specifically to defend the legal standing of French in Manitoba. As he explained to Archbishop Taché, "I have done all I can, I have even gone beyond my sphere in order to remedy the evil."[76] Norquay did not object. Indeed, Royal said that his former colleagues were relieved to throw the matter into Ottawa's lap.[77]

Joseph Dubuc placed the responsibility for the French losses on the Métis: "To struggle against our enemies [the "English"], we do that. It's natural. But to defend ourselves in a struggle to the death against the betrayal of our own people, that gives us heartache. . . . This includes the Hamelins, the Charettes, Benjamin Nault, whose brother nearly died in prison, and

Janvier Ritchot who remained in exile for two years to evade Clarke's persecutions." Was not this disgusting, he asked sarcastically, this conduct of "our *brave and heroic Métis?*"[78] The Michif/French-speaking Métis saw the story differently. Maxime Lépine, a Métis assembly member, allegedly said that those who had started the movement, meaning the two Quebecers, Royal and LaRivière, now were kicking themselves. Dubuc reported Lépine's comment and added "voilà—toute la difficulté." In other words, the situation that provoked the original crisis had not changed. But, in fact, there had been a very important change: the departure of Charles Nolin left the Métis without an assertive, well-placed, Michif/French-speaking leader. The Quebecers were now free to take over the leadership of a francophone Roman Catholic team in the assembly, and Norquay would have to deal with their leader and relinquish the possibility of a renewed Bungee/English alliance with the Michif/French Métis.[79]

There remained one unusual aspect of the ministerial crisis. The 19 June issue of *Le Métis*, Royal's newspaper, reported a rumour that Norquay would be leaving provincial politics and taking a position with the federal government's Indian administration. Politics aside, it said, Norquay would be a good superintendent of Indian Affairs.[80] Royal's ambition and deep-seated racism overshadowed the generous statement. He wanted Norquay gone and he wanted to be premier. His double-majority argument was not irrelevant, though it was undeniably self-serving. At bottom, he saw Indigenous people as his inferiors. In this striking moment of ministerial crisis, however, Norquay emerged the winner. As Lieutenant Governor Cauchon wrote to Bishop Taché, Royal had played his cards too quickly and badly, and Norquay, "seeing himself lost, had played his admirably."[81]

The Election of December 1879

Spring and summer were miserable times for the Métis along the Red River. Snow melt and heavy rain filled rivers and creeks, carried away bridges, and flooded fields. In Ste. Anne, Father Giroux reported that many were buried in debt, had neglected or been unable to work the land, and had been left poverty stricken as freighting contracts disappeared. Several families were disturbed by Nolin's legal troubles and talked of joining him in the North-West. As the Métis moved out, a few French Canadian families moved in, and a noticeable calm descended on the parish. The priest concluded, in the manner of one who cared for his flock but thought that he might be able to upgrade it, that land was for sale at good prices, making this a favourable moment for immigrants from Quebec. Again the gulf between Quebecers and Métis was on display.[82]

Norquay spent the summer engaged in farm work as well as the usual government business. He also took advantage of social occasions to canvass among voters. The *Free Press* gave him generous coverage. When a brave soul shoed "the celebrated mule" on Norquay's farm, a mule that had won fame by running away a year earlier, the newspaper recorded the event and offered a painted photograph to anyone "repeating the experiment." When the premier contributed to a gift for Anglican Bishop Robert Machray, his ten-dollar donation was duly recorded, as was his attendance at the Anglican Church synod meetings in August. His day trip to Emerson and district at the end of the month was noted. So was his week-long excursion with William Ogilvie of Montreal to the area west and north of Portage la Prairie. Also mentioned in newspapers were his presence at a great Masonic banquet, and later at a banquet for two Members of Parliament from England, and his chairing of the great Conservative banquet for Ministers James Aikins and Mackenzie Bowell of the federal cabinet. At the last event Norquay responded to the toast to Manitoba with the comment that it might be the smallest province but it had the largest premier.[83]

The government's daily business continued as usual. One new enterprise, the marketing of Manitoba in eastern Canada, took a step forward when Alexander Begg was dispatched with boxes containing vegetables, cereals, cheese, wood, soil, and clay for displays at agricultural fairs in London, Hamilton, Toronto, and Ottawa. Manitoba's focus on Ontario, not Quebec or the Maritimes, was notable. The tour was a great success. The governor general and his wife twice entered the exhibit, and many business figures also attended it. The accompanying *Free Press* booklet, subtitled *Proving that the Province of Manitoba and the Canadian North-West Is a Fertile Soil for Willing Hands to Work*, attributed to Norquay the role of "prime mover" in the development of the province.[84]

Exhibits at the fall fairs, like his trip to Ottawa in the spring, increased Ontarians' awareness of and interest in Manitoba. Norquay's personal stature grew in the process. When one of the Manitoba cabinet ministers visited Ottawa late in the summer, he received a warm welcome that he attributed to

Norquay's influence: "I was treated in a very kind and hospitable manner & find the Ministers (at least those at home) real jolly fellows. Last night Hon Mr. Pope M. of Agriculture invited me to the Club with the Mayor and Min of Justice, all mighty good fellows. They all spoke highly of you."[85]

Another sign of the new day was a telegram to Ottawa that Norquay co-signed with John Schultz. The two men were encouraging the federal government to consider a member of Elizabeth's family for a junior position in the Indian Affairs branch. This unusual cooperation between two political opponents might be viewed as a minor event, one that merely acknowledged the merits of John Setter, but it had a more significant implication: the telegram signalled that the two long-time opponents were papering over their disagreements.[86]

Most of the English-speaking side of the community accepted Norquay's manoeuvring during these months. Nevertheless, Thomas Scott remained a threat, having positioned himself as a strong supporter of the French as well as of English-speaking Conservatives. Scott had the added advantage of an understanding with Royal. Although he had angered Schultz and the Ontarian Conservatives by joining the plot to overthrow the government, Scott rebuilt those relationships as the months passed and tempers cooled. Schultz's summary of the situation, in a letter to Prime Minister Macdonald, was to dismiss the cabinet crisis as a hiccup and Norquay as an imposter: "Royal will win in the end as the purely Protestant Government [. . .] is of course an impossibility and the attempt is only [a] Norquay effort to retain power."[87]

The various French and Michif factions continued to clash. When Norquay approached Joseph Dubuc at the end of summer with a renewed offer of a cabinet seat, Dubuc told the premier that he should "swallow what he had spit out" by taking Royal back.[88] The search for an acceptable French member of the cabinet eventually led Norquay to Archbishop Taché, who brought up the name of Marc-Amable Girard, a senator and the former premier.[89] The portly Girard was nearly sixty and enjoying his role as a senator, but he was also a loyal son of the church. He had married a wealthy, younger, Montreal widow in the previous year and would have preferred to stay with her and pursue his Senate and business interests rather than return to Manitoba. But he sent a telegram to Norquay declaring that he "would consent to serve country and friends." Norquay then wrote to the archbishop, enclosing Girard's answer and a newspaper clipping on government policy.[90] The premier had found a French-speaking cabinet minister, and though hard feelings remained, the gulf between the two language groups was bridged once again.

Norquay was busy wrapping up loose ends in the late fall. Life at the Parkdale farm continued as usual. He managed to arrange a new life insurance policy, for no less than $2,500, with a Montreal company, at an annual cost of seventy-five dollars.[91] He fielded appeals for payments on his numerous standing accounts, the latest from his friend Reverend Samuel Matheson at St. John's College concerning a "long overdue" bill for his children's schooling.[92] Norquay moved two cabinet members to accommodate the arrival of Girard, dissolved the legislature, and called a general provincial election for 16 December.[93]

Norquay's address to the electors of St. Andrews repeated the guarantees that had undergirded the English partisans in June. As he had done for weeks, he praised Macdonald's National Policy. He spoke warmly of the shift of the transcontinental railway to a route south of Lake Manitoba, and the incorporation of Schultz's "colonization railway," the Manitoba South-Western. After a decade of very slow growth, the promise of three rail lines (the Pacific trunk line, the line to St. Paul, Minnesota, and the MSWR) finally would bring rapid economic development within reach. In defence of his electoral redistribution, Norquay argued that the recent increase in population necessitated new electoral boundaries. Despite the vote of twelve months ago, he said, another election was needed to "give effect" to the new districts. He was on thin ice, as he probably knew, but that was all he could say. No one could be sure whether the new government's English majority, and its non-partisan stance, would survive or whether Thomas Scott would be able to unite Conservatives and push Norquay to the sidelines. The premier spoke of the need to develop roads and suggested that municipal governments, not just the province, should take advantage of their new powers to fund improvements to infrastructure. He also aired familiar issues such as land drainage, an increase in the size of the province, and economy in government. And, finally, he insisted that there should be no party lines in provincial affairs. Rather than engage in partisan debates, Norquay said, the government should seek to advance "the interests of our common country." His platform was consistent with the positions that he had taken throughout the year but with the significant addition of an "English" and pro-development tone.[94]

The *Manitoba Free Press* placed its considerable influence in Norquay's corner. It welcomed his opposition to federal party lines and, interestingly, defended his credentials as a long-time Conservative. One of its key arguments was that federal parties would force local politicians to subordinate provincial interests to those of larger centres and require representatives to submit to the discipline of federal party machines. It urged that local elections be fought instead on "personal and local issues and not on the [federal] Government policy of the day."[95]

The winter campaign was gruelling. Cabinet Minister David Walker nearly lost his life in a blizzard during one campaign outing, and other candidates mentioned the trials of severe winter conditions. The Manitoba wing of the federal Conservative party was divided. One prominent business leader told Prime Minister Macdonald that "Norquay is now a strong Conservative and will gradually have a full Conservative cabinet, but cannot do so yet." Many other Ontarian Conservatives disliked Norquay's reliance on the *Free Press* and the no-party approach. Dubuc, now safely on the bench and allegedly out of politics, recognized and resented the influence of these English business figures: "All these little big men believe themselves the veritable, sole, true Conservatives," he wrote. While the Orange Ontarian partisans relied on Thomas Scott and the *Times* newspaper to lead their opposition to Norquay, Scott was able to make headway only in his Winnipeg riding. The most surprising wrinkle of the campaign was the complaint by a Norquay supporter that the local candidate in Baie St. Paul was "a dry Bugger any how. Why he doesn't either drink or smoke & says he dont know how to tell Lies, either."[96]

Local contests sometimes conformed to federal party lines in the districts populated by new arrivals from Ontario. In Emerson, still hoping to become the metropolis of western Canada, the town's mayor, W. Hill Nash, became the premier's ally during this campaign. Nash won the seat and, shortly after the election, spoke about partisanship: "Party feeling runs so high here that no election can be run on 'no party' policy again in this Division. They have introduced it even in our approaching Municipal election and the devil himself cannot crowd it out."[97] The issue of federal party loyalties could not be avoided forever, but Norquay managed to quell the rumblings, at least for this campaign.

He still had fences to mend among Michif- and French-speaking electors. Their proportion of the total population in Manitoba had been reduced from about half in 1870 to less than one-third in 1879, but they hoped to control about seven seats of the twenty-four. Métis conflict with the St. Boniface elite affected several ridings. Girard had planned to run in Royal's stead in St. François Xavier but was warned that all those who opposed Royal in the past would vote against him: "Je parle des Métis," the priest added pointedly.[98] Dubuc also emphasized the Métis-Quebecer split there, saying that Patrice Breland could campaign successfully on a pro-Métis slogan, "*Métis comme nous autres*." A judicious rearrangement of candidates—Breland ran in St. François Xavier, Girard for the seat next door, Baie St. Paul—ensured that both won by acclamation. Nevertheless, Dubuc was disgusted that Breland would sit in the assembly: "One of the biggest animals among the Métis, he is thick, crooked, venal," he fumed. Why would the Métis choose Breland rather than another Quebecer? "Because he is Métis and has some whiskey. There it is."[99] Dubuc's vexation illustrated the deepening division between Michif-speaking residents and Quebec newcomers, a gulf that Norquay would have to bridge if his government was to represent all groups in the province.[100]

Events in the riding of LaVérendrye, Charles Nolin's old seat, which included Ste. Anne, Lorette, and adjacent districts on the east side of the Red River, illustrated Métis sentiment. There a Quebecer, J. Desautels, was opposed by Maxime Goulet, son of Métis bison hunter Alexis Goulet and brother of the man drowned in the Red River by Ontarian thugs in 1870. As in Ste. Agathe, Joseph Dubuc reported with dismay, the contest pitted "Métis contre Canadiens. C'est vraiment odieux." What was worse, Alphonse LaRivière, the likely successor to Joseph Royal as the French leader in the assembly, campaigned for Goulet, then only twenty-four years old.[101] When Goulet won easily, Norquay appointed him to the cabinet. He was to be a voice for the Michif/French speakers at the centre of the government but, if Dubuc was right, not a strong one. The Métis would miss Nolin's forceful defence of their community.

Travelling by train, Norquay spoke in Emerson on 4 December and near Winnipeg two days later. On 11 December he was in Portage la Prairie, a trip by horse and sleigh of eighty-five kilometres. He encountered warm support at every stop on his English-speaking tour and stayed in Portage la Prairie for several days after his last speech, visiting with his brother-in-law and getting some well-earned rest. When news of his ministry's resounding victory was announced, Norquay accepted an invitation to a banquet in his honour. There he reflected happily on his political career and thanked the people of "western Manitoba" for their support.[102] He could exult in a huge win. The *Free Press* headline read "Victory! Is Ours!" Its story counted seventeen clear Norquay seats, two independents, and one Conservative, that of Thomas Scott, as well as several that could not be allocated to any column. *Le Métis* thought that the government had won eighteen to twenty of the twenty-four seats. And that would include most, perhaps all, of the seven members in the "French party." It also predicted that one of their number, Goulet, would join Girard in the cabinet as the next minister of agriculture.[103]

The results marked a huge change in the province's politics and a shift to a new generation. Eight assembly members, including Norquay, were elected by acclamation. Only six of the twenty-four members were born in Red River/ Assiniboia, whereas seven were from Ontario, three from Quebec, one from New Brunswick, five from England, one from Scotland, and one from Ireland. Ten were farmers, five were lawyers, and five owned businesses.[104] They would pay increasing attention to federal partisanship as the months passed, but for the moment most assembly members claimed to be non-partisan in provincial matters and supporters of the Norquay administration.

The cabinet crisis of 1879, combined with increased in-migration from eastern Canada, contributed to the emergence of a new version of Manitoba. By this time many Michif/French-speaking Métis had left the province, having had to endure violent skirmishes with extreme Ontarians and, lacking other resources, having sold their scrip at bargain prices to speculators. Not only had the Michif/French-speaking districts been weakened, but the province was now heading down a path leading to the loss of official status for the French language and of public financing for Roman Catholic schools, events that came to pass a decade later. The quest for a trans-Canadian bilingual society and state had suffered another serious setback. Whether francophones could have maintained their position in the face of the immigration of anglophones to the province in the 1880s is moot, but their loss of political influence can be traced to the events of 1879 when an English-speaking majority government dedicated to reducing their influence took office. Norquay had not wanted such consequences, however, and held the anti-French forces in check while he retained the premier's chair.

The weakening of the Michif/French-speaking alliance with the Bungee/English-speaking contingent in the legislature could not be reversed. Although the descendants of old Red River retained a sense of community connectedness that crossed language and faith lines during most of the decade, their hard-won harmony ceased to matter in 1879. The province had entered confederation in 1870 as a Métis community: five-sixths of the residents—over one-third Bungee/English-speaking, almost one-half Michif/French-speaking—had been born in the region.[105] By the end of the decade, Indigenous residents—Cree, Saulteaux, Dakota, and those of mixed ancestry—constituted fewer than one-third of the total.[106] Their conflicts with new settlers had been increasing, beginning in the mid-1860s, intensifying during the 1870s, and blowing up in 1879, tearing apart understandings that had stitched the community together for nearly fifty years. The Métis conflict with Quebecers was central to that disruption—"always the old grudges," wrote Joseph Dubuc.[107] In short, the cabinet crisis marked the demise of Red River settlers as a significant factor in Manitoba politics.

Norquay came out of the year in an apparently stronger position and yet, paradoxically, more vulnerable politically than ever. He managed to hold off the introduction of eastern Canadian party lines in local politics and could not be blamed for the cabinet crisis. In the months following that challenge, as well as in the election campaign of 1879, he made honourable compromises with the Michif/francophone community. Although he had had to rely on the lieutenant governor to nullify the assembly's French-language legislation, he had been able to adjust to the enormous growth of English-speaking communities in the province. His new government might have appeared to dominate the assembly, but its loose coalition of French speakers, friendly Grits, and Ontarian Tories was also certain to cause problems within a few years.[108] The deals that Norquay reached with Macdonald in Ottawa released him from responsibility for railway policy in the next year or so, but the absence of a fixed timeline on this arrangement would haunt him eventually. His position may have seemed to be stronger but he could not rest comfortably yet.

CHAPTER 7

Boom Times and Crash, 1880–January 1883

John Norquay started the new term with high hopes. He could feel more confident about his majority in the assembly and was now supported by a more experienced civil service. He had survived exceptional challenges and climbed to the top of what British Prime Minister Benjamin Disraeli called the "greasy pole" of politics. New friends invited Norquay to join their business ventures. The arrival of a baby added much to family life. The children were doing well in school. Manitoba was garnering headlines in the east, and immigrants were beginning to flood into the province. News about difficult conditions on the western plains and in the northern forests, where the fur trade had declined in importance and the bison verged on extinction, was eclipsed by stories about the boom in urban land prices and a rapidly growing farm economy.

The Norquay family continued to be based at the farm in St. Andrews parish. John was less frequently there on weekdays except during the most intense periods in spring and fall. He spent many hours in his office in Winnipeg, ate in a dining room in the government building each day, and stayed in a room in town because the thirty-kilometre trip to Parkdale—whether by horse and buggy, steamboat, or sleigh—was time consuming. For several months each year Norquay travelled. He went to eastern Canada once or twice every year beginning in the spring of 1878 through the fall of 1887. He was frequently on the road in Manitoba, sometimes for hunting trips, sometimes for meetings. When he was in the province he made a point of being home on Sunday, entire weekends if possible. For much of the year Elizabeth managed the Parkdale home with the aid of the children, a hired hand, and sometimes a maid. The older boys and then the girls stayed in college residences during terms. They wrote brief notes to their parents and received letters in return.

An exceptional event took the family by storm just after Betsy turned thirty-nine. On 6 February 1881 she gave birth to their eighth child, Aida Theodora. The other children were old enough to appreciate the occasion and to record their excitement. Bella, age sixteen, wrote to her cousins in The Pas to brag about Aida's "small face, small feet, small nose, small hands," and, as Charles Adams reported, "goodness knows what other admirations, — & everything is 'just like Papas.'" Adams added in this letter to John that "you can't believe how glad yr sister was to hear of your new Tanis [daughter, in Cree] & that poor Elizabeth was getting on well."[1] Adding to such reminders about Elizabeth's health was a question in July from John James Setter in Portage la Prairie: "How is my poor sister this frightful hot weather? I am very anxious about her." In fact Betsy was fine, and so was Aida.[2] Walter Nursey, the provincial auditor and one of Norquay's closest friends, then on a trip to Ontario, mentioned the newborn Aida: "Trusting that yourself, Mrs. Norquay & in particular the 'afterthought' are well."[3]

John wrote to the children frequently when they were in residence at St. John's. Some of their replies remained in his office files along with the many bills for college residence, tuition, and books. The children also began to earn wages. Tom, at sixteen, spent the summer of 1879 as a labourer on a construction crew running a rail line from Winnipeg to Stony Mountain. When he was eighteen he worked briefly near High Bluff. His letter home emphasized resources that his father would appreciate, including the "fine white fish" in Long Lake and "ducks . . . as thick as black birds." Tom also sent greetings to Aida, "that small little sister whose name I cant get my tongue around." Six months later he began a new career as a bailiff in Portage la Prairie. He reported the completion of his first business in January 1882 and added that "I think I can get along allright as there is not mutch about it[.] I am quite well and hope you are the same I remain Your affectionate Son Thos Norquay."[4]

After parish schools, Bella and Caroline Ellen (known by everyone as Nelly) attended St. John's Ladies School at least from 1880 through 1884. A six-year difference in age put them in different social circles. Bella stood near the top of the table in student conduct, third among the thirty-one boarders, Nelly in the middle at seventeenth. Nelly was the better student. Both girls were interested in clothes, sewing, and music, doted on their father, and were said (by Canon John Grisdale) to be "longing for [their father's] return" during one of his absences from the province.[5] The younger boys, like their big brothers, attended St. John's College.

As premier, and as the province's representative among business and political leaders in eastern North America, Norquay paid increasing attention to clothes and fashion. His relationship with Toronto clothier Bernard Saunders grew closer with every expedition eastward, cemented by Saunders's acquisition of land in Manitoba. Norquay's purchases from Saunders in the spring of 1880 included shirts and a "black Berlin coat" and vest. There were more clothing purchases in 1881. John was not a dandy, but on his visits to Ottawa he dressed like the people with whom he was negotiating.[6]

He had become the patriarch of his extended family, the leader to whom one paid respect and directed appeals for help. His services included managing Charles Adams's land, taxes, and statute labour at High Bluff. An engaging correspondent, Adams wrote to Norquay about fur trade returns, practical jokes, the failings of his boss, his interest in obtaining "molasses" (liquor), and thoughtful notes about his wife and their children as well as life in The Pas.[7] John and Elizabeth also maintained close ties with her two brothers, John James and Colin, and her nephew, John.[8]

Numerous Métis friends appealed to Norquay for help.[9] A devastating economic and social crisis had followed in the wake of the disappearance of bison herds from the western plains. Indigenous families faced starvation. One who asked for help was his cousin, John Lazarus Norquay, who wrote in the summer of 1880 with news of his farm near Minnedosa and a request that John support his application to become a farm instructor on the First Nation reserve at Bird's Tail Creek. "You know that I can speak the Lang[uage] and [am] a good farmer." He wrote again two years later, this time for help in establishing his "second" claim to land: "Please doe me the favour and write for me and if I cannot doe as much for you somebody else will."[10]

As Norquay moved in new social circles, his attitude toward alcohol grew more complicated. His initial stance as a supporter of temperance might have been maintained until 1880. In December of that year he served as the chair of a mass meeting at the courthouse in Winnipeg charged with creating a Church of England Temperance Society. He had concluded by then that government-imposed restrictions on alcohol consumption were futile. When, several years later, his school friend, Reverend Ben McKenzie, raised the case of a woman who had been treated badly by a man tormented by alcohol, Norquay promised to do what he could to aid her. But he pointed out that the bigger problem was the management of alcohol in the entire province and confessed that he did not know "how to put down the nefarious traffic" in liquor.[11] The letter was honest and unequivocal. Individuals would have to deal with the problem, in his view, and legal intervention would not help.

His teetotal pledge became a thing of the past. His purchases of alcohol grew more frequent in 1880, and the bills appeared regularly in his office correspondence for the next two or three years. Given the social context of alcohol in that era, the nature of his relations with strong drink mattered. When Norquay visited the town of Emerson, his bill at the Carney House included "1 bottle whisky and 1 brandy," though much of it could have been destined for the entertainment of guests. A letter from William Van Horne, the railway entrepreneur, apologized for missing an appointment with him in Ottawa and added "but the wine will be as good in Winnipeg as there and I look forward to the pleasure of cracking the bottles with you here."[12]

Although his health remained strong, Norquay had an "attack" of what he called rheumatism in the winter of 1881–82 and was in bed briefly with an unnamed affliction during the following winter, but these were minor matters and did not slow him down. He continued to spend considerable sums on life insurance. He changed companies from time to time and allocated several hundred dollars each year in exchange for the guarantee that his family would receive several thousand dollars in payments should he die. The correspondence from the companies included about thirty letters in three years, a measure of his considerable interest in his family's welfare and doubts about his lifespan.[13]

His sociable manner and enjoyment of people made Norquay an attractive, even memorable, personality. He was always in demand as a tour guide and source of information. There were various requests for help: he was asked to find a lost brother, support a deputation from Lord Derby's estate, give "special attention" to a wealthy HBC shareholder from Liverpool, find work for a farm labourer from Orkney, and do favours for dozens of other visitors to Manitoba.[14] An English delegate sent to investigate Manitoba so enjoyed his visit and his time on a Norquay shooting party that he aroused "immense cheering" when he reported back to his sponsors in a Yorkshire farming district.[15] These contacts introduced Norquay not just to individuals but also to speculation and talk of financial gain. It was no coincidence that, when he moved into the premier's office, he embarked on a part-time career as an investor and promoter, partly because he had an obligation to develop the province and partly because he needed the money.

Many more invitations to attend events and join societies now crossed his desk. In 1877, some three years after it was founded, Norquay joined the Manitoba Club, a residence and dining establishment for leading business figures and their out-of-town guests. Although he had trouble keeping up with the twenty-five-dollar annual fee, he settled his account in 1880 and maintained his membership in the following years. Norquay also joined the United Empire Club of Toronto and Winnipeg's Selkirk Club, accepted an honorary membership in the St. Andrews Cricket Club, and subscribed to the library of the Historical and Scientific Society of Manitoba. Bills for these fees, too, appeared in the overdue file from time to time. Norquay also sat on the council of the University of Manitoba, though his attendance was sporadic at best. He belonged to several Masonic lodges but rarely participated in meetings.[16] He was, in short, a very busy, very popular, highly sought-after representative of the province, the government, and a wide variety of more limited identities.

Like public figures everywhere, Norquay was always in demand for special events and frequently offered greetings at formal meetings because it was well known that he spoke fluently and well. When William Tecumseh Sherman, the commanding general of the American army, visited Winnipeg in 1880, Norquay met him at the station, gave him a tour of the city, and later attended a dinner at Government House in his honour. In April 1882 he attended the fourth annual St. George's Society dinner and responded to the usual toast to the government. According to the Conservative newspaper's account, his enthusiastic speech to the fifty gentlemen in attendance won "deafening applause."[17]

The pattern of his public involvement was more focused than the wide range of one-off invitations might suggest. The Anglican Church was central to his religious life, though his thoughts about faith and religion must remain a question. Like most people in Canada in that era, he chose to live his life as a church member, in his case the Anglican church. Some recent scholars refer to the meeting of Indigenous peoples and Christianity as "a site of colonial encounter shot through with uneven relations of power but also animated by agency and contingency."[18] Where he fits in this scale—one that stretches from dependent colonial to independent agent—cannot be established from the available evidence. It is likely that his approach to the Anglican church was shaped by his encounters with Bishop David Anderson and by his regular attendance at Sunday services as well as in committees of church governance. Whether he accepted the church's teachings wholeheartedly, or participated because it served his purposes, or coupled them with Indigenous understandings, remains unknown. He would not have been a cipher.

He became a delegate from the parish of St. John's Cathedral to the church synod in 1874, a member of the council of St. John's College in 1875, and a member of the founding board of St. John's Ladies' School in 1876. He was a lay delegate to the Rupert's Land provincial synod for most of the 1880s, sat on the synod's executive committee, the mission board, and the committee on constitutions and canons. He made donations to church-related enterprises.[19] As an Anglican church representative on the University of Manitoba's governing council, Norquay received many invitations to meetings, and, though he attended less frequently after he became premier, he was called on when delicate matters such as provincial legislation were contemplated.[20] He responded frequently to church requests for aid and would have seen his engagements in church affairs, interventions at meetings, and donations of money as personal choices.

Investing in Land and Coal

The Norquay family should have been at least comfortable in material terms, even relatively prosperous. In the early 1880s, John's annual income as a cabinet minister and assembly member amounted to $3,000, three or four times the amount paid to mid-level civil servants. John sold land, wood, hay, and grain. He rented out the old house on Main Street. He received numerous passes for free travel on railways. But it was never enough.[21]

This phase of his business life began with purchases and sales of land. Norquay assembled five additional "Manitoba Act Grants" between 1876 and 1884.[22] His other purchases included farmland and town lots near sites that he might have judged to be profitable, including Emerson, on the Red River, where the rail line from the United States crossed the border; Selkirk, north of Winnipeg, and the adjacent parishes of St. Andrews, St. Clement's, and St. Peter's Reserve, near a planned transcontinental railway crossing over the Red River; Portage la Prairie, west of Winnipeg, on what became the Canadian Pacific Railway's (CPR) main line; and Rapid City in the west, along another projected railway route.[23]

Norquay also invested in Winnipeg, the scene of an outrageous speculative boom in 1881.[24] He knew that the boom could not last, but while it did he hoped to make some gains. He told a correspondent in Orkney that "there has been a great deal of speculation in our city and prices have gone up in Main Street to $700.00 a foot. Comparative fortunes have been made by keen sighted individuals in the space of six months. There has been a perfect land craze."[25] As a participant in that "craze," Norquay bought four lots in the newest and most promising residential district, the HBC tract, looking over the plains stretching west and north from the Assiniboine River. The transaction gave him a frontage of 200 feet (sixty-one metres) on Kennedy Street directly across from the future residence of the lieutenant governor and the legislature itself. What better site for a premier's home? Or for speculative profits? Although three of the four lots had been purchased by William Bain Scarth's wife and brother for a total of $1,750 in the summer of 1880, Norquay agreed to pay six or seven times as much, over $10,000, in December 1881. To finance the deal, he took out a mortgage of $6,800 with Scarth. The deal illustrated starkly what a boom looked like in action.[26]

His involvement in these financial adventures usually came as a result of personal connections such as that with brothers Alexander and William Ogilvie of the Montreal milling family. The Ogilvies travelled frequently to Manitoba, where they invested in grain, land, and eventually grain elevators at shipping points on the expanding branch line network. They got on well with Norquay from the first and became regular correspondents, chatting about their shared interest in Conservative party politics and the economic prospects of the west. They found Norquay to be helpful and enjoyed his company. William Ogilvie's two young boys, who travelled with their father on one of the trips, were entranced by the premier: "Our boys often speak of you & are not likely to forget you," the Montrealer wrote. Just before Norquay headed to Ottawa in 1879 for the crucial negotiations with Sir John A. on railway policy, Ogilvie sent him a note inviting him to travel on to Montreal when his business in Ottawa was over. The note underlined a growing familiarity: "I am glad you are coming down. You must make me a visit, and we will try to give you a good time. Mrs. Ogilvie in a fit of generosity has just presented me with a daughter. Both are doing very well. The two little boys are growing nicely, they have just had their photographs taken, which I [have] enclosed."[27]

Later that year, while travelling with Norquay on a prairie road, Ogilvie drove horses and buggy directly into a small slough in the expectation that it was shallow and easily traversed. The horses came to a halt, anchored in the lake bottom gumbo for which Winnipeg was famous. Ogilvie climbed down from the carriage seat and, while balancing on the whiffletree in an attempt to unhitch the animals, slipped and fell into the muck. News of the event travelled far and wide. Upon his return to Montreal, Ogilvie wrote to Norquay to say that "your old friends were all inquiring for you, our trip having been chronicled in our newspapers and [Donald A.] Smith had told all about Ogilvie's crossing, and I have been teased a good deal about it, it makes a good story, and I do not object to it." By the time Tom Norquay, John's brother, heard Ogilvie's version several years later, the story was well polished. Tom had asked Ogilvie about John's response to the predicament and whether his brother laughed, to which Ogilvie replied "yes d--- [*sic*] him and what do you think he did next. Why he stripped off his pants shoes &c and waded to the shore, from whence he appeared to enjoy the scene."[28]

The connection with the Ogilvies became closer as their investments in Manitoba increased. William made a point of seeing Norquay whenever he visited Winnipeg, and they continued to exchange letters. In suggesting that Norquay entertain and advise Sir Hugh Allan's son-in-law, or a wealthy Chicago investor, or brothers seeking to set up a stock farm, they were drawing the Manitoban further into the circles of the very wealthy and educating him in matters such as economic growth and sources of wealth. But had they impressed Norquay with stories of risk and loss?[29]

When the prime minister appointed Alexander Ogilvie, William's older brother, to the Senate at the end of 1881, Norquay wired a brief note of congratulations. The new senator thanked him immediately and added a memorable bit of advice:

> I should feel very much pleased indeed to have a long talk with you about Winnipeg matters. I hope that now this big boom is going on, you will make something in lands; for although I know quite well you are always looking first to the good of the country, instead of to your own pocket, yet you should remember it is necessary to lay aside some of the good things of this world while you have an opportunity; and you certainly have given a fair share of your life to the good and success of Manitoba, and deserve something on your own account.

The phrases jumped out: "make something in lands . . . lay aside some of the good things of this world." The dictated note, written by a secretary, the newly named senator's initials scrawled at the bottom, was not the origin of Norquay's investment strategy, but it might have encouraged Norquay to stay in the game while the prairie land bubble was growing bigger and bigger.[30]

One site of his speculative activity was the rich farmland south of Winnipeg, some of which was adjacent to a series of giant marshes that would soon be drained. In 1879 Norquay took ownership of a 640-acre section for a dollar an acre and received the letters patent a year later. It was fertile land and undoubtedly seemed to be a good bet, though it would never earn a large increment above his initial investment.[31]

The real money would be made in townsites, or so many speculators believed. As Norquay ventured deeper into investments in 1880, he struck up a friendship with William Bain Scarth, the brother-in-law of the deputy provincial treasurer, Alexander Begg, one of Norquay's closest associates in the government. Scarth was a cheerful Scotsman who travelled frequently between Toronto and Winnipeg smoothing the flow of British money into the British Empire's newest investment frontier. He was also one of Prime Minister Macdonald's informants on western affairs.[32] It was Scarth who sold Norquay the four lots on Kennedy Street.

Scarth enlisted a Toronto businessman in one of his first townsite speculations and brought Norquay in as a third partner. Scarth was buying a senior politician's influence; in exchange Norquay was offering his knowledge of the province and a modest cash investment in what they planned to call "Norquay City." A few families settled in the district, but two years later the head of the CPR land department was mocking the scheme as "the Southern Manitoba abortion. Where is it, anyway? I can't find it on any map." In 1884 it became clear that the CPR branch line would miss the Norquay townsite by over six kilometres. It was a "hard blow" to local investors and to the farm families who anticipated the imminent completion of rail service.[33]

Another of Scarth's creations was the "Manitoba First Syndicate," a relatively small enterprise that began in 1880 or 1881. It might have been the product of a tour in which James Domville, Scarth, and Norquay visited a number of western districts and came back praising the potential of the territory. Domville, a businessman and New Brunswick Member of Parliament, wanted to secure a huge land grant for "Scarth and his associates" under the federal legislation for colonization companies. Although this plan foundered, the syndicate itself continued, and by the end of 1883 it was divided into thirteen shares. At that point it owned about forty town lots in four different towns, including thirty-four lots in Portage la Prairie, three lots plus a hotel and small store in Rapid City, and four lots in Winnipeg.[34]

The Manitoba First Syndicate failed to strike it rich. All these parcels, which they valued at just under $30,000, were subject to local taxes that had to be paid until the land was sold. Worse, the banks that funded the purchases were unyielding in their insistence on interest payments. The group's "Winnipeg Post Office Lot," purchased for $19,600, sold for over $25,000, far more than the market value of all the other properties together. Despite this one coup, Norquay owed the syndicate nearly $400 at the end of November 1883. The nature of their experience was evident in Scarth's rueful letter to John A. Macdonald: "Like many others, I made losses in the boom and in addition to being cleaned out of money am daily meeting obligations from my income."[35]

In the same months Norquay became involved in a land deal that was to haunt him for years. River Lot 61 in the parish of St. Clement's sat at the northern limit of the parish or just within the southern boundary of the town of Selkirk. It was land that he knew well, a marshy area that would have to be drained, and it might serve as a site for the provincial mental health institution. Norquay's friend, Sam Bedson, warden of Stony Mountain Penitentiary, was negotiating with two owners of the land. Norquay caught wind of the plan, called Bedson in, and asked to be made part of the deal, to which Bedson agreed. But Rice Howard, clerk of the executive council in the Manitoba government, saw an opportunity to make more money by outflanking the penitentiary warden. Bedson was not pleased. Indeed, he was "more than astonished," he wrote to Norquay, by the "*unenviable role*" that the premier and the cabinet secretary had taken by jumping into the purchase ahead of him—and without telling him.[36] Was Norquay implicated in this deal for the asylum site? Yes, though he held only a tiny fraction of the acreage.

Norquay joined yet another of Scarth's town-building ventures during the boom of 1881–82. This scheme had greater promise because it sought to develop a potential station site, to be called Darlingford, on the Manitoba South-Western Railway, John Schultz's branch line that fell into CPR hands in the early 1880s. The five other investors in the Darlingford townsite project were relying on Norquay for several crucial contributions. One of them put their concern bluntly: "We want every *government* [emphasis in original] building we can get." They also wanted to drain a lake and create a river with the approval of government inspectors. In an era when political leaders often invested in economic ventures, these actions crossed an ethical line by contravening the oath taken by assembly members not to participate in votes dealing with personal property. To avoid such issues the opportunists decided that Norquay's name would not appear in the public documents related to their plan.[37]

Norquay had one further role in the Darlingford speculation, a crucial one: he was expected to secure inside information about the railway route. When the CPR was finally ready to build, the company's Winnipeg manager, J.H. McTavish, wrote to the head office in Montreal to ask if the arrangement with Norquay should take precedence over another speculator's interest. William Van Horne replied in a single-word message: "Yes." McTavish then advised Norquay to negotiate with owners of several promising quarter-sections: "Be stiff," McTavish wrote, "& I've no doubt you can get a half interest." He added that the CPR wanted to secure the right of way and station ground within the townsite for free.[38] This was what insider dealing looked like. Norquay and his Darlingford group could make a tidy profit, a less well-informed settler would receive only half of the windfall gains accruing to his quarter-section, and the CPR would be getting free town lots. In the end the railway route changed, the townsite did not occupy the quarter-section owned by the Norquay group, and the original Darlingford investment never paid off. Once again the pot of gold eluded him.[39]

The stories of missed opportunity cropped up several more times during the boom years. Norquay was in at the start of the Great Northwest Telegraph Company in 1880–81 and made overtures to the federal government on behalf of the syndicate. When its charter became a target of larger corporations, his hope of financial gain soared. But he gained very little, if anything, in the end.[40]

Coal seemed to be a sure thing, too, and Norquay heard of several promising deposits across the prairies. In 1880 he proposed an investment in a coal mine to his friend William Ogilvie, but the Montrealer had his hands full with grain elevators and flour mills and declined to get involved. Then, in the summer of 1882, Norquay received a letter from a former High Bluff neighbour, James Sanderson, now a freighter working in the North-West, who told him of a coal seam near the Cypress Hills. Sanderson was concerned that he might not be able to claim the land for himself.[41] This letter might have launched Norquay's involvement in a Medicine Hat coal deposit, though the connection between Sanderson's seam and Norquay's subsequent actions is unclear.

At the end of 1882 Norquay opened negotiations with the federal Department of the Interior for a specific parcel of land in southern Alberta. This tract had been reserved for a Blackfoot community. Moreover, H.H. Smith, a friend of John A. Macdonald, had also applied for the crucial half-section on which the coal seam was located. At this time Norquay secured an unofficial document (extant in his papers) bearing no identifying marks but containing the names and addresses of seventeen individuals, presumably newcomers, allegedly squatting on lands near Medicine Hat. None of these issues—the tract's inclusion within a First Nation reserve, Smith's "prior application" for the parcel that Norquay sought, and the many squatters who might contest the claims of an outside syndicate—deterred him from joining a group that sought a deal of its own.[42]

The Saskatchewan Coal and Transportation Company was founded by three Winnipeg speculators and two others, an Ottawa politician and an Ontarian investor. They did not know how to manage such a complicated enterprise, nor did they possess sufficient money to finance the critical first years of operation. The initial pool of invested capital probably amounted to just over $25,000. Five other individuals received shares that were "not assessable," including Norquay (250 shares with a notional value of $25,000), and two Winnipeg residents, sons of leading Conservative politicians in Ottawa, law partners Hugh John Macdonald and James Stewart Tupper (fifty shares each or $5,000 face value). The founding shareholders' quest for political advantage was plain to see.[43]

Development commenced within months. The *Fort Macleod Gazette* reported in January 1883 that a "strong" company had been organized in Winnipeg to develop a mine near the Medicine Hat coulee, about two kilometres from the CPR route. It was expected that mine operations would begin even before CPR crews built a temporary steel bridge to carry the main line of the transcontinental railway across the South Saskatchewan River, events that led to the birth of Medicine Hat. In the spring Norquay was organizing visits to the mine in the hope of recruiting some well-heeled investors.[44]

As the Red River flooded in the spring of 1882 and the CPR's construction activities moved west, newly surveyed lots in Winnipeg disappeared beneath a shallow lake, land values plummeted, and most of the fortune hunters departed for greener fields. Norquay's friend, the journalist George Ham, said that the real estate crash "left the majority of the pioneers blown off the map financially and otherwise. And few ever 'came back.' Since the boom of 1882, the soul of Winnipeg has never been what it was before." Norquay was one of Ham's "pioneers." Although he was not quite "blown off the map," his serious financial troubles dated from the crazy boom years of the early 1880s.[45]

After the bubble burst, Norquay owed money in his various roles as householder, farmer, investor, and friend, the last because he frequently signed as a guarantor on other people's promissory notes. Letters concerning his many debts took on an ominous tone and became urgent, even desperate, as 1882 ended. Norquay had co-signed a promissory note for the proposed branch railway from Portage la Prairie to the northwest and was asked to hand over $4,000 when the company could not meet its obligations. His Parkdale farm was mortgaged, and, though he met the required $100 payment in July, another payment was due in December. He had commissioned a survey of the plot that he owned in the town of Selkirk, hoping to divide it into town lots, and the surveyor was pleading for payment. His tax bill on the four lots in Winnipeg amounted to $100, and he was being threatened by the city with seizure of his "goods and chattels." A note for over $1,500 was due at the Ontario Bank.[46]

Everyone seemed to know that Norquay managed his money badly. Before the boom had truly begun, one of Sir John A. Macdonald's western informants told the prime minister that Norquay would be the strongest candidate in an upcoming federal by-election, but "I gather he is entirely without means & unless something was done to put him financially in shape he would not do it in any case."[47] Although Norquay might have planted these hints in the hope that Sir John might come to his aid in the forthcoming contest, his need for money was not simply a rumour. In fact he was flirting with economic disaster. He relied on his various government stipends to keep his head above water.

Provincial Treasurer

Norquay took over the post of provincial treasurer in 1879 and set about learning, step by step, what he could do to support the local economy. His contributions to economic policymaking before this assignment involved modest infrastructure projects. In the early 1870s, when the immigration shed was built on the banks of the Red River in Winnipeg, he ensured that local suppliers, including his own woodlot, received contracts. He set the rates for ferry service across several rivers and he supported advertisements recruiting immigrants in eastern Canada and Britain. In doing so Norquay wrote many letters to advertise the province and frequently hosted visitors. But all this remained at an elementary level until he took on the roles of premier and provincial treasurer.[48]

While Liberals held power in Ottawa from 1874 to 1878, Manitoba developed slowly. Its population doubled from about 12,000 in 1870 to about 26,000 in 1876, but the government's straitened circumstances and the lack of a railway led to a widespread perception that Alexander Mackenzie's administration had failed the west. Charles Mair, formerly an Ontarian and Liberal party supporter, described the prime minister as a "Grit Frankenstein" and reported the emergence of a "sullen discontent" in Manitoba that might spawn a "provincial repulsion dangerous and threatening to the permanency of Confederation."[49]

Due in part to a shift in Manitoba's relations with central Canada, important social and economic changes were taking place. Quebecers' interest in the west declined sharply as they took up jobs in the New England states to the south.[50] Many Ontarians, in contrast, looked west when it became impossible to find farmland near their family homes. The direction of trade flows into and out of the prairie west also changed. The new Manitoba economy would be built on farms that sold their products to the world. Its potential staple export was wheat, soon to be described as premium grade Number One Northern hard red spring wheat. The province exported wheat valued at $250,000 in 1882, over $500,000 in 1883, $2.6 million in 1886, and $5 million in 1887. This high-quality, bread-making grain was destined to feed the growing cities of western Europe.[51] Except in relation to the fur trade, Britain's monopoly on Rupert's Land trade ended. American companies soon supplied about one-third of the goods shipped into the province, measured by value. And Ontario buyers, sellers, and shippers set the tone of economic life, dominating Manitoba retail markets and wholesale trade.

The prairies, unlike the provinces of eastern Canada, possessed very little public infrastructure when Manitoba and the North-West Territories entered confederation. The roads and government offices of Ontario, Quebec, and the Maritimes built over the preceding century and more had no equivalents. The Manitoba government was able to spend about $100,000 per year in the 1870s. When Prime Minister Macdonald agreed to grant increases in various accounts in 1881, its budget grew to $200,000. The budget line for one item, the drainage of standing water in rural districts, was then $63,000, nearly 30 percent of the total.

This seemingly unusual priority underlined one of the first objectives of the government, the reclamation of thousands of acres of potential farmland. Viewed as investments, ditches were wonderfully productive. Norquay's minister of public works, Corydon Brown, assembled surveyors, contractors, and labourers to cut waterways through the rich soil. In less than a decade the government excavated nearly 500 kilometres of drainage ditches at a cost of slightly more than $500 per kilometre. The environmental engineering was applauded at the time because it worked a revolution in the productivity of southern Manitoba. Norquay handled the negotiations in Ottawa that secured provincial ownership of thousands of acres of this reclaimed land and another source of income for an administration starved of revenue. One of the main drainage routes, the Norquay Channel, was named after the premier whose government adopted the policy.[52]

Infrastructure needs far exceeded the administration's capacity to deal with them. What could Manitoba do? It could create a new institution of local government, the municipality, which possessed the right to borrow funds and undertake public works to be paid for by the same taxpayers who paid levies to the provincial and federal governments. The assembly passed a municipal act in the session of 1877. It aimed initially at road, bridge, and drainage works, but local developers quickly moved to offer bonuses for branch railway construction. The measure pitted absentee landowners and speculators, averse to paying taxes, against local farmers, who needed railways to get their grain to world markets. Norquay had to balance these pressures, alienating some old friends in the process.[53]

The executive arm of the state was in reasonable shape by the early 1880s, a considerable achievement for which the premier could take some credit. The civil service developed procedures and regulations to cover daily business. It was small, comprising just over thirty individuals in the central government office, all of whom were male. The cabinet met regularly, normally under Norquay's leadership, to deal with questions of policy and to pass orders-in-council. Norquay was the head of the operation, without question, but he did not dominate cabinet discussions. Ministers ran their departments with little interference from his office, though he was consulted on matters of importance. They all understood that the government's spending would be scrutinized by members of the assembly. Cabinet members expected the premier to back them when challenged in debates. In return they corresponded with him in a manner that reflected respect for his position and his person. The dramatic events of June 1879 had ensured that everyone was aware of offsetting powers: ministerial mutinies could unseat a premier, and a premier could easily jettison a troublesome minister.[54]

Norquay lived in a small, sociable, male, club-like circle. Assembly members related to each other informally. During sittings and committee meetings they socialized with senior officials in the civil service, played cards, smoked cigars in the small room behind the speaker's chair, and enjoyed the strong drink available there during evening debates. Business, poker, smokes, and drinks went together. When a rural district dispatched a delegation seeking favourable legislation, one informant sent Norquay some private advice: the group was carrying "some money to spend in treating you Chaps," he wrote, "and you can have all the champagne and Havanas at 20 c[ents] each your whole Government will require for the session if you only work it a little sharp." The informant suggested that the premier meet the group only if wine was served and take care to "introduce them to Begg and Tom Spence [civil servants] and a few more of the boys." A member of the legislature struck a similar note after vetting a job applicant, telling Norquay that he had "not found anything against [Mr.] Lane yet except that he is a Sunday school teacher and President of a Young mans temperance society and though these are very great sins still as it will give a little variety to the Civil Service I think we might let them pass."[55]

Norquay found a reliable, thoughtful colleague in civil servant Walter Nursey, who became one of his closest colleagues.[56] Born in England in 1846, Nursey was educated at Marlborough, a school for the children of Anglican clergy. He moved to Canada in 1864 and to Manitoba shortly after the province was founded. He joined the provincial civil service in 1877, collaborated with Begg in writing *Ten Years in Winnipeg* (1879), and served in the provincial auditor's office. Nursey's cheery, informal letter to the premier from southern Ontario in 1881 bore witness to their close relationship: "You may not readily credit it but after an absence of several years from Eastern Canada, *it falls flat*. There is a marked want of that *lively rush* which characterizes Manitoba, and already am I hungry for a whiff of prairie air. . . . So far I have strenuously avoided all actions that might smack of even a suspicion of impropriety, and hence you will be pleased to hear, have not been charged even with any peccadillo." Nursey was more than an auditor. He quickly became for Norquay a source of political information, a supporter, and a friend.[57]

As minister of finance, Norquay worked closely with all the treasury officials, Alexander Begg in particular. Born in Lower Canada in 1839, Begg attended school in Scotland and moved to Assiniboia in 1867 as an agent for several Hamilton businesses. After reverses in several commercial ventures, he became a civil servant in the late 1870s, acting as sergeant at arms, queen's printer, and deputy provincial treasurer. His strengths were his quick wit and his pen, not his competence as an accountant. His letters to Norquay revealed that Begg looked on his boss as a familiar, one with whom he could speak bluntly and who would carry out favours on request. Adventurous, interested in seeing more of the world, Begg left for London on a secondment to the CPR at the end of 1881.[58] He left behind some financial problems, suggesting that he was out of his depth as deputy treasurer. Norquay demanded that he return to Winnipeg in the summer of 1882 to clear up discrepancies in the official accounts. The shortfall amounted to nearly $4,000, three or four years of salary for someone in Begg's position.[59] Norquay tackled the problem in a severe letter, and Begg addressed the charges immediately. Two brief notes among the orders-in-council passed by the cabinet a year later suggest that this unfortunate chapter came to a rapid close. Begg and his wife deeded "certain lands" to the province to "secure payment of any money that may be found to be owing to the province." On the same day the executive council formally accepted his resignation as deputy provincial treasurer. In the following months Begg also sent regular money orders to Norquay "which will be repeated each month until I hear how you have succeeded in relieving me."[60]

Viewed from a wider perspective, Norquay's decisive intervention revealed that he had a solid grasp of the broad outlines of government finances. He insisted on honesty in the treasury and was scrupulous himself in handling public money. His economic thought focused, first and foremost, on public works policy, what today would be called the development of infrastructure. During his nine years as premier, while farmers plowed their fields and merchants built their main streets, the government constructed the foundations of southern Manitoba, including the initial road, railway, and drainage systems, a network of schools and court districts, the basic land law, the instruments of municipal government, and a pattern of towns and villages that has survived to this day.

Expeditions to Ottawa

Manitoba required immediate changes in the arrangements by which it was governed. How could Norquay impress this necessity on people in the Ottawa establishment who had never travelled west? Having been promised by Sir John A. Macdonald that the boundary would be extended in due course, Norquay wanted to see the province enlarged immediately. Another major policy sphere, that of railway access, depended on joint understandings between federal and provincial authorities. Moreover, many Manitobans complained about one aspect or another of Ottawa's rules on landholding. In addition to those pressing matters, as the only province without control over its lands and resources, Manitoba had to rely almost exclusively on Ottawa for its income. The obvious alternative within the constitutional powers granted to provinces (they were restricted to "direct taxation" by the British North America Act) was some version of personal income tax or sales tax, and, though Norquay talked about that possibility, no one wanted to go down that path.

His solution was unusual: he would conduct annual expeditions to the national capital, supplemented in several years by shorter trips, during which he and his colleagues, including always at least one francophone, would lobby ministers, civil servants, reporters, and anyone else who ventured within earshot. His delegations would make a mark, politically and socially, and ensure that federal politicians simply had to take the province's circumstances into account. En route Norquay frequently stopped to visit with a growing list of acquaintances, during which he publicized the advantages of emigration to and investment in Manitoba. Hotel dining rooms, formal events in Rideau Hall, hurried chats in the lobby of Parliament, five o'clock receptions, evening dances, breakfasts and dinners and bridge parties and poker games became his chosen battlegrounds. Each expedition cost between $1,000 and $4,000 at a time when mid-level civil servants were paid about $1,000 per year. In the nine years from April 1878, when Norquay first travelled to Ottawa, to January 1886, he spent nearly a full year in the capital on ten "better terms" expeditions. The trips were expensive and time consuming, but they achieved results that would not have been possible without such personal representation.[61]

They also changed Norquay. He developed expertise in public finance and mastered volumes of detail in order to present his arguments effectively. He wrote briefs, attended meetings and dinners, made trips into the country, and took in evening entertainments. He enjoyed the contact with a wide array of politicians, civil servants, journalists, lobbyists, and business leaders. Some of the events that Norquay attended were related directly to intergovernmental relations, some could be attributed to Manitoba's pursuit of improved public relations, and some were personal, such as his frequent visits to the Notman photographic studio. He and the other Manitoba delegates often stayed at the Russell House, famous for its dining hall, its bar and sitting room, and a long list of influential guests.[62] In 1881 Norquay paid a livery bill that mentioned carriage services on four occasions in one week, including to the governor general's ball and a visit to the opera. An invoice in 1882 itemized expenses that included forty-three days of board and lodging, plus entries for laundry and carriages. Elizabeth accompanied John on one of these expeditions. On another Horace, then ten, was awarded the trip of a lifetime, documented by a formal photographic portrait.[63]

Norquay observed closely the leading figures in the Canadian government, including John A. Macdonald, and tried to find ways to influence these busy individuals. They were not exactly remote, since he managed to secure conversations with many of them, but it was not easy to pin them down. Norquay was never close to the prime minister, but he exchanged letters with him frequently, and on occasion he dined at the Macdonald home. Norquay learned to define his objectives clearly, to stand resolute in his negotiations, and to settle for half a loaf if he could get no more. He sparred with the prime minister over Canada's imperial rule in the prairie west and over minor matters. In 1881 Macdonald criticized Manitoba's highly restrictive rules for the admission of out-of-province lawyers to the bar. Norquay replied that he would revise the wording, but "I may add that although we don't profess to have a higher standard of Education than in Toronto or Quebec none of those educated with us spell Christ with a K as was the case with some of those applying for admission." Even in 1881 it probably belonged in the category of old jokes, but the pinprick would have been noted in Ottawa.[64]

The expeditions accomplished a great deal. In March 1880 the Manitoba delegation of four addressed no fewer than fifteen items, ranging from the construction of public buildings to drainage infrastructure, a steam dredge, the lowering of Lake Manitoba, and an increased subsidy. Norquay proposed once again that Ottawa extend the province's boundaries. His case for territorial expansion drew from a novel historical interpretation. Building upon intelligence that he had gathered in earlier conversations rather than original sources, he argued that the province's present size, about 100 by 140 miles (14,000 square miles, or 160 by 225 kilometres, roughly 36,000 square kilometres), reflected its Red River Settlement roots. His argument turned on the understanding that the boundary of "postage stamp" Manitoba simply reflected the bounds of the historical HBC District of Assiniboia, the lands within a fifty-mile (eighty-kilometre) radius of Upper Fort Garry (roughly 8,000 square miles or 20,000 square kilometres). In this zone "civil and criminal cases" customarily had been handled by HBC-appointed courts. So it was safe for Ottawa to assume in 1870 that all residents of the District of Assiniboia were familiar with the rule of British law. Norquay claimed that "the Ottawa Government of that day [1870] did not like to go outside the range of country included in this district, fearing to incorporate in the new province more territory than that over which law had obtained already. . . . To do otherwise, might have led to complications with Indians who then claimed title over the whole North-West." Canada had since signed treaties with the Cree and Saulteaux, he argued, and it was now time to make the province into a more effective economic, judicial, and administrative unit. Expansion was a matter of good government. A boost to Manitoba's presence within the Canadian federation would only do justice to its growing national and international profile.[65] The argument became a building block in a Manitoban interpretation of its place within confederation in the years that followed.

The arguments made by Norquay on this occasion did not convince the prime minister to extend the boundaries. Instead, and just as welcome, Macdonald agreed to increase the grant transferred to the province. Norquay received a warm thank you from citizens and the press when he returned to Winnipeg. To ensure that the compliments did not lead to a swelled head, former colleague Alfred Boyd wrote from England to needle him: "I see by the papers, your glory and honour, the entertainments given by 'our Premier.' The remarks made by ditto. The reception in the house of ditto, etc. etc. You must find it almost as good as trading rats [muskrats] up Cumberland quarter."[66]

Norquay tried again to convince Macdonald on the boundary question in mid-October 1880. He led a sizable contingent, made the usual presentations, dined at Government House, and took a trip on the Credit Valley Railway "with a party of Toronto gentlemen." He won a few small concessions from the federal government, including a grant for the construction of public buildings and another small increase in the annual federal subsidy. Although everyone knew that Norquay's object was boundary extension, and though Macdonald was reminded that he had promised to do so, no extension was forthcoming.[67]

The provincial assembly met for a brief session in December 1880, and in early January 1881 Norquay returned to Ottawa, this time with a delegation of ten, to pursue the province's requests for aid. His goal was to secure an extension of the boundary west to the 102nd meridian, north to 53 degrees, and east as far as Thunder Bay on Lake Superior. Macdonald was happy to grant Norquay brief conversations, but he was a busy man, and Manitoba's boundary was not a priority. The biggest issue in national public life, the subject on which the newspapers and the opposition were spending all their time, was the CPR contract. Moreover, both Ontario and a group in the North-West Territories opposed Manitoba's aspirations. But this time Norquay was successful. The governor general assented to the boundary extension bill in mid-March 1881. Norquay had secured a fivefold increase in provincial territory.[68]

Having conceded the western and northern but not the eastern boundary extension, Macdonald believed that he had paid for Norquay's having left him a free hand in railway policy. The annual junkets had to cease. Macdonald had his justice minister deliver a memorandum: "In order to obviate the necessity of yearly visits to the capital as suggested in the memo of the delegates The Privy Council have decided to increase the subsidy." It tarnished Norquay's victory only a little: despite the logjam in Parliament, Macdonald had given Norquay the boundary extension and a doubling of federal grants that he had sought.[69]

Yet he did not relent. A memorandum prepared by the federal government placed the enlarged Manitoba as the third-largest province, behind British Columbia and Quebec but ahead of Ontario.[70] If granted the extensions north, east, and west that it was still seeking, the premier reasoned, it would become a dominant force in the federation. He made precisely that argument when speaking at a gala banquet in Winnipeg celebrating the boundary extension: "It is not unreasonable to suppose that within half a century, or as some more sanguine ones would say, within a quarter of a century, the portion of the Dominion lying west of Lake Superior will give laws to the Dominion of Canada." According to a newly founded newspaper in Kenora, the *Rat Portage Progress*, located on what was then perceived (by Manitobans) to be Manitoba territory, the banquet was a social highlight of the year.[71]

Although the western and northern borders had been extended, Manitoba's eastern boundary remained undefined. Macdonald wanted to limit Premier of Ontario Oliver Mowat's empire, but he wanted Norquay to bear the brunt of the battle. In October 1881 Norquay asked Macdonald how to proceed. If the prime minister thought it wise, Norquay suggested, then he would speak to Premier Mowat about referring the matter to the Supreme Court of Canada "or to any other impartial tribunal that you [Macdonald] may approve."[72] There the matter rested for several years until construction of the transcontinental railway pushed administration of the Precambrian Shield country to the fore.

In February 1882 Norquay and the new provincial secretary, Alphonse LaRivière, signed the register at the Russell House in Ottawa and settled in for another long stay. Norquay met first with John A. Macdonald, once again at his residence. He then spoke with Minister of Justice Alexander Campbell and submitted a lengthy memorandum introducing their requests. He did not mention railway policy or federal disallowance of provincially granted railway charters. Instead, he focused on the need for a larger subsidy, further boundary extensions, additional seats (and influence) in the Senate and House of Commons, and the "energetic prosecution" of plans to build provincial public buildings at federal expense.[73]

For unexplained reasons it took two full weeks for these proposals to reach the desks of Macdonald's cabinet ministers. There they languished. Norquay and LaRivière eventually asked Campbell whether the cabinet had discussed the issues and were told that other business had taken precedence. Norquay complained to the prime minister in a brief note that he had had neither answers nor opportunities to present his case. In the following week Campbell offered a few concessions. Norquay "refused to accept" (his words in his official report to the Manitoba legislature) some of these proposals. Campbell said that he had no authority to go further and suggested that the premier speak to the prime minister. In a brief session the following day, Macdonald and Norquay agreed that the premier would make a presentation to the full federal cabinet on 4 March.

This was his moment to shine. Before the full privy council, as Norquay reported later, he made an "elaborate exposition of the circumstances of the province from its organization up to the present time, comparing its relations to the Dominion with that of the other provinces admitted into the union at the time of Confederation and since." Then he raised the spectre of direct taxation of personal income in Manitoba to meet the dire circumstances of a financial shortfall. LaRivière seconded his arguments. Macdonald praised the premier's statement as a "very lucid presentation," according to Norquay's minute of the meeting.[74]

Three days later they had answers. Manitoba would get an additional senator and several judges, and Ottawa would "second" the province in the negotiations on its boundary with Ontario. On the argument linking lands and provincial revenues, Macdonald came up with an ingenious reply. The other provinces owned their lands before entering confederation, the federal memorandum argued, whereas Canada purchased "the whole of Manitoba" from the Hudson's Bay Company, thereby making it "the property of the Dominion. . . . [It] stands really . . . in the same position as lands in the Territories of the United States, which are not given to new states." The memo acknowledged that the tiny province of Prince Edward Island had not owned its lands either, because the entire province had been cut up by royal grants to absentee landlords a century earlier, and Ottawa had given it a grant to compensate for this shortfall. So, in the Manitoba case, instead of transferring control of public lands to the province, Ottawa agreed to give it a grant in lieu of lands at the rate of $45,000 per year "as was done for Prince Edward Island."[75]

Macdonald was performing a balancing act once again. He could give a little but had to be wary of rousing opposition in other provinces. For Norquay it counted as a significant victory. When presenting the deal to his cabinet colleagues in Winnipeg in early April 1882, he emphasized that the contest would never end. He was "personally aware," he said, "from interviews with prominent members of the [federal] Government," that Ottawa saw "the rapidly changing circumstances of the province" as an emergency requiring immediate support and that "any arrangement now made will have of necessity to be modified from time to time as circumstances warrant." In this official minute he went beyond the federal document itself by declaring that he reserved the right to make the same case again.[76] The very language expressed his sense that Manitoba's arguments had swayed some members of Macdonald's cabinet.

The federal government announced the new set of concessions grudgingly. Both Macdonald and Minister of Finance Leonard Tilly said that the gains would be Manitoba's last for many years—Tilly specified "ten years." Such hard talk might have been good politics in eastern Canada, but the negative, categorical dismissal of Manitoba's unmet claims irritated Norquay a great deal. It also undercut Manitoba's Conservatives during the federal election campaign that followed. It can be seen as the beginning of a rift between the premier and the prime minister that would never heal entirely. Macdonald trusted no one, that was a given, but Norquay, who had wanted to trust the prime minister, now understood that he could not expect Sir John to back him consistently, whatever the strength of the Manitoba case.[77]

The grant in lieu of land ownership represented a significant gain. This issue had rankled with Norquay more than almost any other. As the premier told the assembly in introducing the new financial arrangement a few months later, Manitoba's position differed from those of the other provinces: "When I go East what do I find? . . . [Political leaders] look upon this as an inferior Province—tell us that our lands have been purchased, and we are hindered on all hands instead of being helped. (Hear, hear)." This is why Norquay and many other westerners argued that they were shouldering the cost of the CPR: 25 million acres of land "fairly fit for settlement," perhaps one-quarter of the farmland in the prairie west, had been granted to the CPR, all of it coming from prairie districts. Still, Norquay remained optimistic because, he said, the new financial supports had been adopted to meet a "temporary emergency. . . . It is perfectly understood by the Government below [i.e., in Ottawa] that they will meet the exigencies of the Province as circumstances warrant. (Hear, hear and cheers)."[78] But would they?

Should Norquay have accepted the subsidy increase instead of insisting on the transfer of public lands and resources? In retrospect, the principle appears to have been crucial. But Norquay saw it as a revenue question as well as a constitutional one. He needed money immediately. He planned to renew the struggle in the years to come.[79]

The three years of negotiations in Ottawa taught Norquay the ins and outs of federal-provincial relations. They also cast doubt on the workings of the Canadian federation. He found a sounding board for his misgivings in Victorian Canada's leading curmudgeon, Goldwin Smith, a former Oxford University professor, celebrated Toronto writer on Canadian and imperial affairs, and vigorous critic of John A. Macdonald. In one letter to the Manitoba premier, Smith thanked him for the gift of a book on missions and Indigenous peoples in the districts north of Ontario, then known as Keewatin. The broader point of Smith's missive—and its relevance to Norquay—concerned Manitoba's uneasy place within the federation: "I have contended all along," Smith wrote, "that our statesmen did not see, or if they did see made no practical allowance for, the fact that the time must soon come when Manitoba and the other North Western Provinces would have a will of their own and a word to say about the disposal of their land. Sir John is lighthearted and says 'After me the Deluge.' I suspect his successor will have, if not a Deluge, plenty of difficulties to deal with."[80] Smith's prediction proved to be accurate. His thinking expanded Norquay's horizons. Norquay could see more clearly the structure of the federation and the deep problems that it posed for the prairie west. Still, the biggest crisis in what was becoming an ongoing conflict between the national government and the prairies centred not on land but on Macdonald's handling of railway policy.

Railway Monopoly

While in Ottawa in 1880 and 1881, Norquay heard a great deal about railways. Macdonald and his Conservatives returned to power promising Canadians a "National Policy" of higher tariffs and a transcontinental trunk line. In their first year they enacted the tariff increases and secured Norquay's agreement on their approach to national rail policy. In their second year they looked for a company to lay the tracks. The two first ministers remained on the same page during this period. The Manitoba premier ensured that no charters for railways were passed in the Manitoba legislature's session of January–February 1880 except for a company that planned to develop a Winnipeg tramway.[81] In the summer the prime minister invited the premier to run as the Conservative candidate in a by-election in Selkirk, which included Norquay's home riding. Norquay declined graciously. In his letter he congratulated Macdonald on finding a builder for the national trunk line: "Everything looks favorably in Manitoba now & with the energy recently displayed in pushing the railway ahead the opponents to the Govt policy [are] without a peg on which to hang their objections."[82]

Despite Norquay's initial enthusiasm, the transcontinental contract with the federal government posed a serious problem. Macdonald and Minister of Public Works Charles Tupper had decided that the rail route must be all-Canadian, which meant that the contractors would have to conquer the rock and forest north of Lake Superior. They preferred this solution not only for trade and military reasons but also because it contrasted dramatically with the cheaper, piecemeal approach of Alexander Mackenzie's Liberals, a policy that had relied on a route south of the Great Lakes through the United States. The new Conservative government found a willing builder in the Canadian Pacific Railway Company. Acknowledging the expense and vulnerability of the north shore route, Macdonald agreed to provide the corporation with a very large subsidy. He also guaranteed that the CPR would have a monopoly on rail transport into and out of the prairies. According to clause 15 of the contract, for the next twenty years, or for ten years after completion of the trunk road, the CPR would control "*any* & *every line south*" of its western main line, including the branch railway from St. Boniface to the international border, ownership of which would be transferred from Ottawa to the CPR.[83] This guarantee became Norquay's albatross.

Rumours about the terms began to circulate in early December 1880. According to merchants' gossip in St. Paul, Minnesota, the CPR syndicate had put one over on the Macdonald government.[84] What was worse, the contract perpetuated what seemed like two centuries of corporate monopoly in the northwestern interior of the continent. First had been the royal charter of the Hudson's Bay Company with its exclusive right to trade. Then in the 1870s Norman Kittson and James Hill of St. Paul had allied with the HBC to control steamships on the Red River. Beginning in 1878 Kittson and Hill joined George Stephen of Montreal, Donald Smith of the HBC, and New York financier John Kennedy to complete the first rail line accessing the Canadian prairies, the St. Paul, Minneapolis & Manitoba.[85] Now the CPR's contractually guaranteed monopoly would handicap the western Canadian regional economy again. Moreover, the CPR entrepreneurs would control not only that southern outlet (the line from Manitoba to St. Paul) but also the eastern outlet from Winnipeg to Thunder Bay and eastern Canada. Describing "grave apprehensions" in local circles, even among Tories, Norquay warned Macdonald of the Manitoba fear that the part of the CPR's eastern route above Lake Superior would never get built, or be long delayed, "which to us in the west is of vital importance."[86] The Manitobans wanted two outlets to eastern North America controlled by two different corporations that would be forced to engage in genuine competition over freight rates.

The Manitoba government was not given an opportunity to review the CPR contract. It learned of the terms with the rest of the country and recognized immediately that a new monopoly had been created. Norquay wired Joseph Royal, now the St. Boniface Member of Parliament, in mid-December 1880 asking for "full particulars of [the] arrangement with Syndicate. Great excitement here at what is considered huge monopoly. Do government supporters really all approve arrangements?" He sounded as incredulous as his colleagues in Winnipeg's business community.[87]

Discussion of the contract in Manitoba focused mainly on this matter of competition. The opposition in the Manitoba assembly introduced a resolution on 23 December 1880 calling on the House of Commons to reject the CPR deal. Norquay responded with an amendment: "That this House views with alarm some of the terms of the agreement between the Government and the Syndicate." It passed unanimously. Still, the local government was attacked vigorously by the *Manitoba Free Press* as being too weak in its protests. Editor William Luxton argued that the premier had let Sir John A. visit an "outrage" on the province. A mass meeting in Winnipeg on 29 December attacked the CPR's broad powers while welcoming the decision to route the transcontinental railway through the city. A petition was immediately dispatched asking that "clause 15," the "monopoly clause," be revised so that many companies, including the CPR, could build branch lines to the American boundary, at least "until the eastern section [including the north shore of Lake Superior] is completed." Norquay signed this protest.[88] He and his colleagues believed that, if the cost of the route was the price of the Canadian nation-state, then it would be paid disproportionately by western Canadians. Despite his doubts, in order not to alienate Macdonald and jeopardize the money and boundary negotiations that Norquay was conducting at the same time, he would have to temporize.

On the CPR contract Macdonald did not bend, not then or for the next seven years. Rather, he harked back to their talks of 1879 and insisted that the Manitoba premier had promised not to "allow any legislation infringing on the agreement with the Syndicate." Without saying so specifically, he implied that the pledge should run for years to come, perhaps for the duration of Ottawa's contractual commitments to the CPR. Norquay claimed that the commitment had been for only one session. The disagreement promised trouble, both for the relationship between the two leaders and for the economic aspirations of Manitoba entrepreneurs.[89]

Norquay could not head off the pressure exerted by Manitoba merchants, municipalities, and farm households. The province needed many more kilometres of railway lines, all of them connected to a trunk line that would carry farm-making goods to the prairies and farm-raised products to the world. The Manitoba assembly considered numerous applications for railway charters in these years, and several were granted. At least four of the proposed branch lines might contravene the provisions of clause 15 of the CPR contract by serving as feeders to American trunk lines.[90]

Macdonald told Norquay well in advance that the offending branch line legislation would be disallowed. He scolded Norquay for permitting the passage of these charters: "We who were around the Council table understood that you undertook to discourage and prevent such Legislation." Norquay did not contradict him. Rather, he warned that Manitobans would be very upset and proposed further negotiations. His message carried a hint of compromise: "We can in the meantime keep things quiet. I will be down the latter part of December [1881]."[91] He was angling for a deal, hoping to identify areas in which the disallowance of charters would be offset by concessions of greater importance in other spheres.

Norquay was now talking frequently to eastern Canadians, including the prime minister, about Manitoba politics. He might well have made promises to Macdonald. It is likely that these talks, informal and unrecorded, provided the foundation for the federal grant increases and boundary extension deals of 1881 and 1882. The conversations were conducted cautiously, each party wishing to keep some cards hidden, each reluctant to promise too much too soon. The interests that they pursued and the people whom they served were very different in character. But both leaders were prepared to continue negotiations.[92]

The year 1881–82 stands out as a key moment in Manitoba's railway history. The CPR was beginning to lay tracks on the trunk lines both east and west of Winnipeg. As it did so, and as the monopoly clause demonstrated, its leaders were exceedingly worried about potential American competitors. They feared especially the Northern Pacific Railway, now in the hands of the German American railway tsar, Henry Villard, because it had swallowed up Schultz's Manitoba South-Western and the land grants that came with it. The MSWR, in turn, seemed to be tied to one of Manitoba's recently passed branch line charters, the Winnipeg & South-Eastern Railway, that proposed to build a line from Winnipeg to Duluth and—the serious fear—feed into a transcontinental rail line running both westward, near and just south of the international border, and eastward below the Great Lakes. Because its construction and running costs would be lower than any line running north of Lake Superior, it would defeat the CPR in the competition for Canadian prairie freight.[93] Norquay himself was rumoured to have a financial interest in the Winnipeg & South-Eastern, though no evidence has surfaced to support such a claim.[94]

Ottawa's disallowance of the Winnipeg & South-Eastern charter was announced in January 1882. The key reason given was that its charter conflicted with "the settled policy of the Dominion as evidenced in the contract with the Canadian Pacific Railway Company."[95] Norquay, then en route to Ottawa, reacted calmly to the news, saying in an interview in Toronto that Macdonald's government had acted appropriately and had not infringed provincial authority. He also asserted that the province possessed the power to charter railways within provincial borders. His accommodating tone was probably the result not only of Macdonald's advance warning but also of his own hopes for concessions on boundary and subsidy in the upcoming negotiations. Still, Norquay had to find a way to release the province from the clutches of the CPR/St. Paul, Minneapolis & Manitoba leviathan.[96]

In November 1882 Macdonald disallowed the charters of three more Manitoba rail companies on which he had taken no action months earlier. Within days there were public meetings of protest in Winnipeg. The anger was so strong that even the Conservative newspaper, the *Times*, called for the re-enactment of the charters. Norquay tried to defend the federal action by saying that some of the lines proposed would have gone outside the borders of the province and thus were beyond provincial powers. In the case of a line that made Emerson a terminus, where the provincial government was acting within its constitutional rights, he intended to see the railway completed. He immediately asked his senior civil servants to give him a report on the constitutional powers of the two levels of government.[97]

Taken aback by the hostility in Manitoba, the CPR's George Stephen pressed the prime minister to enact legislation that would prevent the Manitoba legislature from ever again passing charters that contravened the CPR contract. Macdonald replied patiently that Ottawa could not intervene in this way because it would infringe the constitutional rights of the province. He came up with a better idea, one that affected Norquay directly: "One thing must be done. You must have a confidential man at Winnipeg to see the MPPs and *convince* [Macdonald's emphasis] them of the error of their ways if they oppose the great National Railway policy." Newly elevated Manitoba cabinet minister Alphonse LaRivière went unmentioned, but it is likely—as became apparent in the following years—he signed on as the company's secret agent in the province.[98]

John A. Macdonald was losing patience with Norquay. The premier had been too insistent on federal concessions and too unreliable in his support of the national government. In a genial letter to Governor General Lord Lorne at the end of 1882, the prime minister dismissed the Manitoba campaign: "The truth is there is yet no real public opinion in Manitoba. The men who now lead the agitation there are a ring of Land Sharks & Homestead Jumpers. In a year or two the solid mass of Settlers will outvote and override the gang of speculators who now pose as 'The People of The North West.'" Macdonald also predicted Norquay's political demise. Delivered almost in passing, his comment illustrated that neither the province nor the man figured prominently in his thoughts: "There is a little tempest in Manitoba about the disallowance of three Railway Bills. This will soon blow over, altho' it may depose Norquay, who will probably fall from his own vacillation." Viewed from the prime minister's vantage point, the ouster of a Manitoba premier was a matter of little importance.[99] Macdonald would brook no opposition to his railway policies. His primary loyalty was to the nation-state of Canada and to the policies that he and his team had settled on as foundational to its survival and to their party's success.

Norquay concluded that equivocation was the wisest course. He would pass charters sought by railway speculators, then offer a muted response to the federal government's disallowance of the legislation. But how long would this strategy work? Macdonald and Stephen were pressing local Conservatives to get into line. Opposition members in the assembly demanded resistance and "provincial rights." According to the Manitoba Act, which limited the life of any government to four years, a provincial election would have to be held within a year, by the end of 1883. It was time for the premier to consider his future.

Political Parties

Norquay's electoral sweep in the 1879 provincial election had been accomplished on a platform of provincial non-partisanship. But it was no secret that the premier belonged to the federal Conservative party. At a banquet in Winnipeg, he declared that Macdonald's National Policy was "the true policy to build up a great country like Canada." A month later he insisted that the wisest course for the provincial administration was to remain non-partisan, especially in relation to federal matters. For two years after the election, Reformers/Liberals in the assembly ignored federal party lines and gave their support to Norquay.[100]

Dissenters who might undermine his control of the legislature surfaced in 1881, first within the francophone community and then among federal Conservatives and Liberals. Marc Girard simply could not keep his caucus of Michif/French-speaking assembly members in line. Within a year of his appointment, he had been outmanoeuvred.[101] Norquay had little choice but to invite the most influential francophone in the assembly, Alphonse LaRivière, to join the cabinet as provincial secretary and minister of education.[102] From Norquay's vantage point LaRivière's ascendancy introduced as many disadvantages as advantages. The new minister was competent, ambitious, and able to command the faction's five to seven votes in the assembly. But behind the scenes he probably had an understanding with the CPR that provided his newspaper, *Le Manitoba*, with support in exchange for insider information on the cabinet and government.

Norquay faced a different kind of challenge from Orange Ontarian Conservatives, particularly the members of a self-appointed elite in Winnipeg.[103] These party activists grumbled in the background about his leadership but did not have a leader in the assembly to voice their views. Rather, they quarrelled among themselves over appointments and patronage. A by-election in the recently expanded stretches of western Manitoba illustrated their reach. It pitted a Norquay ally, Charles Boulton, one of the leaders of the anti-Riel forces in 1870, against Winnipeg business executive Edward Leacock. Both were Conservatives, and neither would stand down. They split the vote, and a Liberal was elected. But Leacock continued to canvass during the next few months and won the seat in the general election. Boulton's political demise deprived Norquay of a supporter and brought in a fraud. Leacock talked extravagantly, entertained lavishly, and proved to be a fair-weather friend who readily left others in his wake while pursuing his own projects.[104] These two relatively minor events, LaRivière's takeover of the francophone faction and Leacock's sidelining of Boulton, were to cause far greater disruption in Norquay's life than anyone could have anticipated.

The concluding session of the government's term took place in April and May 1882. Although Norquay still enjoyed the support of a comfortable majority, his government was now being criticized by a vigorous opposition under the leadership of Thomas Greenway. A one-time Conservative,

Greenway had abandoned Macdonald and crossed the floor of the House of Commons in the 1870s. He then guided the migration of a large group of Ontario farm families to the rich farmland surrounding Pilot Mound in southern Manitoba. He won a Manitoba assembly seat in the general election of 1879, supported the government briefly, and then parted company with Norquay. They remained on friendly terms, but Greenway became an outspoken critic of Macdonald's National Policy and of Norquay's administration. The first formal announcement of his partisan ambitions came in the 1882 throne speech debate when he introduced a resolution declaring non-confidence in the government.[105]

The atmosphere in the assembly in 1882 was much changed from the three previous sessions. As a member of Norquay's cabinet put it, Greenway "forced Dominion politics on the House."[106] Opposition critics, now calling themselves Liberals, targeted the government's allegedly lax financial management, perhaps having picked up rumours of Alexander Begg's sloppy work. They also focused on the crying need for branch railways in rural districts. According to John Sifton, a new member of the house, Ottawa's disallowance policy breached the Constitution by making provinces subordinate when they were not: "What were we then? Not a Province, surely, but a colony. Not a colony of Great Britain, but a colony of the C.P.R. (Applause)."[107]

Norquay defended his government and claimed that it "steered clear of partisanship." He said that his opponents were mimicking "the old story" of the wolf and the lamb in that these critics, acting as wolf, were tormenting "the unfortunate Government, poor lamb (loud laughter) having to suffer (hear)." Norquay also defended himself against charges that he had lost his connection with old Red River. His words hinted at tensions within the assembly: "Yesterday the statement was made that because I was a native of the country I ought to have taken a special part in defending public interests. Well, I think I have taken such a part. But I hope the day will come when we will all—old settlers as well as newcomers—unite in advancing the public welfare... (cheers)."[108] In public discourse race was not far beneath the surface.

Norquay's language in the debates of the early 1880s was remarkable for its emphasis on capital investment. It was also noteworthy for its appeals to Canadian patriotism: the transcontinental railway project had broad support across Canada, Norquay told the Manitoba assembly in May 1882, because it was "one calculated to foster a great national sentiment. (Cheers)." This was very much the language of Macdonald and federal Conservatives. Norquay added equally persuasive criticisms of Ottawa: "Our province is now equal in size to Ontario with resources as great and affording facilities for settlement superior to that of any other province of Confederation. Yet there is indeed a very hard struggle before us with the Federal Government to induce them to give to us the control of our public domain and thereby place us in the same position as the other provinces of Confederation."[109] Manitoba's position was "a transitional one," he said. His railway deal in 1879 had been "temporary." The province had not received "strict justice." Its protests had been treated by the 4 million other Canadians "as to some extent insignificant."[110] Norquay also had a message about parties, non-partisanship, and the atmosphere in local debate: "He could not close without an expression of regret that hon. Members opposite had directly introduced Dominion party politics into this House. He had all along been desirous to keep the bitterness of party strife outside the Legislature." He lamented that the opposition had introduced a motion censuring the acts of the federal government. As he said, referring to party lines, "the mischief was done," though he refused to commit his own side to alignment with the federal Conservative party.[111]

Norquay was pleased with the reception of his speech in the house, and he remained comfortable in his relations with the national Conservative leader. He wrote to John A. Macdonald after the vote to say that "we had quite a fight in our Assembly in an amendment to address [in response to the speech from the throne]. We carried it last night 17 to 7."[112] Henceforth, as Norquay implied, federal party lines were a factor in local affairs, whether he himself adhered to them or not. In the assembly he could count on about sixteen to eighteen votes, the opposition about six to eight. The Liberal party in Ottawa now had a Manitoba affiliate, the assembly group led by Thomas Greenway. Among Conservatives the lines remained unclear.

Another matter, minor yet potentially disastrous, escaped the government's attention: somehow, in the rush to end the session, Norquay and his colleagues failed to pass a law incorporating the Loyal Orange Association of Manitoba. Seen as a poke in the eye by Orange Order leaders, the omission left the group without the legal standing they coveted. According to one Conservative, Norquay had to bear the responsibility for the lapse. Other accounts, less tinged by Ontarian hostility to Norquay, placed the responsibility on Lieutenant Governor Joseph Cauchon.[113]

Norquay's political course during this three-year assembly can be judged cagey and effective. He asserted Manitoba's authority in the case of branch line charters. Yet he defended the prime minister in debates over federal disallowance of branch line charters. He obtained greater financial support from Ottawa and tried to facilitate as many development projects as possible. Still, he was facing increasingly effective opponents. The Liberal party was moving into provincial politics, and a significant number of outspoken Conservative party members in Manitoba refused to accept his leadership. Given the four-year term permitted by the Manitoba Act, he had to call a general election soon, but before that a federal election would also take place.

Federal Election, June–July 1882, and Provincial Election, January 1883

The federal election of 1882 was held in late June in most of Canada and in early July in Manitoba. The Liberals campaigned effectively in the province, and the Conservatives lost ground, going from victories in three of four Manitoba seats in 1878 to two of five in 1882. As usual, Joseph Royal, re-elected by acclamation, laid some of the blame on Norquay. Although the critique was unreasonable, the criticism illustrated continued divisions in the Conservative ranks.[114]

The fairer observation would be that Norquay had behaved as a loyal Conservative. For every individual who complained about him, several others approved of him. An Ontarian who met Norquay in May 1882 and chatted for an hour reported favourably to the prime minister: "He is very affable and of the right stripe. Mr. Norquay is a thoroughbred Conservative for a certainty." Another business traveller told the prime minister that the local Conservative party was riven by internal disputes and perhaps by corrupt practices but did not include Norquay in his criticism. Macdonald had reached a similar conclusion and decided that a personal campaign visit to the prairies would solve nothing.[115]

Norquay recognized that he would never satisfy some of the Conservative grandees in Winnipeg. An illustration of what he faced appeared in Gilbert McMicken's extraordinary—and fanciful—depiction of the local political scene. McMicken told Macdonald that he planned to "press on the work of ousting Norquay wh[ich] is now the prevailing wish. He has got down to zero in public estimation so that he has no chance of re-election in his own half-breed constituency," a gratuitous slight in itself. This bald-faced attempt to line his own nest and discredit his erstwhile friends was neither credible nor seemly, but it reflected the divided state of Winnipeg Conservatives. As journalist Ned Farrer told Macdonald, "Mr. Norquay is not highly acceptable to old Ontario Conservatives here, but where to get a better man is a question not easily answered."[116]

Once again Norquay faced the decision that confronts every politician as an election nears. Was this the moment to get out of a demanding, uncertain position? He had talked often of leaving politics in the 1870s, had survived a ministerial revolt in 1879, and now was facing a stronger, more confident opposition in the assembly and on public platforms. In late July 1882 Norquay wrote an influential Ottawa acquaintance, John Henry Pope, the minister of agriculture in Macdonald's cabinet, to inquire about the ultimate Canadian political escape, an appointment for life to the Senate. At about the same time Norquay wrote to Sir John A. with the same suggestion. In the letter to Pope he put on a brave front, but the fact of his appeal underlined his unease: "I want the place [the Senate seat] & would like it done soon if the Govt are favourable. . . . The knowledge is of the utmost importance to me here in local politics. . . . I flatter myself that I have earned the position if length of public service is taken into consideration besides which I know that my appointment would be supported by a large majority of the Conservative party."[117]

Pope's reply gave nothing away. The seat was open, Pope said, but he questioned whether Norquay could be spared from Manitoba politics. Besides, the House of Commons, as "a more active House," would be a more attractive venue for a man "of your talent and ability. . . . If I were in your place, I should rather be, at your time of life, in the Commons, or some place other than the Senate."[118] The appointment did not go to Norquay. Instead, Macdonald tapped John Schultz, who had just lost his bid for re-election to the House of Commons and purportedly was near death, to be Manitoba's third representative in the upper house. Norquay could only acquiesce, which he did in a letter to Macdonald a few weeks later: "I don't think you will improve matters by adhering to your decision re senatorship but I suppose gratuitous opinion like advice is never welcome."[119] Schultz lived on to enjoy many more years and several more patronage appointments.

Having to stay in Manitoba and the premier's office, Norquay joined a committee organizing a provincial Conservative convention. The official letter of invitation to delegates noted that federal party lines would impinge on the forthcoming provincial campaign and that Conservatives could not match Liberals' party organization. The invitation also offered an unexpected assurance to the province's rural majority: "Delegates are not asked to meet in Convention to have a policy crammed down their throats. They will number nearly thirty to one as against Winnipeg, and they are asked to adopt a policy of their own making."[120] One might infer that Norquay was asking rural Manitoba Conservatives to attend in large numbers and swamp the Winnipeg Tory elite. Although the real estate bubble had burst, observers believed that Manitoba's economy was still expanding rapidly in the closing months of 1882. Trade (imports plus exports) had amounted to about $8 million in 1880–81, $17 million in 1882, and was predicted to reach at least $30 million in the coming twelve months.[121] But hundreds of farm households and aspiring small-town businesses were complaining, citing their need for branch rail service. Norquay would have to move carefully if he hoped to continue in office.

The announcement in early November that Ottawa was disallowing the three Manitoba railway charters made matters much worse. After two days of deliberation on their response, the "wise men," as Marc Girard described his cabinet colleagues, could not agree. Girard was convinced that Norquay's premiership was going "to bite the dust" and that the federal-provincial conflict could only worsen. Several ministers leaned toward calling a quick session and reintroducing the railway charters. But this path would present a direct challenge to John A. Macdonald and infuriate his Winnipeg loyalists. An early appeal to voters would postpone a confrontation with the federal government, which Norquay clearly preferred. Because the life of the assembly could only be four years, as specified in the Manitoba Act, he would have to call a general election at some point in 1883 in any case. The virtue of a quick election call, from his perspective, was that it would catch the Liberals off guard. After two weeks of reflection the cabinet members agreed to dissolve the house and hold a provincial election.[122]

Conservatives were more divided than ever. Just as Gilbert McMicken voiced the unhappiness of Sir John A.'s loyalists in Winnipeg, so too Joseph Royal, re-elected as a Member of Parliament, furnished the prime minister with a jaundiced view from the Quebecer Conservatives in St. Boniface. Royal was a little kinder to Norquay in that, ironically, he supported him in the short term. But his strategy was to play for a longer transition in which the premier would be ousted *after* winning the election. Royal argued that Norquay was "unpopular for many reasons, yet it is our duty to fortify his position and strengthen his government until better and abler men can be found to take his place and that of his colleagues." There seemed to be little doubt that he saw himself as one of the "better and abler" alternatives. Royal also suggested to Macdonald that any sections of the Mennonite reserve that remained vacant should be opened "to homestead & settlement by white and civilized people."[123] His statements about Mennonite immigrants and Métis offered a St. Boniface supplement to McMicken's racism. Royal concluded a letter to Macdonald with the unusual observation that Norquay "is a Conservative (a halfbreed)." His mention of "halfbreed" in this manner, given that Macdonald would have known that detail, provided another piece of evidence concerning the anti-Norquay prejudice that divided the local party. But Royal, though racist in his dealings with the man who had crushed his attempted party coup in 1879, also said that he would canvass for Norquay: "Let us win victory first; and then we will be able without inconvenience to 'Laver notre linge sale en famille' [wash our dirty linen within the family]." Presumably Norquay, in Royal's estimate, was a stain to be removed.[124]

The election on 23 January 1883 consisted of local competitions rather than a province-wide campaign. Norquay fielded messages from those working on his behalf, writing to allies in many ridings, monitoring the activities of lawyers hired to survey voter lists and challenge individual entries in court, and surveying supporters' efforts to found local newspapers.[125] The campaign itself revolved around railway matters. The Liberals ran on provincial rights, asserted their outright opposition to Macdonald's disallowance measures, and supported an appeal to the imperial government, if necessary, to vindicate the constitutional powers of the province.[126] Norquay had a subtler, more ambiguous, argument. First, he campaigned on "better terms." He claimed that the grants and concessions that Manitoba had won in Ottawa were the result of his friendly relationship with Macdonald. Second, in debates, Norquay tried to be both a defender and an opponent of Sir John's policy. He accomplished this feat by saying that rail lines intended to cross the border to connect with an American line were "beyond local competence" but that lines within the province were a "purely provincial concern." And third, whenever he could get away with it, he added hints about the merits of a non-partisan provincial assembly and the shortcomings of adherence to federal party lines in the local sphere.[127]

This was not a clearly defined, two-party contest. Some candidates could be categorized according to eastern Canada's party lines, but many others could not. On one side of the hustings stood Norquay Conservatives, ultra Conservatives, and Norquay Liberals. On the other stood provincial rights candidates and outright Liberals, all of whom were expected to follow Thomas Greenway, the Liberal leader, in the assembly. William Luxton of the *Manitoba Free Press* devoted his columns to support of the Liberals, but his newspaper reported the election results in two columns under the headings of "Opposition" and "Ministerial." The categories implied that the premier's non-partisan approach to provincial politics would continue in the new legislature.[128]

Norquay and his supporters won a substantial victory in the 1883 contest. His margin in the enlarged legislature (thirty seats) varied a little, but he could count on about twenty supporters, Greenway about ten. The province's politics entered a phase very different from what had existed before. All the Liberals but one were newcomers to the province, five of them born in eastern Canada and four in the British Isles. The Conservatives were more diverse and included four born in old Red River, ten in eastern Canada, four in Britain, and two in Germany.[129] Interpretations of the results varied with the observers. A disappointed William Luxton blamed Norquay's "no party" talk and federal Tory leanings, which, he said, had resulted in voters' choosing "to declare in favour of monopoly." Macdonald, meanwhile, declared the election result in Manitoba a victory for federal government policy. His congratulatory telegram to Norquay, belated and perhaps perfunctory, said the obvious: "Hearty Congratulations Jno A. Macdonald." Neither warmth nor coolness could be read into it. Norquay replied: "Many thanks for your congratulations[,] country safe," implying his allegiance to the Conservative party's federal leader despite the distance between Norquay and Winnipeg Tory notables.[130]

His position was far less certain than it had been in the wake of the 1879 election. Norquay knew full well that his so-called majority depended on uncertain allies, including Macdonald loyalists within the Conservative fold and French-speaking Roman Catholics who would follow LaRivière's lead rather than his own. Still, Norquay could be pleased with his apparent majority and the defeat of the Liberals.

The three years between the elections of November 1879 and January 1883 confirmed that Norquay had become the dominant figure in Manitoba politics. Without question he was the leader of the province and the eloquent champion of its interests. He made impressive gains by introducing the practice of frequent government expeditions to Ottawa, in each of which he played a central role. During these sieges Norquay struck a sufficiently diplomatic tone—not only conciliatory, patient, and genial but also firm—that he obtained a sympathetic hearing and numerous concessions. The civil service remained a work in progress, as evident from the mistakes of Alexander Begg, but it was getting much stronger. Norquay had acquired a familiarity with the range of interests in his rapidly growing province. For the third time in five years, he and his supporters had won a convincing majority in the assembly, where he was acknowledged to be the best-informed and most entertaining speaker. He had yet to adopt a party standard in local politics, however, and both his opponents and some influential Conservatives were pushing him in that direction. Given the province's economic troubles and his personal financial setbacks, Norquay could not rest easy as he entered his third term in office.

CHAPTER 8

The Chief, 1883–February 1885

In the mid-1880s, Canada was sailing headlong toward disaster. The central nation-building project, the Canadian Pacific Railway, faced collapse and appealed to Ottawa for huge cash injections in both 1884 and 1885. Prime Minister John A. Macdonald's policies ran into so much opposition in provincial capitals that disgruntled political leaders in Nova Scotia and Quebec spoke seriously of separating from the Canadian federation. Disputes between Premier Oliver Mowat of Ontario and Macdonald had reached the highest court in the British Empire, the Judicial Committee of the Privy Council. Some recently arrived residents of Manitoba and the North-West Territories, not a majority in either case but significant fractions, talked openly of annexation to the United States. The *Manitoba Free Press* welcomed Premier John Norquay home from his negotiating session in Ottawa in 1885 with an emphatic declaration: "We have already warned the [federal] Government, and we once more tell them, that continued obstinacy on their part will inevitably be followed by the secession of Manitoba from the Dominion."[1] Had there not been an armed resistance movement in the North-West Territories a few months later, a movement that permitted Ottawa to rally all the provinces, the breakup of Canada and the annexation of portions of its territory to the United States could well have taken place. Norquay's stance mattered in these unsettled times, and his ability to balance contending forces marked him as one of confederation's distinguished defenders.

Parkdale

Norquay stood taller in provincial affairs after his election victory in January 1883 and his farm home at Parkdale continued to provide a quiet centre for family life. Little Aida, approaching her second birthday, was a delight and the children were enjoying the novelty of an infant in the house. But suddenly, in April 1883, Aida was stricken with an excruciating pain in her abdomen, probably what has become known as appendicitis. Horace, then fourteen, recalled many years later that he stood behind the door in the Parkdale house and "prayed to God that she might be spared." She died within hours.

Few mentions of Aida have survived the passage of time. There is an entry in the family Bible with her birth and death dates. An invoice in John's office files requested payment of twenty dollars for a "child's coffin." John dictated a letter that explained his absence from a snowshoe club's annual dinner "on account of the recent affliction in my family." In another he apologized for missing the engagement, but "Saturday is the only day that I can get home."[2] Elizabeth, who had been in good health, began to experience weeks of illness once again.

The Norquay children recorded only a few aspects of this period in the family's home life. One child noted in later interviews that they attended church regularly. Another child remembered that "when he [John] was exhausted he would sit in a chair and take a cat nap for 15 minutes, then wake up and be revived and go on with his work." A third said that their father was a great snowshoer. Horace said that the premier was "easy to meet and interesting to talk to. He was good company, and he enjoyed parties and dancing . . . [and] all kinds of reading. In fiction, Dickens and Scott were favourites." The premier also enjoyed facts, all the facts available, and to satisfy his thirst he ordered a twelve-volume version of *Encyclopedia Britannica*.[3]

Norquay stayed at the Parkdale farm less frequently after Aida's death. Unless he was away from the city, he was at the office five or six days of the week. He still regarded Sunday as a day of rest, a day when business was not transacted, and the one day of the week that he had to be home if he was in the province. Norquay welcomed the opening of the railway to Selkirk in August

1883, a service that shortened the journeys home (Parkdale had its own stop) and made family attendance at the St. Andrews Church much easier.[4] He was very busy, his life dominated by both the government's business and his personal investments. This meant that throughout the week he was typically in town, where he found new pastimes to preoccupy him in the hours when he was not working.[5]

Constant attendance in the office left Norquay little time to support Elizabeth. In the language of the day, she suffered from neuralgia, a term that encompassed severe headaches, probably what would be labelled today migraines, and moments of intense pain in specific sites in the body. Some physicians believed that neuralgia could be exacerbated by emotional strain, and it was noted by one that her illnesses sometimes cropped up when John was away. In two separate years, when he was in Ottawa, she lay in bed for days, weakened by pain and fatigue. Doctors attended her on numerous occasions, usually assuring the premier by telegram that the illness was under control and that she would recover.[6]

In February 1884, one of the occasions when John was in Ottawa, twenty-year-old Tom became sufficiently alarmed at his mother's condition that he went to the government offices to ask that his father be informed. Dr. Young of Selkirk was summoned to Parkdale and stayed in touch with the premier by telegraph for the next two weeks. Young's initial report was optimistic: "Since you went away Mrs. Norquay has only had one attack of neuralgia which lasted the usual time, but was followed by a state of great weakness so that she has been confined to bed for the last ten days. I am glad to say however that she is gradually improving. She still feels very weak when she gets up, but as long as she remains in bed feels comparatively well." The premier travelled directly to Parkdale upon his return from Ottawa and stayed with Elizabeth overnight. But the pressures of work did not relent, and he was back in his office a day later.[7] An urban real estate crash and growing rural discontent required his presence, as did rumblings among his own followers in the assembly.

"The Leader of the Great Conservative Party in the Local House"

Most newcomers to Manitoba were Ontarians, and many arrived as dyed-in-the-wool Conservatives or Liberals in federal politics. In their new homes they expressed their partisanship in debates centring on how best to deal with the Conservative government in Ottawa. During the provincial campaign in 1883, party talk had been common, especially among those who claimed to be pure Liberal candidates. After the election William Luxton launched attack after attack on federal Conservative policies in the *Free Press*. It was as if Luxton wished to place all Liberals, and especially recently elected provincial assembly members, on a common policy foundation. Although not as influential or as widely read, the *Winnipeg Times*, also a daily, responded on behalf of federal Conservatives. Norquay's preference, the non-partisan option in local politics, found few advocates.[8]

Norquay called a session of the Legislative Assembly for May 1883. The decisive moments in the birth of Manitoba's party system took place during the next six weeks. The assembly opening took place "with more than the usual éclat" and included "a large turnout of the elite in the city," perhaps because political debate was acquiring a partisan edge that had not been present before. The *Free Press* reported that "flags were flying from a number of flagstaffs . . . and the officers and members of the militia paraded in their uniforms, giving the streets a somewhat martial appearance." The field battery fired the customary salute, and a guard of honour presented arms as the judges, bishops, ministers, and elected members paraded into the assembly's temporary home in the courthouse. The session began with the throne speech, as usual, in French and English. It was delivered by the new lieutenant governor, James Cox Aikins, an Ontarian who had just come to Manitoba after thirty years of service in Ontario and federal politics. Aikins recited conventional words of praise about the "rapid strides" made by the province and listed the promises that Norquay had aired during the recent election campaign. They included plans for a boundary settlement with Ontario, construction of an asylum for the mentally ill, and expansion of the Department of Agriculture and Statistics to meet the demands of the province's burgeoning farm community. But the speech also contained some surprises. The most important was a proposal that Canada should consider revisions to the British North America Act, the basic statute upon which its federal system was constructed. This was a potentially significant departure, probably related to Norquay's insistence on equality among the provinces, and it promised to be controversial within Conservative ranks.[9]

The assembly, seen as a collectivity of thirty, differed considerably from its predecessors. The group was business oriented. Eleven members held commercial roles in their communities, and ten could be described as professionals, including journalists (three), lawyers (three), doctors (two), and surveyors (two), and only eight were farmers.[10] With his many years of experience, Norquay presided over the chamber with ease. He had won the election convincingly and could be expected to dominate proceedings from his seat in the middle of the front row of government benches, where he was flanked by Alphonse LaRivière and Corydon Brown. Norquay intervened in debates with an agreeable and frequently amusing style, spoke forcefully on the major items of legislation, and seemed to be a fixture in the administration of public business in the province. Thomas Greenway again led the opposition. Norquay liked and respected him and was not rattled by his criticisms. The same could be said of all but one of the eight Liberals and provincial rights advocates who sat alongside Greenway. The exception, newcomer Joe Martin, made a difference. He was combative, and his arrival changed the atmosphere of the house.[11]

Norquay believed that he could count on a solid majority. Before the opening session he invited prospective allies to a meeting at which they might "talk over matters." This gathering was the first recorded occasion on which he rallied his caucus in a formal fashion. His message did not mention the Conservative party, a notable omission.[12] It is likely that he hoped to avoid questions about national party affiliation.

In the throne speech debate Greenway and his opposition seatmates focused their attack on Macdonald's National Policy. They criticized Ottawa's disallowance of local railway charters and disparaged its administration of public lands. They claimed to be defending working families required to pay the higher tariffs on imported goods. They also alleged that the local government was corrupt and incompetent. It was clear that the opposition was finding its feet.[13]

In his hour-long contribution to the throne speech debate, Norquay set out the platform that had been part of his electoral campaign. The most important plank addressed rail service for newly settled farm households. Although he supported the immediate construction of branch railways, the premier insisted that Manitoba did not have the constitutional power to charter railways to the boundary where they might connect with an American line. He also elaborated on the paragraph in the throne speech concerning the British North America Act. The confederation statute of 1867, passed by Parliament in Great Britain, was due for a "readjustment," he said, and a convention of delegates from all the provinces should consider the issue. Such a meeting would raise the west's profile in eastern Canada and clarify the constitutional powers of the two levels of government. His approach would also "render uniform the basis upon which subsidies are granted to the provinces." Norquay concluded with the observation that no other member of the Manitoba assembly of 1871, the first in the province's history, was still in the house. The fact that he remained in office showed that "the public had confidence in him." He was not a party leader, but "he had as good, if not a better claim: he had principles, and he was not ashamed to stand by and uphold them . . . (Cheers)." Norquay sat down "amid loud cheers."[14]

His declaration that he was not a party leader surprised some of his colleagues. During the election campaign he had claimed to be both a Conservative and a non-partisan. It was well known that he and William Luxton had worked for nearly a decade to keep parties out of local affairs, claiming that a non-partisan stance would win concessions in Ottawa from either party, whereas a Manitoba government could be left out in the cold if the national administration switched from Conservative to Liberal and back, as it did in the 1870s. But Macdonald had been re-elected as prime minister in 1882, and the advantages of non-partisanship now seemed to be less obvious. That might explain why Luxton had been so fierce in his condemnation of Macdonald's National Policy: Luxton was pushing Norquay to take a stand on national policies and, by implication, provincial party organization.

The premier faced a moment of decision. His allies were telling him that he had to choose, and Macdonald loyalists were spoiling for a fight if he ducked the issue. In truth he was little moved by the partisan loyalties that surrounded him. When an old friend, R.W. Rossiter of Portage la Prairie, fell on hard times, Norquay intervened: "I shall do what I can both as a matter of duty & good will to old Ross, although he is such a great old Grit, which in the matter of friendship, you know, weighs very little with me."[15]

When the assembly was ready to vote on the reply to the throne speech, the key test of the people's confidence in their government, Norquay decided that he had to take the plunge. Henceforth, he told the members, he was a Conservative in local politics. At a public meeting shortly thereafter, he said that he wanted to remove any doubt about whether his was a party government. A *Winnipeg Times* report said that "he made the announcement amid great applause that if there was a doubt in the minds of any with regard to his government he wanted that doubt removed from their minds, as from that day forward his government would be run on strict party lines, and he hoped they would consider him the leader of the great Conservative party in the Local House."[16]

Hugh John Macdonald put a sharper point on Norquay's situation. He explained to his father that "Norquay had a pretty narrow escape on the Address, but as soon as he declared himself a Party man his followers wheeled into line and voted for him like men. He is safe now if he does not intrigue with Greenway & Co." In the division on the reply, Norquay's government was supported by eighteen votes to eight.[17]

Norquay adjusted slowly to the new reality of a party system. Through the summer he supported both major daily papers in Winnipeg, giving printing contracts to each in turn while ignoring their jibes. That even-handedness could not be sustained. His secretary, Arthur Wesley Pritchard, told him in the early autumn that he was losing ground. The federal Conservatives' *Winnipeg Times* was treating him rudely, and Luxton's *Free Press*, always Liberal in outlook, was becoming "very bitter" in its attacks: "It seems presumptuous in me to advise such an old Chief as yourself [Norquay was forty-two, Pritchard twenty-six] and if I am wrong I hope you will overlook it. . . . Luxton may be an old friend of yours personally but politically he is a great enemy and he should not have the patronage." Still, the *Free Press* frequently defended Norquay and spoke kindly of him in the months that followed.[18]

Governing

The government had actually made great strides in managing its affairs despite the partisan atmosphere. One seemingly small event stood out. Norquay's selection of an office administrator transformed the government's inner circle. Arthur Pritchard might have been young, but his experience was impressive. Born in Ontario, he had received rigorous training as a jack-of-all-trades in railway offices and as a secretary for senior executives. He moved to the Manitoba South-Western and then the Portage & Westbourne railways, and entered the premier's office in the spring of 1883. Pritchard became a source of ideas, energy, and discipline.[19] With his arrival, the premier found his work easier and his effectiveness as spokesperson for the province enhanced. The timing could not have been more fortuitous, as it happened, because stormy days were coming.

Flattery and deference accompanied frankness and an ingratiating prose style in Pritchard's dealings with his boss, whom Pritchard addressed in correspondence as "My dear Chief." As office manager, he wrought an important change in the premier's and the government's record keeping. He ensured that files of incoming letters and volumes of onion-skin letterbooks were indexed and readily retrievable. Private correspondence was confined to one letterbook, official government correspondence to another. Pritchard responded quickly to issues, either by transferring a topic to a government department or by dispatching a letter from the premier's office. He explained to the premier, with just a little soft soap, "I am aware that one who is intrusted with the weighty responsibilities of state cannot be expected to give that attendance to minor matters which they may demand and with this end in view I would get a *private book* for filing such matters and if notes or anything which required payment at a certain time remind you of the same when that time arrived." Discretion was his watchword. When he discovered some letters from the former deputy treasurer, Alexander Begg, concerning government bookkeeping, Pritchard assured Norquay that Begg's successor "will keep them under lock and key and from anyone's observation but his own."[20]

The cabinet that Norquay assembled during the 1883–86 term could not be faulted on grounds of ability or strength in the house. Its composition reflected the society that had elected the new legislative contingent. One member had to be a francophone Roman Catholic who had the ear of the archbishop and could speak convincingly in French to that community. Another should represent the largest city, Winnipeg. Yet another should represent the new settlements in southern and western Manitoba peopled mainly by immigrants from Ontario. One should be a lawyer who, by virtue of membership in the Manitoba bar, could fulfill the legal duties of the attorney general. Ideally each of these individuals would have legislative experience. Norquay's choices included Alphonse LaRivière (francophone); Alex Sutherland, James Miller, and Charles Hamilton (Winnipeg lawyers who held the attorney generalship in succession); Dr. David Wilson (southern Manitoba); and Corydon Brown (northwestern Manitoba). Aside from Sutherland, who died after only a few months in office, Norquay was the only cabinet minister to have grown up in old Assiniboia.

The cabinet members were relatively young, articulate, and competent. They worked well together and agreed that the premier should have the final word. Their relations with Norquay constituted another source of testimony concerning his character and comportment. The extant correspondence between ministers and premier, a few dozen letters in total, is marked by informality and respect. The commanding tone evident in the letters to Norquay written by Joseph Royal and David Marr Walker, ministers in the pre-1883 years, was not present in the letters written by the later group. The new cabinet members enjoyed some valuable perquisites, notably passes that railway companies allocated to ministers. Three went on to distinguished careers in later life, Hamilton in St. Paul, Minnesota; Wilson in Vancouver; and LaRivière in the House of Commons and Senate of Canada.[21]

Norquay worked hard on public and private business. He frequently observed that he could not get away from the office and cabinet meetings to enjoy his favourite pastime, hunting wildfowl. As he told a colleague in the spring of 1884, "I wired you to say I can't visit on 4th or 5th. I am so occupied in preparing the work for the session and in other matters that I cannot leave the city even to go home."[22] Norquay maintained regular hours, telling one inquiring visitor that he would be "in my office every day between the hours of 10 and 4 unless something special should call me away." His working language was English, though French and Cree appeared in his files. And he was productive. In three weeks at the beginning of autumn 1885, Norquay dispatched fifty pages of correspondence, all carefully copied into one of his official letterbooks, and another thirty pages into his private letterbook. He took more complete control of the public voice of the government in the summer of 1885 when he ordered that only ministers and deputy ministers were to give out information to the press.[23]

Alphonse LaRivière was the francophone community's representative in the cabinet after Joseph Royal moved to the House of Commons. His relations with Norquay were cordial on the surface and complicated below. The fact that LaRivière and Royal had conspired against the premier, thus precipitating the ministerial crisis in 1879, sowed distrust, but in their correspondence, at least, he communicated with Norquay in a polite, formal, but always friendly manner. He was potentially a source of instability because he leaked news of cabinet discussions to both the CPR and John A. Macdonald.[24]

Although LaRivière acknowledged Norquay's leadership, he could not be counted a sure supporter.

Corydon Brown promoted more development projects and caused more problems than any other member of cabinet. As public works minister he supervised road contracts and excavation of drainage ditches in rural areas, responsibilities that linked him to land speculators, notably eastern entrepreneur William Eli Sanford. Brown also owned several businesses, including a newspaper and a sawmill, and joined others in developing a bank and an important branch railway, eventually known as the Manitoba & North-West. Many of his schemes involved Norquay, whether as investor, director, or political ally. When Brown selected land for the provincial asylum, a site in which Norquay had an interest, he testified blandly before a royal commission hearing: "I try to run my department on business principles and what was in my mind in determining on the site was its eligibility for the purpose." His dealings with the premier were conducted in an amiable, businesslike style.[25] Nevertheless, Brown, like LaRivière, could not be relied on to serve Norquay loyally, as became apparent several years later.

One of this group did not complete the full legislative term. Alex Sutherland, a Winnipeg lawyer, grew up in the Red River Settlement, attended local schools, and graduated from the University of Toronto. First elected to the assembly in 1878 at the age of twenty-nine, he earned his stripes in debate and was invited by the premier to join the cabinet as attorney general in 1882. He did not speak frequently in the assembly, but when he did, he won attention. While Norquay was in Ottawa in February 1884, Sutherland contracted typhoid fever and died. The cabinet called a state funeral, businesses closed, and a huge procession followed the casket to the Old Kildonan cemetery. This vigorous debater and potential leader who possessed significant ties to old Red River became a "might have been." The loss played a part in the premier's trials two and three years later.[26]

Norquay selected David Wilson from among the new cohort of assembly members to join the cabinet in 1884. A medical doctor then practising in southern Manitoba, Wilson had completed two degrees in Toronto, one at Trinity College, where he was a gold medallist, the other in medicine. He got along well with the premier and, perhaps because he was only twenty-nine years old and new to the assembly, deferred to him in a genial fashion. Writing to Norquay from Ottawa, he said that he was enjoying the trip, "but Great

Scott! Everything is dull here." Wilson became a good soldier in the cabinet, supportive, reliable, and capable.[27]

The one serious mistake in cabinet making took place when Norquay filled the vacancy left by Alex Sutherland's death. The appointment and sudden departure of James Miller, a rookie politician, illustrated the instability of the community in the mid-1880s.[28] The flashpoint came when a young man stole some jewellery in a brothel, was arrested, and then tried to break out of the Vaughan Street jail. The young man received twelve lashes in an unpleasant scene witnessed by a group of leading citizens, including new Attorney General Miller, who gave tacit assent if not formal approval to the punishment. The use of the lash was publicized dramatically by the *Winnipeg Times* and provoked a protest meeting. Several hundred citizens heard that Attorney General Miller had ordered the whipping (probably not true) and was present when it was administered (true).

In the following evening, 31 October, a crowd numbering from 2,000 to 4,000 (in a city that could claim only 20,000 residents) gathered on Portage Avenue and marched through the streets singing a local version of an American Civil War tune, "we will hang Jim Miller from a sour apple tree." When they reached the legislature, Norquay spoke to them humorously, noted the attorney general's "good luck" at being out of town at that moment, promised that the cabinet would review the flogging, and won a salute of three cheers. The premier's confident, breezy, good-natured performance delayed the protesters long enough for a militia troop to assemble on Broadway, bayonets fixed. The anger dissipated, and the protesters merely burned an effigy of "Miller the brute," the third likeness to go up in flames that night. They then walked over to the *Free Press* offices, where editor Luxton condemned the jailer's resort to the lash and, well after midnight, the crowd eventually dispersed.[29] The rapid assembling of troops, an unexpected assist from the Canadian Pacific Railway, and Norquay's calm demeanour averted a potentially serious battle in the streets. A month after the event, the popular outcry having remained strong, Norquay dismissed Miller, who found his reward within months when an appointment to a post in the civil service ensured his silence.[30]

What can be taken from the episode? Miller placed a high priority on order and did not like to back down. He continued to defend the punishment and said that he would do the same again. Norquay did not condone the threat of riotous behaviour, acted quickly in the moment of crisis, and conceded that a significant proportion of the public condemned the jailer's resort to the lash. Having taken the time to gauge the community's reaction, Norquay chose to abandon his attorney general. The larger lesson concerned the lash and the crowd. Miller believed that the state had to be seen to be consistent and able to crush dissent. Norquay recognized the necessity of quelling a potential riot. His official thank you to the Canadian Pacific Railway, where the executive officer had delayed labourers planning to join the protest, underlined how volatile the situation had been. His dismissal of the attorney general, taken together with his sure handling of the crowd on the legislature's steps, illustrated his flexibility and his ability to convey authority in the face of potential rioters. His handling of the episode demonstrated that he was, without question, the pre-eminent voice in government. The confidence he projected during the Hallowe'en incident would be required when he faced more difficult challenges, particularly the renewal of negotiations with Ottawa.

Better Terms

Norquay's political calculations continued to centre on John A. Macdonald. How could the premier convince the prime minister not to treat the prairie west as a mere colony? Manitobans were being penalized, he argued repeatedly, because the rest of the country benefited from advantages to which they did not have access. They lost the revenue from public lands and resources that belonged to all the other provincial governments. They paid higher freight rates than eastern Canadians. They were prevented from building branch lines that would introduce better service and greater competition. They had to contend with a distant, rigid lands bureaucracy. The list went on. As a consequence of constitutional arrangements and political decisions imposed during Manitoba's founding months, Norquay's relationships with Macdonald, his ministers, and senior civil servants had become crucial to his political survival. Year after year Norquay faced the same question: which strategy—smiles or threats or outright breaches—would be more likely to produce gains for the province?

Although he had won concessions in previous negotiations, he knew that a renewal of the campaign would not be received well in Ottawa. What Norquay did not know was that Macdonald believed the Manitoba election of 1883 had constituted an endorsement of federal policy. The prime minister argued that the provincial campaign had focused on the CPR charter and the federal disallowance of Manitoba's branch railway charters, not on the administration of the Norquay government. The prime minister wrote to George Stephen, president of the Canadian Pacific Railway, as soon as the results reached him: "Our policy has been sustained by 19 to 11, the House being composed of 30, I believe. This makes plain sailing for us." In the prime minister's mind the Manitoba election had been not a provincial story but a national one. Macdonald had emerged the victor.[31]

Norquay opened the next phase of the "better terms" for Manitoba campaign in March 1883. He worked with his colleagues to create a cabinet memorandum that developed several new arguments, culminating with the statement that increased immigration to Manitoba, though on the surface highly desirable, "would be nothing short of an evil in disguise" because it would increase local government costs. It was an impressive document, judged by historian Chester Martin to be "very able" and worthy to be "classed among the important state papers of the Dominion."[32]

One of the premier's new themes was the interprovincial boundary dispute arising from conflicting claims by Ontario and Manitoba over potentially valuable mines near Lake of the Woods. Another was the relative impact of the federal tariff on each of the provinces. A third, taking direct aim at Macdonald's determination to control land policy, declared that the general election testified to "unanimous opinion" in Manitoba that it should be treated like other provinces in terms of the ownership of lands and resources. The ten-year embargo on further Manitoba talks, publicized in the federal finance minister's budget speech, was declared unacceptable: in the meetings of 1882 "the term of ten years was not mentioned, either in the verbal or written negotiations on the subject." This was good material, expressed vigorously, and it demonstrated Norquay's continuing determination to battle for the province.[33]

The formal statement was followed by a letter from Norquay to the prime minister. It, too, went through several drafts, the first aggressive, the second more restrained though still urgent, and the third, less antagonistic, that was finally dispatched near the end of March 1883. Norquay argued that, in addition to being accorded equal treatment as a province like the others, Manitoba faced exceptional circumstances because there was no historical precedent for the pace or scale of its development. Although newcomers to the province were accustomed to advanced institutions and services, the government could not afford such modernization and was being treated merely as "a creature of the Dominion." Norquay did not assume that success would come quickly. In effect he was opening a new discussion and expected to work on these proposals for some time to come.[34]

The prime minister paid attention to Norquay's pleas. In June 1883, in the face of yet another appeal from Manitoba, this time for an advance on school land revenues, Macdonald sent a note to Minister of Justice Alexander Campbell asking for some help in preparing for cabinet deliberations: "Norquay is insatiable. Will you look into this last demand of Norquay's for Tuesday's meeting of Council. Look at the last agreement & the amounts already advanced on School fund a/c."[35] The note demonstrated that Macdonald was taking the issues seriously and willing to go some distance to support the Manitoba premier.

The two men worked in concert through the rest of the year. One sphere in which they saw eye to eye concerned the boundary between Ontario and Manitoba. Oliver Mowat, the premier of Ontario, proposed that the line should be drawn west of Lake of the Woods, thus expanding his province enormously. Norquay saw little benefit for Manitoba in acquiring the tract, given that Ottawa would control its development and revenues under the present rules concerning prairie public lands and natural resources. Still, he suggested that the line should be drawn at a point 600 kilometres farther east, at Thunder Bay on the western end of Lake Superior, giving his province a more important role in the future confederation. Macdonald claimed to agree. When squabbles broke out between two competing police forces, led respectively by Manitobans and Ontarians at Rat Portage (Kenora, Lake of the Woods), the prime minister wrote to Norquay to say that he was "greatly pleased to see the manly course you have adopted." He labelled Premier Mowat's proposed boundary as "most indecent" and concluded his letter soothingly: "Keep your ground and you will have all the support that I can give you." It was idle talk.[36]

The summer and fall of 1883 were much busier than Norquay had expected. His private coal, gold, and land interests encroached on his time almost daily while the government's administrative duties remained demanding. He wrote to assembly colleague David Harrison that he regretted

> very much that I am so pressed with business here that I cannot devote more time to going through the country for really it is more in accordance with my wishes that I should be roaming over the prairie than be sitting here in an office, but with the Rat Portage election and the war of authority between Mowat and myself raging it scarcely does for me to absent myself for any length of time from the office. By the month of October however one of us [Mowat or Norquay] will have to bite the dust, when I hope to have some duck & prairie chicken shooting with you.[37]

It was a vain hope erased by a deep frost in the farming districts that devastated so many families and challenged the very foundation of agriculture on the prairies.

Farm Province

By the mid-1880s Manitoba had taken on the appearance of a typical North American farming community. In common with its Midwestern American neighbours, it relied heavily on grain and animal exports. Just over 12 million of the 16 million acres of surveyed land available for distribution had been disposed of, and 4 million of the 12 million had actually been "occupied." Furs were still an important export, but the government devoted almost all of its attention to developing a wheat economy.[38]

With the bursting of the speculative land bubble in 1882, Winnipeg's 20–25,000 residents faced an economic recession that did not lift for several years. The nearly 100,000 people in the rest of the province, most of whom had close connections to agriculture, encountered different economic challenges.[39] They needed branch railways and lower freight rates. Their lives were made more difficult by federal tariffs on imports and by prices set by land speculators, grain buyers, money lenders, and millers.[40] These families brought assumptions with them about the environment and cultivation practices that would doom them to heartache and require significant overhaul. They also carried with them political party loyalties. The combination—partisan assumptions and economic challenges—ran headlong into the wall of Macdonald's National Policy. Norquay had to deal with the potent brew.

A deep frost on 7 and 8 September 1883 plunged the province into despair. The freeze devastated ripening field crops. Hopes that exports might reach 2.5 million bushels of wheat (compared with only 500,000 the year before) were dashed. The collapse of the Winnipeg boom, the late-summer frost, low grain prices, high Canadian tariffs on imported goods, and high Canadian freight rates challenged all the fine talk of western wealth. Dozens of farm families left for the United States. Norquay lamented that he was inundated with applicants seeking work and said that he found it "difficult to provide a slight pittance for them all." In turning down the appeal of yet another needy applicant, he cited "the continued depression of business in this City."[41]

James Wickes Taylor, the American consul in Winnipeg and an experienced observer of the transborder region, reported in November 1883 that "public opinion is far from cheerful . . . great disappointment and irritation in many quarters." He hinted that the future of Manitoba and the North-West Territories might yet lie with the United States. Three months later he sent a perceptive assessment of the crisis in prairie agriculture, south as well as north of the border, to the State Department in Washington and offered an important conclusion: "There is no serious purpose of forcible separation from Eastern Canada, although the number who believe that the speediest and surest prosperity of Manitoba would be obtained by union with the United States is greatly increased by recent events." The *Free Press* downplayed talk of secession from the Canadian federation but warned that such sentiments would become more common if the region was relegated to "the lofty purpose of ministering to the avarice of Quebec and Ontario." Prime Minister Macdonald was right to worry about the destiny of prairie Canada in these tough times.[42]

Farmers began to organize in the autumn of 1883, working in two organizations with nearly the same purpose but different leaderships, districts, and focus: the Manitoba and NorthWest Farmers' Union and the Manitoba and NorthWest Farmers' Protective Union. During their first year both groups developed platforms and strategies to defend the newly settled communities in the southwest of the province.[43] In the interim the worries of these new settlers attempting to adapt to prairie conditions stood front and centre in provincial affairs.

A farmers' convention in Winnipeg in December 1883 brought rural issues into sharp focus, particularly the CPR monopoly. The Liberals under Leader of the Opposition Thomas Greenway endorsed the farmers' platform in its entirety. One of Norquay's business colleagues said that the hostility toward the federal government and the CPR was so great that it could end in "rebellion." Manitoba's new lieutenant governor, James Cox Aikins, wrote to the prime minister to warn him of impending trouble.[44] The next alternative, agitators proposed, was a new railway northward to the historic prairie outlet on Hudson Bay. Since so much of the criticism was aimed at Macdonald's National Policy, Norquay, now facing the world as a partisan Conservative, had to navigate these waters carefully. While sympathizing with the farm union delegates, he temporized on the railway to Hudson Bay and rejected their demand for a line to the American border.[45]

Ottawa Negotiations, 1884

The uncertainty associated with political life continued to give Norquay concern. At some point in late 1883 or early 1884, he told his oldest son, Tom, that he was thinking of resigning from the position of premier. The issue might have arisen because, in these very months, rumours abounded about unrest among the Conservative elite in Winnipeg and about Norquay's possible elevation to the federal cabinet. Luxton of the *Free Press* wrote to tell him that "it seems to go by the most common consent here that you are the coming man. . . . I am quite confident that it would be received with very general satisfaction throughout the province."[46]

In January 1884 Norquay travelled to Ottawa, accompanied by rumours that he would soon be called to Macdonald's cabinet. In the eyes of prairie observers, such representation for the province was a "right," and the seniority of the premier made him the obvious choice.[47] That he was taking the rumour seriously can be gleaned from the testimony of a provincial civil servant: "You will remember asking me as regards your chances of election in the city should you conclude to run," he wrote to Norquay. "I have enquired quietly & carefully and the feeling amongst all parties (and the Grits have talked it over) is that you would go in by acclamation."[48]

The premier had three objectives for this expedition: he sought a boundary extension to the north; development of the vast northland, including a railway to and a survey of navigation potential in Hudson Bay; and provincial control of public lands and resources given that the present system was an "anomaly." He emphasized the rise of dissatisfaction among recently arrived families in the hope that this pressure would cause Macdonald to change his course. Norquay gave an interview to a Montreal newspaper that a Manitoba colleague judged to be "vague ominous & foreboding especially in regard to the annexation feeling here. On the whole I think excellent. Stick to it and we cannot fail to succeed."[49]

Norquay had difficulty getting Macdonald to deal with him. The premier cooled his heels for two weeks in Ottawa, biding the time by meeting with civil servants on numerous land issues. He had his photo taken at the Notman studio again. He visited Montreal. And he enjoyed the hospitality of Russell House and the Queen's Hotel, including plenty of oysters, cigars, wine, and whiskey for his large delegation. The summit meeting took place on the morning of 6 February at Macdonald's home, Earnscliffe. Norquay was accompanied by four members of the Legislative Assembly of Manitoba and three of Manitoba's representatives in Ottawa, including one senator and two MPs. The focus of their presentation, Norquay explained, was the claim that Manitoba was Canada's "most profitable" province.[50] This was a new line of argument drawn from calculations of tariff revenue per capita flowing into the federal government's coffers. It might have had some effect. Macdonald then proposed that the delegation meet with a subcommittee of the federal cabinet.

Three more days passed. Telegrams informing John that Elizabeth was unwell convinced him that he should hasten home. He wrote to Macdonald to say that he would have to leave, promising that Manitoba would agree to be bound by a decision of the Judicial Committee of the Privy Council, then Canada's highest court, on its boundary with Ontario. "Excuse me for troubling you today," Norquay wrote, "but I have received word from home that Mrs. Norquay is seriously ill, and will have to leave very probably tomorrow night." He asked Macdonald to "please arrange a meeting for tomorrow" of the Manitobans and some representatives of the federal cabinet. Macdonald acted quickly. Minister of the Interior David Macpherson, Minister of Finance Samuel Leonard Tilley, and Macdonald's Quebec lieutenant, Hector-Louis Langevin (senior ministers all), listened to the delegation's case but made no commitments.[51]

Norquay then waited in the capital for another week. More oysters, soups, partridges, wines, and cigars. Another letter to Sir John A., this time enclosing a telegram from Winnipeg reporting that "the excitement on the extension of the provincial boundaries is intense and seems to be increasing rather than abating." Once again he urged Macdonald to give him "an answer soon." Finally, on 19 February, Norquay sent a note to David Macpherson declaring that "I find that I have to leave for home tonight and would feel extremely obliged if you could have an answer to the memorandum now before the Privy Council, on Manitoba claims." None came, Norquay delayed again, and then he left on 22 February.[52]

When Macdonald sent a telegram to the train, suggesting that he return, Norquay wired back asking for assurance that a deal could be arranged. Receiving none, he continued westward. In an interview with the St. Paul *Pioneer Press* during a stopover, he offered Minnesotans a detailed summary of the protracted visit and responded bluntly to the question of what he might do next. The answer, he said, was to go over the head of the Canadian government and appeal directly to Parliament in the United Kingdom.[53]

A volley of letters and telegrams in February and March 1884 attested to the increasing strength of the protest movement in Manitoba. Even the province's lieutenant governor, James Cox Aikins, warned Macdonald that "the agitation here will not fully subside until the lands in the province are handed over to the local government." Norquay's return "empty-handed," as the *Manitoba Free Press* put it, inspired its scathing editorial about "this section of the Dominion" being administered "solely in the interests of the East." This was the moment when editor Luxton warned that Manitoba could secede from Canada if Macdonald's policies did not change. His *Free Press* called on Norquay to reject the meagre concessions offered by Ottawa.[54]

By refusing to accept Macdonald's terms, Norquay neutralized his local opponents' criticisms. His friend James Colcleugh of Selkirk predicted that the premier would easily win a provincial general election on the issue of provincial rights and better terms. Cabinet Minister Corydon Brown warned Prime Minister Macdonald that the failure of Norquay's mission was serious: "It looked as if the devil was to pay here." He emphasized to Macdonald that "there is grave cause for anxiety" in Manitoba because the Norquay government could fall, leaving "more impetuous men than *even we* [Brown's emphasis]" in control of the province. Brown said that he had been talking to the chief justice and the lieutenant governor and advised Sir John A. to make one key concession: hand over control of public lands and resources to the province. He also emphasized that all the talk of western secession was "bosh."[55]

Norquay saw no sign of a federal cabinet appointment when he was in Ottawa. Pressed about it on his return, he dismissed the idea. As he told a correspondent who had offered congratulations, "I have neither been appointed to a seat in the Government at Ottawa nor am I likely to be. My own opinion is that the report was got up with a view to injure my cause [referring to his canvassing for a ministerial candidate in a recent Winnipeg by-election]."[56]

Within ten days of his getting on the train in Ottawa, Norquay received a wire from John A. Macdonald saying that the Hudson Bay railway would be supported by the federal government. Manitoba submitted another memorandum on its proposals in early March 1884. A subcommittee of the federal cabinet gave it careful attention. Its extensive analysis of the Manitoba arguments demonstrated that Macdonald wished to continue negotiations. The outcome of this process, a document dated 1 April 1884, was closely argued and thorough.[57] His hand was evident in his carefully worded reply.

The prime minister took on Norquay's arguments and offered his own tendentious version of prairie history. In this interpretation the northwestern interior of North America had been owned by the Hudson's Bay Company by grant from the British Crown. With the transfer in 1870 the government of Canada took possession of "all the rights, title, and interest" of the company. Having acquired this vast acreage of real property, Canada then hived off one small part of that territory as the province of Manitoba. The acquisition of the entire region demanded that Canada pay "a large price in cash." Then, because of the resistance movement in 1869–70, Canada spent more money "to obtain . . . peaceable possession," a reference to the military expedition led by Colonel Garnet Wolseley and the subsequent occupation by the Canadian militia. Ottawa also spent money extinguishing Indigenous title and maintaining these communities. In the words of the cabinet document, Canada had "a very large pecuniary interest in the soil, which does not exist in respect to any other of the confederated provinces."[58] The west had been bought and paid for and was owned outright by the rest of Canada, in this interpretation, an imperial view that Norquay had warned listeners about in the preceding months.

Despite subsequent western protests, Macdonald refused to bend.[59] Having paid attention to Norquay's assurances in their meetings, he was convinced that "the great bulk of the people of Manitoba are thoroughly loyal to the Confederation."[60] Besides, Manitoba's agitation did not count for very much in the bigger picture of national affairs. Just how much was evident in a letter that Sir John A. wrote to Lord Lorne, the former governor general. His calm outline of federal-provincial relations began with Quebec, where once again he had "bought off" his "French friends," as he put it; he had satisfied petitioners from British Columbia, and had played a "bold game" to rescue the CPR. "And now," he added, he had "only Manitoba to deal with." In its case he blamed the speculators who fell in the real estate crash plus "some democrats" who "blustered." He told Lorne that he was not much worried about the radicals in the farmers' union who "talked of secession and all that sort of thing." He also said, based upon his correspondents' advice, that "the reaction has set in." He expressed his confidence in Norquay while adding an unexpected qualification: "Norquay who with many faults & weaknesses is loyal to the Dominion has been sustained by an overwhelming vote, 20 to 6, on certain factious amend[men]ts to the speech at the opening of the Manitoba session."[61] The prime minister's emphasis on the premier's loyalty to Canada mattered a great deal. But the phrase "faults & weaknesses" was left hanging in the air without elaboration.

Macdonald's letter to Lorne conveyed two other messages. The prime minister continued to have sympathy for Manitobans' circumstances and to believe that farmers would revise their opinions of national policies when they harvested a good crop: "We are doing all that we can to help them within reasonable limits and on the opening of the spring, when the people are on their farms, the agitation will be forgotten." And he was paying attention to the security situation in the west: "The threat of a Fenian Raid is much more serious as we have no means just now of sending a military force to Winnipeg." He added that, fortunately, there were few Irish Roman Catholics in Manitoba and the Fenians had little or no support there.[62]

Macdonald did try to help Norquay. The federal cabinet subcommittee moved some distance in the negotiations that took place between the beginning of March and mid-April 1884. Ministers decided against increasing the size of the province (they viewed it as very large compared with the others and possibly about to be increased in size, depending on the Ontario boundary settlement), but they would support the Hudson Bay railway with a grant of lands along its corridor, and they agreed to dispatch a seaborne expedition to the Arctic to secure more information about sea ice and shipping challenges. They would investigate Ottawa's financial relations with the Manitoba government and revise the federal grant four times per decade (rather than just once) until the provincial population reached a total of 400,000, the first such revision to take place in the autumn. The request for provincial control over school lands was denied, and so was the request for control over the rest of public lands and resources. But a formal financial inquiry would investigate the claims about lost revenue associated with Ottawa's ownership of the lands and natural resources.[63]

Macdonald had shown flexibility on the details while adhering to his long-standing policy positions.[64] His proposals represented one vision of Canadian development. They showed little interest in Norquay's actual arguments. They did not even address Manitoba's statements about the equality of the provinces. Nor would he consider the idea that provinces, within their separate spheres, possessed powers equivalent to those exercised by the federal government within its sphere.

Rural Disappointment and Secession Talk

The farmers' union scheduled another conference for 5 March 1884, anticipating that it could push the federal government into making concessions. Its campaign came to a screeching halt on the meeting's opening day. By adding to their list of demands a call for cessation of immigration to the prairies (some delegates even advocated outright western secession from Canada), outspoken union members discredited the entire movement. The prime minister's informant in Winnipeg, Gilbert McMicken, immediately advised Macdonald to "be firm[.] Farmers Convention overreached themselves[.] Reaction set in. Look for satisfactory development in few days." The worries in Ottawa, exemplified by a telegram asking Norquay to intervene, suddenly seemed to be overwrought.[65]

Conservatives such as McMicken, Macdonald followers first and Norquay supporters a distant second, took heart. The Manitoba protesters had overstepped the bounds of acceptable debate. But these federal Tory loyalists also looked askance at Norquay's quest for compromises. One of their number, Hugh John Macdonald, scoffed at the "claptrap" uttered by farmers' union "agitators" and said that the talk of secession and rebellion was the work of a small minority. The bigger issue, he told his father, the prime minister, was that Norquay's criticisms of the federal government made the premier "the hero of the hour, and [he] appears to like it. I don't know what his game is and am watching carefully how he plays his cards." Referring to the deal being arranged between Manitoba and Ottawa on the Hudson Bay railway, he offered the sly judgement that Norquay and Corydon Brown "would both take good care to make as much as they could out of it." His jaundiced view of the premier illustrated how difficult it would be for Norquay to hold a majority together in the assembly, let alone in the Conservative party or the wider community.[66]

Throughout these months Prime Minister Macdonald kept a close watch on events in Manitoba. In a series of letters to the governor general, Lord Lansdowne, he underlined the issues that might affect the west's relations with adjacent American states. At the end of February 1884, enclosing an extract from the Chicago *Tribune*, he spoke cautiously about the Winnipeg convention of the farmers' union: "There may be some Fenian movement in connection with this meeting." When that protest fizzled Macdonald sent Lansdowne a copy of a private letter from Lieutenant Governor of Manitoba James Aikins recommending that the American government be warned about "the threats & rumours of invasion" bubbling within its own borders. Macdonald also noted that Aikins warned against permitting American troops to cross the frontier if a Fenian invasion occurred. By the summer of 1884 the prime minister was advising the governor general that "Norquay believes in a secret plot among the Farmers Union to give trouble. The HalfBreeds at Prince Albert are starving and sulky." By late summer Macdonald was more optimistic once again, claiming that a good harvest and sober second thought had taken the farmers out of the grip of speculators who led their union: "It is done," he wrote optimistically. He was wrong.[67]

International notice of Manitoba, which had spiked in the 1870s and during the boom of 1881–82, peaked in 1884. The province would rarely again enjoy such a high profile in the English-speaking world. News of the farmers' union protests reached the eastern United States, where rumours circulated about the possibility of prairie Canada's secession from confederation. A newspaper story sent to Prime Minister Macdonald said that Irish agents, though based in New York, were responsible for unrest in Manitoba. In a letter to Britain's colonial secretary, the Earl of Derby, Governor General Lord Lansdowne mentioned a rumoured Fenian raid on Manitoba. In his unusual reply Derby advised Lansdowne to warn the Canadian cabinet not to take such threats lightly, "as they might be inclined to do." He worried about "Fenians and Irish Americans" who would try to exploit the "weak . . . ties which bind together a newly-made federation, which has no fresh history of common action to look back upon, and has not become habituated to the restraints which federal union imposes. This is a little spark as yet, but it may grow into a great fire."[68] These perceptive thoughts reached Ottawa just a year before violence erupted in the North-West Territories.

Liberal newspapers in Manitoba tried to capitalize on the farmers' plight by blaming Conservatives for rural troubles. Luxton at the *Manitoba Free Press* led the way, arguing that the premier's alignment with the Conservative government in Ottawa betrayed the farm community. The opposition's campaign was especially influential in western and southwestern Manitoba. Distant from Winnipeg, recently settled by families unaware of the history of the Red River Settlement or of political debates during the province's first decade, they found their mouthpiece in the *Brandon Sun*. Describing a meeting between Norquay and farmers' union delegates in the spring of 1884, the *Sun* said that the premier would not speak directly to farmers' suggestions. It mocked "the natural fluency of expression of the Premier, who was characterized more by verbosity of language than acumen." Instead, its report said, he "talked in a circle for an hour or two without having said anything."[69] The paper could scoff, but the premier was proving himself to be a shrewd leader whose national experience and considerable reading produced useful insights into the functioning of the Canadian federation and Manitoba's place within it.

"There Is No Missing Link in That Chain": A Lesson in Prairie History

Norquay went into the session in mid-March 1884 genuinely worried about the challenges presented by the newly organized farmers' union. He also recognized that the political scene was changing rapidly, an awareness that he expressed to an old friend: "I regret very much the radical spirit that seems to prevail largely in the country. It unsettles men's minds without effecting any good and is a great promoter of discontent[,] nine tenths of the agitators not knowing really what they do want." The business of the session centred on whether to accept Ottawa's offer of better terms. Norquay and his cabinet colleagues introduced a series of resolutions that called for revised financial arrangements within confederation that would end the "humiliation of depending upon . . . intermittent increases from time to time." The resolutions passed unanimously. The government also supported construction of railways, one to Hudson Bay and another, a new branch line, in southern Manitoba.[70]

Having left Ottawa abruptly, having insisted that Manitoba had been wronged, and having negotiated aggressively for a further six weeks, Norquay at this point was a local hero. Knowing that he had obtained all the monetary concessions that Macdonald would agree to, he made the province's status within confederation his next rallying point. As provincial treasurer he had the responsibility to record formally the province's financial position and to set out his own spending plans. In the evening of 16 April 1884, the house moved into committee of supply, and Norquay was greeted with cheers as he rose to deliver the budget. He spoke for over two hours that evening and finished his statement the following day. The presentation constituted a landmark in Manitoba history.

Norquay began with the news that the province's financial condition was "stationary."[71] That is, "normal expenditure" exceeded income, and the deficit would have to be addressed. Given that such shortfalls were regarded as unacceptable, he said, he might have to resort to "direct taxation," the only kind of taxing power allocated to the provinces under the BNA Act. Norquay then embarked on a long sketch of Assiniboia and Manitoba history, ranging roughly from the 1830s to the present. This was not a digression. Rather, it set out an alternative interpretation of western and Canadian history. He asserted the justice of Manitoba's demands and disputed the Macdonald government's claims about the status of HBC lands and their annexation by Canada.

The point of this history lesson was to establish that, in the generation or two before confederation, the Red River Settlement, also known as the HBC's District of Assiniboia, was comparable to British North America's other political units in all the ways that mattered. Norquay was building upon a theme that had emerged in Assiniboia between the 1830s and the 1860s. It had been articulated by A.K. Isbister, a distinguished educator then living in England and originally a Red River resident of Cree and Orkney ancestry, and was implicit in arguments presented by numerous others of mixed ancestry, including Louis Riel, Pascal Breland, Johnny Grant, James

Ross, James McKay, and William Dease.[72] The argument might be described as the "Metis as British subjects" school of thought.

Norquay's interpretation contained a bald assertion: "We find that, as far back as 1835, Government obtained in this country to an extent not generally known." In that year, Norquay said, Sir George Simpson, governor of the Hudson's Bay Company, delivered a speech to leading citizens of the "Colony of Assiniboia." He explained that Simpson's speech "appears to have been the first of the kind ever delivered here of which any record is handed down to us; and its tenor indicates unmistakably that those old colonists understood and were resolved to maintain good government." Norquay then quoted Simpson's opening sentences in full, the burden being that the 5,000 souls needed more than "the personal influence of the governor and the little more than nominal support afforded by the police" to maintain "rights of property" and to intervene when "other serious offences" had been committed. These citizens had been asked to ensure that order was maintained in the community and that the justice system functioned effectively. In meeting that challenge they had constituted themselves as the state. They maintained peace, even though they did not have a representative government:

> Here is evidence to show that, long anterior to Confederation there was a community existing on the banks of the Red River, in which obtained the regular forms of Government such as they were—and we know that they were such as met the wants of the community admirably. Law and order were maintained. As British subjects, the settlers enjoyed their rights—they enjoyed, in measure, every right outside those guaranteed by elective and representative institutions. (hear, hear). And in pressing for those rights now as we have done, and as we intend to do (cheers)—we are pressing for that which was ours, in the olden time, and which will be ours yet again. (loud cheers).

Norquay's next argument challenged John A. Macdonald's version of the history of the Canadian west by declaring that Assiniboia was a victim of Canadian aggression. Norquay spoke bluntly: "Manitoba was forced into Confederation, figuratively speaking, at the point of the bayonet, and the people submitted to the conditions imposed on them, not knowing the extent of the responsibilities they were assuming." By a vote of their assembled representatives, the people of Assiniboia did accept the transfer, but they had had limited power to shape the agreement. As Norquay said, the bayonet ruled, and Macdonald had his way. Even though he had been required to negotiate with Red River Settlement representatives, the prime minister had clung doggedly to the thesis that Rupert's Land was an empty vessel harbouring no individuals who had to be consulted, no groups whose interests had to be considered. Then, ignoring constitutional precedents in British North America, he had relegated the northwestern interior to the status of a colony of Ottawa.

Norquay's next argument, echoing statements made by Louis Riel and Members of the Legislative Assembly of Assiniboia in 1870, asserted local residents' faith in the British sense of fair play and in Manitoba's—and Canada's—continued integration within the British constitutional system. As Norquay put it, the people of Assiniboia were "confident that in any event they would be treated with full and impartial British justice in dealing with the Federal authorities." They trusted the incoming system of law, rights, and government because they had lived within such a regime for forty years or more and had been accustomed to asserting their claims and debating their rights. And they knew that, if ever there was a disagreement between Canada and Manitoba, "as the last resort there was the appeal to the foot of the Throne."

Norquay then considered the status of provinces within the Canadian federation and how Assiniboia had been integrated into that system. According to him none other than the federal minister of the provinces, Joseph Howe, had said "that the same constitution the other Provinces possessed would ultimately be conferred upon the country." Manitoba must be treated, Norquay insisted, as a province equal in rights and powers to all the others. He and his fellow Manitobans were asking for "full completion of the promises then and since held out to us, (cheers)." This contention placed ownership of the public domain in a new light.

Residents of this western community, Norquay explained, knew full well what they were negotiating for in 1870 when they joined Canada. The bill of rights "from the old Red River settlement, or colony of Assiniboia," had declared, in its second clause, that they should have admission into confederation as the province of Assiniboia and "with all the rights and privileges common to the different provinces of the Dominion." The eleventh clause of the bill asserted that the "local legislature of the province of Assiniboia shall have full control over all the public lands of the province, and the right to annul all acts or arrangements made, or entered into with reference to the public lands of Rupert's Land, and the Northwest now called the province of Assiniboia." What is more, Norquay said, Manitoba's assembly had a continuous and unbroken record of opposition to Canada's treatment of the province's public domain: "I have endeavoured to show that we never acquiesced in the partial measures of relief accorded to us, but from the very outset we indicated plainly that our position was at once unfortunate and eminently unsatisfactory—a state of affairs resulting from our not having a fair start in the provincial race (hear, hear)." This principle was supported in the first Manitoba assembly session of 1871, he said, when "a minority" (of which he was one) objected to the throne speech "because it contained no assurance that a promise of the restoration of the public lands was held out to the people."

Norquay made his case forcefully. He set out the community's consistent approach to land between 1835 and 1884: "So that from the very inception of representative institutions here, down to the present time, it is clear that this question was never lost sight of, (hear, hear). There is no missing link in that chain, (hear). And for my part I believe that the justice of our cause is such that we will yet triumph, (cheers)." Without a change in circumstances, "then, as far as Manitoba is concerned, Confederation would before long become a thing of the past. (Hear, hear). It is impossible for Confederation to exist unless the provinces generally were placed in a more uniform position. (Cheers)." And "should our right as British subjects be denied us,—we intend to ask that an appeal be next made direct from this House to the foot of the Throne, (cheers)." In that event "the people of Manitoba will separate themselves from Confederation and assume control of their own revenues." Norquay was moving to an extreme, making threats, flirting with the language of the farmers' union. The words were heard across Canada and even reached the august *Times* of London. And they damaged further his reputation among ultra-Conservatives in Manitoba, John A. Macdonald's keenest supporters, from whom Norquay had had only grudging support in the past.[73]

He had delivered a complicated but important history of his community that elaborated the thinking of a generation of Red River leaders. He insisted that Assiniboia had been a colony similar in character to the other British colonies in North America. He depicted Canada as a military aggressor that had refused to acknowledge the wishes of the entire northwest and misled its innocent representatives. He disputed the history of sovereignty in the region as advanced by Macdonald. He argued for the equality of the provinces, particularly in the matter of ownership of public lands and natural resources within a province's boundaries. Finally, he asserted that local residents possessed the rights of British subjects, including the right of appeal to the Crown.

The monarchists among recent Ontario arrivals went along with the premier's emphasis on British principles for their own reasons. But Norquay and the Assiniboians of his generation differed from these newcomers. "Old settlers" who had grown up in Assiniboia before the Transfer of 1870 were not Canadian. They looked in two directions for their governing principles, to their experience in the locality itself and to their inheritance of British institutions: "We are not different from other British subjects in believing that in the end our rights cannot be withheld from us. On the contrary, did we tamely submit to wrong—did we abandon our rights,—we would be less than British subjects, (hear, hear and cheers)." What is more, the provinces that eventually would be carved out of the North-West Territories would face the same issue: "All the more need then for a firm stand on Provincial Rights, (cheers)." In his closing lines Norquay restated his broader themes of Manitoba's British connections and Canada's responsibilities. Must they appeal to the British monarch? They were ready to do so: "If that step has not yet been taken, it is because of the reluctance of the people to take that final step in order to assert their rights (hear, hear)." Instead, they would take their case back to Ottawa, "urging them, too, in such a manner as will, we doubt not, be attended with success (loud cheers)."[74]

Thomas Greenway, leader of the opposition, endorsed Norquay's stand. He noted that Norquay spoke for two hours and that the opposition "were . . . metaphorically speaking supposed to be left without a garment. (Hear and laughter). But I can stand here today and say conscientiously that I am more than gratified to find that my hon. friend did on an occasion of this kind make the speech he did. (Cheers)." Greenway claimed to have arrived at the same position sooner. He agreed with the premier's conclusions: "I have entertained [these views] all along in reference to the great questions agitating the public mind . . . (hear hear)." Greenway said, to cheers and laughter, that

Ottawa had no confidence in the Manitoba government. But "so long as the Premier sits there—and can by any tactics he may use keep himself there—(laughter)—he has a right to the confidence of the people of Manitoba. (hear and cheers)." Greenway insisted that Manitobans must be prepared to leave Canada: "If the treatment is persisted in . . . we should cease to be a member of Confederation. I do not want to say . . . and I shall not say that there is a sentiment in Manitoba in favour of annexation to the country south of us; I do not believe that any such exists extensively." Rather, Manitobans were loyal, but "there is a loyalty that comes home, a loyalty to ourselves and the institutions under which we live. There is nothing in British institutions to compel people to sit silently under such treatment as this. . . . I believe now and say without hesitation that we can get along better without the people of the east than they can without us." The assembly actually held a "joint caucus" at the end of this debate, and members decided to send "an ultimatum" to the federal government.[75]

Norquay's budget speech of 1884 was the most important of his political career, one that developed an original interpretation of the history of the west and a principle concerning the role of the provinces in the Canadian federation. Norquay arranged for a French translation and ensured that copies in both languages were given to federal cabinet members and distributed across the country. In proposing a quite different relationship between Manitoba and Ottawa, he associated himself with a larger group critical of the prime minister's approach to confederation. This school of thought argued that the relationship between central government and province, a crucial matter in any federation, must be based upon the principle that each province is the constitutional equal of the others. Moreover, and more contentiously, relations between Ottawa and the provinces had to be based upon an understanding that the provinces collectively held absolute authority within their constitutional sphere just as the national government was paramount within its sphere. And finally all governments must accede to the principle that the ultimate arbiter in disputes remained the Crown. Norquay had delivered a carefully prepared critique not only of Manitoba's place in confederation but also of the Canadian federal system as Macdonald was administering it.[76]

The two versions of history, the federal memorandum of 1 April and Norquay's speech of 16 April, were equally tendentious. But was one of them a more accurate representation of Manitoba's legal situation? After all, there existed a political entity other than the Hudson's Bay Company that could claim sovereignty in Assiniboia before the negotiations on transfer took place. Indigenous peoples, whether of First Nations or mixed ancestry, believed their claims to the land preceded those of the fur trade company. If their claims had been acknowledged, how would the negotiations in 1870 have been altered? Norquay contended that the residents of the pre-1870 Red River Settlement were the equals of any other free-born Briton, had been governed by an administration that acknowledged this standing, and entered negotiations to transfer sovereignty from Britain to Canada on the understanding that their polity would be treated just as those of the other provinces of confederation were treated. The issue had not been settled in 1870 despite Macdonald's determination to bury it. And it was back on the public agenda in 1884.[77]

Norquay adjourned debate on 30 April, returned home briefly to see Elizabeth, and then on 5 May boarded a train with two members of yet another delegation for renewed discussions with the federal government. En route he called on Governor Lucius Hubbard in St. Paul, Minnesota. From the hotel he wired his office in Winnipeg to request that a dozen copies of his budget speech be sent to him in Ottawa, presumably for distribution when the negotiations resumed.[78]

Stalemate

Norquay's attempt to move the prime minister and his colleagues did not go well. Macdonald was exhausted after months of hard work keeping the CPR alive. The federal cabinet was increasingly impatient with what they saw as Manitoba's stubbornness and the premier's weakness in dealing with the provincial assembly. While they awaited answers, the members of the Manitoba delegation dined with the governor general, Lord Lorne, at Rideau Hall and enjoyed the charms of Ottawa in springtime. The visit was pleasant, but the negotiations ended in a stalemate.[79]

The provincial house had prorogued while awaiting the results of the "better terms" negotiations in Ottawa. Norquay returned to Winnipeg on 24 May 1884, after nearly three weeks on the road, with nothing to show for this latest round of negotiations. He reported to the assembly on 27 May that he had been unsuccessful. Having spent a great deal of time and money on two long expeditions to the capital in the hope of renegotiating the terms of Manitoba's participation in the Canadian federation, he stood before his colleagues empty handed.[80]

Manitoba's political representatives—indeed all sides in public life in Manitoba, from farmers' union members to ultra-Conservatives, with just a few exceptions—reacted with anger. Norquay tabled his report, and two days later, on 29 May, Greenway gave notice of a motion to reject Ottawa's terms as expressed in the memorandum of 1 April. The premier responded that the two sides of the house should work together: this was a new version of the non-partisan stance that he had championed in earlier years, and it won Greenway's reluctant support. Norquay told his colleagues that, "as British subjects, we claim today rights in common with our sister provinces (cheers). . . . One of the main elements of strength [of the confederation]—that which must give it solidity and endurance—was equality of treatment to all the provinces. . . . There must be equal justice. (Hear, hear)." Ottawa had improved its previous proposals but had not gone far enough, "and for that reason their proposition had not been accepted. (Cheers)." An atmosphere of firm resolve prevailed among the assembly members as they talked about Manitoba's secession from confederation.[81]

The next day they laid party differences aside, as Greenway put it, and drafted an ultimatum to the federal government that rejected its terms. Foremost among their reasons was a clause in Ottawa's memorandum stipulating that this would be a final settlement of all claims, a "finality clause" as it was called. The motion of rejection was adopted amid cheers. Only William Wagner, an ultra-Conservative, voted against the motion to reject the federal offer.[82]

Once again Norquay had outmanoeuvred his critics and maintained his hold on the Legislative Assembly. In doing so he had consolidated his position in the province. Even the *Times* of London took notice of his resistance. It chose to feature his most inflammatory statement that, if the province did not receive adequate funds to administer its public affairs, "the people of Manitoba will separate themselves from the Confederation and assume control of their own revenues." The leader of the opposition, Thomas Greenway, said that Norquay was the champion of Manitoba's rights. When the assembly prorogued on 5 June, Norquay was riding high in popular estimation. But could he and Macdonald find a way back to the bargaining table?[83]

The prime minister was frustrated by the premier's rejection of what the federal cabinet regarded as a fair compromise. In the aftermath Macdonald developed two arguments that cast doubt on Norquay's leadership. He repeated them several times and then sat back as they circulated widely among his loyal supporters across the country. The Manitoba premier lacked courage, Macdonald argued, and he lacked parliamentary acumen. He should have put the federal offer to a vote in the Manitoba assembly. A defeat would not have meant the fall of the Norquay government, Macdonald claimed, because it was not a matter of confidence but merely an offer from Ottawa. Norquay did not deserve further Conservative support, he implied, but he left others to draw that conclusion. He said nothing that could be construed as a directive to unseat the premier, but he was distancing himself from the man and the cause.[84]

The failure of the negotiations in 1884 marked an important moment in the Norquay-Macdonald relationship. They now saw each other as adversaries. The prime minister would deal with the premier when issues arose, but his flexibility on Manitoba's revenue problem, now interpreted by Norquay as a constitutional problem, had come to an end. Macdonald would not sweeten the offer that he had made, and he certainly would not relinquish control of prairie lands and resources.

The son of the prime minister wrote to him from Winnipeg to sympathize, saying that he did not "wonder at your being thoroughly disgusted with Norquay, who is utterly unreliable." Hugh John Macdonald listed provincial worries, including the farmers' union (its very existence undercut investors' confidence) and the Manitoba South-Western and Manitoba & North-West Railways (construction on both had stopped). He admitted, too, that even the best Conservatives had been on Norquay's side in this latest skirmish with Ottawa, "and the only man who stood firm was old Wagner, whom I think you know."[85] But he also repeated his father's preferred narrative, saying that a good harvest would change the terms of the debate.

Macdonald proceeded with business as usual. In his correspondence with Norquay he did not express his vexation. The two leaders worked steadily to settle the details of a Hudson Bay railway deal. On that issue the premier insisted that Ottawa, rather than a private, profit-seeking corporation, should determine the freight rates. If the federal administration accepted this responsibility, then his government would "do all in its power to further the enterprise." The lesson of this exchange was that federal-provincial negotiations were never over, the subjects to be settled were infinite in number, and neither party would give in easily.[86]

Macdonald wrote of his frustration frequently. To his new Winnipeg agent, Henry Hall Smith, he spoke bluntly: "*Entre nous* I have no doubt in my own mind that the way to deal with Manitoba is to pay no attention to their grumblings. We shall do what we think is right and if they don't like it we can't help it. I should much prefer myself that Greenway was at the head of affairs instead of Norquay who is really a nuisance."[87]

Suddenly, at the end of June 1884, came the shocking discovery that a full-scale insurrection was brewing among the farm union's angriest members. Norquay sent Macdonald an intercepted letter written by one union leader to another that made rebellion appear to be imminent. The farmer wrote that "there has not been since the commencement of the agitation a better time to strike than the present. . . . I am certain four or five hundred good men will accomplish our object without any difficulty whatever. . . . The military here [in Manitoba] is nothing more than a pack of boys and we have easy access to the [munitions] store rooms."[88]

Having received the news from Norquay while enjoying a working holiday at his summer retreat on the St. Lawrence, Macdonald wired a reply immediately. The premier should warn Winnipeg's military leadership "that arms may be seized & should be guarded."[89] The prime minister added a letter to Norquay on the same day, saying that "I have never heard of such madness as these Farmers Union people are exhibiting." A few days later he told the lieutenant governor not to leave the province. Times were difficult, he said, Louis Riel was back in the country, and Métis unrest in the North-West might spread to Manitoba, "encouraged by the demagogues of the Farmers Union."[90] Whatever the tensions between Winnipeg and Ottawa, neither Norquay nor Macdonald would permit a band of protesters to seize control of the provincial government.

The atmosphere remained feverish for several hot weeks in July. Provincial Police Chief Charles Constantine placed an undercover agent in the ranks of the farm union but, despite a good deal of drinking and talking, the agent discovered nothing of value.[91] By mid-July Lieutenant Governor Aikins concluded that the rumours of revolt were exaggerated. He told Macdonald that Riel, now living in Montana, had visited Manitoba without incident and was now travelling in the North-West Territories. The lieutenant governor did not think that the one-time leader of the Red River Resistance would have any impact there either. What was more, he wrote, the Manitoba farm union appeared to be just another partisan faction. It was "no doubt being run by its promoters as a political machine with the object of getting political control of this Province" and would not become involved in criminal acts. A good crop would allay concerns, and "disappointed speculators" were behind most of the unrest.[92] Such advice encouraged Macdonald to follow the instincts that gave him the title "Old Tomorrow." He did nothing. Unfortunately Aikins did not understand the territory west of Manitoba and had not taken the measure of the problems confronting his own province. In this important dispatch, and despite his sympathy for Norquay's position, Aikins failed to press Macdonald to rethink his policies or review the effectiveness of his agents in the North-West Territories.

Talk of speculators getting their just deserts and of adequate harvests in farm districts encouraged the prime minister to stay the course. He remained alert, however, and asked Aikins to caution Manitoba cabinet ministers about the dangers of connections between Fenians and disgruntled local groups.[93] These were merely words inviting others to keep their eyes peeled, not substantive changes in policy.

It was in this context—straitened economy, Fenian agitation, secession gossip, Métis unrest in Saskatchewan, Cree/Saulteaux and Blackfoot starvation on the plains, and Manitoba's rejection of the Ottawa deal—that Macdonald initiated another round of negotiations with Norquay.[94] Coming as it did only two months after the collapse of talks in May, renewed federal interest was welcome news in Winnipeg. The prime minister presented the usual carrots and sticks. More money would be placed on the table (perhaps as much as $100,000), but an upward revision of population estimates would not happen in the autumn (as had been promised originally), and the finality clause would not be dropped. Several months later he was able to offer Norquay some support in another sphere by ensuring that the premier's Saskatchewan Coal Company secured a charter from the federal cabinet.[95] No one could argue that Macdonald did not want to reach a settlement with Manitoba.

Alongside the renewed conversation between Winnipeg and Ottawa, Macdonald's Conservative loyalists in Manitoba grumbled more loudly about Norquay himself. So steady was the volume of complaints that the individuals acquired a group name, the "old guard." These critics wanted a leader who would defend Macdonald's National Policy. Taking their cues from the prime minister, the dissenters alleged that Norquay lacked courage. If only he was personally stronger, they said, he would have faced down the opposition and carried the federal proposals through the local assembly.[96] They also followed Macdonald's lead in blaming Norquay for having a weak grasp of negotiating subtleties. His only strategy, they said, was to beg Macdonald to come to his rescue, and he could not recognize a good deal when it was offered to him.

The allegation of personal weakness or cowardice was a recent one, originating mainly in the prolonged negotiations of 1884. Another angle of attack, one that had its origin in the resentments of John Schultz and the Ontarians of the 1870s, alleged that Norquay lacked principle. This charge dated from Schultz's failure to win cabinet posts and the success of Norquay in hewing to a moderate line between French and English, Métis and White, during the Archibald and Davis governments.[97] Schultz had never forgotten these setbacks or come to terms with Norquay's defences of old settlers. The Ontarian might have come to Red River in 1861, but he was not an Assiniboian old-timer. He seemed to focus his racism on those of mixed ancestry, whether Bungee/English or Michif/French. His wealth and his elevation to the Senate of Canada ensured his continued access to the highest government circles despite his defeat in the federal election of 1882. Schultz had no sympathy for "the speculative and weakly" (his words) who had lost money in the Winnipeg boom and bust. Having stayed in central Canada during three years of convalescence from a serious illness, he was keen to join the "better element" that had survived the crash. His antipathy to Norquay remained as keen as ever. The same kind of long-standing distrust simmered in St. Boniface, where Joseph Royal would never relinquish his hostility to Norquay.[98]

Public discussion now centred on the claim that Manitoba farm households were being sacrificed to priorities in other parts of the country and to expenditures on a national rail line rather than branch railways. One of Canada's leading journalists, Edward Farrer, as editor of the *Winnipeg Times* and then, in the summer of 1884, the Winnipeg *Sun*, fed this discontent. Watching Norquay contend with the province's limited financial powers and lack of influence in Ottawa, and hearing the arguments in the legislature and public meetings, Farrer decided that Canada, as a country, could not survive.

He concluded that it was destined to separate from Britain and probably to become part of the United States. During his four months at the *Sun*, his biographer has written, the paper's "most notable feature was a consistent, subtle campaign to undermine Confederation and promote either Western independence or annexation." By the end of August, as he was about to move to Toronto, Farrer wrote several blistering editorials on this theme. In one he admitted that the British connection might not be in immediate danger, but "it is as certain as anything can be in human affairs that independence or annexation is the ultimate destiny of Canada.... The birth of a Canadian nation or the bloodless absorption of these provinces by the Republic... is written in the book of fate."[99]

Farrer might also have been responsible for dragging Norquay's name into an unusual and ambitious money-making scheme launched in the summer of 1884: Edward Pew, an Ontario promoter, proposed to sell the Canadian prairies to the United States. To pave the way he proposed the purchase of the three Winnipeg dailies (including the pen of Farrer), payment of bribes to Norquay and his four cabinet ministers, and negotiations for the support of the Roman Catholic Church and Louis Riel (who had just left his home in Montana to join the disgruntled settlers of Saskatchewan). Norquay could be bought, Pew suggested, for $1 million. The entire plan would cost about $25 to $30 million, and the bonds to be issued by the new American state would bring healthy profits to the speculators themselves. No evidence supports the notion that Norquay had any part in the plan. The idea itself vanished in the wind, but it further stoked the fears of official Ottawa.[100]

"A Man Born in That Country": Manitoba's Deal and Norquay's National Celebrity

Norquay dealt with numerous other issues, private and public, during the autumn of 1884. His finances remained worrying. He might have been in Ottawa briefly in early November to deal with his coal mine, and he probably visited New York during this trip. He was living with immense pressures, both in public affairs and in private investments. Still, he found an ideal opportunity to make peace with Macdonald. Despite his low standing among senior Conservatives in Winnipeg, Norquay was nominated to be the provincial party's spokesperson at events celebrating the anniversary of the prime minister's fortieth year in public life. What better way to mend relations with the great man and his government? Norquay would be able to declare his support for and admiration of the prime minister before 4,000 Conservatives in Toronto and again at a gala banquet in Montreal.[101]

Norquay left for the east on 13 December 1884 and stayed six weeks, including during Christmas, an unprecedented absence in his family's experience but one that benefited the province immensely. He told convention delegates in Toronto that he was a representative of the "old settlers" of Red River and pointed out that the institutions of Manitoba had been established by relatives of the people in the audience, pioneers who had migrated westward and were "as nearly like the old ones as possible (cheers)." The Toronto *Mail* praised his presentation as "one of the most notable events in connection with the convention" and said that Norquay "more than once [showed] himself to be the equal, as a powerful and eloquent debater, of any man, bar none in the Dominion." The *Winnipeg Times* noted that Sir John A. Macdonald made special mention of Norquay in his own speech, the prime minister having pointed out that the Manitoba premier was "a man born in that country (cheers)."[102] The oblique reference to Norquay's Indigeneity would have been missed by no one.

The speech marked Norquay's arrival in the public eye as far as Ontarians were concerned. His speaking voice and fluency, combined with his physical presence and well-known ancestry, surprised listeners who had never witnessed the like. The Toronto *News* expressed surprise at his speaking powers and wondered whether Norquay might be a suitable contender to replace the prime minister when the time came. Although it named D'Alton McCarthy as the best easterner for the role, it depicted Norquay as a contender: "But out from the west comes another man, a giant in stature if not in [the public] mind, a born tactician, and a successful leader, Hon. John Norquay, Premier of Manitoba. Personally, almost unknown outside of the Red River valley until within the past few months, he has come down among the eastern party men, has attended two great conventions, addressed two or three immense audiences, has shown cultured oratory."[103] It was a moment of celebrity.

By 22 December Norquay was in the Russell House in Ottawa, receiving word from his office that all was well in Winnipeg except for the temperature, then -53 Fahrenheit, according to Secretary Arthur Pritchard (it was only -39 Fahrenheit according to another report). Norquay was aware that his homeland's accustomed peace and order could no longer be assumed. He received a letter from his old friend William Luxton, who wrote that he planned to cut short his vacation in southern Ontario at Christmas: "These are too anxious times to be away from 'base of operations.'" He spoke of serious worries: "You really can form no idea of the strength of feeling here at present time on '*Manitoba Rights*,' I will call it. . . . I am perfectly sure that unless you succeed . . . in getting nearly *all* demands, not least, extension of boundaries, there will be a big time—I believe a general uprising against Dominion." Still, the editor continued to support him and to speak as a friend: "You have but to *stick* to your position, get your demands, or *resent* not getting them and you are a *hero*."[104]

The Ottawa talks were preceded by Manitoba's submission of another extensive memorandum. Based upon Norquay's budget speech of the previous April, it rejected Ottawa's claim that Canada had "purchased" all the prairie lands in 1870, arguing that such an assertion gave the province an "invidious" status: "The repetition of such a statement should cease," the memo declared bluntly. Norquay restated the province's claims and made a special plea for an extension of the provincial boundary: "It would be advantageous to have a border, and a seaport, on Hudson Bay [because,] . . . having been the channel through which for over two centuries access was obtained to this country, that territory naturally belongs to Manitoba."[105]

Norquay wrote to the prime minister requesting an interview and had a reply from Minister of Justice Alexander Campbell dated Christmas day. The first meeting between the Manitobans and the six ministers on the federal cabinet's subcommittee took place on Boxing Day afternoon. The negotiations continued through the post-Christmas week and were completed by early January. The terms offered in the previous winter were reviewed and accepted. On the tariff, school land, and capital allowance issues, Ottawa would make no concessions. Nor would there be a boundary extension to the north. Still, there was now a charter for a Hudson Bay railway supported by a "liberal grant" of lands. The federal government would pay for an expedition to investigate navigation in the bay itself. On the crucial issue of disallowing railway charters, it went so far as to say that the Canadian Pacific Railway "had intimated that they would not object to any relaxation of that condition [the monopoly clause] in their charter after the completion of the road north of Lake Superior, and that certainly, after 1886, no further objection would be taken to crossing the boundary."[106] This was a remarkable concession that has escaped mention since in the historical literature. Considering the railway battles and political crises that erupted in the next two years, it deserves greater attention than it has received.

The rapid progress of Norquay's negotiations surprised outsiders but not those at the centre of events. In fact the negotiators were merely revisiting the deal reached six months earlier. The quick result also illustrated the advantage of Norquay's timing and the sage advice of John A. Macdonald. As the prime minister had suggested, almost everyone who mattered was in Ottawa during the Christmas weeks. It meant that Norquay was away from home at an important moment in his family's life, but he secured what had been lost in the collapse of the earlier talks as well as a few additional concessions, including an increased grant in lieu of public lands. Minister Alexander Campbell said that this concession was "as large a grant from the Dominion in perpetuity as it [Manitoba] could possibly hope to realize from the administration thereof." With the completion of this agreement, financial demands ceased to be prominent in Ottawa-Winnipeg diplomacy for the next decade, just as Norquay and Macdonald had hoped. John Henry Pope and Norquay signed off on these terms on 10 January 1885, and the Manitoba premier gave in on the "finality clause," agreeing that the deal would serve "as a settlement of all questions in discussion between that province and the Dominion up to this date." If the Manitoba assembly balked, he agreed, then the deal would become "null and void."[107]

In mid-January Norquay travelled to Montreal for the Macdonald banquet and he may have visited Quebec City as well. At the dinner he replied to the toast to provincial legislatures, again praising Macdonald as a "statesman who had the sincerity and earnestness requisite for the development of the great Northwest (Loud applause) . . . [having] never faltered in his faith in the future greatness of that great country." It was another moment when he performed beyond the expectations of his audience, was showered with attention, and was able publicly to applaud the leadership of the prime minister.[108]

Norquay returned to Manitoba via Toronto and was delayed by a snowstorm between Chicago and Minneapolis.[109] A delegation travelled from Winnipeg to the village of Gretna, Manitoba, to welcome him home, and he was the centre of a "grand demonstration" when he stepped off the train in the capital city. The *Winnipeg Times* made much of his successes in the east and repeated the Toronto *News* story recognizing his capacities and elevating him to the rank of prime ministerial candidate. Norquay spoke to the crowd at the railway station, saying that the west was "too little known and so little appreciated in Eastern Canada." He declared that his "whole endeavour has been to lay before the statesmen of Canada the true state of affairs here." He predicted more gains in the coming weeks. A few days later George Stephen announced that the cash-strapped CPR's subsidiary, the Manitoba South-Western, would be extended westward to Whitewater Lake in the coming summer. The increase in the federal grant in lieu of Manitoba's ownership of public land was announced soon after.[110]

Stories about the impact of his speeches in the east preceded Norquay. His friends and colleagues in Manitoba were delighted with the news. Thomas Mayne Daly, the mayor of Brandon, sent greetings: "My Dear Sir[:] Welcome home old man & more power to your elbow."[111] Norquay's brother-in-law, John James Setter, foresaw his "elevation to the premiership of the Dominion, at no very distant day," and noted that newspapers were discussing the prospect of a lecturing tour in England: "Won't you make those 'wise men of the East' stare eh? When they have ocular & auricular demonstration of the products of this great country! Hurrah."[112]

Mixed with the praise came criticism from the usual sources. The *Brandon Sun* judged the negotiations a "failure," mocked the premier's "miserable exhibition" at the Macdonald celebrations, and concluded that Norquay "was more bent on having 'a good time' [in the east] than in attending to the business of his office."[113] Local political debate was only heating up, as the premier had predicted, and Liberal critics were out in force.

Peace in the Conservative Party, Anger in the West

Norquay's relations with Prime Minister Macdonald might have been cooler because of the bruising negotiations during the past eight months, but on the surface the two leaders continued to correspond in a businesslike manner. The prime minister was preoccupied with a crisis at the Canadian Pacific Railway in January 1885. The company faced the high cost of construction on the two segments of the transcontinental line yet to be completed, one on the north shore of Lake Superior and the other in the mountains of British Columbia. It was seeking yet another bailout and threatening disastrous consequences if the money did not flow immediately. To smooth Parliament's passage of a CPR subsidy, Macdonald would have to grant support to railway projects being promoted by several other provinces. As he told Charles Tupper, "the Quebec MPs have the line to Quebec up again. The Maritimes are clamorous for the Short Line & are here blackmailing all round. How it will end God knows, but I think I were well out of it."[114] If Macdonald was bothered by thoughts of Riel's return to the North-West, he was not saying so in public. But he could take pleasure in the agreement that he had negotiated with Norquay.

The view from Winnipeg was similarly positive. Norquay understood more fully the context in which the prime minister had to operate. He spoke with pride about the outcome of the negotiations in Ottawa in the belief that the 1885 deal laid to rest some of the issues that he had been raising for nearly a decade, especially the enlarged federal grant to be paid in lieu of provincial ownership of public lands. In late January Norquay wired Macdonald with congratulations on the opening of telegraphic communications between British Columbia and Ottawa. The final line of his telegram celebrated "the great degree of success attending the unprecedented efforts of the Canadian Pacific Railway in carrying out your farseeing policy." Federal-provincial business was proceeding smoothly.[115]

Tensions within the local party burst into the open in February 1885 when Winnipeg South's representative in the provincial assembly accepted a judgeship and a by-election had to be called. "Old guard" Conservatives launched a canvass in favour of local lawyer Hector Howell. Norquay scotched that plan by naming the recently elected mayor of Winnipeg, Charles Hamilton, to the post of attorney general and putting his name forward for the party nomination. The "old guard" did not take kindly to Norquay's swift intervention. The prime minister's son, Hugh John, told his father of their unhappiness and explained that the sticking point for them was that Hamilton had not been loyal to the prime minister during the Pacific railway crisis twelve years earlier.[116]

Norquay spoke at a large Conservative meeting in early February, acknowledging that "some little dissension" existed in Conservative ranks, "but he hoped that wise judgment would prevail and in a short time the differences that apparently now existed would disappear and all would work together in harmony for the good of the Conservative cause." Privately he took the conflict in stride, telling his brother-in-law that he was "now reaping in Winnipeg the thanks that I expected from my political friends of the 'old guard' who are trying all in their power to down my nominee [Hamilton] and also from those open mouthed well wishers the Grits who take every opportunity to obstruct." The exchange between brothers-in-law revealed their rural Manitoban view of the province. They did not belong to the Ontarian elite of Conservative lawyers and merchants in Winnipeg. The "old guard," now a term in daily use to describe Macdonald loyalists among Manitoba Conservatives, constituted merely one element, and not the most important one, among all the factors deciding political success in Manitoba. After all, rural Manitoba counted for four of every five votes. The premier had concluded realistically that "Winnipeg never was friendly or never will be to me or to my friends."[117]

Then, just when the party divisions threatened to bring defeat in the by-election, John A. Macdonald stepped in and sent a telegram to one of his local informants, William Scarth, asking that Norquay's choice of candidate be respected. The intercession demonstrated once again not just that Macdonald kept close watch on provincial affairs but also that he and his closest advisors on the ground understood the local jealousies that affected so many of the party elite in Manitoba's capital.[118] The Conservative leadership in Ottawa might grumble about Norquay, but he was still seen as better than the alternatives. The prime minister's telegram rallied the party, grumblers and all.

The Winnipeg South campaign was hard fought. Conservative candidate Charles Hamilton followed the Norquay line and had the support of an exceptional electoral machine. The Liberal candidate, none other than *Free Press* editor William Luxton, made a non-partisan "Manitoba rights" appeal and argued that a vote for Norquay was a vote for "eastern provinces having the right for all time to interfere with Manitoba affairs." Luxton said that his desire was "to suppress party issues . . . and unite the people in defence of the rights of the province."[119] Hamilton won 606 votes to Luxton's 529.

The campaign can be viewed as the real beginning of professional party management in Manitoba. Norquay described it as the most difficult that he had ever faced and said that his opponents were "using money unscrupulously."[120] The parties were now operating as professional organizations, employing agents to manage voter contact, organizing volunteers into election day teams, conducting surveillance on opponents' activities, and soliciting donations. The *Manitoba Free Press* said that Hamilton's victory was the result of "the meanest methods," including federal, provincial, and even municipal (Winnipeg) patronage.[121]

Hamilton made a difference in the cabinet. Born in England, he had become a lawyer in St. Catharines, Ontario, and then joined a well-known law firm in Winnipeg. His sober, cautious approach to public affairs was welcome after the upheavals that accompanied James Miller's months as attorney general. Hamilton was forty-one in the spring of 1885, and had recently been elected mayor of Winnipeg on a platform of economy and careful management. He enjoyed two and a half years as attorney general and made the important decision to adopt the Torrens land title system, an arrangement with huge implications for the law related to real estate transactions in Manitoba.[122]

In this campaign Norquay also found the key political manager who could complement Pritchard's office skills and Hamilton's role in cabinet. Alfred Herbert Rennie, who assumed the role of political organizer and jack-of-all-trades, had attended Hamilton Collegiate and Upper Canada College (Toronto) and then worked in a variety of businesses, including ranching, grocery (retail and wholesale), and railway construction. He was only twenty-eight years old, the same age as Pritchard, when he joined Norquay's office. Ambitious, fiercely loyal, and fearless in debate, Rennie had been looking for avenues upward.[123] Norquay's brother-in-law, John James Setter, had employed him briefly in his Portage la Prairie office and was impressed by his abilities. Setter wrote to the premier to say that the young man's most valuable quality was his loyalty: "He is a man who will die for his friends, never hesitates a moment to fire a broadside into any camp of anyone who may dare say a word against any friend of his." Setter could not afford to keep him and welcomed the news that Norquay had placed Rennie on his own staff: "I only wish that my office could stand it, I would never have let him go from me. . . . I am glad that you have found a place for him."[124] Rennie was the final piece necessary to complete Norquay's administration.

If Norquay's position in the party was more stable, despite the carping of Winnipeg's self-styled elite, the economic circumstances in rural households continued to be difficult, and the language of public debate was growing more extreme. In March 1885 the *Brandon Sun* reported on the convention of 300 farmers beneath the headline "Norquay Must Go: The Farmers' Union: An Influential and Successful Convention." It justified its conclusion by pointing to the premier's "corrupt and selfish partyism" and to his membership in the federal Conservative party: "No longer the leader of the people, but of a party; a party kept in power . . . by the votes of a fraction of the people, packed in the corner of the province." The *Free Press* moved from scolding to vituperation. It labelled Norquay "a traitor, a hired betrayer," who might skip out of his responsibilities by accepting a portfolio in the federal cabinet. The assembly members behind him, Luxton's journal warned, exhibited an "unreasoning, cringing, despicable servility and venality."[125]

Liberals in the assembly took advantage of the depressed times to attack Norquay and the government aggressively. Their leadership expanded to include some very effective campaigners. Most prominent, aside from Thomas Greenway (who served as the Manitoba premier from 1888 to 1899), were Charles Stewart (a graduate of Cambridge University), Joe Martin (an MLA and later a member of both the Canadian and the British House of Commons), Clifford Sifton (an MLA, later a member of Wilfrid Laurier's cabinet, and later still a business titan), and Rodmond Roblin (the province's premier from 1900 to 1915).[126] They were strong characters, committed to making the farm country function effectively, and able critics of Prime Minister Macdonald's policies dealing with the west.

Norquay tried to ride out the storm by arguing that it was federal government thinking, not his own, that had to be revised. But he faced renewed trouble in March and April 1885. His secretary warned him about the extreme language in the press. The chief of provincial police, who had placed an agent within the farm movement, heard talk of a link to Louis Riel's activities in the North-West Territories. The intelligence became more urgent when the chief learned that farm union leaders planned to overthrow the government: "The latest is that on Tuesday . . . [31 March 1885] a deputation will wait on the Lieut-Gov and demand a dissolution of the House and that in the event of his refusal will take means to effect it." For the farmers' unions to be considering a *coup d'état*, peacefully if possible but by more aggressive means if necessary, marked an extraordinary development in their campaign. But was it just a hoax?[127]

Talk of a revolution in Manitoba normally might have been described as farfetched. On the surface the government had become much more stable and the established order much more secure during Norquay's third term. The legislature and government precinct in Winnipeg now looked as imposing as those in other provincial capitals and the communications apparatus—railway, telegraph, rural roads, and even, in the city, a few telephones—much more efficient than the media of earlier years. The premier himself seemed to stand above the tumult. Surely a few hotheads could not topple a government by recourse to guns simply because of people's anger at federal policies? But everyone knew that popular unrest in the North-West Territories was approaching the boiling point. The possibility of an equivalent in Manitoba could not be ruled out. Such was the state of affairs in the province in late February and early March 1885.

Norquay's tenacity and shrewdness during the two years of negotiations in Ottawa between March 1883 and February 1885 had won significant gains. By returning regularly to the national capital, waiting in anterooms, making speeches in committee rooms, he simply wore his hosts down. He had diagnosed the Manitoba-Canada problem accurately and reached reasonable settlements. His next budget would allocate $500,000 in spending, five times what he had controlled only six years before when he first entered the premier's office. Norquay was acknowledged to be the central figure in the government. Assembly members and cabinet colleagues saw him as the boss, "the chief," in an administration increasingly well organized, purposeful, and competent. He had won important victories, he told Alexander Begg, "for which I am thanked as usual by the old Conservatives with their virulent opposition. I hope however to be able to pull through as I have lived through many a political struggle before."[128] Despite the unhappiness of Macdonald loyalists in Winnipeg's self-appointed Conservative elite, Norquay was a Conservative and led a Conservative government.

Important questions remained. Were the residents of the prairie west—especially the starving Cree, Saulteaux, and Blackfoot, the Métis beset by uncertainties about land tenure, and the newly arrived farm families living precariously—doomed to wage war against or to secede from Canada?

CHAPTER 9

"An Unfortunate Family Difference," 1885

Communities throughout the western interior were on edge when spring arrived in 1885. The economic problems of households in Manitoba, a consequence of the Winnipeg real estate crash and of farm families' troubled adjustment to an unfamiliar environment, preoccupied political leaders there. In the North-West Territories, many Blackfoot, Assiniboine, Cree, and Saulteaux communities faced starvation. In settler households, uncertainties about land rights and railway service provoked talk of an uprising. The outbreak of violence in March engulfed the farm home of John Norquay's sister, Annie Adams, at Red Deer Hill, NWT. The ensuing troop mobilization reached into Norquay's own home when two of the premier's sons, Tom and Alex, joined the Canadian military expedition.

The story of the "second Riel uprising" might appear peripheral to Norquay's career, but he was affected deeply by the conflict, both in political and personal terms. The armed confrontation provoked important changes in his thinking and affected his standing among influential Conservative party members. What is more, and even more important, though the drastic changes have never been fully delineated and were not much commented on at the time, the events of spring 1885 drew a sharper line between Indigenous and non-Indigenous peoples. That line affected the lives of all Canadians.

Money Matters

By the mid-1880s Norquay clearly belonged in the upper ranks of the province's income earners. He and his cabinet colleagues were paying themselves generously for their government work, in his case between $4,000 and $6,000 in annual salary and stipend.[1] This was four or five times as much as his personal secretary was paid annually. But Norquay's expenditures continued to exceed his income. The collapse of the speculative boom in Winnipeg and the failure of his many investments, combined with expenditures on behalf of family members, cost Norquay dearly. He made matters worse by trying to aid everyone who asked for help.

When dealing with money matters Norquay was both careless and generous. During trips to Ottawa as the Manitoba premier, he simply ensured that a letter of credit was sent by the government's Winnipeg bank to its Ottawa counterpart and then withdrew cash whenever he needed it. At a royal commission hearing into his government's activities, a lawyer asked Norquay about the Ottawa trips: "Did you keep any detailed account of your expenses?" "No I never do." In answer to a further question, he elaborated:

> I may say . . . that I was generally considered the treasurer of the [Manitoba] party and I generally assumed that the charges would be made against me, if we went out for a drive I paid the tab or the hotel bill[,] and other expenses of like nature were generally paid by me and it is in this way that I appear to be charged with a larger sum. . . . I never ask a colleague of mine to make a detailed statement of his expenses as I considered I would insult him[;] as long as the expenditure was within the bounds of reason I would not do so. In travelling on official business it is very much more expensive than travelling any other way. If you send me down as John Norquay I might probably go for about $300.00 but if you send me down as premier of the province it will cost a great deal more.[2]

On 1 December 1884, having endured eighteen months of dismay as he surveyed the premier's finances, secretary Arthur Pritchard took a new tack in trying to manage his spending. By this time Pritchard handled Norquay's personal bills and knew that his boss was flirting with bankruptcy. The concern was a trail of promissory notes that Norquay had signed, sometimes to cover his own debts and sometimes as a guarantor for others.[3] In a formal, stilted letter written on the stationery of the treasury department, Pritchard offered a blunt piece of advice: Norquay should abandon all attempts to manage his own finances. Pritchard proposed to shield the premier from those who came looking for loans. Whenever someone asked Norquay to sign a promissory note, Pritchard wrote, "I then could explain that you had a certain amount to meet on this[,] that or the other and that it would be out of the question for you to attach your name to any more paper and this would throw some of the responsibility of your refusing to endorse on me and relieve you. In your position so many call upon you for monetary assistance thinking you are so well able to bear the brunt when the case is so entirely different." Although Pritchard tried to sugar-coat his words, the message itself and the social distance between them were unmistakable. Norquay's careless approach to decisions about money had to end, and this young man wished to steer the premier clear.[4] Pritchard meant well, and Norquay accepted his advice, at least to some degree. During the next year they allocated small amounts to various outstanding accounts and kept creditors at bay.[5]

One big financial problem was his residence, the farm at Parkdale. Norquay could not afford to keep it going, nor could he afford to leave it.[6] At some point he had taken out a mortgage on the farm. This $2,000 debt probably seemed to be unexceptional in 1880, when it first appeared in his files. As the interest payments came due in the following years, however, the debt took on a menacing aspect. Interest on the renegotiated loan rose from 5 percent to 10 percent. By the end of 1886, on just the Parkdale farm and house, Norquay owed $1,000 in missed payments, plus the current year's payments, plus taxes, and these debts were just the most pressing on a much longer list.[7]

The mounting debts forced Norquay to give up on one of his bigger investments. This was the large plot of land on Kennedy Street in the heart of the future government precinct. He had purchased the tract at a premium from sometime business partner William Scarth in 1881. By 1884 it was no longer the prize that it had seemed at the height of the boom. Norquay sold it, accepting a sizable loss.[8] (In one of history's small ironies, one portion of this land eventually became known as 31 Kennedy Street, today's headquarters of the Manitoba Progressive Conservative party.)

NORQUAY'S PROVINCIAL TROUPE. THE OPENING CHORUS.

FIGURE 28. "Norquay's Provincial Troupe: The Opening Chorus," *Quiz*, 3 February 1879. *Quiz*, a satirical newspaper (the blindfolded court jester in the foreground) was published in Winnipeg in 1878–79. From the left, the musical troupe includes cabinet ministers Norquay (with drum labelled "Spondulics," slang for "money"), David Walker, Corydon Brown (with flute), an as-yet-unnamed minister of "Agriculture," and Joseph Royal (with trumpet). In the centre are the Clerk of the assembly, Lieutenant Governor Cauchon, Joseph Dubuc (Speaker, with top hat raised). Norquay dangles the Speaker's chair, and the $800 stipend that went with the appointment, in front of the "No Policy" opposition members, all of whom are clamouring for the job that Dubuc won. The signs on the fence advertise "tenders for ditching," "charters for railways," and "Norquay's magic oil." The image, proudly described as the first cartoon produced in western Canada, illustrated Norquay's first cabinet, the customary suspicion of government corruption, and the racist tenor of some contemporary commentary (see p. 143).

VALIANT JOHN FALSTAFF NORQUAY!

"A PLAGUE OF ALL COWARDS, I SAY, AND A VENGEANCE, TOO! MARRY AND AMEN!!—*Shakespeare.*

FIGURE 29. "Valiant John Falstaff Norquay! A plague of all cowards, I say, and a vengeance, too! Marry and amen!! – *Shakespeare*," *Grip*, 4 November 1882.

John A. Macdonald carries a document labelled "power of disallowance" and the sign behind him declares: "Syndicate bargain: NO line of railway to be built within 15 miles of boundary sgd John A." The label on Norquay's sword reads: "Manitoba Rights."

FIGURE 30. "'Ministerial' Consolation" *Grip*, 9 December 1882. Maiden Manitoba stands on the trapdoor of the gallows, blindfolded, bound by "monopoly," the noose of "Disallowance" around her neck.

The death warrant, pinned to the scaffold, is a quotation from the Tory newspaper, the *Winnipeg Times*: "Where is the reason in the cry against Disallowance since it is understood to be the settled Policy of the Dominion Government?" Norquay, the clergyman, provides "'ministerial' consolation": "Courage, my dear, you'll not mind it when you get used to it." Lurking behind the pillar, none other than the masked hangman, John A. Macdonald, saying, "I'm sorry, but the 'Bargain' demands it," a quotation from Macdonald's letter to Conservatives in Emerson, Manitoba, who had objected to federal disallowance of Manitoba railway charters.

FIGURE 31. "Advice From Quebec," *Grip*, 2 June 1883. Cartoonist Bengough was intrigued by Norquay's proposal in the Manitoba 1883 Throne Speech to convene the country's first premiers' conference. Here, Quebec's premier (J.-A. Mousseau) advises his colleagues on how to secure provincial rights: "Advice from Quebec: (Probable remarks of the Quebec representative at the forthcoming meeting of Provincial Premiers)—'Federal Interference? Bah! They vill not meddle if your Bleus and your Rouges stand like von man for Provincial Rights as *our* men do. Ze Federal cannot touch Quebec!'"

On the wall: "The Rights of the Provinces are Sacred"

"Every Province shall control its own affairs"

"Provincial Congress"

FIGURE 32. "Norquay's 'Position,'" *Grip*, 12 January 1884. Farmer brandishes "Manitoba Farmers' Manifesto: We demand our Rights."

An elfin Norquay (indicating office with his thumb): "Please don't hurt me, sir. I'm only the caretaker. I can't do anything for you—you'll have to see the Boss!"
On the Manitoba office door: "John A. General Manager"

Picture on wall: "Norquay promises No Disallowance . . . Before Elections"

Vol. XXVII. TORONTO, AUGUST 28th, 1886. No. 8.

GRIP

EDITED BY J. W. BENGOUGH

THE POLITICAL INCUBATORS.

VICTORIA, B.C., August 6.—Mr. Norquay, Premier of Manitoba, arrived last night to have a conference with Sir John A. Macdonald regarding a policy for the North-West. Both are engaged in hatching a surprise policy for that country.—*Despatch to Globe.*

FIGURE 33. "The Political Incubators," *Grip*, 28 August 1886. With provincial and national elections imminent, Bengough's *Grip* speculated that Norquay might get his wish—an end to Ottawa's disallowance of provincial railway charters for lines to the United States border.

FIGURE 34. "Norquay and the python (With acknowledgments to Sir F. Leighton for the design)," *Grip*, 4 June 1887. Norquay, looking strikingly svelte on this occasion, appears to have throttled the python, "Monopoly" (George Stephen), saying "You would, would you?" Tupper and Macdonald look on in dismay.

FIGURE 35. "The First Sod Turned: Manitoba, Saturday, July 2," *Grip*, 16 July 1887. "Hope" dawns. Wasps labelled Sir D.A. Smith, Sir G. Stephen, and Van Horne buzz around a lean Norquay. Charles Tupper pulls on a rope around Norquay's leg in a vain attempt to control the Manitoba premier. Norquay's spade carries "the first sod," thus launching the Red River Valley Railway. John A. Macdonald, attached to a banner quoting his Commons speech five years earlier, "We cannot check Manitoba," dangles from the spade's handle.

FIGURE 36. "Norquay, The Lion King," *Grip*, 13 August 1887. Norquay as lion tamer shows how to control the fearsome animal labelled "Disallowance."

"Hon. John [Norquay]—Ladies and Gentlemen, the Animal's perfectly harmless if you show that you're not afraid of him!" British Columbia in background: "If he can do that why can't I?"

FIGURE 37. "We Cannot Check Manitoba (but we can try mighty hard to)," *Grip*, 24 September 1887. John A. Macdonald, riding the horse "CPR Monopoly," fails to capture Norquay by means of his lasso, "Injunction." The Manitoba premier races ahead on his Red River Valley Railway locomotive, "Provincial Rights."

FIGURE 38. "Manitoba's Foundling," *Grip*, 21 January 1888. Lt. Governor Aikins holds the squalling baby, "New Harrison Govt": "I'm asked to adopt this infant but I want to know about its parentage first."

Norquay: "Don't ask *me!* I know nothing about it, I assure you! I'm sure it doesn't resemble *me* in the least!" [In fact, the baby does resemble Bengough's Norquay in a fighting pose.]

The bemused observer in the background is John A. Macdonald.

FIGURE 39. "The Fall of Cardinal Wolsey Norquay," *Grip*, 28 January 1888. Norquay—"'Had I but served my province with half the zeal I have served John A., I would not now be left'—Shakespeare (amended)." Bengough quotes the lament uttered by the fallen Cardinal Wolsey in Shakespeare's *Henry VIII*: "Had I but served my God with half the zeal I served my king, he would not in mine age Have left me naked to mine enemies." Shakespeare, *Henry VIII*, Act 3, Scene 2.

FIGURE 40. "Norq.Ways That Are Dark," *Grip*, 4 February 1888. "Greenway—'Call yourself a statesman, and leave the Provincial Treasury in this condition?' Norquay—'I always told you, Tom, that the Premiership of Manitoba was an empty honour. Now, perhaps, you'll believe me!'"

The Parkdale home and the Kennedy Street property were not his biggest concerns. That role belonged to two other remarkable chapters in this phase of his life, a gold mine at Lake of the Woods and the coal mine near Medicine Hat. Norquay was involved in these ventures because he had become the recognized face of Manitoba in the rest of the country. Caricatures, some complimentary and others less so, appeared regularly in nationally circulated publications. He had visited businesses in St. Paul, Chicago, and New York, and his name was appearing in British newspapers. His unique political stature as the only elected head of a democratic parliament in this vast, potentially rich region ensured that aspiring investors beat a path to his door. Typically they offered Norquay a seat on a company board, or shares bearing inflated valuations, or both.[9] He wanted to encourage the ventures, and if they succeeded he could put the money to good use, so often he acquiesced.

Norquay originally had steered clear of the excitement surrounding gold exploration at Lake of the Woods, just 200 kilometres east of Winnipeg. When his name was included without his permission in a syndicate being formed by a New York promoter in August 1882, he declined emphatically to contribute $250 for 2,500 shares in the Keewatin Mining Company. The potential participation in the company of William Eli Sanford, a wealthy Hamilton businessman, and cabinet colleague Corydon Brown, as well as the appointment as corporate secretary of his poker-playing friend John Allan, seemed to leave Norquay unmoved.[10] Yet mysteriously, less than six months later, the name of "Hon. John Norquay" appeared on the letterhead of the Keewatin Mining Company as the firm's president. A letter in his files explained his adhesion: M.W. Meagher, an American investment banker, had offered shares in the company to Norquay and Brown, in each case bearing a (mythical) par value of $75,000. Norquay's shares seem to have been a gift; Brown might have paid $500 for his allotment. Most of the other directors, with the exception of Meagher, were Winnipeg merchants, and likely Norquay's name was important to the promoter because the premier had a reputation outside Manitoba, thus adding lustre to the shares then being sold in eastern North America.[11] The company languished for several years, according to Norquay, because it lacked "the judicious application of a little money." He added, with seemingly unquenchable optimism, that the mine "will when developed enrich every person connected therewith."[12] It did not.

The Keewatin gold gamble and a second failed scheme, a copper mine, taught Norquay a little more about his limits as a small investor. When the promoters of a third mining project offered him inducements to join their syndicate in 1885, he spoke more cautiously than before. He would accept a gift of stock "on the distinct understanding that I would not be called upon to pay for the shares allotted me." In place of an investment of cash, Norquay wrote, "[I am] willing to render any aid that lay in my power to promote the interest of the Company." Similarly, when he was encouraged to join yet another syndicate, he replied that "as my experience in mines has not been very profitable hitherto I will let others develop this without my assistance."[13]

At the heart of his business worries was the coal mine. Norquay became the president of the Saskatchewan Coal Mining and Transportation Company in November 1883 and devoted dozens, probably hundreds, of hours to its development over the next three years. To smooth its path he asked Prime Minister John A. Macdonald to "consider favorably" the company's application to purchase five specific sections of land. Norquay claimed that the investors had committed large sums in the preceding ten months: "I promised the members of the Company who by the way are all good workers & of the right [Conservative] stamp that I would make their case a personal one. Therefore I should esteem it a great personal favor indeed if their claim is entertained." He noted that domestic heating fuel was an essential commodity on the prairies and that "the benefit resulting therefrom will be general as well as private." This was the kind of lobbying that his friends had anticipated in bringing Norquay into their group. Thanks in good measure to his activity, the prime minister helped the company to clear several hurdles where it might have fallen.[14]

In November 1883, in a conversation with the Winnipeg manager of the Merchants Bank, Norquay hinted, if he did not promise, that the government of Manitoba would be purchasing the company's coal. A crucial loan, one that enabled the company to carry on through the winter of 1883–84, followed on the heels of that chat. In January 1884, two months after Norquay's conversations with the bank, Corydon Brown took another dubious step. While Norquay was in Ottawa on another diplomatic mission, Brown secured cabinet approval for a $2,000 payment to Saskatchewan Coal based upon an expectation of government coal purchases (500 tons at a bargain price of four dollars per ton). Norquay then spoke to the prime minister and apparently won his support for the company's land claim. Saskatchewan Coal thus secured ownership of the land on which the mine was located.[15] Brown knew they were edging closer to, and probably crossing, an ethical line: "Let us know every move," he concluded his letter to Norquay, "so we can move here too, & you need not be too plain for we will both have to read between the lines."[16]

Was Norquay's behaviour unethical? Politicians frequently participated in businesses. A decade earlier, in a comparable circumstance, Norquay had sold wood from his own land to the government. The Saskatchewan Coal episode was a much bigger story. His defence would be that he had saved taxpayers—and consumers in general—a great deal of money by bringing a competitive source of fuel into the local market. Moreover, the government saved money on its purchases of coal to heat its buildings. Still, assembly members were expected not to vote on matters in which they had "a direct pecuniary interest." His absence when the matter was brought to the cabinet was strategic. He knew that the deal was suspect. Moreover, he had obtained special consideration from the prime minister when a Blackfoot community and local settlers appeared to have prior claims to the land.[17] Anyone could see that the transaction was not at arm's length.

All looked rosy for a brief period, but then, shortly after the Manitoba cabinet decision and Norquay's conversations with Sir John A., the under-capitalized company faced bankruptcy once again. In March and April 1884, when its creditors called a halt to its continued operation, the claims registered against Saskatchewan Coal totalled over $40,000. During this second financial crisis Norquay told a potential buyer that the responsibility for its survival was wearing him down: "For my part I am so tired and worried with the subject that I should be only too glad to retire from the position that I occupy on getting back the money that I put into the enterprise. I have had a lot of hard work and there seems to be no effort put forth by any member of the Company to save it except an attempt to grab all the stock possible without regard to meeting liabilities." This was a fair statement of the circumstances in 1883–84, and his worries only multiplied in the following two years.[18]

The company was reorganized under the direction of another group of Winnipeg merchants and they invited Norquay to continue as its president.[19] The new owners offered no additional investment capital and did not add new partners. Rather, they turned to Norquay and his government as their predecessors had done. In the spring of 1885, during the very weeks that war in the North-West commenced, the principals in Saskatchewan Coal pressed Norquay for another subsidy, which they described as a "bonus." They claimed that they should get a reward for having cut the price of coal in the Manitoba market. But the premier replied that he could go only so far in aiding the company: "[It] would look so much like a personal benefit [he told a fellow director.] I couldn't carry the bonus through with my colleagues." The new owners refused to accept the debt contracted by their predecessors. In the end, to compensate the government for the shortfall on the previous ownership group's promised coal deliveries, and out of his own pocket, Norquay paid the outstanding bill, then about $1,600 (more than a year's salary for a middling civil servant).[20]

Saskatchewan Coal, more than any other single enterprise that engaged his attention, carried Norquay into the world of big business. The entrepreneurs with whom he talked in the course of these three intense years were not the junior speculators of the Winnipeg business community. In Toronto, Montreal, Chicago, and New York, he was encountering individuals who possessed wealth and power. When they surveyed expenses and revenues, they displayed a grasp of entire industries, of interest rates and finances, of payrolls and patents for land, of transportation and marketing costs. Norquay learned as he went along. He might have started out a novice, but by the close of 1886 he had acquired valuable experience as well as debts.[21]

Always attracted to new projects, listening too readily to too many pipe dreams, Norquay stepped beyond the bounds of ethical politics when he took on Saskatchewan Coal. He learned, to his cost, that investors readily transferred risk to the government. By mid-1886, after six or seven years of hopes being repeatedly dashed, he had cooled on these ambitious dreamers. He told a Winnipeg lawyer promoting an iron mine that, yes, there were "large iron deposits" in Manitoba, but it would take considerable capital to develop them: "I cannot understand how it is that the local government is resorted to continually to bolster up enterprises that cannot attract capital on their own merits. It is a mistaken idea to imagine that where people will not invest their money they can induce the government to do so."[22]

The larger lessons of Saskatchewan Coal concerned the relation between his public responsibilities and his private ambitions. Norquay should have declined the invitation to become president of the company. He should never have promised future coal deliveries to government buildings as collateral for a bank loan. He should not have colluded with Brown to secure a government advance for those future deliveries. Saskatchewan Coal went bankrupt twice in the four years that it attempted to work the Medicine Hat seam and market the coal. Now Norquay was finding out what a vigorously partisan opposition could do to blacken his reputation. The attack on his integrity and honour hurt very much.

Daily Life

Norquay moved from confident leader to embattled warrior over the course of these years. But in daily life he seemed to be as cheerful and energetic as ever. His diet ranged widely, and he ate heartily. The tickets marking his presence in the legislature dining room recorded many more meals than days in the week. Either he was frequently entertaining guests, or he was eating several servings at a sitting. He enjoyed all kinds of wildfowl and game, including moose, rabbit, geese, ducks, and prairie chickens. He placed an order for tripe with his friend Samuel Bedson and in return was teased about his taste for it. Norquay spoke with pleasure about bison tongues and asked for some to be sent to Ottawa, perhaps to entertain his negotiating partners.[23] Moments of illness rarely slowed him down. He continued to carry several insurance policies. Between 1882 and the end of 1885, he had dealings with six different companies, held three policies in some years, and paid out at least $100 annually for the promise that his heirs would receive several thousand dollars in the case of his death.[24]

Despite his weight Norquay seemed to be in fine form. Dr. James Edmunds, medical officer of health in London and a visitor to Manitoba in 1884, was quoted in England's *Derbyshire Times* as saying that the premier weighed 310 pounds and stood six feet, one inch tall: "He is a man of Herculean frame, has a grand but soft and controlled voice, and is a most able speaker." Edmunds also observed Norquay's agility: "Taking from one of the Indians a birch bark canoe which was as crank as a cockle shell, he deftly inserted his huge body into it, and handled the paddle in a way which seemed to excite the envy of the Indians whom he ordered to row us after him in an ordinary boat."[25]

Norquay went hunting whenever time permitted. Bills for shot, powder, wads, and cartridge cases arrived in his office regularly, summer and winter. He was invited to become the patron of several rifle associations. Correspondents eager to secure his presence at meetings added details concerning the abundance of ducks and prairie chickens in their area, knowing that this would tempt him to pay a visit. Norquay agreed to attend a government exhibition of field cultivation in the summer of 1884 with such thoughts in mind: "My dear Burrows, I will go out on Saturday if all is well but more to practise Rifle Shooting than to see the plow work."[26]

The intense business of government and the worrying state of his private investments occupied most of his days. But Norquay was beginning to carry himself differently, to convey greater authority, than before. In July 1883, after the successful election and session, he sent a chatty letter to one of his cabinet ministers that offered insights into his thinking about work and leisure. He hoped to visit this colleague's district in the fall, he wrote, "when I intend to (if my health permits) enjoy some sport also. I hope that the ducks & prairie chickens give promise of being very numerous." A postscript illustrated his intellectual reach: "I send you by mail the life and times of Sir John which is very interesting literature[.] I know you will appreciate it. I do." The book in question was the new *Life and Times of the Right Honourable Sir John A. Macdonald*, a 600-page tome by J.E. Collins.[27]

Norquay had moved well beyond the limits of Assiniboia and become a student of Canadian public administration. He spent time reading official documents and seeking experienced observers of public affairs. Having asked his secretary to make a list of the books required to complete his "private library," the reply came back that his collection was fairly complete. The volumes to be acquired were exclusively official publications of the federal government: House of Commons *Sessional Papers* from 1867–68 to 1880; House of Commons *Journals* from 1867–68 to 1879; Senate *Journals* from 1867 to 1880; Canada's *Public Accounts* 1869 and 1870; and *Census of Canada* volume 1, 1881. Norquay also purchased *Canada under the Administration of Lord Lorne*, another work by J.E. Collins. It was a daunting list, not the usual bedtime reading, and it suggested that Norquay was building a reference library to prepare for jousts in Ottawa.[28]

He was invited to many social events each month. In the course of a few weeks in the spring of 1883, he dined with the lieutenant governor, the travellers' association, the Selkirk town council, the St. Andrews society, and two Masonic lodges. In April 1884 the invitations included a reception for a new assembly member at the Bellevue Hotel, the annual ball of the Order of Railroad Conductors at the Princess Opera House, and the St. George's Day gathering organized by England-born Manitobans. At the end of June Norquay presented prizes at St. John's Ladies' College, took part in a shooting competition at the Stony Mountain range, and visited with the Bedsons overnight. In mid-August he visited Portage la Prairie, attended the St. Andrews community picnic, and travelled west, returning for meetings in Brandon.[29] Several weeks later he was entertaining two federal cabinet ministers in Winnipeg, including at a banquet and on a brief rail tour along the southern branch lines.[30]

In the year of Aida's death, 1883, Tom turned twenty, Bella eighteen, John (Jack) seventeen, Alex sixteen, Horatio (Horace) fourteen, Caroline Ellen (Nellie) twelve, and Andrew eleven. They made quite a crew, well-mannered and well-spoken—and costly—young people. Despite the rule that no residents could be older than sixteen, both Tom and John returned to St. John's College in the fall of 1883. In making the exceptions Reverend Matheson proposed that Tom be made captain of the school and "have special privileges owing to his age." But John would "have to be governed by the ordinary rules of the school." This meant that he would have one day per month to leave the college for visits home and one day per week when he could receive visitors in a set two-hour period. The premier wrote back immediately to approve the arrangements: "I do not know what the boys may think of the same, but I am convinced that they will fall in with your views and my only care is that they may show themselves diligent and avail themselves of the chances they get under your training."[31]

Norquay wrote to the children whether he was in Ottawa or at the office. Few of these missives have survived. Because the children were in residence, and subject to strict rules about visitors and absences, they tried to time their visits to Parkdale for days when he would be there.[32] Although Norquay missed Christmas in Manitoba completely in 1884 because of his mission to Ottawa, he was at home for the holiday in 1885, when he made last-minute purchases of gifts for everyone. They included several ladies' cases (for Elizabeth and Bella?), two prayer books, four other books perhaps destined for the younger boys, two "caps" (perhaps for the older boys now in the workforce), and an album, perhaps for a collection of photographs or clippings that Elizabeth was said to be creating.[33]

Bella continued to show evidence of diplomacy and command in her daily life. After the appearance of a newspaper story on a concert that she had helped to organize, she somehow arranged access to her father's office letterbook (and perhaps the drafting skill of his secretary) to dispatch a letter to the editor regretting that "no mention is made in connection therewith of Miss Fulsher our popular teacher and of Mrs. G. Fulsher who were associated with me in getting up the entertainment. In justice to them I beg to say that were it not for the zeal and energy with which they applied themselves to the work there would have been no such event to chair." Caroline Ellen was as ready as her sister to call on her father for assistance: "Please drive up for me on Friday as owing to the change in the train service I can not come otherwise. Be sure to come. Yr loving daughter C.E.N."[34]

When their father was in Ottawa for an extended period in early 1884, the children sent him entertaining letters. Andrew, the youngest, reported on his success in school and on his mother's illness. Horace claimed to be leading his class in math and to be "invincible" in debate, he and his partner having won for the affirmative side on the proposition that an ox was more useful than a horse. Tom, the eldest, offered sober assessments of the policy issues confronting Manitoba and, with hard-headed practicality, noted rumours of his father's elevation to the federal cabinet: "I do not know whether you intend to pursue such a course or not but I think you could not do better," Tom wrote, "especially since you have had notions of giving up the leadership of this party and allowing some one else to run the Government for a while, I should think that it would be just as good to play second fiddle in the Dominion Cabinet for a salary of seven or eight thousand a year, as to do so up here for a salary of two or three thousand." The reference to "second fiddle" must have taken his father by surprise. And the comment about stepping down as premier suggested that the two engaged in frank conversations about important matters.

All of the letters expressed affection for their father. Bella, the most effusive, reminded him of "Mamma's" illness and hoped he would soon come home: "Never mind the business and come back. Kate sends her love to you and Andrew does the same. I also send my love and kisses for my very dear old papa. If you (..) kiss that spot that is where I kissed the paper and it will be like kissing me. I remain dear papa, your loving daughter, Bella Norquay." They were loving children, comfortable in expressing affection for their father, and eager to see him. They also were clear in their understanding that his work required long absences.[35]

Their schooling was expensive. Tuition fees, boarding fees, and book purchases consumed many hundreds of dollars each year, sometimes more than a quarter of their father's government income. John had trouble keeping up with the payments. There were clothing bills, too, as the children graduated from homemade and hand-me-down clothes to wardrobes purchased in stores. In just 1884 and 1885 the new suits and dresses and shoes coming home with the young shoppers added up to more than $250.[36] John passed the bill for one of the men's suits to its owner, son Tom, who had recently taken a job and may have been expected to pay his own way, and he secured a pass for Jack's railway travel, but he couldn't avoid the rest. In 1885 Reverend Matheson made a special appeal to the premier that he pay an outstanding bill at St. John's College: "I am being *dunned* on every hand. Try to send [illegible] . . . to keep me out of prison."[37]

The premier had many other family responsibilities. Perhaps the most onerous was the welfare of his brother, Tom, and Tom's family. Tom had attended St. John's Collegiate School and later taught school in St. Andrews parish while operating a small river-lot farm. Shortly after John became premier, Tom became clerk of the county court at Selkirk, not far from his home. Then, as the province's boundaries were extended westward, he received a promotion to provincial registrar in Virden. He was troubled by alcohol, however, and in the summer of 1884 he acknowledged the problem: "I am happy to state that I have kept to my resolve to quit the cursed drink and once the resolve is made I find the craving leaving me. . . . Since quitting the drink I have been working like a good fellow." The cheery letter seemed to be promising. Within months, however, Tom had weakened, confessing to his brother that he had failed to carry out his official duties.[38] News from the Charles Adams family was a little better, but they also needed help from John.[39] These were difficult times. He did his best to share what he had with those in need, a virtue consistent with the ideals of Indigenous communities, suggesting that he had not left his early days, or his family heritage, behind.

North-West Resistance

Preoccupation with Manitoba politics ensured that Norquay had only glancing connections with public affairs in the North-West Territories.

He was probably surprised in the spring of 1884 to hear that Louis Riel had left his new home in Montana to support a political campaign in the Saskatchewan River valley. Norquay had never met Riel, as far as can be determined, and never exchanged communications with him. The two had had much in common, having grown up in the Red River Settlement, but their paths diverged when they reached their early teens. Riel was sent to Montreal, where he received a classical French Catholic education, while Norquay, by then an orphan, stayed at Red River where he attended the British Anglican school operated by Bishop Anderson. The divergence became more marked in their early adulthood. Far more than Riel, Norquay lived beside, travelled among, and worked with First Nations peoples and countrymen of both Michif/French and Bungee/English ancestry. During the twenty years between 1858, when he left school, and 1878, when he became a full-time premier, Norquay was immersed in the environment of plains, parkland, and Red River Settlement. Riel, in contrast, spent most of those two decades in Quebec and eastern American centres.

Both men became targets of racist jibes, though Riel was subject to far more serious pressure, including having to survive the Ontario government's putting a $5,000 price on his head in 1872. Riel carried the added burden of being French and Catholic at a time of increasing Orange hostility to both, whereas Norquay appeared to fit in with British Canadian ways. In 1875, the federal administration of Alexander Mackenzie officially banished Riel from Canada for five years. Norquay, in contrast, was the subject of subtle whisper campaigns, the kind of racism that hid behind bland faces. In the years after 1878, Riel farmed and taught school in Montana while trying to launch another political movement within that American territory. Norquay worked to reform the Canadian constitution and political system from the inside, taking part year after year in negotiations with federal authorities in the hope that he could secure what he called a fair start for Manitoba within the federation.

The distance between them narrowed in June 1884 when Riel was invited by a group of settlers from the District of Saskatchewan to assist them in their clashes with federal authorities over land regulations, surveys, and political representation. At this point it is clear that Riel knew of Norquay.[40] While conducting his own fact-finding travels through the district in these months, Riel commented that Manitoba's "better terms" campaigns addressed problems similar to those that handicapped residents of the North-West Territories. He praised Norquay's work as premier in a letter to a Prince Albert–area activist: "Mr. Norquay is playing a glorious part, at the head of the Manitoba responsible government. I do not know what he thinks of me. I know I admire him. My intention here is to help his struggle as much as it is in my power." Riel wondered whether Norquay might issue a statement addressed to the Canadian government reiterating Manitoba's unhappiness with the terms of confederation, linking it to the unrest in the North-West Territories, and perhaps noting that Riel was also dissatisfied: "It is that general dissatisfaction that makes our strength. Riel has been ill treated enough to have adopted another Country."[41] There is no record suggesting that he contacted Norquay directly.

After nine months of public meetings and private conversations in francophone and anglophone settlements as well as First Nation communities, and having submitted a petition of grievances to Ottawa without apparent effect, Riel declared the formation of a provisional government on 18 March 1885, a tactic similar to that of 1869–70 though in much-changed circumstances. He also took several hostages to underline the urgency of the situation and rashly threatened "a war of extermination upon all those who have shown themselves hostile to our rights."[42] A week later a Métis force, several hundred strong, under the direction of Gabriel Dumont, intercepted a column of 100 North-West Mounted Police and civilian volunteers heading for Batoche to free the hostages and quell the disturbance. The rattle of gunfire at Duck Lake and the deaths of twelve police and six citizens on the government side, five Métis and one Cree opposing them, roused fears across Canada that a Métis and First Nations uprising would spread across the prairies.[43]

As of 20 March 1885 a Métis-led military confrontation—guided to some degree by Riel and Dumont but involving some Cree communities, some Whites, and threatening to spread to the Blackfoot—challenged Canadian authority in the North-West Territories.[44] Prime Minister Macdonald ordered the militia to mobilize, resulting in the dispatch of no fewer than 5,000 soldiers to the North-West Territories. The huge expeditionary force was expected not only to crush easily the few hundred Métis and their potential White and First Nations allies but also to ensure that the thousands of Cree, Saulteaux, Assiniboine, and Blackfoot in plain and parkland did not join the Métis-led campaign.

Viewed from a European Canadian vantage point, the uprising was an echo of the British Empire's experience in "Queen Victoria's small wars": regiments mobilized, troops marched, soldiers died, and military bands brought out the crowds when the veterans returned. But this time the drama was close to home. Pitched battles took place at Fish Creek, Batoche, Cut Knife Hill, Frenchman's Butte, and Loon Lake. Riel surrendered on 15 May, Poundmaker on 25 May, Big Bear on 2 July. Trials that made a mockery of the principles supposed to guide Canada's justice system took place in Regina and Battleford. Many Indigenous people, including Poundmaker and Big Bear, were sent to prison. Riel was hanged on 16 November. Eleven days later eight First Nations men were executed in a shocking public spectacle at Battleford.[45] Norquay, and Manitoba, had to deal with the fact of a war on their doorstep and with the attitudes toward Indigenous peoples it stirred up.

The Manitoba Government's Response

On 24 March 1885, shortly after the legislative sitting in Manitoba opened, and before the bloodshed at Duck Lake, John Norquay and Thomas Greenway sparred briefly in a debate about railway service. The Liberal leader lamented Ottawa's focus on completion of the Canadian Pacific Railway, arguing that "it would have been better for this province and the C.P.R. itself to have built more slowly and left funds for branch lines." He hoped that the province would "lend tangible aid" to the Hudson Bay railway, a project with more immediate value to Manitoba. Norquay responded that the CPR was not simply a railway for Manitobans but also a national line: "What would Canada be today but for that policy? (Cheers). We hear rumours of serious trouble in the west, and he heard they were well-founded. How would the people of Canada have sent troops to speedily crush this rising but for this railway?"[46] Norquay was merely projecting a plausible scenario at this point, but his assessment of the strategic situation was accurate. His image of troop movements became a reality within days. His decision to stand with Ottawa and Macdonald's Canada, not with his countrymen's resistance, even before the lines had been drawn clearly, stood out.

Then, for several days and evenings in late March 1885, members discussed the "better terms" that Norquay had negotiated in Ottawa and whether to accept the "finality clause." On 29–30 March a late-night debate was interrupted in dramatic fashion by news of the gunfire at Duck Lake.

When copies of the *Free Press* carrying the latest reports arrived by messenger during the assembly sitting, the newspaper's "appearance was greeted with loud applause from both sides of the House. The proceedings were stopped and the news of the disturbances in the North-West was eagerly perused." The members sat until well after 5 a.m., "the longest [sitting] that has ever been held by the Manitoba Legislature." Members then sang "God Save the Queen" and departed.[47]

The assembly continued to debate and legislate while the country, including the people of Manitoba, prepared for battle. In these discussions the premier defended his record by pointing to obvious signs of provincial economic progress. He cited the kilometres of branch lines constructed and drainage ditches excavated and applauded the CPR's completion of the line north of Lake Superior. The latter offered "evidence of the energy with which work on the national highway is being prosecuted, and of the determination of the Central Government and the Canadian Pacific Railway Company, to connect by an all rail route the fertile prairies of our province with the seaboard, and thereby secure expeditious transport of the products of our country to the markets of Europe." This speech in defence of his government won praise, even in the *Free Press*. Norquay had spoken, editor William Luxton said, "with his usual force and effectiveness of oratory. The galleries contained a considerable number of visitors who listened with evident interest and appreciation of the hon. gentleman's speaking powers." But the praise was mixed with censure. When Norquay said that he had won eastern attention for Manitoba's claims, the *Free Press* mocked him, saying that there was a new season in Ottawa now, to go with house-cleaning season and ice cream season, known as "the Norquay expedition season. . . . Mr. Norquay is known to our Eastern friends as the blooming beggar from the blizzard's birthplace." When the settlement reached by the premier and the prime minister in the January 1885 negotiations finally came to a vote, the government's motion passed by the usual margin, seventeen votes to nine.[48]

In the third week of March, after Riel's declaration of a provisional government but before news arrived of the deadly confrontation at Duck Lake, the Saskatchewan troubles seemed to be no more pressing in Manitoba than the continuing agitation by farm unions and Fenians. Then on 26 March, the day of the gun battle, a secret police agent wrote to Norquay that a leader of the farm movement "had been offered money to go West & act in with Riel as a rebel, but [at the] same time watch his (Riel's) movements."[49] Could these farmer and Fenian agitators be trusted, or was the unrest spreading from Métis insurgents in the Saskatchewan River valley to potential rebels in Manitoba?

Rumours of local unrest ran through the province in the weeks that followed. Upon receiving requests from the villages of Griswold and Binscarth, the lieutenant governor wired Ottawa for rifles and ammunition. A citizen in the village of Melbourne, Manitoba, warned Norquay that "for a day or two several very suspicious looking characters apparently of the Fenian stripe about here[,] up and down the railroad track and about Pine Creek Bridge on the CPR. They are bad looking customers and we do not consider the bridge very safe with them about[.] I think it would be well to have it looked after." John James Setter reported from Portage la Prairie that "I have just heard that the Arms, Clothing, &c of the Vol[unteer]s have been wrecked by Fenians, I hope this is not true." The premier was even invited to join an anti-confederation movement that planned to petition the British cabinet for the right to secede from Canada. Anxiety and suspicion bubbled for several weeks.[50]

Norquay was the leader of a government charged with maintaining peace and security in the jurisdiction next door to the North-West Territories. He might have been expected to play a role in the civil war of 1885. Yet he was never asked to intervene. He wired Major General Frederick Dobson Middleton, commander of the Canadian force, with an offer of "fifty-three native scouts" willing to go to the front. They would "require horses[,] arms and accoutrements" but were "just the men for such work as they are acquainted with the kind of warfare likely to take place[.] A dozen will furnish horses on condition of scouts pay guaranteed." The general declined the offer: "At present have scouts enough[.] Will apply to you if men are wanted."[51]

Norquay received news of troop movements throughout the campaign from his friends, a number of whom were senior officers. He heard about the Fish Creek ambush as it was happening and of the victory at Batoche within hours of the event. He knew when troops were heading westward from Prince Albert and eastward from Edmonton in pursuit of Big Bear's people. He might have been relegated to the periphery by the prime minister and officialdom, but the updates that he received were not much different from those reaching Ottawa.

The government did have several immediate tasks. The first was to coordinate locally generated plans for self-defence forces. In early April the Manitoba cabinet approved an order-in-council arranging for "300 stand of arms" to be delivered to newly assembled "home guard" companies. In the same month Norquay appealed several times to the federal minister of militia, Adolphe-Philippe Caron, for guns. In one letter he described a petition asking for arms that he had received from thirteen justices of the peace in the Turtle Mountain district, a comparatively inaccessible region "along our Saskatchewan frontier," over eighty kilometres from the nearest railway station: "What they fear is that before assistance could be rendered them they would all be massacred. I really hope their fears are groundless but must communicate to you their representations." Talk of self-defence forces spread across the province in April and then faded as quickly as it had arisen. Minister of Militia Caron did not approve the creation of such groups and refused to pay for them.[52]

The cabinet also had to handle requests from citizens, notably those in the provincial civil service, who were members of local militia units and clamouring to be part of the expeditionary force. A member of the assembly, Jack Allan, possessed valuable military experience. His vote might be missed in divisions in the legislature, but Norquay decided that Allan, a regular at the premier's poker games, could be accommodated. Norquay also arranged leaves of absence for many civil servants heading into "active service with the various corps to which they belong[ed]." In a note to his supporter Dr. John Pennefather, then at the front, Norquay asked to be remembered to no fewer than eight of their mutual friends (whom he named) marching in the same contingent.[53]

The premier was responsible, too, for ensuring that potential immigrants were not deterred from travelling to Manitoba by reports of warfare in the North-West Territories. Although it flew in the face of local districts' determination to organize armed militias, he secured a resolution in the assembly in mid-April declaring that the troubles in the North-West were far distant, did not affect Manitoba, and should not discourage immigrants, for the province enjoyed "the most perfect security." Norquay immediately wired the resolution to Charles Tupper, now Canada's high commissioner in London, asking him to convey the statement to the people of Great Britain. It appeared the next day in the *Times* of London.[54] Within two weeks of the deaths at Duck

Lake, Norquay had aligned his province with Canada's military operations against the resistance movement. There could be no doubt about his views.

Norquay's Assessment of the Conflict

Norquay was not a stranger to life in the North-West. In addition to bison hunts that had taken him west and south in the 1860s, he had visited the territories on four or five recent occasions: he accompanied federal cabinet ministers to the district near Fort Ellice in the late 1870s, travelled with some land speculators in 1881, entered the Qu'Appelle Valley with the governor general's full-dress excursion in the same year, and visited the Saskatchewan Coal company's mine near Medicine Hat in 1883 and perhaps again in 1884. Norquay recognized looming disagreements among Indigenous peoples over how to accommodate incoming Whites and, after 1879, their trials as they adapted to a land suddenly stripped of bison, hitherto the single most important food resource on the plains. Treaties with the Canadian government (1871–77) introduced reserves, and Canada's Indian Act (1876) imposed extensive supervision of First Nations groups, but many community members, led by chiefs such as Big Bear, resisted the constraints. When Ottawa's initial attempts at control were taking effect in the early 1880s and increasing numbers of First Nations had to accept that bison herds would never return, hunger visited their communities with devastating effect.[55] Norquay understood this context.

His response to the North-West conflict came as much from personal as from official responsibilities. Norquay and his family had direct contact with the war because Tom, then twenty-one, and Alexander (Alick), seventeen, enlisted with the Canadian forces and travelled to the front. Tom served as a junior officer in the contingent sent to Alberta, Alick as postal clerk on the Batoche front. Their parents' thinking as they watched two children heading off to war is not recorded in family lore. But John's concern about Elizabeth's health had surfaced again just before the uprising. John had written to John James Setter, her brother, to let him know that Elizabeth had left the Parkdale farm and was with him in the city: "I shall keep her here [in Winnipeg] until I can go up with her to the Portage and leave her with you for some time."[56]

After the main expeditionary force left Winnipeg, Tom and Alick figured prominently in the premier's correspondence. Their father wrote to them regularly, though these letters have not survived. Several of the boys' replies are in the premier's files. When Alick thanked his father for two recent letters, he added that "you can't tell how good a fellow feels when he gets a letter from home and friends, it sort of braces him up."[57]

Norquay's friends responded generously to his request that they take a special interest in his sons' welfare. Their assurances about the safety of Tom and Alick appeared in numerous letters arriving in his office during the next three months.[58] His own letters reveal his keen focus on his children. "My dear Bedson," he wrote to the Stony Mountain Penitentiary superintendent, now chief transport officer in the expeditionary force,

> I received your kind note today, a thousand thanks for the interest you take in Alick. I am sure his attention to duty will be all that you would wish. I know him well and he will appreciate the interest you take in him. I hope everything will go on all right so that you may all speedily return to us covered with glory if not gore. My best regards to all friends and tell Alick his Mama is getting on all right and she will be pleased to see her soldier boy return with a bronzed face, heavy moustache, and soldier like appearance all around.[59]

Alick accompanied the main force north toward Batoche, driving one of six supply wagons at the rear of the column, about a kilometre and a half behind the ambulance and the foremost troops. Samuel Bedson reported to Norquay on Alick's first experience of battle at Fish Creek, where the Canadian troops endured withering fire: "Had very hot work for over four hours[.] About fifty killed & wounded on our side[.] Rebels loss not yet known[.] Aleck [Norquay], [Walter] Nursey [Norquay's friend in the treasury department], and self OK[.] Let wives know."[60]

Tom moved west with the troops and eventually reached Calgary, where he became part of the Alberta column. Like his younger brother he was very concerned about his family and eager to hear news from home. He was also a team player, neither stepping out of line nor divulging secrets: "About 14 of our boys were run in to the guard tent last night for being drunk[.] Where they got the whiskey is a question I could answer but they got it." Tom was as independent minded as ever, reporting on what he perceived to be the shortcomings of his commanding officers and the internal politics of the command group. He exhibited both a sense of humour and an awareness of the dangers of battle. One of his letters closed with "hoping you are still quite well, I remain, your living son, Tom."[61]

Alick sent the family a long and sobering account of his part in the Fish Creek battle. Written just two days later, when the gunfire was still fresh in his mind, he conveyed the dangers well: "I got through the fight without a scratch thank God, but sad to say nine of our men have been killed and forty-three wounded." His group of five wagons was moving slowly along the trail when he heard a single shot. He and his mates took no notice, "thinking it was a scout firing at a bird or something of that sort. Suddenly I heard a volley fired and I knew we were going to have our first fight. Well to tell the truth I felt nervous and I know I grew pale. I jumped down from the wagon put on my belt and ball pouches which were lying loose on the wagon, put a cartridge in my rifle and got on the wagon again to steady the load which was a very rickety one." They were then told to "hurry up as we might be cut off by a rear flank movement of the rebels." They pushed the horses into a trot but had to stop several times to pick up goods that bounced over the sides, and finally they "caught up to the main column where a zeriba [zareba, a type of corral] had been formed." Alick then headed out "on my own hook for the scene of action which was about half a mile from the zeriba. I arrived there safely and lay down on the brow of the hill of the creek from which the rebels kept up a pretty warm fire. The shooting by this time had become general and wherever the least bit of a rebel appeared the bullets scattered like rain around the spot." Alick closed the letter with a poignant thought: "I hope I may be spared to get back home again. I know my life is in the hands of a Divine Being but if I am not I am happy to say I am prepared to die as a soldier of Christ and doing my duty. Give my love to all at home. Good bye, Your own son, Alick."[62]

Norquay was concerned about the boys' safety and proud of their conduct. He sent a copy of Alick's letter to the bishop of Athabasca, Richard Young, formerly a clergyman in St. Andrews parish, asking that it be shown to Mrs. Young, who had taken "a kind interest" in Alick when he was a child. Norquay added that Elizabeth was "bearing up under her anxieties better than I thought she would have done." In Norquay's correspondence, as this suggests, there were no doubts about the military expedition or his sons' participation in it. Grave worries about the boys' fate, certainly; concerns about his wife's reactions, of course; but no questioning of militia involvement once the campaign began.[63]

Concern about his sister and her family contributed to his unease. The Adams family had left the HBC post in The Pas in 1883 and joined a number of Bungee/English-speaking settlers from High Bluff clearing land for farms around Red Deer Hill, between Prince Albert and Batoche in the North-West Territories. Having left one awkward setting, where Orange Ontarians had made life difficult, they were now immersed in another, where a resistance movement was being organized. When Norquay learned from family letters that Charles Adams and many neighbours had attended "a big 'Riel' meeting at the South Branch" in early March 1885, that 400 Michif/French-speaking Métis had attended another political gathering, and that "there was a talk that Riel was going to be arrested so there were (61) sixty one armed men guarding Riel for a while," he wrote immediately to warn Charles and the Adams boys. Riel could not be trusted, Norquay said, and they should be wary of becoming involved in a movement that they could not control.[64]

Having considered the consequences carefully, Adams and his sons abandoned the resistance movement. But others in the district—including most of the Michif/French-speaking Métis, some Bungee/English-speaking settlers, some Cree, and a few Whites—were not deterred by the prospect of an armed conflict. Adams told Norquay of his decision in mid-April: "My dear Neestaw[,] I suppose you are all interested in the state of affairs out this way, certainly it is a sad state, however we are all safe so far. You were not far wrong in your opinion of that beggar Riel[,] he nearly getting the Eng hf brds [*sic*] in trouble[,] but their loyalty was too strong for his taste & did not go to extremes. The moment he took up arms[,] all with very few exceptions took arms against him."[65]

If Charles Adams remained outwardly composed, his children were becoming increasingly excited. His son Horace struck a dramatic note in his next letter to the Norquays in Winnipeg:

> My dear uncles, aunties & cousins[,] I now once more write you a few lines "perhaps it might be the last time" to tell you that we are in a very dangerous position[.] We all have to go and take up arms tomorrow and fight for the Crown[.] There is no knowing how many of us there is that will live to see the end of this

> Rebellion. But we will pray that God will do what serveth him good and I hope & pray that he will make us victorious in this battle. The Rebels are coming nearer & it is likely we will have to go to war in a few days. . . . I am rather excited just now, but will try & keep cool. H.C.A.[66]

God, the Crown, and rebels: young Horace's language drew on heroic acts familiar from the British Empire's pulpits and schoolbooks.

Norquay replied calmly, though he did not try to hide his worries about the conflict. He reinforced the political choice of the Adams family with his news that two of his sons had enlisted: "My dear Horace[,] I received your letter dated the 28th ult giving me an account of the awkward situation in which you are placed. I hope that you may be able to get out of this trouble without any harm. Tom and Alick are off with the troops and you can imagine my anxiety for their safety. I hope this unfortunate rebellion will soon come to an end. Your affectionate Uncle."[67] Like their Adams relatives the Norquays were concerned about the lives of family members who might soon face gunfire in the Saskatchewan River valley.

Tom and Alick Norquay behaved and thought like their cousins. Tom spoke of their Cree opponents near Fort Pitt as "the devils," and of Big Bear as "the old rascal."[68] He did not doubt the cause for which he was fighting.[69] The premier's many friends who wrote from military camps expressed similar opinions. Without exception they were critical of Riel and the movement that he led. Norquay had a much broader perspective, though his mixed ancestry and public role meant that he faced delicate challenges in speaking about the war. Rather than exult in the crushing defeat of an Indigenous resistance, he deplored the failures of Canada's administration in the North-West Territories.

When news of Riel's initial political activism was still fresh, after Duck Lake but before the final battles, Norquay spoke coldly about the resistance campaign. Later, in a private note to Walter Nursey, his friend and the Manitoba government's auditor, he wrote some of the strongest words that he ever uttered about a matter of public concern: "I hope that this insane movement will soon come to an end and that you will all return safe. But if fighting has to be done my desire is that the Rebels will be knocked to h—l. I only wish I was with you if ever any serious action does become necessary."[70] Norquay expressed similar sentiments to a reporter from the St. Paul

Globe, saying that the "halfbreeds had made a serious mistake in invoking the aid of the Indians." He added a significant qualifier, doubting that First Nations would have entered the conflict had they been treated properly and provided with food, their main concern in the straitened days after the near extinction of the bison.[71]

An exchange of letters with Andrew Spence provides the clearest picture of Norquay's assessment of the North-West Resistance. Spence, Norquay's half-brother (as well as a relative by marriage), had moved west in the early 1880s after failing to resolve his financial troubles. He made several appeals to Norquay for assistance in these years; however, given his own financial situation and the entreaties from so many others, Norquay was unable to help him. Spence reacted unhappily to what he saw as snubs and told one of the premier's sons that he no longer regarded the premier as a friend. However, he aided Norquay's sister and brother-in-law (the Charles Adams family), whose new farm abutted his own, when they arrived in the Prince Albert district. At this point the old High Bluff relationships between Spences and Norquays were renewed.[72]

In 1885 Spence became an activist in the resistance movement and accepted the presidency of a settlers' union in the Prince Albert district. On 14 March, just days before Riel declared the formation of a provisional government, Spence wrote to Norquay appealing for a job. His farm, like that of his neighbour, Charles Adams, was probably in financial trouble. Spence had heard that Norquay was about to secure a portfolio in the federal cabinet and presumably would have the power to distribute civil service appointments. It was a bold and even aggressive appeal, and Spence did not mention his apparent alliance with the Riel insurgency.[73]

Norquay's reply, his most complete statement about the North-West Resistance, was written two weeks later, on 27 March, after Riel's declaration of a provisional government. It was dated the day after the deaths at Duck Lake, but it is unlikely that the news had reached Norquay before he wrote. Rather, he would have known only that farmers in the District of Saskatchewan faced hardship, that his brother-in-law was asking for help, and that by extension Spence faced tough times. Norquay expressed his thoughts in a cool and dignified tone: "My dear Andrew[,] I have not written to you on account of the feeling that you had towards me when leaving Manitoba, which of course was communicated to me by my son to whom you spoke openly in terms that were not flattering to myself and which led me to believe that the friendship which has been so long a matter of mutual gratification between us had come to an end. There is no foundation for the report that I shall be appointed Minister of the Interior." The premier expressed sympathy for the people in northern Saskatchewan who had been left isolated when the railway route and the territorial government's capital were switched far to the south, noting that affairs "must be in a bad shape out in your part of the Territory." Still, he wanted to send words of warning about Riel and the unfortunate strategy, as Norquay saw it, of establishing a provisional government in a land that, unlike Red River in 1869, had a legitimate administration and functioning police force. The premier offered his usual words of caution: "Bad Councils apparently have prevailed. I only hope that no acts of an irreparable character will be perpetrated." These were sentiments of the sort that Norquay had sent to Adams. They conveyed his awareness of both sides' interests and his belief that only careful political protest, not the abrupt break advocated by Riel, would provide help of the sort legitimately requested.

Like Adams, Norquay blamed federal government policies and local officials for the crisis. He denied Spence's assertion that he had abandoned old friends: "I feel for my countrymen because I think they have not been treated as they should be." He argued against the use of threats and violence as negotiating tools and spoke optimistically about the prospects for change: "Under judicious management and a proper course everything will come out all right in the end but I fear very much that the steps that are being taken will retard rather than hasten such condition."

Why had amends not been made sooner? Norquay spoke from experience and with optimism: "I know the government well. They are slow to act but are always open to reason." Canada's western civil service, he argued, must carry the blame: "I can attribute to the conduct of its officials much of the ill feeling that now exists in the Prince Albert district and I think also that were people selected from the different localities in which appointments have to be filled the result would be much more explainable than at present." This last thought echoed the views expressed by Charles Nolin and William Kennedy just a few years before.

The letter was formal in tone, thoughtful, and positive in its expressions of trust in the political process. It suggested how sweeping Norquay's sense of responsibility was for the people of the prairie west. It also conveyed his confidence in his ability to make a difference in their lives. Norquay concluded the letter by expressing his willingness to assist: "I may if able to get away from my official duties in the course of the summer pay a visit to Prince Albert so that I may have the opportunity of finding out thoroughly the wants of the people and if I can in any way advance their interests by an advocacy of their claims I shall only be too happy to do so."[74] The premier had no opportunity to carry out these promises. Once Canada's forces had mobilized, the resistance ended quickly.

The Norquays did not take pleasure in the widespread celebrations of imperial might. Charles Adams gave voice to this disappointment at the end of June 1885 while troops were still in the field. He told his *neestaw* that the rising of "the French" had been "squashed" and added his hope that "the Indians" would soon be defeated. But he was not rejoicing in the victory. Rather, he wrote critically of "the authorities" whose "behavior has all been deceit—& rascality all through." Adams saved his strongest condemnation for his Bungee/English-speaking neighbours (including Andrew Spence, presumably, though he went unnamed) who talked so emphatically about oppression, led others to violence, and then backed away while blaming their erstwhile allies for the consequences: "In my opinion the principals in the Rebellion are those who were first shouting, & who [after the shooting commenced] shouted the loudest—'God save the Queen'![—]& wish to make outsiders believe they were the only *truly loyal* ones." His assessment of the leaders' folly extended to the military commanders who, as "outsiders," failed to understand the country: "[Lieutenant Colonel William] Otter's Cut Knife affair was a great mistake precipitating Ind[ian] war, & it was a defeat—: attacking Indians on reserve!"[75]

During the early days of Ottawa's military organizing, Norquay had offered to help. In a letter to Macdonald on 4 April, anticipating the outcome of the resistance, he called the conflict an "insurrection," assumed that it would be "put down," and offered to assist the federal government in making peace. The process would "require very nice handling," Norquay said, and "if you should require my services in any capacity I will be only too happy to assist in bringing things to a peaceful basis. I know most of the settlers & when I say that I possess their confidence I don't think that I overstep the mark. If you should not require me consider this as unwritten." The missive evoked a diplomatic, perhaps disingenuous, reply written in cipher in which the prime minister asked how the Manitoba premier could be of assistance.[76]

Five months later, at the end of August, Norquay reminded Macdonald of his willingness to serve in the North-West Territories. His letter was brief, phrased as if he was merely responding to the prime minister's question back in April about how he might assist the government. Should the post of lieutenant governor of the North-West Territories become vacant, Norquay wrote, then he was applying for it. He added that assembly member David Harrison could become the premier of Manitoba, the implication being that there was no need for Macdonald to be concerned about Conservative party fortunes in the province. Once again there was no reply from Ottawa. Macdonald was not interested.

There is no evidence that the prime minister was unsure of Norquay's commitment to Canada and, indeed, he had written to the governor general a year earlier saying that Norquay was "loyal to the Dominion." Times had changed, however, and a measure of the change in atmosphere was that, in this time of crisis, the prime minister was ignoring a well-placed leader on the ground.[77] Though relations between the two appeared to be intact, they were a little cooler in the summer of 1885 than in January, when they had reached a settlement on Manitoba's outstanding concerns.[78] The prime minister's failure to use Norquay's services in the year leading up to the conflict or in the weeks immediately after Riel's declaration of a provisional government constituted a significant oversight that had its roots in a more racially charged moment in Canadian public life.[79]

Although he did not support Riel and Dumont resorting to arms, Norquay rejected English Canada's jingoism. Nor did he go so far as Quebec-origin Manitobans such as Joseph Dubuc, Riel's one-time classmate and ally, who referred to Riel in 1885 as "un maniaque dangereux."[80] Rather, Norquay acknowledged the validity of the Métis perspective and, to some degree, shared it. As an experienced public figure, he also understood the realities of statecraft and the discipline of governing. He thought in practical terms and responded to events in a much more sensitive manner than did his sons and their military comrades or the policy makers in Ottawa.

Norquay had behaved circumspectly in this moment of crisis. More than any other individual who identified with the place and the people, including Riel, Norquay understood the state's power and the processes of Canadian governments. He knew dozens, perhaps hundreds, of the Michif/French- and Bungee/English-speaking families in the territories and at least some of the Cree and Saulteaux communities. He presented a fair assessment of the circumstances and offered to take on the task of administering the North-West Territories as lieutenant governor. He would have appointed allies who knew the country and the population to official positions. For the many who did not wish to see more war, he would have provided a plausible reason for hope. Norquay believed that he had a fair chance of winning people's support for a reconstructed territorial government. But his carefully chosen words won little support in Ottawa and even less among the opposition in the Legislative Assembly of Manitoba.

Manitoba Politics: "God Damn You Fellows"

The assembly session in Manitoba in 1885, which took place while troops were marching in the Territories, was exceedingly frustrating for Norquay. The Liberal members doubled down on their determination to defeat him, claiming that they had won a majority of votes in the election in 1883, that they were the true representatives of public opinion, and even that their eight or nine members represented the opinions of nine-tenths of the people of the province. Demanding an immediate redistribution of seats, they claimed that one assembly member from Brandon alone "represented more votes than ten of the smaller constituencies together." As representations of the election results in 1883, these assertions simply were untrue.[81]

It was a busy session. The government introduced changes to the land law, agreed to review the electoral map and the ballot system, addressed branch railway construction, and supported a Hudson Bay rail outlet as a competitor of the CPR. Speaking in favour of an additional "avenue to the seaboard," Norquay emphasized the need for such an "outlet by which the surplus produce of our farmers may be exported and reach the market where the highest prices can be secured." The phrases underlined his adherence to the language and outlook of market-based capitalism. In matters of economic policy he also spoke comfortably about cooperation between the provincial and federal authorities, recognizing that the two levels of government must work together to support large enterprises such as the rail corporations.

While gunfire in the North-West Territories preoccupied the country, his critics in the assembly were undermining Norquay by saying that he was responsible for Manitoba's recession. Cooperation between Conservatives and Liberals, so striking in the assembly's rejection in 1884 of the Ottawa proposals, disappeared. The Liberals blamed Norquay and his government for every problem and did so with unprecedented fire. The anger did not come from the Liberal leader, Thomas Greenway, who got along well with the premier. Rather, it originated in a self-styled Liberal party elite in Winnipeg, who had little respect for Greenway—internal party division was not unique to the Conservatives—and in an irrepressible assembly colleague who simply would not be silenced.[82]

Joe Martin got under Norquay's skin within minutes of his arrival in the chamber. Martin had grown up in Ontario, attended the University of Toronto, and then become a teacher. Switching to law, he moved to Portage la Prairie, where he won a seat in the election in 1883. Within a year he was an unstoppable force in the assembly. He was later described by one who knew him as "pugnacious in disposition, disagreeable in manner, strong in his likes and dislikes, outspoken in his views, imperious in temper."[83] Under Martin's influence, the Liberal caucus in the assembly began to focus attention on Norquay himself. No longer talking mainly about John A. Macdonald and the federal government, they alleged that the premier had given contracts to his friends, had been careless in administration, and had spent extravagantly when travelling on official business. The energized Liberals also objected to Norquay's style in the assembly, mocking his evasiveness and deploring his lighthearted approach to debates. Sittings that had once been congenial and decorous, even in tense moments such as the ministerial crisis of 1879, became rancorous and cruel.[84]

A defensive note appeared in Norquay's oratory in these months, evidence that the personal attacks were hitting home. Norquay began to lash out at both the Liberals across the aisle and, in private correspondence, at the "old guard" detractors within his own party. He reminded his critics of the difficulties that he faced in dealing with the rest of Canada. He told them of his regret that the people of Manitoba "had been overridden by opinions of the eastern section of Canada; and he said so feelingly as one born in this province." As these words suggested, Norquay wanted credit for his effective presentations of the Manitoba case, a sign that he felt the heat generated by his opponents.[85]

At more than thirty sitting days, the spring 1885 assembly stretched from March to May and frequently descended into shouting and catcalling. Joe Martin might have uttered "drunken drivellings," as one source charged, but the accusations levelled by the member for Portage la Prairie echoed throughout the province.[86] The public accounts committee debated the opposition accusations at length, causing Norquay to become very angry with his critics. He happened to enter the committee room when a draft of the report was being read out by a secretary. He exploded: "God damn you fellows, if you put that in you can have my resignation tomorrow if you want it." Cabinet Minister Corydon Brown eventually intervened, proposing that "a modification should be made as he thought it was a little too hard on the old man." The committee members changed a few sentences. As they did so, and while Norquay was in the room, another cabinet member, Alphonse LaRivière, whispered that "these were the facts and we could not help reporting facts." An opposition member who claimed to have heard the aside later claimed that LaRivière also made a more damning assertion: the cabinet had not heard about the government's advance payment for "Norquay's coal" until six months later, and "it would serve the old man a lesson about advancing money without proper authority."[87] The gossipy reports illustrated that Norquay was being undermined not only by the opposition but also by cabinet colleagues LaRivière and Brown.

The public accounts committee introduced a motion of censure against the government, and, to the surprise of the Liberals, Norquay accepted the censure and voted to accept the report. The *Free Press* roared with delight, saying that the government was now "held in popular detestation and contempt." How could its members vote for the opposition's motion when the document was full of criticisms? "The history and contents of that document entitle it to rank chief among the Legislative curiosities of the age. It is the only thing of the kind in the world."[88] Norquay carried on despite the embarrassment.

Then out of the blue, in the last hour of the last day of the session, as the members awaited the lieutenant governor's prorogation of the assembly, Greenway introduced a motion of non-confidence in the government. It was early May 1885, when the military situation in the North-West remained uncertain and when farmers should have been preparing the fields for planting. Seven government members, and only one member of the opposition, had already gone home. A formal vote would be close, perhaps dependent on a few loose fish, including the "old guard" Conservatives who did not like the premier and might desert him. Norquay was angry as well as surprised. Caught off guard he could only argue that it was a "most ungentlemanly, unworthy and unprecedented attack" given that his government had won earlier votes that constituted statements of confidence. "He did not believe," he said, that "such a procedure could be found in the annals of any legislature in the universe—of a motion of such importance ever sprung upon a Government enjoying the confidence of the country."[89]

Norquay then leaped into action. According to the *Free Press* he consulted "several large volumes on Parliamentary practice which he had brought down from the library" in order to prolong discussion. He then "proceeded to hurl a storm of invective and imprecations against the Opposition, directing his vindictive thrusts mainly against Mr. Conklin," who, like Joe Martin, had been promoting allegations of scandal. The *Free Press* report added that "the Premier's senseless denunciations were met with roars of laughter from the Opposition which worked him into a state of passion that must have been painful to his supporters."[90]

Conklin defended the research that underlay what would soon be called the "coal steal and asylum scandal." Norquay, in reply, spoke "in a sarcastic strain," according to the *Free Press*, "using a bitterness of language which indicated that his anger was thoroughly aroused. He said he could scarcely characterize by words strong enough the attempt to spring such a motion upon the House at the last moment... for the purpose of creating an impression throughout the country that was entirely false." As for the charges levied against him, Norquay gave no quarter. The Saskatchewan Coal Company had served the people of Manitoba well: "Had he not been connected with that company he would have advised a gift of $5,000 or $6,000 because of what that company had done to reduce the price of coal." He then addressed a range of issues until the opposition began to ask if he had views on the war in Egypt or the price of wheat.[91]

While Norquay was in full rhetorical flight, Lieutenant Governor James Cox Aikins arrived. Was he thirty minutes early, having made haste in response to an urgent summons to save the government? Or was his presence unrelated to events in the assembly? With his entry, debate ended, and Greenway's motion was not put to a vote. The lieutenant governor proceeded to give assent to the bills that had been passed. He then withdrew, "and the members shortly after dispersed without the usual demonstrations of good feeling on the part of the Government." The *Winnipeg Times* described the afternoon's events as "a contemptible piece of political trickery all through."[92] Norquay had had a close call. If the Liberal attack was beginning to resonate and he could not rely on either the "old guard" Conservatives or some of his cabinet colleagues, then how could he continue in office?

Social Circles and "the Boys"

Public life was increasingly unpleasant and Norquay needed new political friends. Beyond his family he relied first on the people he had grown up with. Despite the complaints by Andrew Spence, Norquay was not guilty of neglecting them, and in turn they regarded him fondly. James Monkman of Peguis wrote to tell Norquay that Jane, his wife, was saving "some good fresh white fish" for him, and their neighbour wanted to shake his hand and hear him tell "some funny yarns." William MacLeod in High Bluff asked Norquay to meet his wife at the train station because she "has no frinds at Winnipeg and never was there before." Several others asked him for a loan or a job. One needed him to cover an interest payment. An easy informality pervades this correspondence, suggesting warm relationships and reliable support.[93]

Norquay also found allies through his membership in a remarkable number of organizations. In 1886 he belonged to the St. Andrews Society and attended a January "grand concert and ball" that featured a reading of works by Robbie Burns. He received invitations to events held by the Knights of Pythias (dedicated to moral uplift and social purification), the St. George's Snowshoe Club (good exercise and lively parties), the Caledonian Club (Scotch and fraternal), the Mounted Infantry mess (military dinners), the Winnipeg Cricket Club (games and gatherings), the Manitoba Rifle Association (shooting competitions), and the Masonic Order (he attended only a few of the many meetings at Prince Rupert's Lodge, Ancient Free and Accepted Masons), among other affiliations. With his role in public affairs Norquay could offer valuable services to the Anglican community and accepted the obligation to do so.[94] He was welcomed at these events, and in attending them he increased his understanding of people's opinions and won a measure of support, or at least sympathy, from them.

Politics and his role as government leader pushed Norquay to make hundreds of new contacts in every part of the province. These relationships differed from the older ones, having a transactional element that preceded whatever deeper personal attachments might develop. In the Norquay City district, where residents were still struggling to keep the town alive, Dr. John Pennefather became one of these associates. Both saw advantages to the relationship, financial on one side, political on the other. In two dozen letters and half a dozen visits over six years, Pennefather sought five different government positions, all with Norquay's approval, all unsuccessful. Pennefather invited Norquay to visit, and the premier replied with a politician's wish: "Remember me to all the boys around."[95]

Norquay found another group of associates among Manitoba's social elite, including business and church leaders and the senior civil servants with whom he worked every day. He selected about thirty colleagues and their wives to receive invitations as his personal guests to the opening of the legislature in March 1885. Top of the list were Messrs. Scarth, Ruttan, Bain, and Alloway, all members of the city's business community and all participants in investments with Norquay. Several Selkirk business owners, including the Colcleugh brothers, and long-time church friends, such as the Kennedys and Thomas Sinclair, as well as Reverend Benjamin Mackenzie of St. Peter's and Archdeacon Abraham Cowley, also made the list. And then there were the civil servants and their wives, including Pritchard from his own office and several from the treasury department. These were the allies on whom Norquay relied.[96] Only a few old Assiniboians figured in this company.

His connections to leading figures in the national sphere never attained the easy familiarity of his friendships in Manitoba. Norquay corresponded regularly with Sir John A. Macdonald and spoke with him annually, but they were negotiating adversaries and party colleagues, nothing more. Sir George Stephen, president of the Canadian Pacific Railway, stood well outside the world that Norquay inhabited. The premier liked William Van Horne, the CPR vice-president, much better and looked forward to frank, flexible dealings with him. The two giants also got on well over a card table. They joined a high-stakes poker game in a hotel room in Toronto where D'Arcy Boulton, a Toronto business leader, lost heavily. Some days later Norquay asked Van Horne to cover Boulton's losses or collect the debt on his behalf. Van Horne's intervention provoked a sharp reply from the Toronto gentleman: "I had overlooked my indebtedness to him [Norquay] and to calm his fears I now enclose my cheque for $49. I am under the impression that I am also a defaulter to you personally & if you will let me know how much I will remit." Van Horne forwarded the letter to Norquay and scrawled on the bottom "Hon John Norquay—D'Arcy says that is a d----d piece of impertinence on your part. WCVH." It was an interesting cameo: had Norquay not pursued the matter, Boulton might not have paid the debt. By breaking an unstated convention and going to Van Horne for payment of Boulton's losses, Norquay was acknowledging that he needed the money and recognizing that he could count on Van Horne, not Boulton, for a fair hearing. This was not mere pocket change. The sum would have been more than a month's pay for a labouring man in Manitoba, and the premier faced serious debts.[97]

The Van Horne exchange represented a new development, an important one, in Norquay's private life. If the premier had not been before, he was now very interested in gambling, particularly games of poker. In 1883–84, for the first time, references to cards appear in his correspondence, typically in letters to men outside his circle of Red River friends. He played cards with a range of individuals and for high stakes on occasion. In a winter 1884 note to Captain Jack Allan, an MLA then residing in Winnipeg's Selkirk Club, he promised to "overhawl my bank account and see if there is anything to my credit" in order to pay off a debt. He added that he had seen one of their friends, a poker player, "and had a small game with him which from its smallness seemed rather to disgust than please him but I was with some straight-laced fellows and they would only go it small." Testifying to his enjoyment of good company as well as gambling—and money troubles—he told Allan that he had later dined with the same friend "and had a good time. He is well fixed[.] I wish to heavens you and I were as well."[98]

The card games could not be separated from alcohol. Whether Norquay drank the beverages that he paid for cannot be proven, but strong drink was now a regular feature of his life. One item in the premier's in-box, a bill for a recently purchased book, reinforced the impression that alcohol pervaded his world even if it was not his own weakness. The volume was *Platform Echoes*, over 600 pages, a classic of the temperance movement written by John B. Gough, published in 1885. It contained Gough's account of losing his wife and child during years of uncontrolled drinking and his painful recovery after taking a temperance pledge.[99] What relation did the book purchase have to his own drinking habits and those of people close to Norquay? It is clear from the comments of colleagues that his temperance pledge, taken in 1875, was a thing of the past. A Sons of Temperance leader noted that Norquay "was not a total abstainer yet he was a firm friend of the temperance cause."[100] He simply enjoyed being with those who took pleasure in his company and with whom he could share conversations, card games, cigars, and drinks.[101]

Drink and gambling defined another social circle among men in that era. Norquay entered more completely into its habits, and the circle itself, at mid-decade. Not that he approved of or shared all its characteristics, but he did participate fully in the banter that was so important to it. George Ham and Edward Farrer, Winnipeg journalists in these years, were mainstays in the Winnipeg chapter. Little wonder that Ham's name is scrawled in three places in Norquay's agenda book for 1885 and, next to it, various sums adding up to just over fifty dollars. Norquay received a letter from Major General Middleton's camp in 1885 signed by "Geo H. Ham N.P. No Poker." They loved to play cards. When they covered stories in Ottawa, Ham said, they "would play Black Jack until three or four in the morning." For a premier what better way to spend empty hours away from home? Card games held the prospect of political talk with Ham and Farrer, well-informed and witty observers of public life.[102]

This male culture was most evident in Norquay's correspondence during the 1885 military campaign, when gunfire intensified friendships and inspired a sense of urgency. The friends who wrote to Norquay from "the front" (their term) offered few acknowledgements of stress and many jocular comments about danger. They did not question the necessity, as they perceived it, of the fighting itself.[103]

Lively letters from George Ham captured the intensity and the excitement of the time. Thrice elected to Winnipeg City Council, a journalist and hail-fellow-well-met, Ham possessed the writing skill and the enthusiastic cordiality that bespoke confidence and manhood in the style expected in Norquay's new circle. His letters were sometimes diary-like, sometimes self-consciously humorous, and always full of energy and reassurance: "Alick [Norquay] and Walter [Nursey] and myself and another galoot camp and mess together. The last one takes the cake for laziness, beating me all hollow. Nursey cooks. I am his assistant. (He says if he had another like me, he would calmly but determinedly ask to die.) Alick and his chum wash dishes, and attend to the wood and water supply."[104] Ham's humour centred on cards and liquor: "My dear Mr. Norquay[,] I feel it my duty to drop you word of the terrible experiences we are undergoing. Thank God—and Major General Bedson—we are here, and although a hostile herd and a dire drought prevail, we are safe. The first deadly peril we encountered was this morning, when we attacked breakfast without a matutinal cocktail. But notwithstanding the great disadvantage we were under, we met the enemy boldly and manfully and we are his. I don't take a drink very frequently. Circumstances over which I have no control, prevent me." This letter was scrawled on the obverse of a sheet entitled "Instructions to Depot Clerks" of the North-West Field Force, a printed form carrying the names of Major General Middleton and Chief Transport Officer Bedson. Ham had carefully amended the report's categories so that instead of "Transport Station" the stationery read "Poker Station," "map" was replaced by "flask," and "supplies" became "drinks or liquor." It was brash and hearty, designed consciously to amuse Norquay and to allay concern about young Alick, who travelled in the same military column.

Ham showed no awareness of the militia's opponents, no apparent interest in the Métis cause or claims, no sympathy for the people who had adopted or been pushed into positions from which they could not back away. Unlike Charles Adams, Ham saw virtue on only one side, the Canadian troops' side. When under fire at Batoche, his only acknowledgement of the opponent was to say that the "Red Devils bothered us like blazes." Much of what Ham wrote to Norquay during these weeks was nonsense, a stream of consciousness designed to allay a father's fears and to sound brave and witty, as if part of the repartee at the poker table.[105]

Norquay enjoyed the banter. He wrote back to express his satisfaction that Ham had swallowed his hard tack biscuits "without a 'cock tail' to give you pluck." He parried Ham's joking requests for card game materials: "I cannot send you the chips as the House is in Session and they are very much required. They are a necessary part of the furniture for Legislation which members will never part with." His comments about the resistance revealed no uneasiness about his own standing: "When you meet Riel and others just tell them Uncle John is well and just as soon as he settles Greenway's hash he is coming up to pay his respects to them." His concluding lines illustrate the male circle's claims to stoicism: "Hoping you may escape with a whole skin so that it will be able to retain the whiskey that you will get when you get back without leaking out. I am yours[,] J Norquay."[106]

The bold talk was an important part of Norquay's world, but it was far from a complete picture of his outlook. Although Norquay joked about the battle, he was much more aware of the people on the other side. Still, Ham and his ilk had become the new majority, the people who reported on his policies, the voters who chose his government, the hearty gamblers with whom he associated on weekday evenings. He welcomed their willingness to include him in their circle and enjoyed the raillery that went with it. By the rules of the game, they accepted him and permitted him to define the terms of his engagement with them. To judge from his correspondence they treated him as the province's premier and, in most cases, as their social equal. But some did not, in some measure because of what they called "race."

Racism

Tensions between French and English speakers, Roman Catholics and Protestants, Indigenous peoples and Europeans reached new heights in Canada during the 1880s. Once the militia moved west in April 1885, news from "the front" made these sentiments far worse. To Norquay's chagrin the Riel-led resistance movement damaged Canadians' confidence in the loyalty of all Indigenous peoples, including the English-speaking Protestants whom he called "my countrymen."[107] He was being pushed to reassess himself and his country.

The day before the Duck Lake battle, during a heated exchange in the Manitoba assembly, Norquay used strong language to condemn the racial discrimination that had occurred in the province in its first years. This statement was out of the ordinary, not the kind of thing about which he usually talked. What is more, in his frustration he used the slighting term "breeds," biting off the word as he criticized the racism of an earlier day.

Ed Hay, assembly member and Norquay's long-time opponent, objected to the premier's statement. He had been living in the west since before 1870, Hay said, and "in these early days the 'Breeds'—as the hon. gentleman called them"—were not, despite the premier's words, "looked down upon and despised by the white settlers. He could not agree with the hon. Premier on that point for then as now the whites entertained the greatest respect for the half-breed population of this country." In making his point Hay claimed that Norquay's nomination in 1870 by acclamation took place at "a meeting composed almost wholly of whites." Norquay was "always willing to change his opinions," Hay scoffed, "when he thought that it was in his own interests to do so (hear, hear)."[108]

Hay's speech was remarkable for its hypocrisy and presumption. He was denying the existence of racist attitudes that had been obvious for years. A Liberal partisan, he was advocating non-partisanship in local politics (a stance that Norquay had championed). His statement about the social composition of High Bluff in 1870 was simply wrong. Adding insult to injury, he concluded with the suggestion that Norquay's followers in the assembly should become Liberals. The bickering illustrated why Norquay was frustrated in 1885. It also laid bare the racist strains lying just below the surface in public life. In this rare (for him) outburst, Norquay had apparently implied (we have only Hay's word for this) that people of mixed ancestry were discriminated against by newcomers (he was referring, presumably, to the "reign of terror" in the early 1870s), and still had to deal with such prejudices. His very use of the pejorative, "breeds," underlined the depth of his anger.

When battle began in the North-West Territories, anti-Métis talk became common in the public sphere. Although French-speaking Manitobans were divided on the actions of Riel in 1885, English-speaking Manitobans unhesitatingly supported the federal government's expeditionary force. Assembly member David Harrison warned the premier that no one in the Minnedosa area sympathized with the uprising: "*Riel must be hanged or shot* [Harrison's emphasis]—or there will not be a Conservative left in the Country." Brother-in-law John James Setter, Norquay's countryman, referred to the Riel forces as "rebs" and "beggars." Norquay's son Tom, usually careful in his choice of words, wrote to his father during the army's pursuit of Big Bear: "We are going into the heart of the Indian country to try if possible to rescue those unfortunate people [including two White women] who had the bad luck to fall into the hands of the devils." "Hanged," "shot," "rebs," "devils": strong terms circulated in prairie Canada, and the talk grew angrier as the weeks passed. A large majority in Manitoba was succumbing to racist clichés.[109]

Race pressed to the fore in Norquay's own thinking. Where previously Norquay might have brushed off the loose talk that racialized his people, now he took offence. European Canadian bias had become too much for him. His revision of a self-authored biographical note in the annual *Canadian*

Parliamentary Companion reflected his change of heart. More than mere coincidence, the change came in the form of a new sentence explaining that he played "a prominent part in all the discussion relating to the Red River Rebellion of 1870, and by the moderation of his views secured the confidence of all parties."[110] Why add this claim at this time? It is likely that the answer lay in the name Riel and the word *race*. As a leader whose ancestry was well known, Norquay felt the need to distinguish himself from Riel's previous and current involvement in resistance movements and to stress what he regarded as his own reasonable, balanced approach to public issues.

Norquay had his own prejudices that had developed during his Red River days. Like other residents of the settlement—White, Métis, Cree, and Saulteaux—he spoke warily of the Indigenous peoples of the plains. His words were probably rooted not in race but in his perceptions of historical enmities and customary approaches to warfare. Norquay knew about the deadly conflicts that had scarred Minnesota in the 1860s, the Cree-Blackfoot battles on the northern plains in 1869–70, as well as George Armstrong Custer's defeat by Sitting Bull at Little Big Horn, Montana Territory, in 1876. The diplomatic and military experiences of those communities differed radically from life in the Red River Settlement, but Norquay and his friends reverted to that earlier language in speaking of their concerns in 1885. Charles Adams, his brother-in-law, and once a neighbour of the Norquay family in High Bluff, put the perception bluntly in a letter to Norquay: Adams wrote that he feared a "general Indian uprising."[111] Norquay used similar words when writing to a federal cabinet minister at the end of the year: "We cannot afford to have an Indian war on our hands."[112] He recognized the existence of a food crisis on the plains but he also was prepared to play on White fears in the hope of moving the national government to action.

His prickly reaction when English-speaking Métis became targets of racism surfaced in relation to his son Tom, who had many stories to tell when he returned from the North-West Territories. One such narrative concerned his treatment by his regimental superiors. Tom had been a second lieutenant in the Winnipeg Light Infantry during his four months of active duty. For much of that time, he believed, he performed the duties of a first lieutenant but was paid at the lower rate of a second lieutenant. His father took up his cause, writing a strong letter to the commanding officer of the regiment. He cited great financial need "as he requires every cent of money that he can scrape to enable him to prosecute his studies and my opinion is that it was well earned." The officer defended his decision not to promote the young man, saying that others ranked above him and that such an act would have appeared to be "gross favouritism." Tom's promotion, he said, would have fomented "discontent through the whole corps."[113]

Norquay was indignant. His words carried more anger than could be explained by the loss of a small sum. He was defending not only his son but also, given the heat of his protest, his countrymen: "Although the difference [in money terms] is not much I am determined to find why there was discrimination made by which he was refused what I think he honestly earned." The premier did not stop with this outburst to the commanding officer. Instead, he went over Osborne Smith's head and appealed for redress to the federal minister of militia, with whom he had had frequent dealings. Sir Adolphe Caron approved the payment of an additional twenty-three dollars to Tom.[114]

The premier was fully aware of the growing racist tide. In attempting to escape from the uncertainties of provincial politics, he had put his name forward for federal appointments several times in the past. Now, in the summer of 1885, he was proposing to take on the lieutenant governorship of the North-West Territories. Norquay recruited several colleagues to write in support. Dr. David Harrison's letter, revealing in its frankness, advised John A. Macdonald that the promotion of Norquay would allay the long-standing unrest in the Winnipeg branch of the Conservative party. Why change the leader? Because Norquay could not rely on "old guard" Conservative support given "his political history and the prejudice against his lineage." There was the story in a nutshell: "his political history," meaning his moderate stance in the culture wars of the 1870s, "and the prejudice against his lineage," meaning anti-Métis racism within his own party, counted against him.[115]

The Conservative "old guard" in Manitoba, whose political loyalty centred on John A. Macdonald, did not want Norquay. Their opinions about race, not commonly found in extant documentation and more likely to be conveyed by whispered asides, found expression in one vivid letter written by William Wagner. A German immigrant, surveyor, prosperous farmer, fifteen-year resident of Manitoba, and one-term assembly member, Wagner warned John A. Macdonald against Norquay's elevation to the federal cabinet. He said that the premier "never was nor is he a faithfull friend to you and I sooner will follow a less able speaker but more true man to our cause—and this is also my strongest reason why I would not advise to take N. into your cabinet." Wagner cloaked his argument in words of apparent sympathy: Norquay was "attached to his family, as all of us are, and I think it would be a cruelty to bring him to Ottawa alone without his family, and Mrs. N. and daughter would be cutting a sore figure amongst Ottawa society—which of course would hurt his feelings." This patronizing, sentimental argument might have been intended to distract the prime minister, but the subtext could not be missed. Because Norquay spoke "English, French, Cree, bongie [Bungee] and some Sioux," and because he was "a very social man [in] particular amongst his own kind," Wagner wrote, "I can see him smoking his pipe of peace with [Cree leader] Mr. Poundmaker . . . which will help you a good deal." Norquay, he said, came from "a race of men and brought up amongst them who only in some few instances perhaps in the third generation may achieve that necessary kind of easy politesse—which we expect from an educated man born on a carpet—but by N. the moccasin will show itself through the finest patent leather boot, you may do what you like."[116] The telltale phrases—"amongst his own kind," "a very social man," "the old settlers," moccasins, "his pipe of peace"—belittled some of the defining qualities of the Red River Settlement. Wagner's phrasing even slighted Norquay's multilingual capabilities. This carefully crafted four-page letter, which Wagner would have described as forthright and dispassionate, represented a race-driven, racist view of Canada and its western interior. It condemned Norquay as unfit to lead White Manitoba.

Such hostile views were not minor inconveniences in Norquay's life. They represented the defining sentiment in the Winnipeg faction of the Conservative party of Manitoba. In light of the conflict in the North-West Territories, such expressions had become acceptable in the province, at least in private conversations in certain circles.[117]

After the North-West Resistance

When the North-West conflict ended, the premier's obligations became ceremonial and memorial. Norquay contributed to planning for a monument "in memory of those who have died in defense of their country." He canvassed for donations and supervised relief payments to veterans' families in need. He joined receptions and made speeches of welcome and thanksgiving to the troops returning home. John and Elizabeth joined hundreds of others in Selkirk to welcome troops who had travelled home via the

Saskatchewan River, Lake Winnipeg, and Red River. While the local band played martial music, two steamboats trailing barges docked, and the troops disembarked. After marching through the streets of the town, the 2,000 soldiers returned to "the flats" beside the river where long tables had been set up to serve lunch. It was a "joyful reunion" for many families, including the Norquays.[118]

The premier renewed his efforts to influence Ottawa's western policy making, but to his dismay the federal administration continued to choose easterners for western jobs. Macdonald and his colleagues seemed to trust only eastern qualifications, especially service to the Conservative party, whereas Norquay believed that they should be looking for strong, judicious individuals who understood the people of the region. He wrote a strong protest to federal cabinet minister John Henry Pope, the minister of railways (and formerly the minister of agriculture), an able ally who had listened carefully to his pleas in preceding years. Norquay's immediate concern was a civil service appointment to the Cree agency in Battleford, where the crisis of the resistance had been compounded by the mass hangings of 27 November 1885. His warning was that "unless you get men that will know exactly where to get proper officers for your Indian Department & replace many of your present ones you may look out for trouble with your Indians in a very short time." Norquay had heard that the Cree in the District of Battleford were likely to be swayed by Gabriel Dumont's continued agitation and remained "as dissatisfied as ever." The flow of whiskey into the country "may be the means at any time of kindling a flame that would with difficulty be suppressed as resistance to authority never mind by whom & from what source would be hailed as the signal for a general Indian uprising[.] Don't for goodness sake send any more Travises out who may be good enough men but not suited to frontier & pioneer exigencies." These were the sentiments of a frustrated ("for heavens sake," "for goodness sake") and well-informed observer who believed that a spark might provoke another serious conflict. Norquay spoke as an experienced and wise observer. Although he directed the appeal to a sympathetic and powerful listener, his words went unheeded.[119]

Norquay had legions of supporters as well as Macdonald-focused "old guard" critics. One distinguished Conservative, Dr. George Orton, the CPR medical superintendent, previously an MP for nine years, and in 1885 a member of the military expedition to the North-West, recanted his initial reservations about the premier. Orton told Macdonald that the troubles in the North-West were just another indication of the federal cabinet's need for a westerner familiar with the wants of the people. The only such person who possessed the "necessary judgment" and would be regarded with satisfaction by the vast majority, he said, was John Norquay. A few ambitious men opposed the premier without good reason, "but with the people at large the confidence reposed in Norquay is practically unanimous." If Norquay had been in the federal cabinet, Orton concluded, then neither the farmers' union nor the Riel troubles would have occurred. An experienced observer who was close to all factions in the Conservative party and had travelled across the west, Orton offered unexpected but convincing testimony about Norquay's abilities and character. This strong vote of confidence was probably forgotten, however, because military activities were consuming all of Macdonald's energy when Orton wrote.[120]

During the Manitoba assembly session in the spring of 1885, while speaking of the better terms deal he and Macdonald had reached in January, Norquay told his colleagues that "Manitoba has had full justice done to her." He corresponded with the prime minister on business matters without apparent tension. In an important speech at a summer picnic in Portage la Prairie in August, Norquay explained the province's "peculiar position." His argument emphasized, once again, the inferior rank assigned to his province by the Manitoba Act. As a consequence of the terms of the Act, he explained, Manitoba did not have "a legal claim" and could ask only for "what was fair." If he had been granted control of public lands, then Ottawa and the rest of Canada would insist that he respect the previously established land policies. Or he could take a much-enlarged grant of money. Which path should he choose? Norquay preferred the extra subsidies, he said, and his listeners cheered.[121] Late in the year, on a public platform, he was once again defending the better terms agreement in a speech said by Lieutenant Governor Aikins to be "a good one."[122] He was making a strong defence of his administration and he was winning the battle for the public mind in Manitoba.

The federal government failed badly in 1885. Sir John A. Macdonald did not recognize the dimensions of the impending crisis in western Canada. Nor did he understand how disastrous were the administrators whom he appointed or how flawed was the advice that they dispatched to Ottawa. Only in the aftermath did he perceive the shortcomings of that intelligence.[123]

One important consequence, as far as Norquay was concerned, was that the prime minister reversed course and supported him against the "old guard" critics in Winnipeg by turning to the fount of partonage, the CPR, on Norquay's behalf.[124] The prime minister wrote from his summer retreat at Rivière du Loup to George Stephen, the CPR president, thanking him for the gift of a grouse and forwarding a letter from the Manitoba premier. This letter cannot be identified but might have discussed some railway matter or it might even have been Norquay's offer to serve as lieutenant governor of the North-West Territories. The conclusion to the letter was what mattered most. Despite the Winnipeg "old guard's" relentless criticism of Norquay, Macdonald would back him: "In these times it is necessary for the quiet of that country that he [Norquay] should be strengthened & have the support of the CPR." It was an important decision because it would guide the railway company's contributions to newspapers and to Norquay's team in the upcoming provincial election campaign.[125] The prime minister feared further problems in the North-West, and—though not willing to trust Norquay with an official role in the Territories—he decided to rely on him as a bulwark in Manitoba.

Norquay was tested during 1885. He endured money troubles and intense political criticisms. Two of his sons faced fire in the North-West Resistance. He was obliged to support imperialists and Orange Ontarians, even though he sympathized wholeheartedly with his countrymen. His offer of help to the prime minister and his thoughtful comments on the war constituted a dignified response to the significant increase in racism in Canada that condemned all Indigenous people to inferiority. Throughout, Norquay remained a politician who depended on broad public support if he was to remain in office. He told one correspondent that he was "pretty well battered but still in the ring." He gathered his strength during the autumn with the thought that he would soon have to face the electorate once again.[126]

His final considered statement on the war in the North-West came in an assembly speech in the spring of 1886. Norquay picked up on a line from his throne speech expressing the province's pride in the volunteer soldiers' contributions "in support of law and order." His nuanced and conciliatory message spoke of "unfortunate troubles that occurred in the west." He acknowledged that the conflict generated "a national feeling" across Canada. He also put his doubts on record. Such a military clash was "still to be deplored" because it was "internecine strife . . . an unfortunate family difference." Then, as in the throne speech itself, Norquay stepped back from a sentiment that might have been viewed by some White voters as too kind to the resistance fighters and insufficiently supportive of Canada's soldiers: "We must give credit to those who rushed forward for the preservation of law and order." He was searching for the middle, declaring sympathy for his countrymen while defending the troops. Three times he used the word *unfortunate* in his depiction of events in the North-West. Even more eye-catching was his selection of two other terms, "family" and "internecine," to define the conflict encompassed both Whites and Métis. Norquay was asserting that his countrymen were the equals of Whites and that the two peoples belonged together in a single community. Would voters accept such a conclusion?[127]

CHAPTER 10

Vindication, 1886

John Norquay turned forty-five in 1886 and was frequently depicted as the "old man." The vigorous enthusiast of earlier years had been succeeded by a more reserved, more determined battler. He remained robust and outwardly cheerful, but the events of the past year, particularly the war in the North-West Territories, weighed on him. He spent hours in the office dealing with correspondence and talking with civil servants and cabinet colleagues. Quarrels over the finances of Saskatchewan Coal left him tired and unhappy. As in the previous year, angry debates in a long legislative session made the floor of the house a challenging and less pleasant place. These were difficulties, not disasters. He travelled more widely than before and dedicated much more time to business ventures. Having acquired contacts in the continental business community and better knowledge of economic trends, Norquay was increasingly preoccupied with investment booms and busts. His conversations with entrepreneurs in Toronto, Montreal, and New York opened a wider world in which he would have liked to have a personal stake. He travelled on the trains they frequented, stayed in the same hotels, and played cards and drank wine and spirits with them.[1] Although he continued to assert his connection to old Red River, Norquay spoke more frequently about other sources of identity in his life, including his Scottish heritage, the Anglican Church, and the western interior of Canada. And three crucial developments—a royal commission, a prime ministerial tour, and a general election—carried him nearly to the peak of his political career.

Home and Extended Family

If the stress of public life affected Norquay greatly, it also pushed him to make decisions that he had been postponing for several years. His finances remained a pressing problem and the Parkdale farm raised concerns that he could no longer evade. Though he made a point of getting home each weekend, the trips were demanding. Elizabeth's health remained uncertain. During much of 1884 and 1885, when the children boarded in the student residences at St. John's College and St. John's Ladies' College, she was frequently left alone at Parkdale with housemaid Jemima Sanders and a farm labourer. Elizabeth's isolation, and the cost of the children's residence fees, finally led them to reconsider life on the farm.[2] A move to Winnipeg would be costly but in the longer term would enable Norquay to economize.

At the beginning of December 1885 he took a lease on a large house on Hallet Street between Main Street and the Red River, a few blocks north of the CPR tracks. This made life simpler because he could be home more frequently, and the children still in school could become day students at St. John's, thereby saving residence fees. At twenty-five dollars per month the Hallet Street house was a bargain.[3] Although the surrounding district of Point Douglas was no longer the city's finest, as it had been a few years earlier, the house was just minutes from the Red River and St. John's Cathedral precinct, ideal destinations for the premier's recreational walks.[4]

The new home, one of three in a terrace, was a suitable residence for a premier's household of constantly changing numbers. Six bedrooms ensured that the children had plenty of space. On the main floor a large reception room and wood-panelled dining room flanked the central hall on one side; on the other, triple doors of black wood opened into a large drawing room stretching the length of the house. It featured massive pillars, also in black wood, that matched the mantel over the fireplace and emphasized its eleven-foot (3.4-metre) height.[5] For Elizabeth there was a cozy second-floor sitting room.[6] When the premier played cribbage with their friend from St. Andrews parish, Eleanor Kennedy, a table was placed in the doorway between them; Mrs. Kennedy sat in the nicely warmed sitting room, and the premier sat in the hall where the air was cooler.[7] The family took delight in one particular aspect of the new home: since they were accustomed to the oil lamps of Parkdale, and before that to the candles of High Bluff days, the electric lights on Hallet Street were a marvel. Just as wonderful was that the premier could now take colleagues home for lunch at noon, and according to one of the children, if Betsy was ill, then Bella acted as hostess; if she too was unavailable, then Nellie would be pressed into service.[8] This was a cheaper alternative than paying for food in the new legislative building's dining room, where Mrs. Smith, the housekeeper, provided modest fare and kept meticulous accounts.[9]

Social life became busier for Elizabeth in 1886 and 1887. She accompanied John to some official events and made the home welcoming for visitors. Spells of neuralgia, however, frequently disrupted her plans. She was ill at Christmas 1885, at the end of January 1886, and again in March. Medicines of various kinds came into the house regularly.[10] In the summer of 1886 Norquay arranged a railway trip to Banff, the new vacation destination on the CPR line through the Rockies, where the hot springs were reported to be health giving. John and Elizabeth enjoyed their stay at the new sanitarium hotel founded by a former Winnipegger, Dr. Robert Brett. It was said that the premier walked at least partway up one of the mountains overlooking the townsite and that his host named the peak Mount Norquay, which it remains.[11]

John and Elizabeth tried to ensure that the children were well situated as they commenced their adult lives. In 1886 Tom, the eldest, was twenty-three, and Andrew, the youngest, was fourteen. Tom enrolled at St. John's College again in 1885 and 1886 but might have failed to finish the academic program, in the former year because he joined the North-West field force, in the latter year because he worked for his father in the election campaign in November. Tom became a clinical assistant at the provincial mental hospital, no doubt owing to his father's intervention. The local newspaper described him as "full of life and spirit, [one] who tactfully attends to his business but is ready for a joke at any moment."[12] The girls remained at home, Bella as Elizabeth's helper and Nellie as a student in St. John's Ladies' School. One of the Norquay boys, probably Jack, went to work as an apprentice machinist in the CPR shops at the age of eighteen in February 1885. Alick, upon his return from the conflict in the North-West, entered the CPR land office and within a year sought a transfer to the freight department to broaden his experience. Horace and Andrew were studying at St. John's College. Both were regarded as fine young men, their conduct described by Bishop Machray as exemplary. Horace had had enough of the closed academic environment of the college, however, and appealed to his father to be permitted to stay home as a day student. Norquay expressed his pleasure that they had "conducted themselves" well and thanked Reverend Matheson for "the kind interest" that he and Bishop Machray had "always taken in their success."[13]

Norquay supported his relatives as best he could. He had to write sternly to his brother-in-law, John James Setter, the sheriff of Portage la Prairie, about transferring the revenue collected in fines to the appropriate agency. Colin Setter was forever appealing for support in one scheme or another. Cousin John Lazarus Norquay sought help in his dealings with bureaucrats. To aid his sister and her husband, Charles Adams, who worried about feeding his family on the farm near Prince Albert, Norquay lobbied successfully for the appointment of Charles as an Indian agent in February 1886. The posting was subject to fierce competition, and despite his best efforts he lost the job to the politicking of others before the year was out. Norquay then intervened with the prime minister and ensured that Adams became a farm instructor in a Cree community, a position that would pay less but offer greater security.[14]

Norquay's own finances remained rocky even though, in 1886–87, he and his cabinet colleagues paid themselves more generously for their government work. The premier received stipends as president of the cabinet ($1,000), as treasurer ($3,000), as provincial secretary for three months ($750), and as assembly member ($612), a total of over $5,300, five times the salary of his secretary.[15] As ever, though, the family's expenditures exceeded his income. The Hallet Street house consumed large quantities of coal and wood. The children's clothing and books and pastimes, not to mention their school fees, put a strain on the family budget.[16] Norquay was involved in a number of investments in real estate, including the moribund Darlingford townsite, none of them likely to bring in revenue.[17] The provincial hospital site, where he owned a tiny portion of the land involved, had become a political football and won the title "asylum scandal" in opposition speeches.[18] Although Norquay leased the Parkdale farm from the beginning of 1886, the finances of that enterprise weighed heavily.

Premiers had many costs that other citizens could control more readily, including memberships in clubs and lodges and associations, requests for donations, invitations to events, and drinks for others at the bar. Then there were his business dealings, none of which was a source of ready cash. According to a memo filed among his papers in 1886, Norquay owed over $2,100 on three different loans on which he was paying 8 percent interest. The cash in his account totalled $500.[19] He would never be free from financial challenges, but these matters seemed not to change his behaviour. Rather, he supported the extended family, gave generously to those in need, and trusted that something would come along to keep the wolf from the door. As long as Norquay remained in high office and could declare proudly that he had not taken advantage of his official position to line his own pockets, he believed that he met the ethical obligations that mattered.

Briton, Scot, Orcadian

Entering the last year of this term in office and the run-up to the general election, Norquay appeared to be vulnerable politically. There were several obvious reasons for the decline in his fortunes. The opposition had found some issues, notably the "coal steal" and "asylum scandal," that hit home. By attacking Norquay personally, rather than the federal government, the Liberals focused attention on his family ancestry as well as his government's finances. In this light the war conducted in the names of Louis Riel, Gabriel Dumont, and the Métis played a part in some of his critics' attacks. Observing the shifts in popular sentiment, Hugh John Macdonald began to doubt that the premier could remain in office. He warned his father not to count on him in the longer term: "Norquay has lost ground tremendously during the last six or eight months and I very much fear he will have a hard time next election unless something turns up in the meantime to discredit the Opposition." The expression of doubt did not mean that Hugh had given up on the premier, whom he professed to respect. He was prepared to await developments—one foot in Norquay's camp, the other on neutral ground—during this period of uncertainty within the party.[20]

As if in response to the racism and the political partisanship that swirled around him, Norquay became more interested in his British family heritage and in Manitoba's ties with Britain. The emphasis might seem to have been out of character for a Bungee/English-speaking product of the Red River Settlement, but it was not. He grew to adulthood as an Assiniboian, not a Canadian. His most influential teachers were British. In the 1860s, when Norquay was in his twenties, Canada was a distant entity, just another colony of the British Crown. He learned much more about Canada in the 1870s, but before his brief official trip to Ottawa in 1878 his closest contact with "the east" came in the form of such émigrés to Manitoba as John Schultz and Joseph Royal, colleagues with whom he had troubled relationships.

Norquay met Governor General Lord Dufferin several times during the vice-regal tour of Manitoba in 1877 and found his Britannic version of Canadian nationalism attractive. Henceforth, Norquay employed similar phrasing, notably in throne speeches in which the British Crown and the life of the royal family received particular attention. The sentiments enabled him to move beyond Orange Ontarians' negative stereotypes of his countrymen and to claim a British heritage. But even that identity could be uncomfortable, as he discovered during another vice-regal tour.

Canada's new governor general, the Marquis of Lorne, Queen Victoria's son-in-law, invited Norquay to join the royal train for a tour of the North-West Territories in 1881. The adventure offered drama and instruction. As the correspondent of the London *Times* explained, "a governor general's passage" to the "extreme end of the world" where workers were laying CPR tracks "is made easier than that of ordinary mortals." What Norquay thought of the attitudes of his fellow travellers, a tone conveyed so well in the *Times* reporter's stories, was not recorded. But the reports illustrated Norquay's knack for public relations. In an informal moment, Norquay and the governor general lifted a heavy wooden tie, carried it to the rail bed, and set it in place. The *Times* correspondent and several others then followed suit and, according to the reporter, "had the proud satisfaction of having lent a hand of what, when completed, will be the greatest, or, at any rate, the longest railway in the world, stretching from the Atlantic to the Pacific, about 4,000 miles."[21]

Demonstrating that the country remained closely knit, a young relative wrote to Norquay with some good news. The premier had had to abandon a horse when he had left the expedition, and it had been found. As John Setter explained,

> I h[e]ard of you visiting Qu'Appelle[.] I wish you came my way [Crooked Lake] you could of killed as many ducks in one day that would kept you the must [most] part of the fall[.] Your horse was braught in to my Place by a Indian a Black horse with a cow Bell on him[.] Tonight the Frenchman that you had told

> about your horse after you put the cow bell on him has told me all the Particulars how it came that you left the horse on the road so by puting the Bell on him saved him [presumably the horse] from dieing[.] I will keep the horse until I here [hear] from you[.] No stamp on the horse.[22]

The stark contrast between John Setter's world and that of the governor general illustrated the divide Norquay had to bridge in daily life. He recognized the realities of plains life. He also understood the stark disaster facing the Plains Cree, Saulteaux, Dakota, and Blackfoot after the buffalo vanished. He dealt, meanwhile, with federal government officials whose failure to respond sympathetically made matters so much worse.

In his book about the tour, Lord Lorne spoke contemptuously about the Cree and Saulteaux events that he attended: "Usually, amid much flowery rhetoric, the speech resolves itself into a demand for more favours, and is, in short, nothing but an exclamatory beggar's oration." In a private letter written in the town of Prince Albert, he explained that "the Indians are horrible savages but are beginning to understand farming. We are giving them presents everywhere as we pass and go through hideous dances 'like Hell.'" In Fort Qu'Appelle, where Norquay was part of the official party, Lord Lorne wrote that "I have a great Indian Council to-morrow. The wretches have been having a sun-dance. . . . All seem very friendly, but all ask for impossible things."[23] Norquay's thinking about these sentiments, if he heard them, has not been recorded. It cannot have been complimentary to Lord Lorne. And yet, though the Manitoba premier might lament the turn of events in the Indigenous west, he had to deal with such attitudes as those expressed by the governor general.

A shift in Norquay's public statements was probably inevitable, given the changing population balance and his need to win votes across the province. Orkney, Scottish, and British references took on a new importance when he was on public platforms. Although he did not disavow his Red River heritage, his mentions of the province's and his own British heritage increased in number. He attended meetings of the Winnipeg chapter of the St. George's Society and, as James Wickes Taylor reported, at one such gathering made an impromptu recitation that "was a surprise to all present." In this "remarkable incident," Norquay "illustrated the worldwide dominion of England by an unbroken enumeration of colonies and dependencies, including every isolated rook and rampart—a wonderful instance of memory and patriotic commemoration." When members of the British Association visited Winnipeg, he presented a carefully prepared statement in which he emphasized the needs of the country and tried to downplay talk of unrest. Saying that he recognized "the great task before us as a people of establishing order & settling the wider expanses of Canada," Norquay emphasized that Manitobans "cherish British institutions and British connections."[24] Aside from the obvious advertising message, his words suggested that he accepted imperial Britain's claim of global leadership.

Just as there seemed to be something deeper in his public statements about Manitoba's British and monarchical heritage, so, too, in his private correspondence, he began to claim a closer connection to Orkney. The change was most evident in his letters to James Thomson of South Ronaldshay, Orkney. After one election, Thomson wrote to tell him that news of the vote's result "has indeed given myself and all friends here very great satisfaction." He promised to entertain a Manitoba visitor by showing him "where at once stood the home of your [Norquay] forefathers finely situated in close proximity to the Pentland Firth." He praised Norquay as "honoured friend & our countryman the *Premier of Manitoba* [Thomson's emphasis]." The grant of "countryman" standing must have given Norquay a start. Norquay stayed in touch with Thomson. The most notable aspect of one of these letters was Norquay's single postscript: "p.s. Convey my sincere thanks to those who take an interest in the success of the Orkney lad. J.N."[25] He maintained his membership in the St. Andrews Society of Winnipeg, ordered a "Scotch plaid" from a clothier in Glasgow, took out a membership in the Orkney and Zetland Association, and bought a copy of the Reverend James Wallace's volume, *A description of the Isles of Orkney*. Writing a Toronto businessman to thank him for some "views of the Old Country," Norquay said he had appreciated the pictures, "especially those from Orkney," and expressed a wish to visit "that very interesting old cathedral which has outstood the wear of time so long." Should the businessman encounter "[James] Thomson of Quoy," the premier concluded, "be kind enough to remember me to him. He is a man who takes great interest in all his countrymen and in all their antecedents. He has two sons in this country who are both doing very well and keeping up the reputation of the energy that characterises our Norsemen of old." His references to "our Norsemen," and to Orcadian "countrymen," and his interest in St Magnus Cathedral illustrated how his language was changing.[26] The world around Norquay on which he depended for his livelihood as an elected representative had become much more British and European and Canadian. He had to ensure that his public image fit the changing times.

Norquay loved to hunt and enjoyed travelling in forest and prairie, but as the years passed he increasingly identified himself with the farms and communities of agricultural Manitoba. It was this Manitoba-ness, an identification with the land that he had known from his earliest days, that became his primary loyalty. It presented him not only with challenges but also with a sense of satisfaction. In winning reforms to Ottawa's colonial approach to the prairie west, Norquay was asserting the province's right to equality with the other provinces and his people's right to equality as citizens of Canada. Whether the voters of Manitoba would recognize his successes and reward him at the polls once again remained to be seen.

A Question of Integrity

Norquay faced a daunting political agenda in 1886. He would have to beat back the Liberal charges of personal corruption. He would have to secure every last dollar that Ottawa had promised to Manitoba. He would have to ensure his party's election preparedness. Though he was confident of his own abilities on the stump, and proud of his personal record in government, he knew that he would face formidable odds if he ran for another term in office.

At the beginning of the year Norquay went to Ottawa yet again, this time to wring the last few dollars out of the deal that he had negotiated twelve months earlier. He decided to risk alienating the prime minister by challenging the federal interpretation of the terms reached in January 1885. Once again Norquay spent a full month in the east. He had expected—and initially told Manitobans that he had won—a total grant of $460,000 per year. However, Ottawa's clauses implementing the deal seemed likely to provide only $441,000, about 4 percent less. He recorded his concerns in a memorandum: the subsidy per head of population was smaller than had been agreed to, he said, the total grant shortchanged the province, and Ottawa should amend its statute to ensure that Manitoba received the full $460,000.

The negotiations did not go well, and Norquay had trouble even securing access to the prime minister. Writing to Macdonald from Russell House at the end of January 1886, after nearly a month in Ottawa, Norquay asked for an immediate interview, adding that he wished "to bring before you a matter of importance to the Province[.] I am anxious to return home as soon as possible and trust that you will be able to see me sometime today." He claimed once again that his trip would have to be cut short because Elizabeth was ill. Privately he received quite different news: Alfred Rennie, his assistant in Winnipeg, sent telegrams on four of the next five days assuring him that Elizabeth was "very much better," "improving," and "no worse" and that their eldest daughter, Bella, would not leave the house while her mother was unwell. Eventually Macdonald gave in, and Norquay won the settlement that he wanted. The federal government agreed to amend its legislation and thereby add a few thousand dollars to the provincial grants. Lieutenant Governor James Cox Aikins, who added his own lobbying effort on Manitoba's behalf when he visited Ottawa briefly, believed that the expedition had secured its goal. Norquay could chalk up yet another victory.[27]

Upon his return he toured several districts in order to assess his party's standing. Travelling by rail and horse-drawn sleigh, Norquay tried to spread good cheer and optimism among the party faithful. He received advice on constituency boundaries and was struck by the depth of popular support for a rail line to Hudson Bay. The tour gave heart to his followers and provided him with encouragement. Upon his return to Winnipeg he spoke more emphatically about his own record and condemned the charges being floated by his opponents. The province had saved money in the so-called coal deal, he insisted. The building of the provincial mental hospital in Selkirk had taken place "with an eye to cheapness and efficiency." Although the Conservative "old guard" in Winnipeg continued to grumble, Norquay believed that his party could defeat the Grits when the time came. Party fortunes were looking up.

Alfred Rennie's appointment to the premier's staff made as much difference to the management of political issues as Arthur Pritchard's arrival had made in office routines. Because the government was entering its fourth year and the Manitoba Act was specific in its declaration that a Legislative Assembly "shall continue for four years . . . and no longer," the premier had to call an election soon. Conservative associations were forming almost spontaneously in western ridings, and talk of party nominations was everywhere. The premier's correspondence focused more and more on electoral preparation, and Rennie became his constant companion. In the first three months of 1886, including the period when Norquay was in Ottawa, he received sixty letters from Manitobans discussing local party operations.[28] Candidate searches commenced, and Norquay was called on to keep the peace. "Like you I have been rather exercised over the knowledge that so many are willing to sacrifice themselves in the interest of their country," he wrote to one local organizer with a touch of irony, but "of course only one can be elected." He was intervening in local ridings, he said, to curb "the insatiable ambition of some and get them all to agree to abide by whoever is the nominee of the convention."[29]

The Liberals established a new theme in these months that they depicted variously as "honest government" and "economy in government." They focused on Norquay's relations with Saskatchewan Coal, targeting his "boldness and impudence" and asserting that the premier was "simply dishonest . . . [in] arranging matters that he might unfairly and unjustly acquire wealth at the expense of others." These criticisms extended to his alleged overstaffing of the civil service and the costs of his trips to Ottawa. Some detractors also argued that the government had received fewer votes than the opposition in the election of 1883 and that Norquay had won only because the constituency boundaries were drawn unfairly. Transcending such issues in parts of western Manitoba was the matter of branch railways. As one party activist told the premier, even a small alteration to an announced rail route would cause "the damdest row you ever heard in that country and a government man needn't show his face there to either Grit or Tory, for their politics are *Railway*."[30]

Norquay showed flashes of irritability. He was being criticized unjustly, he believed, and treated disrespectfully. He complained frequently about the "persistent grumbling" of the government's opponents: "Their sole aim and object appears to be to supplant the Government. . . . [They are] finding fault continually . . . [, and] their whole policy seems to be to rake up filth, keep up agitation and promote discontent." The battle was hardest where Winnipeg's *Free Press* and the *Brandon Sun* were strongest. Despite his protests about stories "beyond the pale in journalistic respectability," the Liberal newspaper campaigns were undermining him throughout the province. He would have to do more.[31]

Norquay conceived a master stroke. On the first day of the legislative session in early March 1886, he announced the creation of a royal commission to investigate his behaviour in office. The opposition would be asked to assemble witnesses to prove their claims, he said, and he would abide by the commission's conclusion. If the opposition's charges were found to be true, then he would step down as premier. It was political theatre, a drama underlining his conviction that he would be found innocent when measured by any reasonable standard of justice.

Who should be the commissioner? Norquay had already spoken quietly to the chief justice of Manitoba, Lewis Wallbridge, about taking on the task. Wallbridge believed that he could perform the required duties "with perfect impartiality" while wondering whether it was wise to accept the appointment. He had been a member of both political parties in his long career, and at the age of sixty he offered the prospect of a fair investigation. But, as he said in a letter to the prime minister in Ottawa, "judges ought to be considered non-political & I would not do so unless with the full consent of the [federal] Govt." He added that "consulting my own feelings [I] would rather not do so." In the end he accepted the assignment.[32]

Other than the announcement of the royal commission, the Manitoba throne speech contained the usual clichés and a few surprises. It celebrated the completion of the Canadian Pacific Railway, the previous autumn's good harvest, the construction of more branch railway lines, and the achievement of a "settlement of the province's claims upon Canada [in the deal of January 1885]." In promising the secret ballot, a franchise extension, and a redrawing of constituency boundaries, the government appeared to be introducing reasonable measures for which the opposition had asked. That the premier was declaring victory in his long campaign to secure equality within confederation stood out as the most dramatic of his announcements. Whether he really believed that the battle was over, and that the recent financial settlement extinguished the need for a transfer of control over public lands and resources, can be doubted. Since Norquay would have to go to the polls within the year, however, it made good political sense to claim success and to smooth over relations with John A. Macdonald.

Debate on the assembly's reply to the throne speech focused on subjects soon to be addressed by the Wallbridge royal commission, including the government's arrangements with Saskatchewan Coal, its selection of the asylum site, and the cost of provincial delegations to Ottawa. Thomas Greenway's motion of non-confidence cited all three. Liberal gadfly Joe Martin quoted a local newspaper's allegation that Norquay was guilty of "personal dishonesty of the grossest kind."[33] Despite the passion of many opposition speeches, no government supporters broke ranks. Norquay's administration was sustained on a motion of non-confidence by sixteen votes to eight.

Wallbridge convened the hearings of the royal commission at the end of March. The judge and his secretary sat at the front of a large room in the recently completed education building, facing rows of chairs filled with reporters, witnesses, and spectators. A team of three lawyers acted as "the promoters" who had to prove the validity of the Liberals' critique. Three Conservative lawyers served as the defence team. Witnesses received subpoenas, were called to the stand, "kissed the book," and gave evidence as they would have done in a court of law. Questions and answers were recorded by a shorthand reporter.[34]

Norquay had laid the ground carefully for the inquiry by embedding the opposition's allegations, using the members' own words, in the commissioner's instructions.[35] Although the excerpted quotations were inflammatory, Wallbridge had not been given a standard by which the premier was to be judged. The chief justice observed that most of the charges made by the Liberals, including statements such as "false vouchers . . . other steals . . . dishonestly used the funds of the province . . . embezzling the public funds . . . having stolen money," were too general or vague to be examined. Two, he said, were specific and could be dealt with: the "coal steal" and the "notorious asylum business." Wallbridge relented later in the proceedings and allowed the critics to address a third subject, expenses incurred by delegations to Ottawa.[36]

Calling the premier to the stand as the first witness, one of the Liberal lawyers asked Norquay about his conversations with the bank manager concerning a loan to the Saskatchewan Coal Company.[37] Did the premier come up with the idea to seek a bank loan of $2,000 against future government orders for coal, or did someone else? Norquay evaded the question: "It was in conformity with an understanding that I had with [the bank manager]." The lawyer tried another tack. Did Norquay assume that coal sufficient to cover the $2,000 advance would *not* be delivered before the maturity of the note on 4 March 1884? Yes, said the premier, he expected that the deliveries would continue throughout the year under the auspices of the coal company's reconstituted management group.[38]

The questions and answers continued: in the following months the company delivered many tons of coal to the government and received payments for the deliveries but refused to count these receipts as part of the $2,000 debt incurred in November 1883. The new ownership group contended that the premier, who remained the president of the company and a shareholder, was personally liable for the government's advance. Norquay had agreed to this stipulation on the condition that the liability would be "one of the first debts to be paid by the company." This was the origin of the shortfall that had brought the entire episode to the attention of the opposition and the public, he said.[39] Subjected to a steady barrage of questions, Norquay remained calm and answered effectively, sometimes with just a word, sometimes with a sentence or two. He emerged from the first day with his dignity intact.

On the second day an issue arose that cried out for further inquiry but, tellingly, roused little interest on either side. Why did the founders invite Norquay to join them on the company's board? "I cannot say what weight they put on my influence. I am not in a position to say what was in their minds." Was he urging the federal government to grant such a patent? "Yes I was." "You were satisfied to do this for the $25,000 stock?" "I would have rendered equal assistance if I had got nothing for it as I thought it a deserving institution." A Liberal lawyer asked about the coal company's patent for the land on which the mine sat. Whom did Norquay see in Ottawa? "I interviewed the Minister of the Interior Sir David MacPherson and also Sir John Macdonald." Was this section of land located on an Indian reserve? "I was informed that it was." When? "It may have been at that time. I think it was a communication addressed to D.B. Woodworth [Douglas Benjamin Woodworth, an MP from Nova Scotia and a coal company principal] from the Department of the Interior." "Then did you ascertain definitely when in Ottawa whether it was on an Indian Reserve or not?" "I did. I think it was corroborated in a conversation with Sir David or Sir John."[40] Remarkable from today's perspective is that no further words were spoken on the subject.

Norquay continued to answer questions briefly, giving the facts as he knew them, including that a patent had never been issued because the company did not have sufficient cash to meet the required payment of ten dollars per acre. "So far as you know the patent has never issued?" "I am not aware that it has." These were significant issues in themselves, though they appeared to be of little interest to the Liberal lawyer. A coal mine had been developed on land that had been set aside as part of a Blackfoot reserve. The federal government had accepted the company's takeover of the tract, though the company had yet to complete the necessary arrangements to make the transfer legal. Norquay, the federal administrators, and the Liberal lawyers all appeared to believe that this enterprise took precedence over the Blackfoot claim.[41]

The Liberal lawyers then turned to "the asylum business." Norquay explained that he had a one-half interest in an eight-acre parcel adjacent to the hospital site, of which three acres became part of the government's purchase. He said that he received "not one cent of money" for this land. Rather, his interest in this acreage was transferred to another party who "would convey an equal amount of land to me for the three acres given by me as part of the asylum site. That is the whole scandal. I have a right to select my three acres in any property owned by Dr. Young in Selkirk. I have not yet selected it."[42]

After a few more questions Norquay's interrogation was over. The premier returned several weeks later, twenty-one Liberal witnesses having testified in the interim, to make a summary statement.[43] His time on the witness stand had occupied two full days and two half days, about twenty hours of rigorous cross-examination. Norquay had acquitted himself well, but he could not deny the transgressions that had provoked all the furor: despite his perfectly reasonable desire to cut fuel costs in Manitoba, he should never have become involved in the coal company's relations with the government. If the interests of friends and local patronage explained his government's choice of the hospital location, as happened frequently in that era, then his ownership of a fraction of the site made the choice wrong. His approach to business and financial accounts betrayed an informality and a lack of interest in details that had become unacceptable in an increasingly exacting administrative context. One question remained: would the premier pay a political price for these mistakes?

Chief Justice Wallbridge wrote his report in the next six weeks, and it was read to the legislature in the last week of May. Its final sentence provided the vindication that the premier sought: "In all of the charges there is nothing which reflects upon the character or conduct of the Hon. Mr. Norquay."[44] To have invited an inquiry into the province's administration, to have given the opposition a free hand in naming witnesses and tabling documents, to have endured legal questioning over four days, and to be absolved of significant wrongdoing made for an exhilarating conclusion. Still, while Norquay stood in the assembly as his supporters cheered, he knew that a quality that he valued above all, his integrity, had been tarnished.

The opposition dismissed the Wallbridge commission as a partisan exercise and continued to claim that Norquay had behaved dishonestly. The *Brandon Sun* described it as evidence of the premier's "loathsomeness. . . . To give a correct representation of such a semblance of a man, would necessitate the use of language that ought not to be heard in refined society." Conservatives did their best to counter Liberals' attacks, and loyal rural newspapers, such as the *Minnedosa Tribune*, insisted that Norquay's reputation remained unblemished. There was a degree of uncertainty, however, in the reactions of many of the urban "old guard" Conservatives. Ed Leacock, for one, chose a line of argument that undercut the premier while seeming to defend him: "The premier was not a businessman and so was an easy prey to the shrewd sharp J.H. Ashdown [an investor in the second iteration of the coal company]." Alphonse LaRivière's partial justification argued that the shortfall in public accounts was only $3,000, not $12,000. Lieutenant Governor James Aikins's measured assessment recognized the chorus of disapproval while judging that the commission would not change the political climate. Aikins wrote to Macdonald that the premier was guilty of insider dealing in the case of the hospital site but only to "the value of $180." The Liberals had been forced to admit "that criminality has not been proved," he said, but "gross irregularity in advancing money as he [Norquay] did on coal has been." Aikins concluded that the premier had escaped without serious political damage: "Greenway & Coy will not make much capital out of it for the elections."[45]

Norquay versus Joe Martin: "Fists Closed and Combs Erect"

For Norquay, the spring of 1886 was filled with gut-wrenching politics. He had to endure not only the Wallbridge hearings but also a legislative sitting that occupied fifty-five days between March and May, longer than the sessions of the three previous years. Assembly members debated more bitterly than ever. The *Manitoba Sun*, in its summary of one week of debate, observed that the session "has been so far remarkable for the number of scenes . . . filled with strong language, insinuations, recriminations, and questions of privilege." The forthcoming provincial election occupied the mind of every legislator.[46]

In their debates, members canvassed the concerns of the province. They weighed the merits of duck hunting against the importance of conservation, prohibition of the sale of alcoholic beverages against strict regulation, the cost of local government, the feasibility of lowering the level of the Assiniboine River, and whether women should be permitted to vote. A discussion of railway policy occupied one full week.[47] That debate had scarcely ended when Ottawa disallowed two more Manitoba charters for branch railways, thus raising the long-running story of federal disallowance once again. Greenway insisted that the Manitoba government could charter railways within the boundary of the old province. He moved that the premier should undertake negotiations with Canadian Pacific Railway to end the monopoly clause. Norquay amended the motion to read that the government of *Canada* should negotiate with the CPR to end the monopoly after the full coast-to-coast line was completed and that charters for branch lines within the original boundary of "postage stamp" Manitoba should then be passed. The premier's amended motion was sustained by seventeen votes to seven. One important new perspective emerged from the railway debates: Norquay argued that when the CPR was "in perfect operation from ocean to ocean it would then be advisable to petition for a withdrawal of the monopoly."[48] The shift in policy—for that is what his statement opened up—became important in the following year.

Branch railway service was a pivotal issue throughout western Manitoba, and both parties knew it. One matter of contention was Norquay's membership on the board of the Manitoba & North-West Central Railway. Was the premier lining his own pockets (the opposition's contention), or was he labouring on behalf of Manitobans (as the premier insisted)? Norquay told the house that "last summer he had gone to New York to ascertain the financial standing of gentlemen with whom negotiations were in progress. . . . His object was to see if there was [a] good prospect of the road going on, and he believed that if certain legislation were secured the road would be in operation some time during the present summer." He expressed dismay that people were blackening his name because of his association with the line.[49]

The premier defended his government's financial record time and again. His administration was doing all that it could to support the province's residents, he said, and choosing wisely in the process: "Take the item of education. This is an item shared in by the richest and lowest. It spreads its beneficial effects on the rich and poor alike." He emphasized that Manitoba spent eighty cents per head on schools, whereas Ontario spent twenty-seven cents and Quebec twenty-six cents. The political jockeying was real enough, as was the anticipation of electoral consequences. Norquay replied to Greenway's attack on local justice costs that the opposition was seeking to make "a lot of cheap capital with which to go to the country, but the result would be the same as at the last election. . . . Defeat met them [then], as it would do now."[50]

During one critical speech at the end of April, Joe Martin referred to the "coal steal." Norquay "interjected a remark that the money was paid back all right. Mr. Martin retorted that it was only paid in the same way a thief would pay when he was caught stealing" and added that the province needed public men "prepared to stand up not for the Government at Ottawa but for the rights of the people of this province." Norquay resorted to a defence that had become one of his favourites: he had been in government for many years and consistently had defended provincial interests. When Martin mocked the reference to fourteen years of service in the cabinet, Norquay retorted that Martin "will never be able to make such a boast." Martin shot back: "That was not a question of importance, but a personal one which should be left entirely out." And then he levelled the charge that Norquay had had to deal with time and again throughout his years in office: "No matter what Government was in power, and though at one time one set of men and one set of principles had prevailed, and at another time another set of men and another set of principles[,] all the time John Norquay was in the Government. That was the reason why Conservatives had lost confidence in him." The Norquay government would lose the next election, Martin declared.[51]

The assembly debates and Judge Wallbridge's conclusions would be major factors in the forthcoming election, but so would the provincial budget. In early May the *Manitoba Sun* observed that the premier had "not been in the House a great deal the last few days, and his absence led to surmises as to the cause. It was learned that the hon. gentleman is preparing to deliver his budget speech one of these evenings. It is said to be the greatest effort of his life, and in order to make it so he has been working away on material for it for some time past."[52]

The speech constituted an election platform folded within a brief history of the provincial government and its expenditures. Speaking as the provincial treasurer, Norquay opened with the now-familiar references to the founding of the province, the costs of administration, the inadequacy of federal financial support, and the rapid pace of development in rural districts. The federal government had been unwilling to increase the subsidy that it granted to Manitoba, he said, yet it had not permitted the province to control its one crucial source of revenue, the land and its resources. This had led to annual delegations to Ottawa and small increases in federal grants. But now, with the latest victory in January 1885, the province had finally made a breakthrough. The federal grant of $100,000 in lieu of lands was a good deal, the premier insisted. He concluded with optimism that "the present is a moment when the people of this country are emerging from the despair that followed the late inflation. . . . The one enterprise which would be conducive [to rapid growth] . . . would be the prosecution and completion of the Hudson Bay Railway. (Cheers)." Norquay sat down to the applause of his supporters.[53]

The opposition expressed disappointment with the weakness of the provincial economy and pressed the charges of corruption raised at the royal commission hearings. Its most extreme representatives employed racist imagery. The *Brandon Sun* managed to hit all these notes when it condemned the government's "carnival of corruption" and warned that Norquay's policies "will, practically, hand the country over to the aborigines." Greenway confined his remarks to criticism of policies and dealt gently with the premier himself, a measure of his warm personal relations with Norquay. Joe Martin delivered a scathing attack. The *Manitoba Sun* (a new Winnipeg daily) delighted in his combative style and observed, probably accurately, that "Mr. Martin does not appear to be a very popular member of the House, although he has his friends. Mr. Norquay does not seem to like him, and in fact most members on the government side declare an aversion for him. But there is little love lost between them. Mr. Martin doesn't seem to care."[54]

Norquay could not block phrases that embedded racialized images in the minds of readers, and not even the chief justice's verdict of "not guilty" in the royal commission report could quiet his critics. On several occasions the premier's usual genial confidence gave way to anger. The *Commercial*, Winnipeg's weekly business newspaper, recorded its impression of such a moment: "Behold the ponderous figure of John Norquay dancing around and sawing the air with his bear-like paws with all the wild excitement of a pugilistic pupil in his first mill."[55]

The assembly session in 1886 wrapped up in dramatic fashion at the end of May. By this point everyone was aware that Martin and Norquay, as the *Manitoba Sun* put it, "cordially dislike each other." When Martin speaks "it is all the premier can do to remain in his seat, and he has a constant look in his face as if he would like to give expression to a well known epithet of his when he is disgusted." Martin, not to be outdone, "seems to regard the premier as the most dishonest man in the world." Norquay walked out of the chamber during Martin's speech on the Wallbridge report. And when he returned, "overcharged" with emotion, "his pent-up hate . . . exploded, and he gave that hon. gentleman a piece of his mind." The *Sun* reported that Norquay "insinuated that he [Martin] was not able to go back to the place he had come from in Ontario. Oh wasn't Mr. Martin mad. . . . He walked up and down uneasily like a she lion when hungry. . . . All he wanted was to call the premier a liar and to call it to his face, at least so he said."

These words ended formal debate in Manitoba's fifth legislature. Then

> the Speaker's silk robe had scarcely swept around the corner out of sight, when Mr. Martin . . . started for his prey. Mr. Norquay had come out from his seat to the middle of the floor and there he was standing when the following consolatory speech was addressed to him by the member for Portage la Prairie: 'Norquay, you're a __ contemptible liar.' It isn't often the Premier is fighting mad, but this riled him, and he struck at Mr. Martin with considerable force. Bantam-like and agile Mr. Martin jumped back and parried the blow, and then with fists closed and combs erect the two men hopped around parrying and threatening for a few minutes. Most of the members had sauntered out of the chamber and those who were nearby were thunderstruck. . . . It is fortunate that this is the last session of the present parliament as a great deal of bad feeling exists among some of the members.[56]

"Old Guard" Again

The clamour of assembly debates slowly faded, but the challenges to Norquay's leadership did not. The premier would have to pull the "old guard" Conservatives into line, but was that possible? He travelled to Ottawa in June 1886 to press once more for a few concessions from the federal government. In these months John A. Macdonald was dealing with several provincial revolts that challenged the very existence of the Canadian federation. Although it seemed that the country might fall apart, the prime minister did not bend. He told a friend that agitation for better terms in Nova Scotia, including an assembly resolution to withdraw from Canada, "looks like blackmail. General election imminent. Hope to secure vote old anti-Confederate party." Quebec's Honoré Mercier seized the leadership of a nationalist protest in response to the execution of Louis Riel and soon became the premier of a Parti National government in Quebec City. Ontario's Oliver Mowat, Macdonald's one-time law student, pressed the prime minister on issue after issue and won time and again.[57] Manitoba's grievances joined the queue, and Norquay had to fall in line behind other premiers from fractious provinces of higher electoral priority.

His delegation to Ottawa, launched just a few months after the premier agreed to the "final settlement" of 1885, had sought only a few thousand dollars. Still, he had to demonstrate that another concession was deserved. Conversations between the premier and the prime minister on 15 June were calm and positive. When they ended Macdonald sent a note to William Scarth in Winnipeg saying that Norquay seemed to be in good spirits. Later that day Macdonald read a letter from Scarth that took him aback. The prime minister immediately replied that it was "perfectly astonishing. I didn't receive it till after Norquay's departure so I had no chance of sounding him.... Could you not speak to him when he returns as to LaRiviere?" Macdonald added that he and Scarth had to get together for a conversation.[58] It is clear that Scarth played the role of intermediary between the prime minister and the premier and that LaRivière's name was associated with rumours that had reached Macdonald.

What was Alphonse LaRivière doing in early June that excited the prime minister's interest? One possibility stood out: the Conservative "old guard" may have decided to unseat the premier. Charles Cliffe, newspaper editor and party agitator in Brandon, wrote privately to Scarth to say that Norquay had to go, citing the scandal charges and "chronic mismanagement" of finances. Charles Stewart, another "old guard" Conservative, offered a similar view: Norquay's "native honesty seems to have been contaminated by his political associations."[59] LaRivière, a member of the St. Boniface elite and Norquay's senior cabinet minister, may have encouraged, or agreed not to oppose, a coup.[60] His willingness to see Norquay ousted would have made the plot feasible. And that may be why his name appeared in the Scarth-Macdonald correspondence.

A sometime business partner of Norquay (and the brother-in-law of Alexander Begg), William Bain Scarth played an influential role in public affairs in Manitoba during the next eighteen months. Born in Scotland, like so many of Macdonald's confidants, he had emigrated to Canada in 1855 at the age of eighteen. He took leading roles in many businesses, starting with hardware, then timber, then land. He went to Winnipeg as the managing director of the Canada North-West Land Company, charged with selling a significant portion of the CPR's land grant, and quickly immersed himself in local politics.[61] Clear headed, amiable, and ambitious, Scarth carefully tended his ties with the CPR head office and with Macdonald. In the spring of 1886 Scarth was renting clubrooms for a Conservative association that he hoped would bridge the old guard/Norquayite divide and unite the party: "There is now very little friction and it would be well I think if there should be none when the local elections come off."[62] Viewed from Norquay's perspective, Scarth remained committed to the "old guard" and Macdonald but was doing his best to paper over differences within the local party.

The prime minister recognized that a Manitoba election had to be held soon, that a federal election would follow, and that some of his Winnipeg supporters wanted Norquay gone. Macdonald asked Scarth to prepare a full report on the quarrel between Norquay and the "old guard." At the beginning of May 1886, before the Wallbridge commission wrapped up and before the Manitoba assembly closed, Scarth wrote a long, dispassionate assessment of the Conservative position in Manitoba. He said that the prime minister's personal standing in the province was high, whereas Norquay's standing was low:

> Well he has not the support of the Conservative party as a whole, and that is where our weakness lies. Hugh [Sir John A.'s son] tells me that you cannot understand the difficulty in keeping united here. Nor did I till I came here, simply because I never before lived where the Conservative leader in a province was believed by a large number . . . of Conservatives not to be a Conservative & was therefore not trusted by them. I had hoped to have been able to overcome this but just as things seemed to

> be harmonizing come the charges of personal corruption with so many & such various explanations.[63]

Scarth sketched three options for the prime minister. Macdonald could appoint Norquay "to some post" and enable the party to run as a new entity, and "we would win." Or he could order party members to "fall into line" behind Norquay, and "we might win." Or the prime minister could encourage the local party to drop Norquay: "His friends would defect: . . . we would probably lose the Local [election] and jeopardize Dominion chances [in the upcoming federal election]." Scarth assured the prime minister that he had no strong preference among the choices: "I am, as always, prepared to follow him [Norquay] or anyone else whom you may advise." These letters contained prediction, advice, and commitment. Like the rest of the "old guard," Scarth's loyalty to Macdonald took precedence over his ties to the Manitoba premier, should the two ever come into conflict.[64]

In late July Norquay called a meeting of thirty Conservative candidates and a number of senior party advisors "to devise the best means to be adopted for carrying the country" in the approaching provincial election. The group decided to hold a party convention in Winnipeg a month hence, during the prime minister's visit to the city, when delegates could consider the platform and generate some good cheer after months of Liberal attacks. Norquay spent the following week, the last week of July, organizing the loyalists and putting out fires among competing factions. Letters left his office at an unprecedented rate as he tried to meet demands for branch line extensions, election workers, campaign funds, and personal appearances.[65] After a two-week holiday with Elizabeth, Norquay returned to his office in mid-August. One of his first acts was to write to presidents of local Conservative associations inviting them to a provincial party convention on 25 August. The event would be "opening at 9:30. The Rt. Hon. Sir John A. Macdonald will be present. Inform delegates."[66]

News of Macdonald's western tour generated excitement in Manitoba. The prime minister would visit the province on his outward journey to the Pacific coast and again on his return to Ottawa, giving the two Conservative factions plenty of opportunity to quarrel over guest lists. The Liberal newspapers enjoyed needling their opponents about such tensions and alleging that the prime minister did not respect the premier.[67] But they could not deny that the two stood side by side on platforms at community meetings and at the rear of a railway carriage as the prime ministerial train steamed through villages in rural Manitoba.

The convention in Winnipeg was a proud moment in Norquay's political career. The premier was hosting the prime minister and presiding over representatives of every faction within the Manitoba Conservative party. Macdonald, now over seventy years of age, was received with rapt attention. Although he claimed to be avoiding commentary on provincial affairs, he endorsed Norquay obliquely and silenced the "old guard" critics. The delegates adopted a compromise platform that conformed to the wishes of federal Conservatives as well as local rights advocates, including Ottawa's CPR policy. They declared "satisfaction with Mr. Norquay's better terms arrangements" and expressed their loyalty to the British connection. They also supported the founding of a new Conservative morning newspaper in Winnipeg. According to one rural weekly, "great unanimity prevailed, and Mr. Norquay, who was present and spoke, was heartily received and endorsed." In the following days he was able to quote Macdonald in cheerful letters to party members: "I can give you no better advice than that tendered by our Old Chieftain who when addressing the convention said 'that while he did not meddle with local politics and was not prepared to give an opinion as to the merits of respective candidates he could always assure them that they would never make a mistake if they elected a Conservative.'" Sir John's presence in the province, and on platforms beside Norquay, boosted the spirits of party members as they headed into an election.[68]

In preparing for the campaign the premier had to address questions about his own government. Corydon Brown, the minister of public works, behaved in the manner of an autocrat and talked more and more confidently about rewards for friends and himself. The attitude extended to his relations with Norquay. When Brown wanted a favour from the premier, he said bluntly that "I must get a land grant from Sir John & you must help me."[69] Such peremptory commands foretold trouble. Norquay invited Dr. David Wilson to take over the department.[70] Brown remained in the cabinet but had to make do with the post of provincial secretary, to which only half the usual ministerial stipend was attached.

To strengthen his team in northwestern Manitoba, Norquay named an additional member, Dr. David Harrison of Minnedosa, as the minister of agriculture, again on a half stipend.[71] Alphonse LaRivière could not be counted a close ally, but he had become the acknowledged political leader of French-speaking, Roman Catholic Manitoba. He accepted a promotion to the important position of provincial treasurer.[72] Charles Hamilton, a reliable and competent ally, continued as attorney general. He took his wife and child on a tour of the five new ridings on the expanded province's western edge, eventually choosing the constituency of Shoal Lake as his new political home.[73] His decision to change ridings opened up Winnipeg South, the constituency that he had won by a narrow margin in a by-election the year before. William Scarth soon became the Conservative candidate in that prominent seat. The nomination of the prime minister's confidant marked another step in Norquay's rebuilding efforts, though it also suggested that the "old guard" was consolidating its position within the government. The premier himself took on a new role as the commissioner of railways, implying further important developments in that sphere. The Conservatives would enter the election campaign with a reinforced front bench and an appearance of unity, crucial factors given the power of the Liberal attack during the preceding months.[74]

One other shock remained hidden from Manitobans. A federal election would take place within months, and candidate recruitment for that event became serious in October and November 1886, complicating the provincial campaign then in progress. Just three weeks before the province's own polling day, Norquay secretly agreed to leave provincial politics and accept a federal nomination. The bombshell underlined the divisions within Conservative party ranks.

What had happened? The most likely explanation is that Scarth, LaRivière, and the "old guard" were once again agitating for Norquay's departure. Norquay decided to take advantage of their influence, thinking that they might smooth his entry into the highest levels of federal politics. In this scenario he would run in the upcoming federal election against the Liberal incumbent in Marquette, the western Manitoba constituency, and be guaranteed a seat in Macdonald's cabinet. Scarth explained that the premier wanted "some assurance of future reward, of being better than [a] private member." There can be no doubt about the seriousness of the scheme. Although concealed in a cypher telegram and never revealed in public, the plan illustrated both the power of the "old guard" and the state of mind of the premier.[75] Norquay's request for preferment carried whiffs of his financial troubles and an overly optimistic assessment of his relations with Macdonald.

None of this impressed the prime minister. Knowing full well that the provincial election would soon clarify the situation, Macdonald simply ignored the telegrams. He would not countenance a provincial leader's abandonment of the party in mid-campaign or the presumption, as he saw it, that lay behind the extraordinary idea.

Election Day, 9 December 1886

To prepare for the December poll, Norquay's office became an electoral machine, the most advanced yet seen in the province. In early July 1886 a Conservative assembly member for Emerson had pressed the premier on "the necessity of some kind of organization at Winnipeg so that we outside members could have some recognized head to telegraph or write . . . when in need of information or a speaker, &c." The suggestion was soon implemented. The person filling the role of campaign chair, Norquay's assistant, Alfred Herbert Rennie, proved to be a godsend. Rennie's rooms at the Queen's Hotel became the coordinating office for local organizers, a clearinghouse for information on issues, and the administrative centre directing the premier's travels. Rennie wrote letters and made especially effective use of a new electoral weapon, the telegraph, as he developed a communications network linking the far-flung districts of Manitoba.[76] He ensured, too, that the party took a more systematic approach to both policy statements and communications tactics.

About 110,000 people lived in the province, over half of whom resided in Winnipeg and the Red River valley. The distribution of seats and voters favoured Norquay's return because, though the number of ridings rose from thirty to thirty-five, the electoral map gave greater influence to voters in the small rural parishes along the Red River.[77] According to the Toronto *Globe*, the average voting population in each of five newly created western constituencies was 4,000, whereas the average in each of five rural seats in the Red River area was only 1,000. Winnipeg voters accounted for over 20 percent (approximately 4,500) of all ballots cast, but their two ridings represented less than 6 percent of the seats in the assembly.

Norquay led a spirited defence of his administration. He developed the arguments employed on the hustings and corresponded with agents in most of the ridings. His decision to condemn Ottawa's disallowance policy and the CPR monopoly on Manitoba rail traffic shocked "old guard" Conservatives.

But his promise to end the railway "blockade" created by Ottawa policies probably defused the Liberal attack in central and western districts. In contrast to his earlier opinion, Norquay had come to believe that patronage, in the form of public works, government jobs, and honorifics could make a difference in the result. He also paid close attention to newspapers, dispensing government advertising and printing to secure their support. In return Conservative newspapers focused on Manitoba's economic progress. The *Portage la Prairie Weekly Tribune-Review*, for one, emphasized that the Norquay government contained experienced individuals who had raised the credit standing of Manitoba and made it one of the most prosperous provinces in Canada: "It stands equal with much older countries."[78]

The key words in the opposition campaign were *bungling* and *boodling*, meaning mismanagement and corruption. The *Brandon Sun*'s list of the premier's sins was typical: "the coal steal, the asylum job, disallowance, the corruption and jobbery that have reigned supreme for some time past, the oppressive tariff, the opposition of Mr. Norquay to the Hudson's Bay Railway, and similar subjects." In summing up its campaign arguments, the *Sun* said that the premier had treated people with "indifference, if not disrespect: . . . Norquay and his gang of parasites have been distributing most lavishly public money among themselves, while taxpayers have been left to sweat and pay."[79]

"Canvassing," the term that covers political conversations designed to establish a voter's intentions and to win support, remained the single most important electoral tactic. Money did play a part in canvassing, but whether it was used to purchase individual votes cannot be proved conclusively. Sir George Stephen, the founding president of the CPR, testified to its presence when writing to John A. Macdonald long after these events: "You know that I have personally & otherwise thro Pope [Minister of Railways John Henry Pope] *alone* spent over one million dollars since 1882." He did not say how Pope allocated the money or whether some of this huge sum found its way into Manitoba Conservatives' hands. But Macdonald's decision to support Norquay in the election, and to encourage Stephen's support of the Norquay government, as well as Norquay's own good relations with Pope, make such a gift not only plausible but likely.[80] It would have been disbursed to newspapers, in particular, and to the central campaign office, where funds for voters' travel expenses received close attention.

As a form of popular entertainment, local campaigns often turned on candidates' performances in public debates. If a candidate could not stand up to an opponent, if arguments became muddled and weak, then supporters would grumble. The premier's role was to back up these candidates. His time in July and again in the autumn of 1886 was taken up with "stumping tours," as his team called them. Norquay travelled not only by rail whenever possible but also by carriage, horseback, and sleigh across the hills and valleys and plains of Manitoba, arriving at a village hall or school where dozens of local men awaited. He shone at these events. People wanted to see him, feel the force of his energy, hear his ornate oratory and ready wit. But these were not easy assignments. One organizer described a sixty-four-kilometre trip in July as "one of the worst drives I ever had. The heat and bulldogs in the lowlands and sand hills between Plum Creek and the Souris was something fearfull." Snowfalls in November produced the opposite effect.[81]

Rennie rationed Norquay's time carefully. As the premier explained to one correspondent, "I don't believe that I shall be able to give more than one [meeting] to each constituency. Remember that there are 35 in Manitoba." The arguments in favour of re-electing his government had to be made again and again. He claimed that he had made "fifty-four speeches . . . often times addressing meetings three times a day and traveling over one thousand miles of country outside of railway travel." The contest, he said, was "the most severe that I ever went through entailing very heavy work physically and mentally."[82] Norquay did not weaken. His blunt honesty and fluent arguments disarmed critics, amused bystanders, and won friends.

Each riding had its distinctive mix of ethnicity, religion, and economic interest. In Souris an able Scotsman agreed to run again in the expectation that Conservative Britons would outnumber Liberal Ontarians at the polling station. In South Dufferin the German-speaking William Hespeler was asked to speak to Mennonites allegedly interested in voting despite the opposition to state-related activities expressed by church leaders. In Oak Lake, a Métis settlement near Brandon, an election worker claimed to have a number of votes in hand but was concerned about Liberal inroads, "especially among the halfbreeds. I will watch them." In Pilot Mound local supporters had to be mollified when a land speculator threatened to move the railway station from their preferred location. In Emerson the sitting Conservative had to overcome the collapse of the local economy and would need funds to bring labourers home from the forests of Minnesota on polling day. In Rockwood the Icelandic settlement's pronounced Liberal bias threatened defeat for the Conservative candidate.[83]

In northwestern districts the need for branch railways took priority in political conversations. To Norquay's advantage, the reorganized Manitoba & North-West (M&NW) Railway, running through ridings stretching from Portage la Prairie toward the town of Russell, was especially solicitous in its treatment of his party's candidates. The M&NW made heroic efforts to grade the route and lay the rails. Would the line reach Russell before the vote? The Conservative candidate, Ed Leacock, warned that "all depends on it as far as I am concerned." Just in time, Norquay received word of a potential celebration at the end of the track. The line's general manager promised that "two entirely new cars" would accommodate Norquay's guests in "pretty comfortable" style as they travelled to Russell and that he had "arranged a bedroom for you [Norquay] in the mail compartment of one of them. I have also put up a little cooking stove so that you will be able to get something to eat and I hope and think that conductor Coffin and my new porter will take good care of you." The expedition smacked of luxury and, best of all, linked Norquay personally with first-time rail access for the villages and farms along the Portage la Prairie–Russell line, six ridings that stretched for 140 miles (230 kilometres) through the enlarged province's northwest.[84]

Evidence that he was making headway first surfaced at a meeting in Brandon in late October. The *Brandon Sun* had been mocking his association with corporate interests by saying that Norquay was just a "thug" and a "boodler" who worked for private gain as one of "the boys." The newspaper's argument centred on his role as a board member of the Manitoba & North-West Railway: "The sole purpose for which the company was organized was that the swag might be secured, and the 'boys' made happy. It did not require much coaxing for 'boy' Beatty [M&NW chair] to induce Mr. Norquay to become a 'boy.'" Speaking at a public meeting in the Brandon rink, and with Greenway on the platform beside him, Norquay tackled the charge head on. He told the large crowd that he went to New York to promote the province and railway, not for private gain. He said that he "was glad to be one of the 'boys,' that he was not ashamed of it." By defending his actions and laughing at his critics, he blunted the charges and won applause. His defiance annoyed the Liberal newspaper all the more. A few days later the *Sun* declared that "it is a standing disgrace to us that he would dare to stand on a public platform and laughingly and boastfully confess that he was one of the 'boys,' and that he only regretted that he had not shared in the 'boodle.'" Viewed from the Conservative camp, the premier had given as good as he got. His combativeness excited his followers and sent them home happy.[85] Most of all it attested to a new phase in the development of Norquay's public image: although the group known as "the boys" lacked precise definition, his embrace of such a fraternity reinforced his chances of victory in these increasingly race-conscious times.

His own election was not a foregone conclusion. Norquay ran in the St. Andrews riding once again, this time against Fred Colcleugh, the mayor of Selkirk, who was receiving extra support from the Liberal party. Unlike in previous elections Norquay could not pay close attention to the details of his local organization, nor could he spend much time in the riding. He had to rely on subordinates, including his son Tom, to do much of the canvassing. His workers went beyond their mandate when they tried to enlist individuals who did not own sufficient property to possess a vote. The unfriendly *Brandon Sun* claimed that seventy-four voters "were struck off the list; other changes were effected, that made a change in favour of Mr. Colcleugh of between 80 and 90." The Liberal paper jeered that Norquay had "descended to the lowest possible level. . . . Among all the corrupt and debauched supporters of the present administration, John Norquay, himself, is the vilest." He replied in time-honoured manner, claiming that the riding had received thousands of dollars in government spending because he was the premier and voters should support him for that and many other reasons.[86]

Late in the campaign, recognizing that they were behind, the Liberals launched a whisper campaign attacking Norquay's native ancestry. The tactic backfired. One of Norquay's countrymen, James Murray, wrote to say that he had been spurred to work harder in the election:

> Seeing that matters are getting beyond endurance . . . I shall from now to the end do all I can for you as I find that the main objection to you is that you are a native of Manitoba[,] the very thing I am proud of you for, and I think the natives of the country ought to be proud that there is one native fit & able to hold the high position you occupy and long may you hold it.

> I know a great many in your constituency and when ever I am able to see any of them I will try and rouse them up.[87]

A few of the St. Andrews voters who had known Norquay in earlier years, especially Bungee-speaking neighbours whose connections reached back to Assiniboia days, sought material help from him, but many more just wanted to see him, to have him stop at their door and sit down for a chat. One supporter lamented jokingly the shortage of adequate lubrication for his dry throat, a condition that, once overcome with a gift of whiskey, would ensure his eloquence:

> Oh boy this is the time for a little to warm my breast to make me talk a little better but I am too poor to have some. People round here say you are getting too rich with government money that its time to put you down but I say no that I am glad that my country boy is the head of the government. Keep the dam Canadians down boy! They are only jealous of you that's what I tell them[.] I hope you will get elected and I will have my fun at them[.] I was down at St Andrews they were nearly getting my head broken. My wife joins me in sending our kindest regards to you and wife & family and accept the same yourself.[88]

By the end of October the Conservative organizers of the central campaign knew where they should focus their attention. The last five weeks became a more intense version of the previous months. The team made good use of telegrams to select events at which Norquay could make a difference. Rennie, often using cypher, arranged transportation for voters and moved workers and speakers with precision. By mid-November several telegrams each day, sometimes as many as five or six, guided speakers and workers. On 20 November Rennie proposed that Norquay attend a "joint meeting [for] Mawhinney & Robinson at Poplar Point Friday twenty sixth [when you are] returning from Russell[.] Robinson making headway." In other words the organizer was anticipating a breakthrough in Lakeside constituency if Norquay lent a hand. The premier's last-minute intervention worked just as they hoped. Robinson wrote a few days before the vote that "your short visit to Poplar Point did me a lot of good. I am fighting my contest straight

Norquay and have knocked Mark Fortune out at every meeting so far." The technology of rail and telegraph made these rapid shifts in focus possible.[89]

Election day planning dealt mainly with transportation priorities. Although such feats had not been possible only two or three years before, the arrival of rail and telegraph made close attention to many more voters feasible. At the centre was Rennie's room in the Queen's Hotel, Winnipeg, where workers kept tabs on the movement of money, volunteers, and voters. Rennie sent packages of instructions to various candidates that contained lists of travelling voters. Those who possessed extra votes through their ownership of several properties had to be moved quickly so that they reached the polling stations before they closed. Train timetables mattered immensely. An agent wrote excitedly that both Brandon seats were now in play and every vote would count. He wanted Rennie to arrange a leave of absence for an employee of the Dominion Lands Commission in Winnipeg, ensure that he voted early in Winnipeg South, and then got a cab to "get to [the] train [station] in time to catch west-bound train. Tell him I will see him when he gets here." Another campaign worker questioned whether Winnipeg residents who had to vote in the city and then reach country points might be accommodated by delaying a train's departure from the city until 9:30 on election day morning. The Carberry agent worried that the twenty voters from Portage la Prairie might not arrive in time. A teller in the Merchants Bank in Winnipeg had no vote there, but his boss should permit him to travel to Brandon, where he did have a vote. The same was true of a machine shop worker in Winnipeg who "could come up free if you could obtain leave of absence for him." Both would have to be shepherded to the train. The Brandon organizer asked Rennie to let one voter, a policeman, stay in Brandon for the ballot, but he acknowledged that, if Norquay needed the man's vote in St. Andrews, where he also qualified as an elector, the premier's riding should have priority. There were always difficult exceptions. One business leader would have to drive all night, eighty-three kilometres by horse and carriage, to cast a vote for the Conservative candidate.[90]

The day before the vote was cold and stormy. Sleet froze on the streets of Winnipeg, and the *Free Press* reported that "a considerable number of individuals interviewed the sidewalk" when they tried to walk around the city.[91] Election day itself was wintry but not forbiddingly cold. About half of all the province's eligible voters turned out. They divided almost equally between the two parties. The Conservatives took just over 50 percent of the 21,000 votes cast, the Liberals just under 50 percent, and 400 votes went to three independent candidates.[92] Three assembly members were acclaimed. Both sides claimed victory. But most of the reports immediately after the count suggested that the new house would contain nineteen Conservatives, fourteen Liberals, and two independents. Reflecting on the campaign, Norquay acknowledged that it had been "a very hard fight." He told James Thomson in Orkney that "the opposition were determined to capture the country and put forth every effort fair and foul, to effect their object."[93]

Tiny margins separated winners from losers. One constituency elected a Liberal by one vote out of 500, another by four votes. The results reflected the parties' geographic strengths and weaknesses. Norquay's Conservatives carried the small Red River valley ridings that had access to railways and were least affected by policies on branch lines. Liberals made gains in the west of the province, including two-thirds of the seats that lay west of the Red River and south of the CPR, where branch railway construction—or its absence—was a crucial factor. Along the M&NW line, Conservatives carried six ridings. In Brandon and Winnipeg the parties split the four seats and the total vote. The turnout in Norquay's seat, 88 percent, attested to exceptional local interest in the campaign, and the premier won by a comfortable margin, 342 votes to 273.[94]

Norquay received many compliments in the following days, both from within the province and across the country. There was a brief telegram from the prime minister: "Hearty congratulations." A few volunteers and candidates wrote to express regrets about local losses. The village of Strathclair invited him to a celebratory supper. His group's post-mortems on the election results provided little illumination. One sensible thought came from an experienced election worker in Pilot Mound: "You may imagine my delight at shouting & hearing others also saying the province is safe. But say my dear old general wasn't it a kind of close call."[95]

The assembly membership illustrated how distant from its Assiniboia roots the new Manitoba had become. Only four of the chamber's complement of thirty-five had been born in old Red River, whereas eastern Canada was the birthplace of sixteen (nine in Ontario, five in Quebec, two in the Maritimes), Britain of fourteen (seven in England, five in Ireland, two in Scotland), and the United States of one. Voters returned all six cabinet ministers, only one of whom—Norquay—had grown up in Assiniboia.

The Liberal *Free Press* spoke of a "revolution" in public opinion and a "crushing defeat" for the government.[96] A more measured judgement came from Lieutenant Governor James Aikins. He wrote to the prime minister that "the agony is over here and Norquay is saved but he has had a close call." Aikins judged that the government would have "a working majority." Significantly he attributed the victory to Macdonald's intervention during his summer expedition: "But for your visit here and your calling on Conservatives to rally for him his Govt would have been defeated." The contest was "a bitter one," Aikins said, and if the opposition had stuck to provincial rights, and not abused the Tories, they probably would have won.[97]

Aikins also picked out a crucial loss, William Scarth, whose defeat he described as regrettable. Not only would the premier miss a strong, respected personality on his front bench, but Scarth owed the loss to the defection of his own friends, "old guard" Conservatives, according to Aikins. The explanation? Scarth had joined Norquay on public platforms in calling for an end to Macdonald's disallowance policy and the CPR monopoly. The "old guard" loyalists had turned "cranky," according to the lieutenant governor, because of Scarth's "so fully endorsing Norquay" and they decided to vote against him.[98] The loss was another of those might-have-beens that shaped the course of events. Without the formal and informal discipline of caucus and cabinet membership, Scarth remained outside the fold and soon resumed his place in the "old guard." That would matter in the coming months.

A Step Too Far

Norquay made an important decision within two weeks of the election. Inevitably it concerned railways. During the campaign, if not before, he had decided that he could not hold off the urgent demands for railway competition. A Hudson Bay railway, it was now widely believed, would offer a third competitive outlet for prairie exports. Why not push that line forward immediately? Although he had never been an outright supporter of the line, Norquay appreciated the arguments for it. The path travelled by his Orkney grandfather had been the lifeline of the fur trade from northern Scotland to Rupert's Land for 200 years. Contemporary estimates declared that Hudson Bay and Hudson Strait would be open for navigation for four to six months per year. The route would cut the rail portion of the present trip to Europe by up to 2,400 kilometres and eliminate several trans-shipments. If only the region could establish competitive economic access to the world.[99]

Manitoba MP Hugh Sutherland won the right to build the Hudson Bay line. He hired contractors Donald Mann, James Ross, and Herbert Holt, then well launched on careers that would carry them to the highest circles of Canadian and international business, to lay the track. Their crews went into action in the fall of 1886 and prepared sixty-four kilometres, though not a completed railway.[100] When the premier met with the Hudson Bay railway team in the week before Christmas 1886, he was glorying in his election victory and expansive in his thinking about another term in office. At this stage Mann, Ross, and Holt had proven their merit as contractors, had worked honourably on the project, and badly needed financial support. They faced one big problem: their preparations were well advanced, but the rail line was far from being operational. Even the president of the line, Sutherland, told the premier that the money should not be handed over because the rail bed was not finished, or so he later claimed under oath. On 20 December 1886, Norquay recommended to his cabinet colleagues that half of the payment for this portion of the line, $128,000, be handed to the contractors. Three of his five cabinet ministers opposed the request. Four days later, a day before Christmas, with the three dissenting ministers away for the holiday, and only Alphonse LaRivière, Corydon Brown, and his private secretary, Alfred Rennie, available to discuss the matter, the premier decided to go ahead and make the interim payment to Mann, Ross, and Holt.[101]

Why Norquay overruled the earlier cabinet vote remains undocumented. It might simply have been that, with the election over and victory secured, he looked on the next four-year term as an opportunity to consolidate his contributions to the province. He might have thought that he was riding high in public esteem and could cast caution to the winds. Assuredly he appreciated the boost that the project had provided during the election and counted on securing the federal government's retroactive approval. Most of all Norquay relied on his judgement of Mann and Holt while trusting his own knowledge of the land. He did have doubts, like those that John A. Macdonald and others had voiced, about the Arctic route. Yet, despite the caveats, Norquay chose the development-minded, aggressive option and delivered the bonds. It was an adventurous, confident decision, a business gamble like several others that he had made in the preceding years. He was to pay a huge price for it.[102]

Norquay had withstood a full year of attacks on his character in 1886. Chief Justice Wallbridge had exonerated him after considering the charges made by the opposition. Macdonald had provided crucial political support. Victory in a hard-fought general election, his fourth win as premier and his sixth as assembly member, confirmed that he held the confidence of many rural Conservative partisans and a wider public. Nevertheless, his assembly majority was narrower than before and the urban Conservative "old guard" maintained a surly opposition.[103] The francophone caucus, led by Alphonse LaRivière, remained susceptible to anti-Norquay appeals. What was worse, several ambitious Conservative members whom the premier had disappointed, including the redoubtable Corydon Brown, seemed to be certain to present a challenge to his leadership. As Norquay attended receptions during the last week of 1886, he could claim that he had been vindicated, but he had to acknowledge that his position was far from secure. In a frank letter to an understanding colleague in the federal cabinet, John Henry Pope, written several months later, Norquay mused prophetically that "it is not unlikely that our present will be a short session followed by an appeal to the country as I can never feel safe in the hands of the bolters who in the meantime have returned to their allegiance but who might rat on any opportunity affording them the chance & upset the Govt."[104]

CHAPTER 11

Defiance, 1887

At the beginning of 1887 John Norquay quietly made plans to tackle the prime minister's veto over Manitoba railway policy. As the months passed and the Manitoba-Ottawa crisis deepened, he fought with increasing desperation to complete a Red River Valley Railway that would end the CPR monopoly. The first ten months of the year brought the highest points in his public career, followed by the most serious challenges to his political survival.

John and Elizabeth celebrated the twenty-fifth anniversary of their marriage in June 1887. Given that life expectancy in Canada at the time stood at about fifty and that several friends had died recently, he might well have wondered about his own future.[1] Elizabeth continued to have both good and bad weeks, and one of the girls was very ill in February, but John remained in robust health. With the move to the Hallet Street home in Winnipeg, the family could be together throughout the week. His income from the government, around $6,500 in 1887, covered most of the family bills. Although he managed to balance his household accounts, payments of larger sums, such as the mortgage on the farm at Parkdale, now in arrears, gave him greater trouble. He did not give up on it, however, and scraped together the interest payment in June.[2]

The relatives who had relied on Norquay in the past continued to put their faith in him. Brother Tom's family required support. Elizabeth's sister-in-law in Portage la Prairie, one of her closest friends, died after an extended illness. The Adams household near Prince Albert managed to survive by sending family members to work in locations far removed from the homestead and wrote cheerful letters welcoming family news in return.[3]

Norquay moved in local society's respectable circles, dealt comfortably with old settlers and newcomers, and was a welcome visitor in the homes of well-known, long-time citizens such as Dr. David Young of Selkirk, the Kennedys of St. Andrews, and Sam and Jemima Bedson of Stony Mountain. Young wrote to Norquay in January 1887, shortly after the new year's festivities had ended, to say that "if you will come down [to Selkirk] I will give you a dance." Norquay received many such invitations to social events, but the pressure of government business reduced the number that he accepted. He continued to field appeals for money from long-time acquaintances and to use his influence to assist them. Through his intervention, William and Eleanor Kennedy petitioned Queen Victoria for a large sum as compensation for the captain's part in the search for Sir John Franklin in the Arctic, though the appeal seems not to have borne fruit. So many of those who shared a Red River background faced difficult times in the new Manitoba, and these services, at least, Norquay could carry out on their behalf.[4]

The few steps that he took on investment matters suggested that he had learned from his mistakes and was no longer as willing to join speculative enterprises. In May Norquay gave up on the Keewatin Mining Company's interest in the gold mine at Lake of the Woods. The Darlingford townsite project came to an end, bringing with it a large loss. Mining activity at the Saskatchewan Coal Company ceased, the shafts filled with water, and this entire chapter was forgotten or misremembered, even in Medicine Hat, the town where briefly it had been important.[5]

Loose Fish

Residents of the prairie west were finding the development of a new economy based upon wheat exports more difficult than they had expected. In 1887 they focused their unhappiness on the clause in the CPR contract protecting the company from competition for twenty years (or ten years after the line was completed). The company's evasion of a principle that governed their own lives—economic competition—seemed to them unacceptable. They argued that construction of the main line had been completed and that the "monopoly clause" should end. The feeling was widespread and urgent; Norquay could no longer hope to dodge responsibility for a Manitoba countermove.[6]

One potential avenue to transportation competition was the Hudson Bay Railway (HBR) Company. It had received $128,000 in bonds at Christmas 1886 and was now pressing for a final instalment, another $128,000, as soon as possible. Norquay, for his part, was obligated to ensure that a 256,000-acre land grant—the land promised by the federal government to the HBR as part of its contract—was transferred by Ottawa to the railway and thence to the government of Manitoba as compensation for the province's bond issue to the railway. Only when this transfer was completed could Norquay justify his leap of faith in giving an advance payment to the HBR. The federal government's chief engineer, having decided that the work was incomplete, argued that the land transfer should not take place.[7] Warned of the problem, Norquay immediately dispatched his finance minister to solve it.

Alphonse LaRivière travelled east in early February 1887 while a federal election campaign preoccupied all the key actors.[8] Norquay instructed him to "explain to Sir John that if land [the subsidy earned by HBR construction] is not turned over to us immediately we will be stuck and it will injure all Dominion Government candidates."[9] After a meeting between the principals, according to LaRivière's version of events, either the prime minister or the railways minister assured LaRivière that Ottawa would transfer the land, as promised in the HBR contract. He wired Norquay on 9 and 11 February to say that the proper arrangements had been made. Given the requisite confirmation, Norquay secured an order-in-council authorizing the payment to the railway contractors.

Months later, when the prime minister denied that such an arrangement had been made, the entire story unravelled. Norquay did not know that the CPR had paid for Minister of Finance LaRivière's ticket, or that the HBR might have given the finance minister a bonus for his support, or, crucially, that LaRivière had failed to obtain any sort of official document attesting to the land transfer.[10] There is no reason to think that Prime Minister John A. Macdonald, preoccupied by the demands of the election campaign, had led him into a trap. But the Manitoba premier was now placed in a vulnerable position, one that LaRivière had helped to prepare and that the prime minister could exploit if he later chose to do so.

Norquay played several important roles in the federal election campaign of February 1887 and helped to ensure that Conservative candidates won four of Manitoba's five seats.[11] He then turned to local politics and the uncertainties caused by some of his opponents in the local Conservative party. Three assembly members, each with an axe to grind, threatened to vote against him when the legislative session opened. The railway issue also posed serious challenges. In early March Macdonald increased pressure on the provincial government by disallowing the charter of yet another Manitoba rail company that might have challenged the CPR. A large fraction of Winnipeg Conservatives responded by declaring absolute opposition to the prime minister. Their defiance, coupled with rural unrest, made Norquay's favoured policy of ambiguity untenable.[12]

Ever the mediator, Norquay obtained cabinet approval for an emergency expedition to Ottawa in a last desperate attempt to sway the prime minister. He was seeking two concessions: federal approval for a rail outlet to the United States, and a boundary extension northward giving Manitoba an outlet on Hudson Bay. If Norquay could not convince Macdonald to bend, then Manitoba would charter a railway from Winnipeg to the American border. If Macdonald once again disallowed the provincial legislation, then the Norquay government would appeal to the British Crown for redress. The battle lines were set.

For ten days in late March and early April, Norquay did what he could to change minds in Ottawa. Some of his allies in the federal cabinet, including Minister of Railways John Henry Pope and Minister of the Interior Thomas White, probably expressed sympathy on the question of the monopoly clause. Not surprisingly, having defended the CPR contract during months of fierce debate in the House of Commons and having seen it endorsed in two general elections, the prime minister refused to budge.[13] Norquay returned to Manitoba, where he was encouraged to lead a provincial rights movement, condemn Macdonald's defence of the CPR, and build another outlet for prairie exports.

Norquay could muster only a tiny margin in the assembly and had to depend on the votes of a few "loose fish" (members who could not be relied on to accept the party whip). The day before the house opened, assembly members gathered in Winnipeg's Grand Union Hotel, where rumours flew fast and furious. Three potential rebels, now called the "new combination," Corydon Brown, John Robinson, and Charles Douglas, all erstwhile Tory MLAs, socialized with Liberals. Brown, said to be "chirpy and pleasant," moved from the lobby to the dining room to the rooms upstairs and stayed until midnight, advocating the defeat of Norquay's government.[14]

The next day, at the opening itself, "an immense concourse of people" filled the legislative building. Seats in the gallery had become the hottest ticket in town. The *Manitoba Sun* commented that the crowds were "doubtless attracted hither by the expectations of a scene in which . . . the government might be defeated." On the assembly floor the "government members" (those expected to vote with Norquay) occupied twenty seats in two rows, plus two for independents, and the opposition sat opposite in two rows with thirteen seats. Norquay had prepared some surprises for the opposition. They began with the naming of David Glass, formerly a Conservative in Ontario, later a Liberal, and now an independent, to become speaker, thereby removing one possible opposition vote and ensuring that Norquay retained all his supporters for divisions in the assembly.[15]

Lieutenant Governor James Aikins read the throne speech, beginning with special mention of the anniversary of Queen Victoria's fiftieth year as monarch. He then came to the bombshell paragraph announcing the government's intention to construct and operate or lease a Red River Valley Railway to the American border at West Lynne and to expedite the completion of the Hudson Bay Railway. He congratulated the house for its work on the extension of branch railways in western Manitoba. He also promised in a dramatic passage that Manitoba would appeal to the imperial government for "relief, should the policy of disallowing railway charters, intended to operate wholly within the limits of the old Province of Manitoba, be persisted in by the Federal authorities." The rest of the speech, including a list of proposed revisions to various pieces of legislation and hinting at plans to cut expenses, seemed to be routine in comparison.[16]

Even before debate on the reply to the speech from the throne commenced, Norquay rose to move first and second readings of the bills providing for more rail service to the United States. He took this step, he said, to address a matter of anxiety throughout the province and to ensure rapid action. Before that day, when "the very fate of this beloved Canada of ours was in the balance, as it were, while that great enterprise, the Canadian Pacific Railway, was being pushed forward to completion . . . we would not have been justified in enacting any such measures." Now, Norquay said, Manitoba's right to legislate for railways within the original boundaries of the province could be acted on: "In doing this we are only conforming with the wishes of a large portion of the community and with the entire community settled within the province of Manitoba. . . . (Cheers)." The dramatic policy shift, announced at a moment when the government's defeat had been anticipated, won him time but cost him dearly, given that the CPR and the prime minister himself would henceforth regard him as an enemy.[17]

Norquay had taken advantage of the rules of debate to wrong-foot the opposition once again. He had promised a huge policy change in the throne speech, appointed an inexperienced speaker, and pre-empted his critics by introducing railway bills before Thomas Greenway could net the loose fish. That, plus some spending cuts and, as the blunt-spoken Thomas Mayne Daly said, "we will have the hypocritical beggars [the Liberals] where the hair is short."[18] Greenway, the Liberal leader, objected lamely to what he described as Norquay's inconsistency. The premier had not proposed a Red River Valley Railway in the election campaign, he said, and had told Manitobans to rest content with disallowance. Having learned belatedly of the people's wish for competition in railways, the government was now reversing direction.[19] After Norquay's brief replies, tempers cooled. Second reading of the railway bills passed before the day was out. Government members "beamed with pleasure" while those on the opposition benches glowered.

The railway bills passed third reading the following day and received royal assent soon after. Two of the members allegedly plotting Norquay's downfall, Charles Douglas and John Robinson, voted with the rest of the Conservative caucus. A third, Thomas Gelley, an independent from the Cartier riding, described by the *Sun* as a twenty-seven-year-old "fun-loving" Quebecer, also voted with the government. As the lieutenant governor informed the prime minister, "Norquay has weathered the storm." Notes congratulating the premier on having secured a majority in the house soon arrived in his office.[20]

Just over a week after the throne speech, Norquay discovered how shaky his majority could be. The opposition introduced a motion critical of Ottawa's disallowance policy. The premier amended it to dilute the attack on Macdonald. Some of his own supporters deserted Norquay, and the government amendment was defeated by eighteen to fourteen votes. The wording that remained spoke of "stagnation in business, of despondency and discontent among the people," and condemned the federal policy "which prevents many coming into the country which they know to be at the mercy of one corporation, and is causing many good citizens to leave it." When the vote was announced, "such a storm of applause went up from the Opposition side as the Legislature has not seen for a long time. Many men in the galleries joined in the applause, which was long continued. Mr. Norquay, Mr. LaRivière and the rest of the ministers wore a very subdued expression on their faces as though they had at last realized that they don't carry the present Legislature in their pocket."[21]

Despite the warning, the debates of the next few weeks reflected Norquay's command of the house. Norquay returned to the confident, teasing style of several years before, waving his arms, speaking softly when he launched into detailed explanations, behaving as if the narrow margin of his majority had no relevance. He occupied the middle desk in the government's front row, a desk that he shared with LaRivière, his commanding physical presence dominating the chamber. The *Manitoba Sun* described one set piece: "Placing his hands in his pockets and grinning good-humouredly, he started in on one of his bluff games" as he "accused 'Tom' Greenway of dying for office." His one-time ally, Liberal William Luxton, warned the premier that the government must be "prepared to stand or fall by every detail; it was not the duty of the Opposition to lead the Government. (Ministerial cheers)." Norquay shot back: "You wish you could." Luxton: "No I don't." Norquay: "I am glad you are satisfied with your position." Luxton: "I do not say I am satisfied. (Laughter)." The atmosphere, so much lighter than it had been a year or even a month earlier, reflected a growing determination among many Manitobans, Conservatives and Liberals both, to throw off the federal yoke and to stand united.[22]

The HBR, of necessity, figured prominently in Norquay's strategy. Recognizing not only its importance to many Manitobans but also that such a risky enterprise might fail, he wanted to secure all-party support for a subsidy. The legislation that he was introducing, he told the assembly, should be seen "more as a tentative measure, more to bring the matter to a focus, . . . and though the Government bring down the measure, they are not wedded to it." Norquay was proposing that opposition and government together should pass a Hudson Bay Railway act. The Liberals objected to the idea, describing it as "a vile act," but in the end they acquiesced. The HBR vote represented another parliamentary victory for Norquay. The pattern continued throughout these weeks. Small majorities of four or five votes enabled the government to emerge unscathed from the eight-week session.[23] Bigger challenges remained: could Norquay overcome the opposition of both John A. Macdonald and the CPR?

Falling for George Stephen's Ruse

Norquay anticipated that he would have to oppose the prime minister and endure a break in what had been a valuable alliance. When travelling to Ottawa in March in his last-ditch attempt to win concessions, he had stopped in St. Paul to meet with Northern Pacific Railroad executives, who controlled considerable operating mileage in the American northwest. They discussed the construction of two possible branch lines that would challenge the CPR's monopoly clause. The lines would run northward, one in the Red River valley, the other from Jamestown (between Fargo and Bismarck), in each case to the international boundary. There they would connect with railways constructed south from Winnipeg and Brandon respectively.[24] The premier had the makings of a deal, though at the cost of a serious confrontation with Ottawa. As he would soon discover, he was underestimating the depth of the bond between John A. Macdonald and George Stephen. Nor did he fully appreciate the power of the nation-state and one of its largest business corporations to shape the outcome of events.

In assembly debates on railway policy during the spring of 1887, Norquay spoke in safe generalities about balancing national and local priorities. He said that he wished to secure fairness for CPR shareholders who had risked their money, for citizens in other parts of the country who had paid the construction bills, and for residents of Manitoba who had the constitutional right to build railways. He claimed to have waited until the CPR enterprise succeeded, and that Manitobans should now receive the benefits of competitive freight rates. Whereas the people of Nova Scotia and Quebec were threatening to break up the Canadian federation, Norquay said, Manitobans should praise the benefits of British and eastern Canadian connections made possible by the CPR: "Had we [Manitoba] not become a portion of Canada our progress would not have been so rapid." He told his colleagues that they should "view that great undertaking [the CPR] not from such a limited . . . provincial standpoint but from the wider and more general application of the term, that of a Dominion standpoint." Norquay also made a resounding commitment: "I do say that every effort of mine within the bounds of the constitution shall be adopted to construct independent lines to the south." The sitting then adjourned to calls of "hear, hear and cheers."[25]

Although Manitoba voters were adamant about the need to erase the monopoly clause in the CPR contract, Norquay himself tried to maintain harmonious relations with the province's largest and most important corporation. He did not deal directly with its president, Sir George Stephen, or key board member Sir Donald A. Smith, but he spoke frequently with local officers of the company and had regular contact with its chief operating officer, Vice-President William Van Horne. Despite their very different backgrounds, Norquay and Van Horne had much in common, including a taste for cigars, card games, good conversation, and late nights. Because Van Horne had lived in Winnipeg in 1882, the first year of his Canadian career, he had met the premier during the period of Winnipeg's great boom and crash. In the years since, they had shared drinks, played poker, and corresponded in friendly fashion. Van Horne looked out for Norquay's interests during the Darlingford townsite speculation. In his turn, Norquay instituted a tax relief measure for the railway in 1883.[26] The cash-strapped CPR built 240 kilometres of branch lines in the southwest of the province during the summer construction seasons of 1885 and 1886 when farm households cried out for such support.

A letter from Van Horne to Norquay in mid-March 1887 suggested that he hoped to visit Winnipeg before the end of the month and "have the pleasure of entertaining you for an evening or two in the old Saskatchewan," his private railway car. Norquay's dalliance with the Northern Pacific, conducted in these very days, put an end to their close relationship. On 27 April Norquay penned a personal note of apology to Van Horne, confessing that he would be building a railway to the border.[27]

In early May, Van Horne ordered cuts in the company's workforce in Winnipeg, cuts in the number of hours worked in the shops, and, if additional labour might then be required, cuts in wages for the new hires. He wanted to make "the anti-disallowance agitators . . . feel some ill-effects from their action." Several days later he threatened to tear up the branch line from Winnipeg to Selkirk if the company was not granted a right of way along the town's riverfront. He also asked his subordinates whether they were still buying coal from Norquay's mine. (They were not.) Van Horne recognized that Norquay faced a great deal of pressure and expressed some sympathy for the premier, who had to deal with the "unsupported and untruthful statements of a few men who only have their own selfish ends in view." The CPR vice-president believed that his real opposition lay in the circle of Winnipeg wholesale merchants, not the broad swath of Manitoba farm families, people whom his company had been trying to reach with branch line service.[28] But his sympathy for Norquay was now overshadowed by his irritation with the pressure groups that the premier of necessity had to represent.[29]

Norquay's fate now depended on the alliance between the CPR and the federal government. Would it remain firm, or would one—or both—of them give in to Manitoba's insistence? Here the crucial actor, besides the prime minister, was George Stephen, president of the railway company.[30] He has long been seen as the great Canadian whose contributions to the transcontinental rail line made possible the country's consolidation at a moment when Canada might well have disintegrated. The CPR itself has been viewed as a "nationalist" project by many Canadians, including historians, an act of resistance to American capital's absorption of the entire continent into a single market and way of life. President Stephen reinforced this outlook in hundreds of letters to the prime minister in the years that followed the government's granting him the contract. He told Macdonald time and again that railway and nation could not be separated while construction proceeded and before the corporation was made secure. Stephen fought continuously to ensure that politicians, company suppliers, construction managers, and headquarters executives held their nerve. But he possessed some less attractive qualities. He mocked his closest colleagues behind their backs. He hated with a vengeance. His ambition, like his extravagant cajolery, knew no bounds, and he did not shrink from using bribes, or *bonifications* (his word), to impose his will. He bluffed, concealed, and duped. Norquay did not know the half of Stephen's thinking. He should not have responded to the apparent fury of the CPR president in the spring of 1887 because, in truth, Stephen's anger was intended to deceive.[31]

Fears about his two closest competitors, Henry Villard's Northern Pacific and James Hill's Manitoba Road (the StPM&M, a corporation separate from the CPR despite having shareholders in common), fed Stephen's overheated correspondence through late April and the first half of May. Having heard about Norquay's Red River Valley Railway ambitions, Stephen wrote to the prime minister to say that "the cheek of these people is something wonderful." He challenged the Manitoba critics to point out a single grievance about rates or facilities: "It is disgusting doing anything for such stupidly ungrateful dogs." Mysteriously, but significantly, Stephen then dropped Jim Hill from his list of enemies. Instead, he focused his anger on the Northern Pacific, warning the prime minister that it was undermining the CPR. He had become discouraged, he said, and never imagined that Canadians would work against his railway in such a fashion.

In mid-May Stephen sent Macdonald two dispatches on the same day. One reported the contents of a wire just received from St. Paul saying that the Northern Pacific had agreed to build a rail line to the international boundary at Pembina or West Lynne, the crossing points on either side of the Red River, if the Manitoba government would build a connecting line from Winnipeg to the border. Not just another bit of gossip, the intelligence was correct. Stephen asked Macdonald to intervene because, he said, the plan had to be defeated, or the CPR would collapse.[32]

Stephen's second dispatch to Macdonald struck an equally dramatic note. As part of a scheme to change the course of local politics, Stephen proposed to bribe the Manitoba premier: "Don't you think it would be a patriotic act to persuade Norquay to resign & take up in *opposition* a really *Conservative* policy [Stephen's emphasis]?" Recognizing that Norquay was always short of cash, Stephen offered a solution: "I fancy the chief obstacle in the way lies in the fact that he has not the means of living without an official salary." The multi-millionaire had a solution: "Looking at the position as it affects the country apart altogether from party politics, I think I might be justified in saying to you that if you saw fit to urge 'resignation' upon Norquay, I would take measures to enable you to say to him that you would see that he got his $2,000 a year for say two years; in case he should be so long out of office. I hear from [illegible] that the 'bread and butter' question settled, Norquay would take a bolder & more patriotic course." Such a plan had to happen "now." Once the competing rail lines had met at the border, Stephen concluded, the CPR line north of Lake Superior "will have to stop running, there will be no use for it."[33]

Stephen then raised the temperature in Winnipeg. On 23 May he sent a telegram to Norquay that constituted the point of no return in relations between the Manitoba government and the CPR. The wire declared that Manitoba's rumoured deal with the Northern Pacific constituted "an act of undeserved hostility towards the CPR" and a "breach of faith" toward its shareholders. If this "mischievous agitation"—in which the CPR was "treated as a public enemy by the people of Winnipeg"—continued, then the company "will at once take steps to establish their principal western shops at Fort William, which, from an operating point of view, has many advantages, leaving nothing in Winnipeg but the ordinary division shops. Pray do not be mistaken. This is not an idle threat, it is a fixed purpose, taken after full consideration."[34]

On the day this telegram went to Norquay, Stephen instructed Van Horne to send a copy to the prime minister. The vice-president duly wrote to the federal minister of railways: "He [Stephen] would be glad if you would show it to Sir John [A. Macdonald]." Van Horne concluded his note with the advice that, "the sooner Norquay is out of office, the better it will be for the Government at Ottawa."[35] The letter represented a new political offensive. By making Norquay the target, the leaders of the CPR were declaring not just that the Red River Valley Railway must be defeated but also that the Manitoba government must fall.

Stephen's talk of bribing Norquay and moving the CPR shops appeared—on the surface—to be the product of someone at wits' end. Stephen complained of his weariness and failure of nerve. But was this truly a case in which the CPR president, having lost all sense of perspective, no longer able to judge events or people, simply lashed out in anger?[36] Or was he intentionally provoking trouble?

Norquay read Stephen's threatening telegram to the legislature. He did so "knowing very well," as the *Winnipeg Call* observed, "that the contents of that telegram would perhaps influence to a large extent the people of Winnipeg." The *Call* recorded Norquay's reply to the CPR threat: "The telegram having been directed to me," Norquay told the assembly, "I sent the following: 'Cannot understand how your company can construe contemplated action of Provincial Government to build a railway to southern boundary as breach of faith to holders of Canadian Pacific Railway securities. Government is acting on behalf of Province uninfluenced by Winnipeg's action to C.P.R. or C.P.R.'s contemplated removal of workshops.' As the hon. gentleman sat down the House rang with applause, which lasted for a number of seconds."[37]

Norquay's response to Stephen's telegram rallied the Manitoba assembly in a manner reminiscent of the better terms debate of 1884. Government and opposition stood united against the outsider. Whatever doubts there had been about building a third rail line (the other two being CPR properties) from Winnipeg to the international boundary suddenly vanished. Two days later at a great public meeting attended by 1,500 people—with Norquay, Greenway, the mayor of Winnipeg, and prominent citizens on the platform—Manitoba fought back. According to a Winnipeg business leader, the audience at the protest meeting included equal numbers of Conservatives and Liberals, "a great many reeves and others from the country," and "representatives of the most important classes in Winnipeg. . . . The Legislature has sunk all questions of side or party, and is thoroughly united as one man. . . . This is now a question of principle viz[:] monopoly or freedom."[38]

Stephen had whipped up a public frenzy. But what was in his mind? Certainly a great deal more than appeared on the surface. Since the completion of the CPR, he had been rethinking his position in the world. In the autumn of 1886 he had succeeded in retaining his seat on the StPM&M Railroad board, despite James Hill's scheme to replace him, thereby gaining time to reflect on the development of railways in northwestern America. During these months he distanced himself from Canada. In the same months Hill was facing his own moments of decision. He believed that he could build a profitable, giant corporation by driving a rail line westward to the Pacific Ocean, using the StPM&M, the "Manitoba Road," as its foundation. The combination—Stephen's ambition and Hill's vision—brought the two men together again.

On 17 May 1887 Stephen wired Hill: "Thanks for message will do what I can." That same day the CPR president asked Macdonald to intervene in the Manitoba case. If Norquay's venture could be held back for sixty days, he told the prime minister, then it would fail. A week later John Kennedy, Hill's investment banker in New York, noted that Donald Smith was moving shares of StPM&M stock. With the passing of another week, Stephen and Smith sent a crucial telegram to Hill. The two Montreal residents apologized that they could not accept Hill's invitation to a meeting (presumably in New York) and tried to set up another one: "We should both be very glad to see you." They suggested that Hill wire them with alternatives "so that we may both be on hand. Want to talk with you particularly about the invasion of Winnipeg by the N[orthern] P[acific]."[39]

Something far greater than a mere Manitoba-Ottawa-CPR battle was under way. Unknown to Norquay or the prime minister, Stephen was leaving

Canada behind. A year later Stephen and Smith assured Hill that they would do whatever was best for the StPM&M, in which "we each have a greater pecuniary interest than we have in the CPR." Stephen was "thoroughly disgusted and for the thousandth time bitterly resent that I ever had anything to do with them [his Canadian associates] or their country. . . . I would like to shake the dust of Canada off my feet and turn my back on the country for ever."[40]

The CPR president was goading the CPR's Manitoba critics in the spring of 1887. Having roused popular resentment, he would now put a high price on the monopoly clause and expect payment from Macdonald for relinquishing it. If his plan worked out, then compensation from Ottawa would secure the future of the CPR for years to come. At the same time Stephen would increase his own financial power manyfold by transferring his attention, money, and influence to Hill's next project, a venture soon to be known as the Great Northern Railroad, and rise yet higher in the hierarchy of global financial titans. It is impossible to establish degrees of motivation in the CPR president's decision making, but his frustration and disappointment, sentiments that might be seen as justifiable, can be juxtaposed with his entrepreneurial talent, creativity, cupidity, and ambition. Add to these factors his taste for vengeance. Stephen had some scores to settle. Norquay figured little in these calculations except as a puppet to be manipulated. In Stephen's view, if the Manitoba government collapsed while attempting to complete the Red River Valley Railway, so much the better.

The Contest

Clause 15 of the CPR contract, the so-called monopoly clause, dominated events in Manitoba in 1887. The promise of a Red River Valley Railway to the United States, a line that would remain outside CPR control, won Norquay widespread support not only in the assembly but also throughout the Winnipeg business community and among many in rural Manitoba. Was the change just another occasion on which he abandoned a principle, as his critics alleged?[41] As ever in politics, that depended on one's starting point. Norquay had changed his recent course, certainly, but he had never accepted the CPR's monopoly clause. His opposition to it, conceived at the moment when the contract was revealed in December 1880, could not be reconciled with loyalty to the prime minister. His argument in 1887 was that the main line of the transcontinental railway had now been completed, and the company should no longer receive such protection. Prime Minister Macdonald himself seemed to be open to this suggestion when he told the Manitoba Conservative convention in August 1886 that the clause "would, he hoped, be given up 'speedily.'" His minister of the interior offered even stronger assurances when he visited Winnipeg in early March 1887. Public opinion in the province overwhelmingly favoured a challenge to the CPR monopoly. Norquay's majority in the assembly was small and unstable. If the premier worried about how the prime minister and the CPR might respond, he kept the reservations to himself. The next moves would be up to Macdonald and the CPR.[42]

The prime minister insisted that the national railway had to be defended against American incursions.[43] Throughout this crucial year he argued consistently that international investors purchased shares in the Canadian Pacific Railway based upon specific promises, including the monopoly guarantee, and that the shareholders would have to agree to its deletion. Macdonald permitted federal candidates in Manitoba to disavow his policy of defending the CPR contract in the campaign of February 1887, but he did not change his own view. Rather, he doubled down on the merits of the Conservative plan for the entire Canadian economy, of which the railway and its contract were important parts.[44]

The Manitoba assembly adjourned early on 2 June 1887 in honour of the twenty-fifth wedding anniversary of John and Elizabeth Norquay. Members of the house presented them with gifts, including two large chairs, a calumet described as a pipe of peace, a box of cigars, and a "costly" dinner set of 150 pieces. Greenway said a few words of congratulation, everyone gave three cheers for "the old man," and members then toured the city in horse-drawn carriages, including visits to the newly founded district of Fort Rouge south of the Assiniboine River and the new City Hall on Main Street. In the evening a huge party was held at the "gaily illuminated" Norquay home on Hallet Street. The grand affair seemed to affirm the people's approval of his leadership. The Norquays received more gifts, including flower stands, canes, goblets, pitchers, and a salad bowl. The program listed twenty-three dances, John and Elizabeth danced a Red River jig, and the celebrations ran late into the night. Nearly all the assembly members were there, the *Free Press* said, along with many "notable citizens." The *Call* added an interesting note: "Mrs. Norquay does not enjoy the best of health at any time, but she was remarkably well last night."[45]

Two weeks later Norquay attended the Presbyterian general assembly in the Kildonan church. The *Canadian Presbyterian* reported that he had "fittingly closed the speech-making of the day in a very happy manner." It was yet another successful appearance in a long string of such moments in the public eye. His letters in these weeks reflected his confidence in his choices. He had faced great pressure in the assembly and had worked out principled stands.[46] When the assembly session closed in early June, Manitobans expected that construction of a rail line to the United States would begin shortly. Within a week the government was negotiating for a $1 million bond issue in London. Several days later it approved a contract with Hugh Ryan, the lowest of three bidders, for "$782,430.00 . . . for the construction and equipment of the Red River Valley Railway." At the same time Norquay had been empowered by an order-in-council to commence negotiations with Winnipeg financier Duncan MacArthur for running rights and operation of the rail line.[47]

Norquay probably had no idea of the depth of deception in his inner circle, but Alphonse LaRivière and Acton Burrows, the former in the cabinet and the latter at the Winnipeg daily, the *Call*, were preparing to betray him. Their reports of the 11 June cabinet meeting galvanized the CPR and the federal government. According to Van Horne, who cited Burrows as his source, Minister of Finance LaRivière was "in a great deal of distress about the financial position into which Mr. Norquay is putting the province."[48]

Stephen responded immediately to the news from Manitoba by dispatching Vice-President Van Horne to Ottawa for talks with the two most powerful federal ministers on railway matters, Charles Tupper and John Henry Pope. At the first of several meetings, Van Horne conveyed a startling new message: the CPR would give up the monopoly clause and accept monetary compensation or a federal government financial guarantee in exchange. His conversations marked the beginning of a year-long lobbying campaign.[49]

Tupper and Pope refused to consider the idea of giving up the monopoly clause, citing Parliament's "recent vote on the disallowance question." They also insisted that Macdonald was "very decidedly of the same opinion." They argued that Norquay's railway was bound to fail. By disallowing any Manitoba charter for a line to the border and preventing "in any possible way his making use of the credit of the province," the federal government would postpone completion of the line until an opportunity arose to crush it forever. Norquay would soon be gone, they assured Van Horne.[50]

On 21 June Van Horne wrote to Stephen to convey an extraordinary piece of news: Macdonald had a scheme to "smash Norquay's railway." No details, just the promise that Norquay would fail. In the view of both the prime minister and the CPR leaders, the premier had sealed his own fate by committing his government to an opposing railway group and by his alleged readiness to enrich associates.[51]

The CPR headquarters now focused on trading the monopoly clause for new money from Ottawa. Stephen began this phase of the courtship with a quiet letter to Macdonald in which he expressed his concern about the news from Winnipeg, suggesting that the "local government seem[s] to be entirely under control of the local ring with whom agitation originated." But his conclusion was plaintive and modest: "Can you say anything to reassure me?"[52]

By then Macdonald had adopted two lines of attack, one constitutional and the other financial. On the first the prime minister contacted Lieutenant Governor James Aikins in Winnipeg to ensure that "authentic" copies of the bills passed by the legislature were sent immediately to Ottawa. The acts had to be disallowed as soon as possible. Macdonald had doubts about Aikins. In the middle of these tense weeks, Manitoba's lieutenant governor wrote a powerful warning to the prime minister that blamed the Thunder Bay shops telegram for the crisis. Had Stephen refrained from such rhetoric, the legislature might have backed down: "But that telegram thrown in their face so incensed them and the people as well that I fear if the matter is not dealt with wisely there may be trouble. . . . I name this as I think you should know the condition of mind and circumstances of the people." Macdonald was unmoved. He disallowed the Manitoba legislation when it arrived in Ottawa.[53]

Eliminating Manitoba's railway charter represented only the first of Ottawa's weapons. The second, cutting off funds, was even more stunning in its speed and effectiveness. In mid-June, about the time that Van Horne was canvassing cabinet opinion in Ottawa, Norquay's government contacted Sir John Rose, London investment banker, in the expectation that the British money market could be tapped by both the Hudson Bay and Red River valley railways. Rose responded positively to the request from Manitoba. Probably on Donald Smith's advice, and foreseeing difficulty, Rose also took the precaution of wiring his old colleague, the prime minister, to ensure that the commitment would not cause problems. Macdonald set him straight immediately. In the flurry of cables that followed, the prime minister convinced Rose not to proceed with the $1 million bond issue.[54]

Macdonald followed up his cables with a long letter to Rose reinforcing his shutdown message, phrasing it as concern for the reputation of Manitoba and Canada. Norquay and his ministers, the prime minister wrote, were "careless of the prestige or prosperity of their province." Because Manitoba's cabinet members "are all impecunious and think only of a continuation in office," he said, they were risking provincial bankruptcy. The "insane" Manitoba legislation involving these expenditures would "in all probability" be disallowed. "Please use this information," Macdonald concluded, "without mentioning my name."[55] Although Rose's firm had already accepted the Manitoba commission, that commitment was soon reversed. The setback was the first of many in a long summer of financial frustrations for the Norquay government.

On 26 June Stephen increased the pressure on the prime minister. In a sentimental letter of the persuasive kind that he wrote so well, he reported the sad news that he had had to leave his flyfishing utopia in Quebec's Gaspé because he was so worried by "Winnipeg events." What made it worse, he said, was that the crisis had been brought on by "the very people the road was chiefly designed to benefit." Stephen then set the hook: could he and the prime minister devise a plan to save the company and the country from further agitation? In this carefully crafted act of persuasion, he declared that no permanent peace was possible until the monopoly clause was ended. Sir John A. should disallow Norquay's bills and then negotiate with the CPR to surrender its monopoly: "We have been damaged more deeply than I dare say on paper, and our great asset—land—is utterly useless now" because of the western agitation.[56] Stephen did not name his price. From this moment on the CPR president inundated the Prime Minister's Office with letters and telegrams in which he railed at the Manitoba government, lamented his own (alleged) nervous exhaustion, and slowly brought the prime minister around to the idea that the monopoly clause had to be abandoned. His letters constituted a master class of deception. In setting a trap for Norquay, Stephen also ensnared the prime minister.

The *Times* of London reported near the end of June that "the excitement" over railway policy in Manitoba was increasing. It quoted Norquay as saying that "the [RRV] railway will be built, no matter what the consequences may be." The premier asserted that "we are not serfs, and will not be found in the background in the event of trouble, which I hope will be avoided, but not at the expense of the railway project." The *Times* also reported that Ottawa was not backing down. The "Ministerial Press," it said, threatened "that force will be resorted to to prevent the construction of the railway to the United States frontier, and all the journals regard the situation as acute."[57]

The London newspaper reported accurately. Winnipeg's business weekly, the *Commercial*, declared that "work will be commenced about the first of July, and the road will be completed to the boundary early in October; in the meantime the Northern Pacific Company are pushing their connecting link northward through Dakota, and their rails will be laid to the Manitoba boundary about the middle of August." The national news magazine *Grip* published a cartoon to celebrate the Manitoba resistance movement featuring a handsome, lithe premier battling a CPR viper named "Monopoly." The snake bore an uncanny resemblance to George Stephen.[58]

At the end of June Norquay paid a second visit to the Northern Pacific Railroad offices in St. Paul, no doubt to affirm his government's commitment. Despite gnawing concerns about finances, he believed that he could complete the railway. Bonds had yet to be floated, admittedly, "but it has been semi-officially announced," said the *Commercial*, that "the funds will be forthcoming at the proper time." In surveying the scene the Winnipeg business journal saw only one cloud on the horizon, the federal government: "There is still considerable uneasiness felt here lest the Dominion authorities should step in and endeavor to stop the work [by adopting] a vigorous and startling line of action." Winnipeggers did wonder, wrote the *Commercial*'s editor, "what can the Dominion do to 'check Manitoba?' If Manitoba be acting within the constitution—and it is claimed she is—dare the Dominion use force to put her down? . . . These and many other questions are constantly debated here, in season and out of season, and wherever two or three are gathered together . . . whilst the Dominion maintains—but let us hope not an ominous—silence."[59]

When James Aikins, Manitoba's perceptive lieutenant governor, blamed Stephen's telegram for passage of the Red River Valley Railway legislation, Macdonald snapped in reply that his CPR policy had been approved by Parliament, "so this policy must be carried out, whatever may be the consequences. I have no fear of these consequences. Your bankrupt population at Winnipeg must be taught a lesson, even if some of them are brought down to trial in Toronto for sedition."[60] Stephen used the policy confrontation between Ottawa and Manitoba to underwrite the consolidation of the CPR and his new investment in Hill's railway through the northern states.[61] When Norquay acquiesced to public sentiment in much of Manitoba, he would have had no idea that he was being used by the CPR president to reverse a federal government policy.

At Daggers Drawn: Manitoba versus the CPR

In Winnipeg the daily newspapers greeted Dominion Day, 1 July 1887, with expressions of regret as well as celebration. The *Free Press* editorial on the country's twentieth anniversary declared that the people were "patriotic, filled with the national spirit, . . . Canadians to the core." But it also pointed out that confederation was still "an experiment" and lamented "all the injustice and tyranny exerted from Ottawa." Many Manitobans, whether Grit or Tory, could not praise Canada unreservedly, it said, while the prime minister's railway policy prevailed.[62] The next day was also memorable. Norquay and his government staged a party, complete with white canvas marquee and hundreds of spectators in holiday attire, to mark a sod-turning ceremony for the railway to the American border.

Norquay's daily schedule remained as busy as ever. The weather was wonderful, the harvest promised to be bountiful, yet the premier could not convince bankers to buy in to the province's railway project. The failure weighed heavily on him. Norquay recognized that he was locked in a battle that would not be settled easily. At the beginning of August he appointed himself to the government's Treasury Board, the key cabinet committee that exercised oversight of spending. He had a falling out with the lieutenant governor in an unpleasant interview that prompted Aikins to send another warning to the prime minister: "It seemed to me as if he [Norquay] did not care who was sacrificed if he could only carry out his plans." In the first week of August some members of the cabinet still harboured hopes of finding an escape from the Red River Valley Railway promise. It was late in the day, of course, and rails were sitting on a dock in Montreal while the grading of the roadbed proceeded. Nevertheless, dissenters such as LaRivière argued that rails were in demand across North America and could be resold, the labour costs associated with the grading were small compared with the next phase of the project, and the CPR's Pembina branch line could be bought or leased for a fraction of the new line's cost.[63]

Norquay's determination to carry on provoked further counterattacks from the CPR. Patronage payments to newspapers and court injunctions to halt construction figured in their strategy. William Van Horne supervised the initiatives within Manitoba. Thousands of dollars went to newspapers, including the *Selkirk Record*, which at that time backed Norquay but, tellingly, also supported federal government policy on the CPR. In Ottawa Stephen and Macdonald continued their long skirmish over the monopoly clause. What is more—a sign that Stephen's campaign was taking a clear direction—the CPR now claimed in conversations with the prime minister that it could not pay for essential improvements to its rolling stock and track. Without such an investment, Stephen said, he feared "great danger." Then, in a letter to the prime minister from his Quebec fishing lodge, he waxed sentimental, inviting Macdonald to visit, get some rest, and "catch a salmon with your own hand."[64]

Macdonald resisted Stephen's entreaties because he feared the consequences of changing a policy that he had defended for so long. If he were to give up the monopoly clause and pay off the Canadian Pacific Railway yet again, after the repeated injections of emergency funding during the crisis years of construction, then he would only inflame the opposition further. He believed in the national and imperial loyalties underwritten by his National Policy, and he wanted to assure stock markets that Canada's word could be trusted. It was a measure of the fluidity of the situation that important figures in the crisis, both in Montreal (Stephen and Van Horne) and in Winnipeg (Norquay, LaRivière), were still debating alternatives at the beginning of August. Some sort of negotiated deal that precluded construction of the Red River Valley Railway might have been pulled off at that late date, but time was running out. Final decisions would have to be made soon.[65]

Could they secure a big loan? Should they lease the CPR's Pembina branch line? Must they start to lay track? Could they keep the public on side? These were the questions facing the premier and his cabinet when they met on 12 August. At that meeting they resolved to go ahead with the Red River Valley Railway. They passed an order-in-council, backdated to 22

July, authorizing the Department of Public Works to complete the railway construction. At that cabinet meeting they also passed orders-in-council authorizing the provincial treasurer to seek a loan of $100,000 and providing "authority to borrow money—$1,000,000."[66]

The Merchants Bank agreed to cover the first part of the shortfall several days later, providing $100,000 credit but on strict conditions and only for current expenditures. The cabinet authorized a payment to release some of the rails on the dock in Montreal. Notions of leasing the CPR's Pembina branch line faded away. The cabinet was now fully committed to ensuring that the Red River Valley Railway was built. The national weekly *Grip* congratulated Norquay, and even *The Times* of London noted that Manitoba's railway project had "entered upon a critical stage." He packed his bags and headed east to find investors for both the Red River and the Hudson Bay railways.[67]

For over a month Norquay travelled with LaRivière in search of funds. He started with meetings in St. Paul, where he was well known, and then Chicago. The *Washington Post* described him in these weeks as "the giant Scotch-Creek halfbreed Prime Minister of Manitoba," presumably mistaking Crees in Canada for Creeks, a Native American group. The interview turned to the potential for violence in western Canada. Norquay admitted that, "yes, there may be trouble, even to the extent of a conflict of arms." His government did not want a quarrel, he said, and he was willing to go to Ottawa to strike a deal. But he was committed to building a rail line from Winnipeg to the United States: "The road undertaken would be completed even at the point of the bayonet. He believed the federal authority would resist them, and of course if such were the case there would be bloodshed."[68] This kind of talk could not have opened the doors of American banks. To make matters worse Manitoba was looking for investors at a very bad time. American money markets were unstable, and many observers feared a financial collapse on Wall Street. It was widely rumoured that the Baltimore & Ohio, one of the potential railway targets of speculators, "teetered on the brink of bankruptcy."[69]

On 20 August Norquay wrote to a cabinet colleague from a hotel on Chicago's Michigan Avenue to report on his meetings. People were interested in Manitoba's progress, he told David Wilson, his minister of public works, but the financial situation was disappointing. He was planning to head for Toronto: "If I can with LaR[ivière] fix up our loan in Toronto I'll go on to New York to fix up the W[innipeg]&H[udson Bay railway] part of the business so that I may not probably be home before ten or twelve days more." The premier spoke of several other current issues: "Good luck & keep the boys at work on the grade[.] We won't pay any more money till we get some material on the line." Money was short, clearly, and Norquay was still trying to keep his options open by postponing the track laying.[70]

He probably went to Toronto in the following week, where he met LaRivière and received only dispiriting replies from bankers.[71] Ten days later Norquay was in New York, writing from a hotel on Fifth Avenue. He seemed to be less optimistic, though he had not given up hope: "I have been here now for several days waiting for the spirit to move the waters in Wall Street pool. I have set matters in train & think will be able to do something before long. I am to see a Mr. Sewards tomorrow who has undertaken to float our loan and if he don't succeed I will have to move in other quarters." Norquay had discovered what people in the metropolis knew well: "Most of New York's financial men are away just now having their holidays and things are very dull around Wall Street. I only met Oakes [vice-president of the Northern Pacific Railroad] tonight for the first time[.] He was away out in the country where my telegrams did not reach him so that I was here without a friend to push matters along."[72]

Norquay had visited New York before, had met a few business figures, and knew the Manitoba financial case well, but he needed introductions to the proper circles, not an easy matter at the best of times. Without the help of Thomas Oakes, Norquay would have been lost. But with that support his mission began to look up. He gave at least one interview to a newspaper, this time emphasizing that the contest with Ottawa would be settled in the courts, not by violence. The premier remained resolute, as he explained in another letter to his public works minister: "I'll be acquainted with some of New York's best men before I go home. LaRivière is here also but like myself he knows nobody. I will likely have to remain here a week or ten days more as this business cannot be forced through with haste. . . . I don't intend to leave before I get the money or at least exhaust every effort to get it." Norquay closed his long letter with thoughts of Elizabeth and the children: "Tell my family I am quite well & wire me how they are all at home when you see any one around from my place."[73]

Norquay stayed in New York from 29 August to 12 September. During these two weeks he received letters and telegrams from his office in Winnipeg. The communications implied that he was making presentations and being asked for documents to support his case. In the middle of this stretch, on 6 September, he sent a telegram to cabinet minister Wilson in Winnipeg: "Will wire you when negotiations are completed." As part of these conversations, Norquay asked his colleague to wire official confirmation that Manitoba would provide 900,000 acres of land as "collateral security" for a loan. A cabinet motion signed by the lieutenant governor and three ministers was dispatched immediately to his hotel.[74] It appeared that Norquay had the makings of a deal. Several newspapers in Toronto jumped the gun by reporting that he had secured "a loan of a million dollars for railway purposes on the bonds of the province of Manitoba. The money will be applied to the completion of the Red River Valley road, the rails for which are now lying at Montreal."[75] And then silence. The investment arrangement, whatever it was and with whom, fell through.

Ten days later Norquay was receiving letters at the Queen's Hotel in Toronto. He had left New York, having failed to secure a loan. Now he and Alfred Rennie, his secretary, recommenced negotiations in the smaller of Canada's two financial capitals. Again Norquay sent a request to colleagues in Winnipeg for documents required to substantiate the province's financial condition. Again he found some interest, this time at two Toronto banks.[76] But he came away empty handed.

The next option was the larger of Canada's financial centres, Montreal. Headquarters for Manitoba's two strongest opponents, the Bank of Montreal and the Canadian Pacific Railway, it had been left to last. LaRivière had contacts within the Roman Catholic Church, some of whom were seeking investments at favourable interest rates. It is likely that talks proceeded with one church group, but the brief visit to Canada's financial capital did not produce a resolution to Manitoba's problems. Norquay then headed back to Winnipeg, arriving there on 26 September, nearly six weeks after he departed. According to the Winnipeg *Commercial*, he admitted in a Montreal interview that the New York quest had been unsuccessful, but he added that he "did not in the least despair of raising the money." The Winnipeg paper cited another story, this one in the Toronto *Mail*, that blamed CPR agents for overturning a nearly consummated New York deal. Norquay also asserted that, if these efforts were unsuccessful, "we have enough resources with the province at our back, to complete the road in spite of all the opposition."[77]

Stephen's campaign to defeat Norquay included several personal attacks and, in mid-September, an accusation that fuelled controversy for several months.[78] In a letter to the prime minister, Stephen accused Norquay of taking money from the "Widows & Orphans money," a trust fund created by the sale of certain Métis lands in Manitoba, to pay for expenses in the 1886 election campaign. The CPR president was simply being his relentless, vengeful self. He also reminded Macdonald of the indisputable fact that CPR shares in London had fallen to £49½, down from £75 a year earlier. He described it as a loss worth more than Winnipeg with all its people thrown in.[79]

Macdonald, famed as "Old Tomorrow," simply waited. He had hinted in late June that he was developing a plan to deal with the Manitoba crisis. In the following weeks he joined his CPR allies in asking the courts for support in opposing the Red River Valley Railway.[80] Now, in mid-September, he intervened more forcefully. His chosen weapon was a blistering letter to the lieutenant governor of Manitoba.

James Cox Aikins, an austere Methodist, was an experienced and thoughtful individual who took his role as lieutenant governor seriously. He had accepted the prime minister's recommendation that he conduct vigorous conversations with his ministers and persuade them to adhere to Macdonald's own policy agenda "without infringing on the principle of Self Government" (Macdonald's phrase). But his sympathy for Norquay, and his recognition of the strength of Manitoba public opinion, led Aikins to send warnings to the prime minister that were not received happily.

Macdonald wanted Norquay to back down and he wanted Aikins to bring about that result. His dispatch of 15 September began with a critique: "Your Government seems to be in an awful fix. Norquay seems quite desperate. I don't think you have acted the Lt Governor sufficiently over these ministers of yours. You are a Dominion officer and as such should act as the G[overnor] G[eneral] does in his capacity as an Imperial officer." Macdonald saw the lieutenant governor as responsible to the prime minister, not the governor general or the monarch. He added that prime ministerial instructions, in general, need not be shown to the premier.[81]

The lecture on the role of lieutenant governor was only part of the reprimand. Macdonald asserted that Aikins had made several significant mistakes. One originated in the lieutenant governor's failure to intervene in February 1887 when the Norquay government delivered bonds to the Hudson Bay Railway. That criticism turned on Sir John A.'s belated, tendentious assertion that he had not met with LaRivière in Ottawa, had not agreed to a land grant to the HBR, and that the Manitoba government had mistakenly financed the railway company without obtaining the federal land grant as compensation. To make this charge a little more convincing, Macdonald added (without attribution) George Stephen's allegations of Manitoba government misuse of public funds, thereby introducing an impression that the wrongdoing was part of a pattern in Norquay's behaviour. In addition to lying about the HBR, Macdonald wrote, Norquay was paying Red River Valley Railway contractors out of their own deposit and purloining widows' and orphans' trust funds "either to pay contractors or for election purposes." Aikins should have prevented these alleged financial improprieties, Macdonald said, any one of which could incur serious, perhaps criminal, charges.[82]

Macdonald was planting rumours of Manitoba government crimes. The first and most outrageous assertion, concerning Ottawa's failure to transfer the Hudson Bay Railway land, he had concocted on his own. This was the "scheme" Van Horne had mentioned in June. The other two came from CPR sources. And what did Macdonald expect Aikins to do? "This information has come to me confidentially," the prime minister wrote: "pray do not mention my name but make quiet enquiries about them." In other words, spread the rumours, talk of potential criminal charges, and see whether some of the charges stick. If a defenestration must occur, the lieutenant governor would be opening the window. Who would push Norquay out? That remained to be seen. At any rate, John A. Macdonald would be able to assert his innocence.[83]

Aikins replied tactfully to the prime minister's aggressive letter. He rejected the criticism that he had been lax, said that he would investigate further, and accepted none of the accusations about Norquay's allegedly corrupt practices. The tension between his office and the Manitoba cabinet was evidence that he had tried to supervise the government appropriately, he said. Aikins did agree that a crisis was developing: "You are quite right in saying that Norquay seems desperate. He is not over thoughtful of the means he employs to accomplish his purpose." The lieutenant governor selected his words carefully and promised only a review: concerning the HBR lands matter, he wrote, "I was not aware of any irregularity"; if payments to contractors came from their deposits, then "it is very wrong"; regarding the cabinet's use of Métis trust funds for ordinary purposes, "I cannot think they would attempt that."[84]

Aikins did not declare that he had lost confidence in his principal advisor. The lieutenant governor wanted to move on, and he refused to dwell on allegations about which he had doubts. His concluding sentences urged compromise: "I do wish this contest was ended[,] nothing but harm can come from it. I have urged on my ministers here and will on Norquay when he returns on Monday next that they stay their hand and cry halt. If he has been disappointed he may be inclined to do so if he could get a compromise to fall on. Can you not suggest a something[?] I would not name the matter to you but that I desire the breach to be healed."[85] As in every other step over the past six months, Aikins's handling of this difficult situation gave evidence of his experience and independence. His refusal to be bullied by the prime minister and his sympathy for Norquay spoke volumes about his own assessment of the facts. In essence he was putting the onus on the prime minister, not on the Manitoba government, to take the next step.

As for the facts, or at least what can be ascertained over a century later, during the summer Norquay had approved the usual expenditures for the printing of sessional bills and signed off on the payment of outstanding accounts. The surviving account books suggest that the government's financial and auditing system remained intact and active through the early autumn. A report produced by the acting auditor on 1 October demonstrated that Norquay's responsibilities, including expenses that fell under the headings of "Legislation" and "Executive Council," were under control. There was no hint within government ranks that the financial situation was in crisis. The auditor listed three pages of expenditures related to the executive council for Norquay's review, and a few days later the premier reviewed the sales of school lands. Nothing seemed to be out of the ordinary, though rumours of financial mismanagement were again circulating, thus reviving a theme struck by Liberal opposition members with their previous accusations of "coal steal" and "asylum scandal." The prime minister's request that the lieutenant governor investigate several specific accounts represented the first serious expression of doubts about the government's money management.

The rumours incited gossip, just as Sir John A. Macdonald and Sir George Stephen had intended.[86]

Macdonald's charges against Norquay were reinforced by letters from CPR headquarters. William Van Horne repeated all the CPR's claims to federal cabinet minister John Abbott. His last lines revealed the identity of the turncoat in the Manitoba cabinet: "My information came from one who as a member of the Government had part of the money, and I cannot afford to say anything that might get him into trouble. I therefore trust to your discretion in the use of this information." Only two Manitoba insiders seem to have contacted CPR headquarters in these months. One was Corydon Brown, suspected for some time of corrupt dealings. The other was Alphonse LaRivière, now the provincial treasurer. As Van Horne explained to Abbott, the widow-orphan fund was "by statute vested in the provincial treasurer and under his control."[87] When later confronted with the charges by the lieutenant governor, Norquay denied knowing of any such activity regarding the Métis fund. If the charges were true, and they have never been proven, then the theft would have fallen under LaRivière's responsibility as minister of the treasury. Whether Norquay knew of or participated in such a distribution cannot be known. In the following months and years, he insisted on his innocence.

The Manitoba crisis seemed to be entering its closing stages. Reports in various journals declared that the railway would not be built. The London *Times* explained at the end of September that "all operations in connexion with the line are practically suspended and its completion will be delayed until next spring." A week after his devastating letter to the lieutenant governor of Manitoba, Macdonald told George Stephen of the CPR that the "excitement is dying out and unless some mistake is made up there, it will disappear." In a second letter to Stephen the same day, he wrote that "'patient firmness' will carry thro' everything."[88]

Although the prime minister was still plotting, he had not yet decided whether to sink Norquay. His comments on the Manitoba situation differed depending on his audience, but his language, usually carefully measured, sometimes became inflammatory. He told his Winnipeg Conservative colleague, William Scarth, that "the issue now is an . . . attempt by the Manitoba Government to break the Constitution and to act as the Southern States did—openly attempting to break up the Dominion. However patience—patience."[89] He would have to choose between negotiation and vengeance, but that decision still lay in the future.

Norquay had been outmanoeuvred. At every turn—London in June, Chicago in August, New York and Toronto in September—he ran into agents of the CPR and the Conservative party who frustrated his plans. At home, public opinion on the railway venture cooled as the weeks passed. The transition in sentiment could be seen in letters to Macdonald written by blunt-spoken Brandon MP Thomas Mayne Daly. In late August Daly said that a strong and determined feeling in favour of Norquay's course prevailed in the province. Not that people opposed Sir John A. himself but that hostility to the Canadian Pacific Railway was "really becoming alarming: . . . The feeling is *all* with Norquay." Six weeks later Daly perceived a dramatic change in public opinion: "The RRV Ry excitement is dying out and a revulsion of feeling against Norquay has set in. . . . I think Norquay is doomed, it is only a matter of time."[90]

The premier's return from the east attracted a crowd to the railway station. Norquay gave a short speech upon his arrival acknowledging that his quest for investors had ended in failure. Forever the optimist, though, he now proposed to mobilize the city's financial capacity and to supplement this capital with support from local investors. News of his comments reached the *Times* in London, which had run several stories on his quest. It observed that Norquay's remarks "were received in silence" and that several Winnipeg newspapers expressed "strong doubts of the Premier's sincerity."[91]

By the end of September the *Manitoba Free Press* had reverted to criticism of the premier, this time because he had failed to float the bond issue. Even his ally in Selkirk, drugstore owner James Colcleugh, wrote soberly about his fall from grace: "Nothing succeeds like success and one false step gets a man the first kick down hill and this failure of Norquay's is taken advantage of by the opposition and the disaffection of his own party to impress the country that he has been always thus." Colcleugh perceived a new stage in the premier's public career. More citizens were inclined to disparage Norquay and to believe that he was dishonest and self-seeking.[92]

The *Commercial*, though never a fan of Norquay or his government, was less critical. In a capsule summary of the Red River Valley Railway project, the Winnipeg business journal reported that rails and iron continued to arrive, "in batches, occasionally"; that construction work had stopped, "probably owing to the fact that the contractors' estimates have not been paid"; that the first injunction case, which would have prevented the railway from crossing one landowner's property, had been dismissed by the court; and that provincial government sources believed the next legal contest, this one occasioned by Ottawa's request for yet another injunction, would also result in a provincial victory. The *Commercial* did not suggest that the premier's setback foretold the end of the railway.[93] What was most remarkable in the month of October was that the attempt to build the line found new life. As long as Norquay carried on, Macdonald and Stephen would be obliged to respond.

Last Gasp

Norquay had to deal with the fallout from Red River Valley Railway problems from the first day of his return from the eastern trip. He met with his five colleagues in almost daily sessions of cabinet and passed a sheaf of orders-in-council. They backed away from a deal with Duncan MacArthur that would have extended the Red River line westward to Portage la Prairie. They cancelled plans for a $1 million bond issue. They agreed to issue debentures to aid the Hudson Bay Railway Company. They agreed to take a $50,000 loan at a steep rate of 6 percent from the Sulpician seminary in Montreal. They approved a formal delegation—Norquay and Attorney General Hamilton—to the upcoming interprovincial conference in Quebec City.[94] Most of all they remained united, at least on the surface, while pursuing new options to fund completion of the Red River Valley Railway.

But they were running out of allies. Duncan MacArthur, president of the Manitoba & North-Western line, criticized Norquay's abandonment of the plan to hook up the M&NW with the Red River railway and threatened to reveal his negotiations with the government during the previous six months. Norquay responded with equal irritation: "Sir[:] After the attitude taken by you towards my government in which you say you will squeak . . . I feel it my duty to return [to] you the annual [pass] sent me by your Company last winter and to inform you that as far as I am concerned you are at perfect liberty to squeak as soon as you please."[95]

Herbert Holt, contractor on the HBR line, revived Norquay's hopes when he stepped into the picture just days later. Holt and his partner, Donald Mann, had the experience, ambition, and familiarity with the Manitoba scene to find a way to complete the line. On 10 October the cabinet passed an order-in-council to sell the Red River Valley Railway, including all completed portions of the line, to Holt. He would have to agree to put it in running order by June 1888, be granted the right to issue bonds for $550,000, guaranteed by the province, and promise not to sell the new company to the CPR or its subsidiaries. The plan was short-lived. By the end of the month, when further financing attempts failed, Holt threw up his hands in disgust: "You people up here talk entirely too much to get a railway. It's a surprise to me if you ever succeed, in view of the way you must talk, talk, talk."[96]

Holt was reacting to the demise of yet another Norquay government attempt to secure funding. The cabinet had launched a drive to sell $300,000 of government bonds to local investors. This scheme, first aired in the summer, would use the city tax base as security for half the issue, $150,000, and the other half would be sold to a "syndicate of merchants." The CPR and the Conservatives, working through John Schultz, challenged the "tax sale" proposal in court. The case was heard in October, and Schultz won. The workers on the Red River Valley Railway who were under contract to Hugh Ryan, the project manager, were "only partially paid" as a consequence. Schultz reported that just a few of "Norquay's 'Shinplasters' as they are called here," amounting to $2,800, were sold.[97] The Manitoba government was running into obstacles at every turn.

The relationship between lieutenant governor and premier remained intact during the early autumn. Aikins had to have a difficult conversation with Norquay about Macdonald's charges, and he did so in early October. His report to the prime minister on this delicate interview illustrated his independence from Ottawa and his wish to make peace. The lieutenant governor reported that Norquay would "gladly get out of the difficulty" of the railway but he added that "it would compromise his political existence to make even an approach towards a settlement of the present difficulty." Having quizzed Norquay about the allegations of misuse of the widow-orphan fund, the lieutenant governor neither accepted nor rejected the prime minister's accusations. Rather, he simply noted for Macdonald that the premier "wished to believe [the fund] had not been improperly used." Aikins added a statement of support: "There is a street rumour that it [the fund] has been [used] but he [Norquay] ought to know."[98]

The source of the Manitoba government's finances and the nature of its railway negotiations remained subjects of speculation. Macdonald then increased the pressure on Aikins. Observing that "Norquay seems to have run himself quite aground in his selfish eagerness to retain his place," the prime minister underlined for Aikins's edification his own view of vice-regal powers: "He [Norquay] will perhaps in his desperation ask you for a dissolution [and thus an election] which he has no claim to and which it will be your duty to refuse. You will I assume not allow your government to take any step which the courts have declared or may declare illegal."[99]

Macdonald turned to the CPR's proposed relinquishment of the monopoly clause and decided that he could finally, and safely, change course. He wrote to President Stephen on 6 October to begin the conversation: "I fancy Norquay has come to the length of his tether and his Government will be very submissive I think, and we must take hold of them while they are down and come to some arrangement with them." Stephen headed for Ottawa. Within days the CPR president and the prime minister had made a secret deal. Macdonald made the crucial concession, agreeing to the CPR plea for a big payday in exchange for giving up the monopoly clause.[100]

The prime minister's temper had become shorter as Manitobans continued to battle. Macdonald told Daly of Brandon that the Manitoba government was engaging in "as deliberate an act of secession" as that of "South Carolina before the American Civil War."[101] He spoke with similar vehemence to former Manitoba cabinet minister Brown, emphasizing that the agitation had "greatly injured" the province as well as the North-West Territories by destroying the possibility of selling land grant bonds or financing the construction of branch lines. He branded a Winnipeg lawyer's defence of Norquay "sedition, if not treason." Macdonald had reached a decision on Norquay. In late October he described his objective to Schultz: "I really hope the RRVR scheme will break down. It is the best way to solve the difficulty." In the same letter he spoke obliquely of his next moves: "We must try to prevent future complications."[102]

Quebec

Norquay had clung stubbornly to his hopes for the Red River Valley Railway and the Hudson Bay Railway through the autumn of 1887. Despite his determined stand, he and his cabinet colleagues had run out of ideas to pay for the two rail lines. To complicate matters the premier was out of the province for two weeks in the last half of October while he attended an interprovincial conference in Quebec City. Moving from hotel to hotel, he received cypher telegrams from Minister of Finance LaRivière in Winnipeg updating him on the growing crisis in the province's finances. In one cable, occasioned by the arrival in Winnipeg of rails that would have to be paid for, LaRivière inquired about arrangements to secure $300,000 for the construction contracts. In another the treasury minister warned that the Merchants Bank was refusing to advance any more money on the provincial government's regular account. A third reported that Holt, the HBR contractor, refused to work on the right of way while a court injunction was in place.[103]

When Norquay reached Montreal, en route to Quebec City and the conference, he completed arrangements for the $50,000 loan from the seminary of St. Sulpice. A month earlier, on hearing that a Sulpician-Manitoba deal had fallen through, Macdonald had simply shrugged, not believing that the priests were "annexationists" (meaning the priests would be unwilling to see Canada's absorption into the United States).[104] His confidence proved to be misplaced. The Sulpicians had an eye for business and welcomed Manitoba's proposed 6 percent interest rate.[105] The cash gave Norquay another few weeks of leeway.

The first ministers' meeting in Quebec City, titled the Inter-Provincial Conference, has long been regarded as an important "first" in the history of the Canadian federal state. The provinces had not gathered formally in the twenty years since Canada came into being. At this moment of serious challenges to the federal government, the premiers agreed to review "the autonomy of the Provinces, their financial arrangements, and other matters of common Provincial interest." Five of Canada's seven premiers attended, along with fifteen of their ministers (the premiers of PEI and BC did not participate), making an official party of twenty around the conference table in Quebec's parliament building.[106] Prime Minister Macdonald refused to join them. In response to Premier of Quebec Honoré Mercier's invitation, he wrote, "I beg to state that it appears to us that it would answer no good purpose to send representatives to this Conference."[107]

The meeting made headlines in Quebec and across Canada. It was conducted in French and English, and Norquay was able to participate in both languages. He told family members upon his return that his hosts judged that he spoke "Parisian French."[108] The delegates approved a series of resolutions followed by a commitment to seek a British law revising the British North America Act. They called for an end to the federal government's disallowance power over provincial statutes. They proposed that courts should decide on the validity of laws passed by either level of government and be empowered to give advisory judgements in advance. They sought a new law to clarify the powers of the lieutenant governor. Noting that Ottawa had recently claimed all Crown lands where no treaty with First Nations had been signed, they asserted that such lands belonged under provincial authority. They condemned the "totally inadequate" federal subsidies to the provinces and requested that the country's financial arrangements be revised and placed out of Ottawa's reach in an "imperial enactment to be final and absolute."[109]

Norquay participated fully in the discussions and supported all the resolutions. He also delighted in the formal banquets and dances, the carriage ride to the Plains of Abraham, the steam yacht voyage past Montmorency Falls, and the tours of the Citadel and Laval University. At Mme. Mercier's reception for 1,500 guests, Norquay saw his name in large letters in the chamber of the upper house beside those of Premiers Mowat, Blair, Fielding, and Mercier. Norquay was accorded the honour of making one of the two formal speeches of thanks at the end of the conference.[110]

His participation in the conference and his support for its conclusions did not originate in the 1887 railway crisis. Nor should his participation be considered, as it often has been, merely a footnote to the concerns of the premiers from confederation's original four provinces. The Manitoba premier had been speaking about constitutional reform for at least five years. He first sought advice on how to change relations between Ottawa and the provinces in November 1882 after Prime Minister Macdonald disallowed Manitoba railway legislation. A few months later he proposed in the post-election throne speech of 1883 the convening of an interprovincial conference that might define more clearly the authority of the national and provincial governments. As he told the Manitoba assembly, he wanted a "readjustment" of the British North America Act.[111]

Norquay had become a student of the federal system and was abreast of discussions then taking place in the other provincial capitals. He strongly supported the equality of the provinces, a principle not adhered to in the Manitoba Act of 1870. He was not a Macdonald centralist. He did not advocate seceding from Canada, as Nova Scotia's William Fielding talked of doing. Rather, Norquay was comfortable within a federation that reserved specific areas of authority to each level of government.[112] He especially wanted to ensure that the Manitoba administration possessed the same powers and received the same financial deal as its counterparts in the other provinces.

In the spring 1887 session of the Manitoba assembly, Norquay had devoted a portion of his speech in the budget debate to just these issues of nation and province. On the surface he was addressing Ottawa's disallowance of Manitoba railway charters. But his approach took him into deeper waters. He explained that the history of the British Empire offered the appropriate context within which to view Macdonald's disallowance edicts. How could such a lesson drawn from international affairs be applied to these local events? The key was responsible government. Britain's willingness to permit the colonies to govern themselves developed only slowly, Norquay said. Now it was eastern Canada's turn to adjust to the west's demands: Manitoba was "undergoing the same ordeal and constitutional experience that Canada underwent before she received responsible government from the Mother Country."[113] Despite the painfully slow evolution of Canada's understanding of its new western territories, this historical interpretation enabled Norquay to present an optimistic picture of Manitoba's current circumstances. The outcome of the federal-provincial deadlock, he implied, would vindicate the province, establish the equality of all provinces, and solidify the constitutional authority of the two levels of government.

The interprovincial conference in Quebec City provided reassurance, even justification, for Norquay. He was cheered to discover that his views on Canada's system of government and the role of the provinces were shared by four other premiers. He was able to speak frankly on a national stage to these experienced leaders and to receive a sympathetic hearing for his own views on the strengths and weaknesses of Canada as a federal state.

That happy moment in Quebec City came to an end all too quickly, however, and he left the conference with the knowledge that he faced a financial and political crisis at home. Norquay and Macdonald were locked in a contest of wills. Fine speeches about the principles of a federal system of government were one thing; funds to pay his own government's bills were another. It should be noted that the constitutional principles defended by Norquay and his four provincial counterparts eventually carried the day—but not during his lifetime.

One of the underappreciated stories in the Manitoba-Macdonald conflict of 1887 concerns the extraordinary persistence of Norquay and the provincial government. The premier would not give up. In early November he was still talking to Mann and Holt about a deal for the following spring. He contacted William Sanford of Hamilton, member of parliament and wealthy industrialist, about taking over the whole project. Norquay also encouraged negotiations between Winnipeg business leaders and railway executives. His cabinet even drew up a new contract to resume construction of the Red River outlet under the General Railways Act.[114]

The Canadian Pacific Railway responded to every threat. Its Winnipeg manager contacted Montreal headquarters on 2 November to warn that the rail line was not dead yet and to urge another disallowance measure. William Van Horne contacted federal minister John Henry Pope to underline the need for action. His letter eventually reached Minister of Justice John Thompson and, by extension, the prime minister. When news of Norquay's latest initiatives arrived, Macdonald again sanctioned the use of court injunctions to prevent construction across federal government lands.[115]

The prime minister's motivation remained unchanged. American challenges to the Canadian railway could undermine the transcontinental nation-state that Macdonald had helped to build. His thinking still focused, as it had in the preceding twenty years, on the danger of losing the northwestern interior to American expansionists. Although he spent less time talking about the issue in public, in his private letters he reverted frequently to expressions of concern about the ambitions of the United States. He wrote to William Scarth in early November requesting copies of Manitoba assembly speeches on the Red River Valley Railway and other evidence of a pro-American, anti-Canadian bias that he believed was present in the province. Scarth replied that Norquay, in an interview in St. Paul or Chicago, had complained about federal government policy that prevented Manitoba from trading with St. Paul, its natural source of supply. Scarth also pointed out that the St. Paul Board of Trade was drafting a motion of sympathy with Manitoba under the oppressive rule of the CPR and Ottawa. By the way, Scarth concluded,

Macdonald should also note the formation of a Commercial Union Club in Toronto and Erastus Wiman's interview (the same Wiman who had plotted to sell the Canadian prairies to the United States several years before), discussing American annexation of Canada.[116] From the vantage point of these Conservatives, national survival could not be assumed, and the Manitoba outlet presented a serious threat.

To feed the flame Stephen continued to emphasize the American menace in his correspondence with Macdonald. The prime minister insisted in reply that the Red River Valley Railway would soon be crushed. In mid-November he declared victory: "I don't think we will hear much more of the Railway this winter." These exchanges should not be read literally. They constituted discreet haggling. Stephen was reinforcing his case for compensation; Macdonald was trying to keep the price down.[117]

The end of the first week of November marked Norquay's arrival at the edge of the precipice. Without money to pay the government's monthly bills, with snow freezing all hopes of the railway's early completion, Norquay spoke of travelling to England "to settle the issue once for all," though whether he was referring to an appeal to the Crown or to a financial rescue for his rail outlet was not clear.[118] He had run out of options. The Red River Valley Railway would not be completed in 1887.

What would happen next? A few Conservative newspapers tried to put a brave face on the project's demise, but even the *Selkirk Record*, the premier's old ally, could not make defeat look like victory. The paper's editor concluded the provincial government had been guilty of "obsequious submission to a few noisy politicians in Winnipeg" when it decided six months earlier to build the Red River valley line. He admitted that the Norquay administration itself was "apparently in a state of chaos." Yet he continued to speak of the premier as the proper leader of the province: "We could not better ourselves by discarding him."[119]

The year 1887 had begun in uncertainty because of Norquay's narrow margin of victory in the provincial election. To consolidate his hold on the assembly, he had abandoned his alliance with Macdonald and united the province on promises of rail outlets to Hudson Bay and the American border. When he and Elizabeth celebrated their twenty-fifth wedding anniversary in June, he stood at the pinnacle of his career. The next five months of unremitting hostilities with George Stephen and the prime minister carried the province close to bankruptcy and brought Norquay close to political disaster. He had not given up his fight against Ottawa's railway policy or his criticism of the constitutional centralization that handicapped his province, but he faced opponents whose wealth and power outmatched his own meagre resources. He now faced the fight of his political life.

CHAPTER 12

Downfall, November–December 1887

The clash between Manitoba and the federal government was coming to a climax. The outcome would be determined mainly by the health of the provincial treasury. In these years federal transfer payments represented by far the largest proportion of Manitoba's revenue. Since John Norquay had authorized huge payments to the Red River Valley Railway builders, he was relying on the regular transfer payment from Ottawa in January 1888 to backstop bank advances covering the administration's daily operations during these last few weeks of the year. But would the banks continue to trust his government? He could do nothing to overcome the vulnerability and was utterly dependent on the goodwill of the bankers and the prime minister.

The board of the Merchants Bank in Montreal became involved in Manitoba's crisis near the end of October when the Norquay government ran out of money. Alphonse LaRivière asked for a $100,000 "temporary loan." Having first denied the request, the bank's board reviewed its response on 28 October but could not reach a decision. It met four days later and again deferred judgement. At a third meeting it decided to proceed only if the federal government agreed to provide a written guarantee that a loan to the province would be repaid out of Manitoba's next subsidy instalment at the start of the new year.[1]

General Manager of the Merchants Bank George Hague then travelled to Ottawa, spoke to the deputy minister of finance, and received an assurance that the federal government would accept any properly authorized order from Manitoba. This promise allayed the bank's concerns, and on 8 November the Merchants Bank board decided to send a formal request for a federal government guarantee covering the bank's commitment. On the same day the Manitoba cabinet passed orders-in-council approving a request for a loan from the Merchants Bank and "authorizing the transfer of [the] semi-annual subsidy from the Dominion Gov[ernment] to the Merchants Bank."[2]

The End of the Road

Once again George Stephen stepped into the picture. He must have been informed in advance of the province's negotiations with the bank, and though the treachery is undocumented it is likely that Manitoba Minister of Finance Alphonse LaRivière was his source. Stephen warned John A. Macdonald of the Merchants Bank negotiations with Manitoba in a pivotal telegram: "It appears Norquay is in extremis and it will be good for him if he is made to feel the effect of his misdeeds. I hope Hague [Merchants Bank general manager] will get no encouragement to make the loan."[3]

The federal finance department suddenly backed away. When Hague submitted the bank's formal request, accompanied by a copy of the Manitoba order-in-council, the department rejected it, arguing it was not a proper application. The board of the bank then passed a motion that it "should not make any further advances to the Government of Manitoba on the security of the Order as it now stood."[4] It was a mortal blow to the Norquay government.

Stories alleging financial fraud within the Manitoba treasury spread quickly. The *Manitoba Free Press* interpretation of events focused on the premier's failure to finance the railway, "a fitting conclusion to the deep-dyed treachery of the Norquay government."[5] To make matters worse, allegations of previous misdeeds then surfaced. Hugh Sutherland, an MP and the president of the Hudson Bay Railway Company, revived Macdonald's tendentious claim that the construction company employed by the HBR had received bonds that should not have been given to it. According to Sutherland, the premier knew that the railway contract had not been completed satisfactorily yet had handed the money to the contractor on Christmas Eve 1886. Sutherland also testified that Norquay had transferred more bonds to the HBR in February

1887 "without first having the land warrants" from Ottawa that would have underwritten the expenditure. The public declaration of that claim, one that clearly originated with Macdonald, demonstrated the reach of the conspiracy to defeat Norquay and his Red River railway.[6]

Hearing these revelations, Lieutenant Governor James Aikins concluded that Norquay had betrayed him. He had signed the order-in-council concerning the HBR deal in February 1887 under the impression that Ottawa had transferred the railway company's land grant to provincial control. Had the land transfer taken place? Although Norquay had shown him telegrams from the east that confirmed the transaction, Sutherland was contradicting the claim. As the lieutenant governor put it in a letter to the prime minister, "the telegrams from LaRiviere were untrue as time showed." What was worse, Norquay "had not told me I had been deceived." Aikins said that he could no longer trust the premier: "This is the first I heard of ½ the bonds being handed over without any authority." His account of the crisis, written on 12 November, revealed not only his despair but also a drastic shift in his assessment of events: "Norquay is desperate and will lay the blame on you [Macdonald] if he can. He is a desperate man and in a dreadful fix. . . . My confidence is all gone."[7]

Imminent Bankruptcy

The province's insolvency could not be concealed. Ottawa's icy rejection of the Merchants Bank appeal for a guarantee and the bank's subsequent embargo on loans brought disaster. Manitoba government cheques for everyday expenditures became worthless. The board of the Merchants Bank received a letter from the manager of its Winnipeg branch "respecting the Government of Manitoba's great straits for money."[8] This report, written on 22 November, revealed the Norquay government's acknowledgement that it faced bankruptcy.

Norquay searched for money in every corner of the government's operations. He pressed the Manitoba & North-West Railway for cash that it owed the government, explaining that "we require the money urgently & I want you to do your best to meet your engagements and as soon as possible." No revenue was forthcoming. He proposed draining money from the government's deposit or trust funds, just as Stephen (apparently prematurely) had alleged several months earlier. The attempt went nowhere, however, because the lieutenant governor refused to sign the order.[9]

The lieutenant governor's sympathy had run out. Aikins told the prime minister that the Norquay government was also "bankrupt politically." The only question remaining was the nature of its collapse. Aikins sought Macdonald's advice: "Ought not the House to meet and consider the situation[?] If Norquay resigns which he may if pressed what then[?] I will be glad to know your thoughts on the situation—and it is a pretty black one."[10]

Norquay had evaded legislators' scrutiny up to that point. After returning from the east he had obtained Aikins's approval for a prorogation of the assembly on a promise to begin a new session on 1 December. In this conversation Aikins warned the premier not to expect a dissolution and an election, just as Macdonald had instructed him to do.[11] Now Norquay was talking of not meeting the legislature until the spring. Instead, he said, he would cross the ocean and seek redress from the British government. Aikins believed that the crisis was too serious to permit such a long delay. At a meeting with him in the last week of November, Norquay requested another prorogation. His explanation of the HBR transaction, outlined in six carefully drafted pages addressed to "My dear Governor," placed the responsibility for his transfer of bonds to the HBR in December 1886 directly on Sutherland, president of the company, and outlined the episode in precise detail. The long memorandum also quoted in full LaRivière's three February telegrams from Ottawa and Montreal assuring the premier that the land transfer had been arranged.[12]

In the last paragraph of this long statement, Norquay referred to his conversation with Aikins the preceding week. He had pressed LaRivière as requested, the premier stated, but the minister would not answer directly when invited to explain the prime minister's denial that a deal had been reached in February. Rather, the treasury minister had requested a delay so that he could travel to Ottawa once again, this time to see the prime minister and railway minister "with whom he had had interviews on the strength of which he sent me [Norquay] the telegrams of 9th, 11th & 18th Feb 1887."[13] The memorandum made plain the premier's sorry position: either Norquay's finance minister had been double-crossed by the prime minister, or his finance minister and the prime minister were engaged in a treacherous plot to remove Norquay from office.

Aikins chose to accept Macdonald's version of events. As an experienced political leader, he probably recognized that the prime minister's duplicity lay at the bottom of the HBR story and that Manitoba's financial crisis could not be resolved by a LaRivière-Macdonald chat about the events of the past February. Aikins no longer trusted his advisors. He did possess limited powers as the lieutenant governor, one of which came to the fore in this circumstance. Aikins wished to preserve the dignity of the Crown and regain the approval of the prime minister, but he did not want to be the immediate cause of his government's collapse. In this tight spot he approved Norquay's appeal for another prorogation. The delay would be for six weeks, and a new session would begin on 5 January 1888.

Macdonald's advice on this very subject arrived in Winnipeg shortly after Aikins made his decision, too late to alter the course of events. The letter did reveal the prime minister's state of mind during the crucial days of the crisis. Macdonald addressed both LaRivière's visit in February and the circumstances in which the Crown might jettison a first minister. On the first point the prime minister repeated his denial: the federal government had never agreed to an HBR deal. The sentence in Macdonald's letter to Aikins was a complicated one: "Norquay's statement to you that Lariviere had got Pope to send for Schreiber and change his report etc etc is all false—not a word of truth in it. Either he must be lying or Lariviere must have lied to him."[14]

The prime minister was offering a single denial to cover at least three allegations: no, he was saying, LaRivière had not made an arrangement with John Henry Pope, the railways minister; no, Pope had not sent for Collingwood Schreiber, the civil servant supervising the HBR contract; no, Schreiber had not changed his report and approved work on the railway. Macdonald's stark conclusion was that one of the two Manitoba ministers, Norquay or LaRivière, lied.[15] The prime minister certainly knew how to dissemble: any single detail might be wrong (perhaps Schreiber was asked to change his report and was told later to delay the revision), yet the bigger picture, as painted by LaRivière, might be perfectly accurate. Aikins could see that both men had plausible cases to make.

As for Aikins's second question, concerning the role of the Crown, the prime minister said that he had delayed his reply to the lieutenant governor to see what would happen in Manitoba's "crise ministerielle." Macdonald made it plain that he wanted Norquay removed. Relying on the words of

Aikins—"my confidence is all gone"—in the 12 November letter, the prime minister could not have been clearer:

> Your position is a very uncomfortable one. So long as Norquay is your advisor, you as a rule must take his advice or rather, if you refuse to take his advice, he must submit or tender his resignation. If there has been any gross impropriety in his conduct you can tell him that he has lost your confidence and that he must resign. On his resignation or dismissal if he refuses to resign—you should send for the man that in your opinion is best able to form a strong and honest government. I am curious to hear the result of all this embroglio.[16]

Macdonald's suggestion—that Aikins should appoint a new premier—had already been outrun by events. Nonetheless, the extraordinary idea that the lieutenant governor had the power to dismiss a premier who had not yet lost the confidence of the house went well beyond the customary powers of his office. It illustrated how far Macdonald was prepared to go in this moment of crisis.

Any observer of public events could see that the premier's reign was in jeopardy. A senior federal government official surveyed the Winnipeg scene in late November and came away shaking his head: "Financially the province is bankrupt—some salary cheques have been refused by the banks." He had discovered, or so he claimed, that the federal subsidy, due on 1 January, was already spent, "leaving nothing for current expenses or to meet the interest coupons of Railway Aid Bonds." Gossip in the city, he said, focused on the "conduct and position of the Government . . . [and was] the only topic" in public discussion. But he had also learned that "Norquay is defiant—says he will have a Royal Comm[issio]n when the House meets and come out victorious."[17]

Amazingly, yet another allegation then exploded in the public sphere, one that originated in the premier's own caucus. Rumours of financial mismanagement had been circulating there for several weeks.[18] Now Edward P. Leacock—erstwhile ally of Norquay, long-time bon vivant, and would-be English aristocrat—delivered a letter to the lieutenant governor naming charges, petitioning for recall of the assembly, and releasing the HBR story to all and sundry.

Leacock's attack shocked the province. He repeated the allegation that LaRivière had misled his colleagues about the HBR bond delivery, added the story of Norquay's Christmas 1886 gift to the HBR, and revealed for all to see the cabinet's attempt on 10 October 1887 to sell the Red River Valley Railway to Herbert Holt. Leacock argued that $1 million of public money had been spent "illegally" and that Norquay had "no asset of any kind to show for the expenditure." He piled the rumours of the government's current financial crisis on top of these shocking revelations: "Your petitioner further shows that the province is without resources, her cheques dishonored, her contractors unpaid, her credit gone, a condition strange to the provinces of the dominion, almost unknown in the history of the colonies of the empire."[19] The charges added up to a public relations disaster.

Why should Leacock have been the one to betray his leader? The explanation lay with the man himself. Larger than life, slippery, prone to self-promotion and self-delusion, he had taken Manitoba by storm from the moment of his arrival at the age of twenty-six in 1879. He claimed to be familiar with the titled and privileged in English society and to have met the leaders who mattered in eastern Canada. He won a seat in the legislature, where he sat for the next six years, but was never invited into Norquay's cabinet, perhaps because his entertaining stories were offset by fibs and name dropping. Leacock lost money in the Winnipeg real estate bust of 1882–83, and his sessional indemnity was being paid directly to a local law firm, testimony to his continuing money troubles. When a merchant bidding for a contract offered him a bribe, Leacock wrote to the premier with contrived shock and genuine disdain: "[Jerry Robinson] had the insolence to offer me money, he was drunk so I did not knock him down but such a man needs a lesson. I therefore ask that all the Departments be notified to give him no orders.... Such insolence must be stopped as it would be horrid to be liable to be insulted by every common person in that way."[20] Leacock's petition at the end of November 1887 was just one more bid for fame and gain. An eager applicant when celebrity beckoned, Leacock had been outspoken in his attacks on the federal government's railway policy. Now he suddenly reversed course, defended Macdonald, and attacked Norquay.

Who had assembled Leacock's long, coherent, and highly partisan document? Only the federal Conservatives and the Canadian Pacific Railway could have supplied the ammunition. What else lay behind his sudden change of heart was not made public. A month later, however, a business weekly claimed to have discovered his motivation: Leacock had been appointed the land commissioner for the Hudson Bay Railway Company, it claimed, at a huge annual salary of $10,000. This sum was sufficient, said the *Monetary Times* with sarcasm, for him to "turn patriot . . . in the service of his country." Leacock was merely the messenger, whereas the authorial role belonged to several others. The federal government and the CPR probably contributed to this chapter of the plot.[21]

While these charges reverberated, the premier and the lieutenant governor met again at the end of November. This time Aikins had more ammunition and Norquay less confidence. According to Aikins, "Norquay was so cornered that he admitted" to paying Holt with the bonds—without cabinet approval—in the undisclosed meeting at Christmas 1886. On the matter of another prorogation, Norquay had no bargaining power. As Aikins reported, "I insisted that the House should be called early in Jan[uar]y." Although his account (written to the prime minister) was self-congratulatory and exaggerated, he reported accurately that Norquay had agreed to a fixed date for the new session.[22]

The premier still hoped to avert disaster. He assured Aikins that he and his cabinet were expecting Ottawa to relent. Two ministers would go to the capital immediately to negotiate a financial rescue.[23] That Norquay did not represent the provincial government on this expedition, the first time that he had not done so in nine years, speaks volumes about his estimate of his standing with Macdonald. But the fact that a deputation was departing indicated that he had not given up yet.

Aikins had another view. In his letter to Macdonald on 30 November, he predicted that "even with the land matter settled they [the Norquay cabinet] will likely be defeated when the opposition will be masters of the situation. What may occur before the House meets time will determine."[24] Despite his coolness toward Ottawa's policies in the preceding months, Aikins now believed that Norquay was doomed.

Everywhere Norquay turned, money problems cropped up, his own as well as those of his government. His personal bank account was empty. He reluctantly wrote Alf Masters, who lived in St. Paul parish, down the road from the Parkdale farm, pressing for repayment of a small debt. He needed "that little difference that you still owe me for the horse," he told Masters. "I am willing to take it in beef or grain[,] that is barley or oats[,] and would feel obliged if you would kindly give the matter your attention."[25] An illustration of his personal problems lay in his correspondence with an old friend, the tailor Bernard Saunders. During his late-summer trip in search of investors for his Red River railway, Norquay had stopped in Toronto for a visit, and he had stopped again in October en route to Quebec City. In the first instance he had purchased a grey Berlin frock coat, waistcoat, and trousers and in the second another pair of black dress trousers. The clothes would have been important to him at those meetings in eastern cities, but he still owed Saunders ninety-nine dollars in December.[26]

The mortgage on the St. Andrews farm presented a much bigger problem. Having made only interest payments in the preceding four years and facing a lofty interest rate of 9 percent on the debt of more than $1,000, Norquay simply gave up. His letter to a law firm on 2 December, a day after the payment was due, conveyed both his disappointment and his awareness that his career in the province's highest office could soon come to an end: "I regret very much that I am not in a position to meet the interest due on Lot No. 8 [the St. Andrews farm]. While I have been able heretofore to meet interest as it occurred I fear in the future I will not be able to do so and although the property is in my opinion worth more than it is mortgaged for I shall be obliged reluctantly to give it up."[27] The letter was accompanied by a signed discharge statement. It was a painful moment: Norquay was acknowledging that his domestic financial troubles would become far worse when the political storm broke. He was giving up on the river lot that he had owned for over a decade. He was surrendering not just a link to his birth parish and his one-time career as a farmer but also a politically advantageous physical presence in the constituency where everyone knew him.

Evidence of the government crisis surfaced in many households. James Colcleugh of Selkirk apologized to his wife, recuperating from an illness in California, for his failure to send her money. The government had paid no member of the civil service for the preceding two months, he wrote, and "we're all strapped." All the public funds had gone to the Red River Valley Railway, he believed, and "no money is paid out for anything."[28]

The premier spent a day in his home parish and Selkirk town during the first week of December. At a St. Andrew's Day dinner in the evening, he visited with old friends and shared political gossip. Colcleugh went away from the festive event believing that Norquay's government was "in rather a tight place and may very likely be defeated when the house meets in January. . . . There is little doubt but there will be an upheaving, resulting perhaps in a general election—and if there is I don't think Norquay will win again." Still, Colcleugh did not imagine that the premier's fate would be a sad one. Political parties looked after their own, he well knew, so he could report optimistically that "it is expected he will get a position of some kind." But that was in the future. For the present he recognized that Norquay "feels a little blue over the situation."[29]

A Ministerial Cabal

How would it all end? Aikins could dismiss Norquay, as Macdonald had advised, making a public spectacle of the event and perhaps generating a crisis over the Crown's role in the government. The assembly could throw Norquay out on his ear, leaving him with his debts and an uphill battle to assert his innocence and recover his honour. He could look for an escape route, perhaps a federal appointment, as Colcleugh predicted, and slide into a comfortable, well-cushioned retirement. The alternatives were few, the precedents fewer, and critics' sympathy non-existent.[30] The Conservative "old guard" and restive assembly members on his side of the aisle were now calling for a change in leadership. Norquay had encountered similar challenges in each of the five preceding years, but the stakes were higher this time and his opponents more powerful. In contrast to those previous occasions, Macdonald himself now wanted Norquay gone.

Norquay continued to perform the duties of premier and railway commissioner during the first three weeks of December, seemingly hoping for a miracle.[31] He told one rural supporter that "the situation looks bluer than ever it did before" but that he hoped "to pull through notwithstanding all the bluster of the opposition." He wrote to a loyal supporter about the opposition's meanness: "It is like their dirty contemptible . . . conduct to go about like their great father, the devil[,] secretly maligning men when they dare not openly attack them. You and the other friends of the Government may rest confident that we are prepared to meet any and all charges that may be brought against us. Thanking you and those who loyally stick by the Government in giving us your support in trying to bust up the monopoly of the C.P.R."[32] As late as 20 December, Norquay orchestrated government tactics and resisted opposition criticisms.[33] On that day his secretary asked the provincial librarian to conduct research in the leading opposition newspaper for proof of Liberal vacillation on railway policy.[34]

If Norquay remained hopeful, it was partly because he had not heard about the backroom scheming of erstwhile allies. Member of Parliament William Scarth voiced the prevailing opinion among "old guard" Conservatives in Winnipeg when he wrote to Macdonald at the beginning of December. Of the premier, whom he had backed a year earlier and abandoned a few months later, Scarth wrote: "I hope you are not going to keep Norquay out of his scrape. He will never be true to you or to any one." Scarth preferred a new Conservative leader "in whom the better class of [Conservatives] . . . could trust—not necessarily a gentleman in the general acceptation of the term—but a staunch true level-headed man." These unusual phrases implied that Norquay had little or no support among the "better class." Scarth then raised the name of cabinet minister David Howard Harrison as a replacement.[35]

One last drama had to play out before the fate of the Manitoba government could be decided. At the request of Norquay and the rest of the cabinet, LaRivière and Harrison travelled to Ottawa at the beginning of December to appeal for a financial rescue and, undoubtedly, to hear Macdonald's suggestions about their next steps. LaRivière would have the difficult task of speaking to the prime minister about the HBR deal that they had struck (or had failed to strike) ten months earlier. Harrison awaited a different but equally daunting conversation. Now depicted as "the hope of the Conservative party" in Manitoba, he faced an informal, off-the-record interview about replacing Norquay. If Macdonald's recollection several years later is accurate, the prime minister actually called Harrison the new premier of Manitoba when they met.[36]

Dr. Harrison possessed credentials sufficient to pacify the "old guard." Forty-four years of age, he was the son of an English immigrant to Ontario. Having first attended the Faculty of Arts at the University of Toronto, he earned a medical degree at McGill University and then moved to Manitoba, where he ran a successful ranch at Newdale, north of Brandon. He entered the legislature in 1883 and the cabinet in 1886. He had enjoyed several duck and prairie chicken hunts with the premier and would have preferred not to undermine him. But Harrison was ambitious, well spoken, and well informed about the prejudices of Winnipeg's "old guard" Conservatives. He was now auditioning for the top job in Manitoba. Whether he would be able to hold the government together at this difficult moment remained a question. His interviews with Macdonald represented the prime minister's attempt to weigh such considerations.[37]

In his two conversations with Harrison, Macdonald sketched a policy for a new government. At this stage the prime minister had not decided how to handle the CPR's relinquishment of the monopoly clause but was reconciled to the idea that a deal would have to be made. He believed that the compensation proposal floated by George Stephen in the preceding months constituted a rewriting of the CPR contract and a breach of faith with stockholders. The latter could successfully petition the British government to disallow such legislation, he said. Macdonald's proposed compromise pivoted on a continuation of the monopoly clause for three years and a promise that the federal government would cease to disallow Manitoba railway charters from 1891. The prime minister accepted Harrison's wish to recruit some "honest members" of the opposition for a coalition government, though he harboured doubts about whether such a partnership was possible.[38]

Macdonald wrote to Lieutenant Governor Aikins on 12 December to say that he had seen "Harrison and Lariviere together and the former alone." The mention of a second interview, in which LaRivière played no part, emphasized the gravity of these sessions. The prime minister repeated his denials of the HBR land deal (LaRivière's account was "*a concocted story*," he claimed [Macdonald's emphasis]) before turning to the heart of the matter: "My impression[,] from my limited knowledge of how things stand in Manitoba[,] is that Norquay & Lariviere should resign and make way for a Harrison Govt." Macdonald accepted Harrison's proposal to allocate two cabinet seats to Liberals and require immediate by-elections ("before your House meets") to put new ministers in office. One advantage of such a plan, Macdonald wrote, was that "with a coalition there will be no necessity for Norquay washing his dirty linen before the House." Finally, if Harrison "can form a Govt on that basis, things will work smoothly till 1891."[39] The lieutenant governor had his marching orders. If Aikins and Harrison could deliver, then Norquay would be relegated to the back benches.

Macdonald's advice to Harrison in their private conversations must have included a word or two about LaRivière. Although LaRivière insisted that the February meeting and agreement on HBR lands had taken place, the prime minister simply dismissed the notion, and Harrison accepted his denial. Alex Norquay, the premier's son, recalled fifty years later that LaRivière "came in for a large measure of [public] censure." Alex's account ended with the Norquay family's assumption that the treasury minister spoke the truth: "In reporting the interview to Mr. Norquay, he [LaRivière] said, when . . . [his December interview with Sir John A.] had concluded, 'Sir John, It's a case of your veracity and mine.'" Norquay appears to have accepted his minister's account. He should not have. LaRivière had betrayed his confidence frequently in the preceding weeks and months; he probably had done so again to provoke the crisis.[40]

Although relatively few documents attest to their activities during their weeks in eastern Canada, the Manitoba ministers won two remarkable victories. Harrison made a deal with the CPR concerning the shipment of rails from Montreal bound for the Red River Valley Railway. LaRivière secured the release of Merchants Bank funds for the provincial treasury. Unlikely as this would have been even a few weeks earlier, the CPR was now cooperating with and accepting the completion of the Red River Valley Railway, and the Merchants Bank was willing to fund the Manitoba government. These successes alone raise suspicions about the two ministers' negotiations in Ottawa and Montreal.

What had happened? The CPR compromise was the result of the company's development of a broader, continent-wide railway strategy. William Van Horne preferred to keep the potential competitor, the RRVR, locked into the route along the Red River rather than see a competitor's attention shift westward to Portage la Prairie or Brandon, where a line to the United States, he said, would "hurt us very much more."[41] George Stephen, having moved his money and personal attention southward, now wanted to keep the Red River Valley Railway alive long enough to ensure that the CPR received compensation for relinquishing the monopoly clause. Given his hope for a lucrative deal, he was happy to reciprocate by giving Harrison, Macdonald's premier designate, a dramatic win.

The Merchants Bank loan must have been the result of Macdonald's direct intervention. What can be documented is that bank General Manager

George Hague spoke to a board meeting in mid-December and told the members that he had had a supportive conversation with Ottawa's deputy minister of finance, who now saw no problem in giving a guarantee on the basis of the Manitoba order-in-council filed previously. This, despite Ottawa's refusal of the same arrangement only weeks before. Given the finance department's change of heart, the bank board agreed to make a significant advance payment to the Manitoba government.[42]

When the ministers returned to Winnipeg in the third week of December, the prime minister's plan to replace the Manitoba government was well advanced. Such a dramatic intervention required a forceful facilitator on the spot. Who should arrive in the provincial capital at this crucial moment but Sir Charles Tupper, federal finance minister, father of confederation, and ablest member of Macdonald's cabinet? Then part of the British delegation in Washington negotiating an agreement on the North Atlantic fishery, Tupper took advantage of a break in the meetings to travel to Winnipeg, where one of his sons worked as a lawyer, for a happy pre-Christmas reunion. His mission remains undocumented. Did he counsel the rebels? Point out how to wrestle the Norquay government to the ground? Stiffen backbones while a new ministry was being set in place? Tupper might have offered nothing more than a clear mind, a steady hand, and the resolve necessary to replace one Conservative ministry with another.[43]

On 19 December, the Monday before Christmas, the Manitoba cabinet passed an order-in-council decreeing yet another postponement of the assembly session, this time until 12 January 1888, one week later than had been agreed. The lieutenant governor approved the delay.[44] Also on that Monday, presumably with cabinet members' agreement, Norquay sent letters to each of eighteen erstwhile colleagues on the government side of the house, including renegades Edward Leacock and Corydon Brown. The brief notes summoned them to a meeting: "You are respectfully invited to attend a caucus of the Conservative Members of the Local House to be held in the Caucus Room Government Buildings on Thursday afternoon [22 December] at 3 p.m. Do not fail to be present."[45]

Two days later, on 21 December, the cabinet met again, this time to consider several thorny railway matters. At this point Norquay might have been absent, at home with a minor illness. But political talk was going on without him. Some of his five ministers (LaRivière, Harrison, Wilson, Murray, and Hamilton), probably with Tupper's advice, were coming to a bold and risky decision. Three of the five, unhappy sailors on a sinking ship, believed that they might stay afloat if they dropped their captain. To that end they sent Norquay letters that either threatened they would resign or demanded his resignation. The letters have not survived. This account fits with the version of the story handed down in the Norquay family. According to the premier's son Alex, "a cabal of his cabinet demanded Mr. Norquay's resignation. At the time, he was ill, at home. He chose to acquiesce, rather than split his party asunder. . . . This is another bit of unpublished history of Manitoba."[46]

Norquay might have hoped to ride out the storm or he might have had his own plans for an honourable transition. According to the lieutenant governor, the premier wanted to remain in office for a few weeks more: "Whether there had been any prompting I don't know but Norquay intended to resign only a few days before the meeting of the House."[47] The matter of "prompting" brings Tupper's presence to the fore. If anyone could deliver prompts, it was Sir Charles Tupper.

Norquay convened the full caucus meeting on 22 December at which members agreed to reconstruct their government under a new leader. They agreed that David Harrison should take on the task and promised to support him when the assembly met. The compromise that he had worked out with Macdonald—a coalition with the Liberals and an end to disallowance in 1891—was rejected "unanimously," according to Harrison. Norquay resisted emphatically the continuation of the CPR monopoly, "in fact refused to be held to support any Govt or party that could not force on the road [the Red River Valley Railway]."[48]

The following day, 23 December, Norquay wrote to Aikins: "I have the honor to tender my resignation as first Minister of the Province & to request that the same may be accepted & would respectfully recommend that the Hon. D.H. Harrison be called upon to form a Government."[49] With this action the Norquay government quietly ceased to exist. Aikins had an anxious moment when he heard of the government's plans because he was not sure of the constitutionality of the new ministry. He wired Macdonald for advice and received approval on Christmas Eve to proceed.[50]

On that day, Christmas Eve, exactly one year after the meeting when Norquay gave $128,000 in bonds to Herbert Holt as part of the HBR grant, his resignation took effect. He had been premier for just over nine years.

During that period he had won a majority in four general elections, become a familiar name in every corner of the province, arranged the extension of provincial boundaries, and secured a five- or sixfold increase in government revenues while administering services for a population that increased by a similar factor. He had also endured unrelenting criticism by opponents while dealing with critics in his own party. Norquay saw the cabinet rebels as a "cabal" (son Alex's term) and the 22 December caucus meeting as a mutiny. He knew that his government was on thin ice, but to judge from the recollection of his son he had not anticipated betrayal. His thoughts on the occasion went unrecorded. After seventeen years during which his intellectual horizons widened and his growing income failed to match his expenses, when he aided both his extended family and dozens of other supplicants, he and his family on Hallet Street now faced straitened finances and uncertain times. Norquay was headed for the backbenches and another round of accusation and vilification.

Why did John Norquay fall from office? His defeat originated in his own policy choice and in George Stephen's abrupt decision to move his investments elsewhere. The conclusion was engineered by John A. Macdonald. The prime minister began to set traps in the spring and again in September of 1887. Macdonald's initial actions only postponed Norquay's railway projects and fostered gossip about the Manitoba government's alleged financial misdeeds. In November, at Stephen's prompting, Macdonald decided to unseat the premier. The prime minister then arranged a financial crisis within the Manitoba government.

The decisions of the Merchants Bank board, based upon pressure from the federal finance department, started the premier's descent. Edward Leacock's broadside on 27 November, and David Harrison's meetings in Ottawa with Macdonald two weeks later, marked key moments in this phase of the plot. Charles Tupper's arrival in Winnipeg, though never linked to these events, must have been more than a remarkable coincidence. Still, even at that moment, Norquay hoped to carry on. Only on 20 or 21 December, when he received letters from cabinet colleagues informing him that they would no longer serve under his command, did he realize that his premiership had come to an end.

Each of the central figures in this drama could claim that, by his own lights, he had behaved in an honourable and far-sighted manner. Stephen could leave behind the carping westerners by trading a monopoly clause of declining value for government financial guarantees solidifying the CPR. Macdonald was able to defend Canada's integrity in international money markets. Harrison and his cabinet rebels could set up a ministerial transition that pinned the blame for the government's past failures on the departing premier and his treasurer while offering a viable path forward for the local Conservative party. Norquay acquiesced, unhappily but calmly, recognizing that he had been outmanoeuvred by Macdonald, CPR officers, the Conservative "old guard" in Winnipeg, and members of his own cabinet.

CHAPTER 13

Dénouement, 1888–89

John Norquay endured great stress after his fall from power. His income cratered and he lost influence. Despite the gloomy circumstances, he encouraged old friends to think positively about the province and to support his party. He received compliments for his far-seeing statements in the legislature and his public lectures on prairie history. He also found sympathy and increasing support during his daily encounters in Winnipeg's business district. His tragic death eighteen months later, when his political fortunes were looking up, came as a shock to Manitobans and prompted expressions of regret from across the country.

The Harrison Hiatus

David Harrison's government took office the day after Christmas. Five days later, on 31 December, the provincial government deposited $34,000 in the Merchants Bank and nearly $92,000 in the Imperial Bank. The lock on the Norquay administration's spending had been broken, and the replacement government could now spend money—borrowed money, admittedly—free from the previous restraints. The federal subsidy, more than $213,000, was deposited in the Merchants Bank on 3 January.[1] It was a remarkable turnabout in the province's finances, due presumably to a prime ministerial intervention.

Norquay had to adjust overnight to a new reality. Letters from old friends expressed sympathy. Bernard Saunders in Toronto blamed "ill luck" and offered the motto "fallen but not vanquished" to describe the new backbencher's position. The staunchest support came from Norquay's home district, where the Selkirk *Record* lamented his departure from office and blamed the Red River Valley Railway, that "ill-starred undertaking," for the loss of "the most able statesman we have in the House." A few weeks later it said that his personal conduct had been distinguished by "sterling integrity and good sense" and named him Manitoba's "first founder and its truest friend." Even Winnipeg's *Commercial*, never a supporter, noted that "the 'old man' is not without friends in the Government following." Norquay responded to one sympathetic letter from a supporter in the village of Killarney with thanks for the expression of confidence and the hope that his relegation to the backbenches might be temporary. He remained convinced that he had nothing to apologize for: "I feel satisfied from the assurance of many others that I have received since I left office that there is a warm spot in the minds of the people for the man who has managed to do something for Manitoba. I trust that you will convey to my friends out there that I thoroughly appreciate their confidence and kindness and it shall be my earnest endeavour always to merit the kind feeling that I know I now enjoy at their hands."[2]

For the first few days Norquay plied his former secretaries with work as if he had not left office, asking them to dispatch letters covering private land transactions and yet another railway proposal, presumably with the thought that these were simply matters outstanding from his days as premier. He agreed to help his cousin, John Lazarus Norquay of Assessippi, to collect an unpaid debt. He had his secretary send letters to the six railway companies that had granted him annual passes in 1887, thanking them for their "kind courtesy" and enclosing the expired passes. These letters written in the two weeks after his fall from power and registered in official correspondence books suggest that Norquay moved slowly to accept his standing as a man who no longer controlled the levers of power. His last dispatch in the official ministerial letterbooks, sent to Thomas Oakes, vice-president of the Northern Pacific Railroad in St. Paul, lamented an Ottawa government attempt to prevent the shipment of Canadian grain in bond on the Northern Pacific line. He suggested that the American company should "bring influence to bear in Washington to remove this embargo." At this point, in mid-January 1888, though no longer in the cabinet, Norquay continued to criticize Ottawa and the CPR.[3]

A painful moment came in the first weeks of transition when his son Tom ran into problems at the Selkirk asylum. Norquay had asked Dr. David Young to give Tom a permanent position as "assistant to the bursar" for $900 per year (a middle-class income) that would carry the rank of junior officer at the institution. Young sought final authorization just as the transition to Harrison's ministry occurred. The new premier said the terms were too generous and made a counteroffer of $720 per year. The reduction angered Norquay, and he tackled Harrison: "Dr. Young writes him [Tom] that he is instructed by you to offer him sixty dollars a month and rations. If he cannot get $75.00 a month and a seat at the mess table of the institution I beg most respectfully on his behalf to decline the offer." His rejection of the appointment meant further embarrassment for the family and greater strain on domestic finances, but Norquay disdained Harrison's intervention.[4]

Conservatives spent the next three weeks blaming each other for the dire state of their party. The "old guard" postured, Norquay glowered, and loose fish swam in all directions. Joseph Royal, now the lieutenant governor of the North-West Territories, in a fawning letter to John Schultz, widely rumoured to be Manitoba's lieutenant governor designate, placed the blame for disunity on his usual targets, including Norquay and Lieutenant Governor James Aikins. But he reserved his strongest words for former minister Alphonse LaRivière, whom he labelled "the evil genius of the whole transaction." Schultz, too, disparaged the new government and blamed Norquay and LaRivière for the party's troubles, saying that they preferred to "'rule in Hell rather than serve in Heaven.'"[5] Schultz and Royal were settling old scores with Norquay, who had beaten them too frequently in the past.

The long-delayed legislative session opened in bitter weather on 12 January, "the stormiest day there has been for years."[6] Although driving snow and wind lashed the city, crowds filled the halls and galleries of the legislative building. Lieutenant Governor Aikins read a hastily prepared throne speech distinguished mainly by its aggressive defence of "Manitoba rights." But the subjects of greater interest to spectators were the fate of the government—would it survive?—and the thinking of its former leader.

Norquay now sat in the back row on the government side: "It looked odd to see him, for over fourteen years the leading figure at the opening of the legislature, take a back seat.... [He] seemed to feel the fall himself for he looked rather flushed in the face under the inquisitive looks of the hundreds in the gallery who were watching him." Premier Harrison, sitting in front of him, looked "worried and appeared to be very nervous; and probably felt that after all there was not so much fun in trying to fill Mr. Norquay's shoes," the *Manitoba Free Press* reported. The Liberal leader, Thomas Greenway, sat at the centre of the front row to the left of the speaker. Near him on the opposition side sat Duncan MacArthur, a business leader, who had defeated a government supporter handily in a by-election just two days before.[7] While ceremonial events were unfolding on the floor of the assembly, newly appointed Conservative cabinet minister Joseph Burke, an anglophone of Quebec origin running in a francophone riding, was losing the by-election supposed to confirm him in office.[8] The government was in deep trouble.

William Scarth believed that the Conservative caucus faced disaster and urged John A. Macdonald to intervene. The Winnipeg MP hoped that a recommendation from the prime minister might encourage assembly members to adjourn briefly while the two parties cobbled together a coalition. Without such a postponement, the government would probably fall on the first vote, he said, and the Liberals would take over. Macdonald took the warnings seriously and tried to prevent the collapse of the Harrison administration. He wired his cabinet colleague Sir Hector Langevin of Trois-Rivières and urged him to intervene with Manitoba's French-speaking assembly contingent. To ensure that his lieutenant understood the importance of action, Macdonald added "now Harrison is better than Greenway. Will you do what you can[?]" If Langevin did try to mediate, his words arrived too late.[9]

The Conservative team simply fell apart. Harrison called a caucus meeting for the evening after the opening of the legislature, ominously Friday the 13th. According to Royal's version, the event was "one of the best circus[es] that many an M.P.P. ever attended. Norquay & Harrison quarrelled and recriminated and fulminated against one another as if they had been enemies. Many others joined in the family fight, and I am informed that the *entente cordiale* no longer exists, if it ever existed before." Edward Leacock and Corydon Brown were threatening (again) to depart; cabinet members Charles Hamilton and David Wilson wanted to leave politics altogether;

and Alphonse LaRivière still asserted his innocence. Norquay defended his course of action in a statement delivered with his customary rhetorical power. The worst moment came when Harrison was forced to admit that he had been told of, or was party to, Norquay's decision at Christmas 1886 on the Hudson Bay railway grant. Relations within the caucus could not recover from this revelation. In a gesture that some would soon regret, the assembled members then invited Norquay to resume leadership of their caucus.[10] Harrison tendered his government's resignation on 15 January. His term as premier had lasted only three weeks.

Thomas Greenway, staying at the Grand Union Hotel, received an invitation to meet with the lieutenant governor and in short order consented to form a government. The house met again on 16 January. Despite the ministerial resignations and Greenway's position as premier designate, members resumed their accustomed seats as the chamber echoed with excited chatter. Harrison formally announced the government's resignation, and the business of the session was postponed again. One press report declared that "Mr. Norquay seemed in high feather. He was in the saddle again; his rival [Harrison] was down in the dark; and not even the immediate prospects of the cold shades of opposition cast a shadow over his joyful feelings." It added the colourful detail that "after the session was over the Conservatives began singing 'There's One More River To Cross' and headed by their leader, Mr. Norquay, marched out of the chamber and power to the lively notes of that once popular air."[11]

On 19 January, their next meeting day, the members formally changed sides. Norquay was the first to move, and others quickly followed him: "For a few moments all was confusion as the members laden with books, papers, etc. crossed the floor; they indulged in a good deal of chaff at the expense of one another, while the galleries joined in and laughed and applauded." The new government counted twenty in its ranks, including the two newly elected members and some former Tories, and Norquay's side numbered thirteen. They met briefly again on 20 January but did no business, instead adjourning for a week while the new government prepared its plans for the coming months.[12]

When the assembly met on 26 January, Norquay introduced a resolution asking for an investigation of the charges that he had colluded with Donald Mann and Herbert Holt, contractors for the HBR line, and had received "consideration therefor." He wished to vindicate his character, he told the house. The motion was carried, though it was never followed up.[13]

Within days "old guard" Conservatives tried to remove Norquay as leader of the opposition. According to the *Manitoba Free Press*, the campaign "has been carefully engineered by some of the 'old guard' of uncompromising Sir John men. . . . Mr. LaRiviere is also singled out for destruction." Their crime, according to this report, was that they had not been "as obedient as they should have been to the great mogul in Ottawa." The newspaper reported that William Scarth, MP for Winnipeg, and Thomas Mayne Daly, MP for Selkirk (the seat that included Brandon and western Manitoba), were leading the movement and that "two caucuses of prominent Conservatives were held yesterday which were attended by a number of the Conservative MPPs for the purpose of discussing a reorganization of the party with new leaders." The *Free Press* concluded its story with an expression of sympathy: "The ex-Premier looked very careworn in the house yesterday, due in all probability to this contemplated act of treachery towards him."[14]

William Luxton and his *Free Press* had the story straight: the Conservatives were splitting into factions. The newspaper reported that three former ministers said that they would not run under Norquay's leadership and claimed to be backed by Conservatives throughout western Manitoba. The eastern part of the province, Scarth guessed, except for the "old guard" in Winnipeg, remained with Norquay and reviled the rebels. Within weeks both Wilson and Hamilton resigned their legislature seats.[15] Although Norquay continued in the role of opposition leader, his faction was much reduced in size and influence.

His political survival irritated the Conservative "old guard." Prime Minister Macdonald wrote frequently in the next month to these Manitoba supporters, disparaging Norquay and casting about for substitutes who would defend his own policies. Macdonald spoke of the need for a "wholesome coalition" that could "save Manitoba from itself. . . . If Greenway goes down Norquay comes up and there is nothing to choose between them." His goal, he insisted, was to secure "new blood and *honest* men."[16] The prime minister's opinion moved very few in Manitoba. As a long-time defender of Macdonald and member of the Tory "old guard" wrote in a private letter, "the general opinion here is that Sir John treated his friends extremely shabilly. . . . In fact the party here that composed 3/5 of the electors in the past is completely annihilated."[17]

The opinion gradually spread that Norquay had been an honest man but that his cabinet had betrayed him, both at the time of his defenestration and in the administration of public affairs. Scarth put the charge bluntly when he told Macdonald that two of Norquay's ministers, Hamilton and Wilson, had been "fattening at the public crib."[18]

Scarth, dead set against Norquay a month earlier, now tried to remove him from the assembly. Knowing that a lack of income posed serious problems for the ex-premier, he wired Macdonald with a vague hint that Norquay was the "only obstacle. Can you shelve him?"[19] Several weeks later he spoke more bluntly, proposing that the immigration agency could be reorganized, a post that would justify an annual salary of $2,000.[20] Macdonald ignored the suggestion.

Opposition Leader

The new Liberal government in Manitoba set to work immediately. Four newly named cabinet ministers had to resign and be re-elected in the then-normal process for ministerial appointments, and all were returned, two by large majorities and two unopposed. Negotiations on the disallowance question commenced in earnest, and Greenway travelled to Ottawa to make his case. The talks moved slowly. When the new premier left Ottawa without a deal, Macdonald wired his train urging him to return "and stay for a few days." It was a crisis staged to persuade a reluctant Parliament to approve yet another financial deal with the CPR. The prime minister agreed not to disallow Manitoba's next railway legislation, the CPR charter was amended by an act of Parliament, and the federal government guaranteed the payment of interest on $15 million of new CPR bonds.[21] Greenway and Stephen got what they wanted, and Macdonald secured a little peace.

Greenway was greeted upon his return to Manitoba with the bonfire, marching band, and torchlight parade that Norquay had anticipated in the previous autumn.[22] The new premier gave a brief report to the assembly, beginning with the boast that, unlike his predecessor, he had been "entirely successful (great applause)." Norquay, seated across the aisle, said that he received the news "with cheerfulness. (Applause)." He trusted that "the bugbear of monopoly has been effectually disposed of." Unable to resist, he added that the result was "largely attributable to the action taken by the government of which I had the honour to be leader during last summer." If he and his colleagues received no credit, "I am not going to record any disappointment but trust to future generations to accord credit to that honourable-mindedness with which myself and my colleagues acted."[23]

The days that followed proved to be a nightmare for Norquay. They began with the government's announcement of a long list of new bills. Greenway promised not only a railway outlet to the United States but a redrawing of the electoral map, broader suffrage rules, and "economy in government," including the firing of government employees. He also announced that civil servants, both federal and provincial, would cease to have voting rights, yet another blow to Conservative electoral fortunes since many incumbents had been appointed by Norquay's government. Norquay devoted his energies in the subsequent debates to salvaging his reputation and defending civil servant colleagues.[24]

The Liberals challenged him at every turn. Why did he install that new invention, a telephone, in his Parkdale house at government expense? Surely the cost should not have been on the public purse? Why did he receive a premier's salary for the last week of December given that he had resigned on 24 December? These examples, they said, were just part of a pattern. Norquay replied honestly but lamely: the phone made his work more efficient, and "he thought that after eighteen years' service he was doing no great sin in taking salary to the end of the month when he resigned." The small details hurt because they reinforced Greenway's "violent attack" on the Norquay government's railway deals. Referring to the HBR deal as a "nefarious transaction," the new premier said that his predecessor had benefited personally in these arrangements. Then the bombshell: the new cabinet was considering whether "they will institute criminal proceedings" against Norquay and LaRivière.[25]

The charges resounded throughout the province. Norquay shot back: "I wish just to state to the Hon. leader of the Government in view of the charge he has stated this afternoon . . . [to] place me under arrest[,] that I am prepared to meet him and to face the court on any question or charge he may prefer against me. . . . I defy him to substantiate those charges." Visitors in the galleries responded with "loud applause." His defiant words were left hanging in the air as this "field day" featuring all the "heavy guns" (the *Free Press* image) came to a dramatic end.[26]

The wrangling continued in the following weeks, but Norquay recovered his balance and defended his record: "No one ever labored with greater earnestness to secure immunity from [railway] monopoly than himself and colleagues." He joked with the other members as in earlier days, noting in one debate that Greenway's planned spending "looked like Satan reproving sin. (Laughter)." But he kept coming back to the railway issue and reminding his opponents that his resistance, and that of the province, had prepared the way for Greenway's success.[27]

When the budget was presented in mid-May, Norquay had to cope with an all-out assault by the new treasurer on his "reckless and dishonest management." Neither Harrison nor LaRivière attended the sitting when Norquay delivered a full reply. John Dafoe, a young reporter, said that Norquay defended himself "with dignity and courage" but noted that he "stood alone on the floor of the house, deserted by those who should have been beside him."[28]

Norquay did not defend LaRivière outright. Rather, he told his colleagues, "he deplored as much as anyone the transactions with which he had been made acquainted, and certain matters[,] if proved under strict investigation[,] he would be in his position obliged to condemn. (A voice, well I should say so.) . . . Before dealing with these he would await the arrival of those who should be here tonight to explain on the floor of the House matters which seemed to him inexplicable. (Applause)." He defended the civil servants who were being "fired summarily." And he attributed his failure to complete the Red River Valley Railway to "the stringency of the money market and the opposition of the Canadian Pacific." Norquay also criticized the new government, particularly its plans to drop the property qualification for voting and to disfranchise the civil service, thus throwing the government "largely into the hands of irresponsible persons having no interest in the country." Greenway then delivered a long speech in which he accused his predecessors of corruption. His government was discussing, he said, "whether it was not a duty that they owed the people to institute criminal proceedings against Hon. Mr. Norquay and his colleague, Hon. Mr. LaRivière, in this connection. (Sensation)."[29]

The sitting of 16 May "was destined to be the field day of the session." According to one newspaper, "the galleries were jammed and the greatest excitement prevailed." Rising on a question of privilege, Norquay read excerpts from a newspaper account of Greenway's speech touching on the HBR bonds and a trip to London undertaken by Alfred Rennie, presumably in relation to financing the railway. The excerpts quoted Greenway as having said that Norquay had "an interest in Mann & Holt's contract," that the Liberal cabinet had considered "the advisability of instituting criminal proceedings against Messrs. Norquay and LaRivière," and that the previous ministry had been involved in "the dividing up of $250,000 worth of HBR bonds among boodlers in which the late Government was a partner."[30]

Norquay asked whether Greenway had made the remarks, and the new premier replied "a portion of them." Had he been reported correctly? "Not entirely." Did he admit the substance of the report? "I admit some of it." Norquay said that the replies should be entered into the house *Journals*. He protested that such accusations should be backed by evidence and again demanded an investigation. Greenway, supported by Joe Martin, argued that Norquay had no right to an inquiry: "Was there ever in the annals of Canadian history anything so outrageous, so nefarious, as the actions exposed the other night, the charges of which were still unanswered[?]" He had received information from "more than one gentleman fully cognizant of the facts." Greenway wondered whether it was worth the expense of "proving what they knew to be true."[31]

Norquay responded instantly: "You don't get out of it that way; that is too cowardly." A newspaper reported that "quite an uproar ensued, members calling out from different parts of the chamber. Mr. Speaker remarked that the member for St. Andrews was using too violent language altogether, and the latter replied that he did not care." Norquay asked what part of the charges did Greenway wish to adhere to? He then moved a resolution containing the newspaper extract as preamble, his denial of the charges, and a statement noting that the premier had not retracted the charges and calling for a commission to report on the allegations.[32]

The debate became even more heated. Norquay insisted that he had a right to defend his "personal honour." The government's threat of criminal proceedings

> was contemptible in the extreme. . . . And if I am found to be that black criminal that I am charged then let me go back to the position which the honourable member had accused me of being—an Indian. That was a most contemptible thing to

> do. He [i.e., Norquay: a newspaper reporter was recording his words] had Indian blood in his veins, and he was not ashamed of it. (Applause). He, too, had Scotch blood in his veins; and he felt that he could meet the Indian or the Scotchman on an equality without being ashamed of either origin. He might, perhaps, have been negligent in discharging his duty; of not having exercised that strict supervision that he should have done, through being engaged in the transaction of his public duties. But the charges against him had gone further; they charged him with being in collusion with railway contractors.

Norquay denied the allegations. The premier should prove his charges or allow Norquay to disprove them, when "he would denounce him [Greenway] as a paltroon and a coward. (Applause)."[33]

On and on the accusations rolled. Martin said that Norquay had appointed a royal commission once before, in 1886, "and the verdict was for him although the evidence was against him." According to the *Call*, "an extraordinary scene then began. Mr. Norquay, who was evidently beside himself with anger, began interrupting Mr. Martin, and being called to order by the Speaker, defied his authority. The Speaker read him a severe lesson." The debate became a battle of wills. Norquay said that "we can stay here as long as you can," and the other side replied "all right." Eventually, at 2:30 in the morning, Martin finally relented, admitting that the government "had considered the advisability of criminally prosecuting" Norquay and LaRivière but had not said "positively that they would take such proceedings; and as Attorney-General he could say that he had not advised such action, and did not intend to do so." After further discussion Martin rose again to say plainly that "the Government had never come to the conclusion to criminally prosecute Mr. Norquay, and they had decided not to do so." Norquay then replied, "I am satisfied with this statement." This portion of the sitting ended at 3:30 in the morning, debate turned to business on the order paper, and discussion finally ended four hours later. The *Call* reported that "at 7:30 in the morning every charge against Mr. Norquay had been exploded."[34]

The session ended on a subdued note and, two months later, the premier asked that the assembly be dissolved. The general election in mid-July 1888 produced an overwhelming victory for Greenway's Liberals. Norquay and his allies managed to field twenty-five candidates in the thirty-eight ridings, barely a respectable showing for the demoralized Conservative party. The Liberals carried thirty-two of the thirty-eight seats, ten by acclamation. Norquay's Conservatives won only five, and there was one independent.[35] The popular vote margin, 55 percent to 40 percent, constituted a Liberal landslide.

Norquay's own campaign proved to be very difficult. The Liberals extended the boundary of the St. Andrews constituency northward to include the large Icelandic settlement around Gimli, where Norquay had fewer allies. The Icelanders' new weekly, *Logberg*, would be backing the Liberal party. He decided not to contest the riding (a Liberal was acclaimed) and shifted his attention southward to a redesigned Kildonan seat, where he faced high-profile banker Duncan McArthur. Still "largely controlled by English half-breed votes," according to newly appointed Lieutenant Governor John Schultz, this district north of Winnipeg proper would be fighting ground for Norquay. Canvassing hard among voters who belonged to "the class he considers specially his own," in Schultz's words, Norquay won by two votes, 305 to 303, the narrowest of any margin in the election.[36]

The result disappointed the Conservative "old guard," who wanted to rebuild the Manitoba party from the ground up, beginning with the removal of Norquay.[37] Scarth told the prime minister that even the Conservatives who won their seats "are no use to the Conservative party. Norquay himself is worse than useless because he is able and unstable and therefore dangerous." Macdonald encouraged anti-Norquay talk, writing bluntly to his Winnipeg confidants that "I am sorry that Norquay did not lose his election as he is the main cause of all the trouble." The prime minister's solution was to build a coalition government containing "honest" individuals from both parties that excluded "the old political hacks," including both Norquay and Greenway.[38]

Not all Conservatives opposed the former premier. Hugh John Macdonald recognized that Norquay continued to have considerable support throughout the province. He explained to his father that "in local politics a strong wing of the party will follow Norquay, and no one else, as long as he remains in the House, and this fact complicates the situation greatly, particularly as the anti-Norquayites have no leader, nor do I see anyone capable of taking the lead."[39]

Schultz, the new lieutenant governor, did all he could to undermine Norquay, both in the election campaign and in the following months. He bragged that Liberals were confiding in him, an unexpected turn of events, but he recognized the reason: "I am known to have disliked and distrusted Norquay for years past." Schultz soon developed a scheme to get the Conservative leader out of the province. Norquay had visited Government House and inquired about his official standing in Ottawa. In telling the prime minister about the visit, Schultz explained that Norquay wanted a Senate seat "on the ground of *long fealty* to the *Conservative party* [Schultz's emphasis, presumably sarcasm] and his being a representative man." Schultz thought that the ex-premier might accept a government appointment, perhaps an "immigrant agency." But the new lieutenant governor preferred a more distant location to ensure that Norquay was well out of the way. Schultz's dismissive phrases included several observations that spoke volumes about his own prejudices: "You know his inordinate vanity and he is very hard up. . . . My own opinion is that he deserves nothing. . . . I told him that if I were beginning life again I would do it at the junction of the Peace with the Great Slave River." Schultz was proposing that Norquay move far to the northwest (1,500 kilometres from Winnipeg), where he could rebuild his reputation and perhaps become a governor in the distant future.[40] Despite this advice, Macdonald did nothing.

As winter closed in, and the Manitoba Liberal government faced heavy criticism for its own recently devised railway plans, the prime minister mused about the possibility of Greenway's government falling. He gave precise advice to Lieutenant Governor Schultz on the constitutional options: "There would be no use in sending for Norquay who has got no following (and who . . . by the way I should be sorry to see in power again)." Greenway's administration survived, however, and Norquay continued to lead the small opposition group. In fact his performance as opposition leader in the assembly and Greenway's troubles in government worked to the former premier's advantage. When Thomas Mayne Daly surveyed the scene at the end of 1888, he advised Macdonald that Norquay was getting stronger than ever and that his friends were rallying around him as the recognized leader. Daly concluded that, until Norquay was "provided for," he would stand in the way of any reorganization of local Conservatives.[41]

In the two legislative sessions that followed the election, in the fall of 1888 and the winter of 1888–89, Norquay's was the only strong voice in the five-member opposition. At first he criticized the new government with his usual energy. As the *Manitoba Sun*'s legislative reporter explained after one performance, "for talking against time Mr. Norquay takes the cake. He managed to take up about three-quarters of an hour."[42] He consistently addressed railway issues, defending his own administration and attacking the choices made by Greenway's government.

In one fluent and effective speech, Norquay outlined a proposal for a government-owned rail line to the border that won the support of several members normally in the Greenway camp. The new premier was not happy that some of his supporters seemed to be wavering and took the opportunity to lecture them on their duty. The *Winnipeg Call* offered a little sketch of the scene: "He [Greenway] literally bellowed forth a reminder that they had been elected to support the government and had better bear that in mind." Norquay taunted him: "That is right, whip them into line." Greenway matched him: "I don't expect to whip you into line, I have most effectually whipped you out of line—Aha!" The *Call*'s tableau ended with Norquay smiling in his chair and "a quiet snicker" echoing in the chamber.[43]

The session ended in mid-October, and a new session commenced in early November. After two weeks of often heated debate, the assembly adjourned until the last day of January 1889. By this time Norquay no longer extended himself in the debates. He had seen enough, had no hope of changing the government's course, and simply left the Liberals to their own devices. As the *Manitoba Sun* observed, "it has seemed like a very one-sided House. A portion of the time Hon. John Norquay, leader of the opposition, was absent, and when he is present he apparently has little fault to find." The *Brandon Sun* came to the same conclusion several months later, noting "evidence that he has lost much of the fire and vigour that at one time characterized him."[44]

Norquay did continue to perform in the various roles that party leadership demanded. At Christmas 1888 he went to Griswold for the opening of the town's new hall and an evening banquet with toasts and music. The *Brandon Sun*, though never a fan of his rhetoric, reported that he gave a "loyal and patriotic speech, full of beautiful sentiment, and expressed in very choice language." The reporter described the "highly interesting and instructive" manner in which Norquay recounted the history of "early Manitoba life" and praised the "beautiful word picture" created by the former premier's comparisons between past and present. The newspaper story concluded on an unexpected note. Norquay had expressed the wish that "at no distant day the ladies would take a more active part in public meetings than they do at present. He retired and was well applauded."[45] These were not the sentiments of someone about to leave public life.

Elder Statesman

Although relegated to the opposition benches, Norquay displayed a breadth of vision and depth of experience that won respect in the assembly and among the wider public. He defended the country's federal system while explaining the distribution of powers between the federal and provincial levels of government. He outlined his preference for an independent, publicly owned rail outlet to the United States that could make contracts with all railway companies, thereby ensuring competition in freight rates and services.[46] His commitment to competitive markets could not be missed, given the prolonged battle over the Red River Valley Railway and his sustained defence of that project in the house. He applauded the Canadian Pacific Railway as a powerful agent of national unity despite its role in casting him into the political shadows. In short, he assumed the mantle of elder statesman in the province.

His speeches in 1888 and 1889 gave evidence that Norquay had moved a considerable distance from positions that he had held a decade earlier. Where once he had looked on eastern Canadians with some suspicion, now he consistently employed Canadian patriotism as a rhetorical weapon. He told his assembly colleagues during one debate that, because of the completion of the transcontinental railway, he had observed among Manitobans the development of "tighter . . . bonds of loyalty that we had to the mother country and feelings of kinship to the eastern portion of Canada. These might perhaps be considered questions of sentiment," he said, but they had to be considered important because "they carried with them weighty results. . . . They carried with them the means of interchange not only of courtesies but of business and commercial relations." During another debate, he listened closely to a speech delivered in French by a newly elected assembly member, Martin Jerome, whose words went unrecorded in the local dailies. Jerome appears to have addressed the development of Canadian patriotism. That prompted Norquay to make his own statement on the subject. He told his colleagues that he supported "the cultivation of a national sentiment, while yielding no right that we possess as a province. Though they were all members of the provincial legislature, they should never forget that they were also citizens of the Dominion" and "should never try to over-ride the rights of the Dominion."[47]

During these assembly sessions, as in previous years, Norquay emphasized the importance of Canada's ties to Great Britain. In the assembly and at public meetings, he often linked mentions of Queen Victoria, the British Empire, and material progress.[48] His statements were undoubtedly designed to establish a feeling of shared political community and to dilute the sometimes bitter partisanship of public conversation in the province. When the Prince of Wales launched an initiative to mark the fiftieth anniversary of the queen's coronation, Norquay adopted its language in his speeches.[49] He spoke of how the province had grown rapidly both in size and in population. A communication network once reliant on boats and carts was now knit into a global web by a transcontinental railway. This progress in communication technology, Norquay said, facilitated the flourishing of the arts and sciences. He was positioning himself as a British subject in these moments, taking pride in the claim that Victoria's reign, as he told his colleagues, was "one of the most eventful of all times."[50]

His political speeches frequently evoked images of "western-ness" or "Manitoba-ness." The theme acquired greater salience when Norquay adopted a new pursuit as author and lecturer. Several reports of his history lectures appeared in Manitoba newspapers in 1888–89 as he sought to remain in the public eye and to earn a little money. With the aid of two influential friends, Norquay was planning a speaking tour of the northern American states in 1889, evidence that he looked at writing and speaking as another source of revenue. For his subject matter he typically drew from the history of the northwestern interior of the continent. He described the Saulteaux community in a brief, impressive, published survey, recalled the prairie bison hunts in another, and outlined two centuries of fur trade and early Red River history in a third. A large portion of the latter text survives in his papers. A talk based upon it was delivered on several occasions to audiences in Manitoba. Norquay was said to be preparing a new lecture on "Imperial Federation" in 1889.[51]

Of his lectures and essays on prairie history, only about 7,000–8,000 words survive in his papers. They offer limited insights into his thinking about his own past and the region's past. These works illustrate how difficult it is to communicate the essence of a culture in prose at a time when few literary models existed. In the extant documents, Norquay employed many expressions that reflected the writings of others, almost all of whom were European. As this suggests, he was more likely to have read about the European side of his community's story—the Orkney and Scottish tales burnished by R.M. Ballantyne, Walter Scott, and Robbie Burns—than to have seen, for example, any of the texts prepared by Louis Riel. The writings of White Europeans and North Americans circulated among his electors, and their perspectives coincided with his electoral interests. As a consequence, the surviving Norquay essays are less valuable as expressions of a distinct Métis perspective than those of his famous contemporary, Riel.[52]

Examples of the gulf between Norquay's experience and his ability to capture it in prose are most evident in the draft essay that Norquay wrote on Red River history. Discussing the conflict at Seven Oaks in 1816 that resulted in the deaths of twenty-one settlers, he refers to Cuthbert Grant's force as "a band of painted savages & halfbreeds instigated by the North West Company." While defending the reputation of Grant, whose "heroic conduct . . . prevented the further destruction of life," Norquay speaks of Grant's followers as "children of nature." He tells a tale about a Métis horseman who shocked the Scots by seizing a newcomer's child, lifting him behind the saddle, and racing away across the prairie before returning him unscathed to his "loving and agonized mother." The phrasing imitates the language of contemporary adventure novels. By adopting it Norquay presumably was pandering to White audiences in order to hold their attention.[53]

Not merely a matter of phrasing and imagery, his reliance on European writing extended to assumptions about law and order. Norquay distinguished the rule of law that developed within the District of Assiniboia from the previous fur trade period when there existed "no means by which justice or redress could be obtained other than what the generosity or scruples of your opponent might dictate." With these words he diminished the customs and enforcement mechanisms within Indigenous communities that he would have known about but had not seen recorded in written texts. In the same vein Norquay defined the political standing of Indigenous peoples in ambivalent terms that relied mainly on European conventions. He wrote that "the Indian chiefs of the Saulteaux and Cree nations" entered into a treaty with Lord Selkirk "whereby he extinguished the Indian title to as much of the lands as he deemed necessary for settlement." The use of the word *extinguished*, and the power attributed to Selkirk, suggest a European rather than an Indigenous way of describing the relationship. But his emphasis on the effect of the treaty, and its necessity, acknowledged that the newcomers recognized and dealt with Indigenous peoples' sovereignty over the land.[54]

Readily available European phrases also crop up in Norquay's depiction of agriculture and hunting as two distinct ways of life. Following Alexander Ross, who developed this contrast thirty years earlier, Norquay wrote that Scottish national character saved the Red River Settlement from a "degenerated" and "semi-barbarian" outcome. When he weighed the relative merits of the alternatives, his preference for hunting and fishing cannot be missed: "This free & untrammelled life of a hunter had a certain charm that the plodding of a farmer's life did not possess." He then reversed ground, perhaps because he was writing and lecturing at a time when bison had been hunted nearly to extinction. Norquay concluded that Scottishness and farms had saved the Red River Settlement. The people of Assiniboia had narrowly escaped the "relapse" that would have accompanied reliance on a hunt-based economy and reduced their settlement to a "transitory home of the nomad of the prairies." What Norquay pictured as an ethnic inheritance—individual farmsteads—had become by the 1880s the fundamental industry of Manitoba. On many public occasions, as these phrases suggest, he emphasized his paternal connection with Scotland. His speeches and writings struck a note that he would have regarded as balanced. He celebrated the development of Manitoba's agricultural society while regretting the loss of a happy past associated with gun, snowshoe, and canoe.[55]

These texts illustrate Norquay's dependence on others' writings while raising difficult questions about his own views of citizenship, race, and law. Given his schooling and his reading habits, Norquay had absorbed works of literature that diminished societies living outside the Western world's social and legal frameworks.[56] Having lived in the Red River Settlement for his first thirty years, he had observed the effective conduct of public affairs in the hunt, fur trade post, parish, and courtroom by people who relied on a limited body of written law. He understood that the people of the western interior, whether they spoke Saulteaux, Cree, Bungee, Michif, Gaelic, or another European language, had participated in ordered communities. The society enclosed within the boundaries of the District of Assiniboia might have differed in character from life on the plains or at trading posts, as his comments on justice in the fur trade suggested, but he recognized that both approaches to public order had achieved their goals. Nevertheless, in the written texts that have survived, he refers only to the inheritance of British and Canadian law.

At Home

Norquay told a reporter in February 1888 that he left office a poor man. It was true: his income dropped precipitously when he moved to the opposition benches. Having to give up the mortgaged Parkdale farm, he could not even draw upon its resources. The loss of free passes on the railway cut off his chance to travel whenever he chose.[57] Norquay had received considerable sums as premier and cabinet minister in the last six months of 1887. From the beginning of January 1888, he received from provincial sources only the sessional indemnity paid to each assembly member when the legislature was sitting, including $300 on 16 January and another $400 in the spring. These amounts did not begin to cover the family's needs. Rent on 18 Hallet Street, twenty-five dollars per month, plus fuel and other household expenses, swallowed up the government stipends. He continued to answer appeals for aid when he could, for both his extended family and a wider network of friends. When his old friend Jock Ross died, Norquay received bills for the coffin, a robe and gloves, the hearse, the grave, mourners' hack fares, and crepe for the door of Jock's house, a total of over fifty dollars.[58] How Norquay shouldered this burden is not apparent.

An illustration of his financial worries emerged during an assembly debate on the Liberal government's plan to change the qualifications for the right to vote. Norquay, ever conservative in matters of the franchise, asserted that people who had no financial stake in the community could not be trusted with the vote. The wealthy farmer Kenneth McKenzie objected to this argument, bluntly asserting that he paid fifteen times more in taxes than the former premier. Norquay replied, as he had before, that he had never taken money inappropriately from the public purse: "Very few men have come out of so many years of public service as I with so little wealth. What property I have suffices my ambition. My ambition has not been in the direction of accumulating wealth; my ambition has been to try and serve my country faithfully and I believe I have done it to the satisfaction of the people, notwithstanding the assertions of my opponents."[59]

Most of the family resided in the house on Hallet Street during the difficult months of 1888–89. The children probably contributed their wages to the household. Tom, now twenty-four, appeared in the city directory as an insurance agent. John Jr. was a "CPR fireman." Alex was listed in one year as "clerk, land department CPR," and in the next as "farmer," having moved west to a newly opened district. Horace was "clerk, Mitchell Drug," and Andrew "telegraph messenger, CPR." Bella might have been working at home, and Nellie was probably still in school.[60]

How could Norquay support the family after his fall from the premier's office? His first thought was to practise law. He had never worked in a law office and never studied as an articling clerk, but he had been close to lawyers and legislation for his entire political career, so he asked a friend to prepare him for the profession. Lieutenant Governor Schultz, a hostile observer, reported that "expremier Norquay is sitting behind a Clerk's desk in the law office of T.S. Kennedy, learning the use of the cyclostyle [typewriter]."[61] On the last sitting day in January 1888, Norquay tabled a petition in the assembly requesting that an act be passed to enable him to qualify as a barrister. The Liberal government promised to deal with the motion in due course. Two weeks later the Law Society of Manitoba considered his application, observed that Norquay had not completed the normal apprenticeship, and turned him down. When the assembly resumed in April, his colleague John Kirchhoffer gave notice of a bill that would authorize Norquay "to practice at the bar in any of Her Majesty's courts of law or equity for the province of Manitoba" after he had taken the usual examinations. The *Manitoba Free Press* explained sympathetically that the bill was intended only to shorten the time to qualify, enabling him to avoid the "usual five years course of study," noting that the measure did not excuse him from the requirement that he pass every exam. Joe Martin and William Luxton argued that the law society had ruled and that by a party vote the assembly had declined to overturn the decision.[62] It was another hard blow.

In his last months in office Lieutenant Governor Aikins interceded to assist Norquay in this time of need. Writing to Prime Minister Macdonald, Aikins explained that Norquay wanted to be appointed to "the position of Indian Commissioner." He observed that Norquay "understands the Cree well and might suit the place and render efficient service," and he added a personal plea: "I feel sorry for him. Had he been surrounded by a better class of men he would not have I think placed himself in antagonism to your Govt and he [is] now out in the cold without much expectation of again leading a Government." People would be happy to see Norquay receive the appointment, Aikins concluded, and the political advantage to the Conservative party would be considerable. When Macdonald rejected the idea in a blunt reply, Aikins acquiesced: "I am nevertheless sorry that one who had such excellent prospects should have blasted them."[63]

Norquay turned to insurance, where he had plenty of experience, albeit only as a client, and in April he became "superintendent in Manitoba and the Territories, of the Mutual Life Insurance Company of New York." Despite kind words in the *Commercial* about his connection to "the most powerful and important insurance company in the world," the story left an impression of his anxiety, not of a lucrative business. Norquay persevered in the role, though it offered only "a precarious livelihood" according to Schultz. One agent who worked under Norquay's supervision was Andy Maxwell, a friend who had suffered terribly in a winter hunting accident a few years earlier. In April 1889 Maxwell wrote from the village of Holland, Manitoba, in reply to a letter from Norquay, assuring his boss that he was talking to people and distributing literature: "As you advise I will stick at them. . . . The country around here has been pretty much canvassed over but most of the agents are here today and away tomorrow and have not the time to make an impression, but I hope by taking it coolly and sticking at them to work up a business yet."[64] The former premier was now in sales, pitching a product that he believed in but making little money and relying on small assembly stipends, a few public speeches, and his children to maintain the household.

Norquay had participated in the speculative land market while in the premier's office, mainly as a means of encouraging wealthy outsiders to invest in the province. One of these ventures involved John Hope, a Montreal merchant, who travelled to Winnipeg in 1879 and bought a great deal of land, more than 1,000 acres, with Norquay's help. During the next decade Norquay assisted Hope by keeping abreast of the legal obligations and tax payments. His files contain more than fifty letters dealing with the portfolio. There is no evidence that he made any money himself, and it is possible that, owing to Hope's death in 1888, Norquay lost an appreciable sum by paying Hope's local tax bill for one extra year. His request for reimbursement was ignored by the merchant's heirs.[65]

Another potential source of revenue was the land that John and the children had amassed. The family's holdings included more than 1,200 acres granted under the Manitoba Act to children of Métis heads of households. Each of the five Norquay children born before 1870 had received a quarter section and an eighth section (a total of 240 acres per eligible child). When he was in Ottawa in February 1886, John visited the Department of the Interior and took receipt of patents for the five tracts located not far from each other in southern Manitoba. Even during the difficult days of 1888–89, John and Elizabeth did not cash in their children's windfall. Each was left to decide how to deal with the land. Although many of the details of subsequent transactions remain obscure, it appears that the children disposed of their 240-acre tracts on their own account over the next ten or fifteen years. John also assisted Alex with the purchase of a quarter section west of Minnedosa, near the just-founded village of Strathclair. John followed up on the taxes on Horace's land to ensure that it did not end up in a tax sale.[66]

Norquay ran through his meagre savings quickly. He had lost the Parkdale farm to a mortgage company in December 1887 when he could no longer cover the interest payments. He possessed two half lots along the Red River, including the adjoining "outer two mile" tracts. These he mortgaged for $2,600 at some point in the decade, perhaps in these very months, and they did not figure in his calculations again. In desperate straits, he gave up two other tracts in March 1888 to cover debts to a friend: "My dear Jimmy[,] Things look so blue that I cannot see my way clear to pay you anything on what I owe you. . . . In fact I do not see how I am even to get a living so I think the best thing I could do was to [transfer] to you my interest in the property and also my interest in lot 7 St. Peters. It is all that I have & the best I can do."[67]

Norquay kept an eye out for any venture that might bring in some extra revenue. In April he spied an article in a local newspaper about a British firm's plan to buy prairie grain. He immediately wrote to inquire about becoming its purchasing agent: "Having been born in the province my experience of Manitoba's production capacity dates from a time long before she became part of Canada." Norquay offered as personal references Lieutenant Governor James Aikins, Roman Catholic Archbishop Alexandre-Antonin Taché of St. Boniface, and the Anglican Bishop of Rupert's Land, Robert Machray.[68] His papers contain no other mention of the prospect. By the middle of 1889

Norquay was flat broke. Happening to bump into LaRivière, he confessed that he "hardly had enough money to live on."[69]

Norquay had more time to visit with people on the streets of Winnipeg's growing business district. He enjoyed the conversations and won many new friends during his walks and lunches. He still attended church and contributed his labour to its committees, both in his local parish, Christ Church in North Winnipeg, and in the Rupert's Land synod. When asked by Bishop Machray to introduce legislation on behalf of the church in the provincial assembly, he readily complied. He received regular notices of meetings in two Masonic lodges, though he rarely managed to attend them. He took his son Tom to the "battlers' ball" in Brandon, responded to the toast to the queen at the medical students' annual banquet, gave a brief, witty speech to the 200 guests at the Northwest Commercial Travellers' dinner, and delivered a much-admired message on commemoration day in St. John's College.[70] His official invitations might have been fewer, but his popularity and his willingness to perform on public occasions continued as before. Norquay was slowly regaining favour as opposition leader while Greenway's government was sinking in public estimation. The summer of 1889 held out the promise of more lectures and further work on a return to political power.

Final Chapter

The last week of June 1889 brought high temperatures to Winnipeg, as much as 100 degrees Fahrenheit (38 degrees Celsius). John Dafoe, at work in the sweltering *Free Press* office, wrote that he was "broiling under a merciless sun and a cloudless sky. However, with some exceptions, the nights are cool and there is always a pleasant breeze from the prairie making life endurable."[71] During that week Norquay travelled west by train to Strathclair to join Elizabeth and the girls, who were helping Alex at his new farm. John returned on Monday, Dominion Day, and as a newspaper noted "appeared much pleased at having seen his people and witnessed the pleasure they were having." He worked during the week in the office with his son Tom and on Thursday "was around town as usual . . . in perfect health and his usual spirits." Feeling a little unwell in the afternoon, he sent Tom out to buy some oranges. He ate four or five and continued to work. John and Tom "took dinner in town, as he had done for some time."[72]

That evening he was racked with abdominal pain and spent a restless, sleepless night, feeling nauseous, vomiting once. On Friday morning, 5 July 1889, he felt better and decided that he had "just a touch of colic." He told his sons that he would be fine, but the cramps continued, so he stayed home, walking about the house, and one or two of the boys stayed with him. By 10 a.m., fearing that the illness might be serious, they sent for Dr. Robert Blanchard. He was at Stony Mountain and did not arrive in Hallet Street until 1 p.m. By that time, Blanchard reported, Norquay was tortured by pain "extending across the upper part of the abdomen with occasional cramps of legs and feet," and he vomited again. The doctor described his patient as being "in great distress, rolling about the bed with each recurrence of pain. . . . There was no evidence of heart disease. Respirations were slightly increased in frequency." Blanchard wrote that, "owing to his great corpulence, there was extreme difficulty attending any accurate examination of the abdomen, though not at the time unnaturally distended." He administered some morphine and "a dose of castor oil and brandy" and left Norquay to sleep. When Blanchard returned a few hours later, "a general collapse had commenced."[73]

According to the *Sun* these hours were filled with torment. The boys could only watch in horror. Norquay talked "as if he felt the end was near, and frequently spoke [with] touching affection about his wife. He seemed to be deeply concerned about his family, and how they would get along after he was taken." As the time passed, the *Sun* reporter wrote, "the patient gradually waxed weaker and weaker. Although he spoke little, being too weak to do so, the doctors say he must have been conscious almost to the last moment. When the end came at last he closed his eyes, turned his head quietly to one side and slowly the breath left the great body. The end at last was peace. The eyes were closed and the saddened doctors and weeping sons left the room."[74] He had lived forty-eight years and two months.

Wanting to know what had caused their father's death, the boys asked for a post-mortem. Dr. Blanchard and three colleagues performed the task. They found a "twist of the bowel . . . forming a sac, about two inches in diameter and four inches in length. This portion and the portion of bowel above were distended with undigested food, chiefly orange pulp. The strangulation was evidently recent." The heart appeared to be normal, and, aside from a good deal of fat about the midriff, Norquay seemed to have been in good health. The doctors told the press that "if in any way this twist could have been taken out the patient would have been afforded instant relief and in ten minutes would have been all right. But in the case of a very corpulent man it is impossible to locate the seat of the trouble, and, even if located, to rectify the evil." These details appeared in the *Northern Lancet*, a new medical journal based in Winnipeg, which devoted several pages to Norquay's death. The journal's editor included both the medical details and a glowing tribute: "In the prime of life, seemingly in perfect health up to a few hours before his death, the loving husband, affectionate father, constant friend, and ablest mind in this Province was summoned to his last long rest."[75]

Elizabeth reached Winnipeg by train within hours of John's death and accepted Greenway's suggestion of a state funeral.[76] She and the family wanted to mourn privately, and Reverend John Grisdale conducted a service at their home on Sunday night. On Monday the copper-lined casket containing Norquay's remains was taken to the legislative building, where it was placed on a bier in the chamber and draped in black. His desk, also draped in black, bore a "beautiful wreath from premier Greenway and a bouquet of prairie flowers gathered by Consul [James Wickes] Taylor." According to the *Manitoba Sun*, hundreds of visitors filed past the coffin: "Everybody seemed to be there, the poor as well as the rich, the young as well as the old, the poorly-clad people, as well as those in rich attire."[77]

After a brief ceremony the mourners departed for St. John's Cathedral: "To say that the funeral procession . . . was the greatest ever witnessed in the west is to speak very mildly; it was simply three or four times greater than any similar event ever seen here. . . . It seemed as if half the province had turned out." The service was long, the congregation filled every corner of the church, and many waited outside the doors for the interment. When the casket was carried out, Norquay's sons stood by the grave, where they remained "until the last spadeful of earth had been placed on their father's remains. The funeral service was closed by singing the . . . hymn 'Brief Life is Here our Portion' after which the benediction was pronounced."[78]

Tributes arrived from across the country and beyond. James Aikins, for five years the lieutenant governor while Norquay was the premier, described him as "a singularly gifted man." The Montreal *Herald* picked out traits that struck everyone: "Bluff in manner and genial in disposition, he was personally liked both by political friends and opponents." Among Manitobans the shock caused by Norquay's death was profound. The *Sun* said that the event "called forth such universal regret and sympathy." It noted that Norquay probably knew twice as many Manitobans as anyone else, "and what was remarkable he was able to call them all by name. His removal creates a greater gap than would the decease of probably any other citizen.... For his personal qualities he was liked from end to end of the province." It also remembered his generosity: "It was said of him that, although a poor man, he never allowed a case of absolute want to pass, if an appeal were made to him, without putting his hand in his pocket and doing what he could to relieve the necessity. Among the French and Scotch halfbreeds he was looked to as a prodigy, and also as a father." One unusual confession stood out: Alphonse LaRivière told a Winnipeg reporter that, "if any sins were committed by the administration of which he [Norquay] was the leader, it was him (LaRivière) who was the sinner and not Mr. Norquay."[79]

Norquay was a beloved, talented public figure and a thoughtful, well-read student of politics and people. The *St. John's College Magazine* reminisced about his being "particularly fond of classics.... It used to be a pleasure to him... when in company with his old fellow-collegians... to repeat passages from Latin authors which he had committed to memory when a boy." It judged Norquay to be "a man of exceptional natural ability and keen observation" who "was often most unjustly criticised" despite "a personal record [that was] stainless and honorable." Walter Nursey, who worked alongside him for a decade, called him "a true and thorough friend." Nursey praised "his mathematical ability, his classical gifts, his flow of language, and marvellous memory, and his keen insight into the latent qualities of the man, or matter, submitted for presentation."[80]

Sir John A. Macdonald ran into political trouble by failing to convey his condolences to the Norquay family. Rumblings about his reluctance soon provoked a response in Manitoba that caused another split in the Conservative party. Prominent lawyer Hector Howell, an avowed "Norquay Conservative," told a newspaper reporter that "he did not see how Sir John could be forgiven for killing Norquay, as he had so cruelly done." Howell explained that Norquay had been a calming force in a moment of national crisis: "The only mistake that Norquay made... was that he declined to go so far as to precipitate rebellion in the province [in 1887]... that was the distance public opinion demanded that he should go." Howell defended the former premier: "I take pleasure in bearing testimony to his honesty in this matter. I remember how bad he felt when he returned from Ottawa after a long battle with Sir John. . . . [He] resolved to resist and it was then Sir John cruelly killed him." Howell also specified the manner of Norquay's defeat: "The word was passed around that Harrison was to be put in his [Norquay's] place and Sir John's bidding carried out."[81] A member of Norquay's inner circle, Howell was providing an accurate public account of the events leading to the premier's fall from office.

Having scorned Norquay for two years, the prime minister simply found it difficult to reverse course. After receiving warnings from Winnipeg, though, he finally did so, sending a letter of condolence to Elizabeth. He also wrote several letters destined for circulation among the party faithful. In one he declared that "I always liked Norquay personally, & regret much his untimely death."[82] Viewed from today's vantage point, the former claim might well have been true, but the latter was not credible.

The family had relied on Norquay and would miss him terribly. He had been a force of nature in the home, an entertainer, a churchgoing, Sunday prayer–leading mentor, an enthusiastic reviewer of teachers' reports, editor of his children's letters, and board member at their schools. John's brother, Tom, spoke of the family's loss, that of Elizabeth in particular. She was "really a wonderful woman, and had contributed a good deal to the successful life of her husband." She followed the press closely, he said, and collected the stories "in such manner as was ever ready for reference when required." Those who knew the family mentioned how much the parents and children enjoyed each other's company and emphasized the loving quality of their relationships. The *Sun* wrote that "the friends who were most intimate say it was the most affectionate family in the city."[83]

Although no one outside the home knew for certain, a rumour circulated in Winnipeg that John had taken out a valuable life insurance policy in the last year of his life and paid a first instalment. According to the *Commercial*, Elizabeth received $10,000 within five weeks of his death. No other record of that policy has been found, and the report probably was not true. His heirs resorted to letters of administration from the surrogate court to deal with his legal affairs because John died without a will. They declared that the estate consisted of only "a life insurance policy in The Standard Life Association of Montreal valued at $2500" plus a tract of land described as a "halfbreed claim." Three years later, in a second court document, Tom, the eldest child, amended the original estimate: his father had not owned a Métis grant at the time of his death but had owned part of a town block in the parish of Portage la Prairie.[84] The details were less important than the small sums involved: these resources would not support the family for long.

They moved a short distance down Hallet Street to a smaller house. Elizabeth and Bella attended the local Anglican church as before and made modest donations to its upkeep. The boys probably contributed to the household budget before moving on. Ten years later, in 1900, a few months after the Conservatives defeated Greenway's Liberals and returned to power, Bella was appointed to the newly created post of assistant provincial librarian. She died at the age of fifty in 1915. Elizabeth then moved in with her other daughter, Nellie, now known by her first given name, Caroline, and formally as the wife of John McAllister, who had purchased the late William Kennedy's fine St. Andrews house. Just a stone's throw from the church, her new home looked over a long, lazy curve in the Red River close to so much of the family's past. Having lost Bella's income, Elizabeth and her daughter asked the provincial government for support, and the new Liberal premier, Tobias Crawford Norris, responded promptly with a grant of fifty dollars per month. In these years Elizabeth was interviewed about her childhood for a volume on Red River women. Her recollections included descriptions of Red River foods, mentions of Saulteaux and Cree use of plants for nutrition and medication, and several recipes for preparing pemmican. Her testimony stood out for its rootedness in Red River practicalities and its connection to Indigenous peoples' ways of life. Elizabeth died at the age of ninety-one in 1933 and was buried beside her husband in the family plot at St. John's Cathedral. After her mother's death, Caroline moved from the Kennedy house to Winnipeg, where she died in 1960.[85] Three of the boys worked in businesses (in Arizona, Toronto, and Vancouver), one became a civil servant (in Edmonton), and one, Horace, became a doctor and served in several Cree and Saulteaux communities before moving back to Selkirk, Manitoba.[86]

Conclusion

> To the memory of the Hon. John Norquay
> who was for many years Premier of Manitoba.
> By his sudden and all too early death
> his native land lost an eloquent speaker,
> an honest statesman and a true friend.
> Born May 8th 1841
> Died July 5th 1889
> This monument is a public expression
> of his sterling worth.
>
> —Inscription on the Norquay memorial, St. John's Anglican Cathedral, Winnipeg

In the year after his death his friends resolved to raise a fitting memorial.[1] They set a donation limit of one dollar, equivalent to the wage earned in a day by a labourer, in the hope that many citizens would be able to participate. Over the next year 1,700 people responded, a design was chosen, and a Winnipeg artist carried out the commission, employing stone quarried near Norquay's birth parish of St. Andrews for base and cap, and red marble from New Brunswick for a five-metre column. The monument was unveiled in a public ceremony before a large audience in 1891.

The Reverend Samuel Matheson, one of his friends, spoke of Norquay's ties to the land on which they stood: "Over the ravine there, in that old building he first attended the parish school. Over this wall and very near this spot he attended St. John's college as a student, where he won great distinction and gave promise of those commanding powers which made him afterwards the distinguished man that he was."

Matheson paid closest attention to character:

> he possessed qualities of head and heart which made him a natural leader of men; and when he had occasion to take his place among Canadian statesmen his native province had every reason to be proud of the man who owed to her his cultured eloquence, his strong personality, as well as his birthplace. . . . If you seek his monument, look around you. Look at the hearts which he won and welded around his own; look at the host of personal friends which he bound to him with ties that even death could not sever. What accomplished that? It was his great heartedness, his unselfish nature, the charm of his personal qualities. On the platform . . . we admired him; in his office or his home, and in our homes we loved him. In public he was a power to admire; in private he was a pleasure to enjoy. Genial and kindly in manner, a mirthful and interesting companion, a staunch friend, we can never forget him.

The clergyman made special mention of the ties that Norquay had maintained with the people of his birth community:

> I take it that I owe the prominent position which I occupy in these proceedings to the fact that I am a native. To us natives he was peculiarly precious. He had no peer amongst us. He was ours and he was our leader; and while we were proud of him as a public man, the poorest and humblest old settler did not gaze at him with a far off reverence. While he distanced us all in ability, he kept close to us in ever sharing with us those predilections which he held in common with us . . . we only had to meet him to find that he was essentially one of ourselves still.[2]

Matheson's words ring true. Throughout his life, Norquay was described as exceptional, a prodigy, full of energy and fun. His speeches in the Legislative

Assembly and on the hustings were ornate and witty but also incisive. In them, he revealed a strategic vision to be realized step by step. The writers of his memorial epitaph chose the term "statesman" to capture his career in a single word. The term is typically reserved for wise, far-sighted public figures whose influential views and policies outlive the individual. The designation fits.

As premier of the only prairie province (Saskatchewan and Alberta were created in 1905), Norquay was a champion of the region when the country's political arrangements were being shaped into formal institutions. By articulating a vision of the northwest's long history and distinct interests, he challenged representatives in the rest of Canada to change some of their fundamental assumptions. His proposals were not merely requests for "more." Through intelligent, tenacious, and repeated negotiations in Ottawa, he established that the national government's treatment of its western partners in confederation was unfair. Equality of the provinces—each with the other—must be a cardinal rule of the federal state, he insisted. He linked this principle with another important claim, that the federal and provincial governments each were paramount within the jurisdictions set out for them by the British North America Act. When they disagreed, he said, the courts should rule, using the constitution as their primary reference source. In the throne speech of 1883, he proposed the convening of an interprovincial conference to review the principles underlying Canada's federation.[3] It was evident then that he had recognized the depth of his differences with the centralizing prime minister.

Norquay perceived that citizens could hold several political loyalties simultaneously, including particularly to province, country, and Empire. The development of this idea, one that has been described as "shared sovereignty," has long been identified with eastern premiers and with Sir John Thompson, the federal justice minister and prime minister of Canada (1892–1894). The idea was as much Norquay's as it was theirs and the product of a western experience.[4]

Norquay presided over Manitoba's crucial decades of development in his six years as a cabinet minister and nine years as premier. During this time the provincial settler population multiplied more than tenfold and the economy grew proportionately.[5] That moment of creation has never faded from sight, marked on today's maps by the townsites, highways, railways, municipalities, court districts, and school districts originating during his years in office. He fought for and won improved financial terms from Ottawa culminating in the federal-provincial agreement of 1885, a way station that he defended—for the moment—as reasonable. He did not accept that the terms in this deal represented a final settlement and he continued to question Prime Minister Macdonald's imperial approach to the ownership of public lands and resources in the prairie west.

Before the conflict in the last year of their official relationship, Norquay had worked effectively with Macdonald, the central figure in the national government, to expand the narrow limits that the prime minister had imposed on Manitoba in 1870. The premier's vigorous presentations in Ottawa contributed to the development of public works appropriate to the province's needs. Macdonald accepted, and indirectly funded, the Norquay administration's land drainage program, an intervention that made tens of thousands of hectares available for cultivation and consolidated one of the world's rich agricultural zones. The premier's lobbying in Ottawa won a boundary extension that made Manitoba Canada's third-largest province in 1881, smaller than Quebec and British Columbia but larger than Ontario and the Maritime provinces. With the British court's resolution of a boundary dispute in 1884, however, Manitoba fell far behind Ontario in size. The prairie jurisdictions were then relegated to a less prominent role in confederation than might have been the case if, as both Norquay and the prime minister preferred, the relative dimensions had been retained.

As a leader in the crucial founding years, Norquay consistently opposed advocates of violence in public life. He favoured mediation and negotiation and was faithful to British parliamentary traditions. He ensured that Manitoba followed the four original provinces in adopting democratic arrangements for the administration of public affairs, including in its newly created municipalities. While sympathizing with those who had been driven to violence in 1885, he rejected the political tactics adopted by Louis Riel, Gabriel Dumont, and their colleagues. A few farm-movement radicals in Manitoba contemplated drastic anti-Canadian action in that tense moment, and again in 1887, but Norquay spoke emphatically against them. When his cabinet and assembly colleagues deserted him, he conformed to the conventions of Canada's parliamentary system by resigning as premier. A month later, when Thomas Greenway's Liberals came to power, he accepted the invitation from his caucus to take the position of opposition leader and performed in that role during three more sessions of the Legislative Assembly.

His "moderation" in 1870 (his word) and his application of the label "insane" to the Resistance of 1885 illustrated that, after the North-West's transfer to Canadian rule, he reacted to the loss of historic Red River conventions very differently from Louis Riel.[6] Both leaders acknowledged that the incomers' pursuit of economic development presented enormous challenges. Riel hoped to build institutional bulwarks that defended a distinct Métis peoplehood against the loss of land, social networks, and community values. Norquay, in contrast, insisted that he and his Red River contemporaries of all backgrounds would have to adjust quickly and far more completely.

Living in an age when a Canadian nation-state dedicated to private property and liberal values took shape, Norquay learned those disciplines and became an advocate for them. Although he gave away or spent almost all the income and material assets that passed through his hands, he treated the principles of the market and private property respectfully. His outlook on public policy questions can be described as a casebook example of possessive individualism.[7] In making this crucial intellectual and emotional choice, he seized on the autonomy of the individual as a fundamental principle. He accepted a liberal, Protestant depiction of society as opposed to the emphasis on Métis collective rights and a version of Catholicism espoused by Riel.

The friends who composed the text on the impressive Norquay memorial chose to mention a handful of qualities, including eloquence and friendship. They also broached the issue of honesty, presumably a response to the intensely partisan politics of the time and to Norquay's own, oft-professed commitment not to profit from his position. Taken in the context of his two decades of public office, he set a high standard for himself and, in the main, lived up to it. His personal poverty and the words of his closest associates can be taken as evidence of his uprightness. But his failures as an investor do not absolve him from having crossed an ethical line on several occasions.

In drafting an epitaph, the memorialists chose to include the phrase "native land." They were writing before the phrase had been embedded in the English-language version of Canada's national anthem, and it seems evident that they were alluding discreetly not just to birthplace or to regional interests but to Norquay's ancestry. They were raising issues of race, Métisness, and Indigeneity.

What meaning should be attached to the word "native" and the phrase "native land" as they appeared in Norquay's life? In childhood he had known people who spoke Cree, Saulteaux, Michif/French, and Bungee/English, and who found it possible to move back and forth across flexible group boundaries. Yet a few years later he acknowledged that Dakota, Cree, and Saulteaux communities would henceforth be recognized as "Indian," and that he and his countrymen were being classified as "Halfbreed" and "Métis." He perceived that both categories of people, First Nation and Métis in today's usage, had become—not by their own choice—distinct from Whites and consequently faced explicit legal boundaries and oft-unstated social limits. As "natives" they belonged in a separate sphere, partially but not entirely citizens of their own country.

Norquay recognized the legal changes as fundamental aspects of life in Canada, but he did not accept the drastic underestimation of Indigenous civilizations or the social inequality that accompanied them. Lamenting the disastrous circumstances prevailing in the North-West in the aftermath of the civil war in 1885, he warned a federal cabinet member that "your Indians"—meaning the First Nations who lived under Ottawa's direct control—might turn to further violence, preferring "to die fighting than starve to death by a slow process which is the present state of affairs."[8] He clearly recognized both the dire straits in which the people lived and their unique political standing. By placing these thoughts on the desk of a powerful member of the Macdonald cabinet, he was making clear his own wish for changes in federal Indian policy.

Other people's thinking about "race" constituted an inescapable presence in his adult life. Although he encountered many examples of racialized thinking and racist action, he pushed these moments to one side and insisted on being dealt with on equal terms. That political enemies such as Joseph Royal and John Schultz saw him as arrogant, and one-time ally Thomas Mayne Daly said that he was "vindictive . . . by nature," merely underscored the tensions accompanying his expectation of equality in everyday social relations.[9]

John A. Macdonald's relation to this thread in Canadian social thought and practice belongs on another plane. In the middle of tense negotiations in 1887, Macdonald reportedly told one colleague that the premier had "too much Indian" in him.[10] The words reveal the language of the time and may have been meant by Macdonald to refer to the premier's tenacity in negotiations, but they also betray the social and political categories in the prime minister's thinking. They pale in significance beside the racism buried within

Macdonald's design for the Canadian federation. Given that the population of the western interior was overwhelmingly Indigenous when Macdonald's "dominion lands" policy was instituted, national control of prairie real estate—Norquay's biggest public policy challenge—can be described fairly as an instance of systemic or structural racism lodged in the heart of Canada's constitution. Seen from the vantage point of government offices in Ottawa, the measure was imperial and appropriately paternal; viewed from the plains and parklands of the western interior of the continent, it was a colonizing instrument that diminished the role in prairie public life and policymaking of such leaders as Norquay, Riel, Crowfoot, Poundmaker, and Big Bear, as well as their countrymen.

How would Norquay respond to today's observers who choose to designate him as "Métis"? He knew details of his family's history for the two preceding generations and embraced his mixed ancestry. He said clearly in one interview that he was of "Orkney stock, slightly blended in two lines of maternal ancestry with Indian blood, and . . . his father was a labourer in the Hudson Bay service."[11] His speeches and letters make plain that he took ownership of the terms "native" and "old settler" and accepted responsibility for his "countrymen" who belonged in these categories. He ensured that his children and members of his extended family received lands allocated by Ottawa to Métis individuals, and he signed legal documents attesting to his and their Indigenous ancestry. But, unlike Riel, he did not adopt the cause of a separate Métis nationhood or peoplehood. As a descendant of Red River and the greater North-West, he found sufficient room for himself and his family within Manitoba, Canada, and British Empire to believe that these polities provided his primary public identities. In accepting his family's mixed ancestry, and the social and political identities that came with it, he also insisted on his equality with other Canadians.[12]

At the time of his death, Norquay was remembered as a leading figure in Canadian public life. Premier Andrew Blair of New Brunswick recalled his presence at the interprovincial conference at Quebec City: "He impressed us all at the conference not only with his very great ability, his many statesman-like qualities, his breadth of information, his moderation and sagacity, but also with his great pride in his own province. . . . Canada loses one of her greatest sons. . . . [It] may well be considered a national loss." The Toronto *Mail*, in addressing his death, spoke of potential: "Had he lived he would undoubtedly have launched into Dominion politics and in time have been recognized as one of our best men."[13] The same observation appeared, with an interesting addition, in Goldwin Smith's *The Week,* the prominent public affairs journal, which judged that Norquay was "the ablest and most influential native leader who has yet appeared. Indeed, the statement would probably be undisputed with the qualifying word 'native,' omitted."[14]

His epitaph? In the language of recently founded Canada, Norquay was a "Halfbreed," a loyal Manitoban, a Canadian patriot, and a British subject in the British Empire. His friends in Bungee/English parishes and in far-flung communities of the North-West might have joined Samuel Matheson in saying that "he was ours and he was our leader," a reference to their shared roots in Red River and to his qualities as a *neestaw*, an engaging ally, and a loving family man.[15] Had Norquay been given the opportunity to write his own memorial, he would have emphasized that he lost his parents early in life, benefited greatly from educational advantages and supportive workmates, and governed honestly on behalf of all the citizens in a rapidly changing province and country.

If one looked for estimates of his impact today, one might find that Métis historians in the academy emphasized Norquay's commitment to *wahkohtowin* to capture his sense of obligation to others.[16] Political economists might say that he adopted the regime of Canadian law associated with markets, Indigeneity, and property more quickly than many of his contemporaries. From any vantage point, Norquay stands out in history for his attractive personality and intellect, for his ability to communicate thoughtfully and humorously with people in all walks of life, for his contributions to the understanding and functioning of Canada's federation, for his encounters with racist behaviour and with the systemic racism buried in the prairie west's founding legislation, and for his leadership during the crucial founding decades of his home province and region.

Acknowledgements

I would like to thank Norquay family members for their assistance on many occasions. Don Norquay, the late Carol Norquay Stoddart, Ian Norquay, Lawrence Norquay, Paul Nielson, Geoff Norquay, the late Mary Norquay Savage, Melissa Tichborne, Deanna Martz, Mary Gair, Joyce Aylen, and Bill Little generously shared memories, references, documentary collections, and notes. Paul read the entire first draft and offered helpful comments. Carol shared her genealogical research. Don spoke thoughtfully about the family and gave me much to think about.

My greatest research debt is to the late Ellen Cooke, who preserved documents, conducted interviews, and placed a trunkful of letters, now known as the Norquay Premier's Papers, in the public domain.

The archivists, librarians, and staff at the Archives of Manitoba and the Legislative Library of Manitoba supported this project in so many ways. I thank all of them, in particular Stuart Hay, Margaret Wilson, Sue Bishop, Louise Ayotte-Zaretski, Louise Sloane, Scott Goodine, Chris Kotecki, Rudy Ramirez, Paula Warsaba, Joan Sinclair, Jason Martin, Julianna Trivers, Rachel Mills, Lisa Friesen, and Oliver Bernuetz.

It has been a pleasure to work with the University of Manitoba Press. I thank David Larsen, David Carr, Glenn Bergen, Jill McConkey, Barbara Romanik, Sarah Ens, Allyn Lyons, Pat Sanders, Dallas Harrison, Adrian Mather, and Jess Koroscil for their labours and many kindnesses.

Paul Vogt, then clerk of the Manitoba Executive Council, and George Hickes, then speaker of the Legislative Assembly, supported a project to collect newspaper reports of debates, unpublished sessional papers, and other source materials. The students who carried out the work included Mackenzie White, Jonas Thor, Gerhard Ens, Robert Hood, Colin Oakes, Lindsay Storie, Roy Loewen, and Leah Morton. It was a pleasure to work with them, and I thank them. The documents are now available in the Legislative Library and the Archives of Manitoba.

I am indebted to the staff at St. John's College, St. Paul's College, the History Department, and Elizabeth Dafoe Library at the University of Manitoba, Graham Library and Robarts Library at the University of Toronto, Toronto Reference Library, and Robinson College Library and the University Library at the University of Cambridge. I would like to thank Ivan Froese, Sandra Ferguson, and Katy Hunt, who helped me frequently in my struggles with computers.

Mel Myers gave me two volumes published by the Legislative Assembly and signed by Norquay that might once have resided on the desk of the premier himself. They have been placed in the Legislative Library in Myers's name.

For translations from Cree I would like to thank Louise Mercredi and Ovide Mercredi. And for reviewing my translations from French, I thank Michel Lagacé.

Many scholars helped me during the preparation of this book. Giving evidence of their stamina and generosity, Jill McConkey, Jim Mochoruk, Gerhard Ens, and Paul Nielson read a much too long initial draft and I am very grateful to them for their advice. Chris Andersen, Tom Brodbeck, Margaret Conrad, Ryan Eyford, Barry Ferguson, Harry Finnigan, Jean Friesen, Norma Hall, Emma LaRocque, Victor Lytwyn, Morris Mott, Adele Perry, Bill Waiser, and three anonymous referees read the next version, and I thank them for their suggestions and support. For advice on many historical points I am indebted to Trevor Anderson, Len Brooks, Sarah Carter, Andy den Otter, Zenon Gawron, Brian Gettler, Gillian Glover, Gord Goldsborough, Sigrid Johnson, James Kostuchuk, Barry Potyondi, Randy Rostecki, Lisa Schaub, Gary Spraakman, Frank Tough, and Tyler Wentzell.

I would like to thank my colleagues in St. John's College, St. Paul's College, the History Department, and the Faculty of Arts at the University of Manitoba, for their encouragement and stimulation. For help away from home, I relied on colleagues at the University of Toronto, especially Carl Berger, Joe Martin, Brian Gettler, Nick Terpstra, and Laurie Bertram, at Trier University and the Free University of Berlin (with special thanks to Petra Dolata, Ursula Lehmkuhl, Wolfgang Helbich, Lisa Schaub, and Wolfgang Klooss), the University of Central Florida (thanks to Rosalind Beiler), and King's College at the University of London (thanks to Peter Busch). I am grateful to David Yates, Morna Hooker, Peter Milloy, and colleagues, who welcomed us to Robinson College, and to Eugenio Biagini and Andrew Preston for introductions to academic meetings in the University of Cambridge.

This book has been a long time coming as Bob, Kathryn, Greg, Sheila, Tom, Ivan, and our tennis partners know too well, and I have appreciated their tactful interest in its completion. My family, Joe and Alex, Ciara and Franca, John, Orla, Giulia, and Ben, Marion and Barry, and Bob and Shelagh, have made the work lighter. Finally, I thank Jean, who shared the entire journey and made it a pleasure.

Gerald Friesen,
Winnipeg, 2024

Abbreviations

CMS	Church Missionary Society Papers
CPR	Canadian Pacific Railway Papers
ECPO	Executive Council Premier's Office
EPRL	Ecclesiastical Province of Rupert's Land Papers
HBCA	Hudson's Bay Company Archives
LLM Hansard	Legislative Library of Manitoba newspaper scrapbook
NPP	Norquay Premier's Papers
SHSB	Société historique de Saint-Boniface
USC	United States Consul Papers of James Wickes Taylor

Keywords

Aboriginal.
The term employed in the Constitution Act, 1982, for "Indian," "Métis," and "Inuit" peoples of Canada.

Cree, Saulteaux, and Sioux.
Terms used by John Norquay for three Indigenous peoples or nations (and members thereof), the Cree (Nehiyaw, Ininew), Saulteaux (Anishinaabe, Ojibwa, Chippewa), and Sioux (Dakota, Lakota).

First Nations.
Applies to communities that have occupied the territories of present-day Canada from time immemorial.

Indigenous.
Contemporary Canadians' term of choice encompassing First Nations, Métis, and Inuit peoples.

Métis.
In the nineteenth century, the term applied mainly to Michif / French-speaking individuals and communities; today, it typically is applied to communities and individuals who choose to identify as having partly Indigenous, partly European ancestry (see s.35 of Canada's Constitution Act 1982).

Natives, countrymen.
Norquay's terms for English-speaking peoples of partly Indigenous, partly European ancestry, many of whom spoke in a dialect of standard English known in the Red River settlement as "Bungee."

White.
The only Canada Census of Manitoba 1870 category for Manitoba residents who were not "Indian" or "Half-Breed"/"Métis." The census directive: "Those who are white, or with no admission of Indian blood."[1]

A Note on Sources

The Norquay Premier's Papers (cited as NPP) constitute the single most important documentary resource for this book. On the basis of scattered clues in the documents themselves, I believe that this valuable collection was prepared by the secretarial staff in the legislature during Norquay's premiership and then tied in bundles with ribbon and packed in a tin trunk shortly after his sudden death. The trunk rested in Norquay family homes for half a century. In 1946 Dr. Horace Norquay or his sister, Caroline Ellen Norquay McAllister, gave it to a historical researcher, Ellen Cooke, who planned to write a full biography. Over the next forty years Cooke interviewed family members, typed copies of hundreds of fading letters, and visited sites of importance in Norquay's life. Her main publication is a mimeographed, fifty-page study of Norquay's ancestors, *Fur Trade Profiles: Five Ancestors of Premier John Norquay* (Winnipeg: published by the author in three editions, bearing the dates 1978 and 1979, the last being the longest version).

Cooke's gift of the entire collection of Norquay papers to the Archives of Manitoba, in 1986, along with a box of her own papers, came with an important condition: the items had to be microfilmed and fully catalogued before they could be made accessible to researchers. Lee Gibson, historian and volunteer archivist, took the dozens of packets of letters and invoices and prepared a carefully itemized list that recorded the basic details of each document on a spreadsheet. Now known as the Norquay Premier's Papers and Executive Council Premier's Office (NPP and ECPO in the endnotes), the treasure includes almost 7,000 items, including letters, official documents, bills, and even some cheque stubs and a little agenda book. I have transcribed much of this material in Word documents and produced a longer manuscript to assist future researchers. It will be housed in the University of Manitoba Archives.

Beginning in 1884, the Legislative Library of Manitoba assembled scrapbooks containing the local newspapers' transcriptions of debates in the Legislative Assembly. This accounts for the references to LLM Hansard in the endnotes.

I am indebted to the creators of a vast storehouse of books and journals on the Web, and especially: Canadiana, https://www.canadiana.ca; *Winnipeg Free Press,* https://www.winnipegfreepress.com/; the Wayback Machine at Internet Archive, https://archive.org/; the University of Alberta's *Peel's Prairie Provinces,* http://peel.library.ualberta.ca/index.html); the *Dictionary of Canadian Biography,* http://www.biographi.ca/en/index.php; the collection of John A. Macdonald Papers at Library and Archives Canada, https://library-archives.canada.ca/eng; the files on "Memorable Manitobans" in Manitoba Historical Society, http://www.mhs.mb.ca/docs/people/index.shtml; Norma Jean Hall's work on the Red River Settlement, https://resistancemothers.wordpress.com/; and the Manitobia newspaper collection at https://digitalcollections.lib.umanitoba.ca/islandora/object/uofm%3Amanitobia_newspapers.

Notes

Introduction

1 Alexander Begg, *History of the North-West* (Toronto: Hunter, Rose, and Company, 1894); George Bryce, *A History of Manitoba: Its Resources and Its People* (Toronto: Canada History Company, 1906), 256, 263; George Bryce, *The Scotsman in Canada: Western Canada, Including Manitoba, Saskatchewan, Alberta, British Columbia, and Portions of Old Rupert's Land and the Indian Territories* (Toronto: Musson, 1911), 31–32; Adrien Gabriel Morice, *History of the Catholic Church in Western Canada, from Lake Superior to the Pacific, 1659–1895* (Toronto: Musson, 1910), 224; Roderick George MacBeth, *The Making of the Canadian West: Being the Reminiscences of an Eye-Witness* (Toronto: William Briggs, 1898), 101–5; Roderick George MacBeth, *The Romance of Western Canada* (Toronto: William Briggs, 1918); John Harrison O'Donnell, *Manitoba as I Saw It from 1869 to Date: With Flash-Lights on the First Riel Rebellion* (Winnipeg: Clark Brothers and Company, 1909), 59–60; Margaret Stovel McWilliams, *Manitoba Milestones* (Toronto: J.M. Dent and Sons, 1928), 109; Joseph Francis Tennant, *Rough Times, 1870–1920* (Winnipeg: n.p., 1921), 172; Thomas McKitrick, *Cornerstones of Empire: The Settlement of Crystal City and District in the Rock Lake Country* (Crystal City, MB: Courier Publishing, 1940), 14; Grant MacEwan, "Honourable John," in *Fifty Mighty Men* (Saskatoon: Modern Press, 1958), 272.

2 Chester Martin, *The Natural Resources Question: The Historical Basis of Provincial Claims* (Winnipeg: King's Printer, 1920), 107, 136; Chester Martin, "Political History of Manitoba, 1870–1912," in *Canada and Its Provinces*, ed. Adam Shortt and Arthur G. Doughty (Toronto: Glasgow, Brook, 1914), 97–143.

3 George F.G. Stanley, *The Birth of Western Canada: A History of the Riel Rebellions* (Toronto: Longmans, Green, 1936), 260–61; Marcel Giraud mentioned only Norquay's grandfather in *The Métis in the Canadian West*, vol. 2 (Edmonton: University of Alberta Press, 1986), 35; first published as *Le Métis canadien: Son rôle dans l'histoire des provinces de l'ouest* (Paris: Institut d'ethnologie, Musée de l'homme, 1945).

4 James A. Jackson, *The Centennial History of Manitoba* (Toronto: McClelland and Stewart, 1970), 131; W.L. Morton, *Manitoba: A History* (1957; reprinted, Toronto: University of Toronto Press, 1967), 219–22, 231.

5 John W. Dafoe, *Sir Clifford Sifton in Relation to His Times* (Toronto: Macmillan, 1931), 12–15; John Skirving Ewart, *The Manitoba School Question* (Toronto: Copp Clark, 1894), 219.

6 Donald Creighton, *John A. Macdonald II: The Old Chieftain* (Toronto: Macmillan, 1955), 472, 493–94; Morton, *Manitoba: A History*, 231; Peter B. Waite, *Canada 1874–1896 Arduous Destiny* (Toronto: McClelland and Stewart, 1971), 195–99;

Richard Gwyn, *Nation Maker: Sir John A. Macdonald: His Life, Our Times II, 1867–1891* (Toronto: Random House Canada, 2011), 543; Bob Beal and Rod Macleod, *Prairie Fire: The 1885 North-West Rebellion* (Edmonton: Hurtig, 1984), 35; an exception is Mary Janigan, *Let the Eastern Bastards Freeze in the Dark: The West versus the Rest since Confederation* (Toronto: Alfred A. Knopf Canada, 2012), 55–80; Gerald Friesen, "Norquay, John," in *Dictionary of Canadian Biography*, vol. 11 (Toronto: University of Toronto/Quebec City: Université Laval, 2003), http://www.biographi.ca/en/bio/norquay_john_11E.html (accessed 23 March 2023); Gerald Friesen, "John Norquay, 1878–1887," in *Manitoba Premiers of the 19th and 20th Centuries*, ed. Barry Ferguson and Robert Wardhaugh (Regina: Canadian Plains Research Center / CPRC Press, 2010), 47–67.

7 Maurice Constantin-Weyer, *Vers l'ouest: Roman* (Paris: La renaissançe du livre, 1921).

8 Aleida Assmann, "Transformations between History and Memory," *Social Research* 75, no. 1 (2008): 52, 63–69.

9 Gerald Friesen, "A Premier, a Tin Box, and a Landlady: Ellen Cooke and the Norquay Papers," *Manitoba History* 77 (2015), http://www.mhs.mb.ca/docs/mb_history/77/norquaygift.shtml (accessed 5 April 2023).

10 Hermione Lee, *Biography: A Very Short Introduction* (2009; reprinted, Oxford: Oxford University Press, 2013), 17–18.

Chapter 1: "A Merry Prankish Youngster," 1841–58

1 John Norquay was baptized on 8 June 1841; see "Baptisms Solemnized in the Rapids Church, Red River Settlement, Prince Rupert's Land 1841," Archives of Manitoba (hereafter AM); HBC, "Notes on Ancestry of Hon. John Norquay," Hudson's Bay Company Archives (hereafter HBCA), E 4/1a, folio 173d, entry 601 (hereafter "Norquay Ancestry"); Ellen Cooke, *Fur Trade Profiles: Five Ancestors of Premier John Norquay* (Winnipeg: self-published, 1978–79), in three editions, the last being the definitive version (hereafter *Five Ancestors*); and Canada, Department of the Interior, "Scrip Affidavit #2501," 24 July 1875; Norquay to H. L. Walton, 20 July 1887, Norquay Premiers Papers (hereafter NPP), Letterbook 5, p 70.

2 Bungee is a dialect of English, Michif a language that borrowed from both European and First Nation languages.

3 I would like to thank Professor Gerhard Ens for material on Oman Norquay; Barry Kaye, "Birsay Village on the Assiniboine," *The Beaver* (Winter 1981): 18–21; on the Red River Settlement, see plates 17 and 18 in R. Louis Gentilcore, ed., *Historical Atlas of Canada II: The Land Transformed 1800–1891* (Toronto: University of Toronto Press, 1993).

4 Norquay used the terms "Cree" and "Saulteaux" throughout his life. Rather than using both modern and historical language, I will adhere to his usage. I employ the linguistic categories "Michif/francophone" and "Bungee/anglophone" as neutral terms that establish an important distinction in Red River society. Norquay did not like the term

"Half-Breed," I believe, but this is more difficult to prove. A learned observer of the Red River's people of mixed ancestry, Alexander Reid, wrote that many of the settlement's residents in the early 1860s, when he lived in the settlement, disliked the label. Alexander Peter Reid, "The Mixed or 'Halfbreed' Races of North-Western Canada," *The Journal of Anthropological Institute of Great Britain and Ireland* 4 (1875): 45–52, with thanks to Donald B. Smith for this reference.

5 Ellen Cooke, "Interview with Jacob T. Norquay 13 November 1965," Ellen Gillies Cooke Papers, file 6; Hudson's Bay Company, "Land Register Book B," HBCA; I would like to thank Lisa Schaub, Trier University, and Jean Friesen for information on this entry.

6 George Bryce, "Among the Mound Builders' Remains," Manitoba Historical Society *Transactions* Series 1, 18 (1885), http://www.mhs.mb.ca/docs/transactions/1/moundbuilders.shtml (accessed 15 February 2023).

7 "Important Statement of Pegowis, the Indian Chief," *Nor'-Wester,* 14 October 1863; I would like to thank Dr. Norma Hall for this depiction of Red River.

8 "Census of the Red River Settlement 1832," HBCA, E 5/6, folio 14, entry 315; Cooke, *Five Ancestors*; HBC, "Norquay Ancestry."

9 On John's father, see HBCA, B.239/u/1, entry 1497; Cooke, *Five Ancestors*; and HBC, "Norquay Ancestry."

10 Donald Ross, "Diary of Donald Ross Oct. 1833–Nov. 1835, Concluded by John Ballenden," entries on 11 April 1833, 11 August 1834, British Columbia Archives (hereafter BCA), Donald Ross Papers, Transcript A/B/20/no83.

11 Jane Vincent to Elizabeth Truthwaite, 1 October 1843, 7 August 1852, AM, Elizabeth Truthwaite Papers; Alfred Savage to James A. Jackson, 2 December 1947, AM, John Norquay Papers, file 2; HBC, "Moose Fort Journal," 17 September 1809, HBCA, B.135/a/97, and "Albany Factory School Journal 1808–1809," HBCA, B.3/a/112, folio 5.

12 HBC, "Norway House Journal, Outfit 1838," records that on 23 July 1838 "Jno. Norquay with his family left here for Red River," HBCA, B.154/1/31; HBC, "Norquay Ancestry."

13 "Censuses of the Red River Settlement, 1840, 1843," AM; Norma J. Hall, "Red River Métis Farming, 1810–1870," https://resistancemothers.wordpress.com/a-casualty-of-colonialism/ (accessed January 2021).

14 Eleanor M. Blain, "The Bungee Dialect of the Red River Settlement" (MA thesis, University of Manitoba, 1989), 2–14, also 240, 251, 285, 309, 317 (I thank Cathy Macdonald for this reference); Margaret Stobie, "Backgrounds of the Dialect Called Bungi," Manitoba Historical Society *Transactions* Series 3, 24 (1967–68): 13; Norn, descended from Old Norse, was a North Germanic language originating in Scandinavia and widely spoken in the Orkney and Shetland Islands until the eighteenth and nineteenth centuries.

15 I would like to thank Mrs. Louise Mercredi and Ovide Mercredi for the Cree translations.

16 Charles Adams to John Norquay, 22 February 1886, Norquay Premiers Papers, C-1415.

17 Charles Adams to John Norquay, 28 December 1879, 4 January 1880, NPP, A-386.

18 Blain, "Bungee Dialect," 2–14.

19 The word *somersault* in Cree is âpocikwânîw; see University of Alberta, *Online Cree Dictionary*, http://www.creedictionary.com/ (accessed 5 December 2022).

20 HBC, "Burial Records, St. Andrews," 18 October 1843, HBCA, E 4/2, folio 131d, entry 147, and folio 133; Paul Hackett, *A Very Remarkable Sickness: Epidemics in the Petit Nord, 1670 to 1846* (Winnipeg: University of Manitoba Press, 2002), 188–89.

21 I would like to thank Don Norquay of Winnipeg for information on Nancy Ward.

22 Canada, Department of the Interior, Library and Archives Canada (hereafter LAC), vol./box 1325, C-14936; HBC, "Baptismal Register, St. Andrews," 1 October 1848, HBCA, E 4/2, folio 65, entry 134; HBC, "Burial Register," 25 October 1848, HBCA, E 4/2, folio 160, entry 294.

23 Gerhard Ens, *Homeland to Hinterland: The Changing Worlds of the Red River Metis in the Nineteenth Century* (Toronto: University of Toronto Press, 1996), 106–10.

24 "Censuses of Red River 1846–7" and "Censuses of Red River 1849," AM.

25 HBC, "Burial Register, Upper Church District, Red River Settlement, 1849," 10 June 1849, HBCA, E 4/2, folio 158, entry 403.

26 Andrew J. Norquay to Ellen Cooke, 7 December 1951, Ellen Gillies Cooke Papers, file 1; Cooke described her as "Jean Norquay Spence," explaining that James Spence was her second husband, in "Premier John Norquay," a short essay presented to the Provincial Archives of Manitoba, 17 December 1985, and filed in Norquay Papers, MG13, C4. Don Norquay, a descendant of Thomas, the premier's brother, suggests that "brothers John and Tom likely did continue to live with their father, John, and his new wife, Nancy, after their marriage, at least until their father's death in 1849, when they were 'orphaned.' They likely continued to live together with their stepmother, Nancy ('the widow Spence'), and half-sister, Nancy [Annie] Norquay, for a (likely short) period of time after their father's death. At some point, for reasons unknown, but likely related to her inability to support her large blended family on her own, Nancy Ward Spence/Norquay gave up custody of her stepchildren (and perhaps her daughter Nancy as well), with Thomas (and possibly Nancy) going to live with his maternal grandparents, the Truthwaites, and John going to live with his paternal grandmother, Jane/Jean Morwick/Norquay/Spence, and her second husband, James Spence (the tailor)." Don Norquay to author, 5 January 2020.

27 David Anderson to Henry Venn, 29 November 1852, 8 February 1853, 30 July 1855, Church Missionary Society (hereafter CMS) Papers, microfilm copy, University of Manitoba Dafoe Library.

28 David Anderson to Henry Venn, 8 February 1853, CMS Papers; William J. Healy, ed., *Women of Red River: Being a Book Written from the Recollections of Women Surviving from the Red River Era* (Winnipeg: Russell, Lang, 1923), 89; "John Norquay: Autobiographical Note," NPP, G8731.

29 Robert Machray, "To the Parents and Guardians of Boys at St. John's College School Jan 23rd 1875," St. John's College (hereafter SJC) Papers, box 22, folio 1; David Anderson, *A Charge Delivered to the Clergy of the Diocese of Rupert's Land, at His Triennial Visitation, in July and December, 1853* (London: Thomas Hatchard, 1854), 32; "First Records of the College" and "Collegiate Board of Saint John's," SJC Papers, box 16; David Anderson to Donald Ross, 10 December 1849, 11 December 1850, 3 June 1851, BCA, Donald Ross Papers; Robert Machray, *Western Churchman* 3, no. 15 (1898): 227–28; W.H.T. [Reverend William Henry Taylor], "Scholarships," "Lists of Scholars," and "Exhibitioners," in Cooke, "Five Ancestors," 40–42; David Anderson to the Governor and Council of Rupert's Land, 12 June 1852, Ecclesiastical Province of Rupert's Land (hereafter EPRL) Papers; "Anderson, David 1849–1851," EPRL Papers, Boon 1505, box P338; Denise Fuchs, "A 'Philanthropist's Bosom' Conflicted: The Reverend John Macallum of Red River Academy," *Canadian Journal of Native Studies* 35, no. 1 (2015): 121–43.

30 Reverend Samuel Matheson, "College and School in the Eighties," SJC Papers, file UA 1, "Mary Kinnear, Photocopies of Archival Material"; "The Red River Academy," EPRL Papers, Boon 1104, box P338, "Gerald H. Wade File"; William John Fraser, "A History of St. John's College, Winnipeg" (MA thesis, University of Manitoba, 1966); John Bumsted, *St. John's College: Faith and Education in Western Canada* (Winnipeg: University of Manitoba Press, 2006); T.C.B. Boon, "The Institute of Rupert's Land and Bishop David Anderson," Manitoba Historical Society *Transactions* Series 3, (1961–62): http://mhs.mb.ca/docs/transactions/3/instituterupertsland.shtml.

31 "Letter from John A. Maggrah, St. John's College, 26 January 1890," *Our Forest Children*, New Series 12, 4, no. 2 (1890): 188; I thank Donald B. Smith, who sent me this document.

32 David Anderson to Henry Venn, 22 November 1849, 30 July 1855, CMS Papers.

33 *Manitoba Free Press*, 30 August 1909; John Venn, *Alumnae Cantabridgiensis* (Cambridge, UK: Cambridge University Press, 1922–54); with thanks to Erica McDonald, Ward Library, Peterhouse, University of Cambridge, and to Professor Martin Brett, Robinson College, University of Cambridge, and Professors David Howarth and Michael Kinnear, University of Manitoba, for their assistance with Cambridge connections.

34 Frits Pannekoek, "Anderson, David," in *Dictionary of Canadian Biography*, vol. 11, University of Toronto/Université Laval, 2003–, http://www.biographi.ca/en/bio/anderson_david_11E.html (accessed 6 April 2023); Nigel Scotland, *John Bird Sumner: Evangelical Archbishop* (Leominister, UK: Gracewing, Fowler Wright Books, 1995), 146; T.C.B. Boon, "A Short History of the Church of England in the Diocese of

Rupert's Land" (typescript, 1951), SJC Papers, file UA 1, "Mary Kinnear: Photocopies of Archival Material"; David Anderson, testimony in UK House of Commons, *Report for the Select Committee on the Hudson's Bay Company* (London: Queen's Printer, 1857), 245–46; David Anderson, *A Charge Delivered to the Clergy of the Diocese of Rupert's Land, at His Primary Visitation* (London: Thomas Hatchard, 1851), 9–10; David Anderson, *Britain's Answer to the Nations: A Missionary Sermon Preached in Saint Paul's Cathedral, on Sunday, May 3, 1857* (London: Thomas Hatchard, 1857), 14.

35 Margaret Anderson to Henry Venn, 23 June 1853, 5 August 1853, CMS Papers.

36 Anderson, *A Charge . . . 1853*, 39–40; Benjamin Mackenzie, untitled memoir, EPRL Papers.

37 Anderson, *A Charge . . . 1851*, 27–30, 33–37; Anderson, *A Charge . . . 1853*, 33, 48–49; David Anderson, *A Charge Delivered to the Clergy of the Diocese of Rupert's Land, at His Triennial Visitation, May 29, 1856* (London: Thomas Hatchard, 1856); David Anderson, *"The Gospel in the Regions Beyond": A Sermon Preached in Lambeth Church, on Sunday, May 3, 1874, at the Consecration of the Bishops of Athabasca and Saskatchewan* (London: Hatchard, 1874), 13.

38 Anderson, *A Charge . . . 1853*, 33; Anderson, *A Charge . . . 1856*, 42–43; David Anderson, *A Charge Delivered to the Clergy of the Diocese of Rupert's Land, in St. John's Church, Red River, at His Triennial Visitation, January 6, 1860* (London: Thomas Hatchard, 1860), 10; also see David Anderson, *The Circle of Light: Or, The Conjuror's Confession* (London: Thomas Hatchard, 1857), 7–10; David Anderson to Henry Venn, 22 November 1849, CMS Papers; and Henry Venn to David Anderson, 3 April 1851, EPRL Papers, box P338.

39 Henry Venn to David Anderson, 3 April 1851, EPRL Papers, box P338; Anderson, *A Charge . . . 1856*, 38; see also Erin Millions, "'By Education and Conduct': Educating Trans-Imperial Indigenous Fur-Trade Children in the Hudson's Bay Company Territories and the British Empire, 1820s to 1870s" (PhD diss., University of Manitoba, 2017).

40 David Anderson to James Ross, 4 February 1854, AM, Alexander Ross Papers; David Anderson to Donald Ross, 3 June 1851, BCA, Donald Ross Papers.

41 Benjamin Mackenzie, "Reminiscences of the Rev. Benjamin Mackenzie," EPRL Papers, 85-59-7593; I thank Dr. Erin Millions, who shared her copy of this text; "First Records of the College," SJC Papers, box 16, file UA 1, "Board 1855–1894."

42 David Anderson to Donald Ross, 9 November 1849, 10 December 1849, BCA, Donald Ross Papers.

43 "John Norquay," NPP, G8731; also see *Nor'Wester*, 14 May, 28 May, and 14 June 1860.

44 David Anderson to Henry Venn, 30 July 1855, CMS Papers; David Anderson to James Ross, 4 October 1855, Alexander Ross Papers.

45 Alexander Sandison, "St. Andrews Recollections," AM, John Schultz Papers, box 16; Mackenzie, "Reminiscences"; Boon, "A Short History of the Church of England";

Margaret Anderson to Henry Venn, 29 July 1853, CMS Papers; Ellen Cooke, "Information from Mrs. Elizabeth Aylen, Daughter of Premier Norquay's Son Alexander, 7 January 1986" (interview in early 1974), Ellen Gillies Cooke Papers, Elizabeth Aylen file.

46 Mackenzie, "Reminiscences"; *St. John's College Magazine*, photocopied page, numbered 10, SJC Papers.

47 Peter Erasmus, *Buffalo Days and Nights* (Calgary: Fifth House, for Glenbow Institute, 1999), 15; "Minutes of the Corresponding Committee and Finance Committee 1850–1876" (typescript copies), 15 May 1855, EPRL Papers, box P338.

48 Andrew J. Norquay to Ellen Cooke, 7 December 1951, Ellen Gillies Cooke Papers, Andrew Norquay file.

49 William Taylor to E. Hawkins, 20 January 1858, in *Reports and Letters of the Reverend W. H. Taylor, 1852–1859*, ed. Anita Schmidt (Winnipeg: self-published, 1972); W.H. Taylor, "Journal of the Rev. W.H. Taylor from Xmas to Lady Day 1858," entry for 1 March 1858, in Schmidt, *Reports and Letters*, 51.

50 William Taylor to E. Hawkins, 27 July 1855, in Schmidt, *Reports and Letters*,13; William Taylor to E. Hawkins, 12 January 1854, typescript copy in Ellen Gillies Cooke Papers, file 13.

51 Taylor, "Journal," 18 May, 27 May, 30 June, 17 July, 29 September, and 31 December 1858, in Schmidt, *Reports and Letters*, and in Ellen Gillies Cooke Papers, file 13.

52 Taylor, "Journal," 20 February 1859, in "Journal Ending March 25 1859," Ellen Gillies Cooke Papers, file 13.

53 William Taylor to E. Hawkins, 27 July 1855, in Schmidt, *Reports and Letters*, 28–30.

54 W.H. Taylor, "Report . . . of Rev. W.H. Taylor . . . for the Qr Ending Sept 29th 1857," in Schmidt, *Reports and Letters*, 28–29, 33–34, 39; W.H. Taylor, entries for August 1859, in "Journal of the Rev. W.H. Taylor of St. James Assiniboia, for the Qr Ending Sept 1859," in Ellen Gillies Cooke Papers, file 13.

55 W.H. Taylor, entry for 13 October, in "Journal of the Rev. W.H. Taylor, . . . for the Qr Ending Dec 1859," in Ellen Gillies Cooke Papers, file 13; David Anderson to Henry Venn, 2 November 1853, CMS Papers.

56 "Journal & Notices of the Rev. W. Taylor for the Quarter ending Dec. 31st, 1857," Schmidt, *Reports and Letters*, 41–50.

57 David Anderson to Henry Venn, 22 January 1850, CMS Papers.

58 Ens, *Homeland*, 82.

59 Quoted in W.L. Morton, "Introduction," in *London Correspondence Inward from Eden Colvile 1849–1852*, ed. E.E. Rich (London: Hudson's Bay Record Society, 1956), xxiii–xxiv.

60 William Taylor to E. Hawkins, 7 August 1855, in Schmidt, *Reports and Letters*, 22–23.

61 Ibid., 22–24; W.L. Morton, "The Battle at the Grand Coteau, July 13 and 14, 1851," Manitoba Historical Society *Transactions* Series 3, 16 (1959–60), http://www.mhs.mb.ca/docs/transactions/3/grandcouteau.shtml.

62 William Taylor to E. Hawkins, 7 August 1855, in Schmidt, *Reports and Letters*, 24–25; Laura Peers and Anne Lindsay, "Governor William B. Caldwell's Souvenir: Exoticism and a Gentleman's Reputation," *Manitoba History* 73 (2013), http://www.mhs.mb.ca/docs/mb_history/73/caldwellsouvenir.shtml.

63 William Taylor to E. Hawkins, 30 June 1858, Ellen Gillies Cooke Papers, file 13; Taylor, "Report . . . for the Qr Ending Sept 29th 1857," in Schmidt, *Reports and Letters*, 32.

64 Taylor, "Journal Ending March 25 1859," 19 and 26 March 1859, Ellen Gillies Cooke Papers, file 13; W.H. Taylor, "Missionary Reports 1859 N. America, West Indies, for the Qr ending Sept 1859," Ellen Gillies Cooke Papers, file 13.

65 J.E. Foster, "The Country-Born in the Red River Settlement, 1820–1850" (PhD diss., University of Alberta, 1973), 145–46; J.E. Foster, "Cockran, William," in *Dictionary of Canadian Biography,* vol. 9, University of Toronto/Université Laval, 2003–, http://www.biographi.ca/en/bio/cockran_william_9E.html (accessed 28 March 2023); Ens, *Homeland.*

Chapter 2: Red River Family, 1859–70

1 William Henry Taylor, "Scholarships," "Lists of Scholars," and "Exhibitioners," in Ellen Cooke, *Fur Trade Profiles: Five Ancestors of Premier John Norquay*, 3rd ed. (Winnipeg: self-published, 1979), 40–42.

2 *Nor'Wester,* 14 June 1860; also see 14 and 28 May 1860.

3 Joe Favell Jr. to John Norquay, 14 December 1879, NPP, A-236.

4 *Nor'Wester,* 28 July 1860; Samuel Taylor, "Samuel Taylor's Journal: A Thing of Shreds and Patches Intended to Afford Amusement to Many, and to Give Offence to None . . . 1849–1863," entry of 1 December 1859, Samuel Taylor Papers; David Anderson, *A Charge Delivered to the Clergy of the Diocese of Rupert's Land, in St. John's Church, Red River, at His Triennial Visitation, January 6, 1860* (London: Thomas Hatchard, 1860), 49.

5 Anderson, *A Charge . . . 1860*, 50–51, 54; Margaret Anderson to Henry Venn, 12 March 1858 (misfiled among 1854 letters), CMS Papers; David Anderson to Robert Machray, 11 December 1865, 28 August 1866, 30 October 1866, EPRL Papers, Boon 2053, 84–87.

6 David Anderson, *A Charge Delivered to the Clergy of the Diocese of Rupert's Land, in St. John's Cathedral, Red River, at His Fifth and Last Visitation, January 6, 1864* (London: Hatchard and Company, 1864), 54; Anderson, *A Charge . . . 1860*, 54; Andrew Bannatyne to Edward Ellice, quoted in J.E. Rea, "Bannatyne, Andrew Graham Ballenden," in *Dictionary of Canadian Biography*, vol. 11, University of Toronto/

Université Laval, 2003–, http://www.biographi.ca/en/bio/bannatyne_andrew_graham_ballenden_11E.html (accessed 6 April 2023).

7 Norma J. Hall, "Red River Métis Farming, 1810–1870," 2015, in *A Casualty of Colonialism: Mothers of the Resistance 1869–1870* (wordpress.com) (accessed January 2022); Hall revises W.L. Morton, "Agriculture in Red River," in *Contexts of Canada's Past: Selected Essays of W. L. Morton*, ed. A.B. McKillop (Toronto: Macmillan, c. 1980), 77–78, 81; David Anderson to Henry Venn, 2 November 1853, CMS Papers; William Taylor to E. Hawkins, 10 August 1857, in *Reports and Letters of the Reverend W.H. Taylor First Rector of the Parish of St. James Church—the Assiniboine Written between November 23, 1852 and August 4, 1859*, ed. Anita Schmidt (Winnipeg: self-published, 1972), 38–39.

8 James McDonald, "Daily Journal Kept by Color Sergeant James McDonald Late R. C. Rifles Coming from the Red River Settlement Hudson Bay Territory to York Factory the H B Company Fort, 12 August to 1 September 1862" (Toronto Reference Library) 4; *Nor'Wester*, 28 May 1860.

9 Taylor, "Samuel Taylor's Journal"; William J. Healy, ed., *Women of Red River: Being a Book Written from the Recollections of Women Surviving from the Red River Era* (Winnipeg: Russell, Lang, 1923), 145–56.

10 Taylor, "Samuel Taylor's Journal," December 1859.

11 Ibid., November 1862.

12 Ellen Cooke, "Conversation with Jacob T. Norquay, 5 June 1965," Ellen Gillies Cooke Papers, file 12.

13 Mrs. John (Caroline Ellen [Nellie] Norquay) McAllister, "Bungee Stories," AM, Inland Audio recording, 1950, tape C386.

14 Taylor, "Samuel Taylor's Journal," 14 July 1855, 11 November 1856, 11–12 June 1859.

15 Ibid., December 1862, summer 1864, June and July 1866; Anderson, *A Charge . . . 1864*, 24–25; Gontran Laviolette, "Tatanka-Najin (Standing Buffalo)," in *Dictionary of Canadian Biography*, vol. 9, University of Toronto/Université Laval, 2003–, http://www.biographi.ca/en/bio/tatanka_najin_9E.html (accessed 6 April 2023).

16 Dale Gibson, *Law, Life, and Government at Red River*, vol. 1, *Settlement and Governance, 1812–1872*, and vol. 2, *General Quarterly Court of Assiniboia, Annotated Records, 1844–1872* (Toronto: Osgoode Society for Canadian Legal History; Montreal and Kingston: McGill-Queen's University Press, 2015).

17 Taylor, "Samuel Taylor's Journal," January 1860.

18 Healy, *Women of Red River*, 148.

19 Ibid., 145–56; Alfred Savage, "John Norquay," John Norquay Papers, file 2; Ellen Cooke, "9 October 1965. Trip to Portage la Prairie with Mr. Jacob Norquay," Ellen Gillies Cooke Papers, file 6; Ellen Cooke, "Interview with Misses Lyda and Ella Setter," Ellen Gillies Cooke Papers, file 6.

20 HBC, "Baptismal Register," HBCA, E 4/2, folio 25d, entry 665; St. Mary's Anglican Church, Portage la Prairie, "Marriage Register," 2 June 1862; "Premier's Bible," photocopied page, Ellen Gillies Cooke Papers, file 7.

21 HBC, "Red River Baptismal Register, 1820–28," 59–62.

22 David Anderson to John Anderson, Peter Garrioch, and others, 25 April 1851 (copy), EPRL Papers, box P338; "Mary Kinnear: Photocopies of Archival Material," SJC Papers, file UA1; T.C.B. Boon, "A Short History of the Church of England in the Diocese of Rupert's Land," SJC Papers, typescript, 1951, n. pag.; Joseph Henry Metcalfe, *The Tread of the Pioneers* (Toronto: Ryerson, 1932), 226.

23 Healy, *Women of Red River*, 145–56.

24 Ibid.; "Minutes of the Corresponding Committee and Finance Committee 1850–1876," EPRL Papers, box P338, 14.

25 St. Andrews Church, "Baptisms 1859–1872": 271, Thomas (6 November 1863); 411, Isabella Jessie Ann (30 July 1865); 473, John George (26 August 1866); Ellen Cooke, "Information from Mrs. J. E. McAllister, March 9, 1946," Ellen Gillies Cooke Papers, file 4; "Norquay, John," Manitoba Historical Society Papers, file 2, 299; St. Mary's LaPrairie, Portage la Prairie, "Baptismal Register 1865–1872": Alexander (29 November 1867); Horatio (November 1869), St. Anne, Poplar Point; Caroline Ellen (March 1871), St. Margaret, High Bluff; Andrew James (August 1872), St. Margaret, High Bluff; "St. Andrews Burials 1870–84": Ada Theodore, 1881, buried 15 April 1883, age one year, ten months; Horace was baptized at High Bluff on 8 November 1869 but probably was born at Duck Bay, as noted in *Selkirk's Seventy-Fifth Anniversary*, ed. Elsie MacKay (Selkirk, MB: n.p., c. 1957), 63; Ellen Cooke, "Andrew Norquay Interview, Vancouver, 1959," Ellen Gillies Cooke Papers, file 1.

26 Healy, *Women of Red River*, 145–56.

27 Ibid., 145–46.

28 High Bluff History Book Committee, *Harvest of History: High Bluff and Area* (High Bluff, MB: High Bluff History Book Committee, 1998), 311.

29 "St. Andrews," Manitoba Parish Lot Files; I thank Roy Loewen for these notes.

30 "Journal of the Rev. W.H. Taylor of St. James Assiniboia, for the Qr Ending Sept 1859," entry of 27 August 1859, Ellen Gillies Cooke Papers, file 13; David Anderson to Henry Venn, 2 November 1853, CMS Papers, reel 31; William Taylor to E. Hawkins, 10 August 1857, in Schmidt, *Reports and Letters*, 38–39.

31 "Letters and Notes of Sr. Curran which Have Been Recopied in 1928: Jan 1868 to August 1885," entries dated August, September, and November 1868, March and April 1869, Ellen Gillies Cooke Papers, file 15.

32 Reverend J. Gardner to William Mactavish, 19 December 1868, and Rollin P. Meade to William Mactavish, 12 October 1868, Gertrude Ann Rhodes Collection, file 140; David Anderson to Robert Machray, 14 September 1868, EPRL Papers, file 2053.

33 *Nor'Wester*, 14 and 28 August 1860; Mary McCarthy Ferguson, *A History of St. James* (Winnipeg: St. James Historical Society, c. 1967), 56.

34 Margaret Arnett MacLeod, "A Note on the Red River Hunt by John Norquay," *Canadian Historical Review* 38, no. 2 (1957): 129–30; "Old Time Sketches: No. 1 The Buffalo Hunt," *Canadian North-West* 1, no. 1 (1880): 2–4.

35 Healy, *Women of Red River*, 149, 152–53, 155–56; George Colpitts, *Pemmican Empire: Food, Trade, and the Last Bison Hunts in the North American Plains, 1780–1882* (New York: Cambridge University Press, 2015), 7–12, 99–113.

36 Colpitts, *Pemmican Empire*, 219–54.

37 Healy, *Women of Red River*, 148–49; *Nor'Wester*, 15 October 1860.

38 Gibson, *Law, Life, and Government*, vol. 2, case 0606; Ellen Cooke, "Andrew Norquay Interview, Vancouver, 1959," Ellen Gillies Cooke Papers, file 1; MacKay, *Selkirk's Seventy-Fifth Anniversary*, 6; Manitoba Executive Council, *Order-in-Council Registers*, 18 December 1872; Margaret E. McBeth, "'Honest John' Norquay: Pioneer Statesman," in Legislative Library of Manitoba, Biographical Files.

39 Ellen Cooke, "Notes from Mr. Glen Stewart, July 1965," in Ellen Gillies Cooke Papers, file 6.

40 Alexander Ross, *The Red River Settlement: Its Rise, Progress, and Present State* (1856; reprinted, Edmonton: Hurtig, 1972); Brenda Macdougall and Nicole St-Onge, "Rooted in Mobility: Metis Buffalo Hunting Brigades," *Manitoba History* 71 (2013): http://mhs.mb.ca/docs/mb_history/71/metisbrigades.shtml.

41 Peter Erasmus, *Buffalo Days and Nights*, ed. Irene Spry (Calgary: Glenbow-Alberta Institute; Toronto: McClelland and Stewart, 1976), 201–4, 228–29; J.W. Taylor to J.L. Cadwalader, 22 July 1875, United States Consul (hereafter USC) Papers; *Nor'Wester*, 22 July 1875; *Manitoba Free Press*, 21 July 1875.

42 *Nor'Wester*, 14 July, 14 August, 28 August 1860; W.L. Morton, "The Battle at the Grand Coteau, July 13 and 14, 1851," Manitoba Historical Society *Transactions* Series 3, 16 (1959–60): http://mhs.mb.ca/docs/people/morton_wl.shtml; *Winnipeg Standard*, 2 June 1876, in J.W. Taylor to State Department, 1 August 1876, USC Papers.

43 E.H. Oliver, *The Canadian North-West: Its Early Development and Legislative Records*, 2 vols. (Ottawa: Government Printing Bureau, 1914), 1–32.

44 "Petitions, January 1863," Gertrude Ann Rhodes Collection, file 155; Gerhard J. Ens and Joe Sawchuk, *From New Peoples to New Nations: Aspects of Métis History and Identity from the Eighteenth to Twenty-First Centuries* (Toronto: University of Toronto Press, 2016), 93–102.

45 Donald Gunn to Philip VanKoughnet, 6 March 1857, Gertrude Ann Rhodes Collection, file 90; Thomas Spence, "Missing Links for the True Story of the Red River Troubles 1869–70 Containing Interesting Speeches by Riel and Others," unpublished manuscript, January 1890, Canadian Héritage, http://heritage.canadiana.ca/view/

oocihm.lac_reel_c1343/44?r=0&s=5 (accessed 17 February 2023); Henry George petition, 5 February 1869, Gertrude Ann Rhodes Collection, file 83.

46 "The Memorial of the Council of Manitobah in Rupert's Land, British North America," in Thomas Spence and the Council of LaPrairie to Lord Monck, 7 March 1868, Gertrude Ann Rhodes Collection, file 132; Spence, "Missing Links," 12; W.L. Morton, *Manitoba: A History* (1957; reprinted, Toronto: University of Toronto Press, 1967), 113–14.

47 Bruce Peel, "Spence, Thomas," in *Dictionary of Canadian Biography*, vol. 12, University of Toronto/Université Laval, 2003–, http://www.biographi.ca/en/bio/spence_thomas_1832_1900_12E.html (accessed 6 April 2023).

48 N.P. Langford to J.W. Taylor, 10/12 July 1870, USC Papers; John Ross testimony in Great Britain, House of Commons, *Report of the Select Committee on Hudson's Bay Company Lands, 1857* (London: Great Britain Colonial Office, 1858), 10–11.

49 Charles Mair to John Schultz, 10 May 1870, John Schultz Papers.

50 W. Mactavish to W.G. Smith, 10 August 1869, HBCA, A 12/45, folio 282–83.

51 W. Mactavish to James McKay, 11 June 1869, University of Manitoba Archives and Special Collections (hereafter UM), Barber-Arkin Collection.

52 Alexander Sandison, "St. Andrews Recollections," John Schultz Papers; John Gemmel to John Schultz, John Garrioch to John Schultz, and John Sutherland to John Schultz, 18 March 1871, John Schultz Papers, 8501–10, 7112, 7124.

53 Cited in W.L. Morton, "The Red River Parish: Its Place in the Development of Manitoba," in *Manitoba Essays Written in Commemoration of the Sixtieth Anniversary of the University of Manitoba*, ed. R.C. Lodge (Toronto: Macmillan, 1937), 97–98; Spence, "Manitoba Missing Links"; *Manitoban*, 12 February 1872.

54 G.A. Gemmill, ed., *Canadian Parliamentary Companion 1887* (Ottawa: J. Durie and Son, 1887), 333.

55 Norma Hall, Clifford P. Hall, and Erin Verrier, *A History of the Legislative Assembly of Assiniboia/Le conseil du gouvernement provisoire* (Winnipeg: Indian and Northern Affairs Canada, Manitoba Metis Federation, Government of Manitoba, c. 2010), 13.

56 "Election Returns, St. Margaret's Parish," Thomas Bunn Papers.

57 Archibald McDonald, "Nomination Meeting, High Bluff, 27 December 1870," in "Elections: Provincial 1870," AM, MG 14 F 1870; *Manitoban*, 4 January 1871; Ellen Cooke, "Norquays in the Red River Disturbances," *Manitoba Pageant* 21, no. 2 (1976): http://mhs.mb.ca/docs/pageant/21/norquays.shtml; T. Alcock to Adams Archibald, 1 November 1870, Adams Archibald Papers.

58 Cooke, "Norquays in the Red River Disturbances."

59 John Norquay [Sr.] to John Norquay [Jr.], 12 July 1876, 12 October 1882, NPP, A-207, A-1139, also 7 January 1886, 23 February 1886, NPP, C-1419, C-1535.

60 John C. Weaver, *The Great Land Rush and the Making of the Modern World, 1650–1900* (Montreal and Kingston: McGill-Queen's University Press, 2003), 18; Chester Martin, "The First 'New Province' of the Dominion," *Canadian Historical Review* 1, no. 4 (1920): 376–77.

61 Frank J. Tough, "Financializing a Junk Charter? British Capital and the Survival of the Mercantilist Hudson's Bay Company during the Age of High Imperialism, 1870–1914," paper presented to the Economic History Society, Keele University, 7 April 2018; Lisa Schaub, "Métis Communities in the Red River Settlement: Territory, Identity, Racialization, 1821–1926" (PhD diss., Universität Trier, 2019); Irene Spry, "The Great Transformation: The Disappearance of the Commons in Western Canada," in *Man and Nature on the Prairies*, ed. R.A. Allen (Regina: Canadian Plains Research Center, 1976), 21–45.

62 George Stanley, ed., "Le journal de l'abbé N.-J. Ritchot," quoted in Thomas Flanagan, *Metis Lands in Manitoba* (Calgary: University of Calgary Press, 1991), 36; the speech by James McKay is in Hall, "Legislative Assembly of Assiniboia," 18.

63 *Manitoban*, 12 February 1872; Adams Archibald to Joseph Howe, 27 December 1870, quoted in Flanagan, *Metis Lands*, 66–67; Ens and Sawchuk, *From New Peoples*, 151–53.

64 St. Andrews parish file, river lot 51, in HBC, Land Register Book B, HBCA; I thank Lisa Schaub, Trier University, for this information.

65 Mary Weekes, ed., *The Last Buffalo Hunter* (1939; reprinted, Saskatoon: Fifth House, 1994); W. Cockran to Secretaries, Church Missionary Society, 25 July 1833, in *The Prairie West to 1905*, ed. L.G. Thomas (Toronto: Oxford University Press, 1975), 35–36; Erasmus, *Buffalo Days and Nights*; Emile Pelletier, ed., *L'espace de Louis Goulet* (St. Boniface, MB: Éditions Bois-Brûlés, 1976); Gerhard J. Ens, ed., *A Son of the Fur Trade: The Memoirs of Johnny Grant* (Edmonton: University of Alberta Press, 2008); John Foster, "Paulet Paul: Métis or 'House Indian' Folk-Hero?," *Manitoba History* 9 (1985): http://mhs.mb.ca/docs/mb_history/09/pauletpaul.shtml; J.J. Gunn, "The Tripmen of Assiniboia," in *Echoes of the Red*, by J.J. Gunn (Toronto: Macmillan, 1930), 24–58.

Chapter 3: "The Transfer Made Us Wise," the 1870s

1 Quoted in Morton, *Manitoba*, 150.

2 James Benson to John Norquay, "Statement of Account 27 March 1876," NPP, A-214; Manitoba Carriage and Sleigh Factory, NPP, 1 October 1876, A-216; 1 June 1877, A-140; 1 September 1877, A-121; 6 January 1879, A-301; Archibald Wright, 3 July 1877, A-120; Andrew McNabb, 30 September 1880, A-586.

3 Ellen Cooke, "Andrew Norquay Interview, Vancouver, 1959," Ellen Gillies Cooke Papers, file 1.

4 Ibid.; William McLennan, trans., *Songs of Old Canada* (Montreal: Dawson Brothers, 1886); Ellen Cooke, "Information from Mrs. Elizabeth Aylen, 7 January 1986," Ellen Gillies Cooke Papers, file 3.

5 Ellen Cooke, "Information from Dr. H.C. Norquay in the Early 1950s," Ellen Gillies Cooke Papers, file 2; Ellen Cooke, "Telephone Conversation with Mrs. Alfred Savage in May 1965," Ellen Gillies Cooke Papers, file 5; Ellen Cooke, "March 1974 Letter from Mrs. Aylen," Ellen Gillies Cooke Papers, file 3; Ellen Cooke, "Andrew Norquay Interview, Vancouver, 1959," Ellen Gillies Cooke Papers, file 1.

6 Robert Machray to John Norquay, 31 March 1875, NPP, A-176; also see in NPP Christmas 1876, A-202; 13 June 1877, A-110; bills in 1877, A-149, A-151.

7 "Fine Character Removed by Death," unidentified news clipping in Thomas Norquay, "Scrapbook," Archives of Manitoba, MG13 C3–4; Bella's school accounts, 1879, NPP, A-167, A-278, A-373, A-501; "Minutes of the Corresponding Committee and Finance Committee 1850–1876," 23 October 1876, EPRL Papers; "Minutes of Council Meetings July 31st 1871–Oct 25th 1888," and "Minutes of College Council Meetings Jan 16 1889–Sept 5th 1923," SJC Papers, box 2, file UA 1.

8 "College Board Record Book, Item #2," SJC Papers, box 16, file UA 1.

9 Bella Norquay to John Norquay, 20 February 1880, NPP, A-397.

10 Ellen Cooke, "Mrs. Alfred Savage, May 1965," Ellen Gillies Cooke Papers, file 5; Alexander and Bryce Co. to John Norquay, 1 July 1879, NPP, A-285.

11 Thomas Norquay to John Norquay, 28 August 1881, NPP, A-794; Charles Adams to John Norquay, 11 and 14 January 1879, NPP, A-383.

12 Ontario Bank to John Norquay, 23 June 1877; NPP, A-132; *Manitoba Free Press*, 4 November 1878, 2 August 1879; *Quiz*, 16 and 27 November 1878.

13 Harris, Son and Company to John Norquay, 14 June 1881, NPP, 718; Lion Rake Company to John Norquay, 14 June 1881, NPP, 721; Marcel Giraud, *Le Métis canadien: Son rôle dans l'histoire des provinces de l'ouest* (Paris: Institut d'ethnologie, Musée de l'homme, 1945), 1127–28.

14 C.P. Brown to John Norquay, 1 November 1876, NPP, A-217; Alexander and Bryce Co. to John Norquay, 1 July 1879, NPP, A-285; J.H. Ashdown to John Norquay, 10 March 1877, NPP, A-141; J.A. Finney and Company to John Norquay, 17 November 1880, NPP, A-569.

15 William J. Healy, ed., *Women of Red River: Being a Book Written from the Recollections of Women Surviving from the Red River Era* (Winnipeg: Russell, Lang, 1923), 145–56; William Chambers to John Norquay, 26 November 1877, NPP, A-134; E.H.G.G. Hay to John Norquay, 31 August 1877, NPP, A-138.

16 Andrew Bannatyne to John Norquay, 31 December 1877, NPP, A-135.

17 A. Howard to John Norquay, 25 March 1878, NPP, A-10; W.N. Kennedy to John Norquay, 8 May 1877, NPP, A-128; Sun Life to John Norquay, 29 April 1876, NPP, A-205, and 12 April 1881, NPP, A-871; also see correspondence with Standard Life, Canada Life, Confederation Life, Equitable Life, Lion Life, and North American Life 1880–82 in NPP.

18 William Kennedy to John Norquay, 17 March 1879, NPP, A-347(a).

19 Charles Arkoll Boulton, *Reminiscences of the North-West Rebellions* (Toronto: n.p., 1886), 18, gives the average for men as five feet six or seven (170 cm). Estimates of Norquay's height varied from six feet one inch to six feet three inches (186 cm).

20 Charles Adams to John Norquay, 13 May 1875, NPP, A-188.

21 *Manitoban*, 8 February 1873; Ellen Cooke, "Telephone Conversation with Mrs. Alfred Savage in May 1965," Ellen Gillies Cooke Papers, file 5.

22 Andrew Spence to John Norquay, 8 April 1875, NPP, A-171; John James Setter to John Norquay, 1 April 1875, NPP, A-187; Charles Adams to John Norquay, 13 May 1875, NPP, A-188.

23 This paragraph is conjecture, not a precisely documented certainty; "Premier's Bible . . . Photocopied Page," Ellen Gillies Cooke Papers, file 7; John Setter to John Norquay, 11 September 1876, NPP, A-210.

24 Charles Adams to John Norquay, 9 January 1878, NPP, A-6; Charles Adams to John Norquay, 23 October 1879, NPP, A-333a; W.W. Ogilvie to John Norquay, 22 April 1879, NPP, A-342; William Kennedy to John Norquay, 1 March 1879, NPP, A-321; Bella Norquay to John Norquay, 8 March 1879, NPP, A-315.

25 Various bills, NPP.

26 *Manitoba Public Accounts* (1871–79); *Manitoban*, 6 May 1871, 26 February 1872, 8 March 1873; Alex Begg to John Norquay, 10 June 1876, NPP, A-206; *Manitoba Free Press*, 11 May 1875, 3 February 1876; as a point of comparison, a janitor in the provincial buildings was paid $300 in 1875.

27 Robert Machray to John Norquay, 13 and 18 June 1877, NPP, A-110; fees noted in NPP, A-149, A-167, A-366, A-373, A-501, A-646.

28 Bernard Saunders to John Norquay, 11 May 1878, NPP, A-30; 25 September 1879, A-332; 1 December 1879, A-330.

29 John Bain to John Norquay, 31 July 1877, NPP, no number; C. Sweeney to John Norquay, 15 October 1879, NPP, A-323; Manitoba Curling Club to John Norquay, 11 November 1877, NPP, A-139.

30 Clarke and McClure Co. to John Norquay, 11 October 1875, NPP, A-180; W.G. Clark to John Norquay, 2 October 1875, NPP, A-166; Mrs. George Bryce, "Historical Sketch of the Charitable Institutions of Winnipeg," Historical and Scientific Society of Manitoba *Transaction* 54 (1899): 4; Michel Duclos to John Norquay, 15 August 1877, NPP, A-109; Daniel Matheson to John Norquay, 28 February 1880, NPP, A-799; James Snell to John Norquay, 18 May 1880, NPP, A-525; I am indebted to Randy Rostecki, who shared with me his research on Norquay's Winnipeg land dealings.

31 A "scrip" was a certificate issued by the federal government that entitled the bearer to a grant of land, in this case under Sections 31 and 32 of the Manitoba Act. These grants were intended to quiet concerns about property rights. J.S. Dennis, "Papers Relating

to Half Breed and Other Claims Received This Day from the Hon Jno. Norquay, 1 February 1881," NPP, A-849. Diametrically opposed interpretations of the federal land policy and its consequences are D.N. Sprague, *Canada and the Métis, 1869–1885* (Waterloo, ON: Wilfrid Laurier University Press, 1988), and Thomas Flanagan, *Metis Lands in Manitoba* (Calgary: University of Calgary Press, 1991).

32 Promissory notes in NPP, A-125, A-196, A-209a, A-211, A-212a, A-212b, A-257, A-356, A-276b, A-571c, and A-789a–c; Norquay signed four notes in the spring and summer of 1876, two in the summer and fall of 1877, one in the fall of 1879, and two in the fall and early winter of 1880, suggesting that the financial problems were more or less continuous; on payment in kind, see R. Gerrie & Co. to John Norquay, 2 November 1876, NPP, A-196, A-197, and A-199.

33 Duncan Setter to John Norquay, 21 March and 28 August 1875, NPP, A-168, A-169; John Setter to John Norquay, 6 April 1875, NPP, A-185; John James Setter to John Norquay, 1 April 1875, NPP, A-187, and 22 November 1880, NPP, A-445; John Lazarus Norquay to John Norquay, 28 November 1879, NPP, A-256; James Adams to John Norquay, 4 March 1878, NPP, A-1.

34 Craig Venter, quoted in Ali Rattansi, *Racism: A Very Short Introduction*, 2nd ed. (Oxford: Oxford University Press, 2020), 37.

35 Ibid., 37; E.J. Hobsbawm, *The Age of Capital 1848–1875* (New York: Charles Scribner's Sons, 1975), 264–68; E.J. Hobsbawm, *The Age of Empire 1875–1914* (London: Weidenfeld and Nicolson, 1987), 32, 252–54.

36 Catherine Hall, "The Racist Ideas of Slave Owners Are Still with Us Today," *Guardian* [London], 27 September 2016; Catherine Hall, "Introduction," in *Cultures of Empire: Colonizers in Britain and the Empire in the Nineteenth and Twentieth Centuries: A Reader*, ed. Catherine Hall (Manchester: Manchester University Press, 2000), 1–33; Adam Gaudry, "Respecting Métis Nationhood and Self-Determination in Matters of Métis Identity," in *Aboriginal History: A Reader*, 2nd ed., ed. Kristin Burnett and Geoff Read (Don Mills, ON: Oxford University Press, 2016), 152–63; David Olusoga, "The Ties That Bind Us," https://www.theguardian.com/news/ng-interactive/2023/mar/28/slavery-and-the-guardian-the-ties-that-bind-us (accessed 1 May 2023).

37 F.W. Chesson, "On Manitoba," in *Proceedings of the Royal Colonial Institute*, vol. 3 (London: Royal Colonial Institute, 1873), 113; Adams Archibald, in *Proceedings of the Royal Colonial Institute 1883–84* (London: Royal Colonial Institute, 1884), 208; I thank Jean Friesen for these references. Margaret Schultz, "Fault Lines: Race and Gender in the Fur Trade Family of Alexander Ross," *Manitoba History* 90 (2019): 15.

38 John Norquay to John A. Macdonald, 19 March 1873, Macdonald Papers; Robert Davis to John Norquay, 18 November 1875, NPP, A-178.

39 David Mills to John Norquay, 18 December 1877, and David Mills to George Bryce, 8 February 1878, Western University Archives, David Mills Papers, Letterbook 2, 615, 926; I thank Dr. Ryan Eyford for copies of these letters; *Manitoba Free Press*, 13 December 1878.

40 Samuel Bedson to John Norquay, 14 March 1878, NPP, A-8; *Manitoba Free Press*, 29 December 1877.

41 John Norquay to John A. Macdonald, 2 April 1879, Macdonald Papers, 164744.

42 Quoted in Nicole J.M. St-Onge, *Saint-Laurent, Manitoba: Evolving Métis Identities, 1850–1914* (Regina: Canadian Plains Research Center, 2004), 31–32; Nicole J.M. St-Onge, "Uncertain Margins: Métis and Saulteaux Identities in St-Paul des Saulteaux—Red River 1821–1870," *Manitoba History* 53 (2006): 1–10; I thank Robert Nelson for information on William Wagner; Robert L. Nelson, "A German on the Prairies: Max Sering and Settler Colonialism in Canada," *Settler Colonial Studies* 5, no. 1 (2015): 1–19.

43 *Manitoba Free Press*, 17 April 1875; Gilbert McMicken to Alexander Morris, "Report of Gilbert McMicken . . . into the Circumstances of the Killing of an Indian [Portage la Prairie] by the Sioux Band on 6 August 1875," Manitoba, GR Series, G8113; Peter Douglas Elias, *The Dakota of the Canadian Northwest: Lessons for Survival* (Winnipeg: University of Manitoba Press, 1988), 37–53.

44 *Manitoba Free Press*, 29 January 1876.

45 *Manitoba Free Press*, 3 February 1876.

46 James McKay to John Norquay, 27 June 1878, NPP, A-20, and 25 November 1878, NPP, A-21; W.W. Ogilvie to John Norquay [1878], NPP, A-194; J.W. Taylor to John Cadwalader, 1 August 1876, enclosed clipping from the *Winnipeg Standard*, 2 June 1876, subsequently reprinted in the Montreal *Gazette*, Toronto *Globe*, and St. Paul *Press*, United States Consular Despatches.

47 William Kennedy to John Norquay, 17 March 1879, NPP, A-347a.

48 J.N. [Norquay], "Sauteaux Indians," *Dominion Illustrated: A Canadian Pictorial Weekly*, 14 September 1889, 166.

49 Ibid.

50 [John Norquay], "Notes on Early Days in Manitoba," NPP, G8731.

51 John Setter to John Norquay, 24 November 1879, NPP, A-371; John Norquay and John Schultz to J.C. Aikins, 12 August 1879, NPP, A-286.

52 John Setter to John Norquay, 1 November 1879, NPP, A-328; Andrew Spence to John Norquay, 6 April 1875, NPP, A-33; 8 April 1875, A-171; 26 February 1878, A-173; S.L. Bedson to J.G. Moylan, 19 February 1879, NPP, A-198; Marchioness of Dufferin and Ava, *My Canadian Journal 1872–8* (London: John Murray, 1891), 327; Alexander Sinclair to John Norquay, 29 March 1879, NPP, A-367.

53 *Manitoba Free Press*, 14 July 1874.

54 *New Nation*, 4 February 1870, cited in W.L. Morton, "The Red River Parish: Its Place in the Development of Manitoba," in *Manitoba Essays Written in Commemoration of the Sixtieth Anniversary of the University of Manitoba*, ed. R.C. Lodge (Toronto: Macmillan, 1937), 97.

55 Nicole J.M. St-Onge and Carolyn Podruchny, "Scuttling along a Spider's Web: Mobility and Kinship in Métis Ethnogenesis," in *Contours of a People: Metis Family, Mobility, and History*, ed. Nicole J.M. St-Onge, Carolyn Podruchny, and Brenda Macdougall (Norman: University of Oklahoma Press, 2012), 59–92; Brenda Macdougall, *One of the Family: Métis Culture in Nineteenth-Century Northwestern Saskatchewan* (Vancouver: UBC Press, 2010).

56 George J. Mountain, *The Journal of the Bishop of Montreal during a Visit to the Church Missionary Society's North-West America Mission* (London: Seeleys, 1849), 57; Henry Venn to David Anderson, 3 April 1851, EPRL Papers, box P338.

57 Gerhard Ens and Joe Sawchuk, *From New Peoples to New Nations: Aspects of Métis History and Identity from the Eighteenth to Twenty-First Centuries* (Toronto: University of Toronto Press, 2016), 87–89.

58 "Petitions, January 1863," Gertrude Ann Rhodes Collection, file 155; Letitia Hargrave to Flora, 7 July 1853, Hargrave Papers, LAC; "Extracts from Governor Simpson's Dispatches of 1825," in "Red River Documents," Archer Martin Papers, file 2/14.

59 James McKay speech, cited in Norma Hall, Clifford P. Hall, and Erin Verrier, *A History of the Legislative Assembly of Assiniboia/Le Conseil du Gouvernement Provisoire* (Winnipeg: Indian and Northern Affairs Canada, Manitoba Metis Federation, and Government of Manitoba, c. 2010), 18.

60 John Schultz, "Indians of the Canadian North-West," in Canada, House of Commons 1873, read into the record in *Canada Senate Debates*, 16 April 1885, vol. 1, 587–96; the issues are considered in Jennifer Hayter, "Racially 'Indian,' Legally 'White': The Canadian State's Struggles to Categorize the Métis, 1850–1900" (PhD diss., University of Toronto, 2017).

61 George F.G. Stanley et al., eds., *The Collected Writings of Louis Riel*, 5 vols. (Edmonton: University of Alberta Press, 1985); Jean Teillet, *The North-West Is Our Mother: The Story of Louis Riel's People, the Métis Nation* (Toronto: HarperCollins Canada, 2019); Ens and Sawchuk, *From New Peoples*, 92–129; M. Max Hamon, *The Audacity of His Enterprise: Louis Riel and the Métis Nation that Canada Never Was, 1840–1875* (Montreal and Kingston: McGill-Queen's University Press, 2020); Max Hamon, "Contesting Civilization: Louis Riel's Defence of Culture at the Collège de Montréal," *Canadian Historical Review* 97, no. 1 (2016): 58–87; Albert Braz, *The False Traitor: Louis Riel in Canadian Culture* (Toronto: University of Toronto Press, 2003); Thomas Flanagan, *Louis "David" Riel: "Prophet of the New World,"* rev. ed. (Toronto: University of Toronto Press, 1996); Thomas Flanagan, "The Political Thought of Louis Riel," in *Riel and the Metis: Riel Mini-Conference Papers*, ed. A.S. Lussier (Winnipeg: Manitoba Metis Federation Press, 1979), 131–60; Gilles Martel, *Le messianisme de Louis Riel* (Waterloo, ON: Wilfrid Laurier University Press, 1984).

62 Sister Curran, "Journal, August 1876," 221, in Ellen Cooke, "Letters and Notes of Sr. Curran [copied in 1928] January 1868 to August 1885," from Archives of the Grey Nuns, St. Boniface, Ellen Gillies Cooke Papers, file 15.

63 In some of his writings, Riel did leave open the possibility of a French-English Métis alliance, notably in infrequent references to a Métis "race" in which was mingled White and Indian "blood"; see George F.G. Stanley, ed., *The Collected Writings of Louis Riel*, vol. 1 (Edmonton: University of Alberta Press, 1985), 88–93, document 1-060.

64 *Manitoban*, 7 December 1872.

65 Ibid.; Sarah Carter, "Macdonald, Allan," in *Dictionary of Canadian Biography*, vol. 13, University of Toronto/Université Laval, 2003–, http://www.biographi.ca/en/bio/macdonald_allan_13E.html (accessed 7 April 2023).

66 *Manitoban*, 7 December 1872.

67 Phillip Buckner, "Whatever Happened to the British Empire?," *Journal of the Canadian Historical Association* (1993): 27; G. Denison to John Schultz, 28 January 1871, John Schultz Papers, box 15; the context is discussed in Carl Berger, *The Sense of Power: Studies in the Ideas of Canadian Imperialism, 1867–1914* (Toronto: University of Toronto Press, 1970), and Doug Owram, *Promise of Eden: The Canadian Expansionist Movement and the Idea of the West, 1856–1900* (Toronto: University of Toronto Press, 1980).

68 Canada, Census of Manitoba 1870, "How the Census Was Collected," https://www.bac-lac.gc.ca/eng/census/1870/Pages/about-census.aspx (accessed 20 March 2020); Canada, The Manitoba Act, 1870, https://justice.gc.ca/eng/rp-pr/csj-sjc/constitution/lawreg-loireg/p1t21.html; Henry Clarke and Ed Hay, speeches in the Legislative Assembly of Manitoba, *Manitoban*, 12 February 1872; Auguste-Henri de Trémaudan, *Histoire de la nation métisse dans l'ouest canadien* (Montréal: Éditions Albert Lévesque, 1935), 379.

69 Robert Ruttan to Archer Martin, 11 July 1894, Archer Martin Papers, box 1, file 5; the sweeping implications of the Canadian nation-state's arrival are noted in Chris Andersen, *"Métis": Race, Recognition, and the Struggle for Indigenous Peoplehood* (Vancouver: UBC Press, 2014), and Bruce Curtis, *The Politics of Population: State Formation, Statistics, and the Census of Canada, 1840–1875* (Toronto: University of Toronto Press, 2002); the broader context is set out in Benedict Anderson, *Imagined Communities: Reflections on the Origin and Spread of Nationalism* (London: Verso, 1991), and James C. Scott, *The Art of Not Being Governed: An Anarchist History of Upland Southeast Asia* (New Haven, CT: Yale University Press, 2009).

70 For example, A.H. Whitcher to Joseph Tait, 29 April 1881, NPP, A-896 and A-819; Robert Adams to John Norquay, 2 November 1875, NPP, A-189; John Norquay to Duncan McLean, 15 September 1885, NPP, Letterbook E, 666; John Norquay to H.H. Smith, NPP, Letterbook E, 667; John Norquay to Thomas White, 21 May 1886, NPP, Letterbook 4, 29–30; John Setter to John Norquay, 28 May 1880, NPP, A-617; and Andrew Spence to John Norquay, 8 September 1875, NPP, A-170, and 6 December 1875, NPP, A-172.

71 The federal government's administration of these lands was judged not to have upheld "the honour of the Crown" by the Supreme Court of Canada in 2013; see https://scc-csc.lexum.com/scc-csc/scc-csc/en/item/12888/index.do (accessed 20 March

2020); Elizabeth's scrip certificate and affidavits are in LAC, RG15-D-II-8-a, vol./box 1323, microfilm C-14931; I thank Gerhard Ens for copies of these documents; Ens and Sawchuk, *From New Peoples*, 145–47.

72 I thank Annette Kaserbauer (Winnipeg) and Sharon Tremeer (Morden), of the Property Registry, who managed these document searches. I also thank Professor Gerhard Ens, of the University of Alberta Department of History, for his advice while I was trying to unravel the details of the Norquay family land transactions. The date of the grant in each case was 17 October 1878. Under "remarks," the clerk wrote "patent handed to the Hon John Norquay 1st Feb 1886." On this date, as other records attest, Norquay was in Ottawa negotiating with Sir John A. Macdonald on several matters. I discuss the outcome in Chapter 13.

73 Hayter, "Racially 'Indian'"; the label "Métis" was more likely to be used as a single term designating the peoplehood with the passage of the repatriated Constitution of Canada in 1982. How to define and establish membership remained a point of debate.

74 The Manitoba assembly sitting of 25 February 1873 passed a resolution directed to the governor general of Canada asking that a land grant be made to "all old settlers and their descendants, of unmixed blood"; *Manitoban*, 8 March 1873.

75 Willie Traill to Annie [1867], in *Fur Trade Letters of Willie Traill 1864–1893*, ed. K. Douglas Munro (Edmonton: University of Alberta Press, 2006), 73; Thomas Spence to William McTavish, 7 March 1868, Archer Martin Papers, box 1, file 34; Gerhard J. Ens, *Homeland to Hinterland: The Changing Worlds of the Red River Metis in the Nineteenth Century* (Toronto: University of Toronto Press, 1996), 127.

76 Henrietta Black to James Ross, [c. 1854], Alexander Ross Family Papers, 495.

77 Charles-Joseph Camper to A.-A. Taché, 24 November 1870, Bishop A.-A. Taché Papers; St-Onge, *Saint-Laurent*, 31–32; St-Onge, "Uncertain Margins," 1–10.

78 F. McPhillips to A.-A. Taché, 6 August 1878, Bishop A.-A. Taché Papers, T20693, and 27 August 1878, T20732 Baptist Spence to John Norquay, 16 June 1875, NPP, A-174.

79 See the words of Donald Smith and Joseph Lemay in the *Manitoban*, 8 March 1873.

80 *Manitoban*, 8 and 15 March 1873; *Le Métis*, 5 April 1873; *Manitoba Free Press*, 21 February 1877; Gerhard Ens, "Métis Lands in Manitoba," *Manitoba History* 5 (1983), http://www.mhs.mb.ca/docs/mb_history/05/metislands.shtml; David Burley, "The Emergence of the Premiership," in *Manitoba Premiers of the 19th and 20th Centuries*, ed. Barry Ferguson and Robert Wardhaugh (Regina: CPRC Press, 2010), 2–28.

81 Kenneth McKenzie, diary entry of 20 February 1877, Kenneth McKenzie Papers; *Manitoba Free Press*, 21 February 1877; Andrew Spence to John Norquay, 8 April 1875, NPP, A-173.

82 R.C. Macleod, *The NWMP and Law Enforcement 1873–1905* (Toronto: University of Toronto Press, 1976), 21–32; Owram, *Promise of Eden*; Donald B. Smith, *Seen but Not Seen: Influential Canadians and the First Nations from the 1840s to Today* (Toronto: University of Toronto Press, 2021); John Schultz, "Indians of the Canadian

North-West," in Canada, House of Commons 1873, read into the record in *Canada Senate Debates*, 16 April 1885, vol. 1, 587–96.

83 George Stewart, *Canada under the Administration of the Earl of Dufferin* (Toronto: Rose-Belford, 1878), 549–50; William Leggo, *The History of the Administration of the Right Honorable Frederick Temple, Earl of Dufferin* (Montreal: Lovell, 1878), 605–6.

84 J.W. Taylor to Secretary of State Seward, 21 and 26 March 1878, United States Consular Despatches; Jacinthe Duval, "The Catholic Church and the Formation of Metis Identity," *Past Imperfect* [University of Alberta] 9 (2001): 69.

85 William Kennedy to John Norquay, 1 March 1879, NPP, A-321, 17 and 18 March 1879, NPP, A-347(a)(b).

86 William Kennedy to John Norquay, 1 March 1879, NPP, A-321; *Manitoban*, 8 February 1873; John Norquay to guests, including Captain Kennedy, 17 March 1885, NPP, E-29; Ellen Cooke, "Information from Mrs. J. E. McAllister, March 9, 1946," Ellen Gillies Cooke Papers, file 4.

87 Henry Clarke speech, *Manitoban*, 22 January 1872, 8 March 1873.

88 Stewart, *Canada under the Administration*, 517 ff.; Marchioness of Dufferin, *Journal*, 344; John Darwin, *The Empire Project: The Rise and Fall of the British World-System 1830–1970* (Cambridge, UK: Cambridge University Press, 2009), 144–52; Berger, *The Sense of Power*; Buckner, "Whatever Happened to the British Empire?"; Phillip Buckner, "The Creation of the Dominion of Canada, 1860–1901," in *Canada and the British Empire*, ed. Phillip Buckner (Oxford: Oxford University Press, 2008), 66–67; Andrew Gailey, *The Lost Imperialist: Lord Dufferin, Memory and Mythmaking in an Age of Celebrity* (London: John Murray, 2015), 121–52; Sarah Carter, "'Your Great Mother across the Salt Sea': Prairie First Nations, the British Monarchy and the Vice Regal Connection to 1900," *Manitoba History* 48 (2005–06), http://www.mhs.mb.ca/docs/mb_history/48/greatmother.shtml.

89 *Manitoba Free Press*, 25 August 1877; Marchioness of Dufferin, *Journal*, 328; Stewart, *Canada under the Administration*, 517–50; Leggo, *The History of the Administration*, 594.

90 Ellen Cooke, "Caroline Savage Interview," May 1965, Ellen Gillies Cooke Papers, file 5; James McKay to John Norquay, 27 June 1878, NPP, A-20.

91 *Manitoba Free Press*, 25 August 1877; Stewart, *Canada under the Administration*, 517–50; Leggo, *The History of the Administration*, 594; Marchioness of Dufferin, *Journal*, 312–68; Barry Potyondi, *Selkirk: The First Hundred Years* (Winnipeg: Josten's/National School Services, 1981), 9–26.

92 Marchioness of Dufferin, *Journal*, 328.

93 James Sanderson to John Norquay, 10 July 1879, NPP, A-338; Charles Adams to John Norquay, 9 and 31 August 1881, NPP, A-772; James Brown to John Norquay, 10 October 1880, NPP, A-485; a "cockie" in this context refers to British Ontarians; in old British usage, the word denoted a farmer.

94 Alexander Sinclair to John Norquay, 29 March 1879, NPP, A-367.

Chapter 4: Public Life: An Introduction, 1871–74

1 James Wickes Taylor to Jefferson Davis, 6 January 1871, USC Papers (microfilm copy).

2 *Manitoba Free Press*, 11 March 1929, citing William Coldwell in *Manitoban*, 15 March 1871; *Report of the Department of Public Works for the Province of Manitoba from 1870 to 30th June 1874* (Winnipeg: Nor'Wester Printing, 1875); David Grebstad, "A Tale of Two Houses: The Rise and Demise of the Legislative Council of Manitoba, 1871–1876," *Manitoba History* 75 (2014): Manitoba History (mhs.mb.ca).

3 Adams Archibald to John A. Macdonald, 7 October 1871, quoted in John T. Saywell, *The Office of Lieutenant-Governor: A Study in Canadian Government and Politics* (Toronto: University of Toronto Press, 1957), 68–69; K.G. Pryke, "Archibald, Sir Adams George," in *Dictionary of Canadian Biography*, vol. 12, University of Toronto/ Université Laval, 2003–, accessed April 8, 2023, http://www.biographi.ca/en/bio/archibald_adams_george_12E.html; Allen Neil Ronaghan, "The Archibald Administration in Manitoba 1870–72" (PhD diss., University of Manitoba, 1987); David Burley, "The Emergence of the Premiership, 1870–74," in *Manitoba Premiers of the 19th and 20th Centuries*, ed. Barry Ferguson and Robert Wardhaugh (Regina: CPRC Press, 2010), 10; *St. Paul Weekly Press*, 6 October 1870; Allen Ronaghan, "James Farquharson—Agent and Agitator," *Manitoba History* 17 (1989): http://mhs.mb.ca/docs/mb_history/17/farquharson_j.shtml; James Wickes Taylor to Jefferson Davis, 21 February and 4 March 1871, USC Papers; *Manitoban*, 4 March 1871.

4 *Manitoban*, 18 March 1871.

5 *Rules, Orders, and Forms of Proceeding of the Legislative Assembly of Manitoba* (St. Boniface, MB: *Le Métis*, 1877). I thank Mel Myers for the gift of Norquay's personal copy.

6 *Manitoban*, 25 March and 1 April 1871.

7 *Manitoban*, 18 March, 29 April, 6 May 1871; Ens, *Homeland to Hinterland*, 140–44; John Schultz to J. McDougall, 23 April 1869, and Charles Mair to John Schultz, 10 May 1870, John Schultz Papers.

8 John James Setter to John Schultz, 19 April 1871, and John Gemmill to editor of *Newsletter*, 12 March 1871, John Schultz Papers; *Manitoban*, 15 and 29 April, 6 May 1871; Dale C. Thomson, *Alexander Mackenzie: Clear Grit* (Toronto: Macmillan, 1960), 132.

9 *Manitoban*, 6 May 1871.

10 G.W. Hill to John Norquay and Francis Ogletree, 17 and 19 May 1871; John Norquay and Francis Ogletree to Adams Archibald, 24 May 1871; John Norquay to Dr. J.H. O'Donnell, 30 May 1871; Adams Archibald to Francis Ogletree and John Norquay, 3 June 1871 (304, 308, 316, 329, 341), all in Adams Archibald Papers; G.E. Greenlay, "Diary," entries for 17, 18, and 19 May and 17 June 1871, G.E. Greenlay Papers; *Manitoban*, 16 January 1872.

11 Sociologist Michael Mann argues that the purpose of the state is to maintain internal order within a bounded community, sustain defence and justice systems, ensure internal communications, and guide economic practices. Michael Mann, *States, War and Capitalism: Studies in Political Sociology* (Oxford: Blackwell, 1988). See also Debra Thompson, *The Schematic State: Race, Transnationalism, and the Politics of the Census* (Cambridge: Cambridge University Press, 2016).

12 John Norquay to Dr. O'Donnell, 30 May 1871, Adams Archibald Papers, 316.

13 William MacTavish to James McKay, 11 June 1869, Harold and Sheila Arkin Collection.

14 John Norquay to Adams Archibald, 27 December 1871, Adams Archibald Papers, 548.

15 *Manitoba Gazette*, 26 June 1871, John A. Macdonald Papers, 77932; *Manitoban*, 3 May, 6 May, 1 July, and 26 August 1871, 26 February 1872; "Draft Pages re Provincial Expenditures and Needed Increases," February 1881, NPP, A-837.

16 Donald A. Smith, "List of Arms, Ammunition and Accoutrements Received by the 1st or Hudson's Bay Rifles, Captain Donald A. Smith, 4 October 1871," BCA, Gertrude Ann Rhodes Collection, file 106.

17 John Norquay, "Letterbook 1879," 107–24, John Norquay Papers, file 1; for context, see Elsbeth Heaman, *Tax, Order and Good Government: A New Political History of Canada 1867–1917* (Montreal and Kingston: McGill-Queen's University Press, 2017).

18 *Manitoban*, 22 April 1871; An Act to Incorporate the Dean and Chapter of St. John's Cathedral Church, *Statutes of Manitoba 1874.*

19 Irene Spry, "The Great Transformation: The Disappearance of the Commons in Western Canada," in *Man and Nature on the Prairies*, ed. R.A. Allen (Regina: Canadian Plains Research Center, 1976), 21–45; for context, see Tim Rogan, *The Moral Economists: R.H. Tawney, Karl Polanyi, E.P. Thompson and the Critique of Capitalism* (Princeton, NJ: Princeton University Press, 2017).

20 A.G. Archibald to Joseph Howe, 27 December 1870, quoted in Thomas Flanagan, *Metis Lands in Manitoba* (Calgary: University of Calgary Press, 1991), 66–67.

21 *Manitoban*, 1, 22, and 29 April 1871.

22 *Manitoban*, 4, 8 March 1873, 4 March 1872.

23 Marc-Amable Girard, "Report of the Select Committee to Enquire into the Causes of the Difficulties in the North West in 1869 and 1870," cited in Burley, "The Emergence of the Premiership," 9–10; R.B. Hill, *Manitoba: History of Its Early Settlement, Development and Resources* (Winnipeg: Russell, Land and Company, 1923), 343; James Wickes Taylor to Jefferson Davis, 4 October and 21 November 1871, USC Papers; L. Wheaton to J.W. Taylor, 12 October 1871, USC Papers.

24 John James Setter to John Schultz, 19 April 1871, John Schultz Papers.

25 Hill, *Manitoba*, 343.

26 "Copy of Resolutions Presented by Delegates to His Excellency the Lieutenant Governor of Manitoba on Friday 1st Decr. 1871," in Adams Archibald to Joseph Howe, 2 December 1871, Dispatch 302, Canada, Secretary of State for the Provinces, AM, reel M24; I thank Dale Gibson for this reference; Gilbert McMicken to John A. Macdonald, 13 October 1871, John A. Macdonald Papers, 25011.

27 "Copy of Resolutions . . . 1st Decr. 1871."

28 Adams Archibald to John A. Macdonald, 13 and 16 December 1871, John A. Macdonald Papers (with thanks to Dale Gibson for this reference); James Wickes Taylor to Jefferson Davis, 1 December 1871, USC Papers; Ronald B.C. Montgomery, "The Premiers of Manitoba," *Canadian Magazine* 9, no. 5 (1897): 386–95; Joseph Dubuc to H. Prévost, 23 April 1871, Fonds Société historique de Saint-Boniface (hereafter SHSB), série documentation, personnages, boite 7, file 256; Diane Payment, "Joseph Dubuc et les développements politiques au Manitoba 1870–1885," unpublished essay, Fonds SHSB, série documentation, personnages, boite 7, file 258, "Joseph Dubuc"; Joseph Dubuc, *Mémoires d'un Manitoban* (Rome: np, 1912), 86, in Joseph Dubuc Papers.

29 Adams Archibald to John A. Macdonald, 25 November 1871, 12 September 1871, John A. Macdonald Papers, 78053, 77948.

30 Adams Archibald to John A. Macdonald, 12 September 1871, 25 November 1871, John A. Macdonald Papers, 77948, 78045; John Finlay, "Boyd, Alfred," in *Dictionary of Canadian Biography*, vol. 13, University of Toronto/Université Laval, 2003–, accessed April 8, 2023, http://www.biographi.ca/en/bio/boyd_alfred_13E.html; *Le Métis*, 23 and 30 November 1871, 11 January 1872; *Manitoban*, 18 November and 16 December 1871; Joseph Royal to A.-A. Taché, 26 November 1871, Bishop A.-A. Taché Papers, T9654.

31 Adams Archibald to John A. Macdonald, 28 May, 9 August, 12 September, and 25 November 1871, 24 February 1872, John A. Macdonald Papers, 77909, 77941, 77948, 78045, 78146; Lovell C. Clark, "Clarke, Henry Joseph," in *Dictionary of Canadian Biography* vol. 11, University of Toronto/Université Laval, 2003–, http://www.biographi.ca/en/bio/clarke_henry_joseph_11E.html (accessed 8 April 2023).

32 Adams Archibald to John A. Macdonald, 13 December 1871, John A. Macdonald Papers, 78066.

33 Finlay, "Boyd"; Adams Archibald to John A. Macdonald, 16 December 1871, John A. Macdonald Papers.

34 "Oath of Office and Oath of Allegiance," John Norquay Papers; Ellen Cooke, "John Norquay Biographical," Ellen Gillies Cooke Papers, file 7.

35 "Norquay's Appointment: From a Canadian Point of View," *Manitoba Liberal*, 26 January 1872.

36 Adams Archibald to Secretary of State for the Provinces, 24 March 1871, John A. Macdonald Papers, 78025; Adams Archibald to Joseph Howe, 24 March and 23 November 1871, Despatches 130 and 301, AM, microfilm reel M24 (a collection of

documents from LAC denominated RG6, C1, vol. 24; I thank Professor Dale Gibson for these references); Adams Archibald to John A. Macdonald, 16 December 1871, John A. Macdonald Papers.

37 *Manitoban*, 16 December 1871; John E. Kendle, "Mulvey, Stewart," in *Dictionary of Canadian Biography*, vol. 13, University of Toronto/Université Laval, 2003–, http://www.biographi.ca/en/bio/mulvey_stewart_13E.html (accessed 8 April 2023); *Le Métis*, 21 December 1871, 11 January 1872.

38 John Norquay to E.L. Barber, 18 December 1871, E.L. Barber Papers; *Manitoban*, 30 December 1871; John A. Macdonald to Adams Archibald, 28 December 1871, John A. Macdonald Papers, LB 16, 687.

39 Henry J. Morgan, ed., *Canadian Parliamentary Companion 1873* (Montreal: Lovell, 1873), 459; Saywell, *The Office of Lieutenant-Governor*, 60–79; Burley, "The Emergence of the Premiership."

40 Carol Norquay Stoddart, interview with author, Toronto, 2012; Ellen Cooke, "Andrew Norquay Interview, Vancouver, 1959," Ellen Gillies Cooke Papers, file 1; "Premier's Bible . . . Photocopied Page," Ellen Gillies Cooke Papers, file 7.

41 *Manitoban and Northwest Herald*, 28 June 1873; George Bryce, *A History of Manitoba: Its Resources and People* (Toronto: Canadian History Company, 1906), 368.

42 Manitoba Executive Council, "Draft Minutes," 1872–73, Alexander Morris Papers, numerous instances in 1757 and 1785; *Le Métis*, 17 February, 2 March, 1 May, 12 June, and 17 July 1872, 5 April 1873; *Manitoban*, 14 September 1872; Louis de Plainval to John Norquay, 12 and 17 February 1872, Manitoba Provincial Police Papers, 29, 32; *Manitoba Free Press*, 14 July 1874; *Manitoban*, 8 March 1873.

43 *Manitoban*, 8 March 1873.

44 *Report of the Department of Public Works for the Province of Manitoba from 1870 to 30th June 1874* (Winnipeg: Nor'Wester Printing, 1875), 1–9.

45 *Manitoban*, 16 and 29 January 1872; Burley, "The Emergence of the Premiership."

46 *Manitoban*, 5 and 12 February 1872; for context, see Robert Tombs and Isabelle Tombs, *That Sweet Enemy: The French and the British from the Sun King to the Present* (London: Heinemann, 2006).

47 *Manitoban*, 5 and 12 February 1872.

48 *Manitoban*, 12 February 1872.

49 *Manitoban*, 22 January and 5 and 12 February 1872.

50 Adams Archibald to Alexander Morris, 17 December 1872, Alexander Morris Papers.

51 *Manitoba Daily Free Press*, 23 October 1875.

52 H. George to Finance Committee, 26 February 1872, EPRL Papers; John Norquay to Alexander Morris, 12 December 1872, Alexander Morris Papers; *Le Métis*, 17 February 1872; *High Bluff Minute Book of L.O.L.* [Loyal Orange Lodge] *No. 1354*, Portage

Collegiate Institute archive. I thank James Kostuchuk for the opportunity to read this rare document.

53 John James Setter to John Schultz, 19 April 1871, John Schultz Papers.

54 J.B. Proulx to A.-A. Taché, 2 February 1871, Bishop A.-A. Taché Papers, T8500; Joseph Royal to A.-A. Taché, Bishop A.-A. Taché Papers, T9817; Jean Hamelin, "Taché, Alexandre-Antonin," in *Dictionary of Canadian Biography*, vol. 12, University of Toronto/Université Laval, 2003–, http://www.biographi.ca/en/bio/tache_alexandre_antonin_12E.html (accessed 8 April 2023).

55 *Le Métis*, 18 and 23 September 1872; Morgan, *Canadian Parliamentary Companion 1873*; "Certificate of Poll Results, St. François Xavier Ouest, 19 Sept. 1872," Louis Riel Papers, 179; John Schultz to Donald Gunn, 20 September 1872, Donald Gunn Papers; *Manitoban*, Extra, 21 September 1872, Robert Cunningham Papers; J.E. Rea, "Cunningham, Robert," in *Dictionary of Canadian Biography*, vol. 10, University of Toronto/Université Laval, 2003–, http://www.biographi.ca/en/bio/cunningham_robert_10E.html (accessed 8 April 2023); John Schultz to Donald Gunn, 23 September 1872, Donald Gunn Papers; A.-A. Taché to Robert Cunningham, 28 March 1873, Robert Cunningham Papers; John A. Macdonald to Adams Archibald, 7 October 1872, cited in Ronaghan, "Farquharson"; Adams Archibald to Alexander Morris, 17 December 1872, Alexander Morris Papers; Amor de Cosmos to John Schultz, 3 September 1873, John Schultz Papers.

56 Alexander Morris, *Nova Britannia; Or, British North America, Its Extent and Future: A Lecture* (Montreal: J. Lovell, 1858); Jean Friesen, "Morris, Alexander," in *Dictionary of Canadian Biography*, vol. 11, University of Toronto/Université Laval, 2003–, http://www.biographi.ca/en/bio/morris_alexander_11E.html (accessed 8 April 2023).

57 *Manitoban*, 8 February 1873; Adams Archibald to Alexander Morris, 17 December 1872, Alexander Morris Papers.

58 Sister Curran, "Entry for 11 December 1872," in "Letters and Notes of Sr. Curran which Have Been Recopied in 1928: Jan 1868 to August 1885," Ellen Gillies Cooke Papers, file 15; Dubuc, *Mémoires*, 15–16; Diane Paulette Payment, "Dubuc, Sir Joseph," in *Dictionary of Canadian Biography*, vol. 14, University of Toronto/Université Laval, 2003–, 2023, http://www.biographi.ca/en/bio/dubuc_joseph_14E.html (accessed 8 April 2023).

59 Alexander Morris to Alexander Campbell, "Honorable John Norquay—Applies to Be Appointed a Stipendiary Magistrate in the Northwest Territories," LAC, RG13-A-2, vol. 31, file 1874-120; Morris did suggest that Norquay might serve as a commissioner in the treaty party heading to Treaty 3: Campbell to Morris, 6 August 1873, Morris papers; with thanks to Jean Friesen for this reference.

60 Lovell C. Clark, "Clarke, Henry Joseph," in *Dictionary of Canadian Biography*, vol. 11, University of Toronto/Université Laval, 2003–,"http://www.biographi.ca/en/bio.php?id_nbr=5436 (accessed 9 February 2024). Gilbert McMicken to John A. Macdonald, 17 July 1872, John A. Macdonald Papers; Clarke, "Clarke."

61 *Manitoban*, 26 February, sitting of 15 February 1872, also 8 and 15 November 1873; *Le Métis*, 15 and 29 November 1873; Donald Gunn to John Schultz, 3 November 1873, John Schultz Papers; Ens, *Homeland*, 144–49; James Trow, *A Trip to Manitoba* (Quebec City: S. Marcotte, 1875), 84–85.

62 *Le Métis*, 29 and 15 November 1873; *Manitoban*, 8 and 15 November 1873; Donald Gunn to John Schultz, 3 November 1873, John Schultz Papers.

63 [John Norquay], "Notes on Early Days in Manitoba," NPP, G8731.

64 Alexander Morris, *The Treaties of Canada with the Indians* (Toronto: Belfords, Clark, 1880), 25–43.

65 Great Britain, British North America Act 1867, Section 91, Subsection 24, https://www.justice.gc.ca/eng/rp-pr/csj-sjc/constitution/lawreg-loireg/p1t1e.html (accessed 21 March 2020).

66 David G. McCrady, *Living with Strangers: The Nineteenth-Century Sioux and the Canadian-American Borderlands* (Lincoln: University of Nebraska Press, 2006), 17–60; John Norquay to Alexander Morris, 8 January and 17 March 1873, in Canada, House of Commons, *Sessional Papers*, No. 23, 1873, 36 Victoria, 14–19.

67 Alexander Morris to Joseph Howe, 11 March 1873, Alexander Morris Papers K.

68 Canada, House of Commons, *Sessional Papers*, No. 23, 1873, 36 Victoria, 14–19; *Manitoba Free Press*, 22 March 1873; "Report of Privy Council Committee, Approved by Governor General in Council," 24 April 1873, Alexander Morris Papers, 1931; Margaret Fahrni and William Lewis Morton, *Third Crossing: A History of the First Quarter Century of the Town and District of Gladstone in the Province of Manitoba* (Winnipeg: Advocate, 1946), 23; "Memo from Morris to Governor General," 30 December 1873, Alexander Morris Papers K; McCrady, *Living with Strangers*, 40–41; Peter Douglas Elias, *The Dakota of the Canadian Northwest: Lessons for Survival* (Winnipeg: University of Manitoba Press, 1988).

69 *Le Métis*, 11 July and 1 August 1874; *Manitoba Free Press*, 6 , 9 , and 14 July 1874, 6 February and 13 May 1875; Alexander Morris to Alexander Mackenzie, 5 and 6 June 1874, Alexander Morris Papers; *A Comparative Statement of the Public Expenditure of the Province of Manitoba under the Clarke and Davis Administrations Respectively, from 1st Jan. 1874, to 31st Dec. 1877* (Winnipeg: Manitoba Daily Free Press Steam Printers, 1878); Burley, "The Emergence of the Premiership"; Gerhard J. Ens, "Lépine, Ambroise-Didyme," in *Dictionary of Canadian Biography*, vol. 15, University of Toronto/Université Laval, 2003–, http://www.biographi.ca/en/bio/lepine_ambroise_dydime_15E.html (accessed 8 April 2023).

70 Canada, Manitoba Act, Sections 5 and 17, Part 1: Manitoba Act—Enactment No. 2, justice.gc.ca (accessed 18 April 2019); M.S. Donnelly, *The Government of Manitoba* (Toronto: University of Toronto Press, 1963), 72; Norman Ward, *The Canadian House of Commons: Representation* (Toronto: University of Toronto Press, 1950), 214–15.

71 *Manitoban*, 4 March 1872; Joseph Howe, quoted in J. McLean, "The Canadian Indian Problem," *Methodist Magazine* 34, no. 2 (1891): 162–71; Ged Martin, "Indian Affairs

in the 1882 Budget," https://www.gedmartin.net/martinalia-mainmenu-3/312-indian-affairs-1882-budget (accessed 28 December 2021); Ged Martin, "How Much Did Canada 'Pay' First Nations for the Prairies?," https://www.gedmartin.net/martinalia-mainmenu-3/313-how-much-did-canada-pay-first-nations-for-the-prairies (accessed 28 December 2021); Ted Binnema, "Protecting Indian Lands by Defining Indian, 1850–1876," *Journal of Canadian Studies* 48, no. 2 (2014): 5–39; John Milloy, "Indian Act Colonialism: A Century of Dishonour, 1869–1969," research paper for the National Centre for First Nations Governance, May 2008, http://fngovernance.org/ncfng_research/milloy.pdf (accessed 28 December 2021).

72 *Manitoban*, 22 January 1872.

73 *Manitoba Free Press*, 15 February 1873; I thank Mrs. Louise Mercredi and Ovide Mercredi for the translation; Jeff Gee [Julius F. Galbraith], "The Incorporation of Winnipeg," in *A Sketch of Both Sides of Manitoba* (1881), republished in *Manitoba Pageant* 5, no. 3 (1960): http://mhs.mb.ca/docs/people/galbraith_jf.shtml.

74 Manitoba, *Statutes, 1874*; *Manitoba Free Press*, 16 July 1874.

75 *Manitoba Free Press*, 16 July 1874.

76 Ibid.

77 Ibid.

78 Hannah Arendt, *The Origins of Totalitarianism* (New York: Schocken Books, 1951), Chapter 9; Ward, *The Canadian House of Commons*, 214; Norma Hall, Clifford P. Hall, and Erin Verrier, "A History of the Legislative Assembly of Assiniboia/Le Conseil du Gouvernement Provisoire," 18, https://www.gov.mb.ca/imr/ir/major-initiatives/pubs/laa%20essay%20eng.pdf (accessed 18 September 2019); Milloy, "Indian Act Colonialism."

79 Gerald Friesen, A.C. Hamilton, and Murray Sinclair, "'Justice Systems' and Manitoba's Aboriginal People: An Historical Survey," in *River Road: Essays on Manitoba and Prairie History*, ed. Gerald Friesen (Winnipeg: University of Manitoba Press, 1996), 49–77; W.L. Morton, ed., *Alexander Begg's Red River Journal* (Toronto: Champlain Society, 1956), 295; Louis Riel Institute and Government of Manitoba, "Legislative Assembly of Assiniboia: Citizenship as Concept and Practice at Red River, 1869–1870," http://www.legislativeassemblyofassiniboia.ca/en/page/121/citizenship-concept-and-practice-red-river-1869-1870#_edn3 (accessed 28 December 2021); *Manitoba Free Press*, 19 April 1888; "The Session" (sitting of 26 April 1888), Legislative Library of Manitoba.

80 *Manitoba Free Press*, 9 and 14 July 1874, 6 February 1875; Saywell, *The Office of Lieutenant-Governor*, 60–79; Burley, "The Emergence of the Premiership."

81 *Nor'Wester*, 8 February 1875.

82 *Manitoba Free Press*, 6, 10, and 13 February 1875, 2 December 1878; *Nor'Wester*, 8 February 1875.

Chapter 5: Senior Minister, 1875–78

1 *Manitoban and Northwest Herald*, 2 November 1874.

2 *Manitoba Free Press*, 14 and 15 July 1874; David Burley, "The Emergence of the Premiership 1870–74," in *Manitoba Premiers of the 19th and 20th Centuries*, ed. Barry Ferguson and Robert Wardhaugh (Regina: CPRC Press, 2010), 1–28.

3 Manitoba Parish Lot Files, "St. Andrews, Lot 8 West, Lot 228 and Lot 229"; I thank Roy Loewen for this research; John Norquay to David Laird, 14 February 1875, LAC, Canada, Department of the Interior Papers, RG 15, D-11-1, vol. 232, file 2927; Andrew Spence to John Norquay, 8 September 1875, NPP, A-170; Ellen Cooke, "Andrew Norquay Interview, Vancouver, 1959," Ellen Gillies Cooke Papers, file 1; Ellen Cooke, "Visit at the Home of Dr. and Mrs. Alfred Savage, 5 June 1965," Ellen Gillies Cooke Papers, file 12; Ellen Cooke, "Interview with Mary Savage, 26 October 1975," Ellen Gillies Cooke Papers, file 12; Kenneth McKenzie, "Diary, 23 December 1875," 65–66, Kenneth McKenzie Papers; Canada, Department of the Interior, Dominion Lands Branch Papers, "Parish of Poplar Point, High Bluff: Half Breed Land Grants, 1876," numbers 174–82; *Manitoba Free Press*, 5 August 1878.

4 *Manitoba Free Press*, 2 and 16 January 1875; *The Canadian Parliamentary Companion 1877*, ed. C.H. Mackintosh (Ottawa: Citizen Printing, 1877), 372; "Events in Manitoba History: Manitoba Provincial Election (1874)," Manitoba Historical Society, http://www.mhs.mb.ca/docs/events/provincialelection1874.shtml (accessed 11 February 2022).

5 Ruth Swan, "Robert A. Davis 1874–1878," in *Manitoba Premiers of the 19th and 20th Centuries*, ed. Barry Ferguson and Robert Wardhaugh (Regina: CPRC Press, 2010), 29–46; *Manitoba Free Press*, 2 and 9 January 1875.

6 Swan, "Robert A. Davis"; Ruth Swan, "Davis, Robert Atkinson," in *Dictionary of Canadian Biography*, vol. 13, University of Toronto/Université Laval, 2003–, http://www.biographi.ca/en/bio/davis_robert_atkinson_13E.html (accessed 8 April 2023).

7 *Manitoba Free Press*, 15 January 1875.

8 *Nor'Wester*, 15 February 1875; *Le Métis*, 6 February 1875.

9 James Wickes Taylor to John Lambert Cadwalader, 4 February 1875, USC Papers.

10 *Manitoba Free Press*, 9 and 12 April, 12 May 1875; *Manitoba Sun*, 27 May 1887; *Winnipeg Call*, 28 May 1887; Kenneth McKenzie, "Diary, 25 February, 8 April 1875," Kenneth McKenzie Papers.

11 Alexander Morris to Alexander Mackenzie, 5 and 15 March 1875, Alexander Morris Papers TB, 219, 224; *Manitoba Free Press*, 2 April 1875; "Ministerial Appointments 11 May 1876, 16 October 1878," in "John Norquay Biographical," Ellen Gillies Cooke Papers, file 7.

12 Donald Gunn to John Schultz, 5 March 1875, John Schultz Papers.

13 *Nor'Wester*, 8 February 1875; James Whiteway to John Schultz, 4 January 1875, John Schultz Papers; *Winnipeg Standard*, 24 April 1875.

14 *Manitoba Free Press*, 6, 10, and 13 February 1875; John James Setter to John Norquay, 1 April 1875, NPP, A-187; John McDonald to John Norquay, 5 August 1875, NPP, A-181.

15 *Manitoba Free Press*, 31 March 1875; Alexander Morris to Lieutenant Governor of British Columbia, 1 April 1875, BCA, Lieutenant Governor of British Columbia Papers, "Correspondence In, 1872–1878."

16 *Manitoba Free Press*, 2 and 3 April 1875; *Le Métis*, 6 March 1875; Alexander Morris to Alexander Mackenzie, 5 and 15 March 1875, Alexander Morris Papers TB.

17 *Manitoba Free Press*, 2 and 9 April 1875; *Le Métis*, 10 April 1875.

18 *Manitoba Free Press*, 12 March, 23 April, 1, 4, and 5 May 1875; *Winnipeg Standard*, 8 May 1875; Ellen Cooke, "Letters and Notes of Sr. Curran which Have Been Recopied in 1928: Jan 1868 to August 1885," January 1876, 206, Ellen Gillies Cooke Papers.

19 *Manitoba Free Press*, 30 April 1875; *Winnipeg Standard*, 22 May 1875.

20 *Manitoba Free Press*, 12 and 31 March, 9 and 23 April, 4, 5, and 10 May 1875, 22 and 25 January, 7 February, 11 November 1876.

21 *Manitoba Free Press*, 31 March, 7 and 29 April, 1 and 12 May 1875, 19 and 26 January 1878; *Winnipeg Standard*, 1 and 29 May, 12 June, 3, 10, and 17 July 1875; Alexander Morris to Lieutenant Governor of British Columbia, 17 May 1875, BCA, "Correspondence In, 1872–1878," Lieutenant Governor Papers.

22 *Manitoba Free Press*, 7 September 1874, 1 May 1875, 18, 20, 26, and 27 January, 4 February 1876; Alexander Morris to Lieutenant Governor of British Columbia, 18 January 1876, BCA, "Correspondence In, 1872–78," Lieutenant Governor Papers; Act Respecting Jurors and Juries, 39 Vict., c. 3, s. 25, 36, 37, and Act to Diminish the Expenses of the Legislature of the Province of Manitoba in Certain Respects, 39 Vict., c. 2; *Le Métis*, 27 January, 10 February 1876; Alexander Morris to Canada, Secretary of State, 12 February 1876, Alexander Morris Papers M; Alexander Mackenzie to Alexander Morris, 3 December 1875, Alexander Morris Papers K; Diane Payment, "Joseph Dubuc et les développements politiques au Manitoba 1870–1885," unpublished essay, Fonds SHSB, série documentation, personnages, boite 7, file 258, "Joseph Dubuc," 373–75.

23 *Manitoba Free Press*, 26 and 27 January 1876; Joseph Dubuc, *Mémoires d'un Manitoban* (Rome: np, 1912), 53–54, in Joseph Dubuc Papers.

24 *Manitoba Free Press*, 30 September, 18 and 23 October, 8, 17, and 22 November 1876.

25 *Manitoba Free Press*, 30 January 1877.

26 *Manitoba Free Press*, 30 January, 1 and 10 February 1877.

27 Laurence Frank Wilmot, "The Christian Churches of the Red River Settlement and the Foundation of the University of Manitoba: An Historical Analysis of the Process of

Transition from Frontier College to University" (MA thesis, University of Manitoba, 1979), 47–48, 86, 108–11; George Bryce, "Obituary: Archbishop Robert Machray," *Manitoba Free Press*, 10 March 1904; I thank Jean Friesen for this reference; *Manitoba Free Press*, 31 January 1876; *Canada School Journal* 8, no. 3 (1883): 168–69; W.L. Morton, *One University: A History of the University of Manitoba 1877–1952* (Toronto: McClelland and Stewart, 1957).

28 Joseph Dubuc to Reverend Paul Benoit, "Memorandum re Mgr. Taché, January 1902," Joseph Dubuc Papers, file 2; *Le Métis*, 18 January, 1 February 1877; *Manitoba Free Press*, 20 February 1877.

29 Cited in Marcel Giraud, *The Métis in the Canadian West*, vol. 2 (1945; reprinted, Edmonton: University of Alberta Press, 1986), 638n25; also see the extended discussion, 375–421.

30 William Coldwell to A.-A. Taché, 17 November 1874, Bishop A.-A. Taché Papers, T15070.

31 Robert Painchaud, "Les rapports entre les Métis et les Canadiens Français au Manitoba, 1870–1884," in *The Other Natives : The Métis*, vol. 2, ed. Antoine S. Lussier and D. Bruce Sealey (Winnipeg: Manitoba Métis Federation Press and Éditions Bois-Brûlés, 1978), 53–74.

32 Diane Payment, "Nolin, Charles," in *Dictionary of Canadian Biography*, vol. 13, University of Toronto/Université Laval, 2003–, http://www.biographi.ca/en/bio/nolin_charles_13E.html (accessed 8 April 2023); Gerhard J. Ens, *Homeland to Hinterland: The Changing Worlds of the Red River Metis in the Nineteenth Century* (Toronto: University of Toronto Press, 1996), 123–38; Gerhard J. Ens and Joe Sawchuk, *From New Peoples to New Nations: Aspects of Métis History and Identity from the Eighteenth to Twenty-First Centuries* (Toronto: University of Toronto Press, 2016), 92–106; Norma Hall, with Clifford P. Hall and Erin Verrier, "A History of the Legislative Assembly of Assiniboia/Le Conseil du Gouvernement Provisoire," 7, https://www.gov.mb.ca/imr/ir/major-initiatives/pubs/laa%20essay%20eng.pdf (accessed 28 December 2021).

33 Painchaud, "Les rapports"; Jacinthe Duval, "The Catholic Church and the Formation of Metis Identity," *Past Imperfect* [University of Alberta] 9 (2001): 65–87; John H. McTavish to A.-A. Taché, 23 November 1870, Bishop A.-A. Taché Papers, T8168; Louis-Raymond Giroux to A.-A. Taché, 9 and 11 December 1874, Bishop A.-A. Taché Papers, T15181; Marcel Giraud, *Le Métis Canadien: son role dans l'histoire des provinces de l'ouest* (Paris: Institut d'Ethnologie, 1945), 1109–16; Gerald Friesen, "Homeland to Hinterland: Political Transition in Manitoba, 1870 to 1879," *Canadian Historical Association Historical Papers* (1979): 33–47.

34 *Manitoba Free Press*, 14 April 1875.

35 Manitoba Executive Council, "Draft Minutes," 14 December 1875, no. 1879, and 16 December 1875, 1880; Manitoba Executive Council, *Orders-in-Council Registers 1870–1891*, 216, 14 December 1875.

36 Manitoba Executive Council, "Draft Minutes," 14 December 1875, no. 1879, and 16 December 1875, no. 1880; Alexander Morris to Alexander Mackenzie, 17 December 1875, Alexander Morris Papers TB, 301; Allan R. Turner, "McKay, James," in *Dictionary of Canadian Biography*, vol. 10, University of Toronto/Université Laval, 2003–, http://www.biographi.ca/en/bio/mckay_james_10E.html (accessed 8 April 2023); Sarah Carter, "McKay, Angus," in *Dictionary of Canadian Biography*, vol. 13, University of Toronto/Université Laval, 2003–, http://www.biographi.ca/en/bio/mckay_angus_12E.html (accessed 8 April 2023).

37 *Le Métis*, 20 December 1877.

38 Charles Nolin to John Norquay, 23 December 1878, NPP, A-24.

39 John Norquay to David Laird, 14 February 1875, LAC, Canada, Department of the Interior Papers, RG 15, D-11-1, vol. 232, file 2927. I thank Dr. Lisa Schaub, who kindly gave me a copy of this petition.

40 *Manitoba Free Press*, 18 January 1876; Manitoba Executive Council, "Draft Minutes," 21 July 1875, Alexander Morris Papers LG, 1865; Andrew Spence to John Norquay, 8 April 1875, NPP, A-173; Ellen Cooke, "Letters and Notes of Sr. Curran, August 1872," Ellen Gillies Cooke Papers, file 15, 113.

41 *Manitoba Free Press*, 16 February 1877.

42 *Manitoba Free Press*, 30 January 1877.

43 *Manitoba Free Press*, 30 January, 10, 15, 21, and 23 February 1877, 4 May 1875; *Le Métis*, 7 December 1876, 11 January, 17 May, 12 July, 9 and 23 August 1877, 9 May 1878; Gerhard Ens, "Métis Lands in Manitoba," *Manitoba History* 5 (1983): http://mhs.mb.ca/docs/mb_history/05/metislands.shtml; D.P. Beattie to John Norquay, 15 November 1879, NPP, A-240; Giraud, *Le Métis Canadien*, 1123.

44 *Manitoba Free Press*, 4 February 1878; William Kennedy to John Norquay, 17 and 18 March 1879, NPP, A-347(a) and (b).

45 Alexander Morris to Lieutenant Governor of British Columbia, 1 April, 17 May 1875, BCA, Lieutenant Governor Papers.

46 *Manitoban*, 8 February 1873; *Manitoba Free Press*, 8, 9, and 13 April 1875.

47 *Manitoba Free Press*, 12 and 13 May 1875, 29 January, 3 February 1876.

48 *Manitoba Free Press*, 2 and 4 February 1878.

49 *Ritual of the British American Order of Good Templars* (London, Canada West: City Press Office, 1860; also published in Montreal: Kyte, Higgins, and Company, 1872), second stanza of the "Opening Ode," 8; E.P. Brown and A.W.J. Phillips, "Certificate," 29 March 1875, NPP, A-182; John McDonald to John Norquay, 29 November 1878, 10 February 1880, NPP, A-22, A-249; for context, see Sharon Anne Cook, *"Through Sunshine and Shadow": The Woman's Christian Temperance Union, Evangelicalism, and Reform in Ontario, 1874–1930* (Montreal and Kingston: McGill-Queen's University Press, 1993).

50 John James Setter to John Norquay, 1 April 1875, 2 December 1878, NPP, A-187, A-31; *Manitoba Free Press*, 13 and 20 March, 22 April 1875; *Winnipeg Standard*, 24 April 1875; Andrew G.B. Bannatyne to John Norquay, 31 December 1877, NPP, A-46; John McDonald to John Norquay, 5 August 1875, NPP, A-181; Andrew Spence to John Norquay, 6 December 1875, NPP, A-172; Charles Adams to John Norquay, 9 January 1878, NPP, A-6; 10 July 1877, A-101; 5 December 1876, A-192; 11/14 January 1880, A-383; 28 December 1879, A-386; Baltimore Oyster Depot (Winnipeg) to John Norquay, 12 February 1880, NPP, A-494 (a) and (b); James Brown to John Norquay, 10 October 1880, NPP, A-485.

51 *Manitoba Free Press*, 22, 24, and 27 February, 1 March 1877.

52 *Manitoba Free Press*, 27 February 1877; *Le Métis*, 1 March 1877.

53 *Manitoba Free Press*, 10 January 1878; Joseph Cauchon to Lieutenant Governor of British Columbia, 18 January 1878, BCA, Lieutenant Governor Papers.

54 *Manitoba Free Press*, 4 February 1878.

55 *Manitoba Free Press*, 4 February, 8 March 1878; Hank McPhillips, "Letter to the Editor," *Manitoba Free Press*, 20 May 1878, NPP, A-156.

56 Alexander Morris to John A. Macdonald, 22 October 1877, John A. Macdonald Papers, 114240. Emphasis in orignal.

57 Robert Davis to Alexander Morris, 9 February 1878, Alexander Morris Papers K, 280; William Luxton to Alexander Morris, 12 February 1878, Alexander Morris Papers K, 281.

58 *Manitoba Free Press*, 18 October, 13 December 1877, 23 January 1878; F.W. Boddy to John Norquay, 28 August 1878, NPP, A-3; John Schultz to John Gunn, 22 February 1875, 7 and 18 March 1878, John Gunn Papers.

59 John Norquay to John A. Macdonald, 16 May, 18 June, 26 July 1878, John A. Macdonald Papers, 160610, 160860, 161067; John Norquay to Alexander Morris, 16 May 1878, Alexander Morris Papers K.

60 Thomas Scott to Alexander Morris, 29 May 1878, Alexander Morris Papers K; J. Colcleugh to G. Colcleugh, 2 June 1878, Colcleugh Papers; W.W. Ogilvie to John A. Macdonald, 6 June 1878, John A. Macdonald Papers, 7696, and copy in John Schultz Papers; Gilbert McMicken to John A. Macdonald, 9 September 1878, John A. Macdonald Papers, 110886; *Manitoba Free Press*, 3, 7, 9, and 10 August, 19 and 27 September 1878, 24–28 January, 5 February 1879; Gilbert McMicken to Alexander Morris, 4 February, 13 March, 29 April 1878, Barber Arkin Collection; Alexander Morris to A.-A. Taché, 21 March, 28 June 1878, Bishop A.-A. Taché Papers, T20150, T20547; Hector Langevin to Alexander Morris, 16 July 1878, Barber Arkin Collection; John Norquay to John A. Macdonald, 3 September 1878, John A. Macdonald Papers, 161568; W.W. Ogilvie to John Norquay, 27 January 1879, NPP, A-339.

61 Alexander Begg to John A. Macdonald, 30 September 1878, John A. Macdonald Papers, 161826; Gilbert McMicken to John A. Macdonald, 9 September 1878, John A.

Macdonald Papers, 110886; Joseph Royal to John A. Macdonald, 28 September 1878, John A. Macdonald Papers, 118172; Frank McPhillips to A.-A. Taché, 6 August 1878, Bishop A.-A. Taché Papers, T20693; F.W. Boddy to John Norquay, 28 August 1878, NPP, A-3.

62 John Norquay to John A. Macdonald, 20 September, 16 October 1878, John A. Macdonald Papers, 161687, 162031; Alexander Begg to John A. Macdonald, 30 September 1878, John A. Macdonald Papers, 161826; Father Joseph McCarthy to A.-A. Taché, 9 September 1878, Bishop A.-A. Taché Papers, T20777.

63 Swan, "Davis, Robert Atkinson," in *Dictionary of Canadian Biography*, vol. 13, University of Toronto/ Université Laval 2003–, http://www.biographi.ca/en/bio/davis_robert_atkinson_13E.html (accessed 10 April 2023).

64 *Manitoba Free Press*, 16 October, 13 December 1878, 18 January 1879; *Manitoba Gazette*, 19 October 1878.

65 *Manitoba Free Press*, 7 August, 7 November, 2 December 1878; Ellen Cooke, "Andrew Norquay Interview, Vancouver, 1959," Ellen Gillies Cooke Papers, file 1.

66 John Norquay to John A. Macdonald, 31 October 1878, John A. Macdonald Papers, 162362; John A. Macdonald to John Norquay, 11 November 1878, John A. Macdonald Papers, Letter Book 21, 122.

67 *Manitoba Free Press*, 15 and 16 November 1878; Manitoba Executive Council, *Orders-in-Council Register 1870–1891*, 11 and 23 November 1878.

68 John James Setter to John Norquay, 2 December 1878, NPP, A-31; *Manitoba Free Press*, 25 November 1878.

69 *Manitoba Free Press*, 16 and 26 November 1878; *A Comparative Statement of the Public Expenditure of the Province of Manitoba under the Clarke and Davis Administrations Respectively, from 1st Jan. 1874, to 31st Dec. 1877* (Winnipeg: Manitoba Daily Free Press Steam Printers, 1878); *Le Métis*, 17 and 24 October 1878; *Manitoba Gazette*, 2 November 1878.

70 *Manitoba Free Press*, 28 November, 2, 7, and 11 December 1878; David Walker to Alexander Morris, 14 November 1878, Alexander Morris Papers K; Alex Murray to John Norquay, 19 November 1878, NPP, A-17.

71 James McKay to John Norquay, 25 November 1878, NPP, A-21, 27 June 1878, NPP, A-20.

72 John McDonald to John Norquay, 29 November 1878, NPP, A-22.

73 Alex Murray to John Norquay, 19 November 1878, NPP, A-17.

74 *Quiz*, 3 February 1879; a copy of the cartoon is in the Joseph Dubuc Papers; *Manitoba Free Press*, 31 October, 14 December 1878, 18 January 1879; David Walker to Alexander Morris, 14 November 1878, Alexander Morris Papers K; John Norquay to John A. Macdonald, 14 November 1878, John A. Macdonald Papers, 167635; Charles Nolin to John Norquay, 23 December 1878, NPP, A-24.

75 *Manitoba Free Press*, 17 December 1878; *Manitoba Gazette*, 21 December 1878; Alfred Boyd to John Norquay, 25 March 1879, NPP, A-246.

76 *Le Métis*, 17 and 31 October, 7 and 14 November, 12 and 19 December 1878; Alphonse Martin to A.-A. Taché, 17 and 28 December 1878, Bishop A.-A. Taché Papers, T21113, T21158; Charles Joseph Camper to A.-A. Taché, 18 December 1878, Bishop A.-A. Taché Papers, T21119; Father St. Pierre to A.-A. Taché, 18 November, 9 December 1878, Bishop A.-A. Taché Papers.

77 *Le Métis*, 13, 14, and 18 December 1878, 17 January 1879; Michel Charbonneau to A.-A. Taché, 18 December 1878, Bishop A.-A. Taché Papers, T21038; *Manitoba Free Press*, 30 January 1879; Kenneth Michael Sylvester, *The Limits of Rural Capitalism: Family, Culture, and Markets in Montcalm, Manitoba 1870–1940* (Toronto: University of Toronto Press, 2001), 109–12.

78 *Manitoba Free Press*, 13 and 28 December 1878; John L. Holmes, "Factors Affecting Politics in Manitoba: A Study of the Provincial Elections 1870–1899" (MA thesis, University of Manitoba, 1936), 29–31; *Manitoba Gazette*, 19 October 1878, 11 January 1879; Joseph Dubuc, "Mémoires 1912," 65–70, Joseph Dubuc Papers.

Chapter 6: Premier, 1879

1 *Manitoba Free Press*, 24 and 26 March 1879.

2 James Mochoruk, "Brown, Corydon Partlow," in *Dictionary of Canadian Biography*, vol. 12, University of Toronto/Université Laval, 2003–, http://www.biographi.ca/en/bio/brown_corydon_partlow_12E.html (accessed 10 April 2023); Bella Walker to John Norquay, 24 January 1885, NPP, C-975; David Walker to John Norquay, 24 February 1885, NPP, C-808; *Manitoba Free Press*, 23 and 29 January 1879; "Draft of Throne Speech," NPP, A-352.

3 *Le Métis*, 6 February 1879; *Manitoba Free Press*, 3, 5, 6, 8, and 10 February 1879.

4 *Le Métis*, 23 and 30 November 1871, 11 January 1872; *Manitoban*, 18 November, 16 December 1871; *Quiz*, 8 February 1879; Joseph Dubuc to Élie Tassé, 1 June 1879, Joseph Dubuc Papers; Joseph Royal to A.-A. Taché, 26 November 1871, Bishop A.-A. Taché Papers, T9654; Alphonse LaRivière to A.-A. Taché, 1 March 1874 (copy), Fonds Société historique de Saint-Boniface, série documentation, personnages, file 541; for context, see Arthur Silver, *The French-Canadian Idea of Confederation*, 2nd ed. (Toronto: University of Toronto Press, 1997); Arthur Silver, "Royal, Joseph," in *Dictionary of Canadian Biography*, vol. 14, University of Toronto/Université Laval, 2003–, http://www.biographi.ca/en/bio/dubuc_joseph_14E.html (accessed 10 April 2023); Arthur Silver, "French Canada and the Prairie Frontier, 1870–1890," *Canadian Historical Review* 50, no. 1 (1969): 11–36; and Gerald Friesen, "Homeland to Hinterland: Political Transition in Manitoba 1870–1879," *Canadian Historical* Association *Historical Papers* (1979): 33–47.

5 *Le Métis*, 15 June, 10 August 1871, quoted in Robert Painchaud, "Les rapports entre les Métis et les Canadiens Français au Manitoba, 1870–1884," in *The Other Natives: The*

Métis, vol. 2, ed. Antoine S. Lussier and D. Bruce Sealey (Winnipeg: Manitoba Métis Federation Press and Éditions Bois-Brûlés, 1978), 58; Jacinthe Duval, "The Catholic Church and the Formation of Metis Identity," *Past Imperfect* [University of Alberta] 9 (2001): 70.

6 Rice Howard to John Norquay, 25 February 1879, NPP, G8729; Manitoba Executive Council, "Draft Minutes, 1872–74," Alexander Morris Papers; *Le Métis*, 17 February, 2 March, 1 May, 12 June, 17 July 1872, 5 April 1873; *Manitoban*, 14 September 1872, 8 March 1873; *Manitoba Free Press*, 14 July 1874; Louis de Plainval to John Norquay, 12 February 1872, Manitoba Provincial Police Papers, 29, 32; for context, see James A. Maxwell, *Federal Subsidies to the Provincial Governments in Canada* (Cambridge, MA: Harvard University Press, 1937); Chester Martin, *The Natural Resources Question: The Historical Basis of Provincial Claims* (Winnipeg: King's Printer, 1920); Jim Mochoruk, *Formidable Heritage: Manitoba's North and the Cost of Development 1870 to 1930* (Winnipeg: University of Manitoba Press, 2004); and Elsbeth Heaman, *Tax, Order and Good Government: A New Political History of Canada 1867–1917* (Montreal and Kingston: McGill-Queen's University Press, 2017).

7 *Manitoba Free Press*, 24 February, 10, 12, and 20 March, 2, 3, and 8 April 1879; W.W. Ogilvie to John Norquay, c. September 1878, NPP, A-194, 27 January 1879, A-339, 5 June 1879, A-318, 18 July 1879, A-243, 7 August 1879, A-259; *Quiz* cartoon described in *Manitoba Free Press*, 8 March 1879.

8 Bella Norquay to John Norquay, 8 March 1879, NPP, A-315; William Kennedy to John Norquay, 1 March 1879, NPP, A-321.

9 James A. Gouin to John Norquay, 31 March 1879, NPP, A-290.

10 "Letterbook 1879," John Norquay Papers; Andrée Désilets, "Masson, Louis-Rodrigue," in *Dictionary of Canadian Biography*, vol. 13, University of Toronto/Université Laval, 2003–, http://www.biographi.ca/en/bio/masson_louis_rodrigue_13E.html (accessed 10 April 2023).

11 Alexander Begg, "Memo," 7 March 1879, and "Memo to Alexander Campbell," in "Letterbook 1879," 52–53, 107–24, John Norquay Papers; John Norquay to John A. Macdonald, 4 and 5 March 1879, John A. Macdonald Papers, 164282, 164284; Manitoba Executive Council, *Orders-in-Council Registers 1870–1891*, 21 February 1879; John Norquay and Joseph Royal to Minister of Finance, "Extract of a Report of a Committee of Privy Council 18 April 1879, in Canada, House of Commons, *Sessional Papers* 44. Alexander Begg, "Memo," 8 March 1879, in "Letterbook 1879," 54, John Norquay Papers.

12 Alexander Begg, "Memo," 8 and 12 March 1879, in "Letterbook 1879," 54, 58–60, John Norquay Papers; Colin Frederick Read, "Dennis, John Stoughton (1820–1885)," in *Dictionary of Canadian Biography*, vol. 11, University of Toronto/Université Laval, 2003–, http://www.biographi.ca/en/bio/dennis_john_stoughton_1920_85_11E.html (accessed 10 April 2023); on land drainage, see Shannon Stunden Bower, *Wet Prairie: People, Land, and Water in Agricultural Manitoba* (Vancouver: UBC Press, 2011).

13 "Note," 10 March 1879, in "Letterbook 1879," 27, John Norquay Papers; Marc Girard to John Norquay and Joseph Royal, 11 March 1879, NPP, A-374; Alexander Begg to Allan Macdonald, 10 and 13 March 1879, and Alexander Begg, "Memo," 11, 13, and 14 March 1879, in "Letterbook 1879," 51, 56–57, 60, John Norquay Papers.

14 *Le Métis*, 13 February 1879; "Notice of Motion" (draft), 11 March 1879, in "Letterbook 1879," 46, John Norquay Papers; William Kennedy to John Norquay, 1 March 1879, NPP, A-321.

15 Alexander Begg, "Memo," 15 March 1879, in "Letterbook 1879," 90–91, John Norquay Papers.

16 John Norquay to John A. Macdonald, 2 April 1879, John A. Macdonald Papers, 164744; Alexander Begg, "Memo," 15 March 1879, in "Letterbook 1879," 90–91, John Norquay Papers; John Norquay to Alexander Campbell, 24 March 1879, in Manitoba, *Annual Report of the Department of Public Works for 1879* (Winnipeg: Queen's Printer, 1880), 175–77; John Norquay and Joseph Royal to John A. Macdonald, 17 March 1879, in "Letterbook 1879,", John Norquay Papers; John Norquay to John A. Macdonald, 21 March 1879, NPP, A-220; John Norquay to D.M. Walker, 21 March 1879, NPP, A-250; John Norquay and Joseph Royal to D.M. Walker, 24 March 1879, in "Letterbook 1879," 101, John Norquay Papers; John Norquay and Joseph Royal to John A. Macdonald, 24 March 1879, in "Letterbook 1879," 99–100, John Norquay Papers; Lawrence Vankoughnet to John A. Macdonald, 8 May 1879, in Deputy Superintendent General Letterbook, vol.1, Department of Indian Affairs Papers (with thanks to Jean Friesen for this reference); Manitoba, *Annual Report of the Department of Public Works for 1882* (Winnipeg: Queen's Printer, 1883); Manitoba, *Annual Report of the Department of Public Works for 1883* (Winnipeg: Queen's Printer, 1884); "Memo: Bridges and Drainage 1878–1886," c. 1886, Executive Council Premier's Office Papers, G8730.

17 John Norquay to William Luxton, 1 May 1879, NPP, A-219.

18 *Manitoba Free Press*, 7 and 26 February 1877, 11 October, 19 November, 18 December 1879.

19 Joseph Dubuc to A.-A. Taché, 27 March 1879, Bishop A.-A. Taché Papers, T21578; John Schultz to John A. Macdonald, 11 March 1879, John A. Macdonald Papers; I thank Alastair Sweeney for this summary; Lovell Clark, "Schultz, Sir John Christian," in *Dictionary of Canadian Biography*, vol. 12, University of Toronto/Université Laval, 2003–, http://www.biographi.ca/en/bio/schultz_john_christian_12E.html (accessed 10 April 2023); William Kennedy to John Norquay, 1 March 1879, NPP, A-321.

20 *Manitoba Free Press*, 17 June, 18 October, 19 November, 18 December 1879; Carman Miller, "Abbott, Sir John Joseph Caldwell," in *Dictionary of Canadian Biography*, vol. 12, University of Toronto/Université Laval, 2003–, http://www.biographi.ca/en/bio/abbott_john_joseph_caldwell_12E.html (accessed 10 April 2023).

21 Joseph Royal to A.-A. Taché, 11 March 1879, Bishop A.-A. Taché Papers, T21539.

22 *Manitoba Free Press*, 12 March 1879; Joseph Royal to A.-A. Taché, 11 March 1879, Bishop A.-A. Taché Papers, T21539; Alexander Begg, "Memo," 12 March 1879, in "Letterbook 1879," 50, John Norquay Papers; Joseph Dubuc to A.-A. Taché, 27 March, 3 April 1879, Bishop A.-A. Taché Papers, T21578, T21624; unidentified newspaper clipping, dated 12 March 1879, pasted in "Letterbook 1879," 50, John Norquay Papers; *Monetary Times and Trade Review* 12, no. 40 (28 March 1879): 1213; John Gunn to John Schultz, 29 March 1878, John Schultz Papers.

23 *Manitoba Free Press*, 28 December 1878, 4, 5, 10, and 12 March, 8 April 1879, 20 July 1881; Joseph Dubuc to Élie Tassé, 13 and 30 September 1879, Joseph Dubuc Papers; Alexander Begg, "Memo," 13 March 1879, in "Letterbook 1879," 57–59, John Norquay Papers; John Norquay to William Luxton, 1 May 1879, NPP, A-219; Phillip Buckner, "Tupper, Sir Charles," in *Dictionary of Canadian Biography*, vol. 14, University of Toronto/Université Laval, 2003–, http://www.biographi.ca/en/bio/tupper_charles_14E.html (accessed 10 April 2023); Luc Dauphinais, *Histoire de Saint-Boniface* (Saint-Boniface, MB: Société historique de Saint-Boniface, 1991); Barry Potyondi, *Selkirk: The First Hundred Years* (Winnipeg: Jostens, 1981); *Emerson 1875–1975: A Centennial History*, ed. James McClelland and Dan Lewis (Altona, MB: Friesen Printers, 1975); Alan F.J. Artibise, *Winnipeg: A Social History of Urban Growth 1874–1914* (Montreal and Kingston: McGill-Queen's University Press, 1975), 64–74; Randy R. Rostecki, "Winnipeg 1870–1886: The Physical Legacy of the Boom" (MA thesis, University of Manitoba, 1980); Alan F.J. Artibise and Henry Huber, "Logan, Alexander," in *Dictionary of Canadian Biography*, vol. 12, University of Toronto/Université Laval, 2003–, http://www.biographi.ca/en/bio/logan_alexander_12E.html (accessed 10 April 2023); Ruben C. Bellan, "Rails across the Red: Selkirk or Winnipeg," *MHS Transactions* 18 (1961–62): http://www.mhs.mb.ca/docs/transactions/3/railsacrossthered.shtml.

24 John Norquay to William Luxton, 1 May 1879, NPP, A-219; *Manitoba Free Press*, 29 May 1879, 24 and 25 March 1886, Legislative Library of Manitoba (hereafter LLM) Hansard, 1886, 153; *Manitoban*, 25 March 1886, LLM Hansard.

25 Theodore David Regehr, "The National Railway Policy and Manitoba Railway Legislation 1879–1888" (MA thesis, Carleton University, 1963), 41–42; Lord Lorne to Privy Council, 18 February 1879, Lord Lorne Papers, additional microfilm, 614; Alexander Campbell, "Excerpt from Report," 4 January 1882, in John A. Macdonald Papers, 54515; Canada, Privy Council Order 486, 18 April 1879; *Manitoba Free Press*, 29 May 1879, 24 and 25 March 1886, LLM Hansard; *Manitoban*, 25 March 1886, LLM Hansard; John A. Macdonald to Martin Griffin, 31 October 1881, John A. Macdonald Papers, Letterbook 21, part 3, 527–28, cited in Regehr, "National Railway Policy," 42; "Petition of the Executive Council of Manitoba to Her Majesty the Queen, 1887," in Canada, *Sessional Papers* 21, 1887, 227–35, cited in ibid., 43.

26 William Notman to John Norquay, April and August 1879, NPP, A-298, A-299; Alfred Boyd to John Norquay, 25 March 1879, NPP, A-246.

27 *Manitoba Free Press*, 18 April 1879; *Quiz*, 5 April 1879; St. Mary's Academy to John Norquay, 30 April 1879, NPP, A-341.

28 John Norquay to John A. Macdonald, 2 and 10 April 1879, John A. Macdonald Papers, 164744, 164852.

29 John A. Macdonald to John Norquay, 18 April 1879, NPP, A-226; William Ogilvie to John Norquay, 22 April 1879, NPP, A-342.

30 J.H. McTavish to A.-A. Taché, 23 November 1870, Bishop A.-A. Taché Papers, T8168; Louis-Raymond Giroux to A.-A. Taché, 9 and 11 December 1874, Bishop A.-A. Taché Papers, T15181; Marcel Giraud, *Le Métis Canadien: Son rôle dans l'histoire des provinces de l'ouest* (Paris: Institut d'ethnologie, Musée de l'homme, 1945), 1109, 1112, 1116; William Coldwell to A.-A. Taché, 17 November 1874, Bishop A.-A. Taché Papers, T15070; *Manitoba Free Press*, 21 January 1876; *Le Métis*, 20 December 1877; Painchaud, "Les rapports," 53–74.

31 Alex Norquay to J. Newbold, 10 November 1935, Ellen Gillies Cooke Papers, file 5.

32 Bishop A.-A. Taché, "Mandement concernant les élections," *Le Métis*, 11 and 16 May, 6 June 1878; C. St. P. ptre to A.-A. Taché, 18 November 1878, Bishop A.-A. Taché Papers.

33 Louis-Raymond Giroux to A.-A. Taché, 29 March 1878, Bishop A.-A. Taché Papers, T20204.

34 *Le Métis*, 17 and 31 October, 7 November, 12 and 19 December 1878; *Manitoba Free Press*, 3 October 1878.

35 Charles Nolin to John Norquay, 23 December 1878, NPP, A-24.

36 A.-A. Taché to F.-X. Kavanagh, 8 February 1879, Bishop A.-A. Taché Papers, T1225.

37 Joseph Cauchon to A.-A. Taché, 27 June 1879, Bishop A.-A. Taché Papers, T22052; *Le Métis*, 7 November 1878; "Memo," 11 March 1879, in "Letterbook 1879," 46, John Norquay Papers; Silver, "Royal, Joseph."

38 Joseph Dubuc to Élie Tassé, 1 March, 1 June, 3 July 1879, Joseph Dubuc Papers; Joseph Dubuc to A.-A. Taché, 6 June 1879, Bishop A.-A. Taché Papers, T21897; *Manitoba Free Press*, 12 February, 27 July 1878 (from *Winnipeg Standard*), 27 January 1879; Fred J. Shore, "Delorme, Pierre," in *Dictionary of Canadian Biography*, vol. 14, University of Toronto/Université Laval, 2003–, 2023, http://www.biographi.ca/en/bio/delorme_pierre_14E.html (accessed 10 April 2023).

39 Louis-Raymond Giroux to A.-A.Taché, 3 July 1879, Bishop A.-A. Taché Papers, T22099.

40 Joseph Dubuc to Élie Tassé, 3 July 1879, Joseph Dubuc Papers.

41 Joseph Dubuc to Élie Tassé, 1 June 1879, Joseph Dubuc Papers; Joseph Dubuc to A.-A. Taché, 6 June 1879, Bishop A.-A. Taché Papers, T21897; Guy Vanier, "La question manitobaine," in *Les cloches de Saint-Boniface* 15, no. 13 (1 July 1916): 212; *L'opinion publique: Journal hebdomadaire illustré* 10, no. 24 (12 June 1879): 280–81.

42 Joseph Royal to A.-A. Taché, 28 May 1879, Bishop A.-A. Taché Papers, T21854.

43 *Manitoba Free Press*, 5 and 6 February 1879; Arthur I. Silver, "La Rivière, Alphonse-Alfred-Clément," in *Dictionary of Canadian Biography*, vol. 15, University of Toronto/Université Laval, 2003–, http://www.biographi.ca/en/bio/la_riviere_alphonse_alfred_clement_15E.html (accessed 10 April 2023); *Quiz*, 8 February 1879.

44 Alex Norquay to J. Newbold, 10 November 1935, Ellen Gillies Cooke Papers, file 5.

45 Manitoba Executive Council, *Orders-in-Council Registers 1870–1891*, 28 May 1879.

46 *Manitoba Free Press*, 30 May 1879.

47 Joseph Dubuc to Élie Tassé, 1 June 1879, Joseph Dubuc Papers; *Manitoba Free Press*, 4 June 1879; a "round-robin" is a written petition, memorial, or protest on which the signatures are affixed in a circle so as not to indicate who signed first.

48 *Le Métis*, 29 May, 4 June 1879; Joseph Dubuc to Élie Tassé, 6 June 1879, Joseph Dubuc Papers; Joseph Dubuc to A.-A. Taché, 6 June 1879, Bishop A.-A. Taché Papers, T21897; Alex Norquay to J. Newbold, 10 November 1935, Ellen Gillies Cooke Papers, file 5.

49 Joseph Dubuc to Élie Tassé, 1 June 1879, Joseph Dubuc Papers; Joseph Dubuc to A.-A. Taché, 6 June 1879, Bishop A.-A. Taché Papers, T21897.

50 *Manitoba Free Press*, 30 and 31 May 1879; *Le Métis*, 29 May, 4 June 1879.

51 *Manitoba Free Press*, 30 May 1879.

52 *Manitoba Free Press*, 31 May, 3 and 20 June 1879; *Le Métis*, 4 and 26 June 1879.

53 Joseph Dubuc to Élie Tassé, 1 June 1879, Joseph Dubuc Papers.

54 Joseph Dubuc to Élie Tassé, 1 and 6 June 1879, Joseph Dubuc Papers.

55 Manitoba Executive Council, *Orders-in-Council Registers 1870–1891*, 4 June 1879; *Manitoba Free Press*, 4 June 1879; R.B. Hill, *Manitoba: History of Its Early Settlement, Development and Resources* (Winnipeg: Russell, Land and Company, 1923), 609.

56 *Manitoba Free Press*, 4 and 5 June 1879.

57 *Manitoba Free Press*, 5 and 6 June 1879; John Norquay, "Memoranda during Session, Speech Notes, No Date" [5 June 1879], NPP, A-352 (a) and (b).

58 Joseph Dubuc to Élie Tassé, 6 June 1879, Joseph Dubuc Papers.

59 Joseph Royal to A.-A. Taché, 11 June 1879, Bishop A.-A. Taché Papers, T21923.

60 *Winnipeg Weekly Times*, 6 June 1879; *Manitoba Free Press*, 5 June 1879; John Norquay, "Memoranda during Session, Speech Notes, No Date" [5 June 1879], NPP, A-352 (a) and (b), A-385.

61 John Norquay, "Memoranda during Session, Speech Notes, No Date" [5 June 1879], NPP, A-352 (a) and (b), A-385; *Manitoba Free Press*, 6 June 1879.

62 Ibid.

63 Ibid.

64 John Norquay, "Memoranda during Session, Speech Notes, No Date" [5 June 1879], NPP, A-352 (a) and (b), A-385; *Manitoba Free Press*, 6 June 1879; Norquay's words, as heard by Royal's camp: "le progrès nous entraîne," *Le Métis*, 12 June 1879; *Quiz*, 6 June 1879.

65 *Manitoba Free Press*, 7 and 20 June 1879; *Le Métis*, 12 June 1879.

66 *Manitoba Free Press*, 19 and 20 June 1879.

67 A.G.B. Bannatyne to John Norquay, 31 July 1879, NPP, A-307; *Manitoba Free Press*, 26 June 1879.

68 *Manitoba Free Press*, 25 June 1879.

69 Joseph Dubuc to Élie Tassé, 6 and 11 June 1879, Joseph Dubuc Papers; Joseph Dubuc to A.-A. Taché, 6 June 1879, Bishop A.-A. Taché Papers, T21897; *Manitoba Free Press*, 6 June 1879.

70 A.A. Cherrier to A.-A. Taché, 10 June 1879, Bishop A.-A. Taché Papers, T21915; Joseph Dubuc to Élie Tassé, 6 and 11 June, 3 July 1879, Joseph Dubuc Papers; Joseph Dubuc to A.-A. Taché, 6 June 1879, Bishop A.-A. Taché Papers, T21897.

71 J.W. Walker to John Norquay, 3 June 1879, NPP, A-380; J.J. Setter to John Norquay, 24 June 1879, NPP, A-263; W.W. Ogilvie to John Norquay, 5 June 1879, NPP, A-318; E. Brokovski to John Norquay, 7 July 1879, NPP, A-244; A.W. Burgess to John Norquay, 31 July 1879, NPP, A-224; D. Girouard to John A. Macdonald, 4 June 1879, John A. Macdonald Papers; *Canadian Illustrated News* 20, no. 1 (5–6 July 1879).

72 John Norquay to John A. Macdonald, 4 June 1879, John A. Macdonald Papers, 165680.

73 Joseph Royal to A.-A. Taché, 11 June, 1 July 1879, Bishop A.-A. Taché Papers, T21923, T22080; Joseph Dubuc to Élie Tassé, 3 July, 24 August, 30 September 1879, Joseph Dubuc Papers; *Manitoba Free Press*, 2 July 1879.

74 *Manitoba Free Press*, 30 June 1879; *Le Métis*, 26 June 1879.

75 *Manitoba Free Press*, 30 June 1879.

76 Joseph Cauchon to A.-A. Taché, 27 June 1879, Bishop A.-A. Taché Papers, T22052; A.A. Cherrier to A.-A. Taché, 14 and 23 June, 4 July 1879, Bishop A.-A. Taché Papers, T21958, T22032, T22109; I thank Michel Lagacé for his help with the translation of these remarkable letters; Frances Russell, *The Canadian Crucible: Manitoba's Role in Canada's Great Divide* (Winnipeg: Heartland Associates, 2003), 147–52, concludes that Macdonald simply let the legislation die; Joseph Cauchon to Lord Lorne, 20 September 1879, Joseph Cauchon Lieutenant Governor Papers, Letterbook M.

77 Joseph Royal to A.-A. Taché, 1 July 1879, Bishop A.-A. Taché Papers, T22080; Joseph Dubuc to Élie Tassé, 3 July, 26 September, 24 October 1879, Joseph Dubuc Papers; A.A. Cherrier to A.-A. Taché, 2 and 10 June, 4 July 1879, Bishop A.-A. Taché Papers, T21879, T21915, T22032; Dugas to A.-A. Taché, 2 and 15 June 1879, Bishop A.-A. Taché Papers, T21875, T21962.

78 Joseph Dubuc to Élie Tassé, 30 September 1879, also Joseph Dubuc to Élie Tassé, 15 July, 24 August, 4 and 30 September, 1, 24, and 25 October 1879, Joseph Dubuc Papers; Joseph Dubuc to A.-A. Taché, 6 June 1879, Bishop A.-A. Taché Papers, T21904; A.-A. Taché to Joseph Dubuc, 18 June 1879, Joseph Dubuc Papers.

79 Joseph Dubuc to Élie Tassé, 3 and 15 July 1879, Joseph Dubuc Papers.

80 *Le Métis*, 19 June 1879.

81 Joseph Cauchon to A.-A. Taché, 27 June 1879, Bishop A.-A. Taché Papers, T22052; A.A. Cherrier to A.-A. Taché, 23 June, 4 July 1879, Bishop A.-A. Taché Papers, T22032, T22109; Andrée Désilets, "Cauchon, Joseph-Édouard," in *Dictionary of Canadian Biography*, vol. 11, University of Toronto/Université Laval, 2003–, http://www.biographi.ca/en/bio/cauchon_joseph_edouard_11E.html (accessed 10 April 2023); F.A. Milligan, "Reservation of Manitoba Bills and Refusal of Assent by Lieutenant-Governor Cauchon, 1877–82," *Canadian Journal of Economics and Political Science* 14 (1948): 247–48.

82 *Le Métis*, 31 July 1879; Louis-Raymond Giroux to A.-A. Taché, 8 August 1879, Bishop A.-A. Taché Papers, T22327.

83 *Manitoba Free Press*, 11 July, 2, 14, and 27 August, 9, 16, and 18 September, 3 and 21 October, 1, 19, and 22 November 1879; a "chromo," the prize, is a painted photograph.

84 *Proving that the Province of Manitoba and the Canadian North-West Is a Fertile Soil for Willing Hands to Work* (Winnipeg: Manitoba Free Press, 1880); "Memo for Estimates," NPP, A-161; Bernard Saunders to John Norquay, 30 September 1879, NPP, A-233; Alexander Begg to John Norquay, 18 October 1879, A-787; Alexander Begg and Bernard Saunders to John Norquay, 11 October 1879, NPP, A-325.

85 Corydon Brown to John Norquay, 9 August 1879, NPP, A-350; *Canadian Craftsman and Masonic Record* 13, no. 10 (15 October 1879): 314.

86 John Norquay and John Schultz to J.C. Aikins, 12 August 1879, NPP, A-286.

87 John Schultz to John A. Macdonald, 24 June 1879, John A. Macdonald Papers, 119904.

88 Joseph Dubuc to Élie Tassé, 15 July, 24 August, 4 and 30 September, 1, 24, and 25 October 1879, Joseph Dubuc Papers.

89 Joseph Dubuc to Élie Tassé, 30 September, 24–25 October 1879, Joseph Dubuc Papers; Joseph Dubuc, *Mémoires d'un Manitoban* (Rome: 1912), 65–70, Joseph Dubuc Papers; Marc Girard to A.-A. Taché, 25 October 1879, Bishop A.-A. Taché Papers, T22672; Édouard Lecompte, *Un grand chrétien, Sir Joseph Dubuc, 1840–1914* (Montréal: Imprimerie du Messager, 1923), 179; G.O. Rothney, "Girard, Marc-Amable," in *Dictionary of Canadian Biography*, vol. 12, University of Toronto/Université Laval, 2003–, http://www.biographi.ca/en/bio/girard_marc_amable_12E.html (accessed 10 April 2023).

90 Marc Girard to A.-A. Taché, 29 October 1879, Bishop A.-A. Taché Papers, T22719; copy of Marc Girard to John Norquay, n.d., Bishop A.-A. Taché Papers, T23066; John Norquay to A.-A. Taché, 30 October 1879, Bishop A.-A. Taché Papers, T22722; *Le*

Métis, 22 November 1879; Winnipeg *Tribune*, 29 October, 1 and 19 November, 5 December 1879.

91 Standard Life Assurance Company to John Norquay, 3 November 1879, NPP, A-348.

92 Samuel Matheson to John Norquay, 25 November 1879, NPP, A-373.

93 *Manitoba Free Press*, 19 November 1879; Manitoba Executive Council, *Orders-in-Council Registers 1870–1891*, 26 November 1879; Lecompte, *Dubuc*, 179–80.

94 "Norquay's Address to the Electors of St. Andrews South," *Manitoba Free Press*, 8 November 1879; Corydon Brown to John Norquay, 14 July 1879, NPP, A-340; Joseph Ryan to John Norquay, 18 September 1879, NPP, A-245; George Leary to John Norquay, 27 August, 9 October 1879, NPP, A-253, A-254; Manitoba Executive Council, *Orders-in-Council Registers 1870–1891*, 26 November 1879.

95 *Manitoba Free Press*, 22 August, 21 October, 5, 7, 14, and 26 November, 2, 4, 6, 10, 15, and 16 December 1879; A.M. Burgess to John Norquay, 29 December 1879, NPP, A-251.

96 William Bathgate to John A. Macdonald, 10 January 1880, John A. Macdonald Papers, 168812; Joseph Dubuc to Élie Tassé, 25 April 1880, Joseph Dubuc Papers; *Winnipeg Weekly Times*, 14, 21, and 28 November, 5, 12, 19, and 26 December 1879; C.W. Allen to John A. Macdonald, 24 November 1879, John A. Macdonald Papers, vol. 311 (I thank Alastair Sweeney for this reference); W.T. Vincent to John Norquay, 27 October 1879, NPP, A-369; Acton Burrows to John Norquay, n.d., NPP, A-247; *Manitoba Free Press*, August–December 1879; David Young to Alexander Morris, 5 November 1879, Alexander Morris Papers K; David Young to Mackenzie Bowell, 15 November 1879, Mackenzie Bowell Papers; J.J. Setter to John Norquay, 29 December 1879, NPP, A-234.

97 W. Hill Nash to John Norquay, 20 September, 1 October, 19 November 1879, 6 January 1880, NPP, A-358, A-381, A-232, A-400.

98 F.-X. Kavanagh to Archbishop A.-A. Taché, 27 November 1879, Bishop A.-A. Taché Papers: "I'm speaking of Métis."

99 *Canadian Parliamentary Companion 1880*, 390–91; Joseph Dubuc to Élie Tassé, 3 and 18 December 1879, Joseph Dubuc Papers.

100 Carl Betke, "McMicken, Gilbert," in *Dictionary of Canadian Biography*, vol. 12, University of Toronto/Université Laval, 2003–, http://www.biographi.ca/en/bio/mcmicken_gilbert_12E.html (accessed 10 April 2023).

101 Joseph Dubuc to Élie Tassé, 18 December 1879, Joseph Dubuc Papers.

102 *Manitoba Free Press*, 4, 6, 15, and 19 December 1879.

103 *Manitoba Free Press*, 17 and 18 December 1879; *Le Métis*, 5 and 22 January 1880; *Winnipeg Weekly Times*, 19 and 26 December 1879, 2 January 1880; Joseph Dubuc to Élie Tassé, 18 December 1879, Joseph Dubuc Papers.

104 John L. Holmes, "Factors Affecting Politics in Manitoba: A Study of the Provincial Elections 1870–1899" (MA thesis, University of Manitoba, 1936), 40–41.

105 Canada, Minister of Agriculture, *Census of Canada 1870–71* (Ottawa: I.B. Taylor, Maclean, Roger and Company, 1873–78): 1870 *population* of Manitoba: 12,228; *religion*: Roman Catholic 5,452; Protestant 4,841; not given 1,935; *birthplace*: North-West and Manitoba 11,298; England 125; Scotland 248; Ireland 49; Canada 60; Ontario 118; other British colony 10; France 9; United States 166; other 27; not given 7; fewer than one-sixth were Canadian or British born in 1870.

106 *Winnipeg Weekly Times*, 30 May 1879, cites Norquay's memo to Canada's minister of finance claiming that the provincial population was close to 55,000; "Census 1881 Manitoba Population, within Former Limits, 48,939," 28 January 1882, NPP, A-875; total in expanded province: 64,814; Manitoba extension: Lake of the Woods 4,261; Lake Winnipeg 2,411; Winnipegosis 1,258; Little Saskatchewan 6,440; Turtle Mountain 1,505; total 15,875.

107 "Toujours la vieille rancune," Joseph Dubuc to Élie Tassé, 3 July 1879, Joseph Dubuc Papers.

108 David Young to Alexander Morris, 5 November 1879, Alexander Morris Papers K; C.W. Allen to John A. Macdonald, 24 November 1879, John A. Macdonald Papers, vol. 311(thank you to Alastair Sweeney for this reference); "Winnipeg Conservative Club: Constitution & By-Laws," Glenbow Library and Archives; David Young to Mackenzie Bowell, 15 November 1879, Mackenzie Bowell Papers.

Chapter 7: Boom Times and Crash, 1880–January 1883

1 Charles Adams to John Norquay, 9 and 31 August 1881, NPP, A-772; Manitoba Vital Statistics Agency, "Ada Theodora Norquay," 29 June 1881, file number 1882, 002199, http://vitalstats.gov.mb.ca/ListView.php (accessed 18 March 2018). The spelling of Ada/Aida varied. Aida seems to have been the version initially favoured by John Norquay. The opera *Aida*, by Giuseppe Verdi, premiered in Cairo in 1871. The official government notice of Aida's death at the age of twenty-two months lists the date as 13 April 1883. I thank Gord Goldsborough for this reference. The details in this paragraph are based upon the genealogical work of the late Carol Norquay Stoddart.

2 J.J. Setter to John Norquay, 4 July 1881, NPP, A-809; Marc Girard to his wife, 17 October 1882, Marc Girard Papers.

3 Walter Nursey to John Norquay, 23 August 1881, NPP, A-650.

4 Tom Norquay to John Norquay, 27 July 1879, 28 August 1881, 19 January 1882, NPP, A-261, A-794, A-1102.

5 Canon John Grisdale to John Norquay, 6 August 1880, 7 March 1881 NPP, A-501, A-566, A-646; E. Cowley to John Norquay, 20 June and summer 1882, NPP, A-1167, A-1497.

6 Bernard Saunders to John Norquay, 11 May 1878, 1 August and 31 December 1879, 1 January, 30 June, 24 September, and 10 November 1880, 1 July and 22 December 1881,

30 June, 15 August, and 8 September 1882, NPP, A-30, A-332, A-295(a) and (b), A-516, A-473, A-419, A-800, A-893, A-989, A-1213, A-995.

7 William Gerrond to John Norquay, 13 May 1879, NPP, A-309; Andrew Spence to John Norquay, 5 August 1880, NPP, A-453; Charles Adams to John Norquay, 11 September 1880, NPP, A-471; John Norquay to Charles Adams, 1881, NPP, A-793.

8 Colin Setter to John Norquay, 19 November 1879, NPP, A-230, also 14 May and 13 December 1880, 3 May 1881, November 1882, NPP, A-611, A-426, A-765, A-1394; Emma Cockran to John Norquay, 9 December 1880, NPP, A-430; band leadership is discussed in Heather Devine, *The People Who Own Themselves: Aboriginal Ethnogenesis in a Canadian Family, 1660–1900* (Calgary: University of Calgary Press, 2004).

9 On appeals for aid, see William Gowler to John Norquay, 3 July 1880, NPP, A-625, A-410, A-411; William Gerrond to John Norquay, 5 August 1881, NPP, A-822; J.A.K. Drummond to John Norquay, 19 November 1880, NPP, A-447; John Norquay to John A. Macdonald, 31 August 1882, John A. Macdonald Papers, 182908-9; James Sanderson to John Norquay, 3 May 1883, NPP, B-497.

10 John Lazarus Norquay to John Norquay, 22 July 1880, October 1882, NPP, A-632, A-1139; Peter Erasmus to John Norquay, 4 June 1882, NPP, A-1169; William Pruden to John Norquay, 13 July 1882, NPP, A-977; John P. Pruden to John Norquay, 14 September 1880, NPP, A-470.

11 John Norquay to Ben McKenzie, 18 April 1883, NPP, Letterbook C; Bernard Saunders to John Norquay, 25 September 1879, 8 September 1882, NPP, A-332, A-995; Loftus M. Fortier to Archbishop A.-A. Taché, 7 December 1880, Bishop A.-A. Taché Papers, T24881.

12 Edward S. Drewry to John Norquay, 1 April 1881, NPP, A-895; Bannatyne store to John Norquay, NPP, A-553, A-540, A-542, A-589; Alex Davidson to John Norquay, 24 October 1882, NPP, A-1494(b); William Van Horne to John Norquay, 27 February 1882, NPP, A-832.

13 H.D. Cameron to John Norquay, 26 January 1882, NPP, A-1103; Charles Adams to E. McDonald, 16 February 1883, NPP, Letterbook C; James Aikins to John Norquay, 2[?] March 1883, NPP, B-62; John Norquay to J.D. Pennefather, c. March–April 1883, NPP, Letterbook D; F.W. Fisher to John Norquay, 30 January 1885, NPP, C-589; J.L. Benson to John Norquay, 1 October 1885, NPP, C-1320; John Norquay to F. Stancliffe, 16 March 1883, NPP, Letterbook C.

14 On letters requesting favours, see NPP, A, 939, 1133, 1148, 1182, 1194, 1212, 1273, 1512, 1585, and B, 22, 35, 412.

15 Canada, Department of Agriculture, "The Report of Mr. George Broderick of Hawes, Wensleydale, Yorkshire," in *Canada in 1880: Reports of Tenant Farmers' Delegates on the Dominion of Canada as a Field for Settlement: Second Series* (Ottawa: Department of Agriculture, 1881).

16 NPP, A-500, A-1498, A-1384, A-1492; Manitoba Club, NPP, A-323, A-581, A-616; Selkirk Club to John Norquay, 3 December 1883, NPP, B-427; Anglican Church, NPP,

A-904, A-911, A-1128, A-1160, A-1165, A-1178, A-1348, A-1349, A-1413, A-1451, B-26, B-30, B-31, B-418, B-424, B-429, B-430, C-8, C-12, C-241, C-293; *Report of the Synod of the Diocese of Rupert's Land. October 19th 1889* (Winnipeg: Manitoba Free Press Printing, 1889); John Norquay to Mackenzie Bowell, 27 March and 10 July 1884, Letterbook C; Robert Machray to John Norquay, 22 September 1884, NPP, C-474, A-1184, A-1413, B-68; Masonic Order, NPP, A-183; Ellen Gillies Cooke Papers, file 7; *Craftsman and Canadian Masonic Record* 6, no. 4 (January 1872): 113; 8, no. 2 (1 February 1874): 60; 9, no. 7 (1 July 1875): 599.

17 *Winnipeg Times*, 24 April 1882, clipping in Charles Acton Burrows Papers.

18 These are terms employed by Mary-Louise Pratt, quoted in Tolly Bradford and Chelsea Horton, eds., *Mixed Blessings: Indigenous Encounters with Christianity in Canada* (Vancouver: UBC Press, 2016) 10.

19 Robert Machray to John Norquay, 2 March 1878, NPP, A-27; Thomas Howard to John Norquay, 28 May 1879, Executive Council Premier's Office (hereafter ECPO), G8729; St. Peter's parish to John Norquay, 1882, NPP, A-1221; Thomas Cook to John Norquay, 27 September 1880, NPP, A-478; *Church Guardian* 1, no. 38 (1 January 1880): 2; 3, no. 34 (8 December 1881): 2; 4, no. 14 (17 July 1882): 4; 4, no. 35 (27 December 1882): 4; 5, no. 4 (23 May 1883): 7; 5, no. 19 (5 September 1883): 5; 5, no. 33 (12 December 1883): 5; 7, no. 11 (24 June 1885): 7; 7, no. 31 (18 November 1885): 6; 7, no. 48 (17 March 1886): 5; 8, no. 14 (3 August 1887): 5.

20 St. John's College, "Minutes of Council Meetings July 31st 1871–Oct. 25th 1888," and "Minutes of College Council Meetings Jan 16th 1889–Sept 5th 1923," SJC Papers, UA 1, box 2; Synod of the Diocese of Rupert's Land, Reports, 1873–1886, University of Manitoba Archives; William John Fraser, "A History of St. John's College, Winnipeg" (MA thesis, University of Manitoba, 1966); George Young, *Manitoba Memories: Leaves from My Life in the Prairie Province, 1868–1884* (Toronto: William Briggs, 1897), 73; Harry Shave, *"Our Heritage": Commemorating the 25th Anniversary of the Present (the Third) St. John's Cathedral, 1926–1951* (Winnipeg: De Montfort Press, 1951), 52; there are many letters in NPP re his membership on the St. John's Ladies' School board and the board of St. John's [Men's] College.

21 Alex Begg to John Norquay, "Memorandum: Salary Statement, Prov Treas & Pres of Council, 1881," NPP, A-853; Legislative Assembly of Manitoba, *Journals*, 1881, Appendix, ccxiii; "Salary Account," 26 July 1882, NPP, A-1510, A-919; "Memorandum, June [1883]," NPP, B-63; Corydon Brown to John Norquay, 30 January 1884, NPP, C-72.

22 Canada, Department of the Interior, "Manitoba Act Grants, Index to Patentees," AM.

23 "Parish and Settlement General Register, Manitoba and North West Territories," AM G-5463; Municipality of St. Andrews to John Norquay, 1884, NPP, A-851; D.J. McInnes to John Norquay, 4 March 1882, NPP, A-961; John Norquay to D.F. Knight, 3 October 1882, NPP, Letterbook C; D.F. Knight to John Norquay, 26 November 1882, NPP, A-1259; Thomas Rosser to John Norquay, 20 February 1882, NPP, A-1211; George P. Vances to John Norquay, 30 December 1881, 9 January 1882, NPP,

A-856, A-1580; A. McDonald to John Norquay, 22 December 1881, NPP, A-860(a) and (b); John Allan to John Norquay, 17 December 1881, NPP, A-865; J.H. McTavish to John Norquay, 31 December 1881, NPP, A-873(a) and (b); A.W. Ogilvie to John Norquay, 31 December 1881, NPP, A-883; J.J. Setter to John Norquay, 24 December 1881, NPP, A-892; Rice M. Howard to John Norquay, 27 and 30 January 1882, and further correspondence re lands, NPP, A-1593, A-1595, A-1174, A-1472, A-954, A-955, A-1577, A-1581, A-1582, A-968, A-969, A-867, A-799, C-1077, A-1537, A-819, A-896 (a), (b), and (c), C-2464, A-975, A-1438, A-987, A-1246, A-1518, A-997, A-1103(a) and (b), A-1098, A-1197, A-1198, A-1209, A-829, A-957, A-1155, A-830, A-1606, A-641, A-816, A-824, A-1214, A-1207, A-1127, A-1508(a), A-1590, A-1591, A-025.

24 On the boom in Winnipeg, see Ruben Bellan, *Winnipeg First Century: An Economic History* (Winnipeg: Queenston House, 1978); David G. Burley, "The Keepers of the Gate: Inequality of Property Ownership during the Winnipeg Real Estate Boom of 1881–82," *Urban History Review* 17 (1988): 63–76; David G. Burley, "Frontier of Opportunity: The Social Organization of Self-Employment in Winnipeg, Manitoba, 1881–1901," *Histoire sociale/Social History* 31 (1998): 35–69; Hartwell Bowsfield, ed., *The Letters of Charles John Brydges*, vol. 1, *1879–1882*, vol. 2, *1883–1889* (Winnipeg: Hudson's Bay Record Society, 1977, 1981); Pierre Berton, *The National Dream: The Great Railway 1871–1881* (Toronto: McClelland and Stewart, 1970); Ellen Cooke, "Letters and Notes of Sr. Curran which Have Been Recopied in 1928: Jan 1868 to August 1885, Entries in September 1881," Ellen Gillies Cooke Papers, file 15; *Report of the Synod of the Diocese of Rupert's Land 1883* (Winnipeg: Manitoba Free Press Printers, 1883), also 1884, 1886; J.W. Harris to John Norquay, 27 March 1880, 11 September 1882, NPP, A-391, A-311.

25 John Norquay to James Thomson, 26 July 1881, Margaret Macleod Papers, file 41, and John Norquay Papers, file 4.

26 Winnipeg Land Titles Office, "Old System Abstract Book, Winnipeg 3 (Abstract 3)," 26, 27, 28k, 29, instruments 25709–10, 25715–18, 31329, 39910, 43628–29, 73348–49, 73351. I thank Randy Rostecki for his detailed research on these land questions; see R.R. Rostecki, "Winnipeg 1870–1886: The Physical Legacy of the Boom" (MA thesis, University of Manitoba, 1980); Bowsfield, *The Letters of Charles John Brydges*; City of Winnipeg to John Norquay, 16 January 1883, NPP, A-1284; John Norquay to Andrews & Corbet Co., 30 May 1885, NPP, Letterbook E.

27 W.W. Ogilvie to John Norquay, c. September 1878, NPP, A-194; 27 January 1879, A-339; 5 June 1879, A-318; 18 July 1879, A-243; 7 August 1879, A-259; 25 August 1879, A-362; 15 September 1879, A-354; 6 October 1879, A-238; 13 December 1879, A-359; 23 August 1880, A-459; 20 September 1880, A-474; 1 June 1881, A-883. The two quotations come from W.W. Ogilvie to John Norquay, 5 June 1879, NPP, A-318, and 27 January 1879, A-339.

28 Tom Norquay to John Norquay 10 July 1882, NPP, A-1441; and W. Ogilvie to Norquay, 6 October 1879, NPP, A-238.

29 W.W. Ogilvie to John Norquay, 6 October 1879, NPP, A-238; n.d. 1878, A-194; 27 January 1879, A-339; 18 July 1879, A-243; 7 August 1879, A-459; 20 September 1880, A-474; Thomas White to John Norquay, 23 August 1880, NPP, A-459.

30 A.W. Ogilvie to John Norquay, 31 December 1881, NPP, A-883; Bernard Saunders to John Norquay, 22 December 1881, NPP, A-893; Allan Levine, "Ogilvie, William Watson," in *Dictionary of Canadian Biography*, vol. 12, University of Toronto/Université Laval, 2003–, http://www.biographi.ca/en/bio/ogilvie_william_watson_12E.html (accessed 11 April 2023); Michèle Brassard and Jean Hamelin, "Ogilvie, Alexander Walker," in *Dictionary of Canadian Biography*, vol. 13, University of Toronto/Université Laval, 2003–, http://www.biographi.ca/en/bio/ogilvie_alexander_walker_13E.html (accessed 11 April 2023).

31 Canada, Dominion Lands Branch, to John Norquay, 30 June 1879, NPP, A-1537; Lindsay Russell to John Norquay, 18 May 1880, NPP, A-615.

32 John A. Macdonald to William Scarth, 24 October 1882, 4 January 1883, John A. Macdonald Papers, Letterbook 22, part 1, part 2; William Van Horne to General Public, 2 January 1882, NPP, A-873(a) and (b); Bank of Montreal, "Minute Book," 21 November and 26 December 1882, Bank of Montreal Papers; *Nor'West Farmer and Manitoba Miller* 5 (1886): 405–6; Frank Austin Carle, *The British Northwest: Pen and Sun Sketches in the Canadian Wheat Lands* (St. Paul, MN: Pioneer Press, 1882).

33 William Scarth to John Norquay, 22 September 1880, 9 July and 3 November 1881, NPP, A-465, A-775, A-779; Richard Munro to John Norquay, 15 and 19 November, 2 December 1880, 9 and 20 June 1881, NPP, A-408(a) and (b), A-448, A-433, A-805, A-808; A.C. Clouston to John Norquay, 11 May 1881, NPP, A-821; John Norquay, "Memo," 10 October 1881, NPP, A-889; A.E. Fisher to John Norquay, 19 October 1881, NPP, A-879; Robert Ruttan to John Norquay, 26 October 1881, NPP, A-783; Merchants' Bank to John Norquay, 22 November 1881, NPP, A-891.

34 John Norquay to John A. Macdonald, 12 October 1881, John A. Macdonald Papers, 176034; H. Cameron to John A. Macdonald, 14 October 1881, John A. Macdonald Papers, 176083.

35 William Scarth to John Norquay, 26 November and 29 December 1883, NPP, B-419, B-454; William Scarth to John A. Macdonald, quoted in Zenon Gawron, "Scarth, William Bain," in *Dictionary of Canadian Biography*, vol. 13, University of Toronto/Université Laval, 2003–, http://www.biographi.ca/en/bio/scarth_william_bain_13E.html (accessed 11 April 2023).

36 Samuel Bedson to John Norquay, 19 January 1882, NPP, A-1105. Emphasis in original.

37 S.W. Farrell to John Norquay, 14 February 1882, NPP, A-1210; 8 February 1882, NPP, A-1216; 24 June 1886, ECPO, G8729; Walter A. Wilkes to John Norquay, 25 November 1882, NPP, A-1312; also A-658 and A-1215(a) and (b); *Rules, Orders, and Forms of Procedure of the Legislative Assembly of Manitoba* (Winnipeg: *Le Métis*, 1877), with thanks to Mel Myers for the gift of this volume signed by Norquay; David G. Burley, "Ross, Arthur Wellington," in *Dictionary of Canadian Biography*, vol. 13, University of Toronto/Université Laval, 2003–, http://www.biographi.ca/en/bio/

ross_arthur_wellington_13E.html (accessed 11 April 2023); S.W. Farrell to John Norquay, 14 February 1882, NPP, A-1216; John Norquay to S. Jameson, 25 October 1882, NPP, Letterbook C.

38 J.H. McTavish to John Norquay and William Van Horne, 26 March 1883, NPP, A-1445(c) and (d).

39 John Norquay to John Egan, 29 March 1883, NPP, A-1392; William Van Horne to John Norquay, 29 May 1883, NPP, A-1356; Robert Ruttan and S.W. Farrell to John Norquay "and others," 1 June 1883, NPP, C-270(a) and (b); John M. Egan to John Norquay, 15 June 1883, NPP, G-8729; John Norquay and James J. Foy to North British Canadian Investment Company, 23 February 1882, NPP, A-697; William Scarth to John Norquay, 31 March and 24 October 1882, NPP, A-988, A-982; A. Bain to John Norquay, 16 November 1882, NPP, C-2171.

40 George H. Ham, *Reminiscences of a Raconteur, Between the '40s and the '20s* (Toronto: Musson, 1921), 66–67; *Monetary Times*, 1 December 1882, 14 September 1883, 29 February 1884, 8 October 1886, 31 January 1887; Edward Leacock to John Norquay, 3 August 1880, NPP, A-452; also A-454, A-477, A-647, A-801, A-804, A-806, A-1599, A-1602, A-1228; for context, see Robert Babe, *Telecommunications in Canada: Technology, Industry, and Government* (Toronto: University of Toronto Press, 1990).

41 James F. Sanderson to John Norquay, 31 May, 26 June, and 21 September 1882, NPP, A-1188, A-1163, A-921.

42 W.W. Ogilvie to John Norquay, 23 January 1880, NPP, A-1613; A. Russell to John Norquay, 10 November 1882, NPP, A-1239; "List of Squatters around Medicine Hat," ECPO, "Misc. Govt" file; Samuel Bedson to John Norquay, 22 February 1883, NPP, A-1465; John Norquay to Wesley Wilson, 4 and 5 April 1884, NPP, Letterbook D.

43 John A. Macdonald to John Norquay, 13 August 1883, NPP, A-1364; Saskatchewan Coal and Transportation Company, "Petition," NPP, C-942; "Letters Patent Incorporating the Saskatchewan Coal Mining and Transportation Company (Limited)," 5 November 1883, recorded 12 November 1883 under the Canada Joint Stock Companies Act, Secretary of State Registers, liber 84, folio 572–75, microfilm C4008; J.E. Woodworth to John Norquay, 16 August 1883, ECPO, G8729; John Norquay to J.E. Woodworth, 10 January 1884, NPP, Letterbook D; J.E. Woodworth to John Norquay, 12 January 1884, NPP, C-35; also B-455, C-239, C-240.

44 *Fort Macleod Gazette*, 24 January 1883; John Norquay to John A. Macdonald (draft), February–March 1883, NPP, A-1432; William Harder to John Norquay, 9 January 1883, NPP, C-250; John Norquay to Dennis Ryan, 24 April 1883, NPP, Letterbook D; Paul Daly to J.P. Lawson, 20 June 1883, NPP, C-832; the late Professor A.A. den Otter kindly helped me with this research; J.W. Morrow, *Early History of the Medicine Hat Country* (1923; revised, Medicine Hat: Medicine Hat Historical Society, 1974); Ellen Cooke, "Saskatchewan Coal Mining and Transportation Company," Ellen Gillies Cooke Papers, file 10; Omer Lavallee, "John M. Egan, a Railway Officer in Winnipeg, 1882–1886: An Account of Canadian Pacific's First Years in the Manitoba Capital,"

Manitoba Historical Society *Transactions*, Series 3, 33 (1976–77): http://www.mhs.mb.ca/docs/transactions/3/eganrailway.shtml.

45 John James Setter to John Norquay, 22 November 1880, NPP, A-445; this correspondence continues, 1880–82: A-425, A-856, A-892, A-922, A-1244, A-1333, A-1461, A-1504; another investor colleague was Samuel Bedson; see NPP, A-1105, A-1116, A-1121, A-1203, A-1210, A-1214; hundreds of bills are included in NPP, including A-507–15, A-978–1000; John Norquay to James Snell, 18 May 1880, NPP, A-525; Ham, *Reminiscences*, 30; Burley, "Keepers," 63–76.

46 Merchants' Bank to John Norquay, 3 May 1882, NPP, A-1500; Ontario Bank to John Norquay, 22 October 1882, 3 January 1883, NPP, A-1505, A-1383; John Watson to James Monkman, 20 June 1882, NPP, C-479; Norquay cheque stubs, 1879–80, ECPO, Miscellaneous, G8730, and July–December 1883, ECPO, Miscellaneous, G8730; for context, see Richard White, "Information, Markets, and Corruption: Transcontinental Railroads in the Gilded Age," *Journal of American History* 90, no. 1 (2003): 19–43.

47 Alfred Boultbee to John A. Macdonald, 25 June 1880, John A. Macdonald Papers, 171637; Edgar Dewdney to John A. Macdonald, 30 June 1880, John A. Macdonald Papers, 89347; "Memo re Norquay Salary," 19 October 1882, NPP, A-919.

48 *Manitoban*, 29 April 1871; *Report of the Department of Public Works for the Province of Manitoba from 1870 to 30th June 1874* (Winnipeg: *Nor'Wester*, 1875), 30; Alexander Begg, *Practical Hand-Book and Guide to Manitoba and the North-West* (Toronto: Belford Brothers, 1877); Alexander Begg and Walter R. Nursey, *Ten Years in Winnipeg* (Winnipeg: *Winnipeg Times*, 1879), 156; *Manitoba Free Press*, 12 and 16 February 1877; Élie Tassé to John Norquay, 19 May 1880, NPP, A-613.

49 Alexander Mackenzie to Alexander Morris, 3 December 1875, 22 and 24 April, 7 June 1878, Alexander Morris Papers K; Charles Mair to George Denison, 28 January, 16 March 1876, George Denison Papers; J.W. Taylor to John Lambert Cadwalader, 15 February 1876, USC Papers; W.L. Morton, *Manitoba: A History* (1957; reprinted, Toronto: University of Toronto Press, 1967), 176–81.

50 For context, see Arthur Silver, *The French-Canadian Idea of Confederation*, 2nd ed. (Toronto: University of Toronto Press, 1997); Robert Painchaud, *Un rêve français dans le peuplement de la prairie* (St. Boniface, MB: Édition des plaines, 1986); Bruno Ramirez, *On the Move: French-Canadian and Italian Migrants in the North Atlantic Economy, 1860–1914* (Toronto: McClelland and Stewart, 1991); Alan Green, Mary Mackinnon, and Chris Minns, "Conspicuous by Their Absence: French Canadians and the Settlement of the Canadian West," *Journal of Economic History* 65, no. 3 (2005): 822–49; J.R. Miller, "Anti-Catholicism in Canada: From the British Conquest to the Great War," in *Creed and Culture: The Place of English-Speaking Catholics in Canadian Society, 1750–1930*, ed. Terrence Murphy and Gerald Stortz (Montreal and Kingston: McGill-Queen's University Press, 1993), 25–48; and J.R. Miller, "Anti-Catholic Thought in Victorian Canada," *Canadian Historical Review* 66, no. 4 (1985): 474–94; an example of the discussion in Quebec is the account of a speech in Montreal by

Joseph Royal, and a rebuttal by A. Gélinas, in *L'opinion publique* 11, no. 22 (27 mai 1880): 253–54.

51 *Manitoba Free Press*, 10 March and 2 April 1879; *Times* [London], 6 October 1879; *Canadian North West* 1, no. 1 (1880): 15; Marquis of Lorne, *The Canadian North-West: Speech Delivered at Winnipeg* (Ottawa: Department of Agriculture, 1881); Gerald Friesen, "Imports and Exports in the Manitoba Economy 1870–1890," *Manitoba History* 16 (1988): http://www.mhs.mb.ca/docs/mb_history/16/manitobaimports exports.shtml; Randy William Widdis, *With Scarcely a Ripple: Anglo-Canadian Migration into the United States and Western Canada, 1880–1920* (Montreal and Kingston: McGill-Queen's University Press, 1998).

52 Manitoba Department of Public Works, *Annual Reports*, 1879–87; "Memo: Public Works Expenditures 1878–1886," c. 1887, ECPO, G8730; *Report of the Minister of Public Works for the Year Ending December 31st, 1881*, and the same publication for 1882 and 1883; Stunden Bower, *Wet Prairie*, 52–56.

53 *Monetary Times and Trade Review* 15, no. 50 (9 June 1882): 1510–11; Stunden Bower, *Wet Prairie*, 31; Alfred Boyd to John Norquay, 23 April and 26 October 1880, 7 September, 29 November, and 23 December 1881, NPP, A-603, A-490, A-641, A-863, A-861; Michèle Dagenais, "The Municipal Territory: A Product of the Liberal Order?," in *Liberalism and Hegemony: Debating the Canadian Liberal Revolution*, ed. Jean-François Constant and Michel Ducharme (Montreal and Kingston: McGill-Queen's University Press, 2009), 201–20; Morton, *Manitoba*, 189.

54 *Winnipeg Times*, 12 July 1884; Corydon Brown to John Norquay, 8 June 1880, NPP, A-619; Manitoba Executive Council, *Orders-in-Council Registers 1870–1891*, 4 June and 26 November 1879, 22 January and 16 November 1881, 2 September 1882, 6 September 1883.

55 John Ralston to John Norquay, 2 May 1881, ECPO, G8729; George Wishart to Government of Manitoba, 5 July 1880, NPP, A-513; Alfred Boyd to John Norquay, 26 October 1880, NPP, A-490; William Winram to John Norquay, 17 June 1881, NPP, A-803.

56 Manitoba Executive Council, *Orders-in-Council Registers 1870–1891*, 11 November 1878; Clerk of the Executive Council, "Letterbook," 4 November 1879–26 June 1884, ECPO, G1044.

57 Walter Nursey to John Norquay, 23 August 1881, n.d., 1 November 1881, 22 August and n.d., November 1882, NPP, A-650, A-780, A-882, A-945, A-1275, emphasis in origninal; "Walter Reginald Nursey," in Manitoba Historical Society, *Memorable Manitobans*, http://www.mhs.mb.ca/docs/people/nursey_wr.shtml (accessed 11 April 2023).

58 Alexander Begg to John Norquay, 5 September 1880, NPP, A-469; also A-443 (a) and (b), A-446, A-640(a), (b), and (c), A-468, A-1150, A-1154.

59 Alexander Begg to John Norquay, 31 August 1882, NPP, A-937; 24 November 1883, B-492; 17 January 1884, C-55; 22 January 1884, C-62; 27 February 1884, C-339; 25

June 1884, C-159; 2 December 1884, C-863; John Norquay to Alexander Begg, 17 October 1883, NPP, Letterbook C; 28 August 1886, Letterbook 4; William Ptolemy to C.A. Bunting, 21 September 1883, William Ptolemy to David Walker, 15 September 1883, and William Ptolemy to Mail Printing Company, 9 October 1883, in Manitoba Treasury Department, "Letterbook 1881–83," F0088, GR1585, G5294; Alexander Begg to John Norquay, 2 December 1884, and John Norquay to Alexander Begg, 9 February 1885, NPP, Letterbook E; Alexander Begg, "Seventeen Years in the Canadian North-West," in *Proceedings of the Royal Colonial Institute*, April 1884 (London: Spottiswoode, 1884), 18; George Broughall, "Report of the Proceedings and the Evidence . . . Wallbridge Royal Commission . . . 1886," *Sessional Papers 1886*, LA009, GR174, G8116, box 6, files 14, 16, Archives of Manitoba, iv–vii, 133–34; William Van Horne to George Stephen, 28 December 1886, William Van Horne Papers, Letterbook 19; Munson & Allen Co. to John Norquay, 25 March 1884, NPP, C-258; Manitoba Executive Council, *Orders-in-Council Registers 1870–1891*, 22 September 1884; William Van Horne to George Stephen, 28 December 1886, William Van Horne Papers, Letterbook 19.

60 Manitoba Executive Council, *Orders-in-Council Registers 1870–1891*, 22 September 1884; Alexander Begg to John Norquay, 2 December 1884, NPP, C-863; John Norquay to Alexander Begg, 9 February 1885, NPP, Letterbook E; John Norquay to Alexander Begg, 28 August 1886, NPP, Letterbook 4.

61 Ham, *Reminiscences*, 232; Manitoba, *Sessional Papers 1886*, "Return to an Order . . . re: Amounts Paid on Account of Delegations to Ottawa," OS, 0017-4, Archives of Manitoba; "Returns Respecting Cost of Trips to Ottawa," *Manitoba Free Press*, LLM Hansard 1886, 207; Manitoba Executive Council, *Orders-in-Council Registers 1870–1891*, 154, 353, 626; for context, see James A. Maxwell, *Federal Subsidies to the Provincial Governments in Canada* (Cambridge, MA: Harvard University Press, 1937), and E.A. Heaman, *Tax, Order, and Good Government: A New Political History of Canada, 1867–1917* (Montreal and Kingston: McGill-Queen's University Press, 2017).

62 Peter O'Leary, *Travels in Canada, the Red River Territory and the United States* (London: J.B. Day, 1877), 66–67; Berton, *The National Dream*, 280–81.

63 Ellen Cooke, "Andrew Norquay Interview, Vancouver, August 1959," Ellen Gillies Cooke Papers, file 1; George M. Pierce to John Norquay, 9 November 1880, NPP, A-570; James Gouin to John Norquay, 15 April 1880, NPP, A-601; 9 March 1882, A-1375.

64 John A. Macdonald to John Norquay, 22 October 1881, John A. Macdonald Papers, LB 21, 513; John Norquay to John A. Macdonald, 4 November 1881, John A. Macdonald Papers, 176516.

65 *Journals of the Legislative Assembly of Manitoba* 10 (1880): Appendix, xcv–cvii; *Letters on the Anomalous Position of Manitoba as a Province of the Dominion* (Winnipeg: n.p., 1881); Manitoba Executive Council, *Orders-in-Council Registers 1870–1891*, 1 March 1880; John Norquay, "Delegation to Ottawa," 28 February 1880, NPP, A-846; "Report

of the Delegates . . . to Ottawa," *Journals of the Legislative Assembly of Manitoba* 10 (1880): xcv–cvii; "Report of the Delegates of the Executive Council of Manitoba to Ottawa," Manitoba Treasury department, "Letterbook 1881–83," 1–75; *Manitoba Free Press*, LLM Hansard, 11 and 13 February 1880; Canada, Dominion Lands Office, "Manitoba before Boundary Extension: Map 1882," NPP, A-1222; for context, see Mochoruk, *Formidable Heritage*.

66 Alfred Boyd to John Norquay, 23 April 1880, NPP, A-603 [probably a reference to the Cumberland House fur post].

67 John Norquay to John A. Macdonald, 17 September 1880, John A. Macdonald Papers, 9589; *Winnipeg Times*, 14 October, 2, 8, and 12 November 1880; John Norquay to John A. Macdonald, 1 December 1880, NPP, A-845.

68 John Norquay, "Memorandum, February 1881," NPP, A-837; John Norquay, "Notes, St. Clement Speech, 1881," NPP, A-755; Mochoruk, *Formidable Heritage*, 105–53; David Walker to John Norquay, 24 January, 10 February, 6 March 1881, NPP, A-839, A-825, A-847; Alexander Campbell to John Norquay, 25 April 1881, NPP, A-756; *Journals of the Legislative Assembly of Manitoba 1881*, cix–cxxvii; John A. Macdonald, speech, in Canada, *House of Commons Debates*, 18 March 1881, 1443–50; Canada, Department of Agriculture, "Memo: Census 1881 Manitoba Population," 28 January 1882, NPP, A-875.

69 John Norquay, "Memo, Interview with Sir Alex Campbell, M[inister] of J[ustice], 25 February 1881," NPP, A-890; John Norquay to John A. Macdonald, with Macdonald's annotation, 5 March 1881, NPP, A-656; David Walker to John Norquay, 5 March 1881, NPP, A-848; John Norquay and Marc Girard to John A. Macdonald, 27 January 1881, and John Norquay to John A. Macdonald, 4 March 1881, John A. Macdonald Papers, 173440, 174023, 174025; John A. Macdonald to John Norquay, 5 March 1881, NPP, A-656; Manitoba, *Journals of the Legislative Assembly 1881*, 7–9, and "Appendix," cix–cxxvii; James Mochoruk, "Thomas Greenway, 1888–1900," in *Manitoba Premiers of the 19th and 20th Centuries*, ed. Barry Ferguson and Robert Wardhaugh (Regina: Canadian Plains Research Center, 2010), 81–83.

70 "Copy of a Report of a Committee of Privy Council, 1 April 1884," in Canada, Parliament, *Sessional Papers 1902*, 83, containing "Return to an Address of the Senate dated 20 February 1902"; (total area of the provinces in 1882: BC, 390,000 square miles; QC, 193,000; MB, 150,000; ON, 109,000; NB, 27,000; NS, 22,000; PEI, 2,000).

71 *Winnipeg Times*, 30 March 1881; *Rat Portage Progress*, 9 April 1881, in "Scrapbook," Charles Acton Burrows Papers.

72 John A. Macdonald to Alexander Campbell, 20 May 1881, Alexander Campbell Papers; John Norquay to John A. Macdonald, 12 October 1881, John A. Macdonald Papers, 176034; Corydon Brown to John Norquay, 17 January 1882, NPP, A-1524; James Mochoruk, "Brown, Corydon Partlow," in *Dictionary of Canadian Biography*, vol. 12, University of Toronto/Université Laval, 2003–, http://www.biographi.ca/en/bio/brown_corydon_partlow_12E.html (accessed 11 April 2023).

73 "Report of the Delegates Appointed to Confer with the Privy Council of Canada, 8 April 1882," AM, GR134, G8113, box 3, files 25 and 31; Norquay, "Memo, 7 February 1882," in ibid.

74 "Report of the Delegates . . . 8 April 1882."

75 Ibid.; Mochoruk, *Formidable Heritage*, 111–21.

76 "Report of the Delegates . . . 8 April 1882."

77 Canada, Privy Council, Order-in-Council 137, 7 March 1882, cited in Theodore David Regehr, "The National Railway Policy and Manitoba Railway Legislation 1879–1888" (MA thesis, Carleton University, 1963), 59–60; *Manitoba Free Press*, 2 May 1882, LLM Hansard.

78 *Manitoba Free Press*, 2 May 1882, LLM Hansard; Regehr, "The National Railway Policy," 62–66; Joseph Hilts, "The Political Career of Thomas Greenway" (PhD diss., University of Manitoba, 1974), 69.

79 Mary Janigan, *Let the Eastern Bastards Freeze in the Dark: The West versus the Rest since Confederation* (Toronto: Alfred A. Knopf Canada, 2012), 68.

80 Goldwin Smith to John Norquay, 13 February 1881, NPP, A-852; also 25 April 1882, A-1111; on the gift book, see Julius Anglicanus, *Missionary Bishops: A Plea for Indians and Immigrants, Particularly in the Algoma District: Being a Letter Addressed to the Right Reverend the Metropolitan of Canada, and the Bishops of Quebec, Toronto, Huron, and Ontario* (Toronto: Willing and Williamson, 1872?), Nicholas Flood Davin to John Norquay, 18 November 1880, NPP, A-441.

81 Manitoba, Legislative Assembly, "Clerk's Records, 1880," AM, G8113, GR 174, box 3, file 13.

82 John Norquay to John A. Macdonald, 17 September 1880, John A. Macdonald Papers, 9589–93.

83 George Stephen to John A. Macdonald, 18 October and 13 November 1880, John A. Macdonald Papers, cited in Regehr, "The National Railway Policy," 32–33, emphasis in original; Donald Creighton, *John A. Macdonald II: The Old Chieftain* (Toronto: Macmillan, 1955), 302, 316; Phillip Buckner, "Tupper, Sir Charles," in *Dictionary of Canadian Biography*, vol. 14, University of Toronto/Université Laval, 2003–, http://www.biographi.ca/en/bio/tupper_charles_14E.html (accessed 11 April 2023); Heather Gilbert, *Awakening Continent: The Life of Lord Mount Stephen,* Vol. I 1829–1891 (1965; reprinted, Aberdeen, UK: Aberdeen University Press, 1976), 268; Berton, *The National Dream*, 346–89.

84 Gilbert McMicken to John A. Macdonald, 3 January 1881, John A. Macdonald Papers, 52943.

85 Henry C. Klassen, "Kittson, Norman Wolfred," in *Dictionary of Canadian Biography*, vol. 11, University of Toronto/Université Laval, 2003–, http://www.biographi.ca/en/bio/kittson_norman_wolfred_11E.html (accessed 11 April 2023); Peter B.

Waite, *Canada 1874–1896: Arduous Destiny* (Toronto: McClelland and Stewart, 1971), 106–8.

86 John Norquay to John A. Macdonald, 2 December 1880, John A. Macdonald Papers, 52657–58; Alexander Morris to John A. Macdonald, 11 December 1880, John A. Macdonald Papers, 52669; Duncan MacArthur to John A. Macdonald, 24 December 1880, John A. Macdonald Papers, 52750; Regehr, "The National Railway Policy," 36–39, 50–51.

87 Joseph Royal to John Norquay, 13 December 1880, NPP, A-427; Joseph Royal to John A. Macdonald, 15 December 1880, John A. Macdonald Papers, 52682, enclosing John Norquay to Joseph Royal, 14 December 1880, John A. Macdonald Papers, 52684–85; John A. Macdonald to John Norquay, 8 December 1880, NPP, A-431.

88 Manitoba, Legislative Assembly, *Journals*, 2nd session, 1880, 15–16; *Manitoba Free Press*, 15, 16, 21, and 23 December 1880; Regehr, "The National Railway Policy," 32–33; "Winnipeg Petition," sent to John A. Macdonald, received 3 January 1881, John A. Macdonald Papers, 52957.

89 John A. Macdonald to Martin Griffin, 31 October 1881, John A. Macdonald Papers, Letterbook 21, part 3, 527–28, cited in Regehr, "The National Railway Policy," 42; "Petition of the Executive Council of Manitoba to Her Majesty the Queen, 1887," in Canada, *Sessional Papers*, 21, 1887, 227–35, cited in ibid., 43.

90 Manitoba, *Statutes, 1881*, 44 Vic., c.1, clause 2; Regehr, "The National Railway Policy," 52–53; Legislative Assembly of Manitoba, *Journals*, 1881; *Manitoba Free Press*, 15 May 1882; T.M. Lewis to John Norquay, 26 May 1882, NPP, A-1179.

91 John A. Macdonald to John Norquay, 5 November 1881, NPP, A-869; John Norquay to John A. Macdonald, 18 November 1881, John A. Macdonald Papers, 176680.

92 John Norquay to John A. Macdonald, 18 November 1881, John A. Macdonald Papers, 176680.

93 John Schultz to John A. Macdonald, 16 April 1880, John A. Macdonald Papers, 119949; John A. Macdonald to Lord Lorne, 7 January 1883, Lord Lorne Papers, vol. 1, 302–6, quoted in Hilts, "Greenway," 69; George Stephen to John A. Macdonald, 15 and 27 August, 15 October 1881, John A. Macdonald Papers, 121882–85, 121226; John A. Macdonald to George Stephen, 19 October, 6, 13, and 28 December 1881, George Stephen Papers; W. Kaye Lamb, *A History of the Canadian Pacific Railway* (New York: Macmillan, 1977); I thank Mr. Jerry Masters and Professor Francis Carroll, who helped me with the history of railways in the northern United States.

94 George Stephen to John A. Macdonald, 10 December 1881, John A. Macdonald Papers, 121906; Gilbert McMicken to John A. Macdonald, 30 October, 10 December 1881, John A. Macdonald Papers, 110914, 110919, and draft reply 118801; Corydon Brown to John Norquay, 3 November 1881, NPP, A-778; Thomas Dowse to John Norquay, 30 March, 6 April 1881, NPP, A-870(a) and (b), A-876; also A-872, A-880, A-956.

95 Regehr, "The National Railway Policy," 57–61; John A. Macdonald to Alexander Campbell, 3 November, 29 December 1881, Alexander Campbell Papers.

96 Toronto *Globe*, 31 January 1882, cited in James A. Jackson, "The Disallowance of Manitoba Railway Legislation in the 1880s" (MA thesis, University of Manitoba, 1945), 31; Regehr, "The National Railway Policy," 58–59; J.H. Pope to John A. Macdonald, 24 August 1882, John A. Macdonald Papers, cited in Waite, *Canada 1874–1896*, 112–13; J.W. Taylor to John Davis, 29 November 1882, USC Papers.

97 Public meetings of protest took place in four Manitoba towns: Emerson, Portage la Prairie, Brandon, and West Lynne. For some protest letters, see NPP, A-1252, A-1263, A-1280; for newspaper coverage, see *Winnipeg Times*, 27 October, 3 and 6 November 1882; *Manitoba Free Press*, 10 November 1882.

98 George Stephen to John A. Macdonald, 8 November 1882, John A. Macdonald Papers, 121972; John A. Macdonald to George Stephen, 9 November 1882, George Stephen Papers; *Monetary Times, Trade Review and Insurance Chronicle* 16, no. 20 (17 November 1882): 544–45.

99 John A. Macdonald to Lord Lorne, 2 December 1882, Lord Lorne Papers, vol. 1, 295–300; John A. Macdonald to Corbet Locke, 9 November 1882, John A. Macdonald Papers, vol. 525.

100 Alexander Begg, *History of the North West* (Toronto: Hunter, Rose & Co., 1894), vol. 2, 350, cited in Regehr, "The National Railway Policy," 49–50; *Winnipeg Times*, 3 September 1880; *Manitoba Free Press*, 2–12 July 1880, 13, 28, and 29 September, 27 October, 14 November 1881.

101 Joseph Dubuc to Élie Tassé, 8 and 10 January 1880, 7 October and 25 November 1881, Joseph Dubuc Papers; Joseph Dubuc, *Mémoires d'un Manitoban* (Rome: n.p., 1912), Joseph Dubuc Papers; Joseph Cauchon to John Norquay, 15 November 1881, NPP, A-885; A.I. Silver, "La Rivière, Alphonse-Alfred-Clément," in *Dictionary of Canadian Biography*, vol. 15, University of Toronto/Université Laval, 2003–, http://www.biographi.ca/en/bio/la_riviere_alphonse_alfred_clement_15E.html (accessed 11 April 2023).

102 John Norquay to Joseph Cauchon, 15 November 1881, NPP, A-885.

103 David Young to Mackenzie Bowell, 15 November 1879, Mackenzie Bowell Papers; Francis Gilmore to John Schultz, 14 January 1880, John Schultz Papers, 7702; John Gunn to John Schultz, 30 March 1880, John Schultz Papers, 7711; John Schultz to John A. Macdonald, 13 October 1880, John A. Macdonald Papers, 119942; Edgar Dewdney to John A. Macdonald, 22 November 1881, Edgar Dewdney Papers, 400–1; Mackenzie Bowell to John Norquay, 10 February 1880, NPP, A-499; John Schultz to John Norquay, 10 February 1880, NPP, A-598.

104 Manitoba Executive Council, *Orders-in-Council Registers 1870–1891*, 523, 7 September 1881.

105 *Manitoba Free Press*, 27 April 1882, LLM Hansard; Regehr, "The National Railway Policy," 62.

106 *Manitoba Free Press*, 9 and 11 February, 13 April, 17 October, 10 November, 19 December 1882; Thomas Peterson, "Manitoba: Ethnic and Class Politics," in *Canadian Provincial Politics*, 2nd ed., ed. Martin Robin (Scarborough, ON: Prentice-Hall Canada, 1978), 61–119.

107 *Manitoba Free Press*, 1 and 3 May 1882, LLM Hansard.

108 *Manitoba Free Press*, 2 May 1882, LLM Hansard.

109 *Manitoba Free Press*, re sittings of 12, 15, 23, 27, and 29 May 1882, LLM Hansard.

110 *Manitoba Free Press*, 2 May 1882, LLM Hansard.

111 *Manitoba Free Press*, sitting of 25 May 1882, also sittings of 15, 25, 27, and 29 May 1882, LLM Hansard.

112 John Norquay to John A. Macdonald, 5 May 1882, John A. Macdonald Papers, 180124.

113 *Manitoba Free Press*, sitting of 15 May 1882, LLM Hansard; Manitoba Assembly, "Reports of Select Committee on Standing Orders," AM, G8113, GR174, box 3, file 22; Frank A. Milligan, "The Lieutenant-Governorship in Manitoba 1870–1882" (MA thesis, University of Manitoba, 1948), 36; J.W. Watkin to John A. Macdonald, 8 March 1883, John A. Macdonald Papers, 186595; William Murdoch to John A. Macdonald, 21 January 1883, John A. Macdonald Papers, 185641.

114 Gilbert McMicken to John A. Macdonald, 12 June 1882, John A. Macdonald Papers, 110924; Alexander Campbell to John Schultz, 16 and 19 June 1882, John Schultz Papers; Joseph Royal to A.-A. Taché, 21, 25, and 30 April 1882, Bishop A.-A. Taché Papers, T26953, T26600, T26613; Joseph Royal to John A. Macdonald, 6 September 1882, John A. Macdonald Papers, 118225; Joseph Royal to Hector Langevin, 11 July 1882, Thomas Chapais–Hector Langevin Papers; Escott M. Reid, "The Rise of National Parties in Canada," Canadian Political Science Association *Papers and Proceedings* 4 (1932): 187–200.

115 J.H. Metcalfe to John A. Macdonald, 5 May 1882, John A. Macdonald Papers, 180120; G. Laidlaw to John A. Macdonald, 7 August 1882, John A. Macdonald Papers, 45542; John A. Macdonald to Charles Tupper, 6 August 1882, John A. Macdonald Papers, 2491.

116 Gilbert McMicken to John A. Macdonald, 13 July 1882, John A. Macdonald Papers, 110932; Ned Farrer to John A. Macdonald, 19 February 1883, cited in Carman Cumming, *Secret Craft: The Journalism of Edward Farrer* (Toronto: University of Toronto Press, 1992), 51.

117 John Norquay to J.H. Pope, 26 July 1882, transferred by Pope to John A. Macdonald, in John A. Macdonald Papers, 182387.

118 J.H. Pope to John Norquay, 1 August 1882, NPP, A-944.

119 John A. Macdonald to John Norquay, 3 August 1882, John A. Macdonald Papers, 182391; John Norquay to John A. Macdonald, 31 August 1882, John A. Macdonald Papers, 182908.

120 Provincial Conservative Association, "Call for a Provincial Conservative Convention, 31 July 1882," NPP, A-1224; Stewart Mulvey to John A. Macdonald, 18 January 1882, John A. Macdonald Papers, 185576.

121 J.W. Taylor to John Davis, 29 November 1882, USC Papers; Friesen, "Imports and Exports."

122 Marc Girard to his wife, 4, 7, 11, 16, and 18 November 1882, Marc Girard Papers; J.A.K. Drummond to John Norquay, 30 November 1882, NPP, A-1269.

123 Joseph Royal to John A. Macdonald, 6 September 1882, John A. Macdonald Papers, 118224; Joseph Royal to John Norquay, 8 and 10 November 1881, 23 December 1882, NPP, A-760(a) and (b), A-897; James French to John A. Macdonald, 16 September 1882, John A. Macdonald Papers, 183125.

124 Joseph Royal to John A. Macdonald, 3 December 1882, John A. Macdonald Papers, 118237; James Aikins to John A. Macdonald, 30 December 1882, John A. Macdonald Papers, 77434; Henry Clarke to John A. Macdonald, 10 May 1883, John A. Macdonald Papers, 187869; W.D.P. to John Norquay, 20 November 1882, NPP, A-1393; Regehr, "The National Railway Policy," 74.

125 George Stephen to John A. Macdonald, 8 and 22 September, 28 October, 8 November, 8 December 1882, John A. Macdonald Papers, 121477, 121496, 121553, 121570, 121615; John A. Macdonald to Lord Lorne, 2 December 1882, Lord Lorne Papers, vol. 1, 295–300; letters to John Norquay re election campaign: NPP, A-1247, A-1271, A-1277, A-1274, A-1248, A-1442, A-903, A-923, A-1254, A-1343; *Commercial* 1, no. 5 (31 October 1882): 86, and no. 7 (14 November 1882): 129–30; NPP, A-864, A-866, A-1343.

126 *Toronto Tribune*, clipping enclosed in W.D. O'Brien to John Norquay, 26 January 1883, NPP, A-1456.

127 *Manitoba Free Press*, 1 January 1883; R.H. Little to John Norquay, 22 August 1881, NPP, A-928; *Church Guardian* vol. 4, no. 30 (22 November 1882): 4; and *Church Guardian*, vol. 4, no. 40 (31 January 1883): 6; Regehr, "The National Railway Policy," 73–74.

128 David Harrison to John Norquay, 2 December 1882, NPP, A-906; other references in A-907, A-1401, A-1262, A-1267, A-1295, A-902, A-1326, A-1328, A-1415, A-935, A-936, A-917, A-1455, A-900, A-1162; Hilts, "Greenway," 75; Regehr, "The National Railway Policy," 74; Jackson, "The Disallowance," 39.

129 John L. Holmes, "Factors Affecting Politics in Manitoba: A Study of the Provincial Elections 1870–1899" (MA thesis, University of Manitoba, 1936), 48–56. A rough tally of the popular vote is registered in the Legislative Library of Manitoba: ministerial total votes: 5,393 and 19 seats; opposition votes: 4,464 and 10 seats; and 1 independent.

130 *Manitoba Free Press*, 25 January 1883; John A. Macdonald to John Norquay, NPP, C-365; John Norquay to John A. Macdonald, 26 January 1883, John A. Macdonald Papers, 185742.

Chapter 8: The Chief, 1883–February 1885

1 *Manitoba Free Press*, 26 February, 1 and 3 March 1884; *Brandon Sun*, 23 February 1884.

2 M. Hughes to John Norquay, 13 April 1883, NPP, A-1544; John Norquay to A.E. Stinson, 20 April 1883, NPP, Letterbook C; "St. Andrews Burials 1870–84," Archives of Manitoba, 409

3 Invoices in NPP, 674, 680.

4 *Commercial* 1, no. 47 (21 August 1883): 995; Barry Potyondi, *Selkirk: The First Hundred Years* (Winnipeg: Jostens National School Services, 1981), 26; John Norquay to William Van Horne, 26 November 1883, NPP, Letterbook D.

5 Ellen Cooke, "Information from Dr. H. C. Norquay in the Early 1950s," Ellen Gillies Cooke Papers, file 2; John Norquay to John Gemmel, 1 April 1884, NPP, Letterbook C; John Norquay to James Fraser, 18 September 1884, NPP, Letterbook E; John Norquay to Colonel Martin, 24 April 1883, NPP, Letterbook C; John Norquay to F. Hill Nash, 3 March 1884, NPP, Letterbook D; John Norquay to W.A. Macdonald, 18 February 1886, NPP, Letterbook E.

6 Chris Alam and H. Merskey, "What's in a Name? The Cycle of Change in the Meaning of Neuralgia," *History of Psychiatry* 5 (1994): 429–74; Janet Oppenheim, *"Shattered Nerves": Doctors, Patients, and Depression in Victorian England* (New York: Oxford University Press, 1991), 86; R. Rowland, *A Treatise on Neuralgia* (London: S. Highley, 1838).

7 David Young to John Norquay, 7 February 1884, NPP, C-90; *Winnipeg Times*, 7 December 1883; telegrams of 10–19 February 1884, NPP, 97–104; also NPP, C-543, C-460, C-332; John Norquay to John Shields, 18 September 1884, NPP, Letterbook D; Ellen Cooke, "Telephone Conversation with Mrs. Alfred Savage in May 1965," Ellen Gillies Cooke Papers, file 5; *Winnipeg Times*, 28 and 29 February, 3 March 1884.

8 *Manitoba Free Press*, 31 January, 5, 10, 12, and 21 February 1883; *Grip* 20, no. 10 (3 February 1883): 2.

9 *Journals of the Legislative Assembly of Manitoba 1885*; *Manitoba Free Press*, 17 May 1883, LLM Hansard; *Grip* 20, no. 26 (2 June 1883): 8; *Winnipeg Times*, 21 May 1883; Norquay explained this position in a speech in a Selkirk schoolroom delivered in December 1882, *Selkirk Herald*, 8 December 1882.

10 *Manitoba Free Press*, 29 May 1886.

11 W.D. O'Brien to John Norquay, 26 January 1883, NPP, A-1456; *Manitoba Free Press*, 28 May 1883; *Canadian Magazine* 13, no. 5 (1899).

12 John Norquay to Henry Tennant, E.F. Gigot, E.L. Fairbanks, D.H. Wilson, Joseph Lecompte, Alex Murray, John Allan, E.P. Leacock, John A. Davidson, Isaiah Mawhinney, William Crawford, William Wagner, D.H. Harrison, and J.E. Woodworth, 8–16 May 1883, NPP, Letterbook D.

13 *Manitoba Free Press*, 17 May 1883, LLM Hansard.

14 *Manitoba Free Press*, 23 May, 21 June 1883, LLM Hansard.

15 John Norquay to W.R. Black, 2 March 1883, NPP, Letterbook C.

16 *Winnipeg Times*, 25 June 1883.

17 Hugh John Macdonald to John A. Macdonald, 31 May 1883, John A. Macdonald Papers, microfilm reel C1499; John Norquay to David Harrison, 15 August 1883, NPP, Letterbook C; John Norquay to Amos Rowe, 24 August 1883, NPP, Letterbook C.

18 A.W. P[ritchard] to Walter R. Nursey, 1 May 1885, NPP, Letterbook D; A.W. Pritchard to John Norquay, 23 August, 16 September 1883, NPP, B-47, and Letterbook C; John Norquay to Amos Rowe, 24 August 1883, NPP, Letterbook C; John Norquay to Edward Farrer, 12 March 1883, NPP, Letterbook C; William Luxton to John Norquay, 26 January 1885, NPP, C-766.

19 *Dominion Illustrated* 6, no. 134 (24 January 1891): 90.

20 A.W. Pritchard to John Norquay, 11 August, 16 September 1883, 5 May 1884, NPP, Letterbook C; 17 December 1883, Letterbook D; 17 December 1884, Letterbook E; *Journals of the Legislative Assembly of Manitoba, 1885*, 34–35; A.W. Pritchard to H. MacDougall, 1 May 1884, NPP, Letterbook C.

21 David Marr Walker to John Norquay, 21 June, 21 November, 13 December 1880, NPP, A-621, A-428, A-818, C-975, C-1797; *Commercial* 10, no. 14 (21 December 1891): 315; John Norquay to F. Hill Nash, 3 March 1884, NPP, Letterbook D; A.W. Pritchard to John M. Egan, 17 January 1884, NPP, Letterbook C; John Norquay to Nicol Kingsmill, 12 February 1885, NPP, Letterbook E; Corydon Brown to John Norquay, 30 January 1884, NPP, C-72; Manitoba Executive Council, "Agenda (Rough Notes) 6 Feb 1882–22 Jan 1885," G 1044; John Norquay to Chalmers, 10 May 1883, NPP, Letterbook D; John Norquay to ?, a rare example of a letter in French, 11 March 1882, NPP, Letterbook C.

22 John Norquay to James Fraser, 18 September 1884, NPP, Letterbook E; John Norquay to F. Hill Nash, 3 March 1884, NPP, Letterbook D; John Norquay to W.A. Macdonald, 18 February 1886, NPP, Letterbook E.

23 On Norquay's office correspondence between 1 and 24 September 1885, fifty letterpress pages in Letterbook E, 634–85, and thirty pages in private Letterbook C, 293–329; on Norquay's office hours, John Norquay to Colonel Martin, 24 April 1883, NPP, Letterbook C; Manitoba Executive Council, *Orders-in-Council Registers 1870–1891*, 3 August 1885.

24 Manitoba Executive Council, *Orders-in-Council Registers 1870–1891*, 6 September 1883; A.I. Silver, "La Rivière, Alphonse-Alfred-Clement," in *Dictionary of Canadian Biography*, vol. 15, University of Toronto/Université Laval, 2003–, http://www.biographi.ca/en/bio/la_riviere_alphonse_alfred_clement_15E.html (accessed 12 April 2023); *Winnipeg Times*, 10 November 1884; Alphonse LaRivière to John Norquay, 27 March, 29 April 1884, NPP, C-206, C-409; 24 December 1884, C-868; 7, 9 June 1885, C-972, C-973; 21 October 1885, C-1493; George Broughall, "Report of the

Proceedings and the Evidence . . . Wallbridge Royal Commission, 1886," in *Sessional Papers 1886*, AM, LA009, GR174, G8116, box 6, files 14, 16, 361.

25 James Mochoruk, "Brown, Corydon Partlow," in *Dictionary of Canadian Biography*, vol. 12, University of Toronto/Université Laval, 2003–, http://www.biographi.ca/en/bio/brown_corydon_partlow_12E.html (accessed 12 April 2023); *Manitoba Free Press*, 10 July 1879; Robert Thomas Riley, *Memoirs* (Winnipeg: n.p., c. 1947), 62–65; Corydon Brown to John Norquay, 17 January 1882, NPP, A-1524; Corydon Brown to John Norquay, 26 January 1884, NPP, C-78(a)(b)(c); also C-564, C-566; Broughall, "Report of the Proceedings and the Evidence," 160–61.

26 W.D. Ardagh to John A. Macdonald, 1 July 1883, John A. Macdonald Papers, 188971; *Winnipeg Times*, 15 June 1883; Alex Sutherland to John Norquay, 22 January 1884, NPP, C-75; W.R. Sutherland to John Norquay, 21 February 1884, NPP, C-458; C. Setter to John Norquay, 26 February 1884, NPP, C-10; John Norquay to A.W. Ross, 7 March 1884, NPP, Letterbook C; Manitoba Executive Council, *Orders-in-Council Registers 1870–1891*, 11 March 1883.

27 John Norquay to David Wilson, 16 August 1883, NPP, Letterbook C; David Wilson to John Norquay, NPP, 27 December 1884, C-909; 25 August 1885, C-1013; 18 November 1885, C-1439; Henry J. Morgan, *The Canadian Men and Women of the Time: A Handbook of Canadian Biography* (Toronto: W. Briggs, 1898), 1089; "Dr. David Henry Wilson," in *Memorable Manitobans*, http://mhs.mb.ca/docs/people/wilson_dh.shtml (accessed 12 April 2023).

28 John Norquay to James Fraser, 18 September 1884, NPP, Letterbook E; James Miller to John Norquay, 17 February 1883, and John Norquay to James Miller (draft), 27 February 1883, NPP, A-1467(a) and (b); also related, A-1409, C-1093, B-51, B-78, B-5, B-6, B-12, B-13, B-15; Manitoba Executive Council, *Orders-in-Council Registers 1870–1891*, 6 September 1883; Lee Gibson, "Miller, James Andrews," in *Dictionary of Canadian Biography*, vol. 11, University of Toronto/Université Laval, 2003–, http://www.biographi.ca/en/bio/miller_james_andrews_11E.html (accessed 12 April 2023); *Brandon Sun*, 14 January 1884; Ed Leacock to John Norquay, 7 January 1884, and C.A. Sadlier to L.W. Cantlie, 7 January 1884, NPP, C-18(a) and (b).

29 *Winnipeg Times*, 30 October 1884 and through November; *Manitoba Free Press*, November 1884; London *Times*, 3 November 1884.

30 *Winnipeg Times*, 15 April 1885; Manitoba Executive Council, *Orders-in-Council Registers 1870–1891*, 14 November 1884; John Norquay to James Aikins, 15 November, 2 and 4 December 1884; James Miller to John Norquay, 3 December 1884; John Norquay to James Miller, 4 and 5 December 1884; James Aikins to John Norquay, 6 and 11 December 1884, all in ECPO, G8729; H. Howell to John Norquay, 26 December 1884, NPP, C-931; J.J. Setter to John Norquay, 4 May 1885, NPP, C-783; James Miller to John Norquay, 10 September 1885, NPP, C-1157; *Manitoba Free Press*, 1 April 1886; *Public Accounts of the Province of Manitoba for the Year Ending June 30th 1887* (Winnipeg: Queen's Printer, 1888), 53.

31 John A. Macdonald to George Stephen, 26 January 1883, George Stephen Papers, 72–73.

32 Chester Martin, *The Natural Resources Question: The Historical Basis of Provincial Claims* (Winnipeg: King's Printer, 1920), 136, 107; Mochoruk, *Formidable Heritage*, 105–23; "Copy of Report re Despatch Better Terms, 2 March 1883," John Norquay Papers, citing advice of John Henry Pope that Manitoba should not seek a "final settlement" of its financial claims.

33 "Memoranda and Statements Prepared by the Hon. the Provincial Treasurer, Manitoba," and "Message Transmitted to the Legislative Assembly . . . in Conformity with an Order in Council," in *Sessional Papers 1884*, LLM, *Sessional Papers* Collection.

34 John Norquay to John A. Macdonald (draft), 15 March 1883, NPP, A-1433, and 23 March 1883, NPP, A-1437; John Norquay to John A. Macdonald, 24 March 1883, John A. Macdonald Papers, 187003; John Norquay to Joseph Royal, 30 March 1883, NPP, Letterbook C; *Winnipeg Times*, 11 May 1883; John Norquay to J.H. Pope, 5 May 1882, NPP, A-1396; A. Caron to John Norquay, 23 February 1883, NPP, A-1459; John Norquay to A. Caron, 2 March 1883, NPP, Letterbook C.

35 John A. Macdonald to Alexander Campbell, 15 June 1883, Alexander Campbell Papers, microfilm M-19; John A. Macdonald to Alphonse LaRivière, 4 March 1885, John A. Macdonald Papers, Letterbook 23; John Norquay to John A. Macdonald, 16 June 1883, and Courtenay (Finance Department) to John A. Macdonald, 21 June 1883, and Alexander Campbell to John A. Macdonald, 18 June 1883, all in John A. Macdonald Papers, microfilm C-1499; Ken Cruikshank, "Macpherson, Sir David Lewis," in *Dictionary of Canadian Biography*, vol. 12, University of Toronto/Université Laval, 2003–, http://www.biographi.ca/en/bio/macpherson_david_lewis_12E.html (accessed 12 April 2023).

36 John A. Macdonald to John Norquay, 17 August 1883, John A. Macdonald Papers, Letterbook 22; Waite, *Canada 1874–1896*, 117–18; Morton, *Manitoba*, 217–19; *Monetary Times, Trade Review and Insurance Chronicle* 16, no. 42 (6 July 1883): 11; John Norquay to John A. Macdonald, 8 January 1884, John A. Macdonald Papers, 48489–91, cited in Regehr, "The National Railway Policy," 83–84; Joseph Royal to John A. Macdonald, 2 January 1884, John A. Macdonald Papers, 118252; Alphonse LaRivière to John A. Macdonald, 21 February 1884, John A. Macdonald Papers, 48493; 22 February, 48497; 1 March, 48511; 14 March, 48518; Gilbert McMicken to John A. Macdonald, 23 February 1884, John A. Macdonald Papers, 110938; Corydon Brown to John A. Macdonald, 26 February 1884, John A. Macdonald Papers, 48501; Donald F. Warner, *The Idea of Continental Union: Agitation for the Annexation of Canada to the United States, 1849–1893* (Lexington: University of Kentucky Press 1960), 169–75.

37 John Norquay to David Harrison, 25 July, 30 August 1883, NPP, Letterbook C; John Norquay to D.H. Wilson, 16 August 1883, NPP, Letterbook C; John Norquay to James Fraser, 25 July 1883, NPP, Letterbook C; James Fraser to John Norquay, 4 August 1883, NPP, B-81.

38 On Manitoba government revenue, *Journals of the Legislative Assembly of Manitoba, 1885*, 34–35; on land distribution, Donald Codd to John Norquay, April 1884, NPP,

C-884; J.W. Taylor to John Davis, 27 October 1884, USC Papers; and Friesen, "Imports and Exports."

39 James Wickes Taylor estimated the population of the western interior of Canada at 100,000 First Nations and 250,000 "civilized population," including northern Ontario (from Lake Superior to Manitoba) 10,000; Manitoba 175,000 (an exaggeration: the *Census of Manitoba 1885–86* reported 108, 640); and the four units of the North-West Territories 65,000 (including Assiniboia 30,000, Alberta 20,000, Saskatchewan 10,000, Athabasca 5,000); see J.W. Taylor to John Davis, 27 October 1884, USC Papers; about 70 percent had been born in Canada and about 17 percent in the British Isles. According to population tables in Canada's 1885–86 regional census of Manitoba, of the 70 percent born in Canada: Manitoba born 31 percent, Ontario born 31 percent, other provinces 8 percent. Of the 18 percent born in the British Isles, England 9 percent, Scotland 5 percent, Ireland 3 percent. In terms of paternal ethnic origin, two-thirds would have described themselves as English, Scottish, or Irish: England 24 percent, Scotland 24 percent, Ireland 20 percent. See Canada, *Census of Manitoba/ Recensement de Manitoba 1885–86* (Ottawa: McLean, Roger and Company, 1887).

40 Donald M. Loveridge, "'The Garden of Manitoba': The Settlement and Agricultural Development of the Rock Lake District and the Municipality of Louise, 1878–1902" (PhD diss., University of Toronto, 1986).

41 John Norquay to Charles E. Torrance, 29 April 1884, NPP, Letterbook C; George Harvey to John Norquay, 31 May 1887, ECPO, G8729.

42 J.W. Taylor to John Davis, 26 November 1883, 28 February 1884, USC Papers; *Manitoba Free Press*, 3 October, 21 and 29 November, 4, 7, 11, 14, and 24 December 1883.

43 Morton, *Manitoba*, 210–15; Brian McCutcheon, "The Economic and Social Structure of Political Agrarianism in Manitoba, 1870–1900" (PhD diss., University of British Columbia, 1974); Jeffery Taylor, *Fashioning Farmers: Ideology, Agricultural Knowledge and the Manitoba Farm Movement, 1890–1925* (Regina: Canadian Plains Research Center, University of Regina, 1994).

44 J.C. Aikins to John A. Macdonald, 30 November, 24 December 1883, John A. Macdonald Papers, 77430.

45 *Nor'West Farmer*, December 1883; *Brandon Weekly Mail*, 9, 15, and 29 November, 6 December 1883, as recorded in Hartwell Bowsfield to J.E. Trevena, 30 September 1963, LLM, Vertical File, "Manitoba and North West Farmers Union"; J.C. Aikins to John A. Macdonald, 30 November 1883, John A. Macdonald Papers, 77427; Regehr, "The National Railway Policy," 83; Manitoba Executive Council, *Orders-in-Council Registers 1870–1891*, 8 August, 22 December 1883.

46 Tom Norquay to John Norquay, 2 February 1884, NPP, C-31; William Luxton to John Norquay, 16 January 1884, NPP, C-51; John Norquay to John Mooney, 4 March 1885, NPP, Letterbook E.

47 *Brandon Sun*, 14 January 1884, reprinting a story from the Winnipeg *Sun*; Hector Howell to John Norquay, 26 December 1884, NPP, C-931; Corydon Brown to John Norquay, 18 January 1884, NPP, C-74; A.W. Pritchard to R.H. Pugh, 16 January 1884, NPP, Letterbook C; *Winnipeg Times*, 16, 22, and 23 January 1884.

48 R.L. Tupper to John Norquay, 23 January 1884, NPP, C- 20.

49 Alex Sutherland to John Norquay, 22 January 1884, NPP, C-75; Corydon Brown to John Norquay, 18 January 1884, NPP, C-74.

50 "Message transmitted to the Legislative Assembly . . . in conformity with an Order in Council," unpublished sessional paper 1884, Legislative Library of Manitoba Sessional Papers collection.

51 "Message Transmitted to the Legislative Assembly . . . in Conformity with an Order in Council," in Manitoba, Legislative Assembly, *Sessional Papers 1884*, 8–11, LLM, Sessional Papers Collection; Manitoba, *Journals of the Legislative Assembly, 1884*, 271–317; *Winnipeg Times*, issues of February 1884; Corydon Brown to John Norquay, 18 and 26 January 1884, NPP, C-74, C78(a)(b)(c); Alex Sutherland to John Norquay, 22 January 1884, NPP, C-75; Alexander Begg to John Norquay, 17 January 1884, NPP, C-55; Begg, "Seventeen Years," 18.

52 J.H. Spencer to John Norquay, 23 January–21 February 1884, NPP, C-488; David Macpherson to John Norquay, 16 February 1884, NPP, C-49; S. Mulvey to John Norquay, 22 February 1884, NPP, C-567; G. Purvis to John A. Macdonald, 4 and 9 February 1884, John A. Macdonald Papers, 46150 and 46170; House of Commons, *Debates*, 4 May 1883, 971; John A. Macdonald to Corbet Locke, 9 November 1882, cited in Regehr, "The National Railway Policy," 70, 76; Lord Lansdowne to Secretary of State for the Colonies, 28 April 1884, cited in ibid., 22–23.

53 St. Paul *Pioneer Press*, 27 February 1884, clipping in J.W. Taylor to John Davis, 28 February 1884, USC Papers; John Norquay to Alexander Campbell, 13 March 1884, NPP, Letterbook C; *Winnipeg Times*, 23–29 February 1884.

54 Lord Lansdowne to David Macpherson, 27 April 1884, and J.C. Aikins to John A. Macdonald, 29 February 1884, both in Lord Lansdowne Papers; James Aikins to David Macpherson, 3 March 1884, James Cox Aikins telegram book, 1881–85; *Manitoba Free Press*, 26 February, 1 and 3 March 1884; Corydon Brown to John Norquay, 18 January 1884, NPP, C –74; Lewis Wallbridge to John A. Macdonald, 23 February 1884, John A. Macdonald Papers, 48504; John A. Macdonald to John Norquay, 3 March 1884, and John Norquay reply, 3 March 1884, John A. Macdonald to John Norquay, 4 March 1884, and John Norquay reply, 4 March 1884, John A. Macdonald Papers, 58002, 58004, 58009, 58010; John Norquay to John A. Macdonald, 7 March 1884, John A. Macdonald Papers, 48514; E.P. Leacock to John A. Macdonald, 4 March 1884, John A. Macdonald Papers, 58011; C.P. Brown to John A. Macdonald, 3 March 1884, John A. Macdonald Papers, 58017; *Brandon Sun*, 25 and 29 February 1884; Gilbert McMicken to John A. Macdonald, 23 February 1884, John A. Macdonald Papers, 110938.

55 Corydon Brown to John A. Macdonald, 26 February 1884, John A. Macdonald Papers, 48501; J. Colcleugh to J. Stephens, 17 February 1884, Colcleugh Papers.

56 John Norquay to John Mooney, 4 March 1885, NPP, Letterbook E; Tom Norquay to John Norquay, 2 February 1884, NPP, C-31; William Luxton to John Norquay, 16 January 1884, NPP, C-51.

57 "Memoranda and Statements Prepared by the Hon. the Provincial Treasurer, Manitoba," "Message Transmitted to the Legislative Assembly . . . in Conformity with an Order in Council," unpublished sessional paper 1884, LLM, Sessional Papers Collection; John A. Macdonald to John Norquay, and Norquay's replies, 3–5 March 1884, John A. Macdonald Papers, 58002, 58004, 58007, 58009, 58010; E.P. Leacock and C.P. Brown entered the negotiations, 3 and 4 March 1884, John A. Macdonald Papers, 58011, 58016, 58017; John Norquay to John A. Macdonald, 7 March 1884, John A. Macdonald Papers, 48514; clippings file, NPP, C-233.

58 "Certified Copy of a Report of a Committee of the Honourable the Privy Council, Approved by His Excellency the Governor General in Council, on the 1st April, 1884," reprinted in Canada, Senate, *Sessional Paper No. 83* (Ottawa: Department of the Secretary of State, 1902).

59 John Norquay to John A. Macdonald, John A. Macdonald Papers, 25 March, 2 April 1884, 48521, 48524, 48527; John A. Macdonald to John Norquay, March 1884, John A. Macdonald Papers, vol. 525, part 1, 243, 360, 364–65, 370–71; Alphonse LaRivière and J.A. Miller to John A. Macdonald, 8 April 1884, John A. Macdonald Papers, 48529; Amos Rowe to John A. Macdonald, 8 April 1884, John A. Macdonald Papers, 48534; Alphonse LaRivière to John A. Macdonald, 9 April 1884, John A. Macdonald Papers, 48539; John A. Macdonald to Alphonse LaRivière and James Miller, 9 April 1884, John A. Macdonald Papers, 48543; John A. Macdonald to Alphonse LaRivière, 10 April 1884, John A. Macdonald Papers, 48538; John A. Macdonald to Alphonse LaRivière, 4 March 1885, John A. Macdonald Papers, vol. 526, part 1, 130; J.C. Aikins to Alexander Campbell, 7 April 1884, James Cox Aikins telegram book, 1881–85.

60 John A. Macdonald to John Binney, 26 March 1884, John Binney Papers.

61 John A. Macdonald to Lord Lorne, 26 March 1884, Lord Lorne Papers, vol. 1, 364–67.

62 Ibid.

63 Lord Lansdowne to Earl of Derby, 1 April 1884, Lord Lansdowne Papers.

64 John A. Macdonald to Alphonse LaRivière, 17 March, 9 and 10 April 1884, John A. Macdonald Papers, Letterbook 22; Manitoba, *Journals of the Legislative Assembly 1884*, 23–24, 26–27, 45–48; John Norquay to Alexander Campbell, NPP, Letterbook C, G8731.

65 Gilbert McMicken to John A. Macdonald, 8 March 1884, John A. Macdonald Papers, 110949; John Norquay to A.W. Ross, 7 March 1884, NPP, Letterbook C; John Norquay to James Fraser, 10 March 1884, NPP, Letterbook C; A. Pritchard to G. Purvis, 3 May 1884, NPP, Letterbook C; J.J. Setter to John Norquay, 19 March 1884, NPP, C-268; A.W. Ross to John Norquay, 12 March 1884, NPP, C-346; also see C-352, C-520, and C-526; John Norquay to John Matheson, 26 March 1884, Letterbook D; A.T. Galt to John Norquay, 6 March 1884, NPP, C-570.

66 Hugh John Macdonald to John A. Macdonald, 5 March 1884, John A. Macdonald Papers, 253186.

67 John A. Macdonald to Lord Lansdowne, 26 February, 6 March 1884 (enclosing J.C. Aikins to John A. Macdonald, 29 February 1884), 17 July, 5 August 1884, Lord Lansdowne Papers.

68 Lord Lansdowne to Earl of Derby, 10 March 1884, and Earl of Derby to Lord Lansdowne, 29 March 1884, Lord Lansdowne Papers; John Rose to John A. Macdonald, 6 March 1884, John A. Macdonald Papers, 117950.

69 *Brandon Sun*, 11 March, 15 May 1884, LLM Hansard.

70 On the new legislature building, see Manitoba, *Annual Report of the Department of Public Works for 1884* (Winnipeg: Queen's Printer, 1885), 59–70; John Norquay to John P. Matheson, 26 March 1884, NPP, Letterbook D; Regehr, "The National Railway Policy," 84–85; *Manitoba Free Press*, 18, 19, and 28 March, 4 and 23 April 1884; and *Brandon Sun*, 20 March, 4 April 1884, all in LLM Hansard.

71 The speech is recorded in *Manitoba Free Press*, 17 April 1884; *Brandon Sun*, c. 17 April 1884; *Province of Manitoba, Second Session, Fifth Legislature: Budget Speech Delivered by Hon. John Norquay, Premier and Provincial Treasurer, April 16th, 1884* (Winnipeg: n.p., 1884).

72 *Manitoba Free Press*, 17 April 1884; *Brandon Sun*, c. 17 April 1884; *Province of Manitoba, Second Session, Fifth Legislature: Budget Speech Delivered by Hon. John Norquay, Premier and Provincial Treasurer, April 16th, 1884* (Winnipeg: n.p., 1884); Tolly Bradford and Rich Connors, "The Making of a Company Colony: The Fur Trade War, the Colonial Office, and the Metamorphosis of the Hudson's Bay Company," *Canadian Journal of History* 55, no. 3 (2019–20): 171–97; "Minutes of a Council Held at New Fort Garry for the Red River Settlement District of Assiniboia Rupert's Land on Monday the 13th day of June 1836," and same dated "16 June 1837," and "27 February 1860," and "Loi d'Assiniboia: Passeé par le gouverneur et le Conseil d'Assiniboia, le 13th April, 1862," and "Memo, 22 October 1889," in Archer Martin Papers; James Taylor to John Norquay, 15 April 1884, NPP, C-199(a)–(f); Ged Martin, "Income Tax in Canada before 1917," https://gedmartin.net/martinalia-mainmenu-3/311-income-tax-in-canada-before-1917 (accessed 12 April 2023).

73 London *Times*, 19 April 1884; *True Witness and Catholic Chronicle* 34, no. 37 (23 April 1884): 4.

74 *Brandon Sun*, c. 17 April 1884.

75 Thomas Greenway, "Province of Manitoba: Its Position in Confederation: Speech on 23 April 1884," in Manitoba, *Sessional Papers, 1884*, Sessional Papers Collection, LLM; *Manitoba Free Press*, 28 March, 17 April 1885; *Brandon Sun*, 21 April 1884, LLM Hansard.

76 For context, see Richard Gwyn, *Nation Maker: Sir John A. Macdonald: His Life, Our Times II, 1867–1891* (Toronto: Random House Canada, 2011), 360–82; Ramsay Cook, *Provincial Autonomy, Minority Rights and the Compact Theory, 1867–1921*

(Ottawa: Queen's Printer, 1969); Paul Martin Romney, *Getting It Wrong: How Canadians Forgot Their Past and Imperilled Confederation* (Toronto: University of Toronto Press, 1999); and Doug Owram, *Promise of Eden: The Canadian Expansionist Movement and the Idea of the West 1856–1900* (Toronto: University of Toronto Press, 1980).

77 Paul Romney, "Mowat, Sir Oliver," in *Dictionary of Canadian Biography*, vol. 13, University of Toronto/Université Laval, 2003–, http://www.biographi.ca/en/bio/mowat_oliver_13E.html (accessed 12 April 2023); Gerald Friesen, "Space and Region in Canadian History," Canadian Historical Association *Report*, New Series, 16 (2005): 1–22; Martin, *"The Natural Resources Question."*

78 *Winnipeg Times*, 5 and 8 May 1884; A.W. Pritchard to John Norquay, 5 May 1884, NPP, Letterbook C; Manitoba Executive Council, *Orders-in-Council Registers 1870–1891*, 1 May 1884.

79 *Manitoba Free Press*, 2 and 4 April 1884; *Brandon Sun*, 5 April 1884, LLM Hansard; *Portage la Prairie Weekly Tribune-Review*, 24 December 1884; *Nor'West Farmer and Manitoba Miller* (May 1886); "Report of Select Committee of Legislature, 27 May 1884," NPP, Letterbook C; Canada, *Sessional Papers of the House of Commons*, 1885, vol. 12, 61; David Macpherson to Hugh Sutherland, 24 April 1884, John A. Macdonald Papers, 58020; John Henry Pope to John A. Macdonald, 20 May 1884, John A. Macdonald Papers, 58022; J. Stewart Tupper to John A. Macdonald, 20 May 1884, John A. Macdonald Papers, 58030; Hugh Sutherland to John A. Macdonald, 22 May 1884, John A. Macdonald Papers, 58035; "Draft Agreement on HBR," John A. Macdonald Papers, 58046; John A. Macdonald to Alexander Campbell, 26 [May 1884?], Alexander Campbell Papers.

80 *Winnipeg Times*, 14, 15, 21, and 26 May 1886; Manitoba, *Journals of the Legislative Assembly, 1884*, 45–48, 135–48, 164–83; London *Times*, 2 June 1884; John Norquay to John A. Macdonald, 8 May 1884, John A. Macdonald Papers, 194588; Alex Murray to John A. Macdonald, 15 May 1884, John A. Macdonald Papers, 48545; John A. Macdonald to Alex Murray, 16 May 1884, John A. Macdonald Papers, 48547; *Public Accounts of the Province of Manitoba for the Year Ending 31 December 1884*, 34–35; *Manitoba Free Press*, 1 May 1886, LLM Hansard.

81 *Manitoba Free Press*, 3 June 1884, LLM Hansard.

82 *Manitoba Free Press*, 31 May, 3 June 1884, LLM Hansard; "Partial Draft Resolution" [late May 1884], NPP, Letterbook C.

83 London *Times*, 19 April, 2 June 1884; J.C. Aikins to John A. Macdonald, 30 May 1884, John A. Macdonald Papers, 48550.

84 John A. Macdonald to J.C. Aikins, 6 June 1884, John A. Macdonald Papers, 48554; John A. Macdonald to C.P. Brown, 4 July 1884, John A. Macdonald Papers, Letterbook 22; P.B. Waite, "McLelan, Archibald Woodbury," in *Dictionary of Canadian Biography*, vol. 12, University of Toronto/Université Laval, 2003–, http://www.biographi.ca/en/bio/archibald_adams_george_12E.htm (accessed 12 April 2023); John A. Macdonald to J.C. Aikins, 28 July 1884, cited in Regehr, "The National Railway Policy," 11.

85 Hugh John Macdonald to John A. Macdonald, 25 June, 24 July 1884, John A. Macdonald Papers, 253190, 253194; John A. Macdonald to George Stephen, 30 July 1884, George Stephen Papers.

86 John A. Macdonald to John Norquay, 13 June 1884, John A. Macdonald Papers, 58040, and Norquay's reply, 23 June 1884, John A. Macdonald Papers, 58043.

87 John A. Macdonald to H.H. Smith, 17 June 1884, H.H. Smith Papers.

88 John Norquay to John A. Macdonald, 24 June 1884, John A. Macdonald Papers, 42273, enclosing a letter from Mack Howes to George Purvis, 18 June 1884, John A. Macdonald Papers, 42774.

89 John A. Macdonald to John Norquay, 1 July 1884, John A. Macdonald Papers, 48558.

90 John A. Macdonald to John Norquay, 1 July 1884, John A. Macdonald Papers, Letterbook 22, part 2; John A. Macdonald to James Aikins, 1 [or 7?] July 1884, John A. Macdonald Papers, Letterbook 23, part 1.

91 J.R. Harris to Chief Constantine, 30 June–14 July 1884, NPP, C-108(a)–(d); George Purvis to John Norquay, 25 July 1884, NPP, C-163; John Norquay to George Purvis, 16 July 1884, NPP, Letterbook C.

92 J.C. Aikins to John A. Macdonald, 30 May, 13 July 1884, John A. Macdonald Papers, 48550, 48560; John A. Macdonald to William McDougall, 30 July 1884, cited in Regehr, "The National Railway Policy," 85.

93 John A. Macdonald to J.C. Aikins, 28 July 1884, John A. Macdonald Papers, Letterbook 23; Earl of Derby to Lord Lansdowne, 29 March 1884, Lord Lansdowne Papers.

94 John A. Macdonald to J.C. Aikins, 28 July 1884, John A. Macdonald Papers, Letterbook 23; Merchants Bank, "Board of Directors, Minute Book, 1883–84," Library and Archives Canada; Bank of Montreal, "Board of Directors, Minute Book, 1884," Library and Archives Canada.

95 John A. Macdonald to John Norquay, 3 November 1884, NPP, C-929.

96 John Norquay to John James Setter, 9 February 1885, NPP, Letterbook D; Corydon Brown to John A. Macdonald, 3 January 1887, John A. Macdonald Papers, 213131; *Brandon Sun*, 29 February 1884; David Macpherson to John A. Macdonald, 23 June 1884, John A. Macdonald Papers, 112728; Ken Cruikshank, "Macpherson, Sir David," in *Dictionary of Canadian Biography*, vol. 12, University of Toronto/Université Laval, 2003–, http://www.biographi.ca/en/bio/macpherson_david_lewis_12E.html (accessed 12 April 2023); George T. Orton to John A. Macdonald, 6 May, 23 June 1884, John A. Macdonald Papers, 194547, 195680; Hector Langevin to John A. Macdonald, 3 July 1884, John A. Macdonald Papers, 97384.

97 Lovell Clark, "Schultz, Sir John Christian," in *Dictionary of Canadian Biography*, vol. 12, University of Toronto/Université Laval, 2003–, http://www.biographi.ca/en/bio/schultz_john_christian_12E.html (accessed 12 April 2023); N.E.A. Ronaghan, "The Archibald Administration in Manitoba 1870–1872" (PhD diss., University of Manitoba, 1986).

98 John Schultz to John Gemmel, 27 December 1884, Frank Gemmel Papers; John Schultz to W.N. Kennedy, 16 December 1884, W.N. Kennedy Papers; A.I. Silver, "Royal, Joseph," in *Dictionary of Canadian Biography,* vol. 14, University of Toronto/ Université Laval, 2003–, http://www.biographi.ca/en/bio/dubuc_joseph_14E.html (accessed 10 April 2023); Joseph Royal to John A. Macdonald, 2 January 1884, John A. Macdonald Papers, 118252.

99 Winnipeg *Sun*, 30 August, 1 September 1884, in Carman Cumming, *Secret Craft: The Journalism of Edward Farrer* (Toronto: University of Toronto Press, 1992), 53–54; Carman Cumming, "The Plot to Buy the Canadian Northwest," *The Beaver* (Autumn 1984): 4–9; Amos Rowe to Edward Farrer, 7 February 1884, NPP, C-427; Alvin Gluek, *Minnesota and the Manifest Destiny of the Canadian Northwest: A Study in Canadian-American Relations* (Toronto: University of Toronto Press, 1965).

100 Cumming, "The Plot"; Cumming, *Secret Craft*, 61; John Norquay to Richard White, 18 November 1884, NPP, Letterbook E; T. Boswell to John Norquay, 17 December 1884, NPP, C-852.

101 Joseph Mulholland to John Norquay, 22 October 1884, NPP, C-401; F.D. Baruyck to John Norquay, December 1884, NPP, C-578; *Winnipeg Times*, 18, 19, 27, 30, and 31 December 1884; *Brandon Sun Weekly*, 11 December 1884.

102 Toronto *Mail*, reprinted in *Portage la Prairie Weekly Tribune-Review*, 24 December 1884; *Winnipeg Times*, 11 and 19 December 1884.

103 Quoted in *Winnipeg Times*, 22 and 28 January 1885; Frederic Nicholls and A.W. Wright, *Report of the Demonstration in Honour of the Fortieth Anniversary of Sir John A. Macdonald's Entrance into Public Life: Proceedings at Toronto and Montreal, 1844–1884* (Toronto: Canadian Manufacturer Publishing, 1885).

104 W.F. Luxton to John Norquay, 17 December 1884, NPP, C-456, emphasis is Luxton's; John A. Macdonald to John Norquay, 5 November 1881, NPP, A-869; *Winnipeg Times*, 30 December 1884, from Peterborough *Review*; John S. Hall to John Norquay, 30 December 1884, NPP, C-917; *Montreal Star* interviews, noted in A.W. Pritchard to John Norquay and W.R. Baker to John Norquay, 23 January 1884, NPP, C-42(a) and (b); Manitoba Executive Council, *Orders-in-Council Registers 1870–1891*, 12 December 1884.

105 Chester Martin, *"Dominion Lands" Policy* (1938; reprinted, Toronto: McClelland and Stewart, 1973), 208–9.

106 Manitoba, *Journals of the Legislative Assembly 1885*, Appendix A.

107 Martin, *"Dominion Lands,"* 208–9; James A. Maxwell, *Federal Subsidies to the Provincial Governments in Canada* (Cambridge, MA: Harvard University Press, 1937), 83–88; James Maxwell, "The Disputes over the Federal Domain in Canada," Canadian Political Science Association *Papers and Proceedings* 6 (1934): 162–74; Manitoba, *Journals of the Legislative Assembly 1885*, Appendix A; W.J. Ptolemy to John Norquay, 24 December 1884, NPP, C-900.

108 *Winnipeg Times*, 20 January 1885; *Grip* 24, no. 7 (14 February 1885).

109 A.W. Pritchard to John Norquay, 23 January 1884, and W.R. Baker to John Norquay, NPP, C-42(a) and (b); Alphonse LaRivière to John Norquay, 8 January 1885, NPP, C-928; St. Paul Metropolitan Hotel to John Norquay, 22 January 1885, NPP, C-864.

110 *Winnipeg Times*, 22, 24, and 27 January 1885; Amos Rowe to John Norquay, 3 January 1885, NPP, C-912; *Manitoba Free Press*, 13 January 1885; *Winnipeg Times*, 29 and 30 January, 23 February 1885.

111 T. Mayne Daly to John Norquay, 26 January 1885, NPP, C-676.

112 John J. Setter to John Norquay, 26 January 1885, NPP, C-662.

113 *Brandon Sun*, 15 January, 12 March 1885, LLM Hansard; W.F. Luxton to John Norquay, 17 December 1884, NPP, C-456.

114 John A. Macdonald to Charles Tupper, 17 March 1885, Charles Tupper Papers, 2826.

115 John Norquay to John A. Macdonald, 24 January 1885, John A. Macdonald Papers 118676; *Winnipeg Times*, 20 and 23 February 1885.

116 Hugh John Macdonald to John A. Macdonald, 4 February 1885, John A. Macdonald Papers, 253199; *Winnipeg Times*, 4 February 1885; Sam Bedson to John Norquay, 3 February 1885, NPP, C-667.

117 *Winnipeg Times*, 4 February 1885; John Norquay to John James Setter, 9 February 1885, NPP, Letterbook D, and 13 February 1885, NPP, Letterbook E; John James Setter to John Norquay, 19 and 21 March 1884, NPP, C-268 and C-782.

118 William Scarth to John A. Macdonald, 4 and 13 February 1886, John A. Macdonald Papers, 119002 and 119013; Gilbert McMicken to John A. Macdonald, 27 February 1885, John A. Macdonald Papers, 110945.

119 *Manitoba Free Press*, 6, 11, 14, 27, and 28 February, 3 and 4 March 1885; J. Lewis to John Norquay, 4 February 1885, NPP, C-874; A.G.B. Bannatyne to John Norquay, Monday n.d. [c. 20 February 1885], NPP, C-683; James Stewart to John Norquay, 25 February 1885, NPP, C-682; Major Lewis to John Norquay, 20 February 1885, NPP, C-1144; *Brandon Sun*, 10 September 1885; John Norquay to J.E. Woodworth, 24, 27, and 28 February, 7 March 1885, NPP, Letterbook D, Letterbook C; J.E. Woodworth to John Norquay, 24 February, 4 March 1885, NPP, C-759, C-673; John Norquay to T.M. Daly, 27 February 1885, NPP, Letterbook D.

120 John Norquay to John James Setter, 23 February 1885, NPP, Letterbook D; John Norquay to John Hope, 7 March 1885, NPP, Letterbook E.

121 *Manitoba Free Press*, 11 February 1885, also 6, 14, 27, and 28 February, 3 and 4 March 1885.

122 *Winnipeg Times*, 9 December 1884; "Charles Hamilton," Manitoba Historical Society, *Memorable Manitobans*, http://mhs.mb.ca/docs/people/hamilton_ce.shtml (accessed 12 April 2023); Greg Taylor, *Law of the Land: The Advent of the Torrens System in Canada* (Toronto: Osgoode Society for Canadian Legal History and University of Toronto Press, 2008).

123 Anthony Sweeting, "Rennie, Alfred Herbert," in *Dictionary of Hong Kong Biography*, ed. May Holdsworth and Christopher Munn (Hong Kong: Hong Kong University Press, 2012), 366–67; Iain Ward, *Sui Geng: The Hong Kong Marine Police 1841–1950* (Hong Kong: Hong Kong University Press, 1991); Hugh Farmer, "Alfred Herbert Rennie," 7 April 2015, The Industrial History of Hong Kong Group, http://industrialhistoryhk.org/alfred-herbert-rennie; "Alfred Herbert Rennie," Manitoba Historical Society, *Memorable Manitobans*, http://www.mhs.mb.ca/docs/people/rennie_ah.shtml (both accessed 7 December 2022); I thank Gordon Goldsborough for several clues about Rennie's career in Hong Kong; *Voices from the Past: Hong Kong, 1842–1918*, ed. Solomon Bard, citing *Hong Kong Telegraph*, 14 April 1908; John Norquay to A.H. Rennie, 23 June 1884, NPP, Letterbook C; A.H. Rennie to John Norquay, 24 July 1884, NPP, C-161; John Norquay to A.H. Rennie, 1 December 1884, NPP, Letterbook D; A.H. Rennie to John Norquay, 8 and 27 December 1884, NPP, C-410 and C-916.

124 John James Setter to John Norquay, 20 February 1885, NPP, C-722.

125 *Brandon Sun*, 12 and 19 March 1885, LLM Hansard; *Manitoba Free Press*, 26–30 March 1885, LLM Hansard; *Manitoba Sun*, 24 and 31 March 1885, LLM Hansard; *Commercial*, c. 10 April 1885; *Journals of the Legislative Assembly of Manitoba 1885*, 1–2; *Winnipeg Times*, 23, 24, 27, and 28 March 1885.

126 Gwyn, *Nation Maker*, 389; Morton, *Manitoba*, 211–13; D.J. Hall, *Clifford Sifton I: The Young Napoleon 1861–1900* (Vancouver: UBC Press, 1981).

127 J.P. Robertson to John Norquay, 26 February 1885, NPP, C-707; Charles Constantine to John Norquay, 27 March 1885, NPP, C-857(a); T.R. to John Norquay, 26 March 1885, NPP, C-857(b); also see C-855, C-1069, C-921, C-650, and C-830; John Norquay to J.H. Pope, 17 February 1885, NPP, Letterbook D; John Norquay to George Purvis, 4 and 27 March 1885, NPP, Letterbook E; John Norquay to J.P. Pennefather, 27 March 1885, NPP, Letterbook E.

128 John Norquay to Alexander Begg, 9 February 1885, NPP, Letterbook E.

Chapter 9: "An Unfortunate Family Difference," 1885

1 Manitoba, Treasury department, "Auditor's Appropriation Ledger, 1886–87," G8706.

2 George Broughall, "Report of the Proceedings and the Evidence . . . Wallbridge Royal Commission, 1886," in *Sessional Papers 1886*, LA009, GR174, G8116, box 6, files 14, 16, 130, 133.

3 Robert Ruttan to John Norquay, 8 January 1883, NPP, A-1373; William Scarth to John Norquay, 29 December 1883, NPP, B-454; S.W. Farrell to John Norquay, 7 July 1884, NPP, C-490; Bank of Nova Scotia to John Norquay, 9 July 1884, NPP, C-513, also 14 and 22 October, 1 November 1884, NPP, C-461, C-402, C-815; Imperial Bank to John Norquay, 11 and 17 November 1884, NPP, C-466, C-379; these issues continue in C-419, C-478, C-1721, C-727, C-984, C-1227; S.W. Farrell to John Norquay, 24 June 1886, ECPO, G8729; C-1265, C-2171.

4 A.W. Pritchard to John Norquay, 1 December 1884, NPP, C-378.

5 John Norquay to J.H.D. Munson, 13 June 1885, NPP, Letterbook E; John Norquay to "Arcade," 30 October 1885, NPP, Letterbook E; John Norquay to Bernard Saunders, 31 October 1885, NPP, Letterbook E; Merchants Bank to John Norquay, November 1885, NPP, C-1179; British Canadian Loan & Investment Company to John Norquay, 6 November 1885, NPP, C-1219; A.W. Pritchard to John Norquay, 30 December 1884, NPP, Letterbook D; also C-918, C-856, C-436; W.R. Richardson to John Norquay, 2 November 1885, NPP, C-1220; Imperial Bank to John Norquay, 12 February 1886, NPP, C-1507; more of the same in C-1507, C-1196, C-1509, C-1463, C-931.

6 St. Andrew's Municipality to John Norquay, 1884, NPP, A-851; on labourers, see NPP, A-794, C-1196, C-1199, C-1294, C-1397, C-256; John Norquay to Alex Howden, 20 April 1885, NPP, Letterbook D; John Norquay to John Haggart, 24 February 1885, NPP, C-680; John Norquay to Colin Setter, 13 December 1885, NPP, Letterbook E; bills in this period included, NPP, C-1205, C-1206, C-1210, C-1211, C-1215, C-1220.

7 There are about sixty documents in the Norquay papers, dated 1882–87, on the farm mortgage debt. Because of financial pressures in 1885 and after, Norquay was unable to answer appeals for help from two friends: John Norquay to Charles Adams, 9 February 1885, NPP, Letterbook D; John Norquay to Andy Maxwell, 8 May 1885, NPP, Letterbook D.

8 City of Winnipeg to John Norquay, 16 January 1883, NPP, A-1284; research on these transactions was conducted by Randy Rostecki, and I would like to express my gratitude to him for his careful report based upon documents in the Winnipeg Land Titles Office, "Old System Abstract Book, Winnipeg 3 (Abstract 3)," 26, 27, 28k, 29, instruments 25709–10, 25715–18, 31329, 39910, 43628–29, 73348–49, 73351; also see Randy Rostecki, "The Growth of Winnipeg, 1870–1886" (MA thesis, University of Manitoba, 1980), and NPP, B-65, C-891, Letterbook E.

9 Archibald Young to John Norquay, 17 January 1884, NPP, C-53; John Norquay to Archibald Young, 13 October 1885, NPP, Letterbook E; John Norquay to H. Swinford, 29 May 1884, NPP, Letterbook C; Duncan MacArthur to John Norquay, 1 December 1884, NPP, C-870.

10 Stephen Knight to City of Winnipeg, 8 August 1882, and W.E. Sanford to John Norquay, 18 August 1882, NPP, A-932(a) and (b); John Allan to John Norquay, 31 July 1882, and John Norquay to John Allan, 10 August 1882, NPP, A-1233(a)(b)(c), A-1600, A-1601; Peter Hanlon, "Sanford, William Eli," in *Dictionary of Canadian Biography*, vol. 12, University of Toronto/Université Laval, 2003–, http://www.biographi.ca/en/bio/sanford_william_eli_12E.html (accessed 13 April 2023).

11 *Monetary Times, Trade Review and Insurance Chronicle* 16, no. 42 (20 April 1883): 1172–73; *Canadian Mining Review*, May 1883, 4, and 24 July 1883, 4; *Engineering and Mining Journal*, 19 May 1883, 287; *Manitoba Free Press*, 8 and 10 May 1883; "Extract from 'Applications for Mining Locations on Hay Island Lake of the Woods,' 1879," NPP, A-1208; Eugène Coste, *Report on the Gold Mines of the Lake of the Woods* (Montreal: Dawson, for the Geological Survey of Canada, 1884); Keewatin

Mining Company Limited, "Statement of Cash Rec'd from Promoters of K M Co," n.d., NPP, A-1376; M.W. Meagher to John Norquay, 14 February 1883, NPP, A-1429; John Norquay to J.J. Johnston, 20 October 1884, NPP, Letterbook D; John Allan to Thomas Spence, 15 June 1883, in Manitoba, Legislative Assembly, Clerk Files, G8113, box 3, file 28, Miscellaneous Papers, 1883, GR174.

12 John Norquay to John Pennefather, 13 December 1883, NPP, Letterbook D; *Kenora Weekly Record*, 9 January 1892; also related, NPP, B-428, C-1056; also see NPP, C-1085, C-1074, C-1046, C-164, C-482, C-1050, C-445 (a) and (b), C-1130, C-1273, C-2185, C-2616; NPP, Letterbook C, 397, 409; NPP, Letterbook D, 35–39, 49–50, 52–53, 67, 159–60, 249; George Harvey to John Norquay, 1 December 1883, ECPO, G8729; *Winnipeg Commercial*, 8 August 1883, 956; *Manitoba Sun*, 24 December 1883; John Norquay to Charles B. Brodie, c. April–May 1883, NPP, Letterbook D; John Norquay to J.G. Ross, 12 October 1883, NPP, Letterbook D; John Norquay to Alex Matheson, 1 November 1883, NPP, Letterbook D; J.J. Johnston to John Norquay, 2 and 10 October 1884, NPP, C-321, C-1056; John Norquay to J.J. Johnston, Letterbook D; L. McMeans to John Norquay, 4 May 1887, ECPO, G8729.

13 Frank W. Robinson to H.J. MacDonald, 23 December 1884, NPP, C-871; John A. Macdonald to John Norquay, 29 December 1884, NPP, C-867; *Canadian Mining Review* 3, no. 3 (1885); Archibald Young to John Norquay, 17 November 1886, NPP, C-2138; John Norquay to H. Swinford, 29 May 1884, NPP, Letterbook C; John Norquay to S.O. Shorey, 24 April 1885, NPP, Letterbook E; John Norquay to C.P. Brown, 8 December 1884, NPP, Letterbook E; John Norquay to J.B. MacArthur, 8 May 1885, NPP, Letterbook D.

14 J.E. Woodworth to John Norquay, 24 and 25 July, 13, 15, 15, and 16 August 1883, NPP, B-67, B-38, B-80, A-1345(a) and (b), B-19; John Norquay to John A. Macdonald, 6 August 1883, John A. Macdonald Papers, 189496; John A. Macdonald to John Norquay, 5 March, 3 November 1884, NPP, C-571, C-929; *Brandon Sun*, 16 February 1884; J. Egan to William Van Horne, 20 April 1885, Canadian Pacific Railway (hereafter CPR) Papers, file 9218; Jacob Klotz to John Norquay, 4 January 1884, NPP, C-244; Jean-Pierre Kesteman, "Galt, Alexander Tilloch," in *Dictionary of Canadian Biography*, vol. 12, University of Toronto/Université Laval, 2003–, http://www.biographi.ca/en/bio/galt_alexander_tilloch_12E.html (accessed 13 April 2023); D. Miller to John Norquay, 5 January 1884, NPP, C-245; J.G. Hargrave to John Norquay, 9 January 1884, NPP, C-17; Jacob Klotz to John Norquay, 11 January 1884, NPP, G8701; John Norquay, "Memo," [1883–84], NPP, C-46; John Norquay to C.S. Drummond, 13 June 1885, NPP, Letterbook D; Broughall, "Report of the Proceedings and the Evidence," 357–58, 188–89; a story on the mine appeared in the 25 November 1883 issue of the *Manitoba Free Press* and the 1 December 1883 issue of the *Selkirk Herald*, LAC.

15 Broughall, "Report of the Proceedings and the Evidence," 4–41; W.J. Ptolemy to John Norquay, 6 October 1885, ECPO, G8729; Jim Quantrell, *Cambridge Mosaic* (Cambridge, ON: City of Cambridge Archives, 1998), 9; Waterloo *Daily Record*, 7 January 1924; *Winnipeg Times*, 5 February 1884, dispatch from Ottawa; Treaty 7

Elders and Tribal Council with Walter Hildebrandt, Dorothy First Rider, and Sarah Carter, *The True Spirit and Original Intent of Treaty 7* (Montreal and Kingston: McGill-Queen's University Press, 1996); I thank Sarah Carter for a copy of her "Population Count and Survey of the Kainai Reserve" via email, 2019.

16 Corydon Brown to John Norquay, 18 January 1884, NPP, C-74.

17 Manitoba, *Rules, Orders, and Forms of Procedure of the Legislative Assembly of Manitoba* (Winnipeg: *Le Métis*, 1877); W.J. Ptolemy to John Norquay, 6 October 1885, ECPO, G8729.

18 John Norquay to Wesley Wilson, 3 March 1884, NPP, Letterbook D; Wesley Wilson to John Norquay, 4 April 1884, NPP, C-205; John Norquay to Wesley Wilson, 4 and 5 April 1884, NPP, Letterbook D; re Saskatchewan Coal's financial crisis of 1884, see Jacob Klotz to John Norquay, 25 January 1884, NPP, C-77; Hugh Macdonald to John Norquay, 11 March 1884, NPP, C-292(c)(d)(f)(h), and Norquay's reply, Letterbook C, 507; John Norquay to Thomas Renwick, 12 March 1884, NPP, Letterbook 3, 98–99; see related documents, C-421–23, C-291, C-238, C-302, C-350, C-438, C-366(c)(d)(e), C-540, C-259, Letterbook C, 518, C-448(a) and (b), C-292(e), C-1058, C-203, C-286, C-292, C-532, C-183, C-850, C-529, C-547–49, C-545, C-179, C-189, C-1138, C-201; Winnipeg City to William Scott, 5 May 1884, ECPO, Miscellaneous Government, G8730; A.W. Pritchard to W.F. Carruthers, 25 March 1884, NPP, Letterbook C; A.W. Pritchard to Hugh Macdonald, NPP, Letterbook C; Hugh Macdonald to John Norquay, 21 June 1884, NPP, C-166; Broughall, "Report of the Proceedings and the Evidence," testimony of Charles Henry Fox, 309–11; D.B. Woodworth to John Norquay, 15 August 1884, NPP, C-432.

19 Broughall, "Report of the Proceedings and the Evidence," 224–29; John A. Macdonald to John Norquay, 5 March 1884, NPP, C-571, C-292(c); A. MacKeand to John Norquay, 13 June 1884, NPP, C-210; J. Egan to William Van Horne, 11 and 20 April, 12 and 15 June, 6 August, 25 September 1885, CPR Papers, file 9218; D.B. Woodworth to John Norquay, 1 July 1884, NPP, C-131; John Norquay to William Van Horne, 4 July 1884, NPP, Letterbook C; William Van Horne to John Norquay, 15 July 1884, NPP, C-349; D. Smith to John Norquay, 8 July 1884, NPP, C-148; John Norquay to J.H. Ashdown, 28 September 1884, NPP, Letterbook D; P.E. Chapleau to John Norquay, 22 July 1884, NPP, C-120; Richard White to John Norquay, 4 August 1884, NPP, C-404; also see C-297, C-432; John A. Macdonald to John Norquay, 3 November 1884, NPP, C-929.

20 John Norquay to S.O. Shorey, 24 April 1885, NPP, Letterbook E; Broughall, "Report of the Proceedings and the Evidence," 77, 79–81; John Norquay to J.H. Ashdown, 17 June 1885, NPP, Letterbook D; A. MacKeand to John Norquay, 31 March 1885, NPP, C-642; S.O. Shorey to John Norquay, 8 and 23 April 1885, NPP, C-606, C-758, and Norquay's reply, 24 April 1885, Letterbook E; J.E. Woodworth to John Norquay, 18 April, 1 May 1885, NPP, C-789, C-1088; Ellen Cooke, "Saskatchewan Coal Mining and Transportation Company," Ellen Gillies Cooke Papers, file 10; Ellen Cooke notes on John S. Ewart, ed., "Galt v. The Saskatchewan Coal Co.," in *Reports of Cases Argued and Determined in the Court of Queen's Bench, Manitoba*, vol. 4, 1887, 304, and vol.

6, 1890, 593, in Cooke papers, file 10; *Medicine Hat Times*, 3 October 1889, 24 July 1890; George Stephen to John A. Macdonald, 4 September 1886, John A. Macdonald Papers, 123224.

21 John Norquay to J.B. MacArthur, 8 May 1885, NPP, Letterbook D.

22 John Norquay to F. Proudfoot, 29 July 1886, NPP, Letterbook 4, 134–35; Archibald Young to John Norquay, 5 November, 3 December 1886, NPP, C-1812.

23 A.M. Wilcox to John Norquay, 2 May, 25 July 1883, June–August 1884, NPP, C-1141, C-521, C-1481; Mrs. Smith to John Norquay, August 1884, 3–28 November 1884, NPP, C-290, C-1366; A.H. Cunningham to John Norquay, 4 December 1884, NPP, C-442, and Norquay's reply, 12 December 1884, NPP, Letterbook D; CPR to John Norquay, 15 November 1886, ECPO, Miscellaneous, G8730; Sam Bedson to John Norquay, 1884, 29 January 1885, NPP, C-468, C-590(a); American Express to John Norquay, 13 December 1884, NPP, C-449; David Harrison to John Norquay, 1 August 1883, NPP, B-76.

24 On insurance policies, see NPP, A-1614, B-57, B-502, C-41, C-82, C-686, C-736, C-799, C-953, C-1173.

25 "crank": weak, fragile, liable to sink; *Derbyshire Times*, cited in *Portage la Prairie Weekly Tribune-Review*, 5 December 1884, and *Selkirk Herald*, 15 December 1884, clipping in A.W. Pritchard to John Norquay, 17 December 1884, NPP, C-876; "Seventy Years Ago—Feb. 3, 1886," unidentified clipping, Fonds Société historique de Saint-Boniface, série documentation, personnages, John Norquay, boite 7, file 701.

26 John Norquay to Acton Burrows, 17 July 1884, NPP, Letterbook D; on guns and hunting, see NPP, A-512, A-1225, A-1297, B-37, B-44; John Norquay to David Harrison, 25 July 1883, NPP, Letterbook C.

27 J.E. Collins, *Life and Times of the Right Honourable Sir John A. Macdonald* (Toronto: Rose, 1883); John Norquay to David Harrison, 25 July 1883, NPP, Letterbook C.

28 G.P. Lancefield to John Norquay, 27 February, 1 May 1885, NPP, C-959, C-793; A.W. Pritchard to John Norquay, 30 December 1884, NPP, C-856; A.W. Pritchard to John Norquay, 30 December 1884, NPP, Letterbook D.

29 *Winnipeg Times*, 9, 15, and 24 April, 25 and 30 June, 3, 7, and 9 July, 14, 19, and 30 August 1884; on the Masonic Order, see NPP, B-420, B-431, B438.

30 John Norquay to James Fraser and A. McDougall, 10 and 18 September 1884, NPP, Letterbook E, 3–4, 8–10.

31 Samuel G. Matheson to John Norquay, 31 August 1883, NPP, B-1; John Norquay to Samuel G. Matheson, 3 September 1883, NPP, Letterbook C.

32 Ellen Cooke, "Interview with Mrs Aylen," Ellen Gillies Cooke Papers, file 7; Ellen Cooke, "Information from Dr. H.C. Norquay in the Early 1950s," Ellen Gillies Cooke Papers, file 2.

33 Alex Taylor to John Norquay, 24 December 1885 and 1 April 1886, NPP, C-1662.

34 Miss Norquay to John Norquay, [roughly December] 1883, NPP, B-403; Robert Richardson to John Norquay, 3 and 29 November 1884, NPP, C-441, C-440, C-285.

35 For the children's letters, see NPP, C-28, C-31, C-27, C-38, C-43, C-846, C-755.

36 For the children's expenses, see NPP, A-1497, A-1368.

37 Samuel G. Matheson to John Norquay, n.d. 1885, NPP, C-743. Emphasis in original.

38 Thomas Norquay to John Norquay, 10 July 1883, NPP, A-1441, and John's reply, 13 July 1883, Letterbook C; Thomas Norquay to John Norquay, 4 August 1884, NPP, C-405; also see A-1276; A.W. Pritchard to Rice Howard, 29 February 1884, NPP, Letterbook C; A.H. Rennie to J.H.D. Munson and T.H. Allen, 26 October 1887, NPP, Letterbook 6; Bella Norquay to John Norquay, n.d., NPP, C-1722; Manitoba Executive Council, *Orders-in-Council Registers 1870–1891*, 5 November 1884 (backdated).

39 Charles Adams to John Norquay, 9 July, 11 October 1883, NPP, B-69, B-470; John Norquay to Charles Adams, 9 February 1885, NPP, Letterbook D; Geordie Adams to John Norquay, 4 April 1885, NPP, C-604.

40 Thomas Flanagan, ed., *The Collected Writings of Louis Riel* (hereafter *CWLR*), vol. 3 (Edmonton: University of Alberta Press, 1985), 578; Gilles Martel, ed., *The Collected Writings of Louis Riel*, vol. 2 (Edmonton: University of Alberta Press, 1985), 420.

41 Louis Riel to W.H. Jackson[?], August 1884[?], in Flanagan, *CWLR*, 56.

42 "Petition to His Excellency the Governor General, of Canada, in Council," in Flanagan, *CWLR*, 41–45; for earlier drafts, see 27–29, 33–36; Louis Riel to L.N.F. Crozier, 21 March 1885, in Flanagan, *CWLR*, 56.

43 John Schultz to Frank Gemmel, 6 April 1885, Frank Gemmel Papers; John A. Macdonald to John Norquay, 27 April 1885, ECPO, G8729; John Norquay to John A. Macdonald, 7 May 1885, John A. Macdonald Papers, 201067.

44 Gerhard Ens, "Gabriel Dumont, Big Bear, and the Indian Rebellion of 1885: The Case of the Peace Hills Reserves, 1884–1885," in *Metis Histories and Identities: A Tribute to Gabriel Dumont*, ed. Denis Gagnon, Denis Combet, and Lise Gaboury-Diallo (Winnipeg: Presses Universitaires de Saint-Boniface, 2009), 25–38.

45 R.C. Macleod, "North-West Rebellion," in *The Oxford Companion to Canadian History*, ed. Gerald Hallowell (Don Mills, ON: Oxford University Press, 2004), 451–53. For context: Stephen M. Miller, ed. *Queen Victoria's Wars: British Military Campaigns, 1857–1902* (Cambridge: Cambridge University Press, 2021).

46 *Winnipeg Times*, 24 March 1885.

47 *Manitoba Free Press*, 30 March 1885, LLM Hansard; *Winnipeg Times*, 14 April 1885, LLM Hansard.

48 *Winnipeg Times*, 24 and 28 March 1885, LLM Hansard; *Manitoba Free Press*, 27 and 28 March 1885, LLM Hansard; *Journals of the Legislative Assembly of Manitoba 1885*, 19 March–2 May 1885; Alphonse LaRivière to John A. Macdonald, 3 April 1885, John A. Macdonald Papers, 48570.

49 "TR" to John Norquay, 26 March 1885, NPP, C-857(b); "Memo," n.d., NPP, C-1687.

50 J.J. Setter to John Norquay, 30 March 1885, NPP, C-784; W.G. Alcock to John Norquay, 15 April 1885, NPP, C-731; James Aikins to A. Caron, 2 and 29 April 1885, James Cox Aikins telegram book, 1881–85; A.H. Attwood to John Norquay, 28 April 1885, ECPO, G8729.

51 John Norquay to Frederick Dobson Middleton, 1 April 1885, and Middleton's reply, 1 April 1885, Coleman Papers, 267, 280. Bishop A.-A. Taché used the term "la guerre civile"; see Dom Benoit, *Vie de Mgr Taché II* (Montréal: Librairie Beauchemin, 1904), 487–88.

52 Manitoba Executive Council, *Orders-in-Council Registers 1870–1891*, 6 March 1885 (backdated from April); John Norquay to A.P. Caron, 22 April 1885, NPP, Letterbook E; John Norquay to Osborne Smith, 4 April 1885, NPP, Letterbook E; John Norquay to Thomas Gilmour, 8 April 1885, NPP, Letterbook E; A.P. Caron to John Norquay, 12 April 1885, NPP, C-919–920; John Norquay to James Lang, 13 April 1885, NPP, Letterbook E; John Norquay to R.J.T. Muckle, 21 April 1885, NPP, Letterbook E; John Norquay to Alf Walker, 19 May 1885, NPP, Letterbook E; John Norquay to A.P. Caron, 25 July 1885, NPP, Letterbook E; John Norquay to A.W. Kent, 25 July 1885, NPP, Letterbook E; Ken Coates, "Western Manitoba and the 1885 Rebellion," *Manitoba History* 20 (1990): http://www.mhs.mb.ca/docs/mb_history/20/1885rebellion.shtml.

53 Manitoba Executive Council, *Orders-in-Council Registers 1870–1891*, 15 June 1885; A.W. Pritchard to R. LaTouche Tupper, 6 April 1885, NPP, Letterbook E; G.B. Bohon to John Norquay, 6 April 1885, NPP, C-744; John Norquay to John Pennefather, 27 May 1885, NPP, Letterbook E; John Norquay to Frederick Dobson Middleton, 31 March, 1 April, NPP, C-749, C-751; Kate Nursey to John Norquay, 1 June 1885, NPP, C-968; John Norquay to J.B. Rutherford, 28 July 1885, NPP, Letterbook E; John Norquay to A.P. Caron, 11 June 1885, NPP, Letterbook E; John Norquay to J.W. David, 17 June 1885, NPP, Letterbook E; John Norquay to Colonel Whitehead, 18 June 1885, NPP, Letterbook E; A.W. Pritchard to Mrs. William Stranger, c. August 1885, NPP, Letterbook E.

54 *Winnipeg Times*, 14 and 18 April 1885; London *Times*, 15 April 1885; John Norquay to Charles Tupper, 4 May 1885, NPP, Letterbook E.

55 James Daschuk, *Clearing the Plains: Disease, Politics of Starvation, and the Loss of Indigenous Life*, 2nd ed. (Regina: University of Regina Press, 2019).

56 Ellen Cooke, "7 January 1986: Information from Mrs. Elizabeth Aylen, 1 February 1974," Ellen Gillies Cooke Papers, file 3; Alick Norquay to John Norquay, 30 March 1885, NPP, C-747; John Norquay to John James Setter, 16 March 1885, NPP, Letterbook D; John McDonald to John Norquay, 30 April 1885, ECPO, G8729; J.J. Setter to John Norquay, 4 May 1885, NPP, C-783.

57 Alick Norquay to John Norquay, 28 April 1885, copy in John Norquay to Bishop Young of Athabasca, 6 May 1885, ECPO, G8729.

58 S.L. Bedson to John Norquay, 29 March 1885, NPP, C-851; also see C-747, C-777, C-776, C-750, C-779, C-756; John Norquay to A. McDougall, 22 April 1885, NPP, Letterbook E.

59 John Norquay to S.L. Bedson, 8 April 1885, NPP, Letterbook D; John Norquay to W.R. Nursey, 7 April 1885, NPP, Letterbook D.

60 S.L. Bedson to John Norquay, 24 April 1885, NPP, C-771.

61 LaTouche Tupper to John Norquay, 24 April 1885, NPP, C-769; Tom Norquay to John Norquay, 11 May/5 June, 3 August 1885, NPP, C-1243, C-1089.

62 Alexander Norquay to John Norquay, 28 April 1885, copy in John Norquay to Richard Young, 6 May 1885, ECPO, G8729.

63 John Norquay to Richard Young, 6 May 1885, ECPO, G8729; Richard Young to John Norquay, 29 December 1885, NPP, C-1333.

64 Charles Adams to John Norquay, 15 April 1885, NPP, C-790; Horace Adams to John Norquay, 3 March 1885, NPP, C-648; Donald B. Smith, *Honoré Jaxon: Prairie Visionary* (Regina: Coteau Books, 2007).

65 Charles Adams to John Norquay, 15 April 1885, NPP, C-790.

66 Horace Adams to John Norquay, 28 March 1885, NPP, C-797.

67 John Norquay to Horace Adams, 8 May 1885, NPP, Letterbook D.

68 Tom Norquay to John Norquay, 11 May/5 June 1885, NPP, C-1243.

69 Alexander Norquay to John Norquay, 28 April 1885, copy in John Norquay to Bishop Young of Athabasca, 6 May 1885, ECPO, G8729.

70 John Norquay to Walter Nursey, 7 April 1885, NPP, Letterbook D.

71 *Winnipeg Times*, 4 April 1885.

72 I am grateful to Don Norquay, Winnipeg, who helped me with the Spence-Norquay family relationship; Ellen Cooke, "Information from Mrs. J. E. McAllister, March 9, 1946," Ellen Gillies Cooke Papers, file 4; Andrew Spence to John Norquay, 6 April 1875, NPP, A-171; 8 April 1875, A-173; 8 September 1875, A-170; 6 December 1875, A-172; 26 February/20 June 1878, A-33; 1 August 1879, A-377; 21 January 1880, A-405; 5 August 1880, A-453; 2 August 1881, A-773; 5 September 1881, A-769; 8 December 1881, A-886; 9–10 June 1882, A-1157; P. Milne to John Norquay, 17 June 1882, NPP, A-1159; Charles Adams to John Norquay, 11 September 1880, 22 October 1883, NPP, A-471, A-1362; Gail Morin, *Metis Families*, vol. 10, 3rd ed., 259, AM.

73 Andrew Spence to John Norquay, 14 March 1885, NPP, C-651; Tom Norquay to John Norquay, 2 February 1884, NPP, C-31; William Luxton to John Norquay, 16 January 1884, NPP, C-51; John Norquay to John Mooney, 4 March 1885, NPP, Letterbook E; *Manitoba Free Press* and *Winnipeg Times*, 28 February 1885; Paget J. Code, "Les Autres Métis: The English Métis of the Prince Albert Settlement 1862–1886" (MA thesis,

University of Saskatchewan, 2008); Bill Waiser, *A World We Have Lost: Saskatchewan before 1905* (Markham, ON: Fifth House, 2016), 522–25.

74 John Norquay to Andrew Spence, 27 March 1885, NPP, Letterbook E; Andrew Spence to John Norquay, 24 November 1885, NPP, C-1229.

75 Charles Adams to John Norquay, 30 June 1885, NPP, C-1024. Emphasis in original.

76 John Norquay to John A. Macdonald, 13 March 1885, NPP, C-764; John Norquay to John A. Macdonald, 4 April 1885, John A. Macdonald Papers, 200447; John A. Macdonald to John Norquay, 9 April 1885, John A. Macdonald Papers, 48573, NPP, C-764.

77 John A. Macdonald to Lord Lorne, 26 March 1884, Lord Lorne Papers, vol. 1, 364–67.

78 John Norquay to John A. Macdonald, 10 June, 6 July, 25 August 1885, John A. Macdonald Papers, 201723, 202189, 46071; David Harrison to John A. Macdonald, 18 May 1885, John A. Macdonald Papers, 201250; John Sutherland to John A. Macdonald, 3 September 1885, John A. Macdonald Papers, 46076; C.A. Boulton to John Norquay, 9 February 1885, NPP, C-726; J.E. Woodworth to John Norquay, 18 May 1885, NPP, C-982.

79 This suggestion was made by George F.G. Stanley, *The Birth of Western Canada: A History of the Riel Rebellions* (Toronto: Longmans, Green, 1936), 260–61.

80 Joseph Dubuc to Élie Tassé, 31 May 1885, quoted in Diane Payment, "Joseph Dubuc et les développements politiques au Manitoba 1870–1885," unpublished essay, Fonds Société historique de Saint-Boniface, série documentation, personnages, boite 7, file 258.

81 *Brandon Sun*, 21 February 1884; *Winnipeg Times*, 28 March, 28 April–1 May 1885; *Manitoba Free Press*, 28 March, 28–30 April 1885, LLM Hansard; *Journals of the Legislative Assembly of Manitoba 1884*, 81; Frank Gemmel to John Norquay, 9 January 1885, NPP, C-697.

82 John Norquay to John A. Macdonald, 9 and 28 March, 23 April 1885, John A. Macdonald Papers, 199792, 200243, 200792; "Speech from the Throne," in *Journals of the Legislative Assembly of Manitoba 1885*; *Manitoba Free Press*, 18 April 1885, LLM Hansard; *Winnipeg Times*, 11 and 15 April 1885, LLM Hansard; Greg Taylor, *Law of the Land: The Advent of the Torrens System in Canada* (Toronto: Osgoode Society for Canadian Legal History and University of Toronto Press, 2008), 9, 132–52; Jim Mochoruk, *Formidable Heritage: Manitoba's North and the Cost of Development 1870 to 1930* (Winnipeg: University of Manitoba Press, 2004); Doug Owram, *Promise of Eden: The Canadian Expansionist Movement and the Idea of the West 1856–1900* (Toronto: University of Toronto Press, 1980); John W. Dafoe, *Clifford Sifton in Relation to His Times* (Toronto: Macmillan, 1931), 16–19.

83 Dafoe, *Clifford Sifton*, 19.

84 *Winnipeg Times*, 15 June 1883; John Norquay to William Kennedy, 9 January, 4 April, 13 and 24 November 1883, NPP, Letterbook C.

85 John Norquay to A. McDougall, 22 April 1885, NPP, Letterbook E; John Norquay to John James Setter, 16 March 1885, NPP, Letterbook D; John Norquay to James Fraser, 24 April 1885, NPP, Letterbook D; William Scarth to John Norquay, 17 March 1885, NPP, C-620; *Manitoba Free Press*, 26, 27, and 28 March 1885, LLM Hansard.

86 *Manitoba Sun*, 20 March 1885, LLM Hansard; *Manitoba Free Press*, 24 and 25 April, 2 May 1885, LLM Hansard; *Winnipeg Times*, 24 April 1885, LLM Hansard; Manitoba, *Annual Report of the Department of Public Works for 1884* (Winnipeg: Queen's Printer, 1885), 40–41.

87 John Headley Bell testimony, in Broughall, "Report of the Proceedings and the Evidence," Manitoba, *Sessional Papers*, 359, 361–76, G8116, box 6, file 16.

88 *Manitoba Free Press*, 2 and 4 May 1885, LLM Hansard.

89 *Manitoba Free Press*, 4 May 1885, 9 March 1886; *Daily Manitoban*, 5 and 9 March 1886; *Winnipeg Times*, 4 May 1885, LLM Hansard.

90 Ibid.

91 Ibid.

92 *Winnipeg Times*, 4 May 1885, LLM Hansard.

93 James Monkman to John Norquay, 5 February 1883, NPP, A-1457; William MacLeod to John Norquay, 3 September 1885, NPP, C-1166; Johnnie McDonald to John Norquay, 3 September 1885, NPP, C-1008; A.E. Forget to John Norquay, 1 September 1885, NPP, C-1169; John Norquay to George Tidsbury, 30 January 1885, NPP, Letterbook E, 134–35. On job requests, see NPP, C-1514, C-1937, C-1936; James Whiteway to John Norquay, 18 January 1886, NPP, C-2071.

94 D.R. Wilkie to John Norquay, 24 November 1885, NPP, C-1459; Jim Hooper to John Norquay, 16 January 1886, NPP, C-1498; John Norquay to Jim Hooper, January 1886, NPP, Letterbook E; John Norquay to John B. Ashby, 9 February 1886, NPP, Letterbook E; St. Andrews Society dues, ECPO, Miscellaneous, G8730, C-1630, C-1398, C-1360, C-2459, C-1705, C-1746, C-1394, C-1397; Masonic Lodge, C-1906, C-22094, C-2130; confederation medal, *Selkirk Record*, 26 November 1885 (with thanks to Henry Trachtenberg for this reference); Anglican Church, Robert Machray to John Norquay, 6 March 1885, and John Norquay to Robert Machray, 6 January 1886, NPP, Letterbook E.

95 John Norquay to John Pennefather, c. April 1883, NPP, Letterbook D, 9–10; John Pennefather to John Norquay, NPP, A-949, C-101–02, C-50, C-185, C-105, C-1165, C-2542, C-2546, C-1638, C-1676, C-1784, C-2002, C-2388, C-2939; John Pyne Pennefather, *Thirteen Years on the Prairies: From Winnipeg to Cold Lake Fifteen Hundred Miles* (London: Kegan Paul, Trench, Trubner and Company, 1892), 1–18; Mary Pennefather to John Norquay, 13 and 28 August 1883, NPP, B-7(a) and (b); *Public Accounts of the Province of Manitoba for the Year Ending June 30th 1887* (Winnipeg: Queen's Printer, 1888), 45; John Norquay to John Parr, 27 July 1883, NPP, Letterbook C; John Norquay to P.J. Haverty, 24 March 1885, NPP, Letterbook E; John

Norquay to Andy Maxwell, 8 May 1885, NPP, Letterbook D; Andy Maxwell to John Norquay, 31 May 1885, NPP, C-1002.

96 John Norquay to Acton Burrows, Mr. and Mrs. Scarth, Whitla, 2 x Colcleugh, Captain Kennedy, Alloway, Whiteway, Ruttan, Mrs. Bain, Bishop Young, Thomas Sinclair, R. Bullock, Archdeacon Cowley, Mrs. and Rev. Mackenzie, Pritchard, Ptolemy, Smith, Mitchell, 1 and 7 March 1885, NPP, Letterbook E.

97 G. D'Arcy Boulton to William Van Horne, 23 May 1884, enclosure in William Van Horne to John Norquay, NPP, C-463; William Van Horne to John Norquay, 8 April 1885, NPP, C-761; John Norquay to William Van Horne, 14 April 1885, NPP, Letterbook E; John Norquay to William Van Horne, 26 November 1883, NPP, Letterbook D.

98 John Norquay to Captain John Allan, 29 February 1884, NPP, Letterbook D; also see NPP, C-254, C-473, C-220.

99 George Bliss to John Norquay, 20 May 1886, NPP, C-1733.

100 *Manitoba Free Press*, 8 July 1889.

101 Re society, poker, and drink, see F.H. Brydges to John Norquay, 31 August 1886, NPP, C-1854; John Norquay, "Agenda Book, 1885," NPP; George H. Ham, *Reminiscences of a Raconteur, between the '40s and the '20s* (Toronto: Musson, 1921); John Norquay to A.H. Rennie, 1 December 1884, NPP, Letterbook D; Ellen Cooke, "Interview with Jacob Truthwaite Norquay," 8 July 1965, Ellen Gillies Cooke Papers, file 6; John Haggart to John Norquay, 2 July 1884, NPP, C-109; also see NPP, C-619, C-628, C-641, C-717, C-839; J.H. Spencer to John Norquay, 23 January–21 February 1884, NPP, C-488, C-666, C-598, C-587, C-723, C-785, C-1184, C-1409; Henry Jameson to John Norquay, 7 March 188?, ECPO, G8729; John Pennefather to John Norquay, n.d., NPP, C-2939; Corydon Brown to John A. Macdonald, 3 January 1887, John A. Macdonald Papers, 213131; David Wilson to John Norquay, 3 January 1887, NPP, C-2428; also see NPP, B-441, C-486, C-11; re Manitoba Club, John Norquay to Acton Burrows, 17 June 1884, NPP, Letterbook C; Acton Burrows to John Norquay, 28 June 1884, NPP, C-265; see also C-367, C-1361, C-997, C-1475, C-1191, C-1230, C-1237, C-1400, C-1407; John Norquay to S.W. Smith, 14 December 1885, NPP, Letterbook E; re clothing, R.J. Devlin to John Norquay, 29 January 1885, NPP, ECPO, Miscellaneous, G8730; John Norquay to Bernard Saunders, 11 April 1883, NPP, Letterbook C, and 31 October 1885, NPP, Letterbook E; Bernard Saunders to John Norquay, June 1883, NPP, B-457, and Bernard Saunders to John Norquay, 5 November 1885, NPP, C-1184; T.H. Allen to John Norquay, 20 February 1886, NPP, C-1736: "I hear that you were one of the greatest attractions at the St. Paul Carnival. I have no doubt of it—*with the girls!*"

102 George Ham to John Norquay, 21 January 1884, NPP, C-61; John Norquay, "Diary 1885," entries for 17 January, 18 March, NPP; Ham, *Reminiscences*, 100, 173–75.

103 LaTouche Tupper to John Norquay, 24 April 1885, NPP, C-769.

104 George Ham to John Norquay, 30 April 1885, NPP, C-985; Ham, *Reminiscences*, 232.

105 George Ham to John Norquay, 5 April 1885, NPP, C-608; also see 30 April 1885, C-985; 6 May 1885, C-980; 8–11 May 1885, C-951.

106 John Norquay to George Ham, 8 April 1885, NPP, Letterbook D.

107 John Norquay to Andrew Spence, 27 March 1885, NPP, Letterbook E; John James Setter to John Norquay, 4 May 1885, NPP, C-783; John Norquay to Henry Muma, 6 November 1885, NPP, Letterbook E.

108 *Manitoba Free Press*, 30 March 1885, LLM Hansard; High Bluff constituency population by birthplace, 1870 census: High Bluff: England 0, Ireland 1, Scotland 4, Canada 0, Ontario 0, MB & NW 139. Poplar Point: England 4, Ireland 5, Scotland 10, Canada 1, Ontario 1, MB & NW 477. "Manitoba 1870: Table IV Birthplaces" pp. 386–387 in *Censuses of Canada 1665–1871: Statistics of Canada IV* (Ottawa: I.B. Taylor, 1876), https://ia903404.us.archive.org/6/items/censusofcana1800cana/censusofcana1800cana.pdf (accessed 16 December 2023).

109 David Harrison to John Norquay, 24 May 1885, NPP, C-895; John James Setter to John Norquay, 4 May 1885, NPP, C-783; *Grip* 24, no. 17 (25 April 1885); Tom Norquay to John Norquay, 11 May and 5 June 1885, NPP, C-1243; Carman Cumming, *Secret Craft: The Journalism of Edward Farrer* (Toronto: University of Toronto Press, 1992), 79; John Norquay to Fred White, 14 September 1885, cited in George Stanley, *Louis Riel* (Toronto: Ryerson, 1963), 366; James Aikins to Frederick Dobson Middleton, 18 and 27 May 1885, and James Aikins to A.P. Caron, 6 July 1885, James Cox Aikins telegram book, 1881–85; J.M. Robinson to John Norquay, 27 November 1886, NPP, C-2313; Joseph Tait to John Norquay, 20 September 1886, NPP, C-1795; James Whiteway to John Norquay, 21 December 1886, NPP, C-2243.

110 G.A. Gemmill, ed., *Canadian Parliamentary Companion 1887* (Ottawa: J. Durie and Son, 1887), 333.

111 Charles Adams to John Norquay, 15 April 1885, NPP, C-790; J.J. Setter to John Norquay, 30 March 1885, NPP, C-784.

112 John Norquay to John Henry Pope, 19 December 1885, ECPO, G8729.

113 Osborne Smith to John Norquay, 26 and 28 August 1885, ECPO, G8729, NPP, C-1040.

114 John Norquay to Osborne Smith, 1 September 1885, NPP, Letterbook E; John Norquay to A.P. Caron, 18 November 1885, NPP, Letterbook E; A.P. Caron to John Norquay, 9 February 1886, NPP, C-1341; Colonel Peebles to John Norquay, 9 February 1886, NPP, C-1385.

115 David Harrison to John A. Macdonald, 20 June, 9 November 1885, John A. Macdonald Papers, 201901, 58084.

116 William Wagner to John A. Macdonald, 18 May 1885, John A. Macdonald Papers, 46072; *Nor'West Farmer and Manitoba Miller* 5 (1886): 338–39; *Manitoba Free Press*, 29 May 1886; Karin R. Gürttler, "Wagner, William," in *Dictionary of Canadian Biography*, vol. 13, University of Toronto/Université Laval, 2003–, http://www.

biographi.ca/en/bio/wagner_william_13E.html (accessed 13 April 2023); Robert L. Nelson, "A German on the Prairies: Max Sering and Settler Colonialism in Canada," *Settler Colonial Studies* 5, no. 1 (2015): 1–19.

117 The Ottawa *Free Press* published a brief note about the Manitoba-Ontario boundary dispute: "'Mowat made one mistake,' said a western gentleman to the *Free Press* representative today, 'He should have seized that half-breed Norquay for disturbing the peace at Rat Portage and clapped him into gaol.'" Reprinted in *Winnipeg Times*, 12 October 1883.

118 Elsie MacKay, ed., *Selkirk's Seventy-Fifth Anniversary* (Selkirk, MB: n.p., c. 1957), 69–70; Alex Norquay to John Norquay, 1 June 1885, NPP, C-970; John Norquay to J.H. Ashdown et al., 30 May 1885, NPP, Letterbook E; John Norquay to Mayor of Winnipeg, 26 June 1885, NPP, Letterbook E; John Norquay to W.H. Jackson, 27 June 1885, NPP, Letterbook E; John Norquay to Donald A. Smith, 7 July 1885, NPP, Letterbook E; G.F. Carruthers to John Norquay, 14 July 1885, NPP, C-1238; also see C-1016, C-1465; *Canadian Military Gazette* 1, no. 15 (18 August 1885): 118; Mary Worsnop to John Norquay, 10 May 1885, NPP, C-2516.

119 John Norquay to John Henry Pope, 19 December 1885, ECPO, G8729; John Norquay to John A. Macdonald, 6 July 1885, NPP, Letterbook E; Thomas White to John Norquay, 2 September 1885, NPP, C-1167; John Norquay to C.C. Setter, 23 September, 14 October 1885, NPP, Letterbook E; John Norquay to Harry Muma, 6 and 11 November 1885, NPP, Letterbook E; John Norquay to Minister of Justice, 25 March 1886, NPP, Letterbook 4; Margaret Stobie, *The Other Side of Rebellion: The Remarkable Story of Charles Bremner and His Furs* (Edmonton: NeWest Publishers, 1987).

120 George Orton to John A. Macdonald, 26 March 1885, John A. Macdonald Papers, 200150; this was exactly the view expressed by G.F.G. Stanley half a century later in *The Birth of Western Canada*, 260–61.

121 *Daily Manitoban*, 17 August 1885; Mary Janigan, *Let the Eastern Bastards Freeze in the Dark: The West versus the Rest since Confederation* (Toronto: Alfred A. Knopf Canada, 2012), 73–74.

122 James Aikins to John A. Macdonald, 3 November 1885, John A. Macdonald Papers, 48578; John Norquay to John A. Macdonald, 1 August 1885, John A. Macdonald Papers; John Norquay to John A. Macdonald, 20 July, 1 and 15 August 1885, John A. Macdonald Papers, 2493, 202786, 3522, 3559, 203032.

123 John A. Macdonald to H.H. Smith, 6 August 1885, H.H. Smith Papers; Sarah Carter, *Lost Harvests: Prairie Indian Reserve Farmers and Government Policy* (Montreal and Kingston: McGill-Queen's University Press, 1990), 130–35; E. Brian Titley, "Dewdney, Edgar," in *Dictionary of Canadian Biography*, vol. 14, University of Toronto/Université Laval, 2003–, http://www.biographi.ca/en/bio/dewdney_edgar_14E.html (accessed 13 April 2023); and E. Brian Titley, "Reed, Hayter," in *Dictionary of Canadian Biography*, vol. 16, University of Toronto/Université Laval, 2003–, http://www.biographi.ca/en/bio/reed_hayter_16E.html (accessed 13 April 2023).

124 John Norquay to John A. Macdonald, 10 June, 6 July 1885, John A. Macdonald Papers, 201723, 202189; Fred White to John A. Macdonald, 1 September 1885, John A. Macdonald Papers, 134934; Macdonald addressed the issue of Ottawa's administration of Manitoba lands in the House of Commons; see Canada, House of Commons, *Debates 1885*, 2782–83.

125 John A. Macdonald to George Stephen, 24 August 1885, George Stephen Papers, 139; George Stephen to John A. Macdonald, 9 July 1885, John A. Macdonald Papers, 122904; John Norquay to George Stephen, 26 January 1885, and Stephen's reply, 27 January 1885, and George Stephen to David MacPherson, 28 January 1885, David MacPherson Papers, files 26 and 27.

126 John Norquay to T.W. Allan, 8 July 1885, NPP, Letterbook E; John Norquay to John Pennefather, 21 October 1885, NPP, Letterbook E.

127 *Daily Manitoban*, 4 March 1886.

Chapter 10: Vindication, 1886

1 Alex Kelso to John Norquay, 11 March 1886, NPP, C-1358; Arthur Hawkins to John Norquay, 14 March, 10 April 1886, NPP, C-1329, C1426; John Norquay to James J. Hill, 18 March 1886, NPP, Letterbook E, and Hill's reply, NPP, C-1314.

2 David Young to John Norquay, 21 December 1885, NPP, C-1397; J. Macdougall to John Norquay, 23 January 1883, 15 January, 10 March 1886, NPP, C-1513, C-1412; also see C-1435(a)(b)(c), C-1424.

3 I thank Randy Rostecki for sharing his "John Norquay Residence, 73 Hallet Street, 1884," unpublished manuscript, 2017, including Lillian Gibbons, "Stories Houses Tell: No 73–75 Hallet Street," *Winnipeg Tribune*, 18 April 1936. The house number was 18 Hallet in the 1890s.

4 John Norquay to W.A. Macdonald, 18 February 1886, NPP, Letterbook E; H.M. Howell to John Norquay, 21 June 1886, NPP, C-1767; also see C-2496, C-1500, C-1410, C-1672, C-1558; A.G. McKenzie to John Norquay, 12 July, 11 September 1886 to April–June 1888, monthly bills, NPP and ECPO, Miscellaneous, G8730.

5 Gibbons, "Stories . . . 73–75 Hallet Street."

6 For invoices, see NPP, C-1205, C-1210–12, C-1215, C-1220, C-1251; ECPO, Miscellaneous, G8730, C-1632, C-1330, C-1448.

7 Ellen Cooke, "Interview with Mrs. J. E. McAllister," Ellen Gillies Cooke Papers, file 4.

8 Ellen Cooke, "Telephone Conversation with Mrs. Alfred Savage [Mary Norquay] in May 1965," Ellen Gillies Cooke Papers, file 5.

9 Mrs. Smith to Norquay, 1 March 1886, NPP, C-1432.

10 James Aikins to John Norquay, February 1886, NPP, C-1431; Bella Norquay to John Norquay, 25 January 1886, NPP, C-1722; Jim Fullerton to John Norquay, 24 October 1886, NPP, C-1873; also see C-1730; Richard Young to John Norquay, 29 December

1885, NPP, C-1333; Alfred Rennie to John Norquay, January–February 1886, NPP, C-1437(c)–(h); Professor Warde to Mr. George, n.d., NPP, C-1584; Dr. William Cowan to John Norquay, 18 June 1886, NPP, C-1296; Corydon Brown to John Norquay, 14 March 1886, NPP, C-1332; W. Whitehead to John Norquay, 1 April, 1 May 1886, NPP, C-1622.

11 Ellen Cooke, "Andrew Norquay Interview, Vancouver, 1959," Ellen Gillies Cooke Papers, file 1, "Telephone Conversation with Mrs. Alfred Savage, May 1965," file 5, and "7 January 1986 Information from Mrs. Elizabeth Aylen," file 3; Aphrodite Karamitsanis, *Place Names of Alberta, Volume 1: Mountains, Mountain Parks and Foothills* (Calgary: University of Calgary Press, 1991), records that the official naming of the mountain dates from 1904; F.C. Harris and G.M. McDougall, "The Banff Sanitarium Hotel," in *Medical Clinics and Physicians of Southern Alberta*, G.M. McDougall et al. (Calgary: McDougall, 1991), 181–204; Patricia Roome, "A Report on Dr. Robert George Brett (1851–1929) and the Sanitarium Hotel," typescript, 1970, Whyte Museum, Brett Family Papers; David J. Hall, "Brett, Robert George," in *Dictionary of Canadian Biography*, vol. 15, University of Toronto/Université Laval, 2003–, http://www.biographi.ca/en/bio/brett_robert_george_15E.html (accessed 14 April 2023); John Norquay to J.P. Alexander, 29 July 1886, NPP, Letterbook 4; Samuel Matheson to John Norquay, 24 August 1886, NPP, C-1665; John Norquay to Thomas Young, 30 August 1886, NPP, Letterbook 4.

12 *Selkirk Record*, 4 June 1886; I thank Dr. Henry Trachtenberg for this reference; Manitoba, "Auditor's Appropriation Ledger 1886–87," AM, G8706; John Norquay to J.H. Conrad, 3 September 1886, NPP, Letterbook 5, and 23 December 1886, NPP, Letterbook 4; Manitoba Executive Council Office, *Public Accounts for Year Ending 30 June 1887* (Winnipeg: Queen's Printer, 1888), 19, GR Series, G8113; Sam Bedson to John Norquay, 8 May 1887, ECPO, G8729; David Wilson to A.H. Rennie, 18 February 1887, NPP, C-2371; D. Young to John Norquay, 13 November 1887, ECPO, G8730.

13 Samuel Matheson to John Norquay, 1885, NPP, C-743; Ellen Cooke, "Telephone Conversation with Mrs. Alfred Savage in May 1965," Ellen Gillies Cooke Papers, file 5; T. Mayne Daly to John Norquay, 1 March 1887, NPP, C-2781; John Norquay to M.R. Reid, c. February 1885, NPP, Letterbook D; John Norquay to J.M. Egan, 7 July 1885, NPP, Letterbook E; John Norquay to Robert Kerr, 6 September 1886, NPP, Letterbook 4, and Kerr's reply, 29 September 1886, NPP, C-1956; John Norquay to Robert Machray, 29 July 1886, NPP, Letterbook 4; Samuel Matheson to John Norquay, 27 July, 24 August, 20 December 1886, NPP, C-1258, C-1665, C-2013; Horace Norquay to John Norquay, 19 March 1886, NPP, C-1425; also see C-1477, C-1367, C-1020, C-1028, C-1473, C-1291, C-1603.

14 John Norquay to J.J. Setter, 10 September, 13 December 1886, NPP, Letterbook 5, and Setter's reply, 3 November 1886, NPP, C-1827; Alfred Rennie to J.H. Munson, 26 October 1887, NPP, Letterbook 6; Colin Setter to John Norquay, 13 March 1886, NPP, C-1346; also see C-1147, C-1405, C-1451; John Norquay to Colin Setter, 13 December 1885, NPP, Letterbook E; also see 18 February 1886, NPP, Letterbook

E; 21 July 1886, Letterbook 4; 28 August 1886, Letterbook 4; also see NPP, C-273, C-1170, C-1639, C-1560, C-1612, C-1616, C-1739, C-1828, C-1837; John Norquay to Thomas Collins, 25 June 1886, and Collins's reply, 25 June 1886, ECPO, G8729; John Norquay to D. Miller, 29 September 1886, NPP, Letterbook 5; D. VanKoughnet to John Norquay, 10 November 1880, NPP, A-418; John Lazarus Norquay to John Norquay, 7 and 23 January 1886, NPP, C-1535, C-1419, and Norquay's reply, 20 January 1886, NPP, Letterbook E; Charles Adams to John Norquay, 27 October 1885, NPP, C-1241(a); also see C-1004(a) and (b), C-1177, C-1241(b), C-1472, C-1415, C-1619, C-1356, C-1645, C-1882, C-1877, C-2318; John Norquay to John A. Macdonald, 1 September 1886, John A. Macdonald Papers, 209896; John Norquay to Charles Adams, 4 September 1886, NPP, Letterbook 5; Norquay also accepted the role of advocate for others in the Métis community; see James Taylor to John Norquay, 18 October 1880, NPP, A-488.

15 Manitoba, "Auditor's Appropriation Ledger 1886–87," AM, G8706.

16 On St. Andrews land, see NPP, C-1384, C-1550, C-1889; on maintenance costs, see NPP, C-1331, C-1195, C-1606, C-1447, C-1754, C-1732, C-1487, C-2086.

17 James Colcleugh to John Norquay, n.d., 18 February 1883, NPP, A-833, A-1480–81; C.S. Farrell to John Norquay, 24 June 1886, ECPO, G8729; also see NPP, C-1407, C-1227, C-1265, C-2171, C-1508; Alfred Rennie to A.H. Whitcher, 3 August 1886, NPP, Letterbook 4, C-2171; also see A-1410; J.W. Jackson to John Norquay, 1 March 1883, and Norquay's reply, 30 March 1883, NPP, A-1547, C-1143; also see C-112, A-1122, A-1125, A-1597, C-413, B-58, B-481, A-36, A-496, C-354, A-1514; further re Darlingford, see NPP, Letterbook C, 37, 86, 122; Letterbook D, 9–10, 77, A-1468, A-1450, A-1445(a)(b)(c)(d), C-270(a) and (b); John Egan to John Norquay, 15 June 1883, ECPO, G8729; also NPP, B-399, B-454, C-478; John Norquay to John Egan, 18 April 1885, NPP, Letterbook D; John Norquay to John Pennefather, April 1885, NPP, Letterbook D.

18 Manitoba Executive Council, *Orders-in-Council Registers 1870–1891*, 31 December 1883; Corydon Brown to John Norquay, 17 January 1884, NPP, C-52; Sedley Blanchard to John Norquay, 5 October 1885, ECPO, G8729; George Broughall, "Report of the Proceedings and the Evidence . . . Wallbridge Royal Commission, 1886," in *Sessional Papers 1886*, LA009, GR174, G8116, box 6, files 14 and 16: 278–83, 294–95, 297–307, 347–51; Samuel Bedson to John Norquay, 22 February 1883, NPP, A-1465; 11 September 1884, C-282; 15 September 1884, C-299; 1 December 1886, C-1888.

19 "Memo of Standing at Bank," c. 1886, NPP, C-1702.

20 Hugh John Macdonald to John A. Macdonald, 4 February, 2 September 1885, John A. Macdonald Papers, 203028, 253199; Hugh John Macdonald to John Norquay, 19 September 1885, NPP, C-1118; *Brandon Sun*, 6, 15, 18, and 24 July 1885; Francis McPhillips to John A. Macdonald, 23 July, 18 August 1885, John A. Macdonald Papers, 202570, 203023.

21 London *Times*, 10 September 1881; John George Argyll, *The Canadian North-West: Speech Delivered at Winnipeg by His Excellency the Marquis of Lorne, Governor-General of Canada, after His Trip through Manitoba and the North-West, during the Summer of 1881* (Ottawa: Department of Agriculture, 1881); P.B. Waite, "Campbell, John George, Marquess of Lorne and Duke of Argyll," in *Dictionary of Canadian Biography*, vol. 14, University of Toronto/Université Laval, 2003–, http://www.biographi.ca/en/bio/campbell_john_george_edward_henry_douglas_sutherland_14E.html (accessed 17 April 2023); William H. Williams, *Manitoba and the North-West: Journal of a Trip* (Toronto: Hunter, Rose, 1882); Robert M. Stamp, *Royal Rebels: Princess Louise and the Marquis of Lorne* (Toronto: Dundurn Press, 1988).

22 John Setter to John Norquay, 14 October 1881, NPP, A-785.

23 Sarah Carter, "'Your Great Mother across the Salt Sea': Prairie First Nations, the British Monarchy and the Vice Regal Connection to 1900," *Manitoba History* 48 (2005–06): 162–63, quoting Marquesse of Lorne, *Canadian Pictures Drawn with Pen and Pencil* (London: Religious Tract Society, 1885), and quoting the Duke of Argyll, *Passages From the Past* II (London: Hutchinson, 1907) 466; W.S. MacNutt, *Days of Lorne: From the Private Papers of the Marquis of Lorne, 1878–1883, in the Possession of the Duke of Argyll at Inveraray Castle, Scotland* (Fredericton: Brunswick Press, 1955), 255.

24 James Wickes Taylor to St. George's Society of Winnipeg, "Notes, v. I," c. 1890, USC Papers, microfilm; John Norquay[?], "Memo: Address to British Association," n.d. 1884, NPP, C-451; Robert Machray to John Norquay, 2 March 1878, NPP, A-27; J.W. Butler to John Norquay, 1884, NPP, C-319; F.M. Harris to John Norquay, 19 April 1884, NPP, C-235; Frederick Young to John Norquay, 5 November 1884, NPP, C-386; also see C-738, C-1554; John Norquay to James Fraser, 18 September 1884, NPP, Letterbook E; "Inventory and Valuation," 1883, ECPO, Miscellaneous Government, G8730.

25 James Thomson to Norquay, 12 January, 17 February 1883, NPP, A-1427, A-1426; Norquay to Thomson, 4, 12 March, 1883, NPP, A-1425; Norquay to James Thomson, 31 January 1887, Margaret Arnett MacLeod papers, file 41.

26 John Norquay to W.F. Munroe, 30 October 1883, NPP, Letterbook C; also see B-59, B-71, C-1171; John Norquay to A.J. Douglas, 14 March 1884, NPP, letterbook D; also see B-452, C-180, C-234(a) and (b); William Brown to John Norquay, 31 October 1883, NPP, B-396; John Norquay to William Brown (Edinburgh), April 1884, NPP, C-439; on St. Andrews Society dinner, see B-409, B-438.

27 *Manitoba Free Press*, 1 May 1886, LLM Hansard; John Norquay to James Aikins, 20 January 1886, NPP, Letterbook E; James A. Maxwell, *Federal Subsidies to the Provincial Governments in Canada* (Cambridge, MA: Harvard University Press, 1937), 79–88; John Norquay to John A. Macdonald, 29 January 1886, NPP, C-2907, C-2908; also see C-1761–63, C-1437(b)–(h); James Aikins to John Norquay, 1 February 1886, NPP, C-1764; John Norquay to Alphonse LaRivière, 21 July 1886, NPP, Letterbook 4; John Norquay to John Pope, 15 April 1887, NPP, Letterbook 5.

28 Ed Leacock to John Norquay, 10 August 1885, NPP, C-1113; Alfred Rennie to John Norquay, November 1885, NPP, C-1458; A.W. Pritchard to Minister of Customs, 22 December 1885, NPP; Letterbook E; John Norquay to John Oliver, 23 July 1883, NPP, Letterbook C; A.W. Pritchard to John Norquay, 8 May 1884, NPP, Letterbook C; Norquay received over sixty letters related to Manitoba political matters and party organizing between December 1885 and May 1886 scattered through documents C-1300–1800, NPP; Daniel J. Meissner, "Theodore B. Wilcox: Captain of Industry and Magnate of the China Flour Trade, 1884–1918," *Oregon Historical Quarterly* 104, no. 4 (2003): 518–41, says that Rennie had been D.A. Smith's and J.J. Hill's assistant in negotiating the "CPR charter," presumably in 1880–81.

29 John Norquay to John Parr, 17 February 1886, NPP, Letterbook E.

30 J. Kirchhoffer to John Norquay, 2 March 1886, NPP, C-1445, emphasis in original; *Brandon Sun*, 21 January, 4 March 1886.

31 John Norquay to A. McDougall, 22 April 1885, NPP, Letterbook E; John Norquay to Robert Rogers, 20 January 1886, NPP, Letterbook E; A.J. McMillan to John Norquay, 25 February 1886, NPP, C-1677; *Portage la Prairie Weekly Tribune-Review*, 21 August, 18 December 1885; *Brandon Sun*, 2 September, 29 October 1885; John Norquay to George Elliott, 23 March 1886, NPP, Letterbook E.

32 Lewis Wallbridge to John A. Macdonald, 4 February 1886, John A. Macdonald Papers, 205501; the final report is published in *Journals of the Legislative Assembly of Manitoba 1886*; the legislative basis of the commission is noted on 189; Bruce W. Hodgins, "Wallbridge, Lewis," in *Dictionary of Canadian Biography*, vol. 11, University of Toronto/Université Laval, 2003–, http://www.biographi.ca/en/bio/wallbridge_lewis_11E.html (accessed 17 April 2023); J.K. Johnson and P.B. Waite, "Macdonald, Sir John Alexander," in *Dictionary of Canadian Biography*, vol. 12, University of Toronto/Université Laval, 2003–, http://www.biographi.ca/en/bio/macdonald_john_alexander_12E.html (accessed 17 April 2023); Tom Mitchell, "1846: Canada's First *Inquiries Act*," *Journal of Canadian Studies* 55, no. 3 (2021): 564–89; Tom Mitchell, "'Ultra Vires and Void': An Executive Inquiry Takes on Manitoba's Legislative Building Crisis (and Wins)," *Manitoba Law Journal* 44, no. 3 (2021): 185–224; I thank Stuart Hay, Legislative Library of Manitoba, and Tom Mitchell for help with this commission.

33 *Manitoba Free Press*, 9 March 1886, LLM Hansard.

34 The "promoters": J.B. McArthur, S.C. Biggs, and John S. Ewart; the "defence": H.M. Howell, N.F. Hagel, and W.R. Mulock; W.R. Mulock to John Norquay, 12 March 1886, NPP, C-1309; Sedley Blanchard to John Norquay, 5 October 1885, ECPO, G8729.

35 *Manitoban*, 5 March 1886; Broughall, "Report of the Proceedings and the Evidence," iv–vii; *Manitoba Free Press*, 21 and 24 August 1885, 17 and 27 February 1886.

36 Broughall, "Report of the Proceedings and the Evidence," 22–23, 25, 28–29, 198.

37 Ibid., 43–47, 58.

38 Ibid., 48–58.

39 Ibid., 63, 68–71, 77, 79–81.

40 Ibid., 96–99.

41 Ibid., 91–103, 106, 111.

42 Ibid., 117–27, 130, 133, 135; John Norquay, cheque stubs, July–December 1883, ECPO, Miscellaneous, G8730; Corydon Brown to John Norquay, 17 January 1884, NPP, C-52; Norquay had applied for a patent on river lot 61 in the parish of St. Clement's in 1882. See LAC, RG15-DII-2, vol. 149, file M.A.2117, microfilm C-14911.

43 Broughall, "Report of the Proceedings and the Evidence," 309–11, 348–51, 389–94; "Judgment, 4 March 1886," ECPO, Miscellaneous Government, G8730; *Brandon Sun*, 22 April 1886; Lee Gibson, "Hagel, Nathaniel Francis," in *Dictionary of Canadian Biography*, vol. 14, University of Toronto/Université Laval, 2003–, http://www.biographi.ca/en/bio/hagel_nathaniel_francis_14E.html (accessed 17 April 2023).

44 Manitoba, *Journals of the Legislative Assembly*, 25 May 1886, 189–95; *Manitoba Free Press*, 1 April, 26 May 1886, LLM Hansard, 252–53; "Report and Evidence of the Royal Commission 1886," in *Sessional Papers 1886*, LA009, GR174, G8116, box 6, file 14; Manitoba Legislative Assembly, *Journals*, 25 May 1886, 195; for context, see Jeffrey Simpson, *The Spoils of Power: The Politics of Patronage* (Toronto: Collins, 1988); T.D. Regehr, *The Beauharnois Scandal: A Story of Canadian Entrepreneurship and Politics* (Toronto: University of Toronto Press, 1990); and T.D. Regehr, "Haydon, Andrew," in *Dictionary of Canadian Biography*, vol. 16, University of Toronto/Université Laval, 2003–, http://www.biographi.ca/en/bio/haydon_andrew_16E.html (accessed 17 April 2023).

45 *Brandon Sun*, 8 April, 10 June 1886; *Manitoban*, 27 May 1886; *Manitoba Free Press*, 28 May 1886; *Minnedosa Tribune*, 28 May 1886; *Manitoba Sun*, 27 May 1886; James Cox Aikins to John A. Macdonald, 21 April 1886, John A. Macdonald Papers, 77452.

46 *Manitoba Sun*, 6 and 8 April 1886, LLM Hansard.

47 *Manitoba Free Press*, 10 March–13 April 1886; *Manitoban*, 25 and 31 March, 9, 10, and 13 April 1886, LLM Hansard; William Scarth to John A. Macdonald, 25 June 1887, John A. Macdonald Papers, 119333; Harold A. Innis, *A History of the Canadian Pacific Railway* (1923; reprinted, Toronto: University of Toronto Press, 1972), 178; Corydon Brown to Alexander Campbell, 25 March 1886, Alexander Campbell Papers; Theodore David Regehr, "The National Railway Policy and Manitoba Railway Legislation 1879–1888" (MA thesis, Carleton University, 1963), 109–16; George Stephen to John A. Macdonald, 24 May 1886, John A. Macdonald Papers, 123170; F.W. Stobart to William Van Horne, 7 April 1886, CPR Papers, file 12466.

48 *Manitoba Free Press*, 1 April 1886, LLM Hansard; *Manitoba Sun*, 27 May 1886.

49 *Manitoban*, 21 and 30 April 1886; *Manitoba Sun*, 30 April 1886; *Manitoba Free Press*, 30 April, 1 May 1886, all in LLM Hansard; file "Newspaper Clippings," 30 April 1886, ECPO, G8729.

50 *Manitoba Sun*, 30 April 1886; *Manitoba Free Press*, 30 April, 1 May 1886; *Manitoban*, 30 April 1886, all in LLM Hansard.

51 Ibid.

52 *Manitoba Sun*, 5 May 1886, LLM Hansard.

53 *Manitoba Free Press*, 4, 12, 13, and 15 May 1886; *Manitoban*, 13 and 14 May 1886; *Manitoba Sun*, 13 May 1886, all in LLM Hansard.

54 *Brandon Sun*, 22 July 1886; *Manitoba Free Press*, 15 May 1886; *Manitoban*, 26 March 1886; *Manitoba Sun*, 6 and 7 April, 5 May 1886, all in LLM Hansard.

55 Winnipeg *Commercial*, 1 June 1886. Thanks to Randy Rostecki for this reference.

56 *Manitoba Sun*, 4 and 27 May 1886, LLM Hansard.

57 Russell House to John Norquay, 11 June 1886, ECPO, Miscellaneous Government, G8730; John A. Macdonald to John Rose, 12 May 1886, John A. Macdonald Papers, 118038; David M. L. Farr, "Rose, Sir John," in *Dictionary of Canadian Biography*, vol. 11, University of Toronto/Université Laval, 2003–, http://www.biographi.ca/en/bio/rose_john_11E.html (accessed 17 April 2023); Judith Fingard, "The 1880s: Paradoxes of Progress," in *The Atlantic Provinces in Confederation*, ed. E.R. Forbes and D.A. Muise (Toronto: University of Toronto Press, 1993), 98–99; Pierre Dufour and Jean Hamelin, "Mercier, Honoré," in *Dictionary of Canadian Biography*, vol. 12, University of Toronto/Université Laval, 2003–, http://www.biographi.ca/en/bio/mercier_honore_12E.html (accessed 17 April 2023); Paul Romney, "Mowat, Sir Oliver," in *Dictionary of Canadian Biography*, vol. 13, University of Toronto/Université Laval, 2003–, http://www.biographi.ca/en/bio/mowat_oliver_13E.html (accessed 17 April 2023).

58 John Norquay to John A. Macdonald, 11 June 1886, John A. Macdonald Papers, 63424; John A. Macdonald to William Scarth, 15 June 1886, William Scarth Papers.

59 Charles Cliffe to William Scarth, 1 June 1886, John A. Macdonald Papers, 119053; J. Kirchhoffer to John A. Macdonald, enclosing editorial of 26 August 1886, John A. Macdonald Papers, 209797; Charles Stewart to John A. Macdonald, 23 August 1886, John A. Macdonald Papers, 209695.

60 William Van Horne to S.C. Biggs, 17 October 1886, William Van Horne Papers, Letterbook 18; William Van Horne to William Whyte, 5 January 1887, William Van Horne Papers, Letterbook 19; William Van Horne to John Egan, 27 June 1886, William Van Horne Papers, Letterbook 17; John Headley Bell, testimony in Broughall, "Report of the Proceedings and the Evidence," 368–70.

61 William Scarth to John A. Macdonald, 9 March 1878, John A. Macdonald Papers, twenty-three letters between 1878 and 1885; John A. Macdonald to William Scarth, 24 October 1882, 4 January 1883, John A. Macdonald Papers, LAC; W.A. Collins to John Norquay, 12 February 1885, NPP, C-718; G. Campbell to John Norquay, 3 December 1886, ECPO, Miscellaneous, G8730; Dennis Bundrit to William Scarth, 14 April 1886, NPP, C-1427(a) and (b); William Scarth to John Norquay, 18 March 1885,

n.d. 1886, 10 March 1886, NPP, C-807, C-1417, C-1758; Zenon Gawron, "Scarth, William Bain," in *Dictionary of Canadian Biography*, vol. 13, University of Toronto/ Université Laval, 2003–, http://www.biographi.ca/en/bio/scarth_william_bain_13E.html (accessed 17 April 2023).

62 Macdonald assured Scarth that he had more influence than "a dozen Alex Galts"; John A. Macdonald to William Scarth, 26 January, 14 October 1886, William Scarth Papers; John A. Macdonald to John Norquay, 5 November 1881, NPP, A-869; Hugh John Macdonald to John A. Macdonald, 4 February 1885, John A. Macdonald Papers, 253199; William Scarth to John A. Macdonald, 4 and 13 February 1886, John A. Macdonald Papers, 119002, 119013.

63 William Scarth to John A. Macdonald, 27 April, 5 May 1886, John A. Macdonald Papers, 119020, 119026.

64 William Scarth to John A. Macdonald, 5 and 15 May 1886, John A. Macdonald Papers, 119026, 119040A.

65 John Norquay to C.E. Hamilton and twenty-nine others, 22 July 1886, NPP, Letterbook 4; William Scarth to John Norquay, 23 July 1886, NPP, C-1277; E.F. Gigot to John Norquay, 26 July 1886, NPP, C-1279; Corydon Brown to John Norquay, 7 June 1886, ECPO, G8729, and 24 July 1886, NPP, C-1276; John Norquay to H.M. Howell, 24 July 1886, NPP, Letterbook 4; John Norquay to John Egan, 26 July 1886, NPP, Letterbook 4; John Norquay to presidents of four Conservative associations in southwest Manitoba, 28 July 1886, NPP, Letterbook 4; John Norquay to J.P. Alexander, 29 July 1886, NPP, Letterbook 4; John Norquay to Robert Rogers, 29 July, 4 September 1886, NPP, Letterbook 4; John Norquay to R.S. Park, 29 July 1886, NPP, Letterbook 4.

66 John Norquay to J.P. Alexander, 29 July 1886, NPP, Letterbook 4; John Norquay to eighteen Liberal and Conservative constituency presidents, 16 August 1886, NPP, Letterbook 4.

67 John Schultz to John A. Macdonald, 25 June 1886, John A. Macdonald Papers, 119992; *Brandon Sun*, 29 July 1886; *Grip* 27, no. 8 (28 August 1886).

68 *Minnedosa Tribune*, 27 August, 3 September 1886; John Norquay to Robert Sutherland, 28 August 1886, NPP, Letterbook 4.

69 Corydon Brown to John Norquay, 11 July 1886, NPP, C-1592.

70 John Norquay to James Aikins, 27 August, 20 September, 26 October 1886, James Aikins Papers, "Correspondence with the Province 1886–1888."

71 *Nor'West Farmer and Manitoba Miller*, September 1886, 600; C.S. Douglas to John Norquay, 6 September 1886, NPP, C-1947.

72 John Norquay to James Aikins, 27 August 1886, James Aikins Papers, P 466/1, "Correspondence with the Province 1886–1888"; William Van Horne to S.C. Biggs, 17 October 1886, William Van Horne Papers, Letterbook 18; William Van Horne to William Whyte, 5 January 1887, William Van Horne Papers, Letterbook 19; William Van Horne to John Egan, 27 June 1886, William Van Horne Papers, Letterbook 17.

73 Charles Hamilton to John Norquay, 17 June 1886, ECPO, G8729; James Paisley to John Norquay, 1 May 1886, NPP, C-1271; E.C. Montague to John Norquay, 19 July 1886, NPP, C-1278; Charles Hamilton to John Norquay, n.d. [1886], NPP, C-1614.

74 John Norquay to Corydon Brown, 20 September 1886, NPP, Letterbook 5; *Manitoba Free Press*, 15 October 1886, LLM Hansard; Winnipeg *Commercial*, 22 June 1886, 792–93.

75 William Scarth to John A. Macdonald, 17 and 22 November 1886, John A. Macdonald Papers, 119130–31, 119139, 119132.

76 C.S. Douglas to John Norquay, 4 July 1886, ECPO, G8729; Robert Rogers to John Norquay, 19 and 21 September 1886, NPP, C-1988, C-1989; also see C-1865, C-2326, C-2327; the party's guide to best organizing practices was outlined in a remarkable letter from John A. Macdonald to H.H. Smith, 25 February 1882, H.H. Smith Papers.

77 John H. Warkentin, "Western Canada in 1886," Manitoba Historical Society *Transactions,* Series 3 (1963–64) http://mhs.mb.ca/docs/transactions/3/westerncanada1886.shtml; *Brandon Sun*, 29 July 1886; *Manitoba Free Press*, 22 May 1886; *Manitoban*, 20 May 1886, all are clippings in LLM Hansard; also see NPP, C-1430(a) and (b), C-1316. The "urban" population included Winnipeg 20,000; Brandon 2,400; Portage la Prairie 2,000; St. Boniface 1,500; Emerson 800; and Selkirk 700.

78 *Portage la Prairie Weekly Tribune-Review*, 13 August 1886; John Norquay to Thomas Young, 30 August 1886, NPP, Letterbook 4; J.P. Alexander to John Norquay, 25 May 1886, NPP, C-1538; also see C-1543(a) and (b), C-1567, C-1570; John Norquay to John Pomeroy, 25 August 1886, NPP, Letterbook 4; John Norquay to John Egan, 26 July 1886, NPP, Letterbook 4; John Norquay to William Van Horne, 27 August 1886, NPP, Letterbook 4; P. McGregor to John Norquay, 19 October 1886, NPP, C-2032; A.W. Pritchard to John Norquay, 16 September 1883, NPP, Letterbook C; *Brandon Sun*, 9 July 1885; William Van Horne to John Egan, 20 July 1885, William Van Horne Papers, Letterbook 12; Acton Burrows to William Van Horne, 29 April 1886, CPR Papers; William Scarth to John A. Macdonald, 3 June, 2 October 1886, John A. Macdonald Papers, 119059, 119086; Hector Langevin to John A. Macdonald, 8 October 1886, John A. Macdonald Papers, 119090; Thomas White to John Norquay, 26 May 1886, NPP, C-1663; John Robinson to John Norquay, 13 June, 5 August 1885, NPP, C-993, C-1038; William Scarth to John Norquay, 13 and 21 September 1886, NPP, C-1830; William Wagner to John Robinson, 13 November 1886, John Moore Robinson Papers; G. Powell to James Aikins, 21 April 1887, James Aikins Papers, "Correspondence with the Dominion January–March 1887"; Mackenzie Bowell to John Robinson, 9 November 1886, John Moore Robinson Papers.

79 *Brandon Sun*, 12 and 26 August, 2 December 1886.

80 Richard Gwyn, *Nation Maker: Sir John A. Macdonald: His Life, Our Times II, 1867–1891* (Toronto: Random House Canada, 2011), 527–28; Michael Bliss, *A Living Profit: Studies in the Social History of Canadian Business 1883–1911* (Toronto: McClelland and Stewart, 1973); John A. Macdonald to George Stephen, 24 August

1885, George Stephen Papers; George Stephen to John A. Macdonald, 14 and 20 September 1887, John A. Macdonald Papers, 123644, 123660.

81 Robert Sutherland to John Norquay, 30 July 1886, NPP, C-1737; W.P. Smith to Alfred Rennie, 23 November 1886, NPP, C-2325, C-2328; John Norquay to H.M. Howell, 30 September 1886, NPP, Letterbook 5.

82 John Norquay to George Morton, 29 July 1886, NPP, Letterbook 4; also see NPP, C-1587, C-1970, C-1974; John Norquay to J.P. Alexander, 4 September 1886, NPP, Letterbook 4; also see NPP, C-1262, C-1868, C-1263, C-1579, C-1601, C-1589, C-1231(a); John Norquay to James Thomson, 31 January 1887, Margaret A. Macleod Papers, file 41, original shown to her by Norquay's granddaughter, Mrs. McAllister.

83 Robert Sutherland to John Norquay, 30 July 1886, NPP, C-1737; also see C-1821, C-1245(a)(b)(c), C-1348; Norman Ernest Wright, *In View of the Turtle Hill: A Survey of the History of Southwestern Manitoba to 1900* (Deloraine, MB: *Deloraine Times*, 1951), 53–54; Acton Burrows to John Norquay, 5 November 1886, NPP, C-1852; H. Tennant to John Norquay, 14 November 1886, NPP, C-2166; also see C-2299, C-2123, C-1947, C-2158, C-1422, C-1489, C-1369, C-1371, C-1428; *Heimskringla*, 2 December 1886.

84 Ed Leacock to John Norquay, 5 September 1886, NPP, C-1923; also see C-1803, C-2301, C-2281, C-2279, C-2347, C-2348, C-2350, C-2324, C-2329, C-2349, C-1939, C-2330, C-2352, C-2292; John Norquay to John A. Macdonald, 22 November 1886, John A. Macdonald Papers, 212085; A.W. Ross to John A. Macdonald, 22 November 1886, John A. Macdonald Papers, 212146; Corydon Brown to John A. Macdonald, 22 November 1886, John A. Macdonald Papers, 212133.

85 *Brandon Sun*, 28 October, 2 and 11 November 1886.

86 *Brandon Sun*, 14 October 1886; John Norquay, "List," n.d., ECPO, Miscellaneous Government, G8730; also see NPP, C-2012(b); "Memo," n.d. [1887], ECPO, Miscellaneous Government, G8730; *Public Accounts of the Province of Manitoba for the Year Ending June 30th 1887* (Winnipeg: Queen's Printer, 1888), 17, 19, 56, 77; John Norquay to J.H. Conrad, 23 December 1886, NPP, Letterbook 5; John Norquay to A.H. Rennie, 12 October 1886, NPP, C-2289; Manitoba, "Auditor's Appropriation Ledger 1886–87," AM, G8706; also see NPP, C-2395.

87 James A. Murray to John Norquay, 12 October 1886, NPP, C-2008.

88 James Whiteway to John Norquay, 13 and 25 October 1886, NPP, C-1804; Joseph Tait to John Norquay, 20 September 1886, NPP, C-1795; George Munroe to John Norquay, 20 May 1885, NPP, C-981; T.A. Cuddy to John Norquay, 15 October 1886, NPP, C-1863; also see C-2014, C-1898, C-2432; Edward Osler, "Electoral Division of St. Andrews: Statement of Election Expenses of Hon. Norquay," 7 February 1887, NPP, Letterbook 5; C.A. Sadleir to G. Bourdeau, 9 February 1887, and C. Graburn to John Norquay, 16 July 1887, in Manitoba Executive Council, *Letterbook of Clerk of Executive Council, 4 Jan 1887–29 Jan 1889*, EC0004, GR1533, 29 A, 84, 236.

89 A.H. Rennie to John Norquay, 26 October 1886, NPP, C-2265; also see C-2268, C-1996; A.H. Rennie to John Norquay, 20 November 1886, NPP, C-2267; John Robinson to John Norquay, 6 December 1886, NPP, C-2311; see fifty telegrams, NPP, C-1997–C-2343; *Manitoba Sun*, 12 November 1888, LLM Hansard.

90 David Harrison to Alfred Rennie, 1 December 1886, NPP, C-2387; Corbet Locke to John Norquay, 22 November 1886, NPP, C-2095; T.W. Gilbert to John Norquay, 1 December 1886, NPP, C-2386; W.A. Macdonald to Alfred Rennie, 22 November 1886, NPP, C-2126; T. Mayne Daly to Alfred Rennie, 14 November 1886, NPP, C-1919; B.M. Armitage to John Norquay, 3 February 1887, NPP, C-2417.

91 *Manitoba Free Press*, 9 December 1886.

92 In the 1886 election, there were 45,000 eligible electors, of whom 21,000 voted; see Winnipeg *Morning Call*, 28 April 1887.

93 John Norquay to James Thomson, 31 January 1887, Margaret A. Macleod Papers, file 41.

94 Manitoba Historical Society, "Events: Provincial Election 1886," http://www.mhs.mb.ca/docs/events/provincialelection1886.shtml (accessed January 2022); John McNeill to John Norquay, 14 January 1887, NPP, C-2105; W.J. Helliwell to John Norquay, 5 January, 30 March 1887, NPP, C-2112, C-2618; Amable Marion to John Norquay, 23 December 1886, NPP, C-2114; A.E. Freeborn to John Norquay, 3 January 1887, NPP, C-2101; Robert Sutherland to John Norquay, 15 December 1886, NPP, C-1823; R. McKay to John Norquay, 11 December 1886, NPP, C-2034; Mayne Daly to John Norquay, 11 December 1886, NPP, C-1917; W.A. Macdonald to John Norquay, 14 December 1886, NPP, C-2041; John Norquay to M.J. Scarry, 2 November 1886, NPP, Letterbook 5; C. Graburn to John Norquay, 16 July 1887, in Clerk of Executive Council, *Letter Book 1887–29 Jan 1889*, EC0004, GR1533, 29 A, 236.

95 Norquay's files contain many notes of congratulation on the election results in 1886, including John A. Macdonald to John Norquay, 12 December 1886, NPP, C-2394; David Harrison to John Norquay, 16 December 1886, NPP, C-2196; Corbet Locke to John Norquay, 7 December 1886, NPP, C-2196; T. Routledge to John Norquay, 15 December 1886, NPP, C-2177; T.S. Menary to John Norquay, 20 December 1886, NPP, C-2178; also see C-1904, C-2042, C-2034, C-1815, C-1823; appeals for patronage appointments and public works, including Joseph Woodworth to John Norquay, 4 September 1886, NPP, C-1813; Norquay also fielded requests for a bridge, a branch line station, a government job, a scrip allocation, an expense payment overlooked by the federal government, and the incorporation of a town; he also exercised oversight of legal battles over election challenges; *Journals of House of Commons, 1899*, vol. 34 (Ottawa: Queen's Printer, 1900), Appendix, "Report of the Select Standing Committee on Public Accounts . . . : Manitoba Election Frauds," 34–35; James Monkman to John Norquay, 5 March 1887, NPP, C-2442; Rennie said that every constituency result had been contested by both the Conservatives and the Liberals: Alfred Rennie to Dave Rodgers, 14 February 1887, NPP, Letterbook 5.

96 *Manitoba Free Press*, 11 December 1886.

97 James Aikins to John A. Macdonald, 11 December 1886, John A. Macdonald Papers, 77458.

98 Ibid.

99 *The Winnipeg and Hudson Bay Railway, Forming with Hudson Bay and Strait, a New Trade Route between America and Europe* (Winnipeg: Manitoba Free Press Printing, 1887).

100 John Norquay to Kingsmill, 9 October 1886, NPP, Letterbook 5; Hugh Sutherland to William Van Horne, 11 October 1886, CPR Papers; James Aikins to Corydon Brown, 30 November 1886, and James Aikins to J.A. Chapleau, Alexander Morris Papers, 133, 134; T. D. Regehr, "Mann, Sir Donald," in *Dictionary of Canadian Biography*, vol. 16, University of Toronto/Université Laval, 2003–, http://www.biographi.ca/en/bio/mann_donald_16E.html (accessed 14 April 2023); T. D. Regehr, "Ross, James," in *Dictionary of Canadian Biography,* vol. 14, University of Toronto/Université Laval, 2003–, http://www.biographi.ca/en/bio/ross_james_1848_1913_14E.html (accessed 14 April 2023).

101 William Scarth to John A. Macdonald, 25 June 1887, John A. Macdonald Papers, 119333.

102 James Aikins to John A. Macdonald, 12 and 30 November 1887, John A. Macdonald Papers, 77505, 77508; John Norquay to Alphonse LaRivière, copy filed between letters dated 2 November 1886 and 23 December 1886 in a now-vanished letterbook, parts of which were typed out by Ellen Cooke; John Norquay to John Pope, 2 February 1887, NPP, Letterbook 5; William Scarth to John A. Macdonald, 25 June 1887, John A. Macdonald Papers, 119333.

103 David Harrison to John A. Macdonald, 9 November 1885, John A. Macdonald Papers, 58084.

104 John Norquay to John Pope, 15 April 1887, NPP, Letterbook 5.

Chapter 11: Defiance, 1887

1 "Nouvelles tables de mortalité par génération au Canada et au Québec, 1801–1991," par Robert Bourbeau, Jacques Légaré, et Valérie Émond, Statistics Canada, September 1997; I thank Eric Sager and Lisa Dillon for guiding me through the information on life expectancy in the nineteenth century.

2 John Norquay to John A. Macdonald, 26 February 1887, John A. Macdonald Papers, 216550; Thomas Mayne Daly to John Norquay, 1 March 1887, NPP, C-2781; Carruthers & Brock to John Norquay, 22 April 1887, NPP, C-2496; A.G. McKenzie to John Norquay, 8 January 1886, NPP, C-1500; Miller Morse to John Norquay, 16 January 1888, ECPO, Miscellaneous, G8730; on life insurance, NPP, C-1326, C-1365, and seven more bills to early 1887; Norquay received $6,301.60 in government payments in 1887, about five times the annual salary of his secretary, Alfred Pritchard; *Public Accounts for Year Ending 30 June 1887* (Winnipeg: Queen's Printer, 1888), and *Public Accounts of the Province of Manitoba for the Year Ending June 30th 1888* (Winnipeg: Queen's Printer, 1889); Norquay also held free passes given to him by at

least six railway companies; the British Canadian Loan & Investment Company held a mortgage and sent him many due notices, including NPP, C-1550, C-2841; John Norquay to R.H. Tomlinson, 1 June 1886, NPP, Letterbook 6.

3 Thomas Norquay to John Norquay, 7 January 1887, NPP, C-2430; Fred Fulsher to John Norquay, 1 February 1887, NPP, C-2507; Munson & Allan Co. to John Norquay, 7 October, 1887, ECPO, G8730, and Norquay's reply, 26 October 1887, NPP, Letterbook 6; Victor Robertson to John Norquay, 10 January 1887, NPP, C-2113; J.J. Setter to John Norquay, 2 and 25 February 1887, NPP, C-1978, C-2580; S.[?] Adams to John Norquay, 15 March 1887, Ann Adams to John Norquay, 15 March 1887, S.[?] Adams to John Norquay, 29 March 1887, NPP, C-2595, C-2596, C-2617.

4 Dr. D. Young to John Norquay, 11 January 1887, NPP, C-2240, and 13 November 1887, ECPO, G8730; Joseph Tait to John Norquay, 14 March 1887, NPP, C-2464; George Ross to John Norquay, 10 October 1887, and Norquay's reply, ECPO, G8730, and Letterbook 5; NPP, C-2512, C-1506; William Pruden to John Norquay, 14 May 1887, ECPO, G8729; John Muir to John Norquay, 3 May 1887, ECPO, G8729; also NPP, C-2460, C-2567, C-2812, C-2854, C-2883; Manitoba Club, NPP, C-1237, C-2174, C-2905; John Norquay to R. Haslam, 7 May 1887, NPP, Letterbook 5; Eleanor Kennedy to John Norquay, 10 January 1887, NPP, C-2535(a) and (b); William Kennedy to John Norquay, 5 March 1887, NPP, C-2776; also NPP, C-2919, C-2934; William Kennedy to John Norquay, 30 November 1887, ECPO, G8730, and draft reply, 2 December 1887, NPP, Letterbook 6.

5 John Norquay to Sam Bedson, 24 December 1886, NPP, C-2075; F. Burpee to John Norquay, 24 January 1887, NPP, C-2197; H.H. Smith to John Norquay, 18 March 1887, NPP, C-2653; Thomas Sinclair to John Norquay, 8 March 1887, ECPO, G8729; L. McMeans to John Norquay, 4 May 1887, ECPO, G8729; S.W. Farrell to John Norquay, 24 June 1886, 22 November 1887, ECPO, G8729; also NPP, C-490; reply, Letterbook D; C-1508; also C-1265, C-2171; Bain, Mulock & Co. to John Norquay, 7 and 10 September 1886, NPP, C-1935, C-1938, and Norquay's reply, 9 September 1886, Letterbook 5; Munson & Allan to John Norquay, 18 September 1886, NPP, C-2009; M. O'Loughlin to Saskatchewan Coal, 30 September 1886, NPP, C-2310; William Van Horne to Redford Mulock, 17 May 1887, William Van Horne Letterbooks, LB 21; Redford Mulock to John Norquay, 19 August 1887, NPP, C-2879; see Ellen Cooke's notes on John S. Ewart, ed., *Reports of Cases Argued and Determined in the Court of Queen's Bench, Manitoba*, vol. 4, 1887, 304, 593, in Ellen Gillies Cooke Papers, file 10.

6 W. Kaye Lamb, *History of the Canadian Pacific Railway* (New York: Macmillan, 1977), 158–59; *Manitoba Sun*, 20 April 1887.

7 Thomas White to Mackenzie Bowell, 2–3 February 1887, Mackenzie Bowell Papers, 2334–36; John Norquay to Alphonse LaRivière, 4 November 1886, NPP, Letterbook 5; John Norquay to Kingsmill, 9 October 1886, NPP, Letterbook 5.

8 *Manitoba Free Press*, 28 January 1887; *Week* 4, no. 11 (10 February 1887): 167–68; John A. Macdonald to John Norquay, 24 February 1887, NPP, C-2579; W.A. Macdonald to John Norquay, 9 and 23 February 1887, NPP, C-2436, C-1799; C.A.

Boulton to John Norquay, 17 January 1887, NPP, C-2108; on Rennie's activities, NPP, C-2410, and fifteen further notes and telegrams, 19 January–21 February 1887; on Norquay's role, NPP, C-2254, C-1984, C-1980, C-2419, C-2380; John Norquay to Samuel Bedson, 7 February 1887, NPP, Letterbook 5, and Bedson's reply, 8 February 1887, NPP, C-1977.

9 John Norquay to Alphonse LaRivière, 6 February 1887, NPP, Letterbook 5, and LaRivière's reply, 7 February 1887, NPP, C-2378.

10 Mackenzie Bowell to John A. Macdonald, 26 September 1888, John A. Macdonald Papers, 148499; LaRivière's version is in 11–16 May 1888, LLM Hansard; Theodore David Regehr, "The National Railway Policy and Manitoba Railway Legislation 1879–1888" (MA thesis, Carleton University, 1963), 133–41; *The [1888] Budget* (Winnipeg: *The Call,* 1888), 19–24, LLM Hansard; Manitoba Executive Council, *Orders-in-Council Registers 1870–1891*, 11 February 1887; D. Miller to John Norquay, 7 February 1887, ECPO, G8729; Alphonse LaRivière to John Norquay, 11 February 1887, ECPO, G8729; William Scarth to John A. Macdonald, 25 June 1887, John A. Macdonald Papers, 119333; William Van Horne to Ogden, 7 February 1887, William Van Horne Letterbooks, LB 20; John Norquay to James Aikins, 25 November 1887, NPP, Letterbook 5.

11 John Norquay to John A. Macdonald, 25 January 1887, John A. Macdonald Papers, 214345; Joseph Royal to Hector Langevin, 23 February 1887, Thomas Chapais–Hector Langevin Papers.

12 Alfred Rennie to John Norquay, 28 March–6 April 1887, ECPO, G8729–30; Alphonse LaRivière to Bertrand, 1 April 1887, Fonds Société historique de Saint-Boniface, série documentation, personnages, file 541; William Scarth to John A. Macdonald, 6 April 1887, John A. Macdonald Papers, 119317; James Aikins to John A. Macdonald, 7 April 1887, John A. Macdonald Papers, 77467; J.J. Setter to John Norquay, 13 December 1886, 12 April 1887, NPP, C-1826, C-2623; John A. Macdonald to William Scarth, 15 June 1886, William Scarth Papers; Alphonse LaRivière to A.-A. Taché, 16 March 1887, Bishop A.-A. Taché Papers, T35446; Mackenzie Bowell to John Robinson, 9 November 1886, and John Robinson to Corydon Brown, 8 February 1887, John Moore Robinson Papers; John Robinson to John Norquay, 6 December 1886, 7, 11, and 22 March, 11 April 1887, NPP, C-2311; also NPP, C-2443, C-2636, C-2647; Acton Burrows to John Norquay, 7 and 11 March 1887, NPP, C-2779, C-2645; James Aikins to John A. Macdonald, 7 April 1887, John A. Macdonald Papers, 77467; *Manitoban*, 6 April 1887; Mackenzie Bowell to John Robinson, 8 April 1887, John Moore Robinson Papers; John Norquay to W.E. Sanford, 26 April 1887, NPP, Letterbook 5; Corydon Brown to John A. Macdonald, 21 October 1886, John A. Macdonald Papers, 211120; 28 January 1887, 214530; 9 March 1887, 217189; 20 March 1887, 217581; 23 April 1887, 218933; 13 June 1887, 220324; I thank Maureen Hoogenraad, LAC archivist, for her decoding of the telegram using, as she wrote, Slater's Telegraphic Code of 1906 (Maureen Hoogenraad to Gerald Friesen, 7 February 1986); James Mochoruk, "Brown, Corydon Partlow," in *Dictionary of Canadian Biography*, vol. 12, University of Toronto/Université

Laval, 2003–, http://www.biographi.ca/en/bio/brown_corydon_partlow_12E.html (accessed 18 April 2023); W.L. Morton and Margaret Fahrni, *Third Crossing: A History of the First Quarter Century of the Town and District of Gladstone in the Province of Manitoba* (Winnipeg: Advocate, 1946), 104; John Norquay to David Wilson, 8 January 1887, and John Kirchhoffer to John Norquay, 17 January 1887, Manitoba, Department of Public Works, Railway Commissioner Correspondence; Corydon Brown to John Norquay, 9 March 1887, James Aikins LG Papers; Manitoba Executive Council, *Orders-in-Council Registers 1870–1891*, 14 March 1887; James Aikins to John Norquay, 11 March 1887, Alexander Morris Papers, 118; Corydon Brown to James J. Hill, 9 March 1887, James J. Hill Papers; W.J. Robinson to John Robinson, 8 April 1887, John Moore Robinson Papers; Regehr, "The National Railway Policy," 120 ff; *Manitoba Free Press*, 31 March 1887, cited in James A. Jackson, "The Disallowance of Manitoba Railway Legislation in the 1880s" (MA thesis, University of Manitoba, 1945), 79–82; Joseph Hilts, "The Political Career of Thomas Greenway" (PhD diss., University of Manitoba, 1974), 97–122; *Commercial* 5, no. 26 (22 March 1887): 537; Alfred Rennie to John Norquay, 28 March 1887, ECPO, G8729; H.H. Smith to John A. Macdonald, 23 March 1887, John A. Macdonald Papers, 217737; J.A. Chapleau to James Aikins, 31 March 1887, and Gédéon Bourdeau to James Aikins, 5 April 1887, in James Aikins LG Papers, "Correspondence with the Dominion January–March 1887"; *Monetary Times, Trade Review and Insurance Chronicle* (hereafter *Monetary Times*) 20, no. 38 (18 March 1887): 1093.

13 Manitoba Executive Council, *Orders-in-Council Registers 1870–1891*, 24 March 1887; *Monetary Times* 20, no. 42 (15 April 1887): 1217; P.B. Waite, "White, Thomas," and "Pope, John Henry," in *Dictionary of Canadian Biography*, vol. 11, University of Toronto/Université Laval, 2003–, http://www.biographi.ca/en/bio/pope_john_henry_11E.html (accessed 18 April 2023); *Manitoban*, 11 April 1887, cited in Jackson, "Disallowance," 81; Russell House to John Norquay, 6 April 1887, ECPO, Miscellaneous Government; Alfred Rennie to John Norquay, 26 March-6 April 1887 [cipher telegrams], ECPO, G8729; *Grip* 28, no. 17 (23 April 1887).

14 Thomas Mayne Daly to John Norquay, 9 April 1887, ECPO, G8729; *Manitoba Sun*, 14 and 15 April 1887; *Manitoban*, 15 April 1887, LLM Hansard.

15 *Manitoba Sun*, 14 and 15 April 1887; Redford Mulock to John Norquay, 14 April 1887, NPP, C-2525, C-2462; *Manitoban*, 15 April 1887; "Diagram of Chamber, Manitoba 6th Legislature," John Moore Robinson Papers; John Norquay to John Pope, 15 April 1887, NPP, Letterbook 5.

16 *Winnipeg Call*, 19 and 20 April 1887; *Manitoba Sun*, 19 April 1887; *Manitoba Free Press*, 19 April 1887, all in LLM Hansard; *Monetary Times* 20, no. 42 (15 April 1887).

17 *Manitoban*, 15 April 1887.

18 Thomas Mayne Daly to John Norquay, 9 April 1887, ECPO, G8729; J. Bedford to John Norquay, 13 April 1887, NPP, C-2485; *Manitoban*, 6 April 1887, LLM Hansard.

19 *Manitoban*, 15 April 1887.

20 James Aikins to John A. Macdonald, 16 April 1887, John A. Macdonald Papers, 77470; *Manitoba Sun*, 15 April, 6 June 1887; *Manitoban*, 16 April 1887; *Winnipeg Call*, 21 April, 2 June 1887; *Commercial* 5, no. 30 (19 April 1887): 608–9; Haley Wilson to John Norquay, 15 April 1887, NPP, C-2528; George Leary to John Norquay, 23 April 1887, NPP, C-2530; J.G. Sturgeon to John Norquay, 21 April 1887, NPP, C-2501.

21 *Manitoba Free Press*, 27 April 1887; *Commercial*, 3 May 1887; Jackson, "Disallowance," 84.

22 *Manitoba Sun*, 19 April 1887; *Manitoba Free Press*, 23 May 1887; *Winnipeg Call*, 29 April, 23 May, 8 June 1887, LLM Hansard.

23 C.S. Douglas to John Norquay, 30 April 1887, NPP, C-2900(a); W. Williams to C.S. Douglas, 30 April 1887, NPP, C-2900(b); Henry Ferguson to John Norquay, 18 May 1887, ECPO, G8729; Hugh Sutherland to John Norquay, n.d., NPP, C-2815; William Scarth to John A. Macdonald, 5 February 1888, John A. Macdonald Papers, 119441; John Norquay to Hugh Sutherland, 16 August 1887, NPP, Letterbook 5; *Winnipeg Call*, 20 April, 27 May, 1, 2, and 7 June 1887; *Manitoba Free Press*, 7 June 1887, LLM Hansard.

24 Duluth and Manitoba Railroad (Dakota Division), "First Mortgage," 1 June 1887, James J. Hill Papers; Jerry Masters, *Northern Pacific Railway in Manitoba* (Naples, FL: Jerry Masters Publishing, 2021); William Van Horne to Thomas White, 23 November 1887, William Van Horne Letterbooks, LB 24; *Manitoba Free Press*, 16 April 1888, LLM Hansard.

25 *Winnipeg Call*, 19 and 20 April, 23 May 1887; *Manitoba Sun*, 19 April 1887, and *Manitoba Free Press*, 19 April, 19 May 1887, LLM Hansard; H. Tennant to John Norquay, 23 May 1887, ECPO, G8729.

26 William Van Horne to William Whyte, 23 February 1887, William Van Horne Letterbooks, LB 20; Acton Burrows to William Van Horne, 31 October 1888, and Van Horne's reply, 2 November 1888, Acton Burrows Papers; William Van Horne to John Norquay, 23 October 1885, NPP, C-1176; also C-1363, C-1642, C-1374, C-1306, C-1643.

27 William Van Horne to John Norquay, 24 February 1887, William Van Horne Letterbooks, LB 20; John Norquay to William Van Horne, 13, 27, and 30 April 1887, CPR Papers, file 15982 (also in NPP, Letterbook 5, 58–60); William Van Horne to John Norquay, 14 March 1887, NPP, C-2533; 22 March 1887, NPP, C-2637; 25 April 1887, NPP, C-2890; William Van Horne to John Norquay, 3 and 16 May 1887, William Van Horne Letterbooks, LB21; William Van Horne to William Whyte, 23 February 1887, William Van Horne Letterbooks, LB20; William Van Horne to J. Kerr, 3 February 1887, William Van Horne Letterbooks, LB20; J.A.M. Aikins to William Van Horne, 16 February, 14 March, 27 April 1887, CPR Papers, file 15982; William Van Horne to J.A.M. Aikins, 24 February, 9 March 1887, William Van Horne Letterbooks, LB20; William Van Horne to J.M. Kirchhoffer, 7 March 1887, William Van Horne Letterbooks, LB20; *Winnipeg Call*, 4 and 9 June 1887; William Van Horne to G. Armstrong, 27 April 1887, NPP, C-2892(b); Hilts, "The Political Career of Thomas Greenway," 97; *Manitoba Free Press*, 4 June 1887; Robert Rogers to John

Norquay, 29 April, 25 June 1887, NPP, C-2607, C-2851; T. Menarey to John Norquay, 13 April 1887, NPP, C-2621, and 31 May 1887, ECPO, G8729; William Whyte to John Norquay, 24 April 1887, NPP, C-2497; James Fraser to John Norquay, 24 March 1887, NPP, C-2602.

28 William Van Horne to William Whyte, 23 February, 8 April, 3 and 17 May 1887, William Van Horne Letterbooks, LB20 and LB21, and 16 May 1887, CPR Papers, file 16805; William Whyte to William Van Horne, 2 May 1887, CPR Papers, file 12210; William Van Horne to J.L. Campbell, 25 February 1887, William Van Horne Letterbooks, LB20; William Van Horne to John Norquay, 3 May 1887, NPP, C-2892(a), and 16 May 1887, William Van Horne Letterbooks, LB21, and ECPO, G8729; John Kirchhoffer to William Van Horne, 2 May 1887, CPR Papers, file 12210, and Van Horne's reply, 6 May 1887, William Van Horne Letterbooks, LB21; W.H. Clendenning to William Whyte, 13 May 1887, CPR Papers, file 16805; George Stephen to John A. Macdonald, 27 April 1887, John A. Macdonald Papers, 123390; William Van Horne to Acton Burrows, 13 May 1887, William Van Horne Letterbooks, LB21; William Van Horne to George Ham, 13 May 1887, William Van Horne Letterbooks, LB21.

29 William Van Horne to William Whyte, 27 April 1887, William Van Horne Letterbooks, LB21; William Whyte to William Van Horne, 6 May 1887, CPR Papers, file 16805; John Norquay to Donald A. Smith, 7 July 1885, NPP, Letterbook E; George Stephen to Lord Lansdowne, 10 June 1887, Lord Lansdowne Papers.

30 Lamb, *History of the Canadian Pacific Railway*, 54–63; Heather Gilbert, *Awakening Continent: The Life of Lord Mount Stephen I 1829–91* (1965; reprinted, Aberdeen: Aberdeen University Press, 1976), 42–52; David Cruise and Alison Griffiths, *Lords of the Line* (Toronto: Viking Penguin Group, 1988), 5–17; Alexander Reford, "Stephen, George," in *Dictionary of Canadian Biography*, vol. 15, University of Toronto/Université Laval, 2003–, http://www.biographi.ca/en/bio/stephen_george_15E.html (accessed 18 April 2023); George Stephen to Sir Arthur Bigge, 16 October 1908, Royal Archives, Windsor Castle, cited in Heather Gilbert, "The Unaccountable Fifth: Solution of a Great Northern Enigma," *Minnesota History* 42, no. 5 (1971): 177; Joseph Gilpin Pyle, *The Life of James J. Hill*, vol. 2 (New York: Doubleday, Page, 1917), 428; Steve Fraser, *Wall Street: A Cultural History*, cited in Alex Preston, "You Eat What You Kill: From Scandal to Catastrophe, the Rise and Fall of the Investment Bank," *New Statesman* 28 (2012): 25, 27.

31 Donald Creighton, *John A. Macdonald: The Old Chieftain* (Toronto: Macmillan, 1955), 308–9, 332, 336; Pierre Berton, *The National Dream: The Great Railway 1871–1881* (Toronto: McClelland and Stewart, 1970), 346–89; Pierre Berton, *The National Dream: The Last Spike* (Toronto: McClelland and Stewart, 1971), 404–10; Anthony Trollope, *The Way We Live Now* (1875; reprinted, New York: Alfred A. Knopf, 1950), 68, 80, 605–8, 667–68; Gilbert, *Awakening Continent*, 42–52; Heather Gilbert, *The End of the Road: The Life of Lord Mount Stephen II 1891–1921* (Aberdeen: Aberdeen University Press, 1977), 3; Cruise and Griffiths, *Lords of the Line*, xvi, 5–17; Lady Ishbel Aberdeen, *Journal*, 15 September 1891, cited in Donna McDonald, *Lord*

Strathcona: A Biography of Donald Alexander Smith (Toronto: Dundurn Press, 1996), 395.

32 George Stephen to John A. Macdonald, letters in 1887, 20 April, 123368; 23 April, 123373; 27 April, 123390; 28 April, 123385; 29 April, 123397; 13 May, 123432; 15 May, 123436; 17 May, 123443; 17 May, 123448; 21 May, 123480; 4 June, 123525; 6 June, 123530; 9 June, 123538; 19 June, 123546; 26 June, 123558, all in John A. Macdonald Papers; Richard Gwyn, *Nation Maker: Sir John A. Macdonald: His Life, Our Times II, 1867–1891* (Toronto: Random House, 2011), estimated that there are 800 letters from Stephen in the Macdonald Papers; William Van Horne to William Whyte, 27 April 1887, William Van Horne Letterbooks, LB 21; John A. Macdonald to William Van Horne, 26 April 1887, CPR Papers, file 16616; Joseph Royal to William Van Horne, 27 April 1887, CPR Papers, file 16694; William Van Horne to William Whyte, 27 April 1887, William Van Horne Letterbooks, LB21; Duncan MacArthur, ed. *Correspondence Relating to the Manitoba Central Railway* (Winnipeg: n.p., 1888).

33 George Stephen to John A. Macdonald, 17 May 1887, John A. Macdonald Papers, 123448.

34 *Winnipeg Call*, 21 May 1887; William Whyte to William Van Horne, 23 May 1887, CPR Papers, and William Van Horne to John Pope, 23 May 1887, William Van Horne Letterbooks, LB21.

35 William Van Horne to John Pope, 23 May 1887, enclosing William Whyte to William Van Horne, 22 May 1887, William Van Horne Letterbooks, LB21.

36 George Stephen to John A. Macdonald, 17 May 1887, John A. Macdonald Papers, 123448; 21 May 1887, 123480; 4 June 1887, 123525; 26 June 1887, 123558; William Van Horne to George Stephen, 17 June 1887, William Van Horne Letterbooks, LB21; George Stephen to John A. Macdonald, July 1889, quoted in Gilbert, *Stephen II*, 25.

37 *Winnipeg Call*, 21 May 1887.

38 C.J. Brydges to D.A. Smith, 26 May 1887, Skene, Edwards & Garson Co. Papers; London *Times*, 30 August 1887; J. Cranter to John Norquay, 21 May 1887, D. Harlow to John Norquay, 27 May 1887, and Thomas Seaman to John Norquay, 15 June 1887, ECPO, G8729.

39 The documentary record on the pivotal decision is thin: George Stephen to James Hill, 17 May, 1 June 1887, James J. Hill Papers; George Stephen to John A. Macdonald, 17 May 1887, John A. Macdonald Papers, 123443; John Kennedy to James Hill, 23 May 1887, James J. Hill Papers; Edward Nichols to James Hill, 3 June 1887, James J. Hill Papers, Correspondence file 20.A.4.4 (1 March–12 July 1887). Donald Creighton, Peter Waite, Kaye Lamb, and Richard Gwyn have all regarded the decision to give up the monopoly clause as a victory of prairie provincial rights campaigners over a reluctant federal government and a disappointed railway company. They did not recognize, as Cruise and Griffiths did, the depth of Stephen's dissembling; Lamb, *History of the Canadian Pacific Railway*, 161–64; Creighton, *John A. Macdonald*, 487; Gwyn, *Nation Maker*, 543; Peter B. Waite, *Canada 1874–1896: Arduous Destiny* (Toronto: McClelland and Stewart, 1971), 197; Cruise and Griffiths, *Lords of the Line*, xvi, 5–17.

40 George Stephen to James Hill, 19 December 1887, James J. Hill Papers; George Stephen to James Hill, 4 and 18 August 1888, cited in Albro Martin, *James J. Hill and the Opening of the Northwest* (1976; reprinted, St. Paul: Minnesota Historical Society Press, 1991), 375–76; George Stephen to John A. Macdonald, 22 April 1888, John A. Macdonald Papers, 123911; Lamb, *History of the Canadian Pacific Railway*, 167–68; Gilbert, *Stephen II*, 17; McDonald, *Lord Strathcona*, 366.

41 *Manitoban*, 15 April 1887.

42 Regehr, "The National Railway Policy," 120 ff.

43 Creighton, *John A. Macdonald*, 303, 462, 474; Harold A. Innis, *A History of the Canadian Pacific Railway* (1923; reprinted, Toronto: University of Toronto Press, 1972), 296–324; *Manitoba Sun*, 5 March 1887; *Manitoban*, 5 March 1887, with thanks to Stuart Hay for copies of these articles.

44 John A. Macdonald to William Scarth, 23 October 1886, William Scarth Papers; Creighton, *John A. Macdonald*, 473–74; Peter George, "Foreword," in Innis, *A History of the Canadian Pacific Railway*; *Monetary Times* 20, no. 38 (18 March 1887): 1093, and 20, no. 42 (15 April 1887): 1217.

45 *Winnipeg Call*, 3, 9, and 10 June 1887; *Manitoba Sun*, 9 June 1887; *Manitoba Free Press*, 3 and 7 June 1887; *Le Manitoba*, 2 June 1887, LLM Hansard; John Norquay to Council of Municipality of Kildonan, 9 June 1887, NPP, Letterbook 5; Mrs. J.E. McAllister to Lillian Gibbons, "Stories Houses Tell," Winnipeg *Tribune*, 18 April 1936.

46 *Canadian Presbyterian* 16, no. 26 (22 June 1887): 411.

47 Manitoba Executive Council, *Orders-in-Council Registers 1870–1891*, 11 and 20 June 1887; *Commercial* 5, no. 40 (27 June 1887): 808–9; George Drummond to Alphonse LaRivière, 16 June 1887, and Alphonse LaRivière to George Drummond, 20 July 1887, Manitoba Treasury Department, Letterbook 1887; Eleanor Stardom, "MacArthur, Duncan," in *Dictionary of Canadian Biography*, vol. 13, University of Toronto/Université Laval, 2003–, http://www.biographi.ca/en/bio/macarthur_duncan_13E.html (accessed 18 April 2023).

48 William Van Horne to George Stephen, 17 June 1887, William Van Horne Letterbooks, LB21; LaRivière was reimbursed by the Manitoba treasury for two trips to Ottawa (in September 1886 and June 1887), with a payment of $300 each time; see "Auditor's Appropriation Ledger, 1886–87," G8706; he also had a pass on the CPR.

49 William Van Horne to George Stephen, 17 and 21 June 1887, William Van Horne Letterbooks, LB21; William Whyte to William Van Horne, 7 June 1887, CPR Papers, file 16805.

50 William Van Horne to George Stephen, 17 June 1887, William Van Horne Letterbooks, LB21; William Van Horne to John Pope, 23 June 1887, William Van Horne Letterbooks, LB22; A.W. Ogilvie to John Norquay, 10 June, 24 August 1887, NPP, C-2802, C-2882.

51 William Van Horne to George Stephen, 21 June 1887, William Van Horne Letterbooks, LB21.

52 George Stephen to John A. Macdonald, 19 June 1887, John A. Macdonald Papers, 123546.

53 John A. Macdonald to James Aikins, 27 June, 14 July 1887, John A. Macdonald Papers, 77481, 77487; James Aikins to John A. Macdonald, 14, 20, and 28 June, 14, 15, and 16 July 1887, John A. Macdonald Papers, 77473, 77476, 77484, 77487, 77489, 77491; James Aikins to Joseph Chapleau, 4 May 1887, Manitoba Lieutenant Governor, Alexander Morris Papers O , 337; Regehr, "The National Railway Policy," 128.

54 Manitoba Executive Council, *Orders-in-Council Registers 1870–1891*, 11 and 20 June 1887; John Rose to John A. Macdonald, 24 and 27 June (with draft reply) 1887, John A. Macdonald Papers, 118092, 118096; Donald Smith [Leanchoil] to John A. Macdonald, 24 June 1887, John A. Macdonald Papers, 120502; David M.L. Farr, "Rose, Sir John," in *Dictionary of Canadian Biography*, vol. 11, University of Toronto/Université Laval, 2003–, http://www.biographi.ca/en/bio/rose_john_11E.html (accessed 18 April 2023).

55 John A. Macdonald to John Rose, 25 June 1887, John A. Macdonald Papers, Letterbook 24, part 1.

56 George Stephen to John A. Macdonald, 26 June 1887, John A. Macdonald Papers, 123558.

57 London *Times*, 29 June 1887.

58 *Commercial* 5, no. 40 (27 June 1887): 808–9; *Grip* 28, no. 23 (4 June 1887); Alexander McLachlan, "Ye Men of Manitoba," *Grip* 29, no. 3 (16 July 1887).

59 *Commercial* 5, no. 40 (27 June 1887): 808–9, and 6, no. 50 (3 September 1888); Manitoba Treasury Department, "Auditor's Appropriation Ledger, 1886–87"; *The Session* (pamphlet), printed by the *Call*, c. 30 May 1888; William Scarth to John A. Macdonald, 25 June 1887, John A. Macdonald Papers, 119333.

60 James Aikins to John A. Macdonald, 20 June 1887, John A. Macdonald Papers, 77476; John A. Macdonald to James Aikins, 26 June 1887, John A. Macdonald Papers, Letterbook 24, part 1; Regehr, "The National Railway Policy," 127.

61 William Van Horne to G.R. Parkin, 8 February 1899, William Van Horne Letterbooks, LB56, 122–25, and cited in John Willison, *Sir George Parkin: A Biography* (London: Macmillan, 1929), 226–27; with thanks to Professor David Hall for this reference.

62 *Manitoba Free Press*, 1 July 1887.

63 James Aikins to John A. Macdonald, 5 August 1887, John A. Macdonald Papers, 77493; John Norquay to L.J. Clarke, 18 and 28 July 1887, James Aikins LG Papers; L.J. Clarke to John Norquay, 19 August 1887, Manitoba Lieutenant Governor, Alexander Morris Papers O, 375 ff.; William Scarth to John A. Macdonald, 25 June 1887, John A. Macdonald Papers, 119333; Saul Engelbourg and Leonard Bushkoff, *The Man Who Found the Money: John Stewart Kennedy and the Financing of the Western Railroads* (East Lansing: Michigan State University Press, 1996), 168; *Portage la Prairie Weekly Tribune-Review*, 9 September 1887.

64 George Stephen to John A. Macdonald, 12 July 1887, John A. Macdonald Papers, 123566; John A. Macdonald to George Stephen, 2 July, 8 August, 31 October 1887, George Stephen Papers, 190, 198, 220.

65 George Stephen to William Van Horne, 1 August 1887, CPR Papers, file 17476, and 2 July 1887, CPR Papers, file 17447; John A. Macdonald to George Stephen, 2 July 1887, George Stephen Papers, 190; William Van Horne to William Whyte, 28 July, 2 and 5 August 1887, William Van Horne Letterbooks, LB22; William Van Horne to A. Manvel, 2 August 1887; to George B. Elliott, 28 July 1887; to Thomas Nickel, 4 and 22 July 1887; and to John Kirchhoffer, 22 July 1887, William Van Horne Letterbooks, LB22; Charles Cliffe to William Van Horne, 30 July 1887, and C. Drinkwater to William Van Horne, 14 July 1887, CPR Papers, file 17941; William Van Horne to John Pope, 1 July 1887, William Van Horne Letterbooks, LB22; William Van Horne to E.B. Osler, 5 and 10 August 1887, William Van Horne Letterbooks, LB22.

66 Manitoba Executive Council, *Orders-in-Council Registers 1870–1891*, 22 July [entered 12 August] 1887; "Articles of Association of the Red River Valley Railway Company," in Manitoba Executive Council, *Orders-in-Council Registers 1870–1891*, 30 August 1887.

67 Merchants Bank of Canada, "Board Minutes," 16 August 1887, LAC; Manitoba Executive Council, *Orders-in-Council Registers 1870–1891*, 25 August 1887; *Grip* 29, no. 7 (13 August 1887), and 29, no. 10 (3 September 1887); London *Times*, 24 and 30 August 1887.

68 *Washington Post*, 23 August 1887; with thanks to Jean Friesen for this reference.

69 Martin, *James J. Hill*, 334–37, 345–47, 349, 364; Engelbourg and Bushkoff, *John Stewart Kennedy*; H.W. Cannon to James Hill, 27 August 1887, James J. Hill Papers; Edward Nichols to James Hill, 27 August, 15 October 1887, James J. Hill Papers; John Kennedy to James Hill, 21, 23, and 26 September, 15 October 1887, James J. Hill Papers.

70 John Norquay to David Wilson, 20 and 30 August 1887, Manitoba Department of Public Works, Minister files (hereafter DPW), Railway Commissioner file.

71 Alphonse LaRivière to T.A. Wade, 20 August 1887, DPW.

72 John Norquay to David Wilson, 30 August 1887, DPW; *Monetary Times*, 2 September 1887.

73 Ibid.

74 David Harrison to James Aikins, 24 August 1887, James Aikins LG Papers; Manitoba Executive Council, *Orders-in-Council Registers 1870–1891*, 12 September 1887; Manitoba Executive Council, "Clerk's Letter Book," 4 January 1887, 29 January 1889, 252–59, including C.A. Sadleir to Alfred Rennie, 29 August 1887, and C.A. Sadleir to John Norquay, 30 August, 5 and 12 September 1887.

75 *Canadian Journal of Commerce, Finance and Insurance Review* 25, no. 10 (9 September 1887): 451, citing a report in the Toronto *Mail*.

76 Manitoba Executive Council, "Clerk's Letter Book," 259–64, including C.A. Sadleir to John Norquay, 23 and 27 September 1887, C.A. Sadleir to Charles Hamilton, 23 September 1887, and C.A. Sadleir to Alfred Rennie, 27 September 1887; George Stephen to John A. Macdonald, 10 September 1887, John A. Macdonald Papers, 123633.

77 *Commercial* 6, no. 1 (26 September 1887): 9; George Stephen to John A. Macdonald, 8 September 1887, John Thompson Papers, 6590; George Stephen to John A. Macdonald, 10 September 1887, John A. Macdonald Papers, 123633; *Brandon Sun Weekly*, 29 September 1887; *Monetary Times* 21, no. 13 (23 September 1887): 397, and 21, no. 14 (30 September 1887): 427.

78 George Stephen to John A. Macdonald, 20 September 1887, John A. Macdonald Papers, 123660; A.W. Ross to John A. Macdonald, 10 September 1887, John A. Macdonald Papers, 222298.

79 George Stephen to John A. Macdonald, 14 and 20 September 1887, John A. Macdonald Papers, 123644, 123660; also George Stephen to John A. Macdonald, 2 and 12 September 1887, John A. Macdonald Papers, 123623, 123637, 123641; John A. Macdonald to George Stephen, 16 September 1887, George Stephen Papers, 199; William Van Horne to William Whyte, 13 September 1887, William Van Horne Letterbooks, LB23; A.W. Ross to John A. Macdonald, 10 September 1887, John A. Macdonald Papers, 222298; Stephen's letter to shareholders, 12 September 1887, printed in the Montreal *Gazette*, 17 September 1887; Gilbert, *Awakening Continent*, 250–51, 280–85.

80 John A. Macdonald to Charles Tupper, 12 September 1887, Charles Tupper Papers, 3565; George Stephen to John A. Macdonald, 10 September 1887, John A. Macdonald Papers, 123633; Thomas White to John A. Macdonald, 9 September 1887, John Thompson Papers, 6593; John A. Macdonald to George Stephen, 12 September 1887, George Stephen Papers, 201; J.A.M. Aikins to John Thompson, 24 September 1887, John Thompson Papers, 6669; Regehr, "The National Railway Policy," 128.

81 John A. Macdonald to James Aikins, 15 September 1887, John A. Macdonald Papers, Letterbook 24, part 1, vol. 527; John T. Saywell, *The Office of Lieutenant-Governor: A Study in Canadian Government and Politics* (Toronto: University of Toronto Press, 1957), 179–83; D.G. Burley, "Aikins, James Cox," in *Dictionary of Canadian Biography*, vol. 13, University of Toronto/Université Laval, 2003–, http://www.biographi.ca/en/bio/aikins_james_cox_13E.html (accessed 18 April 2023).

82 John A. Macdonald to James Aikins, 15 September 1887, John A. Macdonald Papers, Letterbook 24, part 1, vol. 527.

83 Ibid.

84 James Aikins to John A. Macdonald, 25 September 1887, John A. Macdonald Papers, 77496.

85 Ibid.

86 F.R. Burpé to John Norquay, 5 October 1887, ECPO, G8730; George Black to John Norquay, 1 October 1887, ECPO, G8730; J.A.M. Aikins to William Van Horne, 30 October 1887, CPR Papers, file 19097; J.J.C. Abbott to Van Horne, undated October and 29 October 1887, CPR Papers, file 18534; William Whyte to William Van Horne, 30 and 31 October 1887, CPR Papers, file 18534.

87 William Van Horne to J.J.C. Abbott, 31 October 1887, William Van Horne Letterbooks, LB23.

88 London *Times*, 16 and 30 September, 4 October 1887; John A. Macdonald to George Stephen, 22 September 1887 (two letters), George Stephen Papers, 203, 204; "Sir George Stephen to the Shareholders of the CPR Company 12 September 1887," cited in Gilbert, *Awakening Continent*, 250–51, 280–85; *Monetary Times* 21, no. 14 (30 September 1887): 426–27; McDonald, *Lord Strathcona*, 366–82.

89 John A. Macdonald to William Scarth, 1 October 1887, William Scarth Papers.

90 Thomas Mayne Daly to John A. Macdonald, 23 August, 10 October 1887, John A. Macdonald Papers, 221938, 222825.

91 London *Times*, 5 October 1887.

92 *Manitoba Free Press*, 5 and 6 October 1887; James Colcleugh to his father, 8 October 1887, James Colcleugh Papers.

93 *Commercial* 6, no. 3 (10 October 1887).

94 Manitoba Executive Council, *Orders-in-Council Registers 1870–1891*, 23 September–13 October 1887.

95 John Norquay to W.R. Butler, 9 October 1887, NPP, Letterbook 5.

96 Manitoba Executive Council, *Orders-in-Council Registers 1870–1891*, 10 October 1887; "Memorandum of Agreement," c. 10 October 1887, ECPO, Miscellaneous Government, G8730; *Manitoba Sun*, 25 October 1887, quoted in Waite, *Canada 1874–1896*, 196.

97 John Schultz to John A. Macdonald, 25 October 1887, John A. Macdonald Papers, 120010, quoted in Regehr, "The National Railway Policy," 132.

98 James Aikins to John A. Macdonald, 10 October 1887, John A. Macdonald Papers, 77499.

99 John A. Macdonald to James Aikins, 15 October 1887, John A. Macdonald Papers, Letterbook 24, part 2, vol. 527.

100 John A. Macdonald to George Stephen, 6 October 1887, George Stephen Papers, 209; George Stephen to John A. Macdonald, 19 October 1887, John A. Macdonald Papers, 123720, with Macdonald's annotation (it read "see Langevin, Tupper, Pope"), and copied in John A. Macdonald Papers, 123724; *Railway Times*, 22 October, 5 and 11 November 1887; Gilbert, *Awakening Continent*, 216 ff.; George Stephen to Lord Lansdowne, 4 and 30 October 1887, Lord Lansdowne Papers; Lord Lansdowne to George Stephen, 27 October 1887, Lord Lansdowne Papers; Lord Lansdowne to Henry Holland, 12 October 1887, Lord Lansdowne Papers.

101 John A. Macdonald to Thomas Mayne Daly, 18 October 1887, John A. Macdonald Papers, Letterbook 527, part 2, 259–60.

102 John A. Macdonald to Corydon Brown, 17 October 1887, John A. Macdonald Papers, Letterbook 24, vol. 527/part 2, 256–57; John A. Macdonald to John Schultz, 28 October 1887, John Schultz Papers.

103 Alphonse LaRivière [codename Sipi, Cree for "river"] to John Norquay, 17, 18, 20, 21, and 25 October 1887, ECPO, G8730; Queen's Hotel to John Norquay, 18 October 1887, ECPO, G8730.

104 John A. Macdonald to George Stephen, 21 September 1887, George Stephen Papers, 202.

105 Alphonse LaRivière to John Norquay, 18 October 1887, ECPO, G8730.

106 *Proceedings of the Inter-Provincial Conference Held at the City of Quebec from the 20th to the 28th of October 1887 Inclusively*, https://archive.org/details/cihm_07519/page/n17 (accessed 12 October 2021).Honoré Mercier to A.E.B. Davie, 24 September 1887, Premier William Smythe Papers; Gustave Grenier to John Norquay, 5 November 1887, ECPO, G8730; *Manitoba Free Press*, 11 October 1887.

107 John A. Macdonald to Honoré Mercier, 4 October 1887, in *Proceedings of the Inter-Provincial Conference*.

108 Joyce Aylen to Ellen Cooke, March 1974, Ellen Gillies Cooke Papers, file 3.

109 *Resolutions: Respecting Amendments of the British North America Act, Inter-Provincial Conference 1887*, in John Norquay Papers.

110 *Proceedings of the Inter-Provincial Conference*.

111 *Winnipeg Times*, 27 October, 3 and 6 November 1882; *Manitoba Free Press*, 10 November 1882, 17 and 23 May, 21 June 1883, LLM Hansard; *Journals of the Legislative Assembly of Manitoba 1885*.

112 *Winnipeg Call*, 23 May 1887, LLM Hansard; *Commercial* 6, no. 9 (21 November 1887): 169.

113 *Morning Call*, 23 May 1887, LLM Hansard.

114 John Schultz to John A. Macdonald, 25 October, 7 November 1887, John A. Macdonald Papers, 120010, 120005; W.E. Sanford to William Van Horne, 4 November 1887, CPR Papers, file 18634; William Van Horne to W.E. Sanford, 8 November 1887, William Van Horne Letterbooks, LB23; William Van Horne to Corydon Brown, 10 November 1887, William Van Horne Letterbooks, LB23; *Brandon Sun*, 27 October 1887.

115 William Whyte to William Van Horne, 1 November 1887, CPR Papers, file 18700; William Whyte to William Van Horne, 1 November 1887, CPR Papers, file 18567; William Whyte to William Van Horne, 2 November 1887, CPR Papers, file 18598; William Whyte to William Van Horne, n.d. November, 5 and 8 November 1887, CPR Papers, file 18607; William Van Horne to John Pope, 5 November 1887, John

Thompson Papers, 6889; John Schultz to John A. Macdonald, 7 November 1887, John A. Macdonald Papers, 120005; London *Times*, 15 November 1887.

116 William Scarth to John A. Macdonald, 8 November 1887, John A. Macdonald Papers, 119359.

117 John A. Macdonald to George Stephen, 31 October 1887, George Stephen Papers, 220; John A. Macdonald to George Stephen (copy), 19 November 1887, John A. Macdonald Papers, 123759; George Stephen to John A. Macdonald, 25 October, 11 November (two letters), 26 November 1887, John A. Macdonald Papers, 123736, 123744, 123756, 123771; William Van Horne, "Memorandum," n.d. [c. 1 November 1887], William Van Horne Letterbooks, LB 23; John A. Macdonald to William Van Horne, 17 November 1887, CPR Papers, file 18607; William Van Horne to Thomas White, 23 November 1887, William Van Horne Letterbooks, LB 24; Lord Lansdowne to John A. Macdonald, 19 November 1887, Lord Lansdowne Papers.

118 John Norquay to James Hutton, 15 November 1887, ECPO, G8730; John Norquay to Alfred Dozois, 28 November 1887, ECPO, G8730; John Schultz to John A. Macdonald, 7 November 1887, John A. Macdonald Papers, 120005.

119 *Selkirk Record*, 9 December 1887; Toronto *Mail*, 5 November 1887.

Chapter 12: Downfall, November–December 1887

1 Alphonse LaRivière [Sipi] to John Norquay, 20 October 1887, ECPO, G8730; Merchants Bank, "Board Minutes," LAC, meetings of 28 October, 1 and 4 November 1887.

2 Merchants Bank, "Board Minutes," 8 November 1887; Manitoba Executive Council, *Orders-in-Council Registers 1870–1891*, 8 November 1887.

3 George Stephen to John A. Macdonald, 4 November 1887, John A. Macdonald Papers, 123744.

4 Merchants Bank, "Board Minutes," 8 and 15 November 1887.

5 *Manitoba Free Press*, 1 November 1887.

6 *Commercial* 6, no. 8 (14 November 1887): 149; James Aikins to John A. Macdonald, 12 November 1887, John A. Macdonald Papers, 77505; William Whyte to William Van Horne, 11 November 1887, CPR Papers, file 18567.

7 James Aikins to John A. Macdonald, 12 November 1887, John A. Macdonald Papers, 77505.

8 Merchants Bank, "Board Minutes," 22 November 1887.

9 John Norquay to F.H. Brydges, 5? and 10 November 1887, NPP, Letterbook 5; James Aikins to John A. Macdonald, 12 November 1887, John A. Macdonald Papers, 77505.

10 James Aikins to John A. Macdonald, 12 November 1887, John A. Macdonald Papers, 77505.

11 Manitoba Executive Council, *Orders-in-Council Registers 1870–1891*, 29 October 1887; James Aikins to John A. Macdonald, 31 October 1887, John A. Macdonald Papers, 77502.

12 John Norquay to James Aikins, 25 November 1887, NPP, Letterbook 5.

13 Ibid.

14 John A. Macdonald to James Aikins, 23 November 1887, John A. Macdonald Papers, Letterbook 24, vol. 527.

15 "The [1888] Budget, as Reported by *Winnipeg Call*," contains LaRivière's account, probably 12 May, on 19–24, in Manitoba, *Sessional Papers 1888*.

16 John A. Macdonald to James Aikins, 23 November 1887, John A. Macdonald Papers, Letterbook 24, v. 527.

17 Fred White to John A. Macdonald, 23 November 1887, John A. Macdonald Papers, 134980.

18 *Commercial* 6, no. 9 (21 November 1887):169.

19 Edward Leacock to James Aikins, 28 November 1887, James Aikins LG Papers.

20 Stephen Leacock, "My Remarkable Uncle," in *My Remarkable Uncle and Other Sketches* (1942; reprinted, Toronto: McClelland and Stewart, 1965), 14–20; *Canadian Parliamentary Companion 1887*; Edward Leacock to John Norquay, 25 October 1882, NPP, A-1138; 30 October 1882, A-1137; 11 May 1884, C-890; 16 Ma[?] 1884, C-115; A.W. Pritchard to Edward Leacock, 14 January 1886, NPP, Letterbook E; Edward Leacock to John Norquay, 24 July 1886, NPP, C-1286(b) and (c); McArthur, Boyle & Co. to John Norquay, 28 and 30 August 1884, NPP, C-277(a) and (b); Merchants Bank, "Board Minutes," 2 April 1884.

21 *Monetary Times* 21, no. 27 (30 December 1887): 819; Edward Leacock to David Wilson, 16 August 1887, Department of Public Works Papers; John A. Macdonald to William Scarth, 13 September 1887, John A. Macdonald Papers, 119343; William Scarth to John A. Macdonald, 23 November 1887, John A. Macdonald Papers, 119362.

22 James Aikins to John A. Macdonald, 30 November 1887, John A. Macdonald Papers, 77508; John Norquay to Gédéon Bourdeau, 2 December 1887, ECPO, G8730.

23 James Aikins to John A. Macdonald, 30 November 1887, John A. Macdonald Papers, 77508; Manitoba Executive Council, *Orders-in-Council Registers 1870–1891*, 29 November 1887.

24 James Aikins to John A. Macdonald, 30 November 1887, John A. Macdonald Papers, 77508.

25 John Norquay to Alf Masters, 16 November 1887, NPP, Letterbook 5.

26 Bernard Saunders to John Norquay, 31 December 1887, ECPO, G8730.

27 John Norquay to Archibald & Howell Co., 2 December 1887, NPP, Letterbook 6; John Norquay to British Canadian Loan & Investment Company, 5 December 1887, NPP,

Letterbook 6; also A. Bain to John Norquay, 27 October 1886, NPP, C-1889; R.H. Tomlinson to John Norquay, 7 November 1887, ECPO, G8730; John Norquay to Ross & Haggart Co., 5 April 1888, NPP, Letterbook 5; St. Andrews parish files, Deed of Sale for Lot 8, 6 December 1894.

28 James Colcleugh to his wife, 13 and 20 November, 1 December 1887, James Colcleugh Papers; William Kennedy to John Norquay, 30 November 1887, ECPO, G8730, and Norquay's reply, 2 December 1887; Manitoba Treasury Department, "Cashbook E, 1887–1889."

29 James Colcleugh to his wife, 4 December 1887, James Colcleugh Papers; *Selkirk Record*, 21 October, 4 and 25 November, 2 December 1887; John Norquay to John Parr, 5 December 1887, NPP, Letterbook 6, 10.

30 Lord Lansdowne to Macdonald, 19 November 1887, Lansdowne papers, LAC, Microfilm A624; *Brandon Sun*, 8 December 1887; *True Witness and Catholic Chronicle* 38, no. 18 (7 December 1887).

31 James Aikins to John Norquay, 6 December 1887, ECPO, G8730; J.B. McKilligan to John Norquay, 8 December 1887, ECPO, G8730; other business letters on 5, 10, 12, 14, 19, and 20 December 1887 in ECPO, G8730; John Norquay to David Wilson, 14 December 1887, Department of Public Works Papers; John Norquay to J.E. Woodworth, 14 December 1887, NPP, Letterbook 6; J.E. Woodworth to John Norquay, 17 November 1887, ECPO, G8730.

32 John Norquay to J. Henry Tennant, 6 December 1887, NPP, Letterbook 6; John Norquay to J. Sidney O'Brien, 6 December 1887, NPP, Letterbook 6.

33 John Norquay to Alphonse LaRivière, 16 December 1887, NPP, Letterbook 6; John Norquay to W.R. Mulock, 14 December 1887, NPP, Letterbook 6; W. Nursey to John Norquay, 6 December 1887, ECPO, G8730.

34 A. Pritchard to J.P. Robertson, 21 December 1887, NPP, Letterbook 6; P.V. Georgen to John Norquay, 20 December 1887, ECPO, G8730.

35 William Scarth to John A. Macdonald, 2 December 1887, John A. Macdonald Papers, 119366.

36 Zenon Gawron, "Harrison, David Howard," in *Dictionary of Canadian Biography*, vol. 13, University of Toronto/Université Laval, 2003–, http://www.biographi.ca/en/bio/harrison_david_howard_13E.html (accessed 20 April 2023); I thank Zenon Gawron for sharing his notes on Harrison's career.

37 Ibid.; John A. Macdonald to David Harrison, 13 April 1891, John A. Macdonald Papers, vol.28A, 156.

38 John A. Macdonald to Acton Burrows, 13 December 1887, Acton Burrows Papers; John A. Macdonald to William Scarth, 5 January 1888, William Scarth Papers; Gawron, "Harrison."

39 John A. Macdonald to James Aikins, 12 December 1887, John A. Macdonald Papers, Letterbook 527, part 2, 327; John A. Macdonald to H.H. Smith, 10 January 1888, H.H. Smith Papers.

40 Alex Norquay to J. Newbold, 10 November 1935, copied by Ellen Cooke at Mary Savage's house, 27 October 1965, Ellen Gillies Cooke Papers, file 5; Mackenzie Bowell to John A. Macdonald, 26 September 1888, John A. Macdonald Papers, 148499 ff.; LaRivière's version appears in his speech to the Manitoba assembly, c. 12 May 1888, LLM Hansard.

41 William Van Horne to W.E. Sanford, 8 November 1887, William Van Horne Letterbooks, LB23; William Van Horne to Corydon Brown, 10 November 1887, William Van Horne Letterbooks, LB23; William Van Horne to William Whyte, 14 November 1887, William Van Horne Letterbooks, LB23; William Whyte to William Van Horne, 7 December 1887, CPR Papers, file 18914.

42 Merchants Bank, "Board Minutes," 16 December 1887.

43 John A. Macdonald to Charles Tupper, 15 December 1887, John A. Macdonald Papers, Letterbook 24; *Grip* 29, no. 27 (31 December 1887).

44 Manitoba Executive Council, *Orders-in-Council Registers 1870–1891*, 29 October, 24 November, 19 December 1887.

45 John Norquay to David Wilson and seventeen other MLAs, 19 December 1887, NPP, Letterbook 6.

46 Alex Norquay to J. Newbold, 10 November 1935, Ellen Gillies Cooke Papers, file 5; Manitoba Executive Council, *Orders-in-Council Registers 1870–1891*, 19, 21, and 22 December 1887; James Aikins to John A. Macdonald, 28 December 1887, John A. Macdonald Papers, 77518.

47 James Aikins to John A. Macdonald, 28 December 1887, John A. Macdonald Papers, 77518.

48 David Harrison to John A. Macdonald, 17 January 1888, John A. Macdonald Papers, 148469.

49 John Norquay to James Aikins, 23 December 1887, NPP, Letterbook 5.

50 James Aikins to John A. Macdonald, 23 December 1887, John A. Macdonald Papers, 77511, with annotation dated 24 December 1887; James Aikins to John A. Macdonald, 26 December 1887, John A. Macdonald Papers, 77515.

Chapter 13: Dénouement, 1888–89

1 Manitoba Executive Council, *Orders-in-Council Registers 1870–1891*, 26, 27, and 28 December 1887; Manitoba Treasury, "Cashbooks," vol. A (1879–89); I thank Professor Gary Spraakman, York University, for advice on these accounting matters, and Paula Warsaba and Rachel Mills, Archives of Manitoba, who made it possible for me to secure access to the cashbooks through freedom of information legislation.

2 Bernard Saunders to John Norquay, 31 December 1887, ECPO, G8730; Selkirk *Record*, 30 December 1887, 20 January 1888; *Commercial* 6, no. 17 (16 January 1888): 33; John Norquay to Sidney O'Brien, 4 January 1888, NPP, Letterbook 6; John Norquay to Corbet Locke, 30 December 1887, NPP, Letterbook 6.

3 A.W. Pritchard to George Murphy, 26 December 1887, NPP, Letterbook 6; John Norquay to T.B. Pardee, 31 December 1887, NPP, Letterbook 5; John Norquay to Major Bell, 31 December 1887, NPP, Letterbook 6; John Norquay to J. Jackson, 4 January 1888, NPP, Letterbook 6; John Norquay to Elm River Municipality, 4 January 1888, NPP, Letterbook 6; John Norquay to J.D. Gillies, 7 January 1888, NPP, Letterbook 6; John Norquay to William Beech and John Schultz, 7 January 1888, NPP, Letterbook 6; John Norquay to Raymond Dupuy, Thomas Oakes, J. Ledyard, A. Manvel, W.R. Baker, and W.C. Van Horne, 4 January 1888, NPP, Letterbook 6; John Norquay to Thomas Oakes, 13 January 1888, NPP, Letterbook 6; *Commercial* 6, no. 15 (2 January 1888): 289; no. 16 (9 January 1888): 310.

4 David Young to John Norquay, 13 November 1887, ECPO, G8730; John Norquay to David Harrison, 9 January 1888, NPP, Letterbook 6; *Public Accounts of the Province of Manitoba for the Year Ending June 30th 1887*, 67, 77, and *1888*, 56.

5 Joseph Royal to John Schultz, 3 and 16 January 1888, John Schultz Papers; John Schultz to Frank Gemmel, 17 September 1887, Frank Gemmel Papers; John Schultz to John A. Macdonald, 5 and 16 January 1888, John A. Macdonald Papers, 120015, 120018; James Aikins to John A. Macdonald, 28 December 1887, John A. Macdonald Papers, 77518.

6 *Manitoba Free Press*, 12 January 1888, LLM Hansard.

7 Ibid.; William Scarth to John A. Macdonald, 31 December, 14 January [misdated 14 December 1887] 1888, John A. Macdonald Papers, 119378, 119373; James Aikins to John A. Macdonald, 17 January 1888, John A. Macdonald Papers, 148465; William Van Horne to John A. Macdonald, 3 January 1888, William Van Horne Letterbooks, LB24; Donald A. Smith to John A. Macdonald, 2 January 1888, John A. Macdonald Papers, 120510; Alex Murray to John Norquay, ECPO, G8730; John Norquay to Alex Murray, 12 November 1887, NPP, Letterbook 6; Acton Burrows to John A. Macdonald, 11 January 1888, John A. Macdonald Papers, 225063.

8 *Manitoba Free Press*, 12–26 January 1888, LLM Hansard; "The Session," *Winnipeg Call*, c. 30 May 1888, filed in LLM; Raymond Huel, *Archbishop A.-A. Taché of St. Boniface: The "Good Fight" and the Illusive Vision* (Edmonton: University of Alberta Press, 2003), 283.

9 William Scarth to John A. Macdonald, 12 January 1888, John A. Macdonald Papers 119384; John A. Macdonald to Hector Langevin, 14 January 1888, Thomas Chapais–Hector Langevin Papers; David Harrison to John A. Macdonald, 27 January 1888, John A. Macdonald Papers, 225591.

10 James Aikins to John A. Macdonald, 17 January 1888, John A. Macdonald Papers, 148465; William Scarth to John A. Macdonald, 20 January 1888, John A. Macdonald Papers, 148487; David Harrison to John A. Macdonald, 17 and 27 January 1888, John A. Macdonald Papers, 148469, 225591; Edward Leacock to John A. Macdonald, 25

January 1888, John A. Macdonald Papers, 225514 (with thanks to Zenon Gawron for a copy of this letter and for notes on *Emerson International*, 26 January 1888).

11 *Manitoba Free Press*, 12–26 January 1888, LLM Hansard; "The Session," *Winnipeg Call*, c. 30 May 1888, filed in LLM; Manitoba Executive Council, *Orders-in-Council Registers 1870–1891*, 19 January 1888; Thomas Greenway, "Letter to the Editor," London *Financial News*, 15 May 1889, John Schultz Papers.

12 *Manitoba Free Press*, 12–26 January 1888, LLM Hansard; "The Session," *Winnipeg Call*, c. 30 May 1888, filed in LLM.

13 *Manitoba Free Press*, 12–26 January 1888, LLM Hansard; "The Session," *Winnipeg Call*, c. 30 May 1888, filed in LLM; London *Times*, 16 and 28 January 1888; Zenon Gawron, "Harrison, David Howard," in *Dictionary of Canadian Biography*, vol. 13, University of Toronto/Université Laval, 2003–, http://www.biographi.ca/en/bio/harrison_david_howard_13E.html (accessed 20 April 2023); *Portage la Prairie Weekly Review*, 3 and 10 February 1888.

14 *Manitoba Free Press*, 12–26 January 1888, LLM Hansard.

15 Corydon Brown to John A. Macdonald, 26 January, 4 February 1888, John A. Macdonald Papers, 225478, 225806; David Harrison to Thomas Greenway, 24 February 1888, Thomas Greenway Papers; John A. Macdonald to John Schultz, 1 February 1888, John A. Macdonald Papers, 7974; William Scarth to John A. Macdonald, 18 and 20 January, 6 February 1888, John A. Macdonald Papers, 148483, 148487, 119454; James Aikins to John A. Macdonald, 17 January 1888, John A. Macdonald Papers, 148465; Manitoba, *Journals of the Legislative Assembly*, 1888, and Manitoba, *Sessional Papers 1888*, GR174; *Selkirk Record*, 2 March 1888; Stewart Mulvey to John Schultz, 5 February 1888, John Schultz Papers.

16 John A. Macdonald to William Scarth, 17 and 20 January, 1, 3, and 4 February 1888, William Scarth Papers; William Scarth to John A. Macdonald, 20 and 27 January 1888, John A. Macdonald Papers, 148487, 119406; John A. Macdonald to David Harrison, 21 January 1888, John A. Macdonald Papers, Letterbook 24, part 2, vol. 527.

17 Stewart Mulvey to John Schultz, 7 April 1888, John Schultz Papers.

18 William Scarth to John A. Macdonald, 6 February 1888, John A. Macdonald Papers, 119454; William Scarth to John A. Macdonald, 27 January 1888, John A. Macdonald Papers, 119406.

19 William Scarth to John A. Macdonald, 30 January 1888, John A. Macdonald Papers, 119414; William Scarth to John A. Macdonald, 22 January 1888, decoded copy of cypher telegram, John A. Macdonald Papers, 119394; Thomas Mayne Daly to John A. Macdonald, 5 February 1888, John A. Macdonald Papers, 225847.

20 William Scarth to John A. Macdonald, 5 February 1888, John A. Macdonald Papers, 119433.

21 Heather Gilbert, *Awakening Continent: The Life of Lord Mount Stephen I 1829–1891* (1965; reprinted, Aberdeen: Aberdeen University Press, 1976), 217; James A.

Jackson, "The Background of the Battle of Fort Whyte," Manitoba Historical Society *Transactions*, Series 3 (1945–46): http://mhs.mb.ca/docs/transactions/3/fortwhyte.shtml; Harold A. Innis, *A History of the Canadian Pacific Railway* (1923; reprinted, Toronto: University of Toronto Press, 1971), 182–83; Peter B. Waite, *Canada 1874–1896: Arduous Destiny* (Toronto: McClelland and Stewart, 1971), 197.

22 "Report of the Delegates to Ottawa to Discuss the Disallowance Policy and the Abrogation of Monopoly," in Manitoba, *Sessional Papers 1888*, GR174; W. Kaye Lamb, *History of the Canadian Pacific Railway* (New York: Macmillan, 1977), 161–64; Donald Creighton, *John A. Macdonald: The Old Chieftain* (Toronto: Macmillan, 1955), 485–88, 500–1; Waite, *Arduous Destiny*, 195–99; Richard Gwyn, *Nation Maker: Sir John A. Macdonald: His Life, Our Times II, 1867–1891* (Toronto: Random House, 2011), 543.

23 *Manitoba Free Press*, 11 and 12 April 1888, LLM Hansard.

24 James Mochoruk, "Thomas Greenway, 1888–1900," in *Manitoba Premiers of the 19th and 20th Centuries*, ed. Barry Ferguson and Robert Wardhaugh (Regina: Canadian Plains Research Center, 2010), 86; *Monetary Times, Trade Review and Insurance Chronicle* (hereafter *Monetary Times*) 22, no. 3 (20 July 1888): 67; also 22, no. 11 (14 September 1888): 300–1; 22, no. 20 (16 November 1888): 557–58; and 22, no. 21 (23 November 1888): 588; James Aikins to John A. Macdonald, 29 May 1888, John A. Macdonald Papers, 48606; *Brandon Sun*, 26 April 1888; J.P. Robertson, "Ten Years Record," *Marquette Spectator*, 26 October 1898, draft in J.P. Robertson Papers.

25 *Monetary Times* 21, no. 47 (18 May 1888): 1424; "The Session," *Winnipeg Call*, c. 30 May 1888, filed in LLM.

26 "The Session," *Winnipeg Call*, c. 30 May 1888, filed in LLM; *Manitoba Free Press*, 16 April 1888, LLM Hansard; *Brandon Sun*, 26 January, 2 February, 26 April 1888.

27 "The Session," *Winnipeg Call*, c. 30 May 1888, filed in LLM; *Manitoba Free Press*, 16 April, 18 May 1888, LLM Hansard.

28 *Manitoba Free Press*, sittings of 11–16 May 1888, LLM Hansard; John W. Dafoe, *Clifford Sifton in Relation to His Times* (Toronto: Macmillan, 1931), 15.

29 *Manitoba Free Press*, sitting of 11 May 1888, LLM Hansard; Manitoba *Sessional Papers, 1888*, a booklet entitled "Budget Speech 1888: Treasurer Jones' Speech" and "Mr. Norquay" [as reported by the *Call*, 19–24], and "The Premier" [as reported by the *Free Press*, 24–31] and "Mr. LaRivière's Defence" as reported by the *Call*, in LLM, 19–24; "The Session," *Winnipeg Call*, c. 30 May 1888, filed in LLM.

30 "The Session," *Winnipeg Call*, c. 30 May 1888, filed in LLM; *True Witness and Catholic Chronicle* 38, no. 42 (23 May 1888).

31 LLM Hansard, 16 May 1888, re 15 May sitting; "The Session," *Winnipeg Call*, c. 30 May 1888, filed in LLM.

32 LLM Hansard, 16 May 1888, re 15 May sitting.

33 Ibid.; Roderick George MacBeth, *The Making of the Canadian West: Being the Reminiscences of an Eye-Witness* (Toronto: William Briggs, 1898), 104.

34 LLM Hansard, sittings of 11–16 May 1888; "The Session," *Winnipeg Call*, c. 30 May 1888, filed in LLM; "Budget Speech 1888: Treasurer Jones' Speech" and "Mr. Norquay," as reported by the *Winnipeg Call*, 19–24; "The Premier," as reported by the *Free Press*, 24–31; and "Mr. LaRivière's Defence," as reported by the *Winnipeg Call*, in Manitoba, *Sessional Papers 1888*, filed in LLM; James Aikins to John A. Macdonald, 29 May 1888, John A. Macdonald Papers, 48606; *Manitoba Free Press*, 17 May, 3 September 1888; "Handwritten Notes on Nursey," c. 1888, ECPO, G8730; *Manitoba Sun*, 17 May 1888, LLM Hansard; Manitoba Treasury, "Auditor's Appropriation Ledger 1888–1889"; John W. Dafoe, "Sifton," John W. Dafoe Papers, box 4, Miscellaneous.

35 John L. Holmes, "Factors Affecting Politics in Manitoba: A Study of the Provincial Elections 1870–1899" (MA thesis, University of Manitoba, 1936), 79–82; *Manitoba Free Press*, 12 July 1888; John A. Macdonald to George Stephen, 15 June 1888, George Stephen Papers.

36 MacBeth, *The Making of the Canadian West*, 106–7; John Schultz to John A. Macdonald, 20 June 1888, John Schultz Papers (copy), John A. Macdonald Papers, 120029; with thanks to Sigrid Johnson for information on Icelanders' participation in the St. Andrews contest; London *Times*, 14 July 1888.

37 James Aikins to John A. Macdonald, 4 July 1888, John A. Macdonald Papers, 77523.

38 William Scarth to John A. Macdonald, 8 August 1888, John A. Macdonald Papers, 119510; John A. Macdonald to Edgar Dewdney, 12 June 1888, Edgar Dewdney Papers; John A. Macdonald to H.H. Smith, 16 July, 11 December 1888, H.H. Smith Papers; John A. Macdonald to William Scarth, 14 July 1888, 18 May 1889, William Scarth Papers; John A. Macdonald to George Stephen, 7 and 18 July 1888, George Stephen Papers; George Stephen to John A. Macdonald, 5 July 1888, John A. Macdonald Papers, 123965; William Whyte to William Van Horne, 1888 [probably end of July], 1 August 1888, CPR Papers; John A. Macdonald to George Stephen, three letters on 13 August, 22 October 1888, George Stephen Papers.

39 Hugh John Macdonald to John A. Macdonald, 16 October 1888, John A. Macdonald Papers, 253239.

40 John Schultz to John A. Macdonald, 20 and 22 June 1888, John A. Macdonald Papers, 120029, 120041, copies in John Schultz Papers.

41 John A. Macdonald to John Schultz, 3 November 1888, John Schultz Papers; John A. Macdonald to George Stephen, 2 and 7 November 1888, George Stephen Papers; Thomas Mayne Daly to John A. Macdonald, 26 December 1888, John A. Macdonald Papers, 101408.

42 *Manitoba Sun*, 28 and 29 August 1888, LLM Hansard; *Le Manitoba*, 30 August 1888.

43 *Winnipeg Call*, 30 August 1888, LLM Hansard.

44 *Manitoba Sun*, 31 January 1889, LLM Hansard; *Brandon Sun*, 7 March 1889; London *Times*, 23 October 1888.

45 *Brandon Sun*, 26 December 1888.

46 *Manitoba Free Press*, 16 November 1888, 20 February, 4 March 1889, LLM Hansard; *Winnipeg Call*, 8 and 16 November 1888, LLM Hansard; *Manitoba Sun*, c. 19–20 February 1889, LLM Hansard; Jackson, "The Background."

47 *Winnipeg Call*, 19 and 20 April 1887, 13 November 1888; *Manitoba Sun*, 19 April 1887; *Manitoba Free Press*, 19 April 1887, 13 November 1888, all in LLM Hansard.

48 *Manitoban*, 15 April 1887, LLM Hansard.

49 Ibid.; Lord Lansdowne to James Aikins, 5 March 1887, circular letter, containing a printed copy of a speech by the Prince of Wales, 12 January 1887, James Aikins LG Papers.

50 *Winnipeg Call*, 26 April 1887, LLM Hansard.

51 *Manitoba Sun*, 8 July 1889; Ellen Cooke, "Notes on Norquay's Death," containing excerpts from *Manitoba Sun*, 6 and 8 July 1889; *Manitoba Free Press*, 6, 8, and 9 July; and *Winnipeg Siftings*, 13 July 1889, quoting Walter Nursey and James Wickes Taylor, Ellen Gillies Cooke Papers, file 8; *Portage la Prairie Weekly*, 26 June 1889; *Brandon Sun*, 26 December 1888; J.N. [Norquay], "Sauteaux Indians," *Dominion Illustrated*, 14 September 1889, 166; Margaret Arnett MacLeod, "A Note on the Red River Hunt by John Norquay," *Canadian Historical Review* 38, no. 2 (1957): 129–30; [John Norquay?], "Old Time Sketches: No. 1 The Buffalo Hunt," *Canadian North-West* 1, no. 1 (1880): 2–4; [John Norquay], "Notes on Early Days in Manitoba," NPP, G8731 (last file).

52 Aleida Assmann, "Transformations between History and Memory," *Social Research* 75, no. 1 (2008): 49–72; Doug Owram, *Promise of Eden: The Canadian Expansionist Movement and the Idea of the West 1856–1900* (Toronto: University of Toronto Press, 1980), 168–218; Gerald Friesen, "The Collected Writings of Louis Riel," in *River Road: Essays on Manitoba and Prairie History*, by Gerald Friesen (Winnipeg: University of Manitoba Press, 1996), 17–22; Eli Mandel, "Images of Prairie Man," in *A Region of the Mind: Interpreting the Western Canadian Plains*, ed. Richard Allen (Regina: Canadian Plains Research Center, 1973), 201–9.

53 [Norquay], "Notes on Early Days in Manitoba."

54 Ibid.

55 Ibid.; Alexander Ross, *The Red River Settlement: Its Rise, Progress, and Present State with Some Account of the Native Races and Its General History to the Present Day* (London: Smith, Elder, 1856).

56 Even the nineteenth-century British philosopher John Stuart Mill offered the view that Indigenous peoples "do not have the capacity for self-government because of their excessive love of freedom"; quoted in Margaret Kohn and Kavita Reddy, "Colonialism," in *Stanford Encyclopedia of Philosophy* (fall 2017 ed.), ed. Edward N. Zalta, https://plato.stanford.edu/archives/fall2017/entries/colonialism/ (accessed 20 April 2023).

57 *Grip*, 15 February 1888; Alphonse LaRivière to William Van Horne, 20 November 1888, CPR papers, file 21739.

58 Manitoba, Treasury Department, "Cashbook E, 1887–1889," 78, 122; *Public Accounts of the Province of Manitoba for the Year Ending June 30th, 1887* (Winnipeg: Queen's Printer, 1888), 57; *Public Accounts of the Province of Manitoba for the Year Ending June 30th 1888* (Winnipeg: Queen's Printer, 1889), 57; J. Thomson to John Norquay, 12 June 1888, ECPO, G8730.

59 "Report on the sitting of 16 April 1888" in "The Session," *Winnipeg Call*, c. 30 May 1888, booklet filed in LLM; "The Budget" (anon. pamphlet filed in LLM); Alphonse LaRivière to William Van Horne, 20 November 1888, CPR Papers, file 21739.

60 A.G. McKenzie to John Norquay, 29 April, 28 June 1888, ECPO, G8730; *Henderson's Directory 1887, 1888, 1889*, Winnipeg and Western Canada editions, LLM.

61 Stewart Mulvey to John Schultz, 5 February 1888, John Schultz Papers; John Schultz to John A. Macdonald, 17 January 1889, John A. Macdonald Papers, 120130.

62 *Manitoba Free Press*, 12–26 January, 17 May 1888, LLM Hansard; *Le Manitoba*, 9 February 1888; Richard Willie, *"These Legal Gentlemen": Lawyers in Manitoba, 1839–1900* (Winnipeg: University of Manitoba Legal Research Institute, c. 1994); "The Session," *Winnipeg Call*, c. 30 May 1888, filed in LLM "The Session."

63 James Aikins to John A. Macdonald, 26 March, 23 April 1888, John A. Macdonald Papers, 48591, 48603.

64 *Commercial* 6, no. 30 (16 April 1888): 777, and 7, no. 21 (11 February 1889): 495–96; John Schultz to John A. Macdonald, 17 January, 6 May 1889, John A. Macdonald Papers, 120130, 120156; Andy Maxwell to John Norquay, 20 April 1889, ECPO, G8730.

65 Re John Hope lands, Norquay's loss in 1888–89 might have amounted to just over $130. Over fifty documents in Norquay's files record his work on the Montreal merchant's behalf. On the Hope heirs' refusal, see John Norquay to Charles Hope, 10 and 11 June 1889, ECPO, G8730.

66 Canada, Department of the Interior, "Half Breed Allotments No. 1, Alphabetical List of Grantees," RG15, vol. 1478; Canada, Department of the Interior, "Register of Grants to Halfbreed Children under 33 Vic., Chapter 3," Canada, Department of the Interior, RG15, v1478, LAC. The same list, without the details on the specific tracts of land, appears in Canada, Department of the Interior, "Register of Grants to Halfbreed Children under 33 Vic., Chapter 3, RG15, v1476/1477; I thank Annette Kaserbauer (Winnipeg) and Sharon Tremeer (Morden), of the Property Registry, who guided me in this quest. And special thanks to Dr. Gerhard Ens, University of Alberta, who guided me through this complicated set of documents; John Norquay to Hillyard, 19 March and 24 March 1888, NPP, Letterbook 5; John Norquay to Stewart, 19 March 1888, NPP, Letterbook 5; John Norquay to Jackson, 11 April 1888, NPP, Letterbook 5.

67 John Norquay to Jimmy, 23 March 1888, NPP, Letterbook 5; "Parish and Settlement General Register, Manitoba and North West Territories," AM, G-5463; "Deed of Sale, 6 December 1894," Manitoba, St. Andrews parish files.

68 John Norquay to Editor, *Miller*, 8 April 1888, NPP, Letterbook 5.

69 Cooke, "Notes on Norquay's Death."

70 Church of England, Diocese of Rupert's Land, Report of the Synod of the Diocese of Rupert's Land (annually, 1869–89); Church of England, *Report of the Synod . . . 1889*, 12–14; *Church Guardian* 10, no. 47 (20 March 1889): 6; J. Settee to John Norquay, 7 May 1889, ECPO, G8730; *Brandon Sun*, 7 February 1889; *Manitoba, North-West and British Columbia Lancet* 2, no. 5 (1888): 84; *Commercial* 7, no. 15 (31 December 1888): 348; *Monetary Times* 22, no. 27 (4 January 1889): 759; "In Memoriam," *St. John's College Magazine* 5, no. 22 (1889): 354–55.

71 Christopher Dafoe, *In Search of Canada: The Early Years of John Wesley Dafoe* (Winnipeg: Great Plains Publications, 2014), 142.

72 Cooke, "Notes on Norquay's Death"; *Portage la Prairie Weekly Review*, 10 July 1889.

73 "Death of Honorable John Norquay," Manitoba Medical Association *Northern Lancet* 3, no. 1 (1889): 15–16 [previously *Manitoba, Northwest and British Columbia Lancet*, (1887–89), and subsequently *Northern Lancet and Pharmacist* (1890–92)]. I thank Dr. Marion McKay, Nicole Courrier, and Kyle Feenstra for help with these journals.

74 Cooke, "Notes on Norquay's Death"; "Death of Honorable John Norquay."

75 "Post-Mortem," *Northern Lancet* 3, no. 1 (1889): 15–16; Ellen Cooke, "Premier John Norquay: Andrew Norquay Interview, Vancouver, August 1959," Ellen Gillies Cooke Papers, file 8; London *Times*, 8 and 9 July 1889; the full *Times* obituary identified Norquay as being "of Scottish and Indian ancestry."

76 Manitoba, Treasury Department, "Auditor's Appropriation Ledger 1888–1889," July–August 1889, 553.

77 *Manitoba Sun*, 8 July 1889, in Cooke, "Notes on Norquay's Death."

78 *Manitoba Sun*, 9 July 1889, in Cooke, "Notes on Norquay's Death"; one story that featured in newspapers concerned an old Indigenous man who had depended on Norquay for support from time to time and was much affected by his patron's death. He tried to follow the hearse and was eventually told to leave the procession: Mary Savage to Ellen Cooke, 16 February 1973, Cooke papers, file 6; *Portage la Prairie Weekly Review*, 10 July 1889.

79 *Manitoba Sun*, 6 July 1889, in Cooke, "Notes on Norquay's Death"; John W. Dafoe, *Clifford Sifton in Relation to His Times* (Toronto: Macmillan, 1931), 13–15; *Commercial* 7, no. 42 (8 July 1889): 1029; "Death of Honorable John Norquay"; *Manitoba Sun*, 16 August 1889, 3.

80 "In Memoriam"; *Manitoba Sun*, 8 July 1889, in Cooke, "Notes on Norquay's Death."

81 *Portage la Prairie Weekly Review*, 24 July 1889, drawing from *Manitoba Sun*, 20 July 1889.

82 The "letter of condolence" episode can be traced in John A. Macdonald to H.H. Smith, 11 December 1888, 5 and 17 July 1889, H.H. Smith Papers; John A. Macdonald to William Scarth, 4, 10, and 31 July, 3 August 1889, William Scarth Papers; Stewart Tupper to John A. Macdonald, 25 July 1889, John A. Macdonald Papers, 236690.

83 *Manitoba Sun*, 6 and 8 July 1889, in Cooke, "Notes on Norquay's Death."

84 *Commercial* 7, no. 50 (19 August 1889): 1201; *Manitoba Sun*, 6 July 1889, in Cooke, "Notes on Norquay's Death"; Manitoba Surrogate Court, Eastern Judicial District, to Thomas Norquay, 2 and 5 October 1889, 13 and 20 May, 23 June 1892, John Norquay Papers, file 3; "Parish and Settlement General Register, Manitoba and North West Territories," AM, G-5463; "Deed of Sale," 6 December 1894, Manitoba, St. Andrews parish files.

85 Ellen Cooke, "Information from Mrs. J. E. McAllister, March 9, 1946," Ellen Gillies Cooke Papers, file 4; *Manitoba Free Press*, 6 February 1894; *Western Churchman* 1, no. 1 (3 September 1896): 1415; *Church Guardian* 13, no. 29 (30 December 1891): 6; Wishart Furniture to E. Pentreath, 19 and 20 October 1891, ECPO, G8730; "The Late Miss Norquay," LLM, Biographical Scrapbooks and Vertical Files, probably *Manitoba Free Press*, 21 June 1915; Carol Norquay Stoddart, "Genealogical Notes" (unpublished, in author's possession); St. John's Cathedral, "Burial Register #19," 5 August 1933, 154; *Winnipeg Tribune*, 2 February 1931; *Winnipeg Free Press*, 2 and 3 February, 7 August 1933; *Selkirk Record*, 10 August 1933, all in LLM, Biographical Scrapbooks and Vertical Files; W.J. Healy ed., *Women of Red River: Being a Book Written from the Recollections of Women Surviving from the Red River Era* (Winnipeg: Russell, Lang, 1923), 145–56.

86 T.C. Norris to Caroline McAllister, September 1915, Manitoba Premier's Office files, EC0016 GR1665. On memorials to John Norquay, see Parks Canada Papers, files C8400-740 and C8400-50-740; Manitoba Historical Society Papers; *Winnipeg Free Press*, 29 October 1947; Winnipeg *Tribune*, 7, 16, and 23 October 1954; Société historique de Saint-Boniface, Norquay file; LLM, "Biography File: Norquay"; "Notes on Ancestry of Hon. John Norquay" in Hudson's Bay Company Archives; and Shirlee Anne Smith to Gerald Friesen, 17 February 1976.

Conclusion

1 *Manitoba Free Press*, 24 December 1890.

2 *Manitoba Free Press*, 3 August 1891, and *Winnipeg Daily Tribune*, 1 August 1891, in Ellen Cooke, "Notes on Norquay's Death," Ellen Gillies Cooke Papers, file 8; Margaret E. McBeth, "'Honest John' Norquay Pioneer Statesman," 14 pp., Manitoba Historical Society, typed ms., n.d. Though Matheson was the child of Scots parents, he was asserting that all those of Red River origin, whatever their ancestry, should be counted as members of the "native" community.

3 *Selkirk Herald,* 8 December 1882, reports fully on Norquay's speech in a local schoolhouse where he reviewed the historical and constitutional context of Manitoba's place in the Canadian federation.

4 In the spring session of 1888 the Greenway government submitted to the Legislative Assembly the resolutions passed at the Quebec City Interprovincial Conference the previous October. Norquay, though leader of the opposition, voted with the government's motion to approve these principles. *The Times* (London) 10 May 1888; *Winnipeg Call,* 13 November 1888, in LLM Hansard; P.B. Waite, *The Man from Halifax: Sir John Thompson, Prime Minister* (Toronto: University of Toronto Press, 1985), 223–45; P.B. Waite, "Thompson, Sir John Sparrow David," in *Dictionary of Canadian Biography,* http://biographi.ca/en/bio/thompson_john_sparrow_david_12E.html (accessed 12 May 2023); A. Margaret Evans, *Sir Oliver Mowat* (Toronto: University of Toronto Press, 1992), 141–81. Norquay presented a view of the constitution as a living document, an approach that takes into account the "ground" from which it grows; see Peter C. Oliver, *The Constitution of Independence: The Development of Constitutional Theory in Australia, Canada, and New Zealand* (Oxford: Oxford University Press, 2005); Paul Romney, "Provincial Equality, Special Status and the Compact Theory of Canadian Confederation," *Canadian Journal of Political Science* 32, no. 1 (March 1999): 21–39.

5 The First Nation and Métis proportions of the population were drastically reduced, First Nation reserve communities were created, and many people of mixed ancestry moved westward; John H. Warkentin, "Western Canada in 1886," Manitoba Historical Society *Transactions,* Series 3 (1963–64), http://www.mhs.mb.ca/docs/transactions/3/westerncanada1886.shtml#003 (accessed 3 October 2023).

6 J.A. Gemmill, ed., *Canadian Parliamentary Companion 1889* (Ottawa: J. Durie, 1889), 342; John Norquay to Walter Nursey, 7 April 1885, NPP, Letterbook D.

7 Ian McKay, "The Liberal Order Framework: A Prospectus for a Reconnaissance of Canadian History," *Canadian Historical Review* 91, no. 4 (2000): 616–45.

8 John Norquay to John Pope, 19 December 1885, ECPO, G8729.

9 Thomas Mayne Daly to John A. Macdonald, 5 February 1888, John A. Macdonald Papers, 225847.

10 David Harrison attributes the phrase "too much Indian" to Macdonald in his letter to the prime minister, 27 January 1888, John A. Macdonald Papers, 225591–97.

11 "[A]s he told me himself [said the London medical officer of health, Dr. James Edmunds]," in *Derbyshire Times,* cited in *Portage la Prairie Weekly Tribune-Review,* 5 December 1884, and *Selkirk Herald,* 15 December 1884, clipping in A.W. Pritchard to John Norquay, 17 December 1884, NPP, C-876.

12 Norquay would qualify for membership in today's Manitoba Métis Federation (MMF). The criteria set out by the MMF: "a person who self-identifies as Métis, is of historic Métis Nation Ancestry, is distinct from other Aboriginal Peoples, and is accepted by the Métis Nation." Manitoba Métis Federation, Central Registry Office, "Information

on Métis Citizenship and Harvester Identification Card Application Approvals and Associated Processes," https://www. mmf.mb.ca/central-registery-office-cro (accessed 19 April 2023); Tom Brodbeck, "From Humble Red River Roots to Pre-Eminent Manitoba Premier," and "A Red River Settler Through and Through," *Winnipeg Free Press*, 18 August 2023. Such institutions as the MMF and the other provincial Métis associations did not exist in Norquay's lifetime, of course, and he was never required to declare his position in relation to them. But one criterion in contemporary MMF policy requires that he not belong to "other Aboriginal peoples." Some of the Norquay family descendants to whom I spoke say they are of mixed ancestry and choose to be recognized as Indigenous but not Métis.

13 *Manitoba Sun*, 6 and 8 July 1889; London *Times*, 9 July 1889; *St. Paul Dispatch*, all in Ellen Gillies Cooke Papers, file 8. See also *Dominion Illustrated* 3, no. 54 (13 July 1889); Saint Boniface *L'agriculteur* 1, no. 9 (1 January 1890): 132; *Canadian Journal of Commerce, Finance and Insurance Review* 29, no. 2 (12 July 1889): 56; *Canadian Craftsman and Masonic Record* 24, no. 3 (1889): 78; *Hamilton Spectator*, reprinted in *Portage la Prairie Weekly Review*, 24 July 1889; *Minnedosa Tribune*, 11 July 1889; *Brandon Sun*, 11 July 1889; George H. Ham, *Reminiscences of a Raconteur: Between the '40s and the '20s* (Toronto: Musson, 1921), 35–36.

14 *The Week* 6, no. 32 (12 July 1889): 1–2.

15 More than just a family term, *neestaw* (brother-in-law) has a broader meaning, as University of Manitoba scholar Emma LaRocque says in explaining its role in her own Cree/Michif-speaking community: "My dad most always greeted other Métis men with this word, whether or not they were brothers-in-law. It was used as a welcoming or endearing greeting that implied that they were connected, just as everything in the universe is connected."

16 *Wahkohtowin* is a Cree term for the code of conduct that is rooted in kinship obligations and refers more broadly to one's responsibilities within an interconnected universe.

Keywords

1 Though obviously rough-hewn, it gives an approximation of the categories used at the time. In the 1885–86 Canada Census of Manitoba, in "Table III, Origins of the People, Tableau III, Population par Nationalités," the categorization of the population was more detailed. Out of a total population of 108,640, there were 5,575 "Indians/Sauvages," and 7,985 "Half-Breeds/Métis" (the latter in five columns—English, French, Scotch, Irish, and Undefined). There were four columns for residents distinguished as "African/Noir" (19), "Chinese/Chinois" (15), and "Various Other" or "Not Given" (256). Of the other fourteen other columns, English and Scotch residents accounted for nearly 26,000 each, Irish (21,000) German (11,000), French (7,000), and the other ten European categories about 1,000. Canada, Census of Manitoba 1870, "How the Census Was Collected," https://www.bac-lac.gc.ca/eng/census/1870/Pages/about-census.aspx (accessed 15 December 2023), and https://archive.org/details/1886981886F1887engfra/page/22/mode/2up (accessed 15 December 2023), 22–23.

Bibliography

Archival Collections

Archives of Manitoba (AM)

James Aikins [Lieutenant Governor] Papers (Aikins LG)

Adams Archibald Papers

E.L. Barber Papers

George Broughall, "Report of the Proceedings and the Evidence . . . Wallbridge Royal Commission, 1886," *Manitoba Legislature, Sessional Papers 1886*, LA009, GR174, G8116, box 6, files 14, 16

Thomas Bunn Papers

Charles Acton Burrows Papers

James Colcleugh Papers

Ellen Gillies Cooke Papers

Robert Cunningham Papers

Joseph Dubuc Papers

Ecclesiastical Province of Rupert's Land Papers (EPRL)

James Dunlop Gemmell Papers

Marc-Amable Girard Papers

G.E. Greenlay Papers

Donald Gunn Papers

John Gunn Papers

Hudson's Bay Company Archives (HBCA)

W.N. Kennedy Papers

Manitoba Government: Clerk's Office; Executive Council; Legislative Assembly *Sessional Papers* (unpublished, GR174); Lieutenant Governor; Provincial Police; Department of Public Works (DPW); Railway Commissioner; Treasury Department

Manitoba Parish Lot files, St. Andrews

Manitoba Historical Society Papers

Margaret A. Macleod Papers

Kenneth McKenzie Papers

Alexander Morris Papers

John Norquay Papers

Norquay Premier's Papers (cited as NPP), including Executive Council, "Premier's Office, John Norquay Administration, 1882–87, 1887–1889" (cited as ECPO)

T.C. Norris Papers (Premiers' Office files)

Louis Riel Papers

J.P. Robertson Papers

Alexander Ross Papers

John Schultz Papers

Samuel Taylor Papers

United States Consul Papers of James Wickes Taylor (microfilm copy) (cited as USC)

Archives nationale du Québec

Thomas Chapais–Hector Langevin Papers

Archives of the Diocese of Rupert's Land (Anglican)

David Anderson Files

Archives of Ontario

James Cox Aikins Papers

British Columbia Archives (BCA)

Alexander Begg Papers

Archer Martin Papers

Lieutenant Governor of British Columbia Papers

Gertrude Ann Rhodes Collection

John Moore Robinson Papers

Donald Ross Papers

Premier William Smythe Papers

Canadian Pacific Corporate Archives

Canadian Pacific Railway Papers (cited as CPR)

Canadiana Héritage, Canadian Research Knowledge Network

Thomas Spence Papers

Church of England Archives (Lambeth Palace)

David Anderson Letters

Library and Archives Canada

John Binney Papers

Alexander Campbell Papers

Canada Department of the Interior Papers

James Colcleugh Papers

Dufferin, Governor Generals' Papers

Hargrave Papers

Lansdowne, Governor Generals' Papers

Lorne, Governor Generals' Papers

John A. Macdonald Papers

David MacPherson Papers

Merchants Bank Papers

Parks Canada Papers, files C8400-740 and C8400-50-740

William Scarth Papers

H.H. Smith Papers

George Stephen Papers

John S.D. Thompson Papers

Charles Tupper Papers

William Van Horne Papers

Minnesota Historical Society Archives

James J. Hill Papers

National Records of Scotland

Skene Edwards & Garson, Solicitors (Donald A. Smith Files)

Portage la Prairie Collegiate Archives

High Bluff Minute Book of Loyal Orange Lodge No. 1354

Société historique de Saint-Boniface (Centre du patrimoine)

Bishop A.-A. Taché Papers (Corporation Archiépiscopale Catholique Romaine de Saint-Boniface)

Fonds Société historique de Saint-Boniface (cited as SHSB)

Toronto Reference Library
James Cox Aikins Telegram Book, 1881–85
Alex Matheson Papers
James McDonald, "Daily Journal . . . 1862"

University of Calgary, Glenbow Library and Archives
Edgar Dewdney Papers

University Library, University of Cambridge
Royal Commonwealth Society Collection (Bishop David Anderson Sermons)

University of Manitoba Archives and Library (UM)
Barber Arkin Collection
Church Missionary Society Papers [Anglican] (microfilm copy) (cited as CMS)
John W. Dafoe Papers
St. John's College Papers (cited as SJC)

Western University Archives
David Mills Papers

Published Sources

Adese, Jennifer, and Chris Andersen, eds. *A People and a Nation: New Directions in Contemporary Métis Studies*. Vancouver: UBC Press, 2021.

Alam, Chris, and H. Merskey. "What's in a Name? The Cycle of Change in the Meaning of Neuralgia." *History of Psychiatry* 5 (1994): 429–74.

Allen, R.A., ed. *Man and Nature on the Prairies*. Regina: Canadian Plains Research Center, University of Regina, 1976.

Andersen, Chris. *"Métis": Race, Recognition, and the Struggle for Indigenous Peoplehood*. Vancouver: UBC Press, 2014.

———. "Moya Tipimsook ('The People Who Aren't Their Own Bosses'): Racialization and the Misrecognition of 'Métis' in Upper Great Lakes Ethnohistory." *Ethnohistory* 58, no. 1 (2011): 37–63.

Anderson, Benedict. *Imagined Communities: Reflections on the Origin and Spread of Nationalism*. London: Verso, 1991.

Anderson, David. *A Charge Delivered to the Clergy of the Diocese of Rupert's Land, at His Primary Visitation* (London: Thomas Hatchard, 1851).

———. *A Charge Delivered to the Clergy of the Diocese of Rupert's Land, at His Triennial Visitation, in July and December, 1853.* London: Thomas Hatchard, 1854.

———. *A Charge Delivered to the Clergy of the Diocese of Rupert's Land, in St. John's Church, Red River, at His Triennial Visitation, January 6, 1860.* London: Thomas Hatchard, 1860.

———. *A Charge Delivered to the Clergy of the Diocese of Rupert's Land, in St. John's Cathedral, Red River, at His Fifth and Last Visitation, January 6, 1864.* London: Hatchard and Company, 1864.

———. *The Circle of Light: Or, The Conjuror's Confession.* London: Thomas Hatchard, 1857.

———. *"The Gospel in the Regions Beyond": A Sermon Preached in Lambeth Church, on Sunday, May 3, 1874, at the Consecration of the Bishops of Athabasca and Saskatchewan.* London: Hatchard, 1874.

Archibald, Adams. In *Proceedings of the Royal Colonial Institute 1883–84.* London: Royal Colonial Institute, Spottiswoode, 1884.

Arendt, Hannah. *The Origins of Totalitarianism.* New York: Schocken Books, 1951.

Argyll, John George. *The Canadian North-West: Speech Delivered at Winnipeg by His Excellency the Marquis of Lorne, Governor-General of Canada, after His Trip through Manitoba and the North-West, during the Summer of 1881.* Ottawa: Department of Agriculture, 1881.

Armstrong, Christopher. "The Mowat Heritage in Federal-Provincial Relations." In *Oliver Mowat's Ontario*, edited by Donald Swainson, 93–118. Toronto: Macmillan, 1972.

Artibise, Alan F.J. *Winnipeg: A Social History of Urban Growth 1874–1914.* Montreal and Kingston: McGill-Queen's University Press, 1975.

Ashdown, James, and John Robinson. *An Open Letter to the Shareholders of the Canadian Pacific Railway Co.* (n.p.: n.p., 1887).

Assmann, Aleida. "Transformations between History and Memory." *Social Research* 75, no. 1 (2008): 49–72.

Babe, Robert. *Telecommunications in Canada: Technology, Industry, and Government.* Toronto: University of Toronto Press, 1990.

Beal, Bob, and Rod Macleod. *Prairie Fire: The 1885 North-West Rebellion.* Edmonton: Hurtig, 1984.

Begg, Alexander. *History of the North-West.* 3 vols. Toronto: Hunter, Rose, 1894.

———. *Practical Hand-Book and Guide to Manitoba and the North-West.* Toronto: Belford Brothers, 1877.

———. "Seventeen Years in the Canadian North-West." In *Proceedings of the Royal Colonial Institute*, April 1884. London: Spottiswoode, 1884.

Begg, Alexander, and Walter R. Nursey. *Ten Years in Winnipeg.* Winnipeg: Winnipeg Times, 1879.

Bellan, Ruben C. "Rails across the Red: Selkirk or Winnipeg." *Manitoba Historical Society Transactions*, Series 3, 18 (1961–62). https://www.mhs.mb.ca/docs/transactions/3/railsa rossthered.shtml (accessed 19 May 2023).

———. *Winnipeg, First Century: An Economic History*. Winnipeg: Queenston House, 1978.

Benoit, Dom. *Vie de Mgr Taché II*. Montréal: Librairie Beauchemin, 1904.

Berger, Carl. *The Sense of Power: Studies in the Ideas of Canadian Imperialism, 1867–1914*. Toronto: University of Toronto Press, 1970.

Berton, Pierre. *The National Dream: The Great Railway 1871*–1881. Toronto: McClelland and Stewart, 1970.

———. *The National Dream: The Last Spike*. Toronto: McClelland and Stewart, 1971.

Bertram, Laurie K. "'Eskimo' Immigrants and Colonial Soldiers: Icelandic Immigrants and the North-West Resistance, 1885." *Canadian Historical Review* 99, no. 1 (2018): 63–97.

Binnema, Ted. "Protecting Indian Lands by Defining Indian, 1850–1876." *Journal of Canadian Studies* 48, no. 2 (2014): 5–39.

Blain, Eleanor M. "The Bungee Dialect of the Red River Settlement." MA thesis, University of Manitoba, 1989.

Bliss, Michael. *A Living Profit: Studies in the Social History of Canadian Business 1883–1911*. Toronto: McClelland and Stewart, 1973.

Boon, T.C.B. "The Institute of Rupert's Land and Bishop David Anderson." *Manitoba Historical Society Transactions*, Series 3, 18 (1961–62). http://www.mhs.mb.ca/docs/transactions/3/instituterupertsland.shtml (accessed 19 May 2023).

Boulton, Charles Arkoll. *Reminiscences of the North-West Rebellions*. Toronto: Grip, 1886.

Bowsfield, Hartwell, ed. *The Letters of Charles John Brydges*. Vol. 1, *1879–1882*, vol. 2, *1883–1889*. Winnipeg: Hudson's Bay Record Society, 1977, 1981.

Bradford, Tolly, and Rich Connors. "The Making of a Company Colony: The Fur Trade War, the Colonial Office, and the Metamorphosis of the Hudson's Bay Company." *Canadian Journal of History* 55, no. 3 (2019–20): 171–97.

Bradford, Tolly, and Chelsea Horton. *Mixed Blessings: Indigenous Encounters with Christianity in Canada*. Vancouver: UBC Press, 2016.

Braz, Albert. *The False Traitor: Louis Riel in Canadian Culture*. Toronto: University of Toronto Press, 2003.

Bryce, George. "Among the Mound Builders' Remains." *Manitoba Historical Society Transactions*, Series 1, 18 (1885). http://www.mhs.mb.ca/docs/transactions/1/moundbuilders.shtml (accessed 19 May 2023).

———. *A History of Manitoba: Its Resources and Its People*. Toronto: Canada History Company, 1906.

———. *The Scotsman in Canada: Western Canada, Including Manitoba, Saskatchewan, Alberta, British Columbia, and Portions of Old Rupert's Land and the Indian Territories*. Toronto: Musson, 1911.

Bryce, Marion. "Early Red River Culture." *Manitoba Historical Society Transactions*, Series 1, 57 (1901). http://www.mhs.mb.ca/docs/transactions/1/redriverculture.shtml (accessed 19 May 2023).

———. "Historical Sketch of the Charitable Institutions of Winnipeg." *Historical and Scientific Society of Manitoba Transactions* Series 1, 54 (1899). http://www.mhs.mb.ca/docs/transactions/1/charitableinstitutions.shtml (accessed 19 May 2023).

Buckner, Phillip. "The Creation of the Dominion of Canada, 1860–1901." In *Canada and the British Empire*, edited by Phillip Buckner, 66–86. Oxford: Oxford University Press, 2008.

———. "Whatever Happened to the British Empire?" *Journal of the Canadian Historical Association* 4, no 1 (1993): 3–32.

Bumsted, John. *St. John's College: Faith and Education in Western Canada*. Winnipeg: University of Manitoba Press, 2006.

Burley, David G. "The Emergence of the Premiership." In *Manitoba Premiers of the 19th and 20th Centuries*, edited by Barry Ferguson and Robert Wardhaugh, 1–28. Regina: Canadian Plains Research Center, University of Regina, 2010.

———. "Frontier of Opportunity: The Social Organization of Self-Employment in Winnipeg, Manitoba, 1881–1901." *Histoire sociale/Social History* 31 (1998): 35–69.

———. "The Keepers of the Gate: Inequality of Property Ownership during the Winnipeg Real Estate Boom of 1881–82." *Urban History Review* 17 (1988): 63–76.

Canada. Census of Manitoba 1870. "How the Census Was Collected." https://www.bac-lac.gc.ca/eng/census/1870/Pages/about-census.aspx#tab5 (accessed 20 March 2020).

———. House of Commons, *Sessional Papers*. No. 23, 1873, 36 Victoria, 14–19.

———. The Manitoba Act, 1870. https://justice.gc.ca/eng/rp-pr/csj-sjc/constitution/lawreg-loireg/p1t21.html.

———. Minister of Agriculture. *Census of Canada 1870–71*. Ottawa: I.B. Taylor, Maclean, Roger and Company, 1873–78.

Canada in 1880: Reports of Tenant Farmers' Delegates on the Dominion of Canada as a Field for Settlement: Second Series. Ottawa: Department of Agriculture, 1881.

Careless, J.M.S. "'Limited Identities' in Canada." *Canadian Historical Review* 50, no. 1 (1969): 1–10.

Carle, Frank Austin. *The British Northwest: Pen and Sun Sketches in the Canadian Wheat Lands*. St. Paul, MN: Pioneer Press, 1882.

Carter, Sarah. *Aboriginal People and Colonizers of Western Canada to 1900*. Toronto: University of Toronto Press, 1999.

———. *Capturing Women: The Manipulation of Cultural Imagery in Canada's Prairie West*. Montreal and Kingston: McGill-Queen's University Press, 1997.

———. *Lost Harvests: Prairie Indian Reserve Farmers and Government Policy*. Montreal and Kingston: McGill-Queen's University Press, 1990.

———. "'Your Great Mother across the Salt Sea': Prairie First Nations, the British Monarchy and the Vice Regal Connection to 1900." *Manitoba History* 48 (2005–06). http://www.mhs.mb.ca/docs/mb_history/48/greatmother.shtml.

Chesson, F.W. "On Manitoba." In *Proceedings of the Royal Colonial Institute*, Vol. 3. London: Royal Colonial Institute, 1873.

Coates, Ken. "Western Manitoba and the 1885 Rebellion." *Manitoba History* 20 (1990). http://www.mhs.mb.ca/docs/mb_history/20/1885rebellion.shtml.

Code, Paget J. "Les autres Métis: The English Métis of the Prince Albert Settlement 1862–1886." MA thesis, University of Saskatchewan, 2008.

Collins, J.E. *Life and Times of the Right Honourable Sir John A. Macdonald*. Toronto: Rose, 1883.

Colpitts, George. *Pemmican Empire: Food, Trade, and the Last Bison Hunts in the North American Plains, 1780–1882*. New York: Cambridge University Press, 2015.

Constant, Jean-François, and Michel Ducharme. *Liberalism and Hegemony: Debating the Canadian Liberal Revolution*. Montreal and Kingston: McGill-Queen's University Press, 2009.

Constantin-Weyer, Maurice. *Vers l'ouest: Roman*. Paris: La Renaissance du Livre, 1921.

Cook, Ramsay. *Provincial Autonomy, Minority Rights and the Compact Theory, 1867–1921*. Ottawa: Queen's Printer, 1969.

Cook, Sharon Anne. *"Through Sunshine and Shadow": The Woman's Christian Temperance Union, Evangelicalism, and Reform in Ontario, 1874–1930*. Montreal and Kingston: McGill-Queen's University Press, 1993.

Cooke, Ellen. *Fur Trade Profiles: Five Ancestors of Premier John Norquay*. 3 eds. Winnipeg: self-published, 1978.

———. "Norquays in the Red River Disturbances." *Manitoba Pageant* 21, no. 2 (1976). http://www.mhs.mb.ca/docs/pageant/21/norquays.shtml (accessed 19 May 2023).

Coste, Eugène. *Report on the Gold Mines of the Lake of the Woods*. Montreal: Dawson, for the Geological Survey of Canada, 1884.

Coutts, Robert J. *The Road to the Rapids: Nineteenth-Century Church and Society at St. Andrew's Parish, Red River*. Calgary: University of Calgary Press, 2000.

Craft, Aimée. *Breathing Life into the Stone Fort Treaty: An Anishnabe Understanding of Treaty One*. Saskatoon: Purich, 2013.

Creighton, Donald. *John A. Macdonald II: The Old Chieftain*. Toronto: Macmillan, 1955.

Cruise, David, and Alison Griffiths. *Lords of the Line*. Toronto: Viking Penguin Group, 1988.

Cumming, Carman. "The Plot to Buy the Canadian Northwest." *The Beaver* (1984): 4–9. https://www.canadashistory.ca/explore/business-industry/the-plot-to-buy-the-canadian-northwest.

———. *Secret Craft: The Journalism of Edward Farrer*. Toronto: University of Toronto Press, 1992.

Curtis, Bruce. *The Politics of Population: State Formation, Statistics, and the Census of Canada, 1840–1875*. Toronto: University of Toronto Press, 2002.

Dafoe, Christopher. *In Search of Canada: The Early Years of John Wesley Dafoe*. Winnipeg: Great Plains Publications, 2014.

Dafoe, John W. *Sir Clifford Sifton in Relation to His Times*. Toronto: Macmillan, 1931.

Darwin, John. *The Empire Project: The Rise and Fall of the British World-System 1830–1970*. Cambridge, UK: Cambridge University Press, 2009.

Daschuk, James. *Clearing the Plains: Disease, Politics of Starvation, and the Loss of Indigenous Life*. Regina: University of Regina Press, 2013.

Dauphinais, Luc. *Histoire de Saint-Boniface*. Saint-Boniface, MB: Société historique de Saint-Boniface, 1991.

"Death of Honorable John Norquay." *Northern Lancet* 3, no. 1 (1889): 15–16.

Devine, Heather. *The People Who Own Themselves: Aboriginal Ethnogenesis in a Canadian Family, 1660–1900*. Calgary: University of Calgary Press, 2004.

Donnelly, M.S. *The Government of Manitoba*. Toronto: University of Toronto Press, 1963.

Dubuc, Joseph. *Mémoires d'un Manitoban*. Rome: n.p., 1912.

Dufferin and Ava, Marchioness of. *My Canadian Journal 1872–8*. London: John Murray, 1891.

Duval, Jacinthe. "The Catholic Church and the Formation of Metis Identity." *Past Imperfect* 9 (2001): 65–87.

Elias, Peter Douglas. *The Dakota of the Canadian Northwest: Lessons for Survival*. Winnipeg: University of Manitoba Press, 1988.

Engelbourg, Saul, and Leonard Bushkoff. *The Man Who Found the Money: John Stewart Kennedy and the Financing of the Western Railroads*. East Lansing: Michigan State University Press, 1996.

Ens, Gerhard. "Gabriel Dumont, Big Bear, and the Indian Rebellion of 1885: The Case of the Peace Hills Reserves, 1884–1885." In *Metis Histories and Identities: A Tribute to Gabriel Dumont*, edited by Denis Gagnon, Denis Combet, and Lise Gaboury-Diallo, 25–38. Winnipeg: Presses Universitaires de Saint-Boniface, 2009.

———. *Homeland to Hinterland: The Changing Worlds of the Red River Metis in the Nineteenth Century*. Toronto: University of Toronto Press, 1996.

———. "Métis Lands in Manitoba." *Manitoba History* 5 (1983). http://www.mhs.mb.ca/docs/mb_history/05/metislands.shtml (accessed 19 May 2023).

———, ed. *A Son of the Fur Trade: The Memoirs of Johnny Grant*. Edmonton: University of Alberta Press, 2008.

Ens, Gerhard, and Joe Sawchuk. *From New Peoples to New Nations: Aspects of Métis History and Identity from the Eighteenth to Twenty-First Centuries*. Toronto: University of Toronto Press, 2016.

Erasmus, Peter. *Buffalo Days and Nights*. Edited by Irene Spry. Calgary: Glenbow-Alberta Institute; Toronto: McClelland and Stewart, 1976.

———. *Buffalo Days and Nights*. Calgary: Fifth House, 1999.

Evans, A. Margaret. "Oliver Mowat: Nineteenth-Century Ontario Liberal." In *Oliver Mowat's Ontario*, edited by Donald Swainson, 34–51. Toronto: Macmillan, 1972.

———. *Sir Oliver Mowat*. Toronto: University of Toronto Press, 1992.

Ewart, John Skirving. *The Manitoba School Question*. Toronto: Copp Clark, 1894.

Eyford, Ryan. *White Settler Reserve: New Iceland and the Colonization of the Canadian West*. Vancouver: UBC Press, 2016.

Fahrni, Margaret, and William Lewis Morton. *Third Crossing: A History of the First Quarter Century of the Town and District of Gladstone in the Province of Manitoba.* Winnipeg: Advocate, 1946.

Farmer, Hugh. "Alfred Herbert Rennie." http://industrialhistoryhk.org/alfred-herbert-rennie (accessed 19 February 2019).

Ferguson, Barry, and Robert Wardhaugh, eds. *Manitoba Premiers of the 19th and 20th Centuries.* Regina: Canadian Plains Research Center, University of Regina, 2010.

Ferguson, Mary McCarthy. *A History of St. James.* Winnipeg: St. James Historical Society, c. 1967.

Fingard, Judith. "The 1880s: Paradoxes of Progress." In *The Atlantic Provinces in Confederation*, edited by E.R. Forbes and D.A. Muise, 82–116. Toronto: University of Toronto Press, 1993.

Flanagan, Thomas. "The History of Metis Aboriginal Rights: Politics, Principle, and Policy." *Canadian Journal of Law and Society* 5 (1990): 71–94.

———. *Louis "David" Riel: "Prophet of the New World."* Rev. ed. Toronto: University of Toronto Press, 1996.

———. *Metis Lands in Manitoba.* Calgary: University of Calgary Press, 1991.

———. "The Political Thought of Louis Riel." In *Riel and the Metis: Riel Mini-Conference Papers*, edited by A.S. Lussier, 131–60. Winnipeg: Manitoba Metis Federation Press, 1979.

Foster, John. "The Country-Born in the Red River Settlement, 1820–1850." PhD diss., University of Alberta, 1973.

———. "Paulet Paul: Métis or 'House Indian' Folk-Hero?" *Manitoba History* 9 (1985). http://www.mhs.mb.ca/docs/mb_history/09/pauletpaul.shtml (accessed 19 May 2023).

Fowke, Vernon C. *Canadian Agricultural Policy: The Historical Pattern.* Toronto: University of Toronto Press, 1946.

Fraser, William John. "A History of St. John's College, Winnipeg." MA thesis, University of Manitoba, 1966.

Friesen, Gerald. "The Collected Writings of Louis Riel." In *River Road: Essays on Manitoba and Prairie History*, edited by Gerald Friesen, 17–22. Winnipeg: University of Manitoba Press, 1996.

———. "The Evolving Meanings of Region in Canada." *Canadian Historical Review* 82, no. 3 (2001): 529–45.

———. "Homeland to Hinterland: Political Transition in Manitoba, 1870 to 1879." *Canadian Historical Association Historical Papers* 14, no.1 (1979): 33–47.

———. "Imports and Exports in the Manitoba Economy 1870–1890." *Manitoba History* 16 (1988). https://www.mhs.mb.ca/docs/mb_history/16/manitobaimportsexports.shtml (accessed 19 May 2023).

———. "John Norquay, 1878–1887." In *Manitoba Premiers of the 19th and 20th Centuries*, edited by Barry Ferguson and Robert Wardhaugh, 47–67. Regina: Canadian Plains Research Center, University of Regina, 2010.

———. "A Premier, a Tin Box, and a Landlady: Ellen Cooke and the Norquay Papers." *Manitoba History* 77 (2015). http://www.mhs.mb.ca/docs/mb_history/77/norquay-gift.shtml (accessed 19 May 2023).

———. "Space and Region in Canadian History." *Journal of the Canadian Historical Association*, New Series, 16 (2005): 1–22.

Friesen, Gerald, A.C. Hamilton, and Murray Sinclair. "'Justice Systems' and Manitoba's Aboriginal People: An Historical Survey." In *River Road: Essays on Manitoba and Prairie History*, ed. Gerald Friesen, 49–77. Winnipeg: University of Manitoba Press, 1996.

Fuchs, Denise. "Native Sons of Rupert's Land 1760 to the 1860s." PhD diss., University of Manitoba, 2000.

———. "A 'Philanthropist's Bosom' Conflicted: The Reverend John Macallum of Red River Academy." *Canadian Journal of Native Studies* 35, no. 1 (2015): 121–43.

Gailey, Andrew. *The Lost Imperialist: Lord Dufferin, Memory and Mythmaking in an Age of Celebrity*. London: John Murray, 2015.

Galbraith, Julius F. [Jeff Gee]. "The Incorporation of Winnipeg." In *A Sketch of Both Sides of Manitoba* (1881), republished in *Manitoba Pageant* 5, no. 3 (1960). http://www.mhs.mb.ca/docs/pageant/05/winnipegincorporation.shtml (accessed 19 May 2023).

Gaudry, Adam James Patrick. "Kaa-tipeyimishoyaahk—'We Are Those Who Own Ourselves': A Political History of Métis Self-Determination in the North-West, 1830–1870." PhD diss., University of Victoria, 2014.

———. "Respecting Métis Nationhood and Self-Determination in Matters of Métis Identity." In *Aboriginal History: A Reader*, 2nd ed., edited by Kristin Burnett and Geoff Read, 152–63. Don Mills, ON: Oxford University Press, 2016.

Gaudry, Neil. "Fantasies of Sovereignty: Deconstructing British and Canadian Claims to Ownership of the Historic North-West." *Native American and Indigenous Studies* 3, no. 1 (2016): 46–74.

———. "Métissage, and the Métis People as Canada's Mythical Origin." *Aboriginal Policy Studies* 2, no. 2 (2013): 64–87.

Gemmill, G.A., ed. *Canadian Parliamentary Companion 1887*. Ottawa: J. Durie and Son, 1887.

Gentilcore, R. Louis, ed. *Historical Atlas of Canada II: The Land Transformed 1800–1891*. Toronto: University of Toronto Press, 1993.

Geographic Board of Canada. *Place Names of Alberta*. Ottawa: Department of the Interior, 1928.

Gibson, Dale. *Law, Life, and Government at Red River*. Vol. 1, *Settlement and Governance, 1812–1872*, and vol. 2, *General Quarterly Court of Assiniboia, Annotated Records, 1844–1872*. Toronto: Osgoode Society for Canadian Legal History; Montreal and Kingston: McGill-Queen's University Press, 2015.

Gibson, Dale, and Lee Gibson. *Substantial Justice: Law and Lawyers in Manitoba 1670–1970*. Winnipeg: Peguis Publishers, 1972.

Gilbert, Heather. *Awakening Continent: The Life of Lord Mount Stephen*. Vol. 1: *1829–1891*. 1965; reprinted, Aberdeen: Aberdeen University Press, 1976.

———. *The End of the Road: The Life of Lord Mount Stephen.* Vol. 2: *1891–1921.* Aberdeen: Aberdeen University Press, 1977.

———. "The Unaccountable Fifth: Solution of a Great Northern Enigma." *Minnesota History* 42, no. 5 (1971): 175–77.

Giraud, Marcel. *Le Métis canadien: Son rôle dans l'histoire des provinces de l'ouest.* Paris: Institut d'ethnologie, Musée de l'homme, 1945. Translated as: *The Métis in the Canadian West.* 2 vols. Edmonton: University of Alberta Press, 1986.

Gluek, Alvin. *Minnesota and the Manifest Destiny of the Canadian Northwest: A Study in Canadian-American Relations.* Toronto: University of Toronto Press, 1965.

Goldsborough, Gordon. "The Yukon Party from Manitoba." *Manitoba History* 49 (2005). http://www.mhs.mb.ca/docs/mb_history/49/yukonparty.shtml (accessed 19 May 2023).

Great Britain. House of Commons. *Report of the Select Committee on Hudson's Bay Company Lands, 1857.* London: Colonial Office, 1858.

Grebstad, David. "A Tale of Two Houses: The Rise and Demise of the Legislative Council of Manitoba, 1871–1876." *Manitoba History* 75 (2014). https://www.mhs.mb.ca/docs/mb_history/75/legislativecouncil.shtml (accessed 19 May 2023).

Green, Alan, Mary Mackinnon, and Chris Minns. "Conspicuous by Their Absence: French Canadians and the Settlement of the Canadian West." *Journal of Economic History* 65, no. 3 (2005): 822–49.

Gunn, J.J. *Echoes of the Red.* Toronto: Macmillan, 1930.

Gwyn, Richard. *Nation Maker: Sir John A. Macdonald: His Life, Our Times II, 1867–1891.* Toronto: Random House, 2011.

Hackett, Paul. *A Very Remarkable Sickness: Epidemics in the Petit Nord, 1670 to 1846.* Winnipeg: University of Manitoba Press, 2002.

Hall, Catherine, ed. *Cultures of Empire: Colonizers in Britain and the Empire in the Nineteenth and Twentieth Centuries: A Reader.* Manchester: Manchester University Press, 2000.

———. "The Racist Ideas of Slave Owners Are Still with Us Today." *Guardian* [London], 27 September 2016. https://www.theguardian.com/commentisfree/2016/sep/26/racist-ideas-slavery-slave-owners-hate-crime-brexit-vote (accessed 19 May 2023).

Hall, D.J. *Clifford Sifton I: The Young Napoleon 1861–1900.* Vancouver: UBC Press, 1981.

Hall, Norma J. *A Casualty of Colonialism: Mothers of the Resistance 1869–1870.* wordpress.com (accessed 31 January 2021).

Hall, Norma J., Clifford P. Hall, and Erin Verrier. *A History of the Legislative Assembly of Assiniboia/Le conseil du gouvernement provisoire.* Winnipeg: Indian and Northern Affairs Canada, Manitoba Metis Federation, and Government of Manitoba, c. 2010. https://www.gov.mb.ca/inr/pdf/mbmetispolicy/pubs/laa_en.pdf.

Ham, George H. *Reminiscences of a Raconteur, between the '40s and the '20s.* Toronto: Musson, 1921.

Hamon, Max. *The Audacity of His Enterprise: Louis Riel and the Métis Nation that Canada Never Was, 1840–1875.* Montreal and Kingston: McGill-Queen's University Press, 2020.

———. "Contesting Civilization: Louis Riel's Defence of Culture at the Collège de Montréal." *Canadian Historical Review* 97, no. 1 (2016): 58–87.

Hayter, Jennifer. "Racially 'Indian,' Legally 'White': The Canadian State's Struggles to Categorize the Métis, 1850–1900." PhD diss., University of Toronto, 2017.

Healy, William J., ed. *Women of Red River: Being a Book Written from the Recollections of Women Surviving from the Red River Era*. Winnipeg: Russell, Lang and Co., 1923.

Heaman, Elsbeth. *A Short History of the State in Canada*. Toronto: University of Toronto Press, 2015.

———. *Tax, Order and Good Government: A New Political History of Canada 1867–1917*. Montreal and Kingston: McGill-Queen's University Press, 2017.

High Bluff History Book Committee. *Harvest of History: High Bluff and Area*. High Bluff, MB: n.p., 1998.

Hildebrandt, Walter. *The Battle of Batoche: Small British Warfare and the Entrenched Métis*. 1986; reprinted, Vancouver: Talonbooks, 2012.

Hill, R.B. *Manitoba: History of Its Early Settlement, Development and Resources*. Winnipeg: Russell, Lang and Co., 1923.

Hilts, Joseph. "The Political Career of Thomas Greenway." PhD diss., University of Manitoba, 1974.

Hobsbawm, E.J. *The Age of Capital 1848–1875*. New York: Charles Scribner's Sons, 1975.

———. *The Age of Empire 1875–1914*. London: Weidenfeld and Nicolson, 1987.

Holmes, John L. "Factors Affecting Politics in Manitoba: A Study of the Provincial Elections 1870–1899." MA thesis, University of Manitoba, 1936.

Howell, Colin. "W.S. Fielding and the Repeal Elections of 1886 and 1887 in Nova Scotia." *Acadiensis* 8, no. 2 (1979): 28–46.

Huel, Raymond. *Archbishop A.-A. Taché of St. Boniface: The "Good Fight" and the Illusive Vision*. Edmonton: University of Alberta Press, 2003.

Innis, Harold A. *A History of the Canadian Pacific Railway*. 1923; reprinted, Toronto: University of Toronto Press, 1972.

Isenberg, Andrew C. *The Destruction of the Bison: An Environmental History, 1750–1920*. Cambridge, UK: Cambridge University Press, 2000.

Jackson, James A. "The Background of the Battle of Fort Whyte." *Manitoba Historical Society Transactions*, Series 3, (1945–46). http://www.mhs.mb.ca/docs/transactions/3/fortwhyte.shtml (accessed 19 May 2023).

———. *The Centennial History of Manitoba*. Toronto: McClelland and Stewart, 1970.

———. "The Disallowance of Manitoba Railway Legislation in the 1880s." MA thesis, University of Manitoba, 1945.

Janigan, Mary. *Let the Eastern Bastards Freeze in the Dark: The West versus the Rest since Confederation*. Toronto: Alfred A. Knopf, 2012.

Julius Anglicanus. *Missionary Bishops: A Plea for Indians and Immigrants, Particularly in the Algoma District: Being a Letter Addressed to the Right Reverend the Metropolitan of Canada, and the Bishops of Quebec, Toronto, Huron, and Ontario*. Toronto: Willing and Williamson, H. Rowsell and Hutchison. Ottawa: J. Durie, [1872].

Karamitsanis, Aphrodite. *Place Names of Alberta*. Vol. 1, *Mountains, Mountain Parks and Foothills*. Calgary: University of Calgary Press, 1991.

Kaye, Barry. "Birsay Village on the Assiniboine." *The Beaver* (Winter 1981): 18–21.

Kermoal, Nathalie, and Chris Andersen, eds. *Daniels v. Canada: In and beyond the Courts*. Winnipeg: University of Manitoba Press, 2021.

Knight, William. *Memoir of Henry Venn, B.D., Prebendary of St. Paul's, and Honorary Secretary of the Church Missionary Society*. 1882; reprinted, Cambridge, UK: Cambridge University Press, 2010.

Kobrak, Christopher. *Banking on Global Markets: Deutsche Bank and the United States, 1870 to the Present*. Cambridge, UK: Cambridge University Press, 2008.

Lamb, W. Kaye. *A History of the Canadian Pacific Railway*. New York: Macmillan, 1977.

Lavallee, Omer. "John M. Egan, a Railway Officer in Winnipeg, 1882–1886: An Account of Canadian Pacific's First Years in the Manitoba Capital." *Manitoba Historical Society Transactions*, Series 3, no. 33 (1976–77). https://www.mhs.mb.ca/docs/transactions/3/eganrailway.shtml (accessed 19 May 2023).

Leacock, Stephen. "My Remarkable Uncle." In *My Remarkable Uncle and Other Sketches*, by Stephen Leacock, 14–20. 1942; reprinted, Toronto: McClelland and Stewart, 1965.

Lecompte, Édouard. *Un grand chrétien, Sir Joseph Dubuc, 1840–1914*. Montréal: Imprimerie du Messager, 1923.

Lee, Hermione. *Biography: A Very Short Introduction*. 2009; reprinted, Oxford: Oxford University Press, 2013.

Leggo, William. *The History of the Administration of the Right Honorable Frederick Temple, Earl of Dufferin*. Montreal: Lovell, 1878.

Letters on the Anomalous Position of Manitoba as a Province of the Dominion. Winnipeg: n.p., 1881.

Lorne, Marquis of. *The Canadian North-West: Speech Delivered at Winnipeg*. Ottawa: Department of Agriculture, 1881.

Loveridge, Donald M. "'The Garden of Manitoba': The Settlement and Agricultural Development of the Rock Lake District and the Municipality of Louise, 1878–1902." PhD diss., University of Toronto, 1986.

Lussier, A.S., ed. *Riel and the Metis: Riel Mini-Conference Papers*. Winnipeg: Manitoba Metis Federation Press, 1979.

MacArthur, Duncan. *Correspondence Relating to the Manitoba Central Railway*. Winnipeg: n.p., 1888.

MacBeth, Roderick George. *The Making of the Canadian West: Being the Reminiscences of an Eye-Witness*. Toronto: William Briggs, 1898.

———. *The Romance of Western Canada*. Toronto: William Briggs, 1918.

Macdougall, Heather. *One of the Family: Métis Culture in Nineteenth-Century Northwestern Saskatchewan*. Vancouver: UBC Press, 2010.

Macdougall, Heather, and Nicole St-Onge. "Rooted in Mobility: Metis Buffalo Hunting Brigades." *Manitoba History* 71 (2013). http://www.mhs.mb.ca/docs/mb_history/71/metisbrigades.shtml (accessed 19 May 2023).

MacEwan, Grant. "Honourable John." In *Fifty Mighty Men*, edited by Grant MacEwan. Saskatoon: Modern Press, 1958, reprinted *Manitoba Pageant* 5, 3 (April 1960). http://www.mhs.mb.ca/docs/pageant/05/honourablejohn.shtml (accessed 19 May 2023).

MacKay, Elsie, ed. *Selkirk's Seventy-Fifth Anniversary*. Selkirk, MB: n.p., c. 1957.

Macleod, R.C. "North-West Rebellion." In *The Oxford Companion to Canadian History*, edited by Gerald Hallowell, 451–53. Don Mills, ON: Oxford University Press, 2004.

———. *The NWMP and Law Enforcement 1873–1905*. Toronto: University of Toronto Press, 1976.

MacNutt, W.S. *Days of Lorne: From the Private Papers of the Marquis of Lorne, 1878–1883, in the Possession of the Duke of Argyll at Inveraray Castle, Scotland*. Fredericton: Brunswick Press, 1955.

Maggrah, John A. "Letter from John A. Maggrah, St. John's College, 26 January 1890." *Our Forest Children* 4, no. 2, New Series 12 (1890).

Mandel, Eli. "Images of Prairie Man." In *A Region of the Mind: Interpreting the Western Canadian Plains*, edited by Richard Allen, 201–9. Regina: Canadian Plains Studies Center, 1973.

Manitoba. *Proving that the Province of Manitoba and the Canadian North-West Is a Fertile Soil for Willing Hands to Work*. Winnipeg: Manitoba Free Press, 1880.

———. *Rules, Orders, and Forms of Proceeding of the Legislative Assembly of Manitoba*. Saint-Boniface, MB: Le Métis, 1877.

Manitoba. Department of Public Works. *Annual Reports 1871–1888*. Winnipeg: Queen's Printer, and various firms, 1874–1888.

———. Public Accounts. 1871–1888. Winnipeg: Queen's Printer, 1871–1888.

Manitoba Free Press. *A Comparative Statement of the Public Expenditure of the Province of Manitoba under the Clarke and Davis Administrations Respectively, from 1st Jan. 1874, to 31st Dec. 1877*. Winnipeg: Manitoba Daily Free Press Steam Printers, 1878.

Mann, Michael. *States, War and Capitalism: Studies in Political Sociology*. Oxford: Blackwell, 1988.

Martel, Gilles. *Le messianisme de Louis Riel*. Waterloo, ON: Wilfrid Laurier University Press, 1984.

Martin, Albro. *James J. Hill and the Opening of the Northwest*. 1976; reprinted, St. Paul: Minnesota Historical Society Press, 1991.

Martin, Chester. *"Dominion Lands" Policy*. 1938; reprinted, Toronto: McClelland and Stewart, 1973.

———. "The First 'New Province' of the Dominion." *Canadian Historical Review* 1, no. 4 (1920): 376–77.

———. *The Natural Resources Question: The Historical Basis of Provincial Claims*. Winnipeg: King's Printer, 1920.

———. "Political History of Manitoba, 1870–1912," In *Canada and Its Provinces*, ed. Adam Shortt and Arthur G. Doughty, 97–143. Toronto: Glasgow, Brook, 1914.

Martin, Ged. "How Much Did Canada 'Pay' First Nations for the Prairies?" https://www.gedmartin.net/martinalia-mainmenu-3/313-how-much-did-canada-pay-first-nations-for-the-prairies (accessed 28 December 2021).

———. "Income Tax in Canada before 1917." https://gedmartin.net/martinalia-main-menu-3/311-income-tax-in-canada-before-1917 (accessed 28 December 2021).

———. "Indian Affairs in the 1882 Budget." https://www.gedmartin.net/martinalia-mainmenu-3/312-indian-affairs-1882-budget (accessed 28 December 2021).

Masters, Jerry. *Northern Pacific Railway in Manitoba*. Naples, FL: Jerry Masters Publishing, 2021.

Maxwell, James A. "The Disputes over the Federal Domain in Canada." *Canadian Political Science Association Papers and Proceedings* 6 (1934): 162–74.

———. *Federal Subsidies to the Provincial Governments in Canada*. Cambridge, MA: Harvard University Press, 1937.

McBeth, Margaret E. "'Honest John' Norquay: Pioneer Statesman." Legislative Library of Manitoba, Biographical Files.

McClelland, James, and Dan Lewis, eds. *Emerson 1875–1975: A Centennial History*. Altona, MB: Friesen Printers, 1975.

McCrady, David G. *Living with Strangers: The Nineteenth-Century Sioux and the Canadian-American Borderlands*. Lincoln: University of Nebraska Press, 2006.

McCutcheon, Brian. "The Economic and Social Structure of Political Agrarianism in Manitoba, 1870–1900." PhD diss., University of British Columbia, 1974.

McDonald, Donna. *Lord Strathcona: A Biography of Donald Alexander Smith*. Toronto: Dundurn Press, 1996.

McKay, Ian. "The Liberal Order Framework: A Prospectus for a Reconnaissance of Canadian History." *Canadian Historical Review* 91, no. 4 (2000): 616–45.

McKitrick, Thomas. *Cornerstones of Empire: The Settlement of Crystal City and District in the Rock Lake Country*. Crystal City, MB: Courier Publishing, 1940.

McLean, J. "The Canadian Indian Problem." *Methodist Magazine* 34, no. 2 (1891): 162–71.

McLennan, William, trans. *Songs of Old Canada*. Montreal: Dawson Brothers, 1886.

McWilliams, Margaret Stovel. *Manitoba Milestones*. Toronto: J.M. Dent and Sons, 1928.

Meissner, Daniel J. "Theodore B. Wilcox: Captain of Industry and Magnate of the China Flour Trade, 1884–1918." *Oregon Historical Quarterly* 104, no. 4 (2003): 518–41.

Metcalfe, Joseph Henry. *The Tread of the Pioneers*. Toronto: Ryerson, 1932.

Miller, J.R. "Anti-Catholic Thought in Victorian Canada." *Canadian Historical Review* 66, no. 4 (1985): 474–94.

———. "Anti-Catholicism in Canada: From the British Conquest to the Great War." In *Creed and Culture: The Place of English-Speaking Catholics in Canadian Society, 1750–1930*, edited by Terrence Murphy and Gerald Stortz, 25–48. Montreal and Kingston: McGill-Queen's University Press, 1993.

Miller, Stephen, ed. *Queen Victoria's Wars: British Military Campaigns, 1857–1902*. Cambridge: Cambridge University Press 2021.

Milligan, Frank A. "The Lieutenant-Governorship in Manitoba 1870–1882." MA thesis, University of Manitoba, 1948.

———. "Reservation of Manitoba Bills and Refusal of Assent by Lieutenant-Governor Cauchon, 1877–82." *Canadian Journal of Economics and Political Science* 14 (1948): 247–48.

Millions, Erin. "'By Education and Conduct': Educating Trans-Imperial Indigenous Fur-Trade Children in the Hudson's Bay Company Territories and the British Empire, 1820s to 1870s." PhD diss., University of Manitoba, 2017.

Milloy, John. "Indian Act Colonialism: A Century of Dishonour, 1869–1969." National Centre for First Nations Governance, May 2008. http://fngovernance.org/ncfng_research/milloy.pdf (accessed 12 April 2023).

Mochoruk, Jim. *Formidable Heritage: Manitoba's North and the Cost of Development 1870 to 1930.* Winnipeg: University of Manitoba Press, 2004.

———. "Thomas Greenway, 1888–1900." In *Manitoba Premiers of the 19th and 20th Centuries*, edited by Barry Ferguson and Robert Wardhaugh, 79–106. Regina: Canadian Plains Research Center, University of Regina, 2010.

Montgomery, Ronald B.C. "The Premiers of Manitoba." *Canadian Magazine* 9, no. 5 (1897): 386–95.

Morgan, Henry J. *The Canadian Men and Women of the Time: A Handbook of Canadian Biography.* Toronto: William Briggs, 1898.

Morgan, Henry J. [along with C.H. Mackintosh, J.A. Gemmill, and other editors], eds. *The Canadian Parliamentary Companion* [published annually]. Montreal: J. Lovell; Ottawa, Durie, et. al., 1871–89.

Morice, Adrien Gabriel. *History of the Catholic Church in Western Canada, from Lake Superior to the Pacific, 1659–1895.* Toronto: Musson, 1910.

Morris, Alexander. *Nova Britannia; Or, British North America, Its Extent and Future: A Lecture.* Montreal: J. Lovell, 1858.

———. *The Treaties of Canada with the Indians.* Toronto: Belfords, Clark, 1880.

Morrison, J.C. "Oliver Mowat and the Development of Provincial Rights in Ontario." In Ontario Department of Public Records and Archives, *Three History Theses.* Toronto, 1961.

Morrow, J.W. *Early History of the Medicine Hat Country.* Rev. ed. Medicine Hat: Medicine Hat Historical Society, 1974.

Morton, Desmond. *The Last War Drum: The North West Campaign of 1885.* Toronto: Hakkert, 1972.

Morton, W.L. "Agriculture in Red River." In *Contexts of Canada's Past: Selected Essays of W. L. Morton*, edited by A.B. McKillop, 69–86. Toronto: Macmillan, c. 1980.

———. "The Battle at the Grand Coteau, July 13 and 14, 1851." *Manitoba Historical Society Transactions*, Series 3, 16 (1959–60). http://www.mhs.mb.ca/docs/transactions/3/grandcouteau.shtml (accessed 19 May 2023).

———. "Introduction." In *Alexander Begg's Red River Journal*, edited by W.L. Morton, 1–148. Toronto: Champlain Society, 1956.

———. "Introduction." In *London Correspondence inward from Eden Colvile 1849–1852*, edited by E.E. Rich, xiii–cxv. London: Hudson's Bay Record Society, 1956.

———. *Manitoba: A History*. 1957; reprinted, Toronto: University of Toronto Press, 1967.

———. *One University: A History of the University of Manitoba 1877–1952*. Toronto: McClelland and Stewart, 1957.

———. "The Red River Parish: Its Place in the Development of Manitoba." In *Manitoba Essays Written in Commemoration of the Sixtieth Anniversary of the University of Manitoba*, edited by R.C. Lodge, 89–105. Toronto: Macmillan, 1937.

Mountain, G.J. *The Journal of the Bishop of Montreal during a Visit to the Church Missionary Society's North-West America Mission*. London: Seeleys, 1849.

Munro, K. Douglas, ed. *Fur Trade Letters of Willie Traill 1864–1893*. Edmonton: University of Alberta Press, 2006.

Nelles, H.V. "Empire Ontario: The Problems of Resource Development." In *Oliver Mowat's Ontario*, edited by Donald Swainson, 189–210. Toronto: Macmillan, 1972.

Nelson, Robert L. "A German on the Prairies: Max Sering and Settler Colonialism in Canada." *Settler Colonial Studies* 5, no. 1 (2015): 1–19.

Nicholls, Frederic and A.W. Wright. *Report of the Demonstration in Honour of the Fortieth Anniversary of Sir John A. Macdonald's Entrance into Public Life: Proceedings at Toronto and Montreal, 1844–1884*. Toronto: Canadian Manufacturer Publishing, 1885.

[John Norquay]. Manitoba, Second Session, Fifth Legislature, "Budget Speech Delivered by Hon. John Norquay, Premier and Provincial Treasurer, April 16th, 1884." Winnipeg: n.p., 1884.

———. In Margaret Arnett MacLeod. "A Note on the Red River Hunt by John Norquay." *Canadian Historical Review* 38, no. 2 (1957): 129–30.

———. "Notes on Early Days in Manitoba." NPP, G8731.

[Norquay, John?]. "Old Time Sketches: No. 1 The Buffalo Hunt." *Canadian North-West* 1, no. 1 (1880): 2–4.

———. [J.N.?] "Sauteaux Indians." *Dominion Illustrated: A Canadian Pictorial Weekly*, 14 September 1889, 166.

———. [John Norquay?]. "Subject of Sketch Is 2nd Son of the Late John Norquay of St. Andrews. . . ." NPP, G8731.

"Norquay: In Memoriam." *St. John's College Magazine* 5, no. 22 (1889): 354–55.

O'Donnell, John Harrison. *Manitoba as I Saw It from 1869 to Date: With Flash-Lights on the First Riel Rebellion*. Winnipeg: Clark Brothers, 1909.

O'Leary, Peter. *Travels in Canada, the Red River Territory and the United States*. London: J.B. Day, 1877.

Oliver, E.H. *The Canadian North-West: Its Early Development and Legislative Records*. 2 vols. Ottawa: Government Printing Bureau, 1914.

Oliver, Peter C. *The Constitution of Independence: The Development of Constitutional Theory in Australia, Canada, and New Zealand*. Oxford: Oxford University Press, 2005.

Olusoga, David. "The Ties That Bind Us." https://www.theguardian.com/news/ng-interactive/2023/mar/28/slavery-and-the-guardian-the-ties-that-bind-us (accessed 1 May 2023).

Oppenheim, Janet. *"Shattered Nerves": Doctors, Patients, and Depression in Victorian England.* New York: Oxford University Press, 1991.

O'Toole, Darren. "The Red River Jig around the Convention of 'Indian' Title: The Métis and Half-Breed *Dos à Dos.*" *Manitoba History* 69 (2012). http://www.mhs.mb.ca/docs/mb_history/69/redriverjig.shtml (accessed 19 May 2023).

———. "The Red River Resistance of 1869–70: The Machiavellian Moment of the Métis in Manitoba." PhD diss., University of Ottawa, 2010.

Owram, Doug. *Promise of Eden: The Canadian Expansionist Movement and the Idea of the West, 1856–1900.* Toronto: University of Toronto Press, 1980.

Painchaud, Robert. "Les rapports entre les Métis et les Canadiens français au Manitoba, 1870–1884." In *The Other Natives: The Métis*, vol. 2, edited by Antoine S. Lussier and D. Bruce Sealey, 53–74. Winnipeg: Manitoba Métis Federation Press and Éditions Bois-Brûlés, 1978.

———. *Un rêve français dans le peuplement de la prairie.* Saint-Boniface, MB: Édition des Plaines, 1986.

Payment, Diane Paulette. *"The Free People—Otipemisiwak": Batoche, Saskatchewan, 1870–1930.* Ottawa: Minister of the Environment, Minister of Supply and Services, 1990.

Peers, Laura, and Anne Lindsay. "Governor William B. Caldwell's Souvenir: Exoticism and a Gentleman's Reputation." *Manitoba History* 73 (2013). http://www.mhs.mb.ca/docs/mb_history/73/caldwellsouvenir.shtml (accessed 19 May 2023).

Pelletier, Emile, ed. *L'espace de Louis Goulet.* Saint-Boniface, MB: Éditions Bois-Brulés, 1976.

Pennefather, John Pyne. *Thirteen Years on the Prairies: From Winnipeg to Cold Lake Fifteen Hundred Miles.* London: Kegan Paul, Trench, Trubner and Company, 1892.

Peterson, Thomas. "Manitoba: Ethnic and Class Politics." In *Canadian Provincial Politics*, 2nd ed., edited by Martin Robin, 61–119. Scarborough, ON: Prentice-Hall, 1978.

Potyondi, Barry. *Selkirk: The First Hundred Years.* Winnipeg: Josten's/National School Services, 1981.

Preston, Alex. "You Eat What You Kill: From Scandal to Catastrophe, the Rise and Fall of the Investment Bank." *New Statesman* 28 (2012): 25–27.

Proceedings of the Inter-Provincial Conference Held at the City of Quebec from the 20th to the 28th of October 1887 Inclusively. https://archive.org/details/cihm_07519/page/n17 (accessed 12 October 2021).

Quantrell, Jim. *Cambridge Mosaic.* Cambridge, ON: City of Cambridge Archives, 1998.

Ramirez, Bruno. *On the Move: French-Canadian and Italian Migrants in the North Atlantic Economy, 1860–1914.* Toronto: McClelland and Stewart, 1991.

Rattansi, Ali. *Racism: A Very Short Introduction.* 2nd ed. Oxford: Oxford University Press, 2020.

Regehr, Theodore David. "The National Railway Policy and Manitoba Railway Legislation 1879–1888." MA thesis, Carleton University, 1963.

Reid, Escott M. "The Rise of National Parties in Canada." *Canadian Political Science Association Papers and Proceedings* 4 (1932): 187–200.

Rich, E.E., ed. *London Correspondence inward from Eden Colvile 1849–1852*. London: Hudson's Bay Record Society, 1956.

Riley, Robert Thomas. *Memoirs*. Winnipeg: n.p., c. 1947.

Ritual of the British American Order of Good Templars. London, Canada West: City Press Office, 1860; also published in Montreal: Kyte, Higgins, and Company, 1872.

Robertson, John Palmer. *A Political Manual of the Province of Manitoba and the North-West Territory*. Winnipeg: Call Printing Company, 1887.

Rogan, Tim. *The Moral Economists: R.H. Tawney, Karl Polanyi, E.P. Thompson and the Critique of Capitalism*. Princeton, NJ: Princeton University Press, 2017.

Romney, Paul Martin. *Getting It Wrong: How Canadians Forgot Their Past and Imperilled Confederation*. Toronto: University of Toronto Press, 1999.

Ronaghan, Allen Neil. "The Archibald Administration in Manitoba 1870–72." PhD diss., University of Manitoba, 1987.

———. "James Farquharson—Agent and Agitator." *Manitoba History* 17 (1989). http://www.mhs.mb.ca/docs/mb_history/17/farquharson_j.shtml (accessed 19 May 2023).

Ross, Alexander. *The Red River Settlement: Its Rise, Progress, and Present State*. 1856; reprinted, Edmonton: Hurtig, 1972.

Rostecki, Randy R. "Winnipeg 1870–1886: The Physical Legacy of the Boom." MA thesis, University of Manitoba, 1980.

Rowland, R. *A Treatise on Neuralgia*. London: S. Highley, 1838.

Rupert's Land, Diocese of. *Report of the Synod. 1875–1889*. Winnipeg: Manitoba Free Press Printers, and other printers, 1875–1889.

Russell, Frances. *The Canadian Crucible: Manitoba's Role in Canada's Great Divide*. Winnipeg: Heartland Associates, 2003.

Saywell, John T. *The Office of Lieutenant-Governor: A Study in Canadian Government and Politics*. Toronto: University of Toronto Press, 1957.

Schaub, Lisa. "Métis Communities in the Red River Settlement: Territory, Identity, Racialization, 1821–1926." PhD diss., Universität Trier, 2019.

Schmidt, Anita, ed. *Reports and Letters of the Reverend W.H. Taylor, 1852–1859*. Winnipeg: self-published, 1972.

Schultz, John. "Indians of the Canadian North-West." Speech in House of Commons, 1873, read into the record in *Canada Senate Debates* 1 (16 April 1885): 587–96.

Schultz, Margaret. "Fault Lines: Race and Gender in the Fur Trade Family of Alexander Ross." *Manitoba History* 90 (2019). http://www.mhs.mb.ca/docs/mb_history/90/rossfamily.shtml (accessed 19 May 2023).

Scotland, Nigel. *John Bird Sumner: Evangelical Archbishop*. Leominister, UK: Gracewing, Fowler Wright Books, 1995.

Scott, James C. *The Art of Not Being Governed: An Anarchist History of Upland Southeast Asia*. New Haven, CT: Yale University Press, 2009.

Shave, Harry. *"Our Heritage": Commemorating the 25th Anniversary of the Present (the Third) St. John's Cathedral, 1926–1951*. Winnipeg: De Montfort Press, 1951.

Siggins, Maggie. *Louis Riel: A Life of Revolution*. Toronto: HarperCollins, 1994.

Silver, Arthur. "French Canada and the Prairie Frontier, 1870–1890." *Canadian Historical Review* 50, no. 1 (1969): 11–36.

———. *The French-Canadian Idea of Confederation*. 2nd ed. Toronto: University of Toronto Press, 1997.

Simpson, Jeffrey. *The Spoils of Power: The Politics of Patronage*. Toronto: Collins, 1988.

Smith, Donald B. *Honoré Jaxon: Prairie Visionary*. Regina: Coteau Books, 2007.

———. *Seen but Not Seen: Influential Canadians and the First Nations from the 1840s to Today*. Toronto: University of Toronto Press, 2021.

Smith, Goldwin. *An Address to the Electors of Lisgar, Delivered at Selkirk, August 18, 1887*. Winnipeg: McIntyre, 1887.

Spanjaardt, P. "Canadian Newspaper Interviews." *Canadian Magazine* 5, no. 1 (1895): 47.

Sprague, D.N. *Canada and the Métis, 1869–1885*. Waterloo, ON: Wilfrid Laurier University Press, 1988.

Spry, Irene. "The Great Transformation: The Disappearance of the Commons in Western Canada." In *Man and Nature on the Prairies*, edited by R.A. Allen, 21–45. Regina: Canadian Plains Research Center, University of Regina, 1976.

Stamp, Robert M. *Royal Rebels: Princess Louise and the Marquis of Lorne*. Toronto: Dundurn Press, 1988.

Stanley, George F.G. *The Birth of Western Canada: A History of the Riel Rebellions*. Toronto: Longmans, Green, 1936.

———. "The Half-Breed 'Rising' of 1875." *Canadian Historical Review* 17, no. 4 (1936): 399–412.

———. *Louis Riel*. Toronto: Ryerson, 1963.

Stanley, George F.G., et al. *The Collected Writings of Louis Riel*. 5 vols. Edmonton: University of Alberta Press, 1985.

Stewart, George. *Canada under the Administration of the Earl of Dufferin*. Toronto: Rose-Belford, 1878.

Stobie, Margaret. "Backgrounds of the Dialect Called Bungi." *Manitoba Historical Society Transactions*, Series 3, 24 (1967–68). https://www.mhs.mb.ca/docs/transactions/3/bungidialect.shtml (accessed 19 May 2023).

———. *The Other Side of Rebellion: The Remarkable Story of Charles Bremner and His Furs*. Edmonton: NeWest Publishers, 1987.

Stonechild, Blair, and Bill Waiser. *Loyal till Death: Indians and the North-West Rebellion*. Calgary: Fifth House, 1997.

St-Onge, Nicole J.M. *Saint-Laurent, Manitoba: Evolving Métis Identities, 1850–1914*. Regina: Canadian Plains Research Center, University of Regina, 2004.

———. "Uncertain Margins: Métis and Saulteaux Identities in St-Paul des Saulteaux—Red River 1821–1870." *Manitoba History* 53 (2006): 1–10.

St-Onge, Nicole J.M, Carolyn Podruchny, and Brenda Macdougall, eds. *Contours of a People: Metis Family, Mobility, and History*. Norman: University of Oklahoma Press, 2012.

Stunden Bower, Shannon. "The Great Transformation? Wetlands and Land Use in Manitoba During the Late Nineteenth Century." *Journal of the Canadian Historical Association*, New Series, 15, 1 (2004). https://id.erudit.org/iderudit/012067ar (accessed 19 May 2023).

———. *Wet Prairie: People, Land, and Water in Agricultural Manitoba*. Vancouver: UBC Press, 2011.

Swan, Ruth. "Robert A. Davis 1874–1878." In *Manitoba Premiers of the 19th and 20th Centuries*, edited by Barry Ferguson and Robert Wardhaugh, 29–46. Regina: Canadian Plains Research Center, University of Regina, 2010.

Sweeting, Anthony. "Rennie, Alfred Herbert." In *Dictionary of Hong Kong Biography*, edited by May Holdsworth and Christopher Munn, 366–67. Hong Kong: Hong Kong University Press, 2012.

Sylvester, Kenneth Michael. *The Limits of Rural Capitalism: Family, Culture, and Markets in Montcalm, Manitoba 1870–1940*. Toronto: University of Toronto Press, 2001.

Taylor, Greg. *Law of the Land: The Advent of the Torrens System in Canada*. Toronto: Osgoode Society for Canadian Legal History and University of Toronto Press, 2008.

Taylor, James. *Pamphlet Ordered to Be Printed by the Veterans of the Fur Trade Association Showing Their Ownership of 7,455,552 Acres of Land, Being One-Tenth of Lord Selkirk's Estate, in the Country Formerly Known as the District of Assiniboia*. Prince Albert, SK: Advocate Office, 1906.

Taylor, Jeffery. *Fashioning Farmers: Ideology, Agricultural Knowledge and the Manitoba Farm Movement, 1890–1925*. Regina: Canadian Plains Research Center, University of Regina, 1994.

Teillet, Jean. *The North-West Is Our Mother: The Story of Louis Riel's People, the Métis Nation*. Toronto: HarperCollins, 2019.

Tennant, Joseph Francis. *Rough Times, 1870–1920: A Souvenir of the 50th Anniversary of the Red River Expedition and the Formation of the Province of Manitoba*. Winnipeg: n.p., 1921.

Thomas, L.G., ed. *The Prairie West to 1905*. Toronto: Oxford University Press, 1975.

Thompson, Debra. *The Schematic State: Race, Transnationalism, and the Politics of the Census*. Cambridge: Cambridge University Press, 2016.

Thomson, Dale C. *Alexander Mackenzie: Clear Grit*. Toronto: Macmillan, 1960.

Tombs, Robert, and Isabelle Tombs. *That Sweet Enemy: The French and the British from the Sun King to the Present*. London: Heinemann, 2006.

Tough, Frank. *"As Their Natural Resources Fail": Native Peoples and the Economic History of Northern Manitoba, 1870–1930*. Vancouver: UBC Press, 1996.

———. "Financializing a Junk Charter? British Capital and the Survival of the Mercantilist Hudson's Bay Company during the Age of High Imperialism,

1870–1914." Paper presented to Economic History Society, Keele University, 7 April 2018.

Treaty 7 Elders and Tribal Council with Walter Hildebrandt, Dorothy First Rider, and Sarah Carter. *The True Spirit and Original Intent of Treaty 7*. Montreal and Kingston: McGill-Queen's University Press, 1996.

Trémaudan, Auguste-Henri de. *Histoire de la nation métisse dans l'ouest canadien*. Montréal: Éditions Albert Lévesque, 1935.

———. *Hold High Your Heads: History of the Métis Nation in Western Canada*. Winnipeg: Pemmican Publications, 1982, Elizabeth Maguet translation of 1935 volume.

Trollope, Anthony. *The Way We Live Now*. 1875; reprinted, New York: Alfred A. Knopf, 1950.

Trow, James. *A Trip to Manitoba*. Quebec City: S. Marcotte, 1875.

Tuttle, Charles R. *Our North Land: Being a Full Account of the Canadian North-West and Hudson's Bay Route*. Toronto: C. Blackett Robinson, 1885.

Vanier, Guy. "La question manitobaine." *Les cloches de Saint-Boniface* 15, no. 13 (1 July 1916): 212.

Waiser, Bill. *A World We Have Lost: Saskatchewan before 1905*. Markham, ON: Fifth House, 2016.

Waite, Peter B. *Canada 1874–1896 Arduous Destiny*. Toronto: McClelland and Stewart, 1971.

———. *The Man from Halifax: Sir John Thompson, Prime Minister*. Toronto: University of Toronto Press, 1985.

Ward, Iain. *Sui Geng: The Hong Kong Marine Police 1841–1950*. Hong Kong: Hong Kong University Press, 1991.

Ward, Norman. *The Canadian House of Commons: Representation*. Toronto: University of Toronto Press, 1950.

Warkentin, John H. "Western Canada in 1886." *Manitoba Historical Society Transactions*, Series 3, 16 (1959–60). https://www.mhs.mb.ca/docs/transactions/3/westerncanada1886.shtml (accessed 19 May 2023).

Warner, Donald F. *The Idea of Continental Union: Agitation for the Annexation of Canada to the United States, 1849–1893*. Lexington: University of Kentucky Press, 1960.

Weaver, John C. *The Great Land Rush and the Making of the Modern World, 1650–1900*. Montreal and Kingston: McGill-Queen's University Press, 2003.

Weekes, Mary, ed. *The Last Buffalo Hunter*. 1939; reprinted, Saskatoon: Fifth House, 1994.

White, Richard. "Information, Markets, and Corruption: Transcontinental Railroads in the Gilded Age." *Journal of American History* 90, no. 1 (2003): 19–43.

———. *Railroaded: The Transcontinentals and the Making of Modern America*. New York: Norton, 2011.

Widdis, Randy William. *With Scarcely a Ripple: Anglo-Canadian Migration into the United States and Western Canada, 1880–1920*. Montreal and Kingston: McGill-Queen's University Press, 1998.

Williams, William H. *Manitoba and the North-West: Journal of a Trip*. Toronto: Hunter, Rose, 1882.

Willie, Richard. *"These Legal Gentlemen": Lawyers in Manitoba, 1839–1900*. Winnipeg: University of Manitoba Legal Research Institute, c. 1994.

Willison, John. *Sir George Parkin: A Biography*. London: Macmillan, 1929.

Wilmot, Laurence Frank. "The Christian Churches of the Red River Settlement and the Foundation of the University of Manitoba: An Historical Analysis of the Process of Transition from Frontier College to University." MA thesis, University of Manitoba, 1979.

The Winnipeg and Hudson Bay Railway, Forming with Hudson Bay and Strait, a New Trade Route between America and Europe. Winnipeg: Manitoba Free Press Printing, 1887.

Woodcock, George. *Gabriel Dumont: The Métis Chief and His Lost World*. Edmonton: Hurtig, 1975.

Wright, Norman Ernest. *In View of the Turtle Hill: A Survey of the History of Southwestern Manitoba to 1900*. Deloraine, MB: Deloraine Times, 1951.

Young, Brian J. *Promoters and Politicians: North Shore Railway 1854–85*. Toronto: University of Toronto Press, 1978.

Young, George. *Manitoba Memories: Leaves from My Life in the Prairie Province, 1868–1884*. Toronto: William Briggs, 1897.

Illustration and Map Credits

I would like to thank Nathan Kramer of Winnipeg, Heather McNabb and Anne-Frédérique Beaulieu-Plamondon at Montreal's Musée McCord-Stewart Museum, Jason Martin at the Archives of Manitoba, Oliver Bernuetz at the Legislative Library of Manitoba, Annabelle Schattmann and Benoit Longval at Library and Archives Canada, Brian Hubner at the University of Manitoba Archives, Professor Gerhard Ens, the Toronto Reference Library, and Professors Petra Dolata (University of Calgary) and Gord Goldsborough (Manitoba Historical Society).

Figure 1. Red River *Cartes de Visite* Collection, A2013-005, University of Manitoba Archives and Special Collections.

Figure 2a and *2b.* Hall and Lowe Studio, F.P.V. Cowley collection, C112/4, photo 28, Archives of Manitoba.

Figure 3. Ross Studio, Calgary (probably a copy of a Ryder Larsen photograph taken in Winnipeg, c. 1871), CU2122624, Libraries and Cultural Resources Digital Collections, University of Calgary.

Figure 4. Canada Department of the Interior, RG15-D-II-8-a, Volume 1323, C-14931, Library and Archives Canada. With thanks to Gerhard Ens.

Figure 5. P1278, Archives of Manitoba.

Figure 6. Canada, Department of the Interior, RG15-D-II-8-a, Volume 1323, C-14931, Library and Archives Canada. With thanks to Gerhard Ens.

Figure 7. Louis Riel Photograph Collection, PC 107, University of Manitoba Archives and Special Collections.

Figure 8. William James Topley. *The Ottawa Album* (1875), 40. Item 3246598, Library and Archives Canada.

Figure 9. Notman Collection, 1451, McCord Stewart Museum, https://collections.musee-mccord-stewart.ca/en/objects/131358 (accessed 16 January 2023).

Figure 10. Bannatyne Family Collection 90, N14680, Archives of Manitoba. Topley fonds, 1936-270, Library and Archives Canada.

Figure 11. Notman Collection, 1617, McCord Stewart Museum, https://collections.musee-mccord-stewart.ca/en/objects/131575 (accessed 16 January 2023).

Figure 12. Stovel-Advocate collection, photo 165, P7892/5, Archives of Manitoba.

Figure 13a. Notman Collection, II-63884.1, McCord Stewart Museum, https://collections.musee-mccord-stewart.ca/en/objects/103545 (accessed 16 January 2023).

Figure 13b. Notman Collection, View-1384-1, McCord Stewart Museum, https://collections.musee-mccord-stewart.ca/en/objects/131309 (accessed 16 January 2023).

Figure 14. Notman Collection, II-81755, McCord Stewart Museum, https://collections.musee-mccord-stewart.ca/en/objects/106478 (accessed 16 January 2023).

Figure 15a and *15b.* John A. Macdonald Papers, 194588, Library and Archives Canada; and Norquay Premier's Papers, Norquay to Charles Sadleir, c. 1885-87, Archives of Manitoba.

Figure 16. Stovel-Advocate collection, photo 180, original 1888 (copy), P7892/5, Archives of Manitoba.

Figure 17. Stovel-Advocate collection, photo 174, P7892/5, Archives of Manitoba.

Figure 18. P1278, Archives of Manitoba.

Figure 19. Notman Collection, I-63348.1, McCord Stewart Museum, https://collections.musee-mccord-stewart.ca/en/objects/186848 (accessed 16 January 2023).

Figure 20. Supplement to mid-summer *Grip*, 1886, Item 3007728, Library and Archives Canada.

Figure 21. Steele and Wing Studio, Winnipeg, courtesy of John Burchill, Winnipeg.

Figure 22. Félix-Gabriel Marchand, 1968-001, C-011583, Library and Archives Canada.

Figure 23. P1244, Archives of Manitoba.

Figure 24. From Rural Municipality of St. Andrews, *Beyond the Gates of Lower Fort Garry 1880–1981* (1982), 474.

Figure 25. Notman Collection, II-63884.1, McCord Stewart Museum, https://collections.musee-mc-cord-stewart.ca/en/objects/208259 (accessed 16 January 2023).

Figure 26. Grip, Supplement, 17 January 1885.

Figure 27. Dominion Illustrated, 1888.

Figure 28. Quiz, 1879-02-03 (page 3), University of Manitoba Archives, http://hdl.handle.net/10719/2746551.

Figure 29. Grip 19, no. 24, p. 8, https://www.canadiana.ca/view/oocihm.8_06509_493/8.

Figure 30. Grip 20, no. 3, p. 8, https://www.canadiana.ca/view/oocihm.8_06509_498/5.

Figure 31. Grip 20, no. 26, p. 8, https://www.canadiana.ca/view/oocihm.8_06509_523/8.

Figure 32. Grip 22, no. 2, p. 4, https://www.canadiana.ca/view/oocihm.8_06509_555/4.

Figure 33. Grip 27, no. 8, p. 1, https://www.canadiana.ca/view/oocihm.8_06509_691/1.

Figure 34. Grip 28, no. 23, p. 9, https://www.canadiana.ca/view/oocihm.8_06509_731/9.

Figure 35. Grip 29, no. 3, p. 9, https://www.canadiana.ca/view/oocihm.8_06509_737/9.

Figure 36. Grip 29, no. 7, p. 1, https://www.canadiana.ca/view/oocihm.8_06509_741/1.

Figure 37. Grip 29, no. 13, p. 11, https://www.canadiana.ca/view/oocihm.8_06509_747/11.

Figure 38. Grip 30, no. 3, p. 1, https://www.canadiana.ca/view/oocihm.8_06509_764/1.

Figure 39. Grip 31, no. 4, p. 1, https://www.canadiana.ca/view/oocihm.8_06509_765/1.

Figure 40. Grip 31, no. 5, p. 1, https://www.canadiana.ca/view/oocihm.8_06509_766/1.

I would like to thank Julie Witmer, who prepared the four maps, and I am indebted to the following:

Map 1. "Red River." Norma Hall. Mothers of the Resistance 1869–1870: Reconstructing Place, Red River 1870. https://resistancemothers.wordpress.com/.

Map 4. "Manitoba Railways 1887." Rodger Letourneau. "A Pilot Study of the Historical Resources of Manitoba: Railways" (Manitoba Historic Resources Branch, c. 1980).

Index

John Norquay is shortened to JN in subheadings

B

D

G

H

M

N

S